*Every Day
Is Extra*

JOHN KERRY

Simon & Schuster

NEW YORK   LONDON   TORONTO
SYDNEY   NEW DELHI

Simon & Schuster
1230 Avenue of the Americas
New York, NY 10020

First Simon & Schuster hardcover edition September 2018

SIMON & SCHUSTER and colophon are
registered trademarks of Simon & Schuster, Inc.

For information about special discounts for bulk purchases,
please contact Simon & Schuster Special Sales at
1-866-506-1949 or business@simonandschuster.com.

The Simon & Schuster Speakers Bureau can bring authors to your live event. For
more information or to book an event, contact the Simon & Schuster Speakers
Bureau at 1-866-248-3049 or visit our website at www.simonspeakers.com.

Interior design by Paul Dippolito

Manufactured in the United States of America

10   9   8   7   6   5   4   3   2   1

Library of Congress Cataloging-in-Publication Data is available.

ISBN 978-1-5011-7895-5
ISBN 978-1-5011-7896-2 (ebook)

*To my grandchildren—Alexander, Allegra, Astrid,
Isabelle, Jack, Livia and Sloan—to their parents,
to my wife, Teresa, and to the future*

Author's Note

Every Day Is Extra is not just a statement of fact; it's an attitude about life. It is an expression that summarizes how a bunch of the guys I served with in Vietnam felt about coming home alive. It is the recognition of a gift and a mystery. It is a philosophy lived by people who could have died on any given day but didn't when far too many good men did. It is an expression of gratitude for survival where others did not make it. It is a pledge accepting responsibility to live a life of purpose. And it is the recognition that those of us who survived when so many others didn't had better live our extra days in ways that keep faith with the memory of brothers whose days were cut tragically short. Finally, "every day is extra" means living with the liberating truth of knowing there are worse things than losing an argument or even an election—the worst thing of all would be to waste the gift of an extra day by sitting on the sidelines indifferent to a problem.

This book is the story of my journey trying to keep faith with the gift of my extra days.

Contents

There's a battle outside and it is ragin'
It'll soon shake your windows and rattle your walls
For the times they are a-changin'

—Bob Dylan, "The Times They Are A-Changin' "

Every Day
Is Extra

Childhood

"WONDERFUL," MY FATHER said in a soft, hoarse but somehow satisfied whisper, his eyes closed, savoring a bite of the Swiss chocolate he and I both loved since we—decades apart—were young boys in Swiss boarding schools under very different circumstances, young boys who found that rich and sinful indulgence helped fill a void.

It was the last mouthful of chocolate Pa would ever taste.

For nine years, the cancer had been a constant aggressor, but now, in late July 2000, after doctors promised him he would die of something else and advised a "watch and wait" response to his prostate cancer, it had relentlessly, cruelly found its way into his bones. The pain was agonizing. All we could do was liberally pump palliative morphine into his body to bring some measure of comfort—or the next best thing: numbness.

My brother, Cameron, and my sisters, Peggy and Diana, and I were wandering through our childhoods as our father was slipping away, high in a tower of Massachusetts General Hospital, facing the Charles River and the playing fields of the park below. It was a warm, blue-sky July day. I could see a light breeze rippling the trees, while small sailboats dotted the Charles River basin in front of MIT. There was a part of me that yearned to be outdoors, feeling the summer warmth, far away from the reality that my father was about to die. But of course, reality has its harsh way of dragging you back to earth. Coincidentally, just days before, President Clinton had landed his helicopter in the fields below us during a visit to Boston. I had watched from the twenty-first floor while the world of the living, which had no inkling of the personal drama playing out in our lives, went on below. I was one of three finalists under consideration to be Al Gore's running mate. It hit me that my father would never know the outcome of that decision. It was strange to juxtapose what I thought was important with the intimacy and finality of our world in that room.

Pa slipped deeper and deeper into sleep. His breathing became heavier and labored. Now we were just waiting—my sisters, brother and I sitting vigil at his bedside, the day after his eighty-fifth birthday. His breaths grew increasingly shallow. While we were cloistered, quietly and somberly, at Massachusetts General Hospital, our eighty-seven-year-old mother, his wife of more than sixty years, was resting at home, unable to wait with us the long hours for the inevitable. She had said her goodbye a day earlier—a painful bedside farewell in which her last words to him were "I'll see you tomorrow." All of us in the room knew she wouldn't, and the tears in her eyes told us she knew it too. I wondered how you say goodbye like that to someone you've lived with for more than six decades, and I felt enormous pain for my mother, who was clearly overwhelmed by the moment.

I know I was lucky to have parents who lived as long as mine did, and grateful too for all of us to be able to be present to say our goodbyes, but I've learned over time that no matter how old one is, no matter how much longevity there is to celebrate, when a parent dies, we are all of us, no matter what age, still children. Mothers and fathers fall into different categories altogether. Age and illness reverse the role of caretaker. And so it was with us. It fell to the four of us—Richard and Rosemary's adult children—to helplessly wait for our father to die. At one point, we asked one another: Were we really certain he wanted to go? Did he want us to do something, anything—take extra and more extreme steps, however futile they might be—to give him a few more days? Was he really ready to take his leave?

Suddenly, so uncertain were we about Pa's wishes, we went to considerable lengths to wake him to ask what he wanted. "Pa, is there anything we can do? What do you want?" His eyes grew wide and clear. He abruptly sat up in bed and forcefully announced, "I want to die." Those were the last words Pa ever spoke. He lay back on the pillow, closed his eyes once more, and with all of us surrounding him, holding his hands, touching his arms, we watched him slip away.

I suppose for us children trying hard to divine our father's last wish, the certainty of that announcement lifted a burden. It was a relief, a comfort, but it was jarring nonetheless.

Now he was gone. Even after my last-ditch efforts to pull out of him some answers, not just about life's mysteries but about the mysteries of his life, I realized the brief accounts that he had given left me full of more questions than Pa was ever able—or willing—to answer, not just so late in the day but also throughout his life. Some of his reticence to share more, I chalk up to the stoicism of those of the Greatest Generation. Even by that measure, however, Pa or Pop or "Popsicle," as I sometimes teasingly called him, was still a complicated and perplexing man. What I hadn't fully realized as I was growing up was any of the reasons for his emotional reserve.

I wonder to this day what a six-year-old Richard Kerry was like on Wednesday, November 23, 1921. Did he wake up at home in Brookline, Massachusetts, eat his breakfast, hug his parents goodbye, and innocently head off to school carrying a lunch pail? Was he looking forward to Thanksgiving the next day? Did he rush out the schoolhouse doors onto the playground after lunch, chase a ball or find friends to play boyish games, completely unaware that less than five miles away at the Copley Plaza Hotel in Boston, his father, having filed a will eight days earlier leaving everything to my grandmother, was walking straight into the lavatory, pulling out a handgun and shooting himself in the head?

Before the school bell would have rung to call Richard Kerry and the other students back inside, this forty-eight-year-old man, my (unknown to me) grandfather, had died instantly, violently and horrifically.

When did my father learn this? Who told him? What did they tell him? Did someone pull him out of class and rush him home early to be with his mother and older brother in shock and sorrow? Was there a knock at the front door, a policeman and a priest standing stone-faced on the porch to break the bad news to my grandmother?

For years, I had no idea how my grandfather had died. My father had little to say about it. Whenever I asked about my grandfather—when he had died, where he had come from, what he did for a living—all the questions one could imagine—my father was a combination of tight-lipped and seemingly unknowing about his own father.

For a long time, I was simply told my grandfather had been ill. Later I would hear stories of depression, or a business downturn, or womanizing—and God knows it may have been a combination of many things. I think I was sixteen, certainly after my grandmother had died, when someone shared with me that his death had been a suicide, but that was all—no details, no circumstances, just a distant tragedy that was better left in the past. As I grew older I asked my parents and cousins what they knew of his suicide. No one seemed to know any of the details. It was a mystery and seemed destined to stay so. But one thing I do know with certainty: whatever Pa knew and felt, it was a source of pain and some bitterness that he carried with him every day of his life.

Sometime after the suicide my grandmother packed up my father and his older sister, Mildred, and departed for Vienna, where some Kerry family members lived. My father's much older brother stayed behind to continue his own career. No doubt Granny, as we called her, wanted to get away from the swirl of mystery surrounding my grandfather's death. However, as if the burden of the suicide and sudden transformation of life were not already enough, within a year of the trauma, when my father had turned seven, his sister, Auntie Milly, as I came to know her, was stricken with polio.

As my father wrote many years later: "In 1922, when I was 7 years old, my 13-year-old sister came down with a devastating case of infantile paralysis. She was flat on her back for six months and was in a wheelchair for the rest of her life. We were in Europe at the time and spent the best part of the 1920s there."

On top of my grandfather's death, my aunt's sickness was a monumental blow. It consumed my grandmother and clearly left my father grasping for meaning. As I explored my father's beliefs about religion in many later conversations, I learned that his bitterness and profound sadness over the loss of his father and his sister's sudden crippling by a terrible disease crushed whatever faith he had once had.

Though raised Catholic by a mother more than zealous in her faith, my father could never reconcile the tragedies that befell his family with the concept of a merciful God. It was my mother, the Brahmin Protestant, who actually tended to our religious upbringing as Catholics and made certain we learned our catechism, received First Communion, were confirmed, and attended Mass regularly.

Auntie Milly's illness became the focus of all my grandmother's energy. She embarked on a broad search for a cure (or at least improvement) that centered on spas in Europe, and when the family returned from Europe in 1930, their quest ultimately included a stay in the spa town of Warm Springs, Georgia.

It was there that the family met another polio patient by the name of Franklin Delano Roosevelt. When Roosevelt was sworn in as president, my father was invited to the White House with other families of Warm Springs residents. He told me that after the inauguration ceremony, the first group the president met with was his fellow travelers from Warm Springs. My father, then seventeen, recalled with awe the image of curtains being pulled back and Roosevelt standing there in his braces, talking with his friends who shared the same understanding of a life changed instantly by a silent stalker.

Fortunately, first in Chicago and then in Boston, my grandfather had been a successful retail businessman—at least until the moment of his demise. He left enough money to enable my grandmother to live comfortably for the rest of her life. While the crash of '29 had enough impact to curtail the European meanderings and bring the family back to the States, it did not destroy my grandmother's ability to live a good life. She bought a home in Sarasota, Florida, where the weather helped provide comfort for Auntie Milly. She spent summers on Piney Point in Marion, Massachusetts, looking across Buzzards Bay to Naushon Island, which, thanks to my mother's family, would play a large part in my life. She continued occasional travel to Europe and took advantage of her ability to send my father to schools in Switzerland and then Phillips Academy Andover, Yale University and Harvard Law School.

They were not wealthy, but they were certainly always comfortable. When my grandmother died, she provided enough money for my father to pursue his dream of building a sailboat and sailing across the ocean.

My father's passions were introduced to me, his elder son, from the earliest age. He took me skiing for the first time in Davos, Switzerland, when I was eleven or twelve—a place that would become a frequent destination for me as the host city of the World Economic Forum. On my very first day on skis—the old wooden-tipped kind that strapped my cold leather lace-up boots into bear-trap bindings in which there was no margin of safety (fall, and your knee or leg took all the pressure of being locked into the binding)—up we went to the top of the mountain with my father casually saying, "No sweat. Just point your skis forward and down and off you go!"

What my father was thinking I will never know—I asked him many times—but on day one on skis he took me down the Davos Parsenn, not the hardest run but the longest on the mountain. I literally did it mostly on my rear end. My father was an avid fan of the eight-millimeter home movie camera, so I now have reels of humiliation for my grandchildren to laugh at. Despite the embarrassing evidence of my early adventures on the slopes, I remain eternally grateful for his introducing me to mountains and a soaring sport, both of which I love with an exuberance that to this day exhilarates and revitalizes me every time I'm on a snowy mountain.

I can say the same for sailing. For my father, being on the sea became an obsession; for me, sailing was the beginning of a special, unbreakable bond with the ocean.

I vividly recall my early introduction to the magic of wind and sail. It was my baptism of a different kind—holding the tiller and learning the rhythm of the waves, the prance of the bow with a gust of wind, the dipping of the gunwale into the water just enough to challenge gravity but never enough to capsize, the bob of the boat with the swirl of the ocean—feeling the wind and spray in my face. Sailing became a significant part of my life, but not with the same intensity as for my father. Indeed, from college on, there were often large gaps between my time on the water—time spent on one campaign trail or another, or traveling as secretary of state. Despite the intervals between times under sail, I always yearned for the freedom and tranquillity of being at sea. It pulled at me. Even the brief moments when I could get out on the water were peaceful and restorative. Just the memories would feel good.

PERHAPS THE SEA was in our blood—in the DNA of both Kerry and Forbes families. Not only did our passions always stay connected to the ocean, but the original journey by which we came to America by sea, nearly 250 years apart. My Kerry grandparents arrived at Ellis Island aboard the SS *Königin Luise* on May 18, 1905. The "Manifest of Alien Passengers for the U.S. Immigration Officer at the Port of Arrival" lists Frederick Kerry, thirty-two years old, male, married, merchant from Austria, last known address Vienna, destination unknown, passage paid by himself, in possession of more than $50, never before in the United States. Below his name was Ida Kerry, 28, female, married, and below hers, Erich Kerry, 4, male, single—single and noted at age 4, imagine that.

Frederick Kerry's "destination unknown" quickly became Chicago, the first place he chose to make the new beginning. For whatever reasons, that did not last and he moved to Massachusetts, where he ran a shoe manufacturing business. He did very well, settling his family in a comfortable home at 10 Downing Road, Brookline. By all the normal measurements, this immigrant family appeared to be living the American dream. This is the world my father entered.

Ten years after they had docked in New York Harbor, on July 28, 1915, the family welcomed Richard John Kerry's arrival. Sadly, because of my father's distance, both in time and emotion, from his father's experience, my brother and sisters and I—indeed our mother and extended family— never grew up with the narrative of this journey across the ocean to America. It was in every respect the great American narrative—coming to the New World for a new life, experiencing the glorious welcome of the Statue of Liberty, landing at Ellis Island, starting over—but it was lost in the gunshot to the head in the Copley Plaza and, I assume, in other parts of the past that I was not to learn of until I was running for president in 2003.

Later in life I learned the full story of my grandparents' journey to America, and I have often wondered whether my father had inklings of more to their odyssey than met the eye. The line from the musical *Hamilton* comes to mind: "In New York you can be a new man," except maybe you can't completely. Something caught up to my grandfather—what it may have been I will never know for sure. I can only imagine the questions my father must have asked—certainly of himself, if not his brother or his mother—and I can only imagine if he did know more of the story, how that likely would have affected his life choices and outlook. What was clear to me, which became evident in my father's parenting, was that not having a father role model himself had a profound impact on me and my siblings. Basically on his own, his life was privileged and somewhat lonely. His sister was paralyzed, demanding huge attention from my grandmother. His brother was absent, away pursuing his own career. His father had abandoned him in a selfish, violent moment that must have been incomprehensible to this young boy.

When his mother uprooted the family to Europe, hoping to find a cure for Aunt Milly's disease, Pa was plunked down in school in Vienna, their first stop. Every day he would take the streetcar to a school where classes were in German. Later he was sent off to several boarding schools in Switzerland, one near St. Moritz and one near Rolle, on Lake Geneva. My father talked fondly of his time at those schools. I imagine they provided something of a family for him. He once showed me a small picture album he kept with photos of his friends at school, their names handwritten in the margin. I never asked him, but I am certain his good memories of that time contributed significantly to my parents' decision to send Peggy, Cameron—Cam for short—and me to school in Switzerland.

After the wandering family returned to the States, Pa was enrolled as a sophomore in Phillips Andover Academy and, from there, Yale University, graduating in the class of 1937, which included, among other notables, Potter Stewart, who went on to become an associate justice of the Supreme Court, and Texas oil magnate Perry Bass. I found it interesting that the history of the class of 1937 is entitled "A Rendezvous with Destiny."

That destiny seemed to manifest itself quickly. The summer of 1939, before my father's senior year at Harvard Law, he traveled to Saint-Briac-sur-Mer, a small, sleepy French seacoast town in Brittany. The Emerald Coast, as it was known, welcomed vacationers to its beautiful, rocky shore with its interspersed wide beaches during the *grande marée*—the great tides, when the moon's pull is at its greatest. This phenomenon produces thirty feet of ocean rise and fall, stranding small sailing boats and fishing vessels on the harbor bottom and exposing miles of sand when the tide goes out. It is the same gravitational onslaught of ocean that sends the sea rushing in to the famous Mont Saint-Michel at the speed of a galloping horse. As kids, we would visit the Cluny Abbey. We would walk out on the sand as far as we were allowed because of the quicksand, and then we would race in as the tide came up, our own game of tag with a powerful force. Later in life, my cousins and I waited expectantly for every *grande marée* so we could dig in the sand, near the house my mother's family had there, for small sand eels—*lançon*—and search for octopuses in the rocks. Nothing will ever adequately describe the sheer pleasure of bare feet curling into the still-wet tidal sand; the wind, warm and soothing, as we would dart among the newly exposed rocks and probe around in holes with long metal hooks, occasionally pulling a live octopus out and turning it inside out before beating it madly with a wooden hammer to soften the meat. Children can get lost for memorable hours in such activities.

Saint-Briac, France, and Europe more generally had been home for my mother's extended family since 1912, when my maternal grandparents, James Grant Forbes and Margaret Tyndal Winthrop, moved from Boston. Grandpa was working as a partner at William Blair, where he was involved with Pietro Giannini in the founding of the Bank of America. This was the work that most immediately brought him to a life with one foot in England and one in France. In reality, though, I am convinced it was in his blood.

Grandpa was born in Shanghai, China, where his father was engaged in business together with a Chinese partner. The Forbes family had long been involved in the China trade, shipping furs, silver, manufactured goods, cloth, wood—whatever would sell in China in return for loads of tea, silk, porcelain and decorative furniture. It was a lucrative trade, though accompanied by dark references to opium as also being part of the cargo. Much of the history of Boston was built on the courage and tenacity of those who went to sea to find riches in far-off lands. Our family boasted many an adventurer who was part of that history.

Why my maternal grandparents chose to be such longtime expatriates has never been satisfactorily explained to me, and, regrettably, I never explored it as much as I now wish I had. Of course, the 1920s and '30s were filled with the stories of Americans living a high life in Europe, and many a college student since has been affected by the films and books chronicling that period. Indeed, during my years at Yale, I ran with the bulls in Pamplona and attended many a bullfight in search of Hemingway.

What I do know is that Grandma embraced the full measure of aristocratic English country life. She had strong (and expensive) tastes and enthusiastically spent money to support the lifestyle she wanted. We children grew up with wonderful stories of our grandparents' adventures in their young lives—stories that seemed to leap out of the pages of novels and movies. My Forbes grandparents produced four boys and seven girls: James, Jock, Griselda, Eileen, Angela, Rosemary, Ian, Alistair, Iris, Monica and Fiona. Almost *Cheaper by the Dozen*. Grandpa traveled like crazy for business, but he seems to have returned long enough to get Grandma pregnant, and then off he'd go again for more business, leaving Grandma to cope with this large brood.

The family lived in two wonderful and well-known English country houses in Surrey: Squerryes Court and Barrow Green.

During these early years nothing was spared. There were nannies, chambermaids, chauffeurs, gardeners, nursemaids, cooks, butlers and, of course, horses and dogs—multiple dogs! In effect, the children were raised by nannies, which was thought normal among families of means, so parenting was more of an organizational task than a hands-on operation. Nannies would make sure the children took their baths, dressed in their matching pajamas and nightgowns and then presented for their good-night hugs and acknowledgments. They wore made-to-order clothes from London's best children's stores, including beautiful velvet capes with their names embroidered in them, each of which later was folded away in the playroom of the restored house my generation was privileged to stay in. We would dress up and play in their no longer wearable or suitable treasures from an earlier age.

When it came time to go on vacation, Grandma would rent three houses on the Brittany coast of France. The children would pile into a rented bus to travel to the ferry and then another bus would collect them across the channel, and off they went to the villas and a regimen of beach calisthenics, great meals, games and tea—and, of course, all the adventures of a sprawling family at play.

Sometime in 1928 my grandfather bought a beautiful property on a promontory in Saint-Briac-sur-Mer, the next town over from the rented villas. He named the property Les Essarts (which means "the Clearing" or "the Open Space"). The house boasted then, and still does, what I am convinced is one of the great views in the world, looking west through a Japanese tree my grandfather planted, across a rocky bay to the far cliffs of the Cap Fréhel peninsula and, beyond that, the peninsula that is Brittany itself, jutting out to form the southern border of the English Channel. The house looks directly at Fort La Latte, a medieval castle that was prominently used as the site of climactic battles in the Kirk Douglas–Tony Curtis film *The Vikings* (1958). For years, we children would make a pilgrimage to the fort and, with our cousins, my sister Diana and I would reenact the final battle scenes on the top of the turret, jumping around and terrifying onlookers with our erstwhile derring-do!

Les Essarts became the center of prewar life for my mother and her family. From 1928 until the German invasion of Poland, the family enjoyed idyllic times with a household of teenage energy bursting at the seams. The home itself was an enormous, rambling Victorian structure. In the pictures I've seen of it, I thought it was dark and foreboding, but the family loved it. Grandpa was particularly attached to it. It was at his insistence that it was eventually rebuilt after the war. My mother never had formal schooling. While the boys in the family went off to Eton, my mother and her sisters were tutored in a little house on the property. Today that house is used as a spillover room when the main house gets crowded. She and her siblings led an active and adventuresome life, carefree and, yes, even spoiled, though for that generation, at that moment, it wasn't thought of in the same way we would characterize their upbringing today.

It was into this household that my father appeared in 1939. He had visited Saint-Briac as a younger boy and now was back to study sculpture during his summer break before his last year of law school. It was there that he was introduced to Rosemary Isabel Forbes, the middle sister of the Forbes girls, all of whom were enjoying a summer interlude. And it was there that my mother and father fell in love. It's hard to imagine how they would not: a dashing young law student from Harvard studying sculpture and a beautiful, somewhat shy but engaging young American living abroad with the winds of war blowing in the background. Their meeting seemed destined to be more than a passing acquaintance.

My mother's sister Angela, a drop-dead gorgeous, intelligent and independent soul, had just married Frederick Winthrop from Hamilton, Massachusetts. She was living on the Winthrop farm called Groton House, named after the town in England from which our great-grandfather eight times over, John Winthrop, departed on the *Arabella* to become the first governor of the Massachusetts Bay Colony. It was he who, several days out from Boston, delivered the famous sermon saying, "We shall be as a city upon a hill," a sermon quoted by John F. Kennedy and later by Ronald Reagan.

During this same summer just before World War II started, Angela and Fred also visited Les Essarts. Rosemary casually asked Angela to stay in touch with Richard Kerry. She did, inviting him to Groton House for Easter lunch the next spring. It was there that my father confided to Angela that Rosemary had accepted his proposal, showing her a telegram that said simply: "Yes with love. Rosie."

I REMEMBER THE sound of broken glass crunching beneath my feet. I was holding my mother's hand, walking through the ruins of Les Essarts. In the summer of 1945, my mother's beloved home had been bombed and burned by the German army as it was being driven out of Saint-Briac. It was now

1947. I was four years old. This was my mother's first visit back to France, only two years after the war ended. It was my first trip out of the United States, and at a quite young and tender age. I didn't really know where I was or what was happening, but I distinctly remember some of the sights and sounds, as well as certain feelings and emotions. Everything was new and clear in these earliest moments of my memory—the very reason I am sure of my few memories of this long-ago time.

My mother was crying, which upset me. I had never seen her cry. I didn't know why she was so distressed, but I dutifully walked alongside her. A stone staircase rose up into the sky. It stood alone at one end of the rubble. A chimney similarly pointed into the sky above the ruins at the opposite end of what had been the house. That's it—all I remember—but this image of destruction and my mother's tears stayed with me, later developing into a powerful impression of the consequences of war. As I went on in life, I was extremely conscious of my journey from the war of my parents into the war of my generation. This earliest of introductions to the consequences of war was an improbable beginning for anyone, but in our family it seemed normal.

OUR HOME WAS Millis, Massachusetts. My father practiced law at Palmer & Dodge in Boston, while Mama was a hands-on mother, taking care of Peggy and me.

A Boston suburb, the town was more rural than urban back then. We lived adjoining a small farm, called South Farm. I distinctly remember swimming in the pond and being terrified of eels, which I thought were snakes, a phobia that haunts me to this day. Millis was home to the Cliquot Club Company, a soda bottler. The factory filled the air with wonderful smells. I wondered what happened inside, and I dreamed of growing up to become the Eskimo who appeared on the labels. My sister Peggy and I dressed up in our heavy snowsuits in the middle of summer to play Eskimo. It's a wonder we didn't pass out from heatstroke. Other days, I sat in the lap of the farmer driving the tractor, his skin leathery from the sun, his vocabulary marked by a colorful string of expletives any time the tractor backfired or the oil leaked. I was proud of this early education in cuss words—magical phrases my parents said I should never use and quickly forget, a certain incentive to judicious deployment at the appropriate time. I remember sitting for hours in his lap as we plowed or harrowed a field. I was mesmerized by the constant growing rows of plowed earth, expanding outward in neat lines. Later I would get to drive a tractor at Groton House, and to this day I could be very happy just plowing away, measuring the progress as I went. I found it enormously satisfying. Occasionally Pa would plop me on his lap so I could steer the Jeep up the driveway using the rhododendron bushes as guideposts. Life was simple and fun.

These days I have a warm, visceral sense of life in Millis. It was a Main Street America sort of town where people knew each other. Our babysitter was Helen Cassidy, the daughter of the folks who owned the farm just down the street—Cassidy's Farm. We would stop off there for one thing or the other, and I would walk around the farmyard near the barn. Once I witnessed the beheading of a chicken. I'll never forget the sight of all the other chickens running around the yard squawking in protest. I stayed away from the barn after that. The Cassidys were wonderful neighbors. Years later when I was running for office, they would reappear in my life and remind me of some of the adventures of those early days.

Suddenly, one day, all that ended and we were off to Washington, D.C., where Pa took on new challenges, first at the Navy Department and then, shortly thereafter, in the Foreign Service, as Secretary of State John Foster Dulles undertook a major expansion of the State Department. I knew none of that at the time. All I knew was that I hated saying goodbye. Goodbyes were to be a running thread throughout my childhood.

In Washington, D.C., we first lived in Georgetown at 2725 Dumbarton Street, directly opposite the home of the noted columnist Joe Alsop. He had a wonderful parrot that I was privileged to taunt occasionally. I started school a few blocks away at Jackson Elementary School on R Street and ultimately went on to St. Albans School by the National Cathedral.

St. Albans was demanding. I remember distinctly what happened when we got unruly: a certain Mr. Spicer would grab us by the neck in a pincer vise between his thumb and forefinger and squeeze us into submission. It was painful and served its purpose of quickly taming whatever boisterous enthusiasm I or others may have been pursuing. There was a demerit system of some kind and it was possible, with enough demerits, to earn Saturday morning attendance at school to walk off your demerits in the courtyard. I earned my way into several Saturday sessions.

I played seventy-five-pound football in the fall, wrestled in the winter and played baseball in the spring, an early introduction to a three-sport cycle that would mark my years through college. I was, thanks to my mother, an avid Cub Scout. At some point during my mother's years in England she had met Lord Baden-Powell, the founder of Scouting. She became a huge believer, promptly enrolling Peggy as a Brownie and then a Girl Scout and me as a Cub Scout. But Mama didn't just throw us in and watch from the sidelines. She was also my den mother, the leader of our pack. Future

Fox News journalist Brit Hume was in my Cub Scout den, and I must have done something very bad to him that would go on to haunt my political career. But I loved Scouting, embracing the projects with huge enthusiasm and earning my way up to Webelos ("We'll Be Loyal Scouts"), which is the jumping-off point from Cub Scouts to Boy Scouts.

My father had an elaborate set of tools from Sears, Roebuck. They took over the basement at 3806 Jenifer Street, where he would disappear for hours working on bookshelves and cabinets. My great achievement at that age was gaining sufficient confidence from him to be allowed to use the band saw by myself. I would busy myself carving out jigsaw puzzles and making unusable objects. One sad day it came in handy, though, when I found my beautiful Cairn puppy, Sandy, run over and dead in the gutter of Reno Road, just around the corner from our house. Sandy was my first pet—the first animal I knew that I saw dead. I remember when I picked him up out of the gutter how stiff, cold and motionless he was. I wondered about a living thing going from such bubbling energy to cold and motionless. My mother and I had the first of several conversations about death.

I built Sandy's coffin with my father's help. We all got up early one morning and drove out to Virginia, where my mother had helped the Potomac School develop a nature trail—which is still there today—and we buried him on a peaceful rise overlooking the trail. I have a wonderful picture of Sandy and me sitting in Pa's chair, quite content with ourselves. I have always remembered Sandy as my pal, my very personal friend. He was a wonderful companion, and because of him I have always had a dog whenever I can since that time—including on my boat in Vietnam.

Religion entered my life. I had attended Mass with my grandmother and with my parents, but like most kids, I was looking around the church and waiting to be sprung from the service. It was that period when practicing families shared the experience and habit of attending but without much meaning. It wasn't until I began to prepare for my First Communion at Blessed Sacrament in Chevy Chase, Maryland, that I started thinking about what we were doing and why—which is exactly the reason children begin to prepare then. I remember being genuinely, deeply moved at receiving First Communion. The preparation, which in my case included being slapped by a nun when I was roughhousing in line while waiting to march to a classroom, gave me a genuine sense of anticipation for this moment when I would be able to experience bringing Jesus into my soul. I knew nothing about transubstantiation, but I was convinced that taking Communion was going to bring me closer to God, which was important to me and everyone in my group. When the day arrived, I was resplendent—or so I thought—

in my white suit. Along with the rest of the recipients, I felt an incredible sense of well-being when the moment finally came. I felt like things were right and good and the way they were meant to be. The same was true later of my confirmation at Blessed Sacrament, with the same sense of anticipation and of good and enriching things happening to me. At confirmation, the bishop stood in front of us and asked questions. At the first question, my hand shot up along with others, but lo and behold, His Excellency called on me. I stood up and almost shouted the answer. My parents were shocked but proud.

I was settling into a new childhood home, which I loved. I dreamed of being old enough to start a paper route delivering the *Washington Evening Star*, with my red wood-slatted wagon to stack the newspapers in. I was on the cusp of starting Little League, a huge deal for a kid who would plead with his dad—not a baseball fan—to take him to Griffith Stadium to watch the Senators, where I obsessively followed Eddie Yost and even snagged his autograph on my baseball, which I still have.

Then—just like that—it was time to move again. Pa announced he was being sent abroad to Berlin to serve as the legal advisor to the high commissioner of Germany. I never got to become a Boy Scout, have an *Evening Star* paper route or experience Little League. None of this is to complain, but there were milestones meant to be part of a young boy's life, and these began to create expectations and hopes in me, but I didn't have a vote in the matter.

I don't think it ever occurred to my parents that because we were going off to Europe, there were things we were leaving behind that actually mattered to me. Later, when I came back to the States to attend high school, I watched my younger cousin Robby Winthrop's Little League games and thought what fun it would be to be playing.

I grew up in a wonderful adventure, but it was not the everyday adventure of most people my age. Despite my remarkable opportunities and life-shaping experiences, a part of me longed for the comforts and consolations of familiarity, for one neighborhood, one school, one backyard and the same neighbors from one year to the next.

Now it was on to Berlin and a new life in a place that had great meaning to my parents. In the summer of 1954, we set off on the great adventure, packing up completely, leaving our home and going to live in Germany. Somewhere along the way, I was told I was going to school in Switzerland. That was it, no discussion and no choice. I just accepted that this was what you do when you pull up stakes, leave your home and go to another country. Pa had gone to school in Switzerland, so at least there was a certain historical rationale. My younger siblings were headed to Berlin to be with my parents. At the time I wasn't too sure where Switzerland was or how far I would be from my parents. I certainly didn't think about what it meant to be leaving the security of home with mother and father and siblings. For the moment, what excited me was the prospect of crossing the ocean on one of the great liners of the time, the SS *America*. It was smaller than the SS *United States*, which held the transatlantic speed record and which we traveled on in 1958 en route to Norway, but it was a beautiful vessel with great lines and accommodations. Believe it or not, in those days, U.S. diplomats traveled first class. So, much to my surprise, we traveled in style.

Somehow my mother got us organized to leave—big trunks packed to the rim with all that my sister Peggy and I would need at our boarding schools. My father was already in Paris, where he had been teaching at the NATO Defense College. As usual, Mama was picking up the pieces. We took the train from Washington to New York City. There we stayed for a day or so before boarding the *America*. Drop-off car rentals had yet to be invented, and flying was out of the question with all our luggage. Mama had arranged a huge treat for the night before we boarded. We went to see *Peter Pan* on Broadway starring Mary Martin. To this day I remember the thrill of seeing a flying Peter Pan swing out over the audience suspended by nearly invisible wires. Captain Hook terrified me to no end, even causing me to dream for a while of crocodiles with a clock ticking away. New York was amazing and quite a grand start to the adventure of a lifetime we were embarking on.

The next day we boarded the SS *America*. If ever an eleven-year-old had been given a paradise for a playground, this was it. I loved every minute of the voyage and started exploring from the moment we stepped aboard. I remember racing from one deck to another and was surprised when I confronted a gate marked with second- or third-class signs. It seemed weird. Occasionally, I found a way through them, but mostly I explored the complex of decks and salons that made up first class. There were shuffleboards, Ping-Pong tables, swimming pools, gyms, stores and endless corridors in which to get happily lost.

Dinner was a big deal. Everyone got dressed up to appear at the appointed hour for a multicourse meal in a large dining room with a lower and upper tier of tables, all covered in white tablecloths and sporting beautiful silverware. A live orchestra played each night. The ship's captain had his own table but would circulate to chat with all the passengers and make them feel important and welcome. There was at least one special night that included party hats, streamers and balloons. Since then, every movie I've ever seen that has a scene of a meal on an ocean liner brings back memories of those carefree, fun dinners.

One early morning the ship slowed and the air changed. You could smell land as we quietly slid into the bay that enveloped the harbor of Cobh, on the southern side of Great Island in Cork Harbour. The ship stopped altogether. A small, fast boat approached us, came alongside, and a man was lifted up into the ship through a hatch door that had been opened on the ship's side. I learned he was a "pilot" who was going to guide the ship up the channel. The beautiful green hillsides were magical, sloping up from the water, my first introduction to the stunning green and beauty of Ireland.

I knew only the broad brushstrokes of Irish history and the background of emigration. I knew there was a County Kerry, which fascinated me in a parochial way. Little did I know I was looking at the place the *Titanic* made its last port of call after Southampton and Cherbourg as it set out on its fateful voyage. We slid into the beautiful harbor, where a large vessel came alongside to collect those passengers disembarking. I happened to notice a young man and a beautiful young woman, possibly college students, whom I had seen hanging out together, embracing before she got off in Ireland. Peggy and I had caught them kissing on the lower deck one night after dinner. I was filled with youthful curiosity about their relationship. Yes, despite my age, I had begun to notice enough about the opposite sex to be intrigued by this relationship. Had they just met on board? How serious was this deal? What was going on? I was totally captivated by this goodbye. The image of these two beautiful people in their romantic world was indelibly stamped in my imagination.

The next morning, we arrived in the bustling port city of Le Havre. There we were met by my mother's sister Eileen. She was jabbering in French to the porters, who were all dressed in blue overalls. In fact, back then, for a young lad's first look around, it seemed almost everyone was dressed in blue overalls. They were busy, under the chaotic direction of my aunt, separating the luggage, and all I could hear was the frequently uttered phrase "walla, walla." Later I learned it was a staple of the French language—*"voilà voilà,"* which roughly translates to "here it is," but when barked out by my aunt many times in a row and very fast, the repeated word clearly meant something like "Here you are, and I'm so relieved to have found you!"

From Le Havre we drove straight to Les Essarts, which had been rebuilt and opened the year before. It was exciting to return, seven years later,

to the place I had first been introduced to as a ruin while holding Mama's hand. We drove past the beaches of Normandy where the great D-Day invasion took place, past Mont Saint-Michel, one of the wonders of the world, and arrived at the "new" Les Essarts. Although the house had been immensely important to my mother and her immediate, but large family, from the day I arrived at the new house right up to this day, for me and my extended family, and down to a few more generations now, the house and its environs have been a hugely special place in our lives.

My grandmother put the house at the full disposal of all family members. She had her own property in town, called Plaisance. She would walk up to the main house every day surrounded by her corgis, sit in the garden and hold court. She was a graceful woman with a head of white hair accented by a streak of blue. I thought she exuded wisdom and a quiet elegance.

Les Essarts became a gathering spot for the offspring of her children, who had produced plenty of their own children. Those offspring, myself included, now manage the house as a refuge for the next generations. But it was so much more too. It became the place that provided much of the glue for those in the family who, because of Grandma and Grandpa's introduction to life abroad, found their lives playing out where they had been raised. And for those of us in America, it was the magnet for our staying connected. All twenty-nine of us first cousins were in many ways more like brothers and sisters. We literally grew up together and shared in one another's development—the victories and the tragedies.

In summer we would go together to calisthenics class on the beach; have great picnics; learn about teatime and the splendor of a midafternoon snack of biscuits and chocolate, tea or Orangina; play tennis; explore the surrounding villages and history of the war; ride bicycles for miles into the French countryside; and eat exotic foods like crêpes and galettes on the ramparts of Saint-Mâlo. We put on plays we wrote to entertain the adults and ourselves. It was idyllic. Grandma made certain of that. It was always very hard to leave at the end of a stay.

On this first excursion into living abroad, I began to dread the separation from family. I was going to boarding school for the first time. That fact was beginning to sink in. After working through the painful goodbyes with all my cousins, we took the train to Paris, where we met Pa. Then from Paris we drove to the German part of Switzerland en route to Zug. When we stopped in Zurich, parking the car by the train station so my parents could change money, my sister Diana and I distinctly remember practicing our German from a *How to Speak German* book. From the car window we would ask passersby for the time: *"Wie spät ist es?"* It became a great game

as to who would ask. The problem was that people actually understood our question and answered. Their rapid-fire answer left us looking at each other dumbfounded because we couldn't understand a word they said. We would break out into raucous laughter until the next victim came along and repeat the exercise. Then, to add insult to injury, a big bus that was blocking the view pulled out, and there was an enormous clock hanging from the station displaying the time for all to see. We laughed hysterically. Even today we still say *"Wie spät ist es"* to each other.

That night was my last with the family before they dropped me off. We stayed in a hotel in Zug at the base of the mountain Zugerberg, where my school was perched at the top. That first night in Switzerland was also my introduction to an eiderdown that, for a boy who was used to being tucked into bed with sheets and a blanket, struck me as a strange way to stay warm. The next morning as we headed off to the new school, I felt as if I were going to prison or to the executioner. We drove into the courtyard of Institut Montana Zugerberg, a school that is still thriving. There I was introduced to the headmaster and the dormitory chief. My clothes were unloaded. The minutes ticked by. The moment came for goodbyes. The tears I had held back came pouring out. I could see my mother was upset too. Then, when I had sufficiently pulled myself together, my parents got in the car with my siblings and vanished down the mountain to take my sister Peggy to her school near St. Gallen. I was alone. A huge emptiness engulfed me. For three weeks I moved on automatic pilot, thinking of home, missing my family, trying to make friends and adjust to a very alien experience. I alternated between sorrow, stoicism, tears and a brave face.

It was a rude awakening but also fascinating. Soon friendships began to form. I liked my American roommate, Barry Eldridge. A routine set in. My dorm supervisor had persuaded me that the time until Christmas, when I would go to Berlin, was not that far away. I began to count the days and settle in. I had been sent there to learn German, but with 150 Italians, 50 Germans and 3 Americans, I mostly learned Italian—especially colorful swear words. It was the only way to get food passed at the table. Days ticked by. We few Americans were tutored separately in a small class. The fall came fast on top of the mountain, which boasted a stunning view down onto the large Lake Zug, called the Zugersee in German. There was a funicular station close to the school. It was our connection to Zug and the outside world. On Saturdays we were allowed to take it down into town, wander around and spend our allowance. This is when I fell in love with Swiss chocolate. Occasionally we took a field trip to Zurich, and I remember that when Thanksgiving came we Americans were treated to a gathering with

other Americans at a hotel nearby. I waited with keen anticipation for letters from my mother. I loved the moment when this blue envelope with her distinctive, meticulous script would appear and I would read and reread her accounts of life in Berlin.

Fresh from my Catholic confirmation in Washington, I would pray a lot at school. It gave me strength and comfort. There was a tiny chapel below our second-floor window in the dorm. On Sundays I would attend services. At night, I would sometimes kneel at the window and say a Rosary. Occasionally Barry joined me. Then one day I remember coming back to my room and Barry was gone, and I mean gone, with no trace of him left behind. The bed was stripped. I was told just that he'd gone home, with no real explanation. It was as if he had died. I was dumbfounded by his departure and felt abandoned. We had become friends. He was my American connection. How could this friend just vanish?

From the seeming constancy of the pain of goodbyes to my family to the later loss of friends in the war, I have always had a terrible time with any separations and goodbyes. I still do. School in Switzerland—despite all the positives about the experience—is where it all started.

One day in the fall, we were in our classrooms, when outside we noticed a large number of uniformed soldiers with guns running through the campus. They were darting around and behind buildings, taking cover and running across open spaces as if avoiding enemy fire. It was the Swiss army conducting exercises. Naturally, we poured out of the classrooms to watch. There we were, an entire school of boys, gawking at these guys trying to pretend they were at war, defending their country, while sarcastic taunts from Italian and German teenagers were hurled at them. I think the whole school played hooky for a while following the maneuvers. I was fascinated. Playing soldier seemed like such a magnificent escape from the real world. Of course, at eleven, I had little to no understanding of what war really was.

IN SEPTEMBER 1957, I was deposited at St. Paul's School in Concord, New Hampshire. I arrived with my trunk of labeled clothes per the admissions instructions, ready for a new adventure. I was in the eighth grade, and it was my seventh school. (At one, Fessenden School in Newton, Massachusetts, I met Dick Pershing from New York City, who, like me, was doing a year of transition before going off to secondary school—in his case, Exeter. Neither of us had any inkling that our lives would be intertwined, but we enjoyed each other's company at this early age. Dick helped make boarding school fun and sometimes mischievous.)

It's fair to say that I arrived at St. Paul's somewhat lost. I had moved so often that it was hard for me to connect to one culture or place, let alone make lasting attachments with many friends. But I had learned some good moves on a soccer field in Europe. And I did gain great independence and confidence during my travels in Europe. After all, how many kids get to travel alone at age eleven by train from Switzerland to the divided Cold War city of Berlin and stay up all night to journey through East Germany and watch Russian soldiers rap the muzzles of their guns on the compartment windows when they caught you peeking out?

I felt confident, but I didn't understand the ebb and flow of the dominant current of St. Paul's. The majority of my classmates appeared to come from Philadelphia, New York City, Long Island and Connecticut. Many knew each other from country day schools or urban schools with long pedigrees. With that came a pretty automatic pecking order. A good part of the humor and vernacular was alien to me. Whether it was madras jackets or Peal shoes, they seemed to have similar points of reference.

So St. Paul's took some adjusting to, but despite my own missteps and awkwardness, I came to cherish the intimacy of the classrooms; the extraordinary beauty of the campus with the magical change of seasons (with the notable exception of the time between winter and spring, known as mud season); the intellectual give-and-take between teachers and students, and friend to friend; the tranquillity of a Channing Lefebvre organ recital at Evensong in the school's stunning chapel; learning to play hockey and enjoying the uniqueness of black ice on the ponds; throwing a lacrosse ball around or playing Ultimate Frisbee in the long, lazy light of warm spring evenings when we procrastinated before study time; the deep friendships made, some of which survive to this day and two of the best that were lost on the battlefields of Vietnam. St. Paul's did a lot for me—which is what a school should do—and I am forever grateful for the tutelage of special teachers such as Andre Jacques, Herbert Church and Reverend John Thomas Walker.

In the fall of 1960, I traveled one November day to Boston for a visit to the orthodontist. I took the train from Concord to Boston's North Station, dutifully and painfully went to my appointment in Kenmore Square and then was planning to catch a late-afternoon train back to Concord. When I arrived at North Station I noticed an unusual hustle of people, many of them carrying "Kennedy for President" signs or wearing plastic hats with "Kennedy" emblazoned on the brim. It was the eve of the election—November 7, 1960, and I learned that Senator John F. Kennedy was due to arrive shortly for the final rally of the campaign before going to Hyannisport to await the returns.

Coincidentally, I was due to make a presentation the next morning before the daily post-chapel school assembly, arguing the case for Kennedy while my schoolmate class president Lloyd Macdonald was going to speak for Nixon. There may have been all of twenty-five Democrats at St. Paul's, and the straw poll taken after our presentations was lopsidedly for Nixon, but we Democrats were, nevertheless, a stalwart, determined lot. My Democratic bona fides had been forged in 1952, when I dutifully followed my sister Peggy around Georgetown while she went door-to-door carrying a cup, collecting contributions for Adlai Stevenson. If my older sister was a Democrat, then I was a Democrat at age nine. I believe both my mother and father approved, he quietly since he was at the State Department. But I liked Jack Kennedy and I didn't trust Richard Nixon even back then. I felt he was shallow and opportunistic.

With a quick decision, I purposefully missed the train and spent time soaking in the atmosphere and, most important, collecting literature that enabled me to write my speech for the next morning while traveling back to Concord. Unfortunately, the candidate was delayed and I had to leave for school before he spoke, but I have always felt it was special to be there, to feel the extraordinary excitement and pride of Massachusetts in that historic rally.

My final months at St. Paul's were spent luxuriating in the warm spring of New Hampshire while awaiting word on admission to college. Most of my family, over many years, had attended Harvard. The notable exception in this lucky line was my father and his older brother, who were Yalies. I hoped to go to Yale because I didn't want to be quite so close to home, and when I visited the campus, it just felt right. I was excited when Yale chose me as well. It made the last months at St. Paul's completely carefree. My classmate Lewis Rutherfurd and I served as proctors for fourth formers in one of the small dormitory houses. When graduation finally arrived, he and Peter Wyeth Johnson took off with me to Bermuda, where we served as crew for my dad's last leg of his transatlantic sailing voyage back to Newport. It was a wonderful ending to the constraints of boarding school and opening to the freedom of college.

WELL BEFORE PRESIDENT Kennedy was elected in November 1960, it was evident to anyone following politics in Massachusetts that Ted Kennedy, the youngest of the three living brothers, was destined to run for Jack's Senate seat. "Destined" is probably a soft word. It was ordained and organized. It was really not a choice. It was what Teddy had to do and no doubt wanted to do. He was the easiest, most natural politician of the three brothers. Naturally gregarious, outgoing, he thought nothing of charging up a room or a crowd by bursting into a rousing rendition of "Molly Malone" or "My Wild Irish Rose." He loved a good story, a good laugh, always tried to find a way not to take things too seriously but could bear down with amazing discipline when the moment called for it. He worked as hard as anyone around him.

The race pitted two extraordinary Irish families and political dynasties against each other. In the summer after my graduation from high school and before heading off to college, I volunteered for the Kennedy campaign. He was running against Edward McCormack, the Massachusetts attorney general and nephew of the Speaker of the U.S. House of Representatives. I started working regularly at the Tremont Street headquarters in Boston. Not to be outdone, the McCormack campaign rented an office building only a few doors down—the two biggest political families duking it out on the biggest commercial street in the city. It was a race with big stakes and national focus.

I threw myself into the campaign with all the energy and enthusiasm of an eighteen-year-old free from books and exams and about to enter the great adventure of college. Everything was new and fresh. In the beginning I worked like every other volunteer, addressing envelopes, stuffing mail, collecting signatures, running errands, sometimes pounding out hours working at one of the tables in the first-floor main entrance room. Over time I got to know some of the regular staff, particularly Terri Haddad, who worked near the volunteers on the first floor; Eddie Martin, the press secretary; Albie Cullen, who ran the volunteers; and even Ted Kennedy's brother-in-law Stephen Smith, who was basically running the show. At this early time all of these folks loomed large in the organization and seemed out of reach to the average volunteer, a category I fell into for sure, but over time, by working hard, being present and getting odd tasks done, I earned some measure of trust. I think during the whole course of the campaign I probably shook Ted's hand and said hello two or three times. I doubt very much that he remembered me at all, but that's the nature of campaigns.

In a very strange juxtaposition of my life outside the campaign with my life inside it, I actually spent more time with the president of the United States, Ted's brother John F. Kennedy, than I did with the candidate I was working for. That first meeting came about in the oddest way. Janet Auchincloss, Jackie Kennedy's half sister, had become a friend of mine. I met her through my roommate at St. Paul's, who had dated her for a while, but they had broken up—at least temporarily. Janet invited me to the family home, Hammersmith Farm in Newport, during the summer, and it turned out to be a weekend when President Kennedy was visiting to watch the America's Cup yacht races.

I remember driving down from Boston and stopping to make a phone call to tell Janet I was running late. Janet said I should hurry up because the president wanted to go out sailing and they were waiting for me to arrive. What?! The president of the United States is waiting for this wide-eyed, green young volunteer in his brother's campaign? Can't be. . . . But I got back in the car, floored it and drove like a madman, figuring that if I got stopped I would try to make the police officer believe I was going sailing with the president. If I was pulled over, I was sure to end up in the loony bin.

I arrived at the imposing driveway to Hammersmith Farm where, believe it or not, a single Secret Service guy waved me through. I drove up to the front door under the covered entryway and told one other Secret Service agent who I was and then walked into the house—no identification requested, nothing.

There was no one in the large foyer, but off to the right I could see someone in white pants and a blue polo shirt standing by the large dining room windows with a glorious view down the lawn to the water and the narrow spit that marks the entrance into Narragansett Bay and Newport. The person turned around and walked toward me, hand outstretched to say hello. It was President Kennedy. I reached out and said, "Hello, Mr. Kennedy." I did not know to call him "Mr. President." That's how fresh and naive I was. He didn't flinch but said, "Hi," and asked me what I was up to. I told him, "I'm working for your brother in the Senate race." He said, "That's terrific—I think it's going pretty well," or something close to that. Then he said, "Where are you going to college?" I told him Yale and rolled my eyes with a laugh as if to excuse myself that it wasn't Harvard. He smiled and without missing a beat said, "Oh, that's okay—I'm a Yale man myself now." He had just received his honorary degree at Yale and made his famous comment: "I now have the best of two worlds—a Harvard education and a Yale degree."

To this day I am grateful for the conversation we had and for the grace and ease the president showed to this young volunteer and friend of a relative of his. We spent a memorable afternoon on the Coast Guard yawl sailing around Narragansett Bay. I sat in the cockpit, eating lunch with the president, soaking in the conversation about politics, issues and the world. The president clearly reveled in the peacefulness of the moment. He lay in the sun, smoked a cigar and occasionally sat on the foredeck alone, thinking about God knows what. Later that day we enjoyed a wonderful dinner with the members of the family and then sat in the living room with music playing, some dancing and lots of conversation.

Still later, when I went back to the front office of the campaign, I had a story I was sure I couldn't share with anyone because, first, they probably wouldn't believe me, and second, if they did, I knew it would create a barrier between me and the folks I was working with. It was an unexpected early lesson that sometimes life puts you in situations you are just better off not talking about—they are meant for you and you alone.

One of the places I never talked about a lot was a blessing hard to describe and a privilege difficult for many to digest. I was introduced to it at three years old and it would play a key role in my life—Naushon Island. Naushon is one of the five Elizabeth Islands including Penikese Island, in Buzzards Bay off the south coast of Massachusetts. Starting at Woods Hole, situated off the mainland of Upper Cape Cod, Naushon, seven miles long and a mile and a half wide, is the first island of the five, running west from there to the small island of Pasque, then Nashawena, Cuttyhunk, where there is a small town with a few year-round residents, and, finally, Penikese. John Murray Forbes purchased Naushon in 1843 (Pasque and Nashawena followed later), and ever since then, it has been a summer gathering spot for the extended Forbes family. My mother was a goddaughter of J. M. Forbes's direct descendant William Cameron Forbes (my grandfather's cousin after whom my brother, Cam, was named) and a distant cousin herself, so we were incredibly lucky to be able to rent one house or another of the few houses built for summer occupation at the eastern end of the island. Most of the island remains as shaped by Mother Nature, with the guiding hands and labor of Forbes work parties that clear roads, cut back catbrier and act as extraordinary stewards of history. The lion's share of my initial passion for the environment, my involvement with the oceans and climate change, comes from lessons I learned on Naushon, the example I saw of the Forbes family's commitment to preserve and conserve. My mother instilled in all of us not just appreciation for the beauty and mystery of wilderness, but a deep sense of responsibility to care for it. Naushon remains an extraordinary example of responsible stewardship.

It also was—and remains—a paradise for kids. There are no cars on the island. No paved roads. Only several dirt and sand roads extending the length of the island or winding through glens and fields. There is a farm with a tractor, truck and maintenance vehicle. During our early years, there were hundreds of sheep being raised on the island. Every August there would be an enormous sheep drive from the west end of the island to the farm on the east so the sheep could be shorn. It was an island-wide activity, but you had to be twelve years old to qualify for this big event called a "sheeping." Today there is a hugely reduced, small herd of sheep, because coyotes found their way to the island and decimated the herd.

Naushon remains a place of rare beauty. The light is magical. The painter Jamie Wyeth once visited and raved to me about the quality of the light. Around every corner there is an island secret—a tree with a name, an old graveyard, a stunning beach, a grove of birches, a pasture full of horses, sheep wandering a field, a bridge over an estuary with a massive current running under it.

Throughout history, remarkable people have passed through as guests of the family. Presidents Ulysses Grant, Teddy Roosevelt, Calvin Coolidge and Bill Clinton all visited and all left hats behind, which still reside on the island. Emperor Akihito, then crown prince of Japan, came in September of 1953. Ralph Waldo Emerson's daughter married John Murray Forbes's son. Oliver Wendell Holmes visited and wrote an original poem in the guest book. Herman Melville . . . Indeed, countless artists, authors, philosophers, raconteurs, musicians and military men have spent time on the island. After World War I, General Black Jack Pershing wrote his official report on the war while staying as a guest of William Cameron Forbes at Mansion House.

Colonel Robert Gould Shaw, who led the first all-black regiment during the Civil War, spent time at Naushon and famously wrote during the war how much he wished he could be on the island at Christmastime. Soon after this letter, he was killed leading his men in an assault at the Second Battle of Fort Wagner.

Visiting Naushon was a gigantic and magical step back in time. Arriving by boat from Woods Hole, family and guests would be greeted at the dock by a collection of horses and carriages waiting to take baggage and passengers to the houses. That sight alone was enough to slow the pace of life and invite you into another world. For me and my cousins, it was a place to be safe, to be free to roam, create adventures and revel in summer. We kids would walk around for a month without wearing shoes, unless we rode horses or went to the mainland to shop. We sailed, swam, caught shrimp, dug clams, collected mussels, fished, hiked, picnicked, sang at bonfires, played charades and capture the flag, aquaplaned, water-skied, raced model boats, cleared brush, jumped off a bridge into the racing current, did treasure hunts, listened to scary ghost stories from older cousins—there was limitless testing of the imagination—especially in a world without television, which it was and, for the most part, still is. As I said—paradise on earth.

CHAPTER 2

Bright College Years

I ARRIVED IN NEW Haven in my 1962 Volkswagen Beetle—the beautiful original—chockablock full of the stuff you think you need but could do without. Driving an early Bug was a unique experience. With its tiny cockpit and front end sloping away from you, it felt like an overpowered toy, leaving little between you and the road—or trucks—in front of you. It was like driving an expanded go-kart, which is why it was fun. The trip to New Haven was an exercise in momentum management. I would floor the accelerator the minute I hit the Massachusetts Turnpike and, except for the most urgent traffic situation, basically not let it off the floor until the exit for New Haven. Sometimes you felt like you needed to get out and push the car up a hill, but it was reliable and affordable. I am grateful I never tested the crash resistance.

I unloaded the car amid the chaos of parents and furniture moving onto the Old Campus, where all the freshmen lived. I was assigned to Bingham Hall, with an entryway opposite the statue of Nathan Hale, a reminder to all the hazards of rebellions. I met up with my roommate, Dan Barbiero, a friend already from St. Paul's. Danny and I remained together as roommates throughout Yale and we have remained lifelong friends.

A steady, calm soul, Dan was a great check on some of my enthusiasm. He had grown up in North Valley Stream, Long Island, a member of a proud and close-knit Italian American family. His father was a wonderful, engaging patriarch who had worked through the labyrinth of New York politics from assemblyman to district court judge. Danny was musically gifted and had won a coveted place in the St. Thomas Choir School—a forty-boy school for St. Thomas Church on Fifth Avenue in Manhattan. He sang in the choir there as both he and I did at St. Paul's. He was also a talented pianist who could play almost anything by ear. I remember he would sit for hours at the piano in the Jonathan Edwards Common Room, playing for his own pleasure. After Yale, and after the Marines and Vietnam, where he served with distinction, he took time off to decompress, during which he spent a few years working as a recording engineer in New York City, where he recorded Stevie Wonder's *Innervisions* and John Lennon's *Mind Games* before going on to a successful career in real estate and finance.

Freshman year flashed by. The transition from St. Paul's was seamless. I was used to a campus and to making choices about study and play. I joined a few extracurricular activities, enjoyed the parties, learned how to make the most of weekends and occasionally studied. Sadly, I was not a hugely motivated student at that point in my life and I'm definitely not proud of that. Someone should have kicked me in the butt to remind me why I was there, but no one did. I have often wondered why I was so indifferent to the academic opportunity of Yale.

At one time I blamed it on St. Paul's but, on reflection, that wasn't fair. I think I just needed a strong mentor who would motivate and inspire me early on to understand and value the importance, immediacy and excitement of history or literature that seems so obvious and compelling now. Today I can't read enough or narrow down my ever-growing list of books to be read. It's particularly fun to pick up a book first read long ago and now notice things I missed previously or even understand better themes that once seemed remote or incomprehensible. The virtues of age and experience.

Nowadays, I find myself dueling with the crush of time and the desire to know more than I do. I see and feel connections to history and life that I never felt while at Yale. I know that's not unusual. What I too often saw as a chore back then, I now see as a window on the world that those college years always were, an invaluable insight into human behavior that is timeless and fascinating. I would have been the perfect candidate for what is now called a "gap" year. I kick myself to think that the time I now steal to spend luxuriating and learning by reading books and articles was available to me every day of those four years. It wasn't until law school that my brain really switched on and I began to learn to think.

In October of freshman year, President Kennedy came to town to give a speech literally just outside our room on the New Haven Green. He was campaigning for Senator Abe Ribicoff and the Democratic ticket, helping the powerful party boss John Bailey deliver the state. We gathered on the green to listen to the speech. The president mounted a podium just below our building and spoke, the familiar accent filling the speakers, drowning out a few Republican hecklers. One heckler particularly caught my attention. I went over to ask him to quiet down and saw Danny standing with him. Danny introduced me to Harvey Bundy, nephew of McGeorge "Mac"

Bundy, President Kennedy's national security advisor, and Bill Bundy, the assistant secretary of state for Far East affairs. Evidently Harvey came from the sole Republican wing of the family. I confess I was momentarily annoyed, but it was quickly forgotten.

Harvey became a close friend of Danny's and mine. We drafted him to be our third roommate for the next year when we moved into Jonathan Edwards College. Harvey hailed from Manchester, Massachusetts, where his family had resided for several generations. Unlike the majority of our class, Harvey seemed to have come to Yale knowing exactly what he wanted to do in life. He was whip smart, great with numbers and already tracking a career in business. I was always impressed by how clear Harvey was about the road he was on and how disciplined he was in pursuit of his choices. No surprise, he met his wife-to-be, Blakely, freshman year. He knew almost immediately—or so it seemed—this was the person for him. They pretty much moved in together—as much as one could or did back then—so that in effect there were four roommates, three from Yale and one from Wheaton. Harvey and Blakely married right after our June graduation in August 1966. That fall, the newlyweds headed off to Tuck Business School at Dartmouth, and from there, they moved to Chicago, where Blakely was raised. Harvey eventually became the chief analyst for William Blair and Company in Chicago, where he and Blakely live to this day, reveling in their grandchildren.

Our freshman year, the Harvard-Yale football game was in Cambridge. I drove up in the Bug, got outrageously inebriated in the stands of the stadium, somehow found my way to campus, where at some point in the evening I passed out. When I came to I figured it was time to go home. I got in the Bug and started to drive, when I at least had the presence of mind to know that this was not a good idea. I was not going to make it home. So I somehow parked the car and made my way back to my cousin's room in Eliot House, where I fell asleep among the many making a regular parade to throw up in the bathroom.

When I woke up in the morning, I smelled bad enough to scare myself. I drove home to Groton, where I worked through a three-day hangover. I am happy to say that only once since then—in Vietnam—did I ever pass out from drinking again, and I have never had even a sip of the same hard liquor since 1962. The aroma alone is enough to bring back bad memories.

Sometime in that first fall at Yale, I met David Thorne. We were walking on the Old Campus near our rooms. The conversation quickly focused on his attendance at Groton School and his family's life in Rome, Italy, where his dad was the publisher of the *Rome Daily American*. David was the first person I met at Yale who shared the experience of going to school in Switzerland while his family was overseas. We quickly compared notes only to find we had remarkably similar reactions to being sent to boarding school abroad at a very young age. Given the commonalities in our backgrounds—the European connection, our passion for soccer, our high school experiences and a similar view of the world—we struck up a fast and close friendship.

Over spring vacation of freshman year, David and I decided to make the first of what would become many trips together. The civil rights movement was increasingly grabbing our attention as marches or sit-ins challenged the shame of segregation. It was hard to believe that we lived in a country that asked a black man to go fight for his country but wouldn't allow that same person to vote, or go to a certain school, or use a bathroom or lunch counter the same way whites did. I still find it hard to digest that in my lifetime we were a segregated nation.

David and I decided to take a spring break trip through the segregated South to Florida and then race back to Vermont for a few days of skiing. It was more than slightly crazy, but many of us enjoying the first freedoms of college wore that label proudly.

We crossed the line between North and South, where we both saw "White Only" and "No Colored" signs for the first time in our lives. It was incredibly jarring. At St. Paul's, in the Senior Year Speaking Contest, I had delivered the winning speech in a hard-hitting summary of events in the South. I had talked about the "revolution" in our own country, but now, a year later, here I was walking into a building where a "White Only" sign was prominently displayed, seeing human beings actually forced to separate on the basis of skin color, taking in the expressionless look on the faces of the African Americans I saw go into "their" facilities—it all turned my stomach and made me wonder even more how this could be the United States of America in 1963.

Through North Carolina and Georgia and into Florida this scene repeated itself. It seemed impossible to me that anyone thought they could prevent the inexorable yearning of people to be free, to enjoy the same full rights as others in the same country living under the same Constitution. Little did I know what I would witness in the turbulent and violent next years. The screaming, mad-dog looks of white students shouting insults at young black women trying to walk into school, protected by state troopers or federal troops, infuriated me. And when Bull Connor unleashed the dogs and billy clubs, I felt ashamed for all of us.

• • •

DURING THE SUMMER of 1963, right after my freshman year, I came mighty close to being killed. It was luck that I wasn't. Harvey and I had flown to London to pick up the Austin-Healey 3000 his father had given him in recognition of his successful transition from Groton to Yale and the completion of his freshman year. We planned to drive through England and France—and who knows where else. We picked up the car and drove 45 mph for five hundred miles, because in those days cars needed to be broken in. We had the car serviced after the break-in period and then departed for the ferry in Portsmouth. From Le Havre we drove to Paris for Bastille Day and then on to Switzerland, Liechtenstein and Austria, driving through the night to arrive in the morning in Lech, where I had learned to ski. I wanted to surprise my boyhood ski instructor, Othmar Strolz, but we arrived so early that we had several hours to kill.

Instead, as dawn lit up the mountains, we decided to climb one. For several hours we struggled up a steep and unbeaten path. When we seemed to have gone high enough and killed enough time, and could see the car as a miniature in the road below, we turned around and plunged downhill, jumping and leaping from foothold to foothold. It was exhilarating and exhausting.

We then paid a wonderful early-morning visit to Othmar, an extraordinary man who had become far more than a ski instructor. He was a philosopher of the mountains and life. He loved the fun that came with skiing, but he taught me to respect the power and majesty of the mountains. He would tweak me when I got tired, saying, "Johnny, life is hard in the mountains," goading me on to find more reserves in my body. I owe Othmar a lot for the joy of climbing well above the lifts to find pure, virgin, granular spring snow and then the rush of swooping down from one gully to another and winding up breathless on the valley floor, exhilarated by the vertical descent.

Othmar gave me one other memorable, precious moment, which I have passed on to my children. Climb to the top of a mountain and just sit there. When the heaving of your breath has calmed down, stop and listen carefully to the silence. He is the only person who taught me to listen to silence.

From there we went to Monte Carlo and then drove up to Brittany to spend time at Les Essarts. One night I had driven to Dinan, a beautiful, historic town twenty miles from the family house. I was accompanied by Peter Kornbluh, a classmate of Harvey's and mine who was staying with us briefly at Les Essarts. We were driving back from a nightclub and were almost home, perhaps three miles from the house. As we approached a relatively pronounced left curve in the road that I knew pretty well, a car came from the other direction somewhat jutting into our lane. I moved over slightly to the right, and before I knew it my right wheels were trapped in the hedgerow ditch that ran alongside the road. The dirt began to pile up in front of the car, and suddenly I felt the back of the car lift up and move end over end to the front. We were flipping over. I felt the centrifugal force push against the seat belts with the dreadful realization that we were crashing and were about to be upside down. I have no recollection of how we landed or what happened as we hit the ground. I do think I heard a massive scraping sound and then a skid along the road for a few yards, followed by total silence.

When I came to, I heard people yelling that the car might blow up. I reached for Peter but didn't feel him next to me. I undid my seat belt, felt my body drop to the ground and crawled out of the car. I walked a few yards away and lay down on the ground. I heard people again talking about how the car might catch on fire. I got up and walked back to the car to take the keys out of the ignition. I checked on Peter, who was sitting on the ground too but seemed to be okay. He was incredibly calm and collected. Then I lay down again and waited for an ambulance to come.

I never feared that I was so wounded I was in jeopardy, but I was furious at the oncoming car, horrified for Harvey at what had happened to his beautiful Austin-Healey. It was totaled. We were quickly transported to the hospital. Peter was released almost immediately, but the doctors kept me for an extra day, during which a regular parade of my cousins marched through the Dinard hospital to inspect the example of what not to do.

A few weeks later I returned to the States to start fall term. I have never stopped thinking how lucky I was to be alive. I had flipped over and landed upside down in a convertible. If my head had been in the wrong place as we went over the front end, it would have been crushed in the landing. Or Peter or I could have been thrown out of the car and been killed or paralyzed. For years, because of this or Vietnam or any number of other close calls, I have never stopped being grateful for the grace of God that spared me. It was the first time I became aware I was lucky to be living extra days.

Freshman year I had avoided soccer in order to focus on ice hockey. I made the freshman hockey team, played center on the second line, got my numerals at the end of the season, but in the end, I decided I missed playing soccer. So in the fall of sophomore year, I tried out for varsity soccer. David Thorne and I had missed connecting during the summer, but he invited me to his family's place on Long Island before reporting to practice in

New Haven, where he was pretty much assured a place on the team, having played as a freshman.

In late August I rolled up to the Thorne house in my borrowed family VW bus. I had so much junk I was taking to Yale that it could only fit in the bus—plus my faithful friend Faustus the parakeet, who lived with us freshman year. I was a little embarrassed by my traveling circus—but not that much. David walked out of the house to greet me, but my eyes were on a dark-haired girl in a small bikini who walked out behind him. "John, this is my sister Judy—Judy, my friend John Kerry." I was instantly intrigued. More powerfully so when we cruised around the property with Judy hanging on to the roof rack while standing on the rear bumper of the moon-equipped VW David and I had driven down south, all the while singing "500 Miles" at the top of her lungs. I was impressed and curious about this woman who lived in New York and Italy.

This was my first encounter with Julia Thorne. We saw each other a few times in the course of sophomore year. I grew more interested, but our lives were on totally different schedules, she working in Italy for RAI, the Italian TV station, and me stuck at Yale, three years from even beginning a life beyond school. She was jetting back and forth to Rome. I was living in New Haven, making friends of a lifetime in a small universe. Sophomore year was punctuated with sporadic Julia sightings and brief rendezvous that just whetted my appetite.

At Yale, the tryouts for the soccer team were brutal. We were doing double practices, meaning two sessions a day. Between the morning and afternoon sessions my muscles would tighten up, and by the time evening rolled around, I could barely walk. It was even worse the next morning, in part because I had shown up in the worst shape I'd ever been in as a result of my accident in France just a month before returning to school. Somehow, I made the team.

One of the unexpected benefits of playing soccer was reuniting with Dick Pershing. We had last seen each other at Fessenden School. Dick had gone on to Phillips Exeter Academy and then a postgraduate year at Lawrenceville. Dick shared with David Thorne and me the experience of a too-young exposure to boarding school in Switzerland. All of us had been introduced to soccer there—football, as they called it, the Beautiful Game. I didn't have much interaction with him freshman year, but now that we were playing on the same team, we began to hang out. "Persh," as we called him, was an incredibly gifted, natural athlete. He was also something of an iron man, capable of drinking beer, smoking cigarettes, staying up late and partying and yet never giving out on the playing field, always running as hard and playing as energetically as anyone. None of us knew how he did it. He was also a great prankster, livening up practice with antics that kept even our taciturn Scottish coach smiling. One day, we memorably stuffed Persh into a laundry hamper, carried him out to the field on our shoulders while chanting some absurd made-up war chant on the way and deposited the basket in the middle of the field to watch the top slowly open and Persh rise to cheers and jeers. The moment was pure nonsense, but the smiles and laughter were worth the absurdity.

Friday, November 22, marked the beginning of Harvard-Yale weekend. It began innocently enough. A headline in the *Yale Daily News* was calculated to get your attention: "Miss USA to Smooch Smoochers When 'News' [the *Yale Daily*] Beats Harvard." A picture of Miss USA made sure you at least glanced at the story.

Sometime in the midmorning, I took the athletic department bus out to the Yale Bowl to change into my soccer uniform and warm up for the game against Harvard—the most important game for either team. Beat Harvard and you ended the season on the right note.

Autumn was at its New England best, boasting a clear, bright, crisp fall day. I was excited to be playing my first varsity matchup with Harvard. A dynamic Nigerian named Chris Ohiri played for Harvard. He was a formidable player, the high scorer of the Ivy League, reputed to have knocked out a goalie with the force of one of his kicks.

Sometime after 1:30, I was substituted and returned to the bench. We were about twenty-five minutes into the game when a murmur went through the crowd. It built to a crescendo that ended with voices calling out, "The president's been shot!" The words struck like a shot itself. No one seemed to believe it at first, even as the words were repeated endlessly.

At 1:36, ABC Radio issued a national bulletin: President Kennedy had been seriously wounded when shots had been fired at his motorcade. Four minutes later, CBS TV followed with the first nationally televised report of an assassination attempt. Before long there was complete consternation in the stands, a kind of controlled chaos, with stunned faces looking around blankly, clearly not knowing what to do next. It was impossible to focus on the game or even imagine that we were going to play on.

President Kennedy was pronounced dead at Parkland Hospital in Dallas, Texas, at 1:00 p.m., Central Standard Time—2:00 p.m. our time. The news was incomprehensible, and we all looked at each other for answers and consolation.

Until I sat down to write this account I did not remember who won the game. I didn't even remember if we finished the game. I looked in the *Yale*

Daily News archives and learned that we lost 3–2. The story said, "The game was not cancelled because it had been in progress for 25 minutes when President Kennedy's assassination first became known."

From the minute we returned to our room after the game, Danny, Harvey and I spent the next three or four days hardly moving away from the small black-and-white TV in the living room of our suite. We were transfixed. Each image from those sorrowful days was indelibly imprinted in our minds forever—the live shooting of Lee Harvey Oswald by Jack Ruby; the president's coffin lying in state in the White House and the Capitol; the Kennedy family and world leaders marching behind the caisson; John Jr. saluting his father from the steps of the cathedral.

My cousin Serita Winthrop, who was attending college nearby, knew I had met the president and worked for Ted Kennedy, so she jumped in her car and came to Yale to share in the shock of what had happened. We walked around and around the immediate streets surrounding the college, talking into the wee hours of the morning, trying to understand what had happened. I remember saying to her that no matter what, we all had an obligation to work to make this right—whatever it took. That is the night I made a commitment to myself that I would pursue a life in public affairs. I didn't know what I would do or how I would make a difference, but I vowed I would.

As THE SUMMER of 1965 approached, I was already thinking about graduation one year away. While I didn't know specifically what I wanted to do afterward, I was pretty certain this would be my last "free" summer, a time when I could indulge my thirst for the "freedom of the road"—an instinct I first enjoyed riding my bike in Berlin and later through England and France.

I had worked my tail off the previous summer, selling *Collier's Encyclopedia* door-to-door in Massachusetts. It was tedious, even hard work, walking a neighborhood in the dead of summer with dogs and kids nipping at your heels, carrying a briefcase filled with demo books and performing the carefully choreographed presentation Collier's field office taught its salespeople to employ.

There I was, decked out in jacket and tie, briefcase and all, walking door-to-door in unfamiliar neighborhoods. I felt there were two worlds: the one where they were enjoying a warm summer's night at the drive-in and the one where I was knocking like crazy on doors, waiting to see whether an unfriendly oddity answered and rudely sent me packing.

As tedious and challenging as it was, selling encyclopedias was a wonderful "people" education. We salesmen would each develop our own style, plugging in variations on the rote sales pitch we had been taught. We would do everything possible to convince Mom or Dad that these reservoirs of knowledge were going to empower their kids to do anything they wanted. It's hard even to imagine this in the current world of the internet, but without the modern-day availability of unlimited information, having your own encyclopedia was a gold mine. I was able to spice up my presentation by talking about my own experience with our encyclopedia at home in Washington. I did love it and used it all the time. The reality is, without the internet or a trip to the library, it provided an instantaneous journey to far-off places. My conviction was genuine.

I learned a lot from this job. Walking into someone's home unannounced—if they let me in—was an amazing inside view of a daily, completely impromptu slice of life. In fact, just getting into a house required establishing some measure of trust. The presentation—depending on how far you got—took from forty-five minutes to an hour. During this time, there were usually a dozen interruptions for dogs, children, friends and personal stories. Sometimes people wanted to unload about their lives or life itself. Later, when I was running for office, I thought about the lessons I learned on this job. It taught me a lot about listening, watching body language, understanding someone's realities and knowing when to fold, pack up my bags and leave. It was good training for anyone.

The Gulf of Tonkin—both the incident and the congressional resolution—had been in the headlines just a few weeks before I came back to New Haven for early soccer practice in late August of '64. But I didn't dwell on it. I had a season to get ready for, friends to catch up with and a long list of extracurricular activities. Besides, it was a presidential election year. Lyndon Johnson was poised for a historic landslide against Barry Goldwater, and Johnson's words on the evening news were crystal clear: "We are not about to send American boys nine or ten thousand miles from home to do what Asian boys ought to be doing for themselves."

By the spring of '65 he was doing exactly that—and my circle of close friends had decisions to make in a hurry. Suddenly, the draft had meaning for all of us. Our lives were thrown topsy-turvy. A whole lot of guys who hadn't considered the immediacy of military service now confronted that choice. I was one of them—a distracted student who had thought about journalism or business or possibly the Foreign Service—and suddenly I had decisions to ponder. Graduate school, study abroad? There were options and each of us thought about them, but ultimately, many of us came back to a shared belief: We were kids of World War II parents. We'd been Cold War teenagers. We believed in the ethos of the age, of President Kennedy's challenge, put forward in his 1961 inaugural address, to "pay any price, bear any burden."

But first, with my stash of encyclopedia earnings from the summer before, David Thorne and I decided we would go to London, pick up a cheap set of wheels and drive where whim and fancy took us. We had already planned to visit Spain, which neither of us had been to, but we also had the specific notion of taking in the Festival of Saint Fermín in Pamplona. I wanted to tune into the nostalgia of *The Sun Also Rises*, go to some of the places Hemingway had described and see how they measured up. I had read a lot about the running of the bulls. Experiencing a few bullfights would satisfy a lot of curiosity, an excursion into a different, romantic slice of life. With responsibility looming ahead, we reasoned that soon we might not have similar opportunities to be quite so footloose. So off we went.

Once we arrived in London we embarked on a search for the perfect ride. David had the brilliant idea of trying to find a retired London taxi and make that our traveling home. There was something magical about the look and sound, and the spacious passenger area would make it perfect for piling in people and stuff. Besides, how many London cabs have ever been seen outside London? The idea was appealing to our wallet and our vanity.

With a few phone calls and several cabbie conversations, we found the London graveyard for taxis. Spread out before us in a remote London suburb was this huge lot of black cabs supposedly in their final resting place. The lot master thought we were nuts, but he helped us pick out a beast with soul and an engine that worked.

We tooled around London for a couple of days, waving off people who tried to hail us. We wanted to get to Le Mans for the "24 Hours," the world's oldest sports car endurance race, then in its forty-second year and still going strong today. One night around midnight, realizing we had some ground to cover to make the race, we looked at each other and simultaneously decided we had to get out of London immediately. Our further adventures needed to begin.

I remember driving out of Knightsbridge and Mayfair almost precisely at midnight. David drove the leg from London to Dover while I slept curled up on the comfortable back seat of the cab. To this day I remember the smell of leather and the gurgling chugging of the engine. We had made a reservation on the first ferry of the morning. It was a blustery day, with a roiling, churning sea—a classic channel crossing. Literally, as fast as the ferry cleared the breakwater, the motion of the boat became so violent and so irregular that myriads of people were queuing up for the loos in order to throw up. The whole ferry became an upchuck disaster zone. David and I were both seasoned sailors so we luckily avoided seasickness, but the stench of vomit and the pools of puke covering the floor in and near the toilets were enough to inspire abandoning ship. I have never before or after seen so many people throwing up at one time.

Arrival at Le Havre in France did not come too soon. From there we drove directly to Le Mans, listened to the deafening roar of engines well into the night and early morning, and then drove quietly to Les Essarts, where we intended to stay for a few days before heading south to Pamplona and the Costa del Sol of Spain. We set up a deck chair next to the driver's seat in the cab and it became the seat of choice. It was a luxury to sit with feet extended out onto the left fender, reading a book or watching the countryside roll by in the open air. I was reading a Winston Churchill biography, which prompted us to detour slightly to take in the invasion beaches of Normandy en route to Les Essarts.

David had never been to these beaches. I had been privileged to go several times, beginning with the visits with my family when we first came to Europe.

The cemetery on the Omaha Beach bluff, a patch of deeded American land in France, is sacred. The story of D-Day is one of an extraordinary gift of freedom and sacrifice. It takes my breath away. I would soon learn what it is like to be shot at, even to know you will be shot at well before the ambush takes place, but to this day I am convinced that the unknown element of a shot that comes from a mangrove or bunker on a river in Vietnam is light-years away from the experience of knowing that at any moment a door will drop on a tiny boat and half the people—perhaps all—who are with you will be dead in seconds. Think about it. Think about what it's like to see a whole Higgins boat, a landing craft, next to you blown up as you approach the beach. Think about the huge bluffs ahead of you in the haze of smoke from weapons seemingly everywhere, with gigantic concrete fortresses, each filled with machine guns, mortars and artillery. Think about being pinned down and trying to find cover where it is nearly nonexistent. Still, those guys on that beach pushed on, up the bluff, over the hill and painstakingly, ultimately, on to Berlin. Almost 2,500 Americans died on Omaha and Utah Beaches and in the paratroop drops behind the lines just on D-Day alone. David and I moved quietly among the crosses and Stars of David, in total awe of what that small piece of America means to all of us.

Next stop was Les Essarts. Within days of our arrival the taxi had acquired a name—Baxer. It was derived from the hit song "The Name Game," which had come out the year before. "Taxi" produced "Taxi, Taxi, bo-baxi, banana-fana fo-faxi, fee-fi-mo-maxi—Taxi!" "Baxi" became "Baxer." And, yes, we were slightly nuts, but we were as untethered as we'd imagined and hoped we'd be at the outset of this exotic adventure.

Baxer gained an immediate, strong following at Les Essarts. On one occasion, about ten cousins piled in the back on the floor, the jump seats and the bench seat. We were like the clown car in the circus, and before long we *were* a circus—pointless jokes, laughing hysterically, being generally obnoxious. We were happily cruising along when Baxer decided to stop and freeze in the middle of the road. The emergency brake wire had snapped, engaging the brake in a locked on position. Baxer just plain wasn't moving anywhere. Traffic started to pile up behind, in front and beside us since we were in the middle of a major intersection.

Pandemonium ensued. Cousins piled out trying desperately to manage the emotions of stymied drivers who had gotten out of their cars and were surrounding Baxer and us. Epithets were flying. I left the task of responding to the angry motorists to the cousins who spoke perfect French. One cousin was out in the middle of the street trying to direct traffic around us, her arms waving in one direction and then the next, looking more like a cheerleader than a traffic cop. Whatever she was doing contributed mightily to the chaos.

During this circus going on around us, we discovered two huge proboscises protruding beneath Baxer's chassis. Needless to say, despite the fact that whatever was down there was sort of tubular in shape, someone immediately joked about Baxer's big balls. We found a way to lower them, which lifted the rear wheels off the ground. Then we were able to get under the car and free the emergency brake. We pushed Baxer to the side of the road, where the brake was repaired; exactly how, I have no memory. We avoided bodily harm by hordes of extremely upset French drivers wondering what kind of British assholes had upset their day. All in all, a great adventure, and we avoided American culpability by hiding behind Baxer's classic British body.

From Les Essarts, with a few stops along the way, we drove south to the Pyrenees and on to Pamplona, where David and I would see if Hemingway was right about the bulls, the bullfights and the fiesta. How many people have made that same voyage, I don't know, but I am sure that nobody had more fun.

The Festival of Saint Fermín began in medieval times and included bullfights even then. Running with the bulls started around the seventeenth century, and the first bullring was built in the middle of the nineteenth century.

There were always foreigners taking part in the festivities, but the main attraction became hugely popular after Hemingway discovered the fiesta. Ever since the publication of *The Sun Also Rises*, the more modern festival has steadily developed into the extravaganza it is today.

When David and I arrived in 1965, the fiesta still held much of its original charm. I think we were up most of the night, eating, drinking and carousing with people we had never met before. There were students, the young and old, tourists from all over Europe, the United States and Canada, and, of course, loads of Spaniards who delighted in this centuries-old celebration.

The spirit was contagious—and exhausting. In the wee hours of the morning we decided for sure we would run with the bulls. We found our way to the beginning of the run, where hundreds of young guys were decked out in their white pants and shirts with red bandannas. David and I were conspicuous for our blue jeans and denim shirts and lack of bandannas.

The bulls were due to be released from their pen at 7:00 a.m. We originally positioned ourselves at the beginning of the narrow street heading toward the bullring, but then we felt we wouldn't get the full run so we moved closer to the paddock where they release the bulls. We thought that because we were training for our senior-year soccer season, we were both in good shape and could outrun any bulls. Little did we know what was in store for us.

A rocket flare was fired into the air warning of the release of the bulls. There was a stir among the runners, with some starting to take off. I remember saying to David not to go yet because we'd get too far ahead. Right then, a second flare went off signaling the release of all the bulls from the pen. We started running. I turned around and saw these muscular black bulls charging up the hill. I yelled at David to run for his life. I thought we were surely going to die.

I glanced back several times while running at full speed, only to see that I was definitely not going to outrun these monsters. I began checking exit strategies. Several doorways were already crammed with people. Nowhere to go. I had lost track of David and was certain I was imminently going to be gored, so I leaped for the next doorway, bounced off the bodies already jammed in it and fell to the sidewalk. As I looked at the horde of four-legged beasts hurling toward me, I curled up into the smallest fetal ball I could and waited for the worst.

Lo and behold, the bulls were not yet isolated or distracted, and they were so fixated on rushing along that they jumped right over me. I looked up to see the entire herd had gone past. David was off to the right of me on the other side of the street. He had succeeded in getting crunched with other bodies into a doorway, protecting himself and his camera. Not wanting to miss out on getting into the bullring, I got up and immediately started sprinting after them—an entirely new twist on running with the bulls. In fact, at one point, I grabbed the tail of one of the oxen released to guide the bulls, and I got pulled along. I was the last person to make it into the ring when they shut the doors behind me.

When the bulls run into the ring, they run straight through and into a corral where they will await the bullfights that evening. Meanwhile, the bullring fills up with the runners, who await the subsequent release of small bulls or cows who charge through the crowd, throwing anyone in their way up in the air to the delight of the spectators. David made it into the arena with a second wave of runners after the bulls were in the corral. We were standing there comparing notes when a small bull with tennis balls on its horns was released into the melee. It charged full speed into the arena. We watched while one person got pummeled with a direct hit. He flew across the bullring and lay motionless on the ground. We watched people tossed above the crowd, one after the other, to descend to a crescendo of olés and cheers. At one point I had a near miss but brushed against the passing bull and got covered in bullshit—a probably worthy metaphor for the whole scene. It was great fun, assuming you were not among the injured.

We were young and on an adventure. There is no good rationale for wanting to do such a dangerous thing. It's emotional and romantic and, yes, there are other adjectives, but of course there's always a potential consequence of daring to do something risky. But that's life . . . there are plenty of things we choose to do that don't make sense. This obviously was one of those escapades. To this day, I am glad we did it, but I have no intention of recommending it to my grandchildren.

The best was yet to come. After changing out of our putrid clothing, we explored Pamplona, ate a great lunch of paella with an appropriate amount of wine. Then we joined the throngs heading to the bullring for the evening fights. It was a first for me, and I was curious. I had read a lot but never seen a live fight. Bullfighting today is controversial. Some traditional sites have banned it—Barcelona for one—only to have courts overrule the decision. I was fascinated by bullfighting and wanted to understand the various primal forces that were at play in the course of this no-holds-barred public display of man against beast. Could the artistry of the matador be so powerful that it superseded or rendered inconsequential any bloodlust in the spectators? I cannot deny I find aspects of the ritual—the courage, the grace and the metaphors—all intriguing, but I understand the dissenters. On this evening, in this particular place, however, there were no dissenters. The arena was jammed. The excitement level at a fever pitch.

I believe the matador was Manuel Cano Ruiz—El Pireo. He enthralled the crowd, putting on a display of elegance and abandon that kept our hearts in our throats, the olés rising in the dusk with increasing intensity. The whole stadium swayed with every pass, a low-throated olé growing into a massive shout of approval for bull and man. Together, bull and matador performed pass after pass as if choreographed. The courage and daring of each matched the other. At one point, El Pireo was down on his knees, drawing the bull between him and the wall of the arena, with not a millimeter margin of error. His passes were each closer than the last, each performed with the elegance of a ballet, with bull and matador both executing their moves with determination. In the end, you could almost say there was a level of mutual respect.

When the fight was over the arena exploded in thunderous applause. Seat cushions were thrown from every level, piling up in the arena. Live chickens, roses, hats—all found their way to the sandy ground. Nothing was spared. Then, unsatiated, the crowd itself spilled into the arena, placed the matador on its shoulders, and proceeded to march him to a series of bars, where he was serenaded with drinks raised on high. It was an evening of complete abandon.

I don't know who lasts for seven days at the festival, but I know we didn't. We decamped and headed for the Costa del Sol and its beaches, sun, water and no threat of bulls. After a few welcome days of genuine R&R, we headed back to Les Essarts via the most scenic, restful route we could find. There we settled in for a period, until David drove Baxer to the Thorne home in Italy. Within a few days Julia came from Italy to visit Les Essarts for the first time. We shared an extraordinary time exploring Brittany, enjoying the routine of Les Essarts and visiting the local markets. Too quickly the days of August slipped by. Julia flew back to Rome. I headed back to the States to spend some time with my family, then off to Yale for senior year.

CHAPTER 3

Raising My Right Hand

MY FATHER WAS one of the very first cadets in 1939 who volunteered to fly in Europe. Even though tuberculosis kept him from combat, I still cherished the creased black-and-white photo of him in his Army Air Corps aviator gear and loved the story of my mother volunteering as a nurse to treat the refugees at Montparnasse before the Nazis rolled into the city. At Yale in 1965, my friends and I were still definitively the children of the Greatest Generation. They, and their times, passed on to us, almost unconsciously but inescapably, a sense of responsibility. We shared their idealism about service, duty and country. But we were only just beginning to focus on Vietnam. In the fall of 1965, we had questions but not objections. For all the back-and-forth in long discussions that went on most nights, for any flirtations with graduate school or studying abroad or time spent parsing the implications of the draft, when it came right down to it, my friends David Thorne, Dick Pershing—the grandson of General Black Jack Pershing, who had served as the commander of the American Expeditionary Force in World War I—Danny Barbiero and others felt compelled to serve.

In my limited exposure to the war while at Yale, two men in particular influenced me. As I have mentioned, my roommate Harvey Bundy was the nephew of McGeorge and Bill Bundy—two standouts among President Kennedy's "best and the brightest." The Bundys were often hard to tell apart, with their round faces, slicked hair and thick glasses, but that's where the comparisons ended.

I'd met McGeorge in Washington, D.C., when Harvey and I went there to secure speakers for the Yale Political Union. He insisted we call him "Mac," even though he was a famous presidential advisor who had lunch with the president every Tuesday. For all his serious public demeanor, he was pretty laid-back and funny in our meeting. As he showed us the Oval Office, he joked about our standing in the center of power. We also saw his office with his desk stacked high with papers and cables, evidence of what many called a "miniature State Department" run out of his cramped space in the bowels of 1600 Pennsylvania Avenue. Mac was a man of enormous intellect—and he knew it. When he was an undergraduate at Yale, he wrote on an English test that the question was silly, answered his own question instead and still passed.

Bill was no intellectual slouch but a little harder to get to know. He kept up the same buttoned-down appearance as Mac. He could famously dance the Charleston and do a brilliant imitation of his colleagues. The only thing you didn't want to get wrong in front of Bill was politics. He was a Democrat down to his toes. When a newspaper once mixed up the Bundy brothers' politics, Bill called and demanded a correction.

While serving as assistant secretary of state for Far Eastern affairs, he visited Yale to deliver a speech. Afterward, he hung out in our room and drank a few beers with us. We grilled him about his perceptions of Vietnam. Nothing is more important, he said. Vietnam is the domino theory in action. He also told us that we were critical to this effort. The United States needed its young men to go serve abroad in the armed forces. "This is the thing to do, boys," he said. "We need you." Both Bundys left us with a personal sense of responsibility to serve.

The question I was wrestling with wasn't so much whether to serve, but which service. I have vivid memories of a few recent graduates returning for a weekend to visit with friends or take in a hockey game. I asked them about the choices they made. Each said the same thing: "Look, you're better off choosing the service you want to go into than just getting drafted." I'd always loved the ocean, ships and boats of almost any kind. I had been around the sea all my life. The die was cast. In the early fall of 1965, during the first semester of my senior year, I decided to apply to Officer Candidate School. Given the draft, getting into OCS had become more competitive. It felt like applying to college all over again but with even more paperwork. Happily, I was accepted. On February 18, 1966, I raised my right hand and took the oath to enlist in the U.S. Naval Reserve.

As senior year chugged along, Vietnam crept more and more into our conversations—as a question, as an issue and, for many of us, a possible destination. Draft cards were now being burned on campuses. Midterms brought headlines about the Battle of Ia Drang Valley. We wondered how both sides could claim victory when American firepower was so dominant. As we headed into Christmas, in order to give diplomacy a chance, President Johnson announced a temporary halt to Operation Rolling Thunder— our sustained aerial bombardment of North Vietnam.

As for me, I was heeding the words of Mark Twain, who said, "Never let school get in the way of an education." I took those words to heart, even as we crept collectively closer to graduation, when we would exchange our mortarboards for helmets. I was consumed by a wonderful distraction: flying an airplane, practicing takeoffs and landings out at Tweed Airport, three miles outside New Haven.

I had grown up on stories about my father in the Army Air Corps. When I first arrived at Yale in '62, I learned that as World War I broke out, a group of students formed the first Yale flying club and volunteered to become America's first naval aviation unit. They were our eyes in the skies, scouting enemy troop movements, locating mines, tracking submarines. On November 14, 1916, the *Yale Daily News* said they were doing the "work of the pioneer." Because they believed they had a responsibility to country, some gave their lives to a cause bigger than any of them as individuals.

Inspired by these early pioneers, by my father and by my friend and classmate Fred Smith, the future founder of FedEx, who already had his pilot's license, I asked my parents for flying lessons as a graduation present. After a little hemming and hawing, they agreed. I think I made it hard for my father to say no. Getting a license required forty hours of instruction, a combination of learning landings and takeoffs, regulations, and cross-country and instrument flying. I loved every minute of it. The precision, the navigating, the test of crosswinds and landings—they all combined to appeal to boyish interests in all things with an engine and controls. I hate to say it, but the premise of the gift—graduation—was almost sidetracked by the gift itself. I wasn't studying hard and wound up graduating with the worst one-year record of my four years.

As if learning to fly wasn't time-consuming enough, I spent a lot of time with my friends in one of Yale's so-called secret societies, called Skull and Bones, and in the spring of senior year, I was inspired to play lacrosse, which I had last played at St. Paul's and which I loved. I reported for spring practice as a walk-on and managed to make the team. It turned out we were one of the top teams in the country, beating Maryland, Johns Hopkins, UVA, UNC Chapel Hill and Army. We were ranked nationally until we lost a couple of key games, one of which I still remember for the goal I missed and the shot I failed to block. It's amazing how more than a half century later you can remember every move and the agony of losing an important game.

During the lull after final exams, David Thorne, Persh and I took a few days to decompress, sailing around Buzzards Bay and Nantucket Sound in my father's thirty-nine-foot Concordia yawl. Lending it to us was a generous gesture, ratifying the notion that with graduation from college comes greater responsibility. Whether it meant that or was simply acquiescence to my pestering I never learned, but those few days were memorable. We sailed into Hadley's Harbor at Naushon Island, where we anchored for the night. Because it was late May, few if any summer residents were on the island. Most houses were still shut for the winter. But we nevertheless conducted a vital raid on Mansion House, a big gray clapboard home that sits in a dominant position on a hill above the harbor. After dark, we snuck up to the house, climbed up on the roof above the front porch, found an unlocked window and proceeded to slip inside. Our objective was the "hat room" on the first floor, where General Black Jack Pershing, a friend of Cameron Forbes, had spent time recuperating and writing his report to the nation at the conclusion of World War I. When he completed his report, he left behind his hat, which now sits in a glass box. Dick was elated to touch this piece of his grandfather's history. I was delighted to be able to show it to him, even if it meant breaking and entering to make it happen. We sailed on from there to Nantucket and then drove back to New Haven.

The week before graduation, the size of the change about to consume us hit me with newfound clarity and even urgency. Months before, a committee had selected me to be the Class Day speaker based on my hastily written, clichéd, claptrap address of the kind usually associated with graduation exercises. I wasn't excited about what I was about to share with my classmates. However, during the last week between final exams and graduation festivities, a certain reality started to sink in for all of us. About nine or ten of us, including Pershing and Thorne, had disappeared to an island in the St. Lawrence Seaway for a final fling at a rustic retreat—no electricity in the cabins, swimming in the river, a fair amount of beer, poker, lots of swaggering stories and trash talk.

I remember looking around the table while it sank in that a number of us were about to be scattered to the different branches of the military, others off to graduate school of one kind or another. We started talking about the war. I was struck by how we were unable to articulate what American foreign policy was—even as we were about to become the pointed end of its spear. If you had told us as freshmen that four years later we were going to be carrying a gun and fighting the communists, we would have assumed that we'd be fighting in Havana or back in Europe countering the Red Army. Vietnam? How did that happen? How had two hundred thousand American troops ended up supplanting the French in the jungles of what we still remembered as Indochina? And at some point, I realized I couldn't go through with a run-of-the-mill speech on Class Day, when so much needed probing, poking and parsing. I stayed up in the cabin, furiously writing. My mind was roiling. I was conflicted but unsure of all the reasons why. I had lots of questions.

At Class Day in the yard on the Old Campus on a beautiful, sunny afternoon, I posed some of those questions in my speech, even though I didn't yet have all the answers. I concluded with a blanket statement summarizing the revolution to come: "We have not really lost the desire to serve. We question the very roots of what we are serving."

Later that afternoon, at each of our individual colleges, Yale handed us our diplomas. Our real education was about to begin.

I WAS DOG-TIRED—AND perhaps slightly hungover—when I got out of the car in Newport, Rhode Island, to report for Officer Candidate School. It was the morning after Harvey Bundy's wedding, August 21, 1966, a little more than two months after graduation. I sleepwalked up to the induction center in my civilian clothes—my white shirt totally wrinkled, with open collar, no tie. I was immediately yelled at to "button those buttons!"

This was the first of many seemingly arbitrary orders to come. I had little time to worry about how stupid my dress shirt looked buttoned up to the chin without a tie. I was in for a far more humiliating introduction to military life. Minutes later, I sat in the barber chair watching my hair being shaved off—all my hair. I could see scars I didn't know I had. It was about a ninety-second haircut, and I was the baldest I've been since the day I was born. I do not have a head that was made for no hair. Thank God they didn't have selfies in those days. If some think I look like a pterodactyl now, they should have seen me then. What a coming-down-to-earth moment, but I thought, *What the hell, everyone else looks pretty ridiculous too.*

We all went through the supply lines, where we were issued a uniform, shoes and boots—or "boonies," as we called them. I benefited enormously from the "mustangs," the guys in my OCS class who had served as enlisted men. The mustangs taught me how to spit shine my shoes. I was stunned by how interminable rubbing with cloth, polish and water built up a gloss that made boots look like patent leather. They also taught me how to make my bunk the Navy way. We'd use a dollar bill to measure the fold over the sheet. No wrinkles. I mean, this had to be a bed you could bounce a quarter on, with the corners carefully tucked. It was all somewhat fascinating. Then we marched. *Hup, two, three, four!* Fall in, fall out. We marched everywhere at OCS. Even when you were alone, you had to march and turn square corners.

Although I could have done without the shorn head, I otherwise took to military life. I was in Quebec Company 702, living in the World War II wooden barracks at Newport Naval Station. Everyone seemed to become a caricature of every character I'd seen in the movies, including a lot of guys who were serious and rigid, clean-cut and ready to go. Others had trouble getting things right. We were all just trying to get by, but we learned quickly that no one prospered unless everyone prospered. One of the great lessons of the service is that no one does well or right by doing alone. Teamwork is everything. It probably sounds corny, but it felt good to be part of a time-honored tradition, doing the same things, learning the same things, literally following in the footsteps in the same buildings and classes as the guys who won World War II.

I enjoyed the new subjects—engineering, the steam cycle, navigation, naval history, military protocol—and learning basic tools of the trade about ships, flag signals and Morse code. We had contests with the other companies and spectacular relay races. It was a combination of indoctrination, psychological preparation, hazing, initiation and equalizing. It was breaking things down to build them up. Every movie you ever saw on boot camp got it right. At OCS the only reward for a good training session was more training. Despite two bouts of pneumonia, on December 16, 1966, I received my commission and I proudly walked out of the ceremony, received my first salute from the chief petty officer who trained us, gave him the traditional dollar for that honor and then set out for home to prepare for shipping out to my first duty station. After a family-filled, delicious Christmas Day lunch at Groton House, I headed to Treasure Island, California, a raw ensign who at least understood that what I had really earned was the right to learn how to be a good officer.

My father planned to drive me from Hamilton to Logan Airport in Boston. Shortly after we set out, his car broke down. We limped into a gas station on historic, overly developed Route 1. We were running late. It looked like I was going to miss my plane. A guy was filling up next to us. I asked him, "Hey, man, can you drop me off at Logan?" Pa and I said our good-byes right there at the gas station, impromptu and too hurried, as I made my way to the airport and flew to San Francisco with high hopes and a great sense of adventure. I was a twenty-three-year-old kid going off to duty on a ship. What was there not to be excited about? My father was more somber. He wouldn't say it, but I knew he didn't believe in the war. He didn't see an end in sight. For the first time in my life, I could see that the sadness behind his eyes had something to do with me. He hugged me and off I went.

When I got to Treasure Island Naval Station, it really hit me: "Holy cow, how am I this lucky? Is this for real?" Here I was on an island in San Francisco Bay, living in a place called the "bachelor officer quarters" with a room looking out at the profile of San Francisco with all its allures and, beyond it, the beautiful Golden Gate Bridge. The city was incandescent. The Summer of Love and kaleidoscope dancing were kicking into gear and, before I departed, were in full blossom.

On January 3, 1967, I started Damage Control School in an old World War II wooden building on the island. It seems almost oxymoronic to say that studying damage control was a lot of fun, but it was. What a strange contradiction: I was training by day for something that could get me killed, and by evening I was enjoying the nightlife of San Francisco, far away from thoughts of danger or war.

On day one I met another Massachusetts native assigned to the same program, a delightful guy with a thick mixed Boston-New York accent and a passion for talking politics. Paul Nace and I became fast friends, hanging out together both in and out of classes. We feasted on the sights, frequented Italian restaurants near Fisherman's Wharf, replete with checkered tablecloths and endless supplies of wine. We took in the Grateful Dead at the Fillmore and heard them play some of my favorites, "He Was a Friend of Mine" and "Stage Banter." Neither of us could believe that our early lives in the Navy were in fact what the Navy was all about. Perhaps someone had made a mistake, and we pinched ourselves to make sure the pleasure of our beginning days on active duty as young ensigns—the lowest officer rank in the Navy—was real.

While at Treasure Island, Paul and I would occasionally rent a plane down the peninsula near Palo Alto. We would fly out to the beach or take friends sightseeing. Increasingly, the war was becoming a constant hum in the background of American life. I had developed a healthy skepticism about what was unfolding, but in early 1967, I wasn't yet against the war. I was thinking about it in policy terms, reading Bernard Fall's 1963 book, *The Two Viet-Nams*, and his more recent book from 1966, *Viet-Nam Witness, 1953–66*, and a lot of Graham Greene. I was particularly struck by the war reports from David Halberstam. They sounded grim. One account he'd written stayed with me for years to come: "The pessimism of the Saigon press corps was of the most reluctant kind: many of us came to love Vietnam, we saw our friends dying all around us, and we would have liked nothing better than to believe the war was going well and that it would eventually be won. But it was impossible for us to believe those things without denying the evidence of our own senses. . . . And so we had no alternative but to report the truth. . . ." It resonated as credible.

I had no idea what Vietnam had in store for my generation, but I had my hopes. I hoped that the political differences would be resolved without the war becoming even more intense. I felt a sense of curiosity and anticipation as a young person who thought about war in the context of World War II. Here I was in uniform training to fight. Guys were getting shot out of the skies and ambushed on the ground, and many of America's finest were coming home in body bags. I felt a generic sense of risk, but as with a lot of young people, I was comfortable cloaking myself in a veneer of invincibility. And duty on a ship on the gun line was further removed than other assignments. The risk and the war still seemed far away.

Each day at school, we'd put on our work uniform of khaki pants and shirts and drill down on the do's and don'ts of damage control. A prime early focus was firefighting. Fire on a ship at sea is no joke. Fuel, ammo and other flammable items are everywhere. There's no place to run, no fire department to call—we were the fire department. So, in training, we put on fireproof clothing, an oxygen breathing apparatus—a diver's air tank—and a mask and then, when a wood and diesel fire was started, we manned incredibly powerful fire hoses to put it out. Holding one of the hoses was like trying to hold on to an agitated python. It was jarring to crawl through smoke and experience just how blinding and suffocating it could be. It was also intriguing to learn the practical realities of an electrical fire versus a chemical fire versus an oil-based or fuel fire. We took this part of schooling seriously. The training gave me eternal respect for firefighters because we learned firsthand how extraordinarily dangerous and physically demanding their jobs are.

Our instructors hammered into us warnings about the immediate threat of fire at sea. As if to underline the lesson, the aircraft carrier *Forrestal* caught fire in the Gulf of Tonkin in July, not long after we left Treasure Island. A young naval aviator, Lieutenant (JG) John McCain, had to scramble out of his aircraft to avoid the inferno. Front pages across the country showed a crippled carrier—one of the most imposing ships ever built—trailing smoke, with its iron flank ripped open and crumpled like paper. Hundreds of young men had died in the flames. Even as it steamed into harbor a few days later, the sailors had to rush below from time to time to put out fires caused by smoldering mattresses in the ship's mangled stern.

Yes, the threat of fire was real. It may not have been something I foresaw in the context of fighting the Vietnamese, but it was critical training for any naval officer. I was glad to get it under my belt.

There were lighter moments too. In a certain phase of training we learned how to patch a hole in the side of a ship. We'd climb down into a damage control training simulator—a pretend destroyer engine room—and respond to the loudspeakers blaring: "Battle stations! All hands man your battle stations!" The simulator would fill up with water, bells would go off, and a guy on a loudspeaker would shout, "We've been hit, we've been hit—

there is a major hole in the side. Patch it up now." The water poured in like a river. Before we could catch our breath, it came up to our waists. Paul and I would look at each other: "How the hell did we get here?" We went from checkered tablecloths, Italian wine and good food in the evenings to being half up to our necks in water trying to stuff a mattress in a hole to keep an artificial ship from sinking in a swimming pool. After a particularly tedious day of training, one glance and we agreed, "Let's get back to the Old Spaghetti Factory." I think the point of this exercise was to show everyone how hard and scary it can be trying to patch a hole, which to my recollection no one ever did adequately. We were laughing most of the time and then enjoying a great night in San Francisco.

Later in the spring of 1967, after damage control, Paul and I reported for nuclear, biological and chemical training, also on Treasure Island. NBC School is serious business, but my buddies and I still managed to laugh our way through some of it. We really couldn't believe some of the scenarios thrown at us, threatening as they were. I'm sure the instructors weren't thrilled, but Paul and I weren't the only ones who thought we were tilting at windmills. We were going to Vietnam to fight guerrillas on the ground. As far as we knew, the Viet Cong didn't have a Navy threatening the United States, but we were learning to patch up a ship after a torpedo strike. We shouldn't have been so dismissive. The skills we were learning were important for any officer serving at sea, but we were a wee bit cynical about dreary training routines. It was easier to get through the day cracking jokes.

The most realistic exercise in NBC School was donning chemical suits and being exposed to a whiff of CS gas, essentially similar to tear gas. Our throats burned like crazy. It was hard to breathe. Our eyes welled up. The instructors didn't expose us for long. They weren't trying to hurt us, just help us understand the effects. Message received loud and clear by everyone. We also learned how to measure radioactivity. I was fascinated to learn about nuclear attacks, the dimensions of throw weights, areas of damage and how you calculate the size and potential effect of mushroom clouds.

In the early summer of 1967, the Summer of Love, Paul's and my idyllic stay in San Francisco came to a close. Paul had to report to his ship, a landing ship tank (LST) that was going to deploy to Vietnam. I had more training. Paul and I said a sad farewell, pledging to reconnect when we got back to Massachusetts.

On June 8, 1967, I began my official tour of duty on USS *Gridley*. It was an introduction to hands-on responsibility. The first thing I noticed when I stepped aboard was how big and clean it was. The *Gridley* was a DDG, a new guided missile destroyer and a state-of-the-art ship. I was lucky compared with David Thorne, who had reported for duty aboard USS *Maddox* of Gulf of Tonkin fame. It was a destroyer built in 1943, long enough ago that we used to call it (not so affectionately) "The Shitbox." Long Beach was home port for *Gridley* and *Maddox*, which were in the same squadron. Both our ships, and we individually, were slated for more training before deploying to the gun line off the coast of Vietnam.

David's quarters were incredibly cramped, but while in port he was permitted to find an apartment in town, which he did promptly. I was blessed. My quarters were spacious for a combat vessel. I shared it with a married lieutenant who lived onshore, leaving me the quarters until we went to sea.

I took my *Gridley* responsibilities seriously. One of the most important lessons learned in OCS is that you don't walk in as the new kid with a pair of bars on your shoulder and start ordering people around. I've seen so many guys screw up, thinking that just because they're an officer, they're automatically in charge. Wrong. The bars represent an opportunity to learn how to be an officer. Some guys don't see it that way, and folks resent the hell out of them. The sergeants in the Marines, and the chief petty officers in the Navy, are the guys who know the ropes. You just have a college degree and four months of OCS; you really don't know anything, especially compared with chief petty officers twice your age who have been in the Navy for twenty years. To be successful, listen to them.

I may not have appreciated it as much at the time, but the military was giving me a great education in leadership. I learned about accountability and self-measurement, as well as punctuality, despite my near tardiness on the first day of OCS. I learned about the importance of leading, not by telling people what to do, but showing them by example. It's easy to come up with a long list of lessons I absorbed, but these lessons shaped my views on leadership in fundamental ways.

From the first day I stepped aboard *Gridley*, I was focused on becoming qualified to take the "con"—that is, to drive the ship. I spent weeks learning where everything was located and memorizing manuals about propulsion, communications and shipboard procedures. When we went to sea for training exercises, I looked forward to being assigned responsibilities as the junior officer on the bridge. I watched, listened and learned. Once you're qualified to drive the ship, you can take the con and you're responsible for making sure the ship is going where it's supposed to until you're relieved. Of course, you're not alone. There are layers of responsibility. If you have any doubts, you first check with the officer of the deck, your immediate superior and the officer to whom the captain has delegated the full authority to run the ship. If he has doubts, he'll call the captain and say, "Sir, I need you to check this out." You have a team supporting you. You've got a navigator, a Combat Information Center and an engine room. But you learn how to manage it all—and you learn when you need to ask for advice and when you don't. Even if you're qualified to drive the ship, you're not qualified to be officer of the deck (OOD). But, as OOD, from the moment you say, "I relieve you, sir," and the other guy responds, "I stand relieved," and salutes, you're in charge. I'd been around boats all my life. I couldn't wait to qualify.

I also learned in those early days on *Gridley* that this was not the type of seagoing experience I wanted for all four years. *Gridley* was 510 feet long with some 380 men and officers on board. I started out as first lieutenant, the officer-in-charge of the division responsible for the ship's appearance and everything that happens on deck—principally the docking lines, the lifeboats, the paint job, anchoring. I was also—no surprise—the damage control officer and flight officer responsible for helo operations on the fantail (the rear end of the ship). It was challenging at first, but the size and routine quickly made me restless to be on a smaller vessel with less formality and more responsibility. That's one of the reasons I later put in for Swift boats. Patrol Craft, Fast (PCF) vessels and their smaller cousin the Patrol Boat, River (PBR) were the only boats where I could be in command as a lieutenant (junior grade). I wanted command responsibilities and also a measure of independence different from big-ship naval routine. I also wanted to see up close what the war was really all about. As I wrote to the chief of naval personnel more than six months later, on February 10, 1968: "I request duty in Vietnam. My billet preference is 'Swift' [Shallow Water Inshore Fast Tactical] boats with a second choice of Patrol Officer in a PBR Squadron. . . . I consider the opportunity to serve in Vietnam as an extremely important part of being in the armed forces and believe that my request is in the best interests of the Navy."

While we were training to go to the war, the war was increasingly coming home to America. Protests were growing. Later that summer, President Johnson visited Century City in Los Angeles. David and I were curious what the reaction to his visit might be, given the increasing public agitation about the war. Navy tradition frowns on talk of politics in the wardroom. Nobody was debating Vietnam on *Gridley*, but among friends, on quiet evenings out with fellow junior officers or nonmilitary friends, there were whispers. I remember one guy on *Gridley* who'd been in Da Nang, a port in the northern part of South Vietnam, as harbormaster. He told me that we were on a fool's errand and we'd be lucky to come out of there alive.

It was the summer of liberation, of Ken Kesey, Haight-Ashbury. My friends all shared a sense that something big was happening. You could feel it in the air. Protests were increasing. I wanted to see for myself what the anti-war movement was all about. We were in uniform, after all, removed from the real street currents surrounding the Vietnam issue. Neither David nor I wanted to get caught up in a protest. But we were also curious and beginning to question the fundamental premises of the war we were about to be part of. We decided to go and observe the people who had gathered to protest LBJ's appearance. Late in the afternoon, we arrived at the Century Plaza Hotel. The first thing we saw was a bunch of folks peacefully chanting. All that changed when the speeches began. H. Rap Brown, an outspoken Student Non-Violent Coordinating Committee leader, put it starkly: "I can't believe Lyndon Johnson is more humane than Hitler," he roared. "Hitler gassed people to death. Lyndon Johnson bombs them to death." David and I looked at each other with a mutual sense of foreboding.

The crowd started to get restless. The police moved in hard. What began as a peaceful movement turned chaotic as Los Angeles cops broke it up and whacked the crap out of people. The crowd was shouting, "Gestapo!" Organizers stood on the flatbed of a truck urging the crowd to link arms so the police couldn't break their ranks. David and I had the same instinct: "Let's get the hell out of here." So we bolted, but the entire scene stayed with me.

It jolted me. Here I was about to deploy, and here was my country increasingly tearing itself apart over the war.

WHEN WE SET out from San Diego in February 1968, I was full of anticipation for the adventure. We sailed away from the California coast in a four-ship group—one frigate, *Gridley*, and three destroyers—steaming in formation to Pearl Harbor. Just getting one or two nights away from the coast was magical. In all our training runs we had stayed pretty close to California. Now we were cranking up speed, heading west across the Pacific Ocean, honking along with the ship plowing through rolling waves as the sunset lit us up in bursts of crimson and orange. We created an enormous wake. I stood on the fantail feeling the ship vibrate and churn beneath my feet, watching the ocean race by at a pretty good clip.

We were the squadron flagship for this convoy, so we took the lead position in a diamond formation. Standing on the bridge on a 535-foot Navy frigate moving at over 20 knots; sensing the harmony of ship, ocean and sky; feeling the ship shudder as it rises and falls with the waves; and watching the sun set into the horizon and looking for a green flash is a pretty damn good moment. It's why people go to sea and never get over it, why,

as John Masefield wrote, men "must go down to the seas again, for the call
of the running tide, / Is a wild call and a clear call that may not be denied."

I had previously developed a good sense of relative motion on the ocean.
Sailing had taught me about winds, storms and squalls. Ducking beneath
the stern of a competitor sailboat in a race taught me a lot about measuring
distance, speed and time. It all came in handy as I learned the ropes. I also
learned that it can get tedious when you're steaming steadily in one direction. But a ship to the right and the left and then one behind will keep you
on your toes. The challenge in convoy is holding the proper distance between ships. It's particularly difficult at night when all you can see are dim
lights outlining the shapes of the ships. I loved that part of the job. It was
a lot of fun, a constant challenge. It felt like being part of the World War II
documentary TV series *Victory at Sea*, with its triumphant music and the
dramatic pictures of convoys with sea pouring over the bows and spray flying through the air, lights on the bridge flashing Morse code as they signal
each other. If you'd asked me as a teenager what I thought military service
would look like, this was it.

A few days later we pulled into Pearl Harbor, where the history of the
"Day of Infamy" surrounds you. As we glided slowly through the channel,
battleship row and the memorial to USS *Arizona* off to our left, and the lush
Hawaiian hills in the direction of the first planes of the Japanese attack on
December 7, 1941, I was moved by our proximity to such a gigantic moment of history. I couldn't take in enough fast enough. A number of World
War II–era buildings on the airfield, including the tower building, were still
standing. I made sure to visit as many of the historical sites as possible. We
spent several laid-back days in Pearl Harbor, during which I explored the
whole island in a rented Jeep, had a few umbrella drinks in tourist traps and
surfed briefly at Waikiki. Then we departed again.

I had assumed additional duty as the ship's public affairs officer, so as
we steamed farther west, the captain suggested I share some history with
the crew as we passed key battle sites. Particularly as we went by Midway
and through Leyte Gulf, I gave short one- to two-minute summaries over
the ship's loudspeaker describing two key battles of World War II so everyone could share in the significance of the moment. I thank my parents for
always reminding us how closely connected we were to the past. They instilled in me a love of history for all it teaches us about the present.

HISTORY, HOWEVER, HAS a painful way of catching up to us when we
least expect it. In February, after departing Pearl Harbor and shortly after
we steamed past Midway, the executive officer approached me with an

ashen look on his face and asked me to sit down. I could tell immediately that the news was bad. "Do you know a guy named Dick Pershing?" he asked. I knew right away what had happened and everything went black all around me. It was a punch to the gut as I read the telegram:

"Richard Pershing . . . killed due to wounds received while on a combat mission when his unit came under hostile small-arms and rocket attack while searching for remains of a missing member of his unit."

I was excused and walked off the bridge and cried. The shock and disbelief were overwhelming. I tried everything I could to get a helicopter or plane to take me back home, but there was no way to make it happen. David Thorne and I, both on duty stations, missed the funeral. I felt more empty and alone than I ever had in my entire life.

When I wrote home, I didn't hold back. I was desperately sad. I just didn't believe life was meant to be this cruel and senseless. With the loss of Persh, something changed in me and, I dare say, I think in all those who knew him really well. He was so much a part of our shared life at Yale. He was an unbelievable spark for all of us who were close to him. He was irreverent—fun-loving and fun-making. He was always ready to test the limits of institutional expectations. At that age we all took for granted that we would always be together, crashing through life with confidence and perhaps even bravado. We'd grown up together, gone to middle school together at Fessenden. Never a serious student, Dick knew better than anyone how to push the boundaries of just getting by, but he did so with a charm and self-awareness that negated judgments about the irresponsibility of his choices. He lived large and clearly had a glorious time doing so. To all his friends, including me, this gifted natural athlete was invincible. Now he was gone.

Persh's death increased my skepticism about the war. Right or wrong, it made more immediate and sensitive the growing doubts about the truth of what we were being told. It was a blow to whatever idealism about the war remained in me. Suddenly there was a personal cost none of us in our little world had paid thus far. I wrote a letter to my parents that clearly reflected anger: "If I did nothing more, it will be to give every effort we can to somehow make this a better world to live in and to end once and for all this willingness to expend ourselves in this stupid, endless self-destruction." As big and perhaps grandiose as that may sound today, it was a twenty-four-year-old's honest reaction to the sudden death of one of his closest friends.

At the same time, the home front was increasingly waking up. Tet brought about a sea change in American attitudes. The spectacular attacks in more than one hundred cities and hamlets and even the U.S. Embassy in

Saigon stunned the American people. We all watched the drama on television: broadcasts of Viet Cong rockets and mortars pounding cities across the country; U.S. troops fighting to protect the embassy and its breached walls; the wounded being ferried away on stretchers. It all played out across our screens. The U.S. and South Vietnamese armies ultimately declared Tet an allied victory, but psychologically and politically, it was a disaster. The offensive undermined confidence in our approach and knocked all of us on our heels. For President Johnson and the Army commander in Vietnam, General William Westmoreland, the remedy was simply to throw another million troops in theater. They knew they had the numbers; whether they had the strategy was another question.

I didn't focus on America's chances at this point. The war was happening and I had a job to do. I had previously always imagined that we'd succeed because we were the United States of America. There was no way to know how simplistic that conviction was until I got on the ground and could see and feel the deceptions—the free-fire zones, the difficulty of separating Viet Cong from the general population, the brutal nature of guerrilla warfare, the weakness and demoralization of South Vietnam's army and the corruption of its government. I very quickly realized that we—like the French and others before us—had, to use a trite but true phrase, bitten off more than we could chew. This wasn't some set-piece war where an army could move tanks around and come in with airpower. It was a very different animal, which is why the concept of "winning hearts and minds" became such a burning, telltale description of the challenge. I began to feel that much of what we were doing led directly not to winning hearts and minds but alienating them. We had a body-count mentality, and the Vietnamese civilian population was paying the price. Three years after the Tet Offensive, in 1971, I would protest the war, but even then I had no idea about the extent of the lying, the falsification of reports, the exaggerations and field deceptions. It wasn't until I read Neil Sheehan's *A Bright Shining Lie*, more than twenty years after I served, that I realized how deep the rot had already gone and how early it had begun.

AFTER CROSSING THE Pacific we spent a few days in harbor at Subic Bay, Philippines. It was a unique sailors' port. Suffice it to say the stories are legendary. From there we steamed into the Gulf of Tonkin, where we spent a couple of months operating with the aircraft carriers from which our Navy and Marine pilots were bombing North Vietnam. It was from one of these carriers that John McCain had taken off for his ill-fated mission on October 26, 1967, when he was shot down over Hanoi. Our job was to provide missile protection for the carriers and to act as plane guard—a ship that follows steadily five hundred yards back in the wake of the carriers, prepared to pick up a pilot if there is a failed catapult or a crash on takeoff or landing. Whether at night without any lights or day, during all flight operations, we were on station behind the carrier. The roar of the engines at night when you could barely see in the pitch dark was as deep and majestic as the full-throated roar of a lion in the jungle, primal and exhilarating. It was the one time I sometimes wondered if I should have signed up for flight at OCS. My father's advice that flying would become a job and not a passion had kept me from signing up—that and the prospect of a six-year hitch.

In March, after a couple of months in the Gulf of Tonkin, we were dispatched to Da Nang. We went there for in-person briefings that I was never privy to, but, as first lieutenant in charge of the gig, the captain's boat, I was delighted to be able to get ashore when we ferried the captain and the doctor in.

My first order of business was to make a phone call. I hadn't been ashore since Persh died, so I had zero direct communication with anyone about him or anything else. I wanted to try to reach Julia on the Military Auxiliary Radio System—the MARS telephone system. I stood in line for thirty minutes and got to talk with Julia for about two. It was a more than frustrating exercise—well intended, but the connection was terrible and the brevity made me miserable for what I was missing. Besides, it was harder than hell to talk on a line that sounded like you were talking into a tin can on the moon and the whole world was listening.

I also knew my roommate Danny Barbiero was serving in a Marine detachment somewhere in the vicinity—or so I thought. I hoped to be able to find him, though it was a long shot at best. Da Nang was a huge Marine base.

But in a "finding a needle in a haystack" moment, Danny happened to be in the very communication hut we connected to: I found him serving as the communications officer for his Marine unit near Quang Tri, north of Da Nang. He was stunned. It was an amazing moment. When we said goodbye at Yale, we didn't know when or where we'd see each other again, but on this first day of my being on the ground in Vietnam, it was so good to hear a familiar, friendly voice. After the call, I was about to go back to the ship when I suddenly wondered if my eyes were deceiving me: twenty yards away, a bunch of Viet Cong bodies were stacked like a woodpile. It was a shock. The dead bodies I had seen before—at a wake, at a funeral, in a casket laid out in their Sunday best—were nothing like this: cold, stiff, distorted, heaped one on top of the other. Where the hell was I?

The day in Da Nang sparked my curiosity. I'd been onshore for a few hours, but just that brief visit made me want to know more about what it was like to really be there, to feel the currents of daily life for the Vietnamese and see what was working and what wasn't. I felt a palpable energy in the Marine hut, on the street, in the coming and going of troops and support personnel. I was intrigued and from that moment looked forward to returning as a Swift boat skipper.

We returned to our repetitious plane guard duty in the Gulf of Tonkin, occasionally running missiles out on the launchers when North Vietnamese MiGs approached too close to our shoot zone. But they always turned back at the last moment after playing a dangerous game of chicken.

On April 4, 1968, we learned Martin Luther King Jr. had been gunned down in Memphis. I still remember talking with my father about Dr. King's speech in Detroit, Michigan, in June 1963, known later as his original "I Have a Dream" speech. He'd used an interesting word—"maladjusted." My father pointed out that the term was normally used in a negative sense to describe someone who didn't fit in with society. But Dr. King directed that term right back at himself. He said he was proud to be maladjusted because he could never live comfortably amid racial discrimination, religious bigotry, unreasoning hate and the self-defeating effects of violence. I thought of those words on the day I learned of Dr. King's death. I thought about what it meant to be "maladjusted" to violence and about my duties to the country as an officer in the Navy. I didn't have any answers. But I started to feel the importance of applying the same sense of conscience—the same guts, the same determination—to ask the right questions.

Toward the end of April, we were relieved from plane guard duty in order to represent the United States at the Coral Sea celebration in New Zealand. First we pulled into Subic Bay to provision. The captain was so insistent the ship be painted for the visit to Wellington that my entire division was denied liberty in order to remain on board, day and night, with buckets of paint everywhere. Needless to say, two solid months at sea and no liberty did not sit well with the crew. Ultimately, after getting bruised and beaten in the ancient ceremony of crossing the equator at sea, when "pollywogs"—as the uninitiated are called—are transformed into "shellbacks," we enjoyed a spectacular long weekend visit in Wellington. It was the best liberty of my time on *Gridley*. I still have the sheepskin rugs I bought in the lush New Zealand countryside. Then we started the long trek back to California.

As we approached the coastline off Long Beach after this first tour of duty, on the night of June 5, I was working late with the public affairs team as we picked up the first crackling radio reports on the California primary. I listened to Bobby Kennedy's victory speech from the Ambassador Hotel. For a moment, it felt like the dreams of his brother Jack might be ascendant once more. Then the frenzy of .22-caliber handgun shots changed everything once again. We docked in the early morning. I could see David and Julia standing among the well-wishers and families assembled to welcome us home. When David caught my eye he made a finger-gun signal with shrugged shoulders and a roll of the eyes, as if to say, "Oh my God—another incomprehensible moment—things are crazy." I thought, *Jesus Christ, I just left Vietnam, where there's a lot of madness and killing. And here I am coming home to the United States and it's the same over here.* David, Julia and I spent days holed up in David's apartment, watching the drama of mourning and burial play out on TV much as it had at Yale when the president had been murdered. I will never forget the crack in Ted Kennedy's voice when he talked of "my brother," reminding us of the words (from George Bernard Shaw) by which RFK had lived: "Some men see things as they are and ask why? I dream things that never were and ask, why not?"

During the passage back to the States I had received my orders for Swift boats. I was delighted, and within days of returning, I separated from *Gridley*, taking time for leave before reporting in August to Coronado Amphibious Base for Swift boat training. I went home to Boston for a few days of R&R.

Curious about the political currents, I bought a ticket to a Eugene McCarthy rally at Fenway Park. I wanted to see and feel what his campaign was all about. I'd been away for enough time in such a completely different world that I felt strangely disconnected from everything at home— particularly the politics of 1968. I knew there was some bitterness between the McCarthy and Kennedy camps, but I had no feel for where the race was after Bobby's assassination. McCarthy was now carrying the anti-war flag by himself. I wondered whether he could be a legitimate threat to Vice President Humphrey, who had still not separated from Johnson on the war. None of this, I thought, was being properly analyzed. The day before the rally, all the press could discuss was whether McCarthy would be able to fill the Red Sox's ballpark. Volunteers lined the streets of Boston, hawking one-dollar tickets less than twenty-four hours beforehand, to make sure he did.

When I arrived on the night of the rally, it was bedlam. Young people packed Kenmore Square. An improvised dance hall was hopping. Kids who had gone "clean for Gene" were wearing "Eugene" neckties and shoving petitions such as "Food for Biafra" into any hand that would take them. The

warm night, the pleasant breeze, the music, the masses of young people—
it all felt like I was back in San Francisco.

Fenway was packed. People crouched in the aisles. Thousands stood in
the parking lot, craning their necks to catch a glimpse of the closed-circuit
televisions that McCarthy's staff had jury-rigged as thousands of supporters
streamed up Brookline Avenue. Some even hung from the billboards to take
in the scene.

Many spoke, but Pete Seeger sang. He took the stage and belted out,
"Tonight, you and I have a war to stop," and the audience lost it, singing "If
I Had a Hammer" with him by the end. Forty thousand voices joined as one.
You could hear the sing-along all the way across the Charles River in Cambridge. Alan Arkin and Leonard Bernstein spoke, and the cheering began
again. It started a full three minutes before McCarthy took the stage. "We
want Gene," the people roared. And they got him.

McCarthy entered like royalty. He stepped out from the shadows below
the center field bleachers flanked by Boston policemen on horseback. The
crowd exploded as he approached second base, where the stage was set
up. McCarthy wasn't exactly an inspirational speaker. His voice was flat.
He rarely got excited. His message, however, was crystal clear. He wanted
America to become "an America of confidence, an America which trusts
its own judgment." At one point, a police horse reared and whinnied and
the microphone caught it. "Even the horse approves, I think," McCarthy
said to laughter. When he turned to Vietnam, he called it a "holy war" and
accused the Johnson administration, which was then engaged in talks with
the South Vietnamese government, of following a doctrine of "infallibility."
They were too busy suppressing "heresy" to make the right decision. "We
must undertake to pass a judgment on the war in midcourse," he said under
the glare of the floodlights. "To say we think what we are doing is unwise,
even to admit it was wrong."

I suddenly felt out of place among my peers. I used to pass through their
number without issue in San Francisco and at Yale. Now I was a sailor. More
than that—I was heading to the war, to Vietnam, and while I had reached a
point of seriously questioning the war, I didn't yet know the things I would
soon learn that would make me furious. I had reservations. I was increasingly hearing things that fed doubts. I sensed that the war represented a profound failure of leadership, and I could certainly see that our country was
coming apart at the seams. But I needed to know more to be convinced of
how we stitch it back together.

• • •

IN LATE JULY 1968, five officers and crews arrived at the U.S. Navy Amphibious Base in Coronado, California, for four months of training prior to deploying to Operation Market Time in Vietnam. I rented a beachfront apartment on Mission Beach, a few miles away on the Pacific Ocean, south of La Jolla. Each day I would ride my bicycle to the Coronado training base accompanied by a new friend, an intelligence officer named Giles Whitcomb, who was assigned to the language school with the rest of us. Giles found an apartment farther south down the beach, but each day we would rendezvous near the amusement park and practice our Vietnamese as we rode through the Marine Corps Recruit Depot, a convenient shortcut to the ferry to Coronado. We must have been quite a sight—two Navy officers in our khaki uniforms on French racing bikes, riding through a bunch of Marine recruits doing their push-ups and marching from one evolution to another, while we were working on the daily lesson in Vietnamese.

In off-hours we were free to make the most of San Diego: surf on the beach, visit the famous Hotel del Coronado, where *Some Like It Hot* was filmed, and go to dances at the Marine Corps Recruit Depot. During our classroom studies we learned everything about Swifts—their engines, communications procedure, armament—and most important, we met the crews that we'd be teamed with in 'Nam. It was great to finally get on a Swift boat; these stubby, fifty-foot-long, aluminum-hulled gunboats were about to become our home away from home. The boats were not designed for the job. They were created as water taxis for the offshore oil rigs in the Gulf of Mexico. But when it became apparent some new vessel was needed for shallow-water work along the Vietnamese coast, the boats were snatched up by the Navy.

Each boat was manned by a crew of six men. One officer, usually a lieutenant (junior grade), was the officer-in-charge, or OINC. The boats were armed with twin .50-caliber machine guns on top of the pilothouse and a single .50-caliber machine gun on top of the 81mm marine mortar on the stern. Supplementing these were several M-79 grenade launchers, M-16 rifles, antipersonnel and concussion grenades, .38-caliber revolvers, a riot gun and any other weapon that the men could beg, borrow or steal. The boats were powerful, driven by two 480-horsepower diesel engines, but because of the amount of ammunition carried on board, they seldom attained speeds over 25 knots, a little less than 29 mph. There were accommodations for four men—two up forward under the pilothouse and two in the main cabin. A small stove and icebox provided a fairly rudimentary several-days-away-from-base capability.

It was a good feeling when we first sortied, initially under the watchful eye of experienced Navy petty officers and then alone. It was satisfying to be in command—exactly what I had anticipated. Everyone on board seemed to enjoy the independence, the more relaxed atmosphere and the responsibility that came with it. We familiarized ourselves with various maneuvers in San Diego Harbor, then went out to sea before taking overnight trips, where we boned up on our navigation skills and, for the first time, shot the mortars and machine guns.

Before any of us could depart for Vietnam, we were required to pass the SERE course—survival, evasion, resistance and escape training. It was a combination of survival training and a mock prisoner-of-war experience. Here's the drill: We gathered on a Sunday evening at the base in Coronado, wearing full uniform and jacket, with a big Ka-Bar knife dangling at our sides. We rallied on the beach near the hotel, after being dropped off in buses up near the North Island Naval Air Station. At dusk the instructors gave us a lecture on how to find a fish or clams or catch a seagull. Then we marched off, looking for food. After the stark realization that there was no food to be found on this well-combed beach, we bedded down in the rocks, freezing, and tried to sleep. At about 4:00 a.m., after waking up to no food, we took off in buses to go to a place in the desert called Warner Springs, where the main SERE training was held. Once there, we spent the next four days in the desert doing two things and two things only: walking around listening to instructors and surviving. The instructors even taught us how to catch and skin a rabbit. One night, someone did produce a rabbit. I think it was bought and provided for the demo purposes, but never mind—one rabbit, properly skinned and gutted, was plunked into a pot of steaming water over a warm fire. That unlucky Bugs Bunny provided soup for the whole group and it tasted great.

The vast majority who made it to Thursday were rewarded with escape and evasion drills. There are two teams of instructors at SERE—a Blue Team and a Red Team. The Blue Team are the good guys who tell you what to do, how to find food and how to evade, resist and escape. The Red Team are the enemy—big, fit, well fed and well rested. Early in the morning on Thursday, the Blue Team gathered everyone into a defined area, with a dried-up streambed on one side and sage brush and trees on the other. We were lined up at the far end of the terrain and told we had a certain number of minutes to get to home base, three miles away. If you managed to get there within the allotted time, you had a choice between enjoying a sandwich or an orange—not both—and a half hour of respite. To make things more interesting, they released the Red Team enemy troops into the area after ten minutes, so you had to get camouflaged fast, move and pick a route to evade these guys, all dressed in uniforms with red epaulets to look like the Soviets or Chinese Communists or North Vietnamese army regulars. They knew how to play their role. They were serious, mean-spirited guys—at least for the moment—who were out to get us. When captured, you were transported to a prisoner-of-war camp nearby in the desert. There you were put to the test of the Code of Conduct—your name, rank, serial number and endurance for the next twenty-four hours. Everything was evaluated. No sweet talk, no hand-holding.

Because I used to play a lot of capture the flag on Naushon and I hunted, I felt relatively experienced at camouflage, movement and stealth. Since we were operating as individuals, not teams, I thought it was important to outmaneuver the Reds by controlling my environment as much as possible. That meant moving quickly away from the crowd and going it alone. At one point, I heard the enemy troops draw close. I crunched up in my best Pamplona fetal ball again, playing dead in a bush. I can still see one guy's boots walking four feet away from me. I didn't move. I became part of the environment, and they didn't see me—or they gave me a break for effort and pretended. What I was most terrified of was meeting a rattlesnake crawling through the rocks and brush.

Around me I could hear some other guys getting captured, but I managed to make it to home base. There were four or five other men already there enjoying their reward. I chose the orange. I turned out to be the only officer and therefore in charge. We were relaxing, joking around about the whole exercise, when a Jeep came rolling up at the end of half an hour. A bunch of guys got out dressed in their enemy uniforms and feeling their oats. They got rough with one of the enlisted men. My job was to stand up and protect him—so I said something stupid but mandatory: "Hey, listen, I'm the senior officer here and you're not allowed to do that." Next thing you know, I'm coldcocked, lying facedown in the sand with a foot on my back and a rifle on my neck, and the officer says, "Shut the hell up." They then proceeded to waterboard the poor guy to extract information. Soon we were put in the back of Jeeps and taken to the prison camp, where we were ordered to strip completely. They took our clothes, substituting prison uniforms for them, and assigned us to a tent bungalow with a bunch of other guys.

Around lunchtime, we were all taken out to dig a hole six feet deep and then immediately fill it back in. Meanwhile, an airplane flew over us sounding an air-raid signal. Everyone scurried back into the hut. Throughout the exercise, the instructors were tough, smacking us around, picking people off one by one for interrogation. Everyone got called, so I waited my turn. Amazingly, even knowing this was only an exercise and it would end in twenty-four hours, some guys turned and came out wearing enemy uniforms and started bossing the rest of us around. I never found out whether that was a trick, but it had its effect. Some folks just did not make it, however. They flunked out during interrogation or just couldn't handle the isolation.

When it was my turn, I went into a dark room with a guy sitting at a desk. He asked me what my unit was. I gave my name, rank and serial number. At one point, I smirked, which was a huge mistake. Obviously, I was not sufficiently in role. I was promptly slammed on the ground and told to do push-ups till I caved. Then they put me alone in a "tiger cage," a narrow box. I couldn't move right or left, up or down—and I stayed like that for forty-five minutes, my head and face crammed down into my knees, my back inches from the lid of the box. I get claustrophobic and had to work major mind games to get through it. I get the willies just recalling it now. I pushed my mind to visualize sailing or skiing—nice things, but then I realized, *Whoa, there aren't any nice things. I'm in a fucking box. I can't move, and my back is hurting. I'm bent over and I can't breathe.* Had the ordeal lasted much longer, I felt sure I would have gone crazy. Every five minutes, the guards came by and knocked and asked me if I was all right. With no more than a grunt, I acknowledged that I was and hung in there. Then they put me in a bigger box with multiple people all crammed into a tiny space, arms and legs crisscrossing each other, heads jammed into someone else. The togetherness thing wasn't half as bad as being in a box alone. Actually I was one of the lucky ones. I'm told other guys got put in a coffin.

So we went through this grueling process for what seemed an interminable time, with the guards trying all the time to break you, in part by playing one of us against the others. During the night I tried to escape over a roof and then over the fence, because escape would win you a sandwich and another respite, but I never made it beyond the roof. When it became clear to me this was not a good route, I backed off the roof and slid into my hut. So the night went. There were a few successful escapes. Then at some point late the next morning they lined us all up in the courtyard facing north. A siren went off. We were ordered to turn around, and there, beautiful and liberating, was the American flag flying in the sun. I was surprised by how welcome and even emotional a moment it was. We knew we'd survived. The weeklong ordeal was over. We were bused back to the base at Coronado. I raced home to the beach apartment to enjoy the best meal and longest, most welcome shower I'd ever had.

I learned something about myself in SERE training. I didn't want to get captured, especially by the Viet Cong, because I felt sure they'd skin me alive. And when it came to resisting torture, I knew I would do my best, but I had had a taste of how tough it would be over time to keep the code. The experience of just twenty-four hours taught most of us that ultimately—certainly for most people—there probably is a breaking point. I admire beyond belief what John McCain and the other POWs put up with to survive—all that solitude and pain just to stay alive. But one of the great lessons of that period was the limitations of the code itself. As a result of the Vietnam experience, the official prohibitions against torture became even stronger. At the time that we were about to deploy to Vietnam, we had learned you do what you can. If your mind is strong and your body half strong, you might make it through, but what was reinforced in me at SERE training was that I did not want to be taken alive. Soon, in combat on the rivers of the Mekong Delta, something else was reinforced in me: I would do everything in my power to keep my crew and myself alive.

In the last weeks before I was to leave for Vietnam, Julia came out to California. We luxuriated in a soft journey by car up the coast of California—Highway 1—one of the great roads anywhere. Julia and I had loved the quiet intimacy of the 1967 movie *Two for the Road*, where Audrey Hepburn and Albert Finney drive through the South of France. We meandered through extraordinary California countryside, sometimes aimlessly, sometimes purposefully, but never rushed and always free to change our minds and do something else. It was idyllic, stopping where we wanted to, visiting Hearst Castle, Carmel, ultimately San Francisco. Somewhere along the way, Julia turned to me and started talking about getting married. It just happened—not a proposal, but a natural segue from our conversation. Before either of us fully digested what was happening, we had decided we were going to get married. In San Francisco we stayed at the Mark Hopkins, splurging on a suite, knowing departure day was around the corner. As I think back on those special days, it seemed in certain ways that time stood still—only it didn't. Everything seemed to be in slow motion except the clock. We made our farewell after calling our parents to tell them we were going to get married when I came back, but we wanted to keep it quiet because of what had happened to Dick Pershing, who had been engaged when he died. We were superstitious.

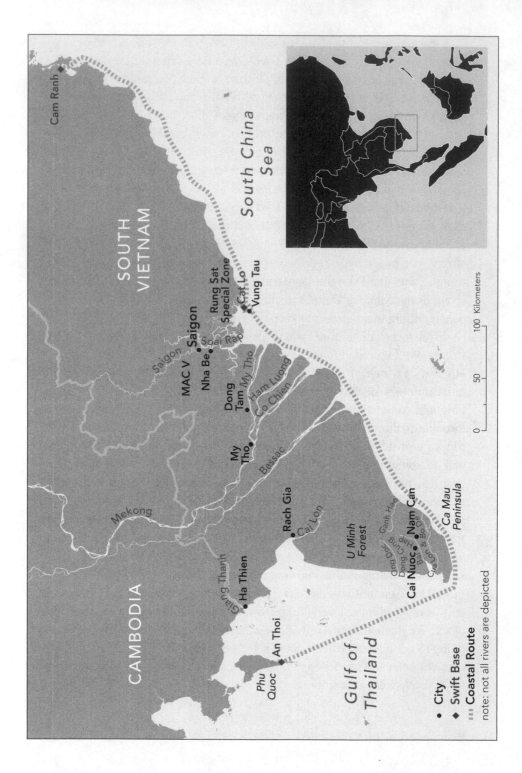

CHAPTER 4

War

"GOOD LUCK, SUCKER," an anonymous soldier smugly proclaimed.

"You're in for a year of fucking hell," said another dismissively.

We had landed to refuel at an air base outside Tokyo after the long flight from Tacoma, taking us to Vietnam. Barrier fences in the terminal separated the line of troops heading to war from those going home. The men leaving looked tired and haunted, their eyes sunken into their sockets, worn-out souls.

They were greeting us with a warning we chalked up to gallows humor.

I arrived in Vietnam in time for Thanksgiving. Ironically, as we were on approach to Cam Ranh Bay, descending through the clouds, a huge rainbow extended its bow down onto the airport itself, striking me as one mocking display too many by Mother Nature. It was impossible to conjure up any notion of a pot of gold waiting in Vietnam. When the aircraft door opened and we disembarked, a blast of warm, moist wind of the monsoon season blew across the runway. It had just been raining.

The airport was clogged with camouflaged Air Force planes. A battalion of Vietnamese Rangers disembarked from a C-130 near us, their dark faces and tiny bodies straining under packs almost as big as they were.

In the distance was a field high on a hill. My first instinct was to think how great it would be to explore it. It looked peaceful, but the illusion of tranquillity was shattered by the reality that we were now in a war zone. Just about any Vietnamese could be a Viet Cong ready to kill you. We were entering an unknown world, which I later learned was in some ways unknowable.

A truck arrived to transport us to the Swift boat headquarters. As we drove through the sprawling Army/Air Force base, it struck me that only Americans could have built such a facility in a time of war. The various buildings stretched for miles along a vast white beach, with row upon row of wooden barracks and a PX that would put Macy's to shame, with a sauna and massage parlor, enlisted men and officers' clubs, and most any service imaginable. For an instant, I wondered where the war was.

We arrived at the Swift boat base. I presented my orders, learning to my initial disappointment I was to be assigned to Coastal Division 14 (CosDiv 14) right at Cam Ranh itself. CosDiv 14 was commonly referred to as the "Fun in the Sun and Surf Division," tucked away from the real life of Vietnam. I had anticipated something more than Cam Ranh's reputation promised. I asked the administrative officer of the squadron if I could instead go to Cat Lo, at the mouth of the Saigon River, or to Da Nang.

"The names were drawn from a hat and it's decided. You're staying here," he told me.

We met with the squadron commander, Commodore Charles Horne. He was young, energetic and enthusiastic. You couldn't miss the captured gun mounted like a stuffed swordfish on the wall above him. He called each of us "skipper," an unfamiliar but flattering title, especially to us new kids on the block who had not yet been assigned a boat. We listened attentively while the commodore expounded on Operation Sealords, a joint operation between the United States and South Vietnam to disrupt enemy supply lines from the North.

A week passed. I began to settle in. I lived in a single room, a luxury in Vietnam. Showers were fifteen yards from the barracks. Water was plentiful. Beer was available at the officers' club. The beach was beautiful, the water warm. Most important, my mail arrived on time. I received the tape my mother sent of the entire Harvard-Yale game, which the *Crimson* famously chronicled with the headline "Harvard Beats Yale, 29 to 29." Harvard had come from two touchdowns behind to tie the game with about a minute and a half on the clock. It was painful to listen to: college seemed such a world away from Vietnam.

Each morning, a truckload of Vietnamese, crowded together like cattle, pulled into the base, their faces peering through the slats on the sides of the truck. Out of the back would pour chattering women and wizened old men who did all the service work, from cleaning the barracks to maintaining the roads. The women would take our uniforms home to wash and iron them for a price. I often looked for some expression that would tell me how these people felt, cleaning up behind us as we waged war in their countryside, but they never gave away their thoughts.

I was told that the officers' club was the best in Vietnam. Folklore informed us that nurses from Saigon used to be flown in for wild parties. Finally, one of the enlisted men got so angry at missing the fun, he wrote his mother, who wrote her congressman. The parties stopped. USO shows still came through, including one starring Chinese girls bumping and grinding in a sloppy, unchoreographed way, out of sync with everything around us.

Some sat comfortably at the officers' club swapping stories of their patrols. A few expressed doubts about the mission or the war itself, stating curtly, "Can't see how anything over here is worth getting shot at for." I don't think I met anyone who wasn't obsessively focused on counting the days until he went on R&R or went home. Short-timers would count the days out loud: "Only twenty-nine more days in this shithole." The bar was a good place to pick up stories of close calls on patrol or the big night of combat when a trawler was intercepted with a major arms haul. It was a high point of the division's engagements.

ABOUT TEN DAYS later, I was still waiting to be assigned my own boat. The operations officer, Lieutenant Schacte, asked me if I would like to take part in an operation they were planning for that night—a so-called skimmer op. I didn't know precisely what it entailed, but I knew it was a small boat operation and a break in the monotony of early indoctrination patrols. I said yes.

We departed the base on a Swift boat, heading north, towing a small thirteen-foot Boston Whaler behind us. Night fell just as we arrived at the target area. Lieutenant Schacte had recruited two enlisted men, Bill Zaladonis and Pat Runyon. I had never met Runyon, but he and Bill knew each other from service prior to arrival in Cam Ranh. Each volunteered hoping to see some action before his tour was up.

We lowered an outboard engine into the Whaler, positioning it on the transom. Then we placed an M-60 machine gun on the flat, forward deck of the Whaler. Finally, we lowered a radio and prepared to head inland. Schacte instructed us to go toward the shoreline, maneuver up through a small inlet between the peninsula and an island, and take any violators of the curfew under fire if need be. There was a simple rule: if someone was there, they were enemy in a free-fire zone.

Three grown men could barely fit in the Whaler. I was jammed in the middle while Zaladonis manned the engine in the stern and Runyon worked the M-60 machine gun in the bow.

Schacte assigned our boat the call sign "Robin." He and the Swift boat would be "Batman." They would hang back in the bay to provide fire support if needed. Zaladonis, Runyon and I spent most of the night inching up the inland shoreline to intercept Viet Cong. Again and again we were startled beyond description by one or two Vietnamese at a time, who, sitting quietly in their sampans, suddenly took shape out of the dark. We had no choice but to take them into custody, then retrace the entire distance traveled in order to deposit them on the Swift boat so they couldn't warn anyone we were coming. To complicate matters, the steering cable broke and the engine needed to be manipulated from the stern.

Several hours later, when we finally got close to the shore, we shut the engine down. We started to paddle stealthily. By now we were in a tiny passage of water with jungle rising up about five to ten yards away on either side. All we could hear was our own breathing. We came slowly around a bend when suddenly, yards in front of us, there was a sampan with a man in the stern. Then, suddenly, another man jumped out from under a tarp, scaring the hell out of Runyon in the bow. Runyon was so surprised he instinctively pulled the trigger on his machine gun. Fortunately for the two men, the gun's safety was still on. Had he fired, the men would have been blown overboard, dead for certain and likely shredded by a machine gun only yards away. Our initial impression was they were fishermen, stupidly or wittingly in a free-fire zone, fishing in a no-fishing area after curfew. I learned soon thereafter that deaths in a free-fire zone were almost always tallied as Viet Cong killed in action, and so they would have been had that gun gone off.

Runyon was so shaken by the near miss that he changed places with Zaladonis and drove the boat for the rest of the mission. We detained the fishermen and again made the trip all the way back to the Swift. There they confirmed their bona fides as genuinely innocent fishermen who didn't know where one zone began and the other ended. Their papers were perfectly in order. So far in our mission, a lot of time was chewed up playing prisoner taxi. Finally, very early in the morning, while it was still dark, we reached the point up the coast designated as our objective. There, through the magnified moonlight of the infrared starlight scope, I watched, mesmerized, as two sampans, with several people in each, glided in toward the shore. We had been briefed that this was a favorite crossing area for VC trafficking contraband. I turned the radio off so that we would not receive an unwanted voice that could be picked up by our new targets.

We paddled in closer to shore while the Vietnamese pulled their sampans up on the beach and began to unload something—we couldn't tell what. I illuminated them with a flare. The entire sky exploded into daylight. The men stood up, stiff and erect, momentarily frozen. Then, with panicked leaps, they ran for cover. We opened fire. My M-16 jammed, and as I bent down in the boat to grab another gun, a stinging piece of heat smacked into my left arm above the elbow. The inside of my arm burned. I presumed I had been hit by shrapnel or small-arms fire. I had no idea where it had come from. By this time, Runyon had started the engine, which had been resisting his best efforts. We passed by the empty beach to our starboard side, strafing it. Then it was quiet.

We fired a couple more flares to determine if anything besides the sampans was visible on the beach, but there was no way to do it without putting too much light on us as well, so we stopped. We beached briefly and considered recovering whatever the VC had been transporting, but most of our ammunition was gone and our engagement had alerted any VC for miles around of our presence. We were not in a good position to fend off a counterattack. Runyon ensured the sampans were unusable by filling them with holes from the M-60 machine gun. Then, with a warning from the cover boat of a possible VC ambush, we departed the area, taking a different route.

I was a little frustrated. Taking so many fishermen as prisoners had chewed up much of the night. I wondered what might have unfolded if we could have set up an ambush earlier at the upper end of the inlet. I thought we had improvised pretty effectively. The vision of VC running like spooked deer stayed with me. Zaladonis couldn't see the people clearly when he first started firing. The .30-caliber bullets kicked up the sand way to the right of them as he sprayed the beach, slowly walking the line of fire over to the left, where the men had been leaping for cover. I had been shouting directions and trying to unjam my gun. Runyon was locked in a personal struggle with the engine, trying to start it. There were moments when each of us felt his heart in his throat. It occurred to me many years later that Navy SEALs train for a long time for similar operations. Two of us had never even said hello before that night. We operated out of instinct. When I got back to the Swift boat, the adrenaline subsided; I curled up on the afterdeck and slept while we transited back to Cam Ranh.

The doctor at the medical facility took the piece of metal out of my arm and bandaged me up. The next day I was sent on a regular Swift boat indoctrination patrol with an officer who was nearing the end of his tour. It was uncommonly boring. We slowly steamed north and south for the length of our patrol area. There were no sampans, much less Viet Cong freighters. The boat pounded uncomfortably in the monsoon waves. As it got dark, we anchored in a small cove and relaxed over dinner.

Then, as we patrolled through the night, we saw the lights of fishing junks moving through a curfew zone. The OINC of the Swift showed me how to tell the Vietnamese where they can and can't fish. We went alongside a creaky wooden junk that reeked of stale fish. The officer made a lot of threatening noises in his best Vietnamese, learned quickly and often less than adequately at the Coronado Naval Amphibious Base. He motioned the fisherman to go away: *"Di di mau."* Go away quickly. The fisherman apparently didn't move fast enough to pull his nets in. So the officer took out a knife and cut the nets off where they came over the gunwale into the junk. Hundreds of feet of net still dragging behind the junk sank to the bottom of the sea. I watched the fisherman's face sink with it, clearly seeing his investment go down into the deep. Without nets, his job, his income, his ability to make a living were now all at risk. A small boy who had been watching silently from the bow of the junk pulled up the weight they'd used as an anchor. The junk moved off into the darkness. I know the officer was within his authority to cut the nets, but I thought it was a counterproductive exercise of authority over a defenseless fisherman and a great recruitment tool for the Viet Cong.

The officer, a lieutenant, turned to me and said, "If you think they've been in a no-fish zone several times, just shoot a notch in the junk so you'll recognize it next time you see it. Then, if they keep on doing it, just shoot a hole in the boat below the waterline—that really gets 'em." I was left wondering what the little boy would think ten years from then and how receptive he would be to America's policy of winning hearts and minds.

Two AND A half weeks after my arrival in Vietnam, the division operations officer asked me, "How would you like to go to An Thoi?" An Thoi was the home of Coastal Division 11 (CosDiv 11), the southernmost Swift boat base. The headquarters was a floating barracks ship off Phu Quoc Island in the Gulf of Thailand, near the border with Cambodia. I realized quickly that it was an assignment, not an invitation. The officer smiled. "You wanted to go a few weeks ago so you came to mind. Besides, there's no one else. You're leaving in two hours. We're giving you PCF-44. You can pick up your charts and orders after you pack."

An Thoi—the word carried many meanings.

I immediately pictured Vietnamese army generals and colonels flying into a one-strip airport, hoping for a swim in the turquoise water of the bay and stocking up on nuc mam, a fragrant local delicacy, to be traded later for services rendered on the mainland; a nearby prison camp detaining more than fifteen thousand Viet Cong; and our out-of-the-way Navy base, remote from civilization.

Most ominously, to Swift crews, An Thoi had quickly become a synonym for Operation Sealords. It meant being in the rivers more often than not. It meant operating in the heart of VC strongholds. In the early stages of Sealords, An Thoi had taken the brunt of the casualties.

My early curiosity regarding my posting was now being rewarded.

A quick inspection of a map shows the huge Mekong Delta spread out over a vast network of rivers and canals in the southernmost portion of Vietnam. The Mekong is one of the great rivers of the world—originating in China, running south through Laos, Thailand and Cambodia, and finally spilling out into a spiderweb of rivers large and small, all charging toward and ultimately emptying into the South China Sea. There are few roads. Because of its poverty and difficult geography, it became a Viet Cong stronghold against first the French and then us Americans. Unless large numbers of troops were deployed to hold territory, the only way to have a presence in the delta was to patrol and control the waterways.

Operation Sealords was started officially in November 1968. It began unofficially when earlier, two Swift skippers—tired of doing board and search missions—made unauthorized runs through major rivers in the southern part of the Mekong Delta. These unauthorized raids sparked the imagination of the squadron commander, Captain Hoffmann, and suddenly Swift boats went from the South China Sea to Mekong Delta rivers. It quickly grew into a joint operation between U.S. and South Vietnamese forces to disrupt enemy supply lines in and around the delta.

In early December, the pace and intensity of Sealords raids in the delta had picked up significantly. So had the casualties, since the boats were more exposed to danger. They were conducting raids nearly full-time in the rivers of the southern delta. Two boats had now been ordered south to fill in for damaged boats and wounded crews: my newly assigned boat—the 44—and the 57. The OINC of the 57 was Ted Peck, a lieutenant (junior grade) recently shifted to Cam Ranh Bay from CosDiv 12 in Da Nang. Ted had been stationed north of Da Nang with the detachment of Swifts at the small outpost of Chu Lai—the Chu Lai Tigers, as they were called, or called themselves. He was an action-oriented, no B.S. OINC, and sitting at Cam Ranh cramped his style and sense of duty. When no one else volunteered to go to An Thoi, Ted said he would.

So it was that in early December 1968, late in the afternoon, after packing and provisioning, PCF-44 pulled away from the pier with its new crew and with me, its new skipper. It joined PCF-57 as they pointed their bows toward the southernmost tip of Vietnam and ultimately to Phu Quoc Island in the Gulf of Thailand.

I WAS FILLED with curiosity and anticipation for this new but potentially dangerous assignment. The first thing I wanted to do was get to know my crew and have them get to know me. They'd been through a lot before they inherited me. We were thrown together from different backgrounds, with a hodgepodge of accents that would have confused the hell out of the best translators. We were from Arkansas, Illinois, the Florida panhandle, upstate New York—and yours truly from Massachusetts by way of far too many far-flung places.

Two of the sailors on board were especially raring to find some action. I met them for the first time only minutes before leaving. One was my leading petty officer—the enlisted man who acted as second-in-command. He was an extremely capable radarman second class with only one remaining month on his tour in-country. He had a round face with a toothy smile, accented by large, dark-rimmed glasses and a healthy shock of blond hair. His enthusiasm for everything we were doing was contagious.

He volunteered to go with me because his previous eleven months had bored him stiff. He'd become remarkably proficient in Vietnamese, able to jump into a junk and converse easily with the locals during board and search. But that didn't satisfy him. It was too passive for his adventurous spirit. His dream was to get into a river and see some action before he went home. "Give me just one good firefight and I'll be happy," he used to say. His name was Wasser—James Wasser.

The other new man was Drew Whitlow, a boatswain's mate third class. He was a shy person, decent to the core. The guys loved to rib him. They had their long-running sitcom sequences—many of which involved good-natured teasing, especially when Drew was perpetually five minutes late for a meeting on a fifty-foot boat that took ten seconds to walk end to end. He was good company.

The gunner's mate, Stephen M. Gardner, had at one time been a petty officer, but after a clash of one sort or another, he was reduced to seaman. Since then, he enjoyed a seesaw relationship with promotions and demotions. He had a short-timer's attitude. Where guns were concerned he was capable. He worked hard, and, like Wasser, he waited for the day when he could try those guns on an enemy.

The engineman, Bill Zaladonis, a petty officer third class, was laid-back and quiet. I knew and admired him from our earlier patrol. He was as competent as anybody on the boat. Under-spoken, understated and, on occasion, undernourished, he religiously saw to it that the engines always ran at top performance, that the oil was at the right level and that he got to eat on time. He was super-skilled with an engine. If there was a way to get more out of our nearly 1,000 horsepower, Zal was able to do it. We depended on him to keep the twin 480-horsepower General Motors 12V71 marine diesels running 24/7. Other than that, the war could go right on being fought and it wouldn't faze him at all. "Man, I don't give a shit," he would say.

The final crew member was also a boatswain's mate, like Whitlow. Stephen Hatch was incredibly competent and calm. He helped round out a terrific crew. Steve delighted in telling me and everyone else on the crew that he had only thirty more days in-country and "it was high ho and off on the fucking freedom bird and back to the States."

Everyone dreamed about the freedom birds, the big, beautiful Pan Am and Northwest and other charter jets that we could see climbing away from Vietnam heading for home. Hatch and Wasser kept telling me that with them on board the 44, I had nothing to worry about. Had I known more about how capable they all were, I would have heartily agreed. But we were new as a team and yet to be tested. As we continued down the coast of South Vietnam toward the rivers of the delta, miles away from the nearest freedom bird, I hoped they were right.

THE NEXT MORNING, after taking a teeth-jarring beating in the huge South China monsoon seas, we stopped for fuel at Coastal Division 13 in Cat Lo. Then we were off again, out through the narrow river, past small huts sticking high up out of the mud on the riverbank, past rickety old junks piled to the gunwale with nets and manned by rail-thin Vietnamese fishermen, past the once-upon-a-time carefree resort of Vung Tau and out through the shallows into the deep water six miles off the coast.

From there, navigation was precarious unless one stayed well out to sea, following the line on a chart showing a constant ten fathoms—the deep water. To our right, as we moved southward, was the Mekong Delta, flat for miles, barely providing a radar presentation. Occasionally, tufts of green mangrove could be seen rising on the horizon. Even when we were cruising along several miles out from the shoreline, the water depth could occasionally drop to six inches. In many places it seldom reached more than four feet, except in scattered channels, where the current sliced out in ever-changing patterns. Each time we passed one of the big mouths of the several branches of the Mekong that actually shaped the delta—the Co Chien, the Bassac, the My Tho—the water would roughen. The boat would rock uncomfortably through muddy brown waves. We did a good job of putting the seaworthiness of Swift boats to the test.

Throughout the day, we headed south to the point of land at the very southern tip of Vietnam. At midnight, four miles from the line where we'd cross from the South China Sea into the Gulf of Thailand, we rendezvoused with a landing ship tank (LST). Huge fenders were lowered over the sides of the LST to permit the Swifts to tie up. Nestled comfortably alongside, we refueled. We continued south firmly pinioned to our large friend. I looked up about twenty feet to the deck of the ship and saw a ladder come tumbling down with an invitation to come aboard. We quickly accepted.

The captain interrupted a late-night showing of a movie to welcome Ted and me with coffee and conversation. Something about the exchange was foreboding: he described a recent bloodbath involving his ship and the Swifts. Weeks before, in a predawn raid, within minutes of the Swifts entering the Bo De River, the Viet Cong had taken five boats under fire from both banks and cut them to ribbons. The LST had been criticized for missing its targets while trying to provide cover to the Swifts. It was a miracle that no one was killed. But seventeen men wounded had earned the operation the name "Bo De Massacre."

As the captain of the LST worked hard to exonerate his ship for its role in the pre-raid bombardment, I sat there thinking about the fighting I was about to confront. I thought about the officer on that raid who lost his leg just six weeks after arriving in-country. For centuries people have wrestled with, philosophized about and debated the psychology of combat. Generation to generation, most of the people hungry for action are the people who haven't seen what war looks like up close. They want to test the warrior ethos—whether as a testing of self, or the completion of a duty, or an expression of the youthful delusion of invincibility. Probably everyone comes at it somewhat differently, even as they surrender to age-old instincts. In any event, we had an obligation to live up to.

Whatever the rationale, it doesn't take long to understand how much luck interacts with character to determine the outcome. And it doesn't take long to realize how senseless the experience can be. And yes, when we arrived in An Thoi, we requested that we be sent on a mission, more evidence that the youthful zest for action is irrepressible. It pulls at you in a tug-of-war between the rational and emotional, between common sense and adventuresome youth.

BY THE TIME I arrived in An Thoi, a pall had fallen over the division. Only a day or so earlier, an ambush claimed the life of one of the enlisted crewmen. Sealords was new enough that people were still feeling their way through the initial emotions that come with fighting and with death. People still carried themselves with outward bravado, which was the unspoken rule, but underlying everything—meals, jokes, drinking—there was a tension that was inescapable.

It didn't ease matters that we were living on a floating barracks ship anchored several hundred yards offshore. About thirty officers shared one another's dreams and aroma in one crowded bunkroom. The room was hot. Occasionally, concussion grenades dropped in the water reverberated against the barracks hull, preventing enterprising VC from swimming up and sabotaging our home.

Compounding the difficulties of sleeping were the Swift boats themselves. They were tied up alongside the barracks, "nested" one alongside another. When the sea got rough, which it sometimes did at three in the morning, the whole nest would thump against the metal barge. If the pounding got bad enough, the officers whose boats were on the outside of the nest were roused from their slumber to move their craft.

The next four days raced by. Another raid was scheduled for the Bo De River, a repeat of the mission that had been thwarted a few days earlier. To a man, my crew expressed a desire to be included. We wanted to see the rivers for ourselves.

Lieutenant Bill Locke, the ops officer for CosDiv 11, was intelligent and capable. To Bill fell the unpleasant task of assigning boats to missions, keeping up with a schedule that was shuttled down to him in messages from the desks in Saigon. It was a tough job sending out men knowing they might not return alive.

Bill listened to our request. He must have quietly thought that we were naive for wanting to get into a river. He told me it wouldn't be long before I would have rivers up to my neck. I didn't realize how true those words would be. Instead of the Bo De, we were sent up to the northern tip of Phu Quoc Island, right on the Cambodian border, to patrol the waters separating Vietnam from Cambodia. The international water boundary lay at one end of the patrol area. If a navigational error didn't get you in trouble, your curiosity and imagination could.

The patrol, however, was uneventful—not surprisingly, since that particular patrol was always uneventful. The most exciting thing that happened was the meeting of Swift boat and hidden rock. One officer hit the same rock several times, thereby ensuring it was named for him. Except for hitting his rock and occasionally finding new ones to hit, the only other occurrence on the R&R patrol was a request to fire a harassment and interdiction mission—H&I, as it was known. The purpose was merely to let the Viet Cong know that we were thinking of them—literally to harass and stop movement along the waterways. If someone else happened to be in the target area—an area cleared for firing because there were no friendly troops of record in the vicinity—then so be it. Any unlucky, innocent passersby or bystanders were also harassed and interdicted. If hurt or killed, they were viewed as collateral damage.

When we returned to An Thoi, we loaded extra ammo on board. Zaladonis applied his considerable skill to tuning the engines in the hope that maybe we'd soon make the run through the Bo De River. While we were waiting for this assignment, one of the boats operating to the south of An Thoi had a serious enough engine problem to necessitate its return to base. Another boat was shifted from the patrol area nearest to it, and we, in turn, were ordered to fill the vacated patrol area, not far from the U Minh forest, where five hundred French paratroopers had been dropped during the French-Indochina War, never to be heard from again. The U Minh was a patchwork of rivers, streams and canals; it had never been under the control of any government. It was considered hard-core VC territory. We never ventured into it—at least while I was in Vietnam. We did feel a certain intrigue in being so close to an area of such mystery, but beyond the legend and the excitement, there was nothing else to shout about. Hundreds of junks fished along the shore. We spent the entire day boarding and searching them, a tedious undertaking.

Each junk was crowded with children. Often families greeted us with toothless smiles and unintelligible phrases. Their nets stretched out behind them, and in baskets on the decks were various kinds of fish and shrimp of all sizes. Several times our propellers became tangled in their nets. We had to stop dead in the water, put a man overboard to cut the nets free and then continue on. When this happened, we gave the boss-fisherman as many cans of our C-rations as it took to get him smiling again. I would profusely shower him in my best Vietnamese—*"Xin loi, xin loi, quí ông"* (Excuse me, mister), a necessary sentence in any foreign soldier's lexicon—and we would depart for another job of boarding and searching.

Unlike the mainland delta, most of the offshore islands were friendly. When we finished searching every visible junk and sampan in our patrol area, we would drop anchor at one of the smaller islands that kept beckoning to us from a distance. We quickly identified a favorite island. It was a Pacific paradise—the kind you dream about.

We would anchor in a small inlet with several lush beaches, rows of wild palm trees sprouting up along them, forming an idyllic border from one end to the other. No invitation needed to be extended to turn the crew into explorers. Gardner, the gunner's mate, had the life raft in the water before anyone said a word. He and Wasser, my leading petty officer, paddled off toward the beach like two shipwrecked men who had sighted land after weeks at sea. They took some candy and a first-aid kit to woo anyone they met. Hatch swam after them, while Whitlow and I remained on the boat to cook the shrimp we traded our C-rats for with fishermen during board and search. An hour passed. I was lying in the sun when I heard laughter coming across the water. I looked up to see a Vietnamese fisherman in a large sampan towing Wasser, Gardner and Hatch out to the boat: three U.S. Navy sailors, sitting precariously on the tiny life raft like three Robinson Crusoes, being towed to safety. The fisherman responded to their candy with a gift of coconuts. As they neared the Swift, the raft tipped over at least ten times. The fisherman didn't know what to think of the crazy Americans. Nor did we watching from the boat.

While we passed the lunch hour in this unique fashion, a radio call ordered us to return immediately to An Thoi. We transformed from pleasure craft back to gunboat and headed out at high speed.

WHEN I CLIMBED up to the CosDiv 11 operations office, one of the officers came up to me and said, "Have you heard the latest? Two boats are being sent to Cat Lo and you're one of them." I couldn't believe it. I ran up to the operations office and asked Bill Locke. Sure enough, Captain Hoffmann, the squadron commander, had ordered an increase in the Cat Lo patrol force for a few weeks. My boat had to go because Bill couldn't divert any of the boats on assignment and we were "junior" to boot.

It was an early lesson in the power of a seniority system, good training for twenty-eight years to come in the U.S. Senate. Our boat was the last into An Thoi and therefore the first out. Someone had to go. We knew our mail was sure to be thoroughly lost in the shuffle and, having just weathered the monsoon trip down, we also knew the trip back into the wind and sea would be even worse. It promised to be a struggle.

The OINC of the Swift accompanying us was being transferred because he'd seen too much of Sealords. Each time he departed for raids, he would pull one of his fellow officers aside and point out where his very personal belongings were located in the event that he didn't return alive. Often, he would sit in the wardroom, staring at a wall while chain-smoking, his hands shaking. He couldn't have been a nicer guy. His only problem was too much thinking combined with too much imagination.

Hemingway warned that the combination of thinking and imagination in combat areas is not conducive to tranquillity:

Danger only exists at the moment of danger. To live properly in war, the individual eliminates all such things as potential danger. Then a thing is only bad when it is bad. It is neither bad before nor after. Cowardice, as distinguished from panic, is almost always simply a lack of ability to suspend the functioning of the imagination. Learning to suspend your imagination and live completely in the very second of the present minute with no before and no after is the greatest gift a soldier can acquire.

I thought Hemingway's warning was an important one. I wanted to keep thinking and not shut down entirely. It was important to have balance, to be a good soldier and a good observer, to stay sane and alive.

From what I'd seen so far, the U.S. position was ill-fated. The Vietnamese themselves seemed pretty adept at playing everybody off each other. It was a war of slow attrition for a long-term gain that always remained in doubt. Sometimes it even seemed we cared more about winning than our South Vietnamese allies. We seemed to see the war differently, which makes sense when you consider how long the Vietnamese had coped with other countries fighting in their land.

The start of the trip from An Thoi to the tip of the Cà Mau Peninsula was pretty smooth, but once we rounded the cape and met the northeast monsoon seas head-on, things became tough. Swift boats were designed for the calm waters of the Gulf of Mexico, not the South China Sea. With a short bow, we'd crest a wave and, before the bow could pop up, it would run into the next one head-on, with each wave smashing against the pilothouse, breaking over the guntub and cascading back along the boat. The guntub was fitted with only a canvas cover. Seawater would seep through, spraying inside, dripping on whoever was steering the boat. Ultimately everything was soaked. We did everything we could to tighten the hatches but nothing worked. The humidity was 100 percent and the windows dripped with water.

The Swift boat traveling with us had started the journey with a nonfunctioning radar. No sooner did we round the point into the South China Sea than a huge wave swept over the bow, knocking out our radar too. It was such a black night that it remained impossible to judge the size of the oncoming waves. The key was to find the right speed, to try as best as possible to stay above the wave, but the waves often came at different intervals and heights. When there was a moment of hesitation on the crest of a wave, an extra push upward, we knew that the boat was going to slam down with a resounding crash, sending our spines through our skulls, inspiring a cacophony of four-letter words from the men hanging on to the decks below. The helmsman's seat had a seat belt, keeping him from levitating every time the boat hit a wave. If you were standing, the force of the crash could drive you to your knees. The only way to be half comfortable was to try to lie absolutely flat and arch slightly at the moment of contact.

The compass lights eventually shorted out. Both the forward and the aft watertight compartments filled to the brim, and our small pumps were unable to keep up with the water coming in, necessitating an emergency rendezvous with one of the Coast Guard cutters to borrow their more powerful pumps. The searchlight shorted out along with the rest of the electrical system. Each time something went wrong or the boat hit a wave with exceptional impact, groans of "only twenty more days" rose from the depths of the cabin. Clothes and books and codes were strewn over the deck, mixed with food that had spilled out of the storage locker.

We kept well offshore as we hammered steadily north to Vung Tau, home base for CosDiv 13. As we approached the bay off Vung Tau, because the waters were shallow for miles, we remained glued to the fathometer to ensure we didn't run aground. Hours later, our two boats reached the protected waters shielded by the peninsula. We were finally able to dry out while watching large cargo ships steaming toward the mouth of the Saigon River.

The trip to Cat Lo seemed to take forever. In reality, it took thirty-five hours. When Zaladonis, the engineman, stuck his head through the pilothouse door and yelled, "Hey, goddamn, I'm gettin' hungry," we knew that the trip was almost over. Spirits picked up immediately.

As we slid by Vung Tau, we began to run low on fuel. We turned in to and limped up the Dinh River, which led to Cat Lo, where CosDiv 13, food and sleep were waiting. Regulations required that all boats docked during the night be fully fueled in the event of attack. Dying for sleep, we spent another hour refueling and then, finally, checked in at the division headquarters. The men were assigned bunks in the enlisted barracks. I was led to the officers' quarters, where the operations officer gave me a rack for the night. I fell on it and woke up the next day, thirteen hours later.

CAT LO WAS a small Swift base on solid ground, near the Vietnamese tourist city of Vung Tau. Unlike An Thoi, it came under VC mortar attack from time to time. Whenever there was an attack, boat crews sped out of the confined spaces of the Swift base for the relative security of the bay.

Toward the end of 1968, infiltration through the barrier of the Coastal Surveillance Force (activated for Operation Market Time) had been so curtailed that for the Swifts the biggest battle to fight while on patrol was against boredom. For those boats stationed along the delta coastline there was, however, natural and immediate entertainment at hand—a quick dash up one of the Viet Cong–infested rivers with guns ablaze, all in the name of excitement. Among a small group of officers, these excursions into the rivers became a regular game, an unconventional way to make the war bend to one's own pace.

In Cat Lo, I thought back to the relative comfort and safety of the floating barracks, which reminded me of our colleagues in CosDiv 11. I remembered a conversation I'd enjoyed with another OINC named Mike Bernique.
Mike had lived in France and studied at the Sorbonne, and he was gutsy: He
had little reservation about challenging the rivers. In fact, if he had had a
chance, he would have beached his boat and chased after Ho Chi Minh himself. He and I kicked the war around frequently, my skepticism a foil to his
certainty. He would say, "Don't you see how if we were to leave here the
whole of Southeast Asia would fall?" And I'd say, "No, I don't, and even if
that did happen, how does that threaten us?" We debated in particular about
our allies. I pointed out how difficult it was to discern "that South Vietnamese leaders want to win as much as we want them to."

His retort was always something along the lines of "But it's not the
South Vietnamese that we're really trying to help anyway, it's ourselves.
We have to beat back communist advances. This is where we have to make
a stand."

Then a group of us would ask him why we had to make the stand in
South Vietnam, and how we were really helping ourselves, and what it
meant for us to be in South Vietnam. It was a circular argument. The discussion was never acrimonious. It was always taken with a grain of salt, good
humor and respect. I think everyone was looking for answers.

Mike's fervor had a good deal to do with the Swifts' participation in
river warfare. Without authorization, he'd race into the Cua Lon River leading out of the delta. Many rivers were fortified with multiple bunkers along
the banks, some hidden in the thick jungle foliage. Looking at the map,
Mike figured if he went up the Bo De on one side of the tip of the peninsula, he could connect with another river that would empty into the Gulf of
Thailand on the other side. Indeed, he made the river run without incident,
probably since the VC never thought Swifts would be daring enough to try.
Obviously, his trip alerted them to the reality. The Viet Cong were ready for
future runs.

While Mike and I had some differences on the geopolitics of our enterprise, we found common ground on river strategy. Boarding and searching
boats, looking for VC, weapons and ammo, made sense to us, but just running up a river, guns blazing, taking on targets of opportunity, which frequently were simply thatched huts, seemed to be serving ourselves up to a
potential ambush as a flotilla of floating targets. Given the noise of our twin
engines, everyone within miles could hear us coming, giving them plenty
of time to prepare to shoot at us from bunkers. If it was upstream, the Viet

Cong knew that we had no choice but to come back at least partly the same way. They were patient and disciplined. They'd be waiting.

In the early summer of 1968, the command of the Coastal Surveillance Force changed hands. Policy was quick to change with it. Captain Hoffmann, a veteran of World War II, did not intend to be caretaker of a passive organization. It was wartime, and war is when you take the initiative. Military reputations are made in doing so. He wanted the Navy—Swift boats in particular—to play a larger role in the war. If Viet Cong were operating in the vicinity of his jurisdiction, he wanted to go after them. He would back up anybody who showed resourcefulness in the pursuit of Viet Cong. I admire those instincts. They are legitimate—providing they are strategized and resourced properly, neither of which I thought was happening.

For the first few months, the tempo of operations changed only slightly. Then, in the middle of October, the quick dashes into the rivers for excitement transitioned from clandestine game to public policy. Lieutenant Mike Brown, operating from CosDiv 11, made a run through the Cua Lon River in the southernmost tip of the Mekong Delta. Entering the Cua Lon on the Gulf of Thailand side of the Cà Mau Peninsula, he transited the length of the river through Viet Cong country, turned in to the Bo De River and exited into the South China Sea, but not without incident. Near the exit, the boat was taken under fire and Lieutenant Brown and several of his men were lightly wounded.

At first, an attempt was made to keep the excursion a secret, but word inevitably leaked out. When it reached the commanding officer in Cam Ranh Bay, Lieutenant Brown was recommended for the Silver Star. The concept of river penetrations had obviously found a welcome ear in Captain Hoffmann.

Ten days later, Mike Bernique made a dash up a small river that designated the Vietnam-Cambodia border at the north end of the Gulf of Thailand, near the Vietnamese town of Ha Tien. With the help of Army troops who were riding in his Swift, he overran a Viet Cong tax station that had been extorting funds from the local citizens. He succeeded in killing several of the Viet Cong and capturing their weapons.

Unfortunately, because the action had taken place so near to the Cambodian border and because several of the dead had fallen on the other side of the international dividing line (which at the time was still observed), the incident was not so easily swept away. The next day, Mike was flown to Saigon, where the Naval Forces Vietnam Command argued whether he should be court-martialed or decorated. Lieutenant Bernique was recommended for the Silver Star. The small river he had successfully transited became known as "Bernique's Creek."

BEFORE TOO LONG, my crew on PCF-44 was seeing action on the Soi Rap River, south of the Long Tau River, not far from Saigon. It was not a Sealords raid but a patrol that got us there. We were glad to be on a river at last, mixing with the population, seeing the delta for ourselves. An unearned feeling of invincibility accompanied us up the Long Tau shipping channel, probably because we hadn't been shot at yet, and men who haven't been shot at are inclined to be cocky.

Patrolling up our first river, we were too busy loading machine guns and laying M-16 rifles out on the deck to think much about the surroundings. We just knew that the riverbanks of mangrove could light up at any moment with tracers from heavy-caliber machine guns. We'd learned enough to know if we were ambushed, our reaction had to be instantaneous. The only way to ensure that was to know without question where everything was situated on the boat. We felt a healthy respect for what might happen even as we felt confident we knew how to respond.

The Soi Rap River stretched through the bleak mudflats of the Rung Sat Special Zone (RSSZ), also known as the Forest of Assassins, an area that had been specifically structured for extra defense because of its proximity to Saigon and to the cargo ships carrying war supplies. Thoroughly defoliated by thousands of tons of Agent Orange, the banks of the river looked like an atomic wasteland, bleak and brown, like Verdun and the trenches of World War I. The American command decided the easiest way to eliminate the dangers of the jungles near the river was to eliminate the jungles themselves. With the jungles stripped of their greenery, the chances of ambushers using the undergrowth for cover while they poured rockets on the freighters would be minimized. At least, so they calculated.

No sooner did we assume our patrol station in the Soi Rap River, a few miles downstream from a military headquarters at Nha Be, than some would-be assassins used the cover of the Rung Sat mud to fire rockets at a freighter, hitting it twice. The thousands of tons of herbicides evidently didn't faze the guerrillas. Headquarters at Nha Be ordered several PBRs— shallow-draft river patrol boats—to move into the area. We were asked to move from our position to cover them while they searched in several small estuaries of the Long Tau. We jammed the engines forward to full speed and raced up the river with anticipation that we would fight the whole war in those few moments. The high was short-lived. Nothing suspicious could be found anywhere in the vicinity of the reported attack zone. We relaxed.

When we finished looking around the banks of the river for some traces of the attackers, we returned to our patrol area. It occurred to me that while we were gone, if anyone wanted to cross the river with contraband goods, it would have been the easiest thing in the world. All they had to do was wait on a bank of the river until we disappeared around a corner, then slip their sampans from the mangrove cover and glide quickly across to the other side, a maneuver that consumed five minutes at most. During this time, we would be continuing merrily down the stream. Even at idle speed our engines could be heard for a considerable distance, warning anyone about to cross that it was not the wisest moment.

Events piled up on top of one another with magnetic tenacity. Not long after we returned to the patrol area, an air strike began a few hundred yards away from us. There was no warning—nothing. We had been sitting quietly eating peanut butter and jelly sandwiches when the scream of a jet a couple hundred feet above us sent everyone scrambling for cover. The initial reaction was to duck and then look. Then—*kaboom*—a billowing cloud of flame and black smoke exploded into the sky. More screams of jets as they dive-bombed down in graceful, silent arcs, silent until right above you when the black speck that was an airplane—any plane—became a bomber and it loosed its load and then drove almost straight upward into the sky, gaining altitude as quickly as possible and rolling out from a nearly vertical position as it reached the maximum point of its climb. From where we were, we could see the black eggs being lobbed from the belly of the jet. Just after the pilot pulled upward, he would let go of his load and the momentum and angle of climb would lob the napalm or high explosive onto a target somewhere a few hundred yards ahead. By the time the bombs hit, the plane was usually well into its climb away from the scene.

I called our boss at the tactical operation center and asked him politely if an air strike had been scheduled in my area. He answered, "Yes, there is one. Disregard it." And so, with jets diving a few hundred yards away, we disregarded it.

I never found out whether my life had been saved from something I didn't know about or whether it had almost been taken by something I did. There was reason to want to know what was going on. Not too many months before I'd arrived, one of the Swift boats had been shot right out of the water by an Air Force jet mistakenly identifying the Swift as a North Vietnamese PT boat. The jet fired one rocket into the boat and only the skipper and one crewman survived. The skipper had been physically challenged ever since. We had the best pilots in the world, but still we could feel nervous when a jet made a low pass for identification purposes or just for pleasure.

That night found us supporting a Popular Reconnaissance Unit. The PRUs, as we called them, were made up largely of VC defectors who were paid by the kill or by the number of weapons captured. In the unit that we worked with that night, the commander told me that five of his men had been decorated for bravery by Ho Chi Minh himself, prior to their defection. Now their job was shooting their former comrades.

The fact that men could so easily be brought to shift their allegiances in their own country prompted even deeper doubts about the eventual success of our policy. As long as there were jets and napalm and vast resources of ammunition and guns and hospital supplies, of course it must have been inviting to fight on the government's side. But when these were exhausted, which they had to be someday, then what? Would they shift back to the other side if they began to believe that the guerrillas were gaining? I wondered, while we helped this former VC to land in supposed enemy territory, where he and his comrades would hunt for the present VC.

For an hour or so, we sat in the night not far from where the PRUs had been dropped off by two PBRs. We had shut down our engines and were nestled into the shore on the bank opposite the landing point. Only our generator's clatter broke the silence. Two men kept an intense lookout on the shore side to see that no one crept up on us. The rest of us sat silently with M-16s close by, waiting either to be attacked or to hear from the PRUs.

Suddenly, a red flare shot into the sky from their position, calling for emergency extraction. The two PBRs sprang to life and started up a small estuary leading to the PRUs. The PBR skipper was on the radio to headquarters, yelling, "Emergency extraction requested—moving in now— emergency extraction requested—moving to coordinates."

We started the engine and pulled off the bank as fast as possible. We'd never worked with PBRs and knew only what we had read in the operation order given to us that morning, when we had assumed the patrol area. I carefully headed up the estuary in the wake of the PBRs. Swifts, designed for the ocean, with a three-and-a-half-foot draft, risked running aground, whereas the PBRs could float in inches of water. It was so dark we couldn't see where they were. Wasser started yelling, "Over there, skipper, over there," and he pointed to an even smaller stream that disappeared around a corner. We could hear the noise of the PBRs once we slowed down.

"Hey, skipper—I saw someone move in that hut over there," Gardner yelled down from the guntub.

"Where?" I asked, and then I looked out the other door to see that we were only ten feet from the bank and that ten yards in from the bank was a long thatch hut with a light on in it. At the same moment, shots came from the vicinity of the PBRs. There were a few bursts of M-16 and then the .50 calibers started firing in earnest. Some of the tracers flew over our heads.

I started up the small stream. Fish stakes spanned it from one side to the other. For a moment, I hesitated and then said, "The hell with it." We smashed right through the wooden poles. They broke on contact with the bow. We still couldn't see the PBRs. The shooting was sporadic by this time. The stream had narrowed so that we barely had room to turn around. I was wondering if we should continue when the decision was made for me. We began to feel ground beneath us. A few more shots were fired. I ran outside the pilothouse and took the controls at the outdoor aft helm, where it was easier to see. Slamming the gears first into reverse and then spinning the boat on its axis by working the engines against each other—one full reverse, the other full forward, with the wheel fully turned—we avoided the mud bank. I turned the boat around, hoping the PBRs wouldn't come screaming around the corner and crash into us, creating a gallery of sitting ducks for whatever had prompted the shooting originally. We moved into the larger estuary, where we waited for the PBRs. I was momentarily frustrated the Swifts couldn't operate in shallower water. Wasser said, "Shit, I was hoping we could've gotten up there and seen something."

Eventually, after long moments of uncertainty while waiting in the dark as we drifted near the bank of the river, the PBRs appeared from the small stream where we had nudged the mud. They were moving very slowly with a sampan in tow, confident the shooting was over for the evening. Hatch nursed the Swift alongside the PBR. I jumped aboard to talk with the chief petty officer in charge.

"What happened?" I asked. He told me that the PRUs were patrolling through the area when they came on a hut with two people in it—a man and a woman. They went in, found the woman writing a letter to her VC boyfriend, so they took them into custody. As they were coming back, they spotted a sampan with four people in it. "They took 'em under fire and that's it."

"Were the people killed?" I ventured timidly.

"Hell yes. PRUs don't miss when they shoot."

"But the people in the sampan didn't fire or anything?"

The chief just talked on. "It was a free-fire zone. They shouldn't have been there. Besides, one of the PRUs says they had guns, but the sampan tipped over and the guns were lost in the water."

I looked at the face of the woman who was squatting in the rear of the

PBR. She was defiant. She was very calmly watching the movements of the men who had just blasted four of her countrymen to bits. She glared at me. I wondered where her boyfriend was fighting us.

I could see the terror, perhaps hatred, in her eyes. I wanted to tell her that things would work out, but I wasn't confident they would. I knew I did not like the feeling of making someone look at us that way.

While we exited back into the Soi Rap River, the PRUs moved excitedly among themselves, talking about the action that had taken place. One mocked and mimicked the expression and position one of the dead had assumed at the instant he was blown away. They laughed. I was taken aback, but maybe it was just their way of relieving tension. Bottom line—the four dead were just four more casualties of war. Statistics. The body count was now higher.

I WAS SUPPOSED to be on a quick reconnaissance flight to view some of our patrol area from a helicopter, but it was diverted into a medevac. We arrived at a skeleton base at the foot of the Long Tau River where a tiny Vietnamese soldier was ushered into the seat next to me. He had been hit in the face. His entire head was swathed in gauze. By the time the helo arrived, the gauze was a saturated dark red. I didn't learn anything about what had happened—how he got hit. He kept feeling the bandage with his hands and lolling his head around uncontrollably. Occasionally, his head would drop for an instant against my shoulder. I was nauseated. His agony was affecting all my senses. His blood rubbed off onto my uniform.

We diverted to the base, where we helped the soldier into a waiting ambulance. Then we were off again, over the delta area I had seen so often on Huntley-Brinkley reports, over the Rung Sat Special Zone, over miles of mud and canals that wove forever through the RSSZ. The trip was peaceful. Only the vibration of the helicopter up and down with the singular *whoop-whoop* of a Huey engine and the brown mud below reminded us that we were in fact riding over the Mekong Delta of South Vietnam. We inspected the bunkers from the air, then returned to base.

In the afternoon, a helicopter cover team arrived to give us support, and I took PCF-44 to the Soi Rap and entered the river, which earlier that day had looked so peaceful from the air. The tactical operations center had read its tide table incorrectly. There were ten foot tides in this area, and at low tide, we could barely see over the high banks on both sides, which created the effect of being in a small canyon. It was impossible to see bunkers from where we were. I kept thinking how incredibly easy it would have been for the VC to shoot down on us and tear the boat to shreds. Only the helicopters gave us some sense of security. Since we couldn't see the bunkers, one of the helos spotted for us. We fired a few mortar rounds with the hope that one or two might land on a target.

Midway through the firing, one of the helos developed mechanical problems, so both left us and returned to base. We retraced our earlier steps with no air cover and luckily exited without a shot being fired. The Viet Cong had missed a prime opportunity to decimate a lone exposed Swift boat.

LATER IN THE afternoon, in the same river, we received a call asking us to move some Vietnamese troops from the base at Nha Be to a small village near the end of the Soi Rap River. Among the soldiers was a U.S. Marine captain who was acting as advisor to the Vietnamese. His name was Tim— I don't remember his last name, but he was reaching the end of his tour in Vietnam and the end of his rope as well.

"What's it been like?" I asked.

"Kinda varied," he said. "There's no way to sum it up really."

I asked him how he would describe the war generally. I was fishing with the hope that I would learn something about the war I hadn't seen.

"I dunno," he said. "It's been pretty bad. . . . We had a job to do. We did it as best as possible, I guess."

He really didn't want to talk, at least not to a stranger. He stood in the pilothouse thinking, looking down with deep furrows in his brow, squinting against the sun. Then he came out of his thoughts and said, "I can't really say it was worthwhile. I mean, I can't see what we've gotten done. We've torn up a lot of villages . . . killed a lot of people that probably shouldn't have been killed. We've lost a lot of good men too. I dunno. It's hard to say. I sure as hell know that we can't ever win over here . . . nothing to win anyway. You run through a fucking village cleaning out the VC and then you come back a few weeks later and they're all in the same place again. You walk over booby traps—booby trap after fucking booby trap—and there's nothing you can do about them. Just keep going and hit some more. I dunno. I'll be glad to get out of here and forget."

"Were you always down in this area?" I asked.

"No. I was up around Da Nang for a while. Then they shifted me down here to take on this advisory bit. Man, that was a scene up there. We used to sit around on some mountaintop waiting for weather to lift with battalions of North Vietnamese regulars closing in on us. That was hairy. You felt alone out there. Just sitting on a hill waiting for the gooks to sneak up and shoot your head off. That was a hell of a setup. But we got out of it. Lucky, I guess."

"What do you do down here?"

"I've been helping these guys"—he pointed to the Vietnamese sitting around the boat—"to set up a perimeter defense for their village. But it's harder than hell because no one wants to sit out on the perimeter and man a gun. They all insist on coming into the village at night because they feel safe. . . ."

We deposited the Marine and his entourage at the village. I didn't envy him having to stay there overnight, but it was clear he'd been through a lot worse.

During the night, we found that it was almost impossible to patrol effectively. If we tried to shine a light on the banks of the rivers to detect camouflaged sampans waiting to cross, we were providing them with an ideal target.

Despite their dangers, the rivers were an unending source of pleasure. They were a way of life for the Vietnamese. By patrolling them each day, we were given an opportunity to share that life in a unique manner. The rivers were the interstate highways of the delta. Junks were their trucks. Some junks were so large and so laden with goods of one sort or another that there was no way to move the goods and inspect thoroughly. It was all very well to have the special routine for searching a junk we had learned at San Diego, but in the rivers of South Vietnam, it just didn't work.

The junks were overflowing with grandmothers, grandfathers, children, animals, bicycles. It would have taken half the day to inspect the identification papers of the people alone. We learned to simply scan the passengers and interrogate any males who appeared of fighting age.

We would ask the peasants for their papers, and they would dutifully hand them over. Wasser and I would pretend that we were reading them carefully for errors and for legitimacy. My Vietnamese was not sufficient to make much out of their answers. I learned to interpret their body language, including hand motions, and long speeches of protest. Wasser was capable of gleaning a lot more. With much pronounced head nodding, muttering something here and there to show approval or disapproval, we would feign full comprehension.

We examined their papers to see whether they had done their military service, whether they had a fishing permit or whether they carried the identification papers authorized by the government. If not, we would detain them as VC or as deserters for interrogation by intelligence.

One day we came across a large, very suspicious-looking junk. It was loaded down from gunwale to bilge keel with sand. Wasser climbed on board and started to dig away at the sand, hoping to find a hidden shipment of AK-47s. After an hour's digging, and aided by the friendly men aboard the junk, we gave up. While we'd been digging on this one junk, twenty-five or thirty others passed us. The percentages were hardly in our favor.

To try to cover as many junks as possible, we would anchor in the middle of the river and hail everyone over as they passed. If a sampan tried to slip by pretending not to notice us, we would fire an M-16 across the bow and it would immediately veer toward us. One couldn't help but think about what it would be like to be cruising down a Los Angeles freeway or the Connecticut Turnpike and have a Mexican or a Canadian who was helping the U.S. government search automobiles fire a shot across the front of your car to make you stop.

There were times when we had as many as twenty junks and sampans alongside. It would have been easy for the VC to get us if they had wanted to—just float down on a barge and, when we were tied up with a mass of sampans, jump us in our confusion.

Wasser, Hatch and Gardner took the most pleasure out of boarding and searching. They would swarm over the chickens and the market produce, sticking their hands incredulously into everything. The Vietnamese would laugh at them as they stumbled over the passengers or possessions. We'd laugh back. Sometimes the girls would flirt with the crew. In the end, it was impossible to tell whether we'd searched them or they us. I remember once a chicken bit Wasser, and he was so surprised that he fell backward and landed prone in the vegetable produce. In one day, we might inspect hundreds of junks and sampans, visually and by hand, and in the few weeks we weren't carrying out Sealords raids, we only once found a piece of contraband—a stolen U.S. Navy anchor that had somehow found its way onto one of the barges.

The Army periodically gave us a blacklist of Vietnamese to watch out for: If we came across someone whose name matched that on the list, we were to bring them into the headquarters for interrogation. Unfortunately, the names on the lists that they gave us invariably didn't have the accent marks on the right letters or they had no accent marks at all. One name could be confused with one hundred people. Nevertheless, they expected us to bring in the blacklist people we found.

One day on the Soi Rap River we found a young man we thought was on the blacklist. We couldn't take him off the ferry because he was the only helmsman and pilot. Wasser was convinced the man was on the blacklist. From the top of the ferry, Wasser yelled down, "Mr. K., we've got to take this guy in. I know he's on the list and he's mighty crooked looking." So we took the entire ferry into custody, and with Wasser remaining on board to guard the helmsman while he steered, we stuck the nose of the Swift right on the ferry's stern and herded everyone up to the base at Nha Be.

From our position in the rear of the ferry, we were able to look directly into the kitchen. We watched, fascinated, while a little, old Vietnamese lady prepared food. She in turn watched us and, to our surprise, handed bowls of rice to us from the window. The sight of this comic parade from the banks of the river had to be hilarious—Wasser standing with his rifle behind the helmsman, a crowd of passengers staring at him, and a Swift boat passing food back and forth through the rear window, almost pushing the ferry toward its rendezvous with the interrogators at Nha Be, where we found that the accentless list was responsible for one more case of mistaken identity. The ferry was allowed to go on its way.

On another occasion, one of the junks approaching us to be searched came alongside too fast and started a panic among those already tied up. People started running around untying lines and shouting, and the result was a crash that put about three people in the water with chickens all over the place and little kids laughing and old men swearing at each other. I think it was the only time I saw them get honestly upset over anything.

Funnier than the way in which we conducted our job of boarding and searching was the manner in which the Vietnamese patrolled. Several of our new Swift boats had been turned over to them in Cat Lo, but I rarely saw them go out on patrol. They spent most of the time painting the boats and getting them ready for something. They were very good at waving as we passed them going to or returning from a river. Generally, however, they were anchored and everyone aboard was asleep. When this was the case, we would occasionally go by them at full speed, passing about a foot or two away. With delight, we would watch as our wake washed into them, waking up the crew. One of them always poked his head out of the hatch to see what was happening and then, *kerplunk*, he disappeared from view. When they weren't asleep they were usually fishing. Although we joked about our allies' work ethic, it was an ominous contrast to those who were running up and down patrolling their rivers.

The situation came to a crescendo in An Thoi, where the Vietnamese Swifts were finally persuaded to make a river incursion. Each Swift carried an American advisor. The Swifts were ambushed. One of the advisors was blown overboard. The boats refused to stop in or near the ambush to look for the advisor. Instead, they retreated completely out of the river before even considering a search. Once out of the river, they decided that they didn't want to go back and look for the man because they didn't want to be ambushed again. They refused even though the advisor might be alive in the water somewhere.

When notification was received at the An Thoi base, several American crews were detailed to leave and initiate a search at an ungodly hour of the morning. The advisor was never found, although a piece of his skull was picked up off the deck of the Vietnamese Swift. It was some time before anyone wanted to work with the Vietnamese again.

On the night of our last day on patrol near Nha Be, we got a call to pick up a Vietnamese woman who needed emergency transportation to the Navy base. At full speed, through the darkness, we raced down the Soi Rap River to a prearranged rendezvous with another Swift. There was something very special about answering this call. We were racing to save a life rather than take one. We sensed this. It lent purpose to all the hours spent cruising slowly up and down the river boarding and searching.

When we reached a point known as the French Fort, the other Swift showed up on the radar, a yellowish electronic flash, moving closer to us each time the sweep illuminated it with its mesmerizing 360-degree arc. We slowed, turned around to face upriver and waited for our sister ship to come alongside. As soon as it was close to us, we transferred the stretcher bearing the woman and then we shot off into the night to deliver her to professional medical hands in Nha Be.

The woman was in great pain. Before separating from the other Swift, they had told us she had an extrauterine pregnancy and was close to death. Her mother or possibly just a friend came aboard with her. They held hands, and both seemed awed by the concern and effort that was being made to do something for them. We had called ahead to the base at Nha Be. They said they would be expecting us.

Doctors were hovering over the stretcher as soon as we passed it to the pier. I last glimpsed the woman as she disappeared in the dark with a covey of curious soldiers and doctors scurrying around her. I never found out whether she lived, but that night I felt the patrol had been worthwhile.

Night was a time of fascination. We were only seven miles from Saigon. The horizon in that direction was always bright and inviting. Throughout the night, aircraft were flying around and around the city, dropping flares to watch for movement in the dark, lending security to the city's perimeter defenses. From where we sat in the river, there was a constant ballet of flickering light as the flares ignited high in the sky and drifted slowly to the ground. I would play a game, betting against myself which flares would hit the ground still burning. Sometimes helicopters, flying a support mission for a night ambush, would open up on a target and we could watch a steady stream of red tracers curve toward the ground. If the burst of fire was long enough, a straight line of red seemed to connect the helicopter with the target below it. Everyone knew that the guerrillas were moving at night. That thought alone brought a certain excitement to patrol.

When the patrol finally came to an end, we tied up at the pier at Nha Be, waiting for our relief to arrive. I went into the tactical operations center to speak with the officer on watch. I was curious to see how our missions were devised. It turned out that the center was shared by the Americans and the Vietnamese. The Americans couldn't make a move without checking with their counterparts, and the officer told me that their counterparts seldom knew what was going on. He said, "Whenever you want to get a plan moving, you explain to them the details of an idea. After proposing one or two alternatives, you wait for the Vietnamese to say, 'Why don't we do this?' It's usually the first thing that you've proposed. If they don't suggest it, nothing happens. When they finally do, you congratulate them on their good thinking and move on to the next problem."

I asked him if there were any waterway restrictions on traffic to Saigon. He said no. An idea that had been germinating in my head for several days became a reality. When the relief boat assumed the patrol, we set off from the pier, and entering the Saigon River, we made a brief curiosity foray into Saigon.

The river from the South China Sea to Saigon was a highway, with ships from all over bringing cargo to the capital. It was a mixture of U.S. and Vietnamese warships, cargo junks, sampans and ferries. The river was key to the U.S. military supply chain. Every morning, U.S. minesweepers steamed the length of the river to ensure that no mines had been placed overnight. To further protect the traffic, the U.S. Air Force had dropped Agent Orange along both banks, killing all the vegetation for a mile back to ensure that no insurgent force could hide in the foliage. The VC were determined, however. They would dig bunkers in the mud and jump up to fire a B-40 at a passing warship, then disappear before fire could be returned. Once, though, a VC made the mistake of firing at a ship that was carrying soldiers from the Republic of Korea. The senior ROK officer ordered the ship's captain to make a hard turn into the bank and hundreds of their soldiers streamed off. It was reputed that no other VC tried to shoot at passing ships for months afterward.

It was only a few miles upriver to Saigon. We covered them at full speed until we reached the outskirts of the city. Saigon was a world apart, a world of freighters tied up at docks, of barges housing refugees, of gaudy advertisements on billboards, of cars and buses weaving in and out of traffic, of large government buildings that dominated the waterfront, of countless huts raised above the mud banks on wooden poles, of dilapidated Navy ships belonging to the Koreans and docked in front of the Vietnamese Naval Headquarters, of water taxis skirting across the harbor, and, on this day, of one U.S. Navy Swift boat parading boldly through the middle of the city on a quick sightseeing tour. For a few moments, Saigon and Vietnam were connected in a way they hadn't been. We promised ourselves that we would return.

When we arrived back at the Cat Lo base, we were greeted with the news that one of the boats had been hit badly on a river patrol. Lieutenant (JG) Bob Emory had been medevacked. One of his men was killed. His boat had been towed back to the base. I walked over to see it. A huge hole ran through the pilothouse and down into the main cabin. The ambush occurred toward the end of a mission in a small river. Emory's boat had been playing one of the psyops tapes over the boat's loudspeaker. His engineman went below to turn off the tape machine. At the moment he turned around to walk back up into the pilothouse, a B-40 rocket went right through the hull into the main cabin and blew the man's head off. The shrapnel from the rocket tore into Bob's legs. Others were wounded too.

We arrived to see Bob's boat pulled out of the water, resting in skids on the floating dock where the repair work was done. Several men were on board cleaning up. I watched one of them make a face of disgust as he picked some hair and teeth out of the ceiling. The brief inspection of Saigon and the pleasurable side of the rivers evaporated instantly. The war was suddenly very real again.

Two days later, we were operating in the close vicinity of Dong Tam, the home base of the Ninth Infantry and the Riverine Force. I was trying to find a way to get into the Bob Hope USO Show and I was really low on fuel. I see this LST anchored in the middle of the river with a floating dock at its side. A couple PBRs were refueling there. I pulled up at the dock, tied up and was looking around for someone to ask for fuel. Suddenly this distinct mix of Brooklynese and Boston yells to me, quite authoritatively, "Hey! You can't tie your boat up here! Get your damn boat away from my ship!" I knew that voice immediately. I looked up and there was Paul Nace, whom I hadn't seen since we left Treasure Island. A year and a half had gone by. Paul hadn't recognized me—little did I know he was the officer in charge of the dock and, at that moment, my future. Suddenly, Paul recognized me and broke out into a big shit-eating grin—a wonderful moment of reunion in the middle of war, in the middle of the Mekong Delta. I'll never forget that moment and the improbability of a random meeting in a river with a friend in Vietnam. I also vowed never to let him forget that his first instinct was to deny me fuel! It was the only negative thing Paul ever said to me.

DAYS LATER, WE were assigned to take part in a Riverine Force attack up several small streams not far from Dong Tam. We rendezvoused with a massive Riverine armada. Monitor-like vessels, troop carriers with massive steel reinforcements on their sides and sandbags were everywhere. We looked puny and exposed beside them. At one point I heard someone yelling, "Mr. Kerry—Mr. Kerry—hello!" I looked over to see one of the enlisted men from *Gridley* waving to me from one of the carriers. I shouted my well wishes as we slid away from them. We were supposed to be doing an exhibition assault for the benefit of Secretary of Defense Melvin Laird, who was scheduled to observe from helicopters above us. At the last minute, our coordinates were changed to a different location because the initial assault zone was too hot. I will never forget this staged mission, which inevitably filled the secretary with a contrived view of what was taking place on the ground.

A few days later, we were operating with a small group of PBRs during another assault. As we nosed up a small side river we came under brief fire, and I heard Gardner yell from the guntub, "I'm hit!" The fire subsided quickly. We exited into the larger river. Gardner had a light wound in his arm. We departed immediately to the medical facility at the Ninth Infantry headquarters.

When I walked Gardner into the field hospital at the Dong Tam base, I found myself witness to a struggle for life in the triage area. A severely wounded man lay on a stretcher. He was Vietnamese. He was completely nude. His small, bony body was stretched out on the brown plastic mat covering the operating tables. Figures in green pushed in and out through the two doors that marked the pre-operating section of the Third Surgical Division, U.S. Army. An eerie, makeshift but still professional fluorescent light shone down on his chest, which was moving up and down with each trying breath, up and down with no rhythm and with very little strength. The tent was very cool, and my eyes caught the plastic tube for air-conditioning that ran across the overhead and that dominated all the other septic trimmings of the emergency ward, reminding me starkly and harshly that was where I was. Three or four operating tables, glass cabinets with surgical tools and battle dressings, oxygen bottles and resuscitators all congested to paint an ugly picture for an eye that was already transfixed and shocked.

When they took Gardner off to patch him up, I remained fixated on the struggle of the young Vietnamese infantryman. I watched while a very young boy with concern, hope and inexperience in his wide eyes prepared another pint of blood for transfusion. He quickly and meticulously pulled the plastic blood bag into an inflatable net and rubber container and, after breaking the seal, inserted a tube into the bag. Then, pumping on the kind of hand pump that a doctor uses to take blood pressure, he squeezed the blood from the bag into a small receptacle, and from there it ran into the limp body lying at the mercy of those who stalked around it.

With each thrust of his hand, slowly pushing the blood through the tube, I wanted so badly for life to be driven into the courageous figure that lay there so helplessly. Now and then the feet of the wounded man would twitch and his arm would try to move up toward his head—movements that were strangely disconnected from the rest of his body and from normality. I will call him Nguyen, because he could well have been and if he wasn't, he still needs a name. He was a Tiger Scout, a pathfinder for one of the platoons of infantrymen at Dong Tam. Whispers said that he had walked into a booby trap. Other murmurs said that he had been hit by gunfire. From where I was, I could see that his neck was bleeding. His head was arched back and his eyes, only half-open and dazed, were searching for something. There was nothing familiar here for this man. This was a moment of complete loneliness, I thought. No one to hold on to. No one to talk to, because he could not speak English and we could not speak Vietnamese, and, anyway, how does one bridge such a gap at a moment like this?

His left hand was wrapped in gauze that had turned almost completely red, soaked as it was with his blood, his red badge of courage. A pool of red had gathered on the table below the green Army stretcher on which he lay. Large transparent plastic tubes surrounded his legs, inflatable splints, and these too showed an increasing hue of dark red as his life flowed through them. I felt weak and my stomach began to twist. Beads of sweat poured all over me. I was hot and cold at once. I sat down on the floor because I thought I was going to be sick.

Nguyen's right hand, with long, sensitive fingers, occasionally reached up and swayed in the air. I wondered if he was trying to find something that we might understand or to reach out and touch something a man touches before he dies. Tears came to my eyes. I wanted to hug this little man who was so alone in his personal battle. His chest still moved up and down and with the movement remained the hope that he would win. I wanted so much for him to win. Once or twice his hand moved over to one side and his head slowly followed, allowing me to see the strong features of his face, a face hardened by years of war, suffering and uncertainty.

Then his right arm moved upward and out toward nothing but air. A doctor quickly took his pulse and his blood pressure. His toes, sticking out from the plastic splints, twitched back and forth. He tried to raise his head to look—maybe to ask for something, or perhaps in a last effort to fight for life. Then he was quiet. His right hand came slowly down on his chest and his other arm, bandaged and absent, lolled over the side of the stretcher. Nguyen was gone. No words. No cry. No sound of a breath. I prayed that I would never be as alone as he had been those last moments. I never learned his name. I don't think anyone in the tent did.

It seemed so absurd—a man dying alone in his own country. I wanted to cry, but I thought that I couldn't let myself, and so tears just welled up in my eyes.

The next two weeks passed quickly. We patrolled through several of the main rivers of the Mekong, experiencing a remarkable insight into the busy, beautiful life on the rivers, the main highways of South Vietnam. We shot duck with the riot gun from the bow of the boat, we traded C-rations for fresh shrimp, we boarded and searched countless junks, we interacted with the seemingly endless parade of very young children who would beg for a handout—any handout—as they would yell "You number one." We soaked in a bucolic but bustling life, somehow capable of producing its own tranquillity on a brown river running fast with a heavy current toward the sea. It was something to behold. Occasionally a few shots were exchanged here or there, but no serious firefights.

EARLY IN JANUARY 1969, we returned from a several-day patrol to be informed we were to return to An Thoi to resume our assignment with CosDiv 11. Back we went, retracing our journey around the southernmost point of Vietnam, the Cà Mau Peninsula, then the straight shot north to Phu Quoc Island, through the deep turquoise waters of the Gulf of Thailand. The demarcation between the muddy brown water of the South China Sea and the gulf was stark, as if a painter had drawn a bold, clear line across a canvas, one color on one side, a different one on the other.

An Thoi was the same as when we left, except the number of raids had grown. With experience under our belts in Cat Lo, we were immediately cycled into the rotation. Most of the members of my initial 44 boat crew had timed out on their year in Vietnam. Those who hadn't were detailed to fill individual slots on boats as other vacancies opened up.

On January 29, Ted Peck, one week after shifting with his whole crew to the 94 boat, was part of a six-boat operation up the Cua Lon River, led by a Commander Connolly, a desk officer from Cat Lo. It was hard to understand what a desk guy from Cat Lo was doing leading an An Thoi raid, but Peck and his crew, distinctly not thrilled at having been rousted early in the morning from a sound sleep, went to work. Soon, Commander Connolly instructed Peck and another boat to head up a small side canal to hunt for VC. Peck, I later learned, had haunting premonitions about what was to follow.

It was low enough tide that the boats were literally looking uphill, up the muddy gray banks of the canal. Conversely, anyone shooting at them was shooting down at a sitting duck in a bathtub. Moreover, the crew had no extended vision beyond the lip of the hill. Abruptly, an explosion went off under the 94, lifting and rocking it in the water. Del Sandusky, the boatswain's mate, remembers seeing a spider hole on the left side. Before he could shoot, Peck was seriously wounded by machine-gun fire from the banks. Bleeding and in pain, he managed to get off some shots while Sandusky miraculously managed to turn the boat and head out of the canal. Sandusky barely had room to turn in. He had to spin the boat at full power, nestling the bow in the mud on one side of the canal while the stern just cleared the other. He churned the props through the mud while ordering David Alston, the twin .50-caliber gunner, to stay in the guntub and keep firing. Peck then got hit again with a bullet in his ankle, breaking his leg. Alston kept firing. A bullet grazed his head and another hit him in the arm, but he kept up a furious barrage of the twin .50s. Once they got out in the main river, free from the intense firefight, help arrived to find that Ted Peck, despite the pain and being half-conscious, remained as tough as nails. Ted was transferred to an emergency medical unit, where he underwent surgery. He was then medevacked to the hospital in Saigon. We were told it was touch and go. Ted's pluck, combined with every man on that boat doing what he was supposed to in a hellish moment of surprise but certainly terror, saved all their lives.

Because Ted was to be sent back to the States, I was the lucky OINC who took over the 94 boat and its extraordinary crew. We bonded quickly.

My second-in-command was Del Sandusky, the boatswain's mate who had so skillfully maneuvered the boat out of danger. There is no doubt in my mind or that of any of his crewmates that Del's remarkable seamanship in turning that boat under intense fire saved the lives of the entire crew.

Gene Thorson, nicknamed "Thor," was our engineman. It was our good fortune that he was one of the best in the business. The last thing you wanted to ever experience was engine failure in the middle of an ambush. With Thor's talent, we never did.

Tommy Belodeau, the forward gunner, a radarman, hailed from Massachusetts. He and I felt an immediate connection, from Red Sox to accent.

Tommy had already seen serious action prior to the latest ambush. He had been decorated for capturing a prisoner on the riverbank after a chase.

Mike Medeiros, a boatswain's mate from San Leandro, California, was a jack-of-all-trades. He and Thor would swap responsibility for the aft .50-caliber machine gun. He was shorter than the other crew members—five foot six—but he was strong, calm and extremely capable at whatever he did. He served as my radioman in some operations. You could always count on Mike to be in the right place.

The final member of our crew was our rock-steady gunner's mate, David Alston. David was the most exposed of all—sitting up in the gun turret above Del and me, who were in the main pilothouse. He manned the massive twin .50-caliber machine guns, which were the heavy firepower of our boats. In the ambush that incapacitated Peck, the guntub he sat in was riddled with bullets. When the boat was being repaired in the skids out of the water back in An Thoi, several of us counted the holes. There were more than 160. A majority were in the guntub. How they missed Alston was nothing short of a miracle. Earlier in January, he had been wounded and was medevacked on that occasion. He told me he was saved then by his King James Bible in his pocket. David never had any doubt that God saved him again.

Over the next weeks we engaged in the highest operational tempo to date. We were in the rivers far more than we were out. There was an extraordinary range to the missions we undertook. On one occasion we ferried huge, heavy balloons of fuel for the Navy SEALs who were beginning to operate regularly in the area. It was called Operation U-Haul. We dragged the balloons twenty yards or so behind the boats, hoping they would not be exploded by rockets from the banks of the river. On the same mission we loaded our boats from top to bottom with lumber to deliver to the Vietnamese military base at Cai Nuoc for construction. When we arrived, kids helped us unload, and I marveled at how industrious they were as they diverted a good percentage of wood into their homes.

There was no limit to the variety of missions we took on: we picked up platoons or companies of local Popular Reconnaissance Forces to deposit them on riverbanks for sweeps along the river; we set ambushes along well-advertised VC routes and lay in wait for multiple sampans moving supplies at night; we went on tense night missions with units of SEALs in which we would insert at one location and then lie in wait for an extraction signal or a rendezvous at predetermined coordinates; we pulled prisoners out of the water after an ambush, taking them out to the Coast Guard cutter for interrogation; and time after time, we ran through rivers with varying numbers of boats, shooting at "targets of opportunity" and more often than not being shot at; we shuttled defenseless women, children and the elderly from the danger of being caught in cross fire or being targets of opportunity themselves to the safety of the cutter for transfer to a securer location.

Early in my days on the 94, we were assigned to run a SEAL team up to Cai Nuoc with Bob Hildreth and the 72 boat. As we approached fish stakes at the entrance of the Bay Hap River, Hildreth told me to take the left opening. I did so. We passed through holding our breath but without incident. Hildreth followed. *Boom*—the 72 was engulfed in water and smoke. It rocked back and forth as the riverbanks exploded with gunfire. A number of rocket-propelled grenades (RPGs) were fired simultaneously. I could see one fishtail by us in front of the boat to explode harmlessly off to starboard. As we cleared the area another mine exploded off our bow, spraying us but with no other effect. When we reached Cai Nuoc and inspected our boats, the tally was sobering: our lifelines had been shot in two; there were several bullet holes through the hull, one in the flag and two more just inches above my head near the pilothouse door. Bob's boat, the 72, had its flagstaff shot in half. There were a number of bullet holes in the hull that appeared to be heavy-caliber rounds. In addition, Bob's engines had been unable to produce high RPMs on the way to Cai Nuoc, an obvious result of the high concussion under the boat. The episode reminded all of us how much Lady Luck played a daily role in our lives. Not wanting to press that luck too far, we spent the night at the dock in Cai Nuoc.

On another day we carried out an extraordinary Sealords mission about fifteen miles up a river the Swifts had never ventured into, deep in Viet Cong territory. We carried psychological operation materials for distribution to the locals and goodies for the kids. While transiting up the narrow river, we played tapes—so-called psyops tapes—with a message to the citizens about the virtue of turning against the VC and loving the government of South Vietnam. We told them how they could be safe.

The river turned and curled around itself, winding through the flat delta so intensely that at times you could see only the radar mast of a Swift ahead, which seemed to be going in the opposite direction around a turn you couldn't see. If someone had fired a rocket between the boats, there was a chance the boats might have opened fire on each other. We were lucky on two counts that day. First, not a shot was fired. And second, we traded C-rations for a little, pesky runt of a dog slated for someone's meal. We called him VC—for Viet Cong. He became a lucky, albeit far from housebroken, mascot on our boat.

Days later, we were on another psyops mission, traversing beautiful countryside in a long file of Swift boats. Technically it was a declared free-fire zone, but every skipper and every boat crew on this run held their fire when they saw a woman running for cover with a child in her arms, or an old farmer looking for cover behind a tree or hootch. One of the two helicopters providing cover for us on the way in was hit by small-arms fire, so both choppers returned to base, leaving us without an important deterrent on the way out. We fired occasional recon fire, random bursts of the .50 calibers to keep ambushers at bay. As we passed through the final stretch of heavy foliage and trees just before turning back into the wider Cua Lon River, a man off to our left was seen running and ducking just as an RPG exploded off the port side. I was standing half in and half out of the port door to the pilothouse when a piece of shrapnel ripped into the back of my left leg. Almost immediately we were past the turn into the wide expanse of the Cua Lon.

When we returned to the Coast Guard cutter, they informed me the X-ray machine wasn't working, so after the doc probed my hamstring for a while, they sent us back to An Thoi for an X-ray. After the X-ray, which showed a small piece of metal lodged deep in my muscle, the doctor decided to leave it in. He thought it would be more trouble than it was worth to take it out. Apparently shrapnel can work its way to the surface over time—or so he said. We headed right back to the rivers.

This journey through such an extensive free-fire zone raised lots of questions in my mind about our strategy. Who decided what was a free-fire zone? Who made the call? What were the criteria? On what basis did someone declare that anyone moving in a certain area was the enemy and could be killed? How could we trust in this when we saw women, children and the elderly all moving around in the normal course of life? No one set out any rules for discretion in a free-fire zone. I'm proud that Swift boats and Swift officers applied their own common sense, but I can't say it was a process devoid of moral hazards. In these zones, you didn't need to get clearance from headquarters before opening fire, but the fact is Swifts were never able to fire first at the opposition. The engines made so much noise that the boats could be heard approaching from miles away. The local citizens almost always hid before an encounter was possible. Generally, from the moment they entered the rivers, the boats were targets, forced to wait and shoot only when they'd been shot at, so they could tell where the enemy was. The casualties suffered were high. Almost no boat was left unscathed.

February 28, 1969, was the day I decided to change the dynamic of just cruising up a river serving as a magnet for an ambush. I thought we had better strategic options.

We were transiting up the Bay Hap River with two other Swifts skippered by my friends Bill Rood and Don Droz. The plan was to move north toward an insertion point on the Dong Cung Canal after we stopped in Cai Nuoc to pick up local troops. I was the skipper in tactical command of the other boats. I had told Bill and Don that if the circumstances were correct, I'd consider beaching our boats to go after the enemy. If we weren't aggressive, we'd be like sitting ducks in a shooting gallery. We all knew the odds. Our nerves were on edge. We shared a pretty good sense the Viet Cong were waiting to ambush us.

Shortly after we left the dock at Cai Nuoc and turned right up the Dong Cung, we came under fire. My ear had learned to distinguish between heavy- and small-caliber weapons, between machine guns and AK-47s. I didn't hear any heavy-caliber automatic weapons fire coming at us—at least not yet. All I heard at first was the *clack, clack, clack* of AK-47s and Chicom (Chinese Communist) carbines. We were perhaps fifteen to twenty yards at most from the riverbanks from which we were taking fire. I grabbed the radio and shouted the order: "Turn zero-niner-zero. All boats turn zero-niner-zero. Head into the beach. All boats turn 0.9.0." To Bill's and Don's eternal credit, they didn't hesitate. It was as if we had practiced it a hundred times. The boats turned in unison, utterly surprising the ambush. We turned the full power of three twin .50 calibers and countless M-16s on the beach as we rammed into it with our bows raising slightly upward as they pushed into the mud.

The minute we were lodged against the bank, I ordered all the troops on board to charge ashore and overrun the ambush. They poured over the bow. Within minutes it was over. Those enemy who weren't killed fled into the jungle. Six Viet Cong were lying dead where they had fired on us. We collected their weapons and searched for any documents.

While the troops were mopping up after the attack, guarding the perimeter, I heard more shots coming from upstream. I instructed Don Droz to remain at the location of the initial ambush to provide fire support to the troops now ashore, while Bill Rood joined me going upstream to investigate. We maneuvered around a right-hand turn, perhaps several hundred yards farther upstream. Suddenly, a B-40 rocket exploded off the port side of the boat, blowing out the windows. I immediately ordered Sandusky to head straight into the riverbank where there was a slight opening—our best estimate of where the shot had come from. We needed to move fast before the shooter had a chance to reload.

With his normal, immediate and unquestioning response, Del beached the boat on the right spot. A Viet Cong fighter, ten yards or so in front of us, leaped out of a spider hole and pointed a grenade launcher right at us. When he saw a Swift boat just yards away, staring him down, he froze. Then, just as suddenly, to our astonishment, he turned and ran toward the path and toward a hut off to the left. I knew we couldn't let him get behind the hut where he could hide, turn and take out the boat, so I immediately raced across the bow, jumping over Tommy Belodeau, who was firing the M-60 machine gun from the forward tank.

Tommy covered me, clipping the Viet Cong in his leg. He fell but got up immediately and started to run again. I then took him out with my M-16 from my vantage point on the path. The man fell just to the right of the hootch. The B-40 rocket fell by his side. After we had secured the area, I picked up his B-40 launcher, confident it was obviously not booby-trapped since he had just been using it against us.

No one prepares you for what it's like to take a life. But in that instant, I didn't have a scintilla of doubt in my mind. This man was armed. He had just tried to kill us and by the grace of God had missed. He was ready and willing to fire at us again. As a soldier, I had been trained to take action, and even more important, I had been trained to take whatever action necessary to eliminate the enemy. I knew I'd made the right call that day and I had the right crew backing me up when it mattered. Del Sandusky proved again that he had nerves of steel and could react without hesitation.

After the operation, it's fair to say that all of us were more than a little jacked up. We debriefed Will Imbrie, who was our overall supervisor on the Coast Guard cutter. We killed ten Viet Cong (confirmed) in that operation and uncovered a network of underground tunnels that was used to store supplies, including ammunition, Viet Cong flags and Ho Chi Minh posters.

Our commanding officer at the time, Lieutenant George Elliott, recommended everyone for decorations. Up and down the chain of command, all three boat skippers and their crews were congratulated on a superb operation. Admiral Elmo Zumwalt made a point of intercepting the recommendation for my award and decided to make an immediate "impact" presentation of the highest award he was allowed to designate—a Silver Star. He flew down to An Thoi with Captain Hoffmann to personally pin medals on each uniform of the eighteen men who fought together that day.

Any pride we felt was tempered by the realization of how close we all came to meeting our maker that day, but the fact that we hadn't steeled us for the weeks to come.

ON SUBSEQUENT MISSIONS we worked with Nung troops, an ethnic minority from the north and the highlands. On one of those missions we shared a moment of chaos and a moment of improbable comedy. The chaos came when four Swift boats were operating in the vicinity of a very narrow canal that connected the Cua Lon and Bay Hap Rivers. We had inserted Nung troops to conduct a sweep and were waiting to pick them up. Larry Thurlow, the extremely able skipper of the 53 boat, had just experienced a near miss when a mine went off close to the bow of his boat. Bill Rood in the 23 boat was nearby. Don Droz in the 43 was at the mouth of the canal where the Nung had been inserted.

As we pulled alongside the 53 boat, a huge explosion rocked us. Larry and the 53 boat were engulfed in smoke and mud. The 94 similarly was jolted by the blast. The 53 rocked over so hard, it smashed against us. We could hear the familiar *clack* of AK-47s as we were taken under fire. Our gunners opened up in two directions to suppress the fire. The Viet Cong had obviously done a hell of a job of planting remote-triggered mines in the canal and planning an ambush. Then, through all the gunfire and smoke, came this horrifying shout over the radio: "This is 23—I've lost my eye—I can't see." It was Bill Rood. I could see Bill's boat yards away from us in the canal. We moved quickly alongside, where I saw Bill bandaged with a large battle dressing over his head and eye. His pilothouse windshield had been shattered in the ambush. Shards of glass had gotten into his eye. I radioed Don Droz to join us from the point at the entrance of the canal where he was waiting for the Nung to exit.

The ambush ended almost as quickly as it began. We moved out of the canal to the wider river, where we could regroup and get Bill medical attention. It was then that we noticed VC, our newly minted mascot, was nowhere to be found. We presumed we had lost him in the ambush. Then, from one of the other boats, we heard this yapping—there was VC on another boat, barking at us. During the blast under our boat, both engine covers had been blown open by the explosion. Obviously, VC had been standing on one and was catapulted over to the next boat. There he was like nothing had happened, yapping away. What were the chances of that? We knew now he really was good luck: Bill Rood had not lost his eye and, after healing, would be able to see again.

February and the first two weeks of March were defined by almost daily forays into the rivers. We lived Sealords. The day after Bill Rood was injured, March 13, we took the Nung up another narrow canal and inserted them for a sweep. It was a five-boat operation.

Rich McCann's boat had some engine problems, so we loaded his troops on the 94. With the extra soldiers on board, we churned through a tiny river with multiple wakes careening off the riverbanks to create a bathtub effect, the boats sloshing around, difficult to control. Finally, we arrived at the location of a prior ambush, where we wanted to start the sweep.

Not long after the Nung were unloaded, we heard an explosion in the direction they had taken. The radio crackled with the message: "Can you send someone in to pick up a body. One of my guys got killed by a booby trap." Mike Medeiros and I went ashore with several guys from other boats—I believe Larry Thurlow was among them. We quickly came upon the crumpled body of Bac She De, the Nung who met his fate when he foolishly reached for a booby-trapped trophy of war. It was hard to relate the remains we found to the live person we had known; Bac She De had been a practical joker among the Nung, always the ringleader for their antics. His stomach was completely hollowed out, his body almost in two separate parts, held together by spine and some sinew. A huge hole went through his mouth and nose out the other side of his head. Mangled flesh and bone—a nonperson. Two of our men scooped him into a couple of ponchos. As we carried him out we were fired on again. We ducked down in some already existing ditches until the fire had been suppressed. We called headquarters, asking for helicopters to join the fight, but none was available. I then called Sandusky and asked him to reposition the 94 boat slightly closer to where we were.

Eventually we got Bac She De back on board. We tried to excite the Regional Forces and Popular Forces (RFPF)—nicknamed Ruff Puffs—to go after the Viet Cong. They wouldn't have anything to do with it. Mike Miggins, the local Army advisor, told me that he thought the RFPFs didn't want to fight alongside the Nung, ethnic mercenaries. We were treated to a great education that morning. We stood by while the Vietnamese army guys engaged in a debate. Eventually, the mercenaries decided to fake a firefight, thinking that might stir the RFPFs into action. No dice. At one point, the Vietnamese, tired of just milling about and having decided they weren't going to fight, just went back to the boat and sat down. It was a terrible moment for the whole theory of Vietnamization of the war. I know Miggins, a dedicated and courageous Army advisor, felt awful.

Eventually we needed to leave. We wanted to deposit our nonfighting RFPF forces back in their village and head out to the LST. The trip back down the Dong Cung was tense but uneventful. We thought for sure the narrowness begged another ambush but it didn't come. We arrived in the much wider Bay Hap without further incident, disembarked our Ruff Puffs—who today had earned their nickname—and then took the Bay Hap to return to the LST and Coast Guard cutter. I did observe something strange. Normally when we arrived in Cai Nuoc, even after the ambush of February 28, which had occurred close to the village, the dock was filled with kids and townspeople. This day, there were none. I should have processed that—but it probably wouldn't have changed our options. We still had to transit the river, as we did every day, in order to get home.

At the same spot where we had previously been hit on the Bay Hap, a massive explosion went off right under PCF-3. The whole boat went a couple of feet up in the air, wrapped in mud and spray, and then splashed back in the river to begin a weird zigzagging course, drifting downstream. At the same time, we came under small-arms fire from the banks. We started to turn toward the bank with the intention of attacking the ambush, but Sandusky, who'd been focused on the 3 boat, said it looked to be in really bad shape. We veered back toward the 3 boat when another mine went off right beside us on the port side where I was standing. The blast threw me backward into the sharp edge of the doorframe, smashing my lower arm around the wrist. During our maneuvering, Army Lieutenant Jim Rassmann, the lead advisor to the Nung, was thrown overboard. Rassmann said he instinctively swam to the bottom to avoid our props and Droz's boat behind us. While on the bottom he shed his heavy backpack and weapons.

Sandusky maneuvered us closer to the 3 boat. One of the crewmen, Ken Tryner, was in the doorway and bloodied, firing an M-79. I could see the twin .50-caliber machine guns blown up and out of their swivel. Larry Thurlow and his crew were heroically wrestling to get the crippled 3 under control. It seemed every man on board had been wounded.

Then the chaos was penetrated by a shout of "Man overboard!" Fred Short, from his higher vantage point in the guntub, had looked back upstream and could see Jim Rassmann in the water maybe two hundred yards back, under fire from the nearest bank. We immediately turned the 94 and raced back to provide cover fire and try to rescue Jim.

We could see little splashes in the water near where Jim was sighted. He kept diving down to avoid the bullets, trying to minimize the target for the VC, only to reappear, grab a breath and go down again. Sandusky skillfully went from full speed to almost a dead stop, fighting to make sure he didn't run over Rassmann. Fortunately, we had our landing nets hanging over the bow from the insertion of the Nung, so there was a ready way to get someone aboard. Jim was so exhausted from swimming and diving that the only way to get him aboard was to lean over the bow and grab him. I ran out, praying that the larger target I provided on the deck would not attract a bullet, and then lay on the deck, reaching down to pull him up. My wrist hurt enough to make it hard to grab, but with my adrenaline pumping and his, I got Rassmann rolled on board and we took off.

One of the Swifts transferred the wounded from the 3 boat out to the

LST. The 94 and another boat tied up on each side of the 3 boat to help sta-
bilize it, while people were bailing like crazy to keep it afloat. After what
seemed like ages, we neared the LST. A damage control team came aboard
to relieve the exhausted sailors who'd been bailing. During this entire episode, Bac She De's body, scrunched in the ponchos, had been lying on the
fantail of our boat. His head, what was left of it, had slipped out to make the
scene just a little more macabre. Jim Rassmann told me that as he climbed
up the rope netting to get to the deck of the LST, Bac She De's blood dripped
on him from the poncho above. As Jim climbed onto the deck of the LST a
Filipino steward said to him, "Sir, get out of your uniform and I'll wash it
for you." Jim felt it was the most decent moment of an indecent day.

All the wounded were treated back on the LST or Coast Guard cutter.
They X-rayed my arm—no breaks, no fractures as we had feared, but it
had been badly ripped against the sharp edge of the door. The arm was bandaged and then off we went. Once again, we were all lucky. The boat was
far more wounded than any of us. Similarly, the 3 boat had been even luck-
ier. What could have been catastrophic turned out to be bad, but not fatal.

Four days later the 94 boat and its crew were back in An Thoi. The boat
was undergoing repairs. It was March 17—St. Patrick's Day. We celebrated
with a blowout party onshore at the small base. Commander Elliott informed me I was going home under the "three times wounded and you're
home rule." Don and Skip Barker both counseled me that it made sense and
it was the right thing to do, particularly since I was guaranteed my crew was
going to be transferred to Qui Nhon, far from Sealords.

War has always contrasted the real with the absurd. Vietnam was complicated in the motives Americans brought to the fight. Some went there
believing they were fighting to save a country or a people. Others were
skeptical that we could make another country "safe" for democracy. But
for all, it was a tour of duty. We had joined the service. We had taken an
oath. We had a job to do and we did it, which meant that the absurdities all
around us struck us even more vividly. One moment there was beauty and
silence, and the next moment there was horror and chaos. The days melded
one into the other. We learned how to put emotions on automatic pilot and
not vary the course no matter the input.

By March 1969, I'd seen more of the misery of war—the killing, the
faces of terrified civilians, the destruction of homes and hamlets—than I
had ever anticipated, enough for a lifetime. On several occasions, I'd come
within a whisper of having my own life ended in a random instant. While I
carried out my orders—patrolled, boarded and searched junks, returned fire
when ambushed—I found myself in good company with many who ques-

tioned our tactics. What were we accomplishing on the rivers? How were we winning over the civilians we came in contact with? What were we securing for the long haul? How could we measure the impact of a psychological operation in which ten boats pushed miles up uncharted VC territory to hand out flyers and small packets to children?

What I did learn through interpreters and Army advisors who were living with Vietnamese in outposts and villages was that the average Vietnamese fisherman and farmer, along with their families, were apolitical. They didn't support the VC or the government. They just wanted to be left alone. When we roared up the rivers and canals, swamping their boats, burning their homes, destroying rice crops, I feared we were inadvertently convincing them that the VC were correct. We were losing hearts and minds.

It was difficult to fit what we were doing into a viable overall strategy in Vietnam. The domino theory, or whether Ho Chi Minh was a communist or a nationalist—it all seemed distant from basic common sense and was being contradicted daily. The blind repetition of missions, which by design couldn't accomplish much and which were inadequately conceived and supported, was symbolic of our whole failing commitment to a war that I was now convinced was wrong. I began to see Vietnam with the vision of the critical observer rather than the participant. I asked myself what it would be like to be occupied by foreign troops, to bend under force to the desires of fighters from half a world away who could not possibly know what really counted in my country. I was heading home with truths to share, if anyone would listen.

CHAPTER 5

The War at Home

I BOARDED THE FREEDOM Bird, a World Airways charter, at Cam Ranh Bay on March 26, 1969. On takeoff, a restrained clapping echoed through the plane as we left behind the sand dunes, turquoise water and, I thought, the war. With the benefit of the Date Line transition, I arrived in Tacoma, Washington, on the same day. I transferred to the civilian airport and flew to San Francisco to reunite with my younger sister, Diana, before flying to New York City to rejoin Julia.

San Francisco stood out in my memory as a bridge back to more innocent times, training for the Navy by day and overindulging in music, laughter, food and friends by night. But as I taxied into the city from the international airport, I felt like a stranger, disconnected from everything: from the traffic, from people living normal lives. How often did they think about the war where American kids were being killed and killing in their name? Emotionally, I was a lifetime away from that twenty-two-year-old newly minted naval officer who had excitedly taken a similar taxi ride to Treasure Island a little more than two years earlier.

Early the next morning I boarded a flight to New York. I was traveling in uniform since I was on military orders. My arm was still bandaged around my wrist area from the injury I received in the last ambush. I had the entire row to myself and gratefully stretched out to sleep. At some point the plane shook a little in turbulence. I woke up with a start, shouting, "Look out! Get down. . . . Move!"—only to find that I was on a half-full airplane and nothing out of the ordinary was happening. The smoke and haze in the air wasn't from machine guns or wood fires, but from carefree passengers smoking cigarettes. I was hugely embarrassed for my startled outburst, but even more so as I absorbed the stares of folks seated near me and particularly when several people moved seats to be farther away. No one reached over and tapped my forearm to ask "Are you okay?" No offer of help. "Can I do anything?" Message received—they were moving away because the guy in the uniform might be nuts and might hurt you. I felt strangely disconnected and guilty, feeling for a moment that maybe I belonged back on the rivers, or at least somewhere else. I didn't allow myself to fall asleep again for the remainder of the flight. Julia greeted me at the gate with the longest hug I had ever experienced.

On the East Coast, the next days were filled with reunions, first with Julia and Peggy in New York and then with my parents and brother, Cam, in Massachusetts. The contrast between being in Vietnam and being home was jarring. "Adjustment" isn't even the right word. It wasn't some abstract disconnect; it was concrete: to go from life-and-death choices, daily tension, constant adrenaline, the emotional ups and downs of a week on patrol, while surrounded entirely by brothers in combat who understand without even a spoken word everything you're experiencing—and then suddenly, it all turns off, to be replaced not just by the love and affection of family, but with the freedom to choose where you go and what you do at any given hour of the day, while surrounded by people you love unconditionally but who weren't there with you on those boats. That was a shift I may have dreamed about but wasn't really prepared to accept. I certainly wasn't prepared for how it happened so instantly. It was impossible to put aside the intense relationships we had formed in the rivers, and I didn't want to. I was home, but my friends and fellow sailors were not, and my opposition to the war had crystallized so firmly that I wanted to find a way to tell the story of what was happening in Vietnam.

I wanted to help end the war and bring my friends home. It wasn't intended to be cathartic, but in my mind it was purposeful. I channeled all those pent-up energies and emotions onto paper—long legal pads and notebooks filled up with my sideways, slanted, prep school penmanship. Day and night, I wrote furiously, mostly stream-of-consciousness memories of my time in Vietnam while events were still fresh and raw in my mind. What I wrote in those first few months after coming home was neither eloquent nor structured, but it was the freshest of "fresh recollection"—a term of art I was to learn later at law school reflected the best evidence of memory.

My service wasn't concluded yet. I had been assigned the plum position of aide to Admiral Walter F. Schlech, commander of military sea transport for the East Coast. A desk job. No one shooting at me, no one lurking in mangroves or spider holes waiting to pick me off. I was lucky to be alive, all my limbs intact; lucky enough to have returned home to Julia, who feared I would come home in a box like Persh. But within two weeks the reality of what I had left behind found me again when I ripped open a letter at the apartment Julia and I were sharing in New York. I was stunned to read that one of my closest friends from Coastal Division 11, Don Droz, had been killed. Donald "Dinky" Droz—one of the really good guys with whom I had shared a lot of time, thoughts and hopes was dead. Once again, fate seemed to play out with crushing, grotesque unfairness.

Don was a wonderful human being. He'd grown up in Missouri in a small town where patriotism ran deep, where Memorial Day and Fourth of July parades were command performances. He graduated from the Naval Academy in 1966 just as I was finishing up in New Haven. We became fast friends in-country, went through a lot together on the rivers, and, as I departed, we made plans to reconnect after the war. Don was a short-timer. He knew the end of his tour was in sight and he had a lot of reasons to make it home soon. He had just been accepted to a graduate studies program at Dartmouth. We celebrated the news together before I left Vietnam.

He had married his wife, Judy, shortly before going to Vietnam. His daughter, Tracy, was born while he was deployed. In an unexpected gift, only weeks before he was killed, Don was reunited in Hawaii on R&R with Judy. There, in the sweetest encounter of all, he met his newborn, Tracy. He was brimming with plans he shared with Judy for their life after the war: a permanent home, more kids, so much ahead of them. Before he left Hawaii, he kissed Tracy and said, "Be good for Mama, smile pretty." It was the last time he'd see either of them.

I am always grateful that Don was with me during the battle where we beached our boats and overran the ambushers.

When I opened the letter from Lieutenant Skip Barker, explaining the operation that claimed Don's life, the pain turned toward anger—deep anger. Don could have been me and I could have been Don:

Dear John,

Thank you for your letter received today. I have been trying to write you since the 12th of April when Don was killed but have found it to be quite difficult to write at all—my mind has suffered a degree of numbness as relates to thinking of my present environment—perhaps a natural, protective response to such an utterly frustrating and infuriating situation about which I seem so unable to effect a reconciliation. I seem now to be just floating along, pushed at will by the whimsical orders of seemingly inhumane superior officers. I have finally learned—or perhaps just realized what it is to be a pawn—an asset—in the hands of authorities whose primary concern seems to be the use of war to further their careers. We, like most men here, are statistics and statistic producers.

I am not sure what all Bill Rood told you of the Battle of the Duong Keo—but as an eye-witness I would like to give you my account—for I would like to have on record with one who cares, what I consider to be a classic example of the completely incompetent leadership that the men of this division are made to endure.

HE WENT ON to describe how twelve Swift boats with two companies of Vietnamese marines embarked were to insert in the Duong Keo River and sweep up along the banks to clear the area of Viet Cong. Skip's boat was designated tactical command with three key officers on board, including Coast Guard Commander Yost, who'd been in-country for two weeks. It was his "christening" as officer in tactical command, assigned by Captain Hoffmann, even though he had no Swift operational or river warfare experience. A first wave of Swifts entered the river and put marines ashore to start sweeping.

Skip, in a second column of Swifts, said he repeatedly suggested to the three officers in his pilothouse it was time to put their troops ashore and sweep the banks. He wrote: "I began continuously recommending that we beach and begin sweeping. I informed the three officers . . . of the many bad experiences we'd had in the Duong Keo previously and pointed out the many bunkers and trenches we were passing." Commander Yost kept passing the decision down the chain. Skip got in an argument with the Vietnamese lieutenant, who said, "Keep going." He told Skip he would check if it "looked dangerous."

That's when the banks of the river erupted. Claymore mines detonated; a rocket exploded near Skip's boat. His forward gunner was hit by an AK-47 round in his lower back that exited his stomach, but he fired throughout the ambush. Because Yost never gave the order for the last boats in the column to turn back, each of them ran the gauntlet of the ambush—or kill zone, as we called it. It was five hundred meters long. As soon as they cleared the zone, Skip recommended beaching and sending the marines after the enemy. Yost said nothing. The Vietnamese lieutenant said to keep going. They finally beached four kilometers upstream, where they could get their wounded medevacked.

At that moment they were informed the 43 boat—Don's boat—had been hit badly. It was aground at the ambush site! They needed to go back. Skip asked Yost for some troops to put a perimeter around the 43, but Yost told him no, that the Vietnamese lieutenant wanted them all where they were— at the landing zone. So two boats, Skip in the 31 and Bill Shumadine, OINC of the 5 boat, with dead and wounded on board, barely able to man their guns, headed back to the stricken 43 boat.

Skip described what they encountered:

When we arrived on the scene I was met with the most sickening sight of my 25 years. PCF-43 had run up on the left bank at full bore. 9/10ths of the boat was out of the water. It was listed to the starboard 50 degrees and all survivors, 14, were in the mud and water under her starboard side trying to hold off the VC who were trying to rush them. When we arrived with guns ablaze, the VC re-manned their bunkers and opened up on us—but with little effect. PCF-5 took position slightly downstream astern of 43 to provide cover. 31 went in to the beach alongside 43 and began pulling people on board. My forward gunner was in a constant duel with a .30 caliber emplacement 20 meters off my starboard bow. His shooting was superlative and eventually the .30 caliber was firing at the sky.

As we pulled alongside the 43 the first man I noticed was a grinning Pete Upton—in mud and water to his chest. He started getting the wounded on board. Then we got the bodies of Don and the UDT Chief Corpsman. Don had been killed almost instantly by a B-40 in the pilothouse. The Chief, on the fantail, was hit in the stomach by a B-40. By this time, Captain Hoffman [*sic*] was overhead in a Seawolf. He radioed down for us to stop firing so the helos could come in to fire—this order was relayed to me by Yost. I told him Bull Shit—"I'm not going to stop firing until we [are] out of here"—and I didn't. So Captain Hoffman had the helos strike behind the bunkers which almost did us in—but for those strikes and his valiant directions he is being given the Silver Star.

After what seemed an eternity, we pulled out and headed up stream. By this time, the 43 was on fire. Darkness was upon us and all night we could hear her death throes as her fuel, ammo and 800 lbs. of C-4 blew up. We barely got all of the wounded out before darkness. Don spent his last night in a river on the fantail of my boat. The next morning a helo came in and carried out our dead—3 US, 4 VN—and with the Marines sweeping ahead we began a funeral-like procession downstream—out to the LST. In the ambush area, the bodies of two VC were found—although the Press (UPI) later reported we had killed 24 of the enemy. Towing two boats, we reached the LST at 1600 the afternoon of the 13th. Besides the complete loss of PCF-43, 5 boats had been hit by B-40s, two of these by two rounds. Every boat had numerous bullet holes—AK-47 and .30 caliber and every boat had blood on her decks.

• • •

I THANK GOD Don, Judy and Tracy had that time to share in Hawaii—even though Tracy would only know about it from her mother. The promise of his life to come with his new family juxtaposed with his bloody, muddy death in a river in Vietnam has always been a heavy burden to bear for all who knew Don. Judy would later lead a march in Washington against the war—and, in a sign of the times, be criticized by other war widows for doing so. It was a bitter pill to swallow because Don had often written home about the significant shortcomings of Operation Sealords and his opposition to the war itself.

Twenty years later I had the pleasure of offering Tracy an internship in my Senate office, where I was touched to be able to help her get to know her dad. I was so happy I could do that. It was a way of keeping faith with Don. Tracy went on to produce a wonderful documentary called *Be Good, Smile Pretty*, the story of discovering her father. Today, she is a well-respected documentary filmmaker.

The letter from Skip triggered a combination of anger and purpose in me. Rage at the way Don died turned to rage about the reasons he died. Everything I had been writing reflected my belief that every man who had served on the riverboats on the Mekong Delta was as courageous as every man who had jumped out of a Higgins boat to take Omaha Beach at Normandy. But this was a different war from World War II.

Don's death was the spark. I could also feel the anger and frustration of Skip and other friends. But they could not speak out. I could.

My months in-country, beginning with the first moments after I walked off the plane at Cam Ranh and observed the division of labor, steadily instilled in me a sense of the absurdity of our engagement. Like cement drying in the sun, my impressions had hardened into convictions. The guys I served with were amazing. I remain hugely respectful of their sacrifices for our country. They were courageous and innovative, the best our country summoned to service, but the war itself wasn't right. There was no standard by which it constituted a justifiable use of brave young men's lives.

Don's death punctuated those feelings with urgency. It forced me to act. I moved from thinking I had time to write a book to feeling compelled to get out and tell the story of the war publicly. It was then I knew I had to become an activist to try to end the war. I felt a fundamental responsibility to do something. But what—and how?

My sister Peggy was a great connector. She embodied the sixties—and still does. She's a "movement" person, actually more committed over a lifetime to the women's movement than anyone I've known. In the fall of 1969, she was spending most of her time in the run-down offices of a grassroots organization dedicated to ending the war, the Vietnam Moratorium Committee at 150 Fifth Avenue in New York City. Peggy connected me with Adam Walinsky, one of the band of brothers who had been with his boss, Robert Kennedy, in Los Angeles when RFK was assassinated.

Walinsky was continuing to speak out for peace, as Kennedy had. A day of events—rallies, teach-ins, vigils—was planned for October. There were politicians on the playbill, including Gene McCarthy and New York's Republican senator Charles Goodell, and Yale's activist chaplain, William Sloane Coffin, whose eloquence against the war defined just how much the Old Campus had changed since I'd graduated in '66. It was the young activists, though, who were most stirring, not just Walinsky, but my contemporaries, notably Sam Brown, David Mixner, Marge Sklenkar and John Gage, who showed remarkable leadership and helped change the course of history. They literally organized the country's campuses against the war. All of them became great friends on the long journey ahead.

Walinsky needed a pilot to get him around New York to speak at as many of the events as possible, but this was the peace movement on a shoestring budget. The group could afford to charter a tiny plane, but it needed a pilot. Peggy knew exactly who to volunteer for the job. Those carefree days spent taking flying lessons at Tweed New Haven Airport during my senior year were about to lead me into an experience I never could have predicted. I took a vacation day and soon enough was flying Walinsky around New York—from the Hudson Valley to Albany and up to Buffalo and Syracuse—usually wherever there was a big campus population. We soared over the fall foliage, dipping into tiny airports in a single-engine plane, then driving to each event while Walinsky, his tie sporting the PT-109 tie clip given to him by RFK, scribbled notes on a dog-eared legal pad, updating the speech he was about to give. In between rallies, I enjoyed listening to Adam talk about the road he had traveled.

Together with Jeff Greenfield, Adam Walinsky had become one of the most important aides to RFK. A graduate of Yale Law School, he was one of a vanguard of young, thoughtful activists committed to changing the country. His passionate, forceful advocacy for justice and an end to the war in Vietnam earned him the nickname "Adamant Adam," a moniker I would have been proud of in those turbulent times.

I didn't speak at any of the events. I didn't even contemplate it. I was there to observe. I was in my civilian clothes, enjoying the anonymity of standing off to the side of the crowd, just absorbing the scene. For the first time since I'd left Vietnam, I felt a sense of common purpose. The feeling of being part of a movement took me back to more innocent days on campus, hearing Allard Lowenstein speak on civil rights, challenging us to care about a cause beyond the comfortable confines of campus. But everything was so different in so many other ways. The Al Lowenstein I first met exhorting us to action on the Yale campus was now a young congressman fighting to end the war in which I'd fought. We'd gone from the excitement of the New Frontier to the political revolution of the McCarthy and Kennedy insurgencies, and yet somehow Richard Nixon had been elected president and seemingly brought at least some of the country back to the 1950s.

Now, the great enterprise of grassroots democracy was in the hands of people like Adam Walinsky, still in his thirties. The times had changed and, as always, the music reflected our mood. Peter, Paul and Mary had gone from the hopeful "If I Had a Hammer" during the civil rights marches when I was a sophomore, to the wistful "Leaving on a Jet Plane" in 1969, with an entirely different meaning for those of us who had boarded planes to the war in Southeast Asia. I looked out across the crowds: young faces, older faces, tears and chants—"End the war." "Bring them home." Occasionally an unmistakable whiff of marijuana would waft across the sea of humanity. There was palpable excitement in the air, a feeling that young people could change the world if we organized. It was refreshing to feel a surge of idealism after Vietnam had ripped apart so many of my assumptions and hopes. In a transition that felt a little strange, the next day I put on my uniform and went back to work.

I also continued to write. The idea came to me to turn all my scribbles into an open letter to America, an attempt to lay out the truth I had witnessed in Vietnam and the lies people were being fed at home. Peggy introduced me to the incomparable Pete Hamill, the columnist for the *New York Post*. We met at the Lion's Head, Pete's hangout in the Village. He read my "manuscript" and told me he thought I was onto something, that my personal recollections, details from my journal written when I was in-country and factual input could be an important addition to the debate. But he also had a gentle way of telling me that no book or article, however passionate, was going to make the difference I hoped for. Few writers had that kind of impact. I loved the meeting. Pete was direct and tough. He had no patience for the war and even less for the politicians who seemed at a total loss for what to do with Nixon at the nation's helm, keeping his secret plan for peace a secret.

One weekend when I was home in Massachusetts, my father invited me to talk to the Groton Rotary, where he was a member. I think he and the audience were a little surprised by the critique that I delivered, just speaking from my gut and from my own analysis, at once the son of Foreign Service Officer Richard Kerry as well as a fully formed twenty-six-year-old whose views of the war had been shaped not in Foggy Bottom but on the Cà Mau Peninsula. It felt right, that I should speak out and that someone should hear it.

My brother, Cam, in 1968 had worked as an organizer for an anti-war candidate who had run against Massachusetts congressman Philip Philbin, a war hawk, twenty-eight-year veteran, and powerful member of the Armed Services Committee. Cam wrote me a letter suggesting I might do the same in 1970. Long shot as it would be, the fight itself could be important. It would be a way of telling the story of Vietnam. If everything broke our way, I'd be there in 1971 with Congressman Lowenstein on the floor of the House, working to end the war. On the other hand, if it landed with a thud, I would have at least spoken out. What's the worst that they could do to me? Send me back to Vietnam?

There was, of course, one hurdle to running for Congress, and it was formidable. I was still very much in the Navy. I approached Admiral Schlech and asked him if he would support my request for an early release from the Navy so I could return home and start running. He could not have been more supportive. A wonderful "old salt," a submarine skipper from World War II, he bent over backward to facilitate my departure. I was lucky to have such a boss. He put in the papers right away. I still had obligations to fulfill in the Navy, which I did, even as my mustering-out date crept up fast. I began to look ahead to a wild but exhilarating adventure in Massachusetts.

Just deciding to run without having engaged in many of the normal base-building activities of politics was a little crazy, but I was convinced that I could make the case about the war and, more important, that I had an obligation to do so. Although I enlisted filled with a sense of duty and service, I was now outraged at the deception and immorality of much of the war. I felt I had lived so much change so quickly. When I had signed up it was 1965. I was a son of World War II, and like so many others of my generation, I had been taught bedrock values of service and sacrifice. However, 1968 and 1969 had a profound transformational impact on me: they changed me as they changed my generation and the country. Few were immune to those years.

I had lost too many good friends—from high school, Peter Wyeth Johnson, who loved to read and write poetry and developed a beautiful calligraphy script with which he wrote superb essays at St. Paul's; Steve Kelsey, the son of Army parents stationed in Paris who traveled with me on motorbikes through the Loire Valley of France, where we learned more than we could ever find useful about the beautiful châteaus of the region; Dick Pershing, friend from prep school and college; John White, my debate team partner, who shared hours with me plotting arguments against Princeton and Harvard; Bob Crosby, my classmate from Swift training in Coronado and fellow Massachusetts citizen; and Don Droz—all of whom were heroes to me. But the rationale for the war, the flawed execution of an unsound strategy, the failures of leadership, both political and military, and the stubborn, myopic impulse that dug us deeper and deeper—none of it ever lived up to the example of their sacrifice.

I was always struck by the fact that Robert McNamara, one of the principal architects of the war, never matched the courage of the men who put their lives on the line. McNamara was smart enough to come to understand the war was wrong, but he, like many others, left the battlefield to slink off to the World Bank, where he remained silent as thousands continued to sacrifice and die, even as his own son protested the war. Why hadn't he spoken up when it could have mattered? There was in this realization a bitter taste, a leaving behind of the near-mythological awe with which the "best and the brightest" had been welcomed to Washington to set the nation on its new course in the New Frontier. It was jarring that Bill Bundy, the uncle of my roommate and the man I had sat with and been impressed by as a senior at Yale, had been so wrong about a country and a war that cost so many lives and set us on such a disastrous course.

I began to reach out and introduce myself to activists in my congressional district. For Julia, this was about as full immersion as one gets: from the freedom of Italy to the rigors of a campaign in Massachusetts. Here she was, not yet married, being plunged into my passion for ending the war. She took it on heart and soul, knowing how much it mattered with her older brother Lanny serving in the Marines near the demilitarized zone along the border of North Vietnam. We had decided to wait to get married until Lanny returned from Vietnam. By any measure, Julia was remarkably accepting of a completely alien experience.

On January 1, 1970, I received my honorable discharge and was released from active duty as a full lieutenant in the U.S. Naval Reserve. I had just learned that Father Bob Drinan, the dean of Boston College Law School, was being urged by several anti-war Democrats to get into the race for the same congressional seat. Before I knew it, I was in a pitched organizational battle against some formidable veterans of Massachusetts politics. Jerry Grossman, who was supporting Father Drinan, was an activist's activist. Deeply involved in the Council for a Livable World, he was a force in liberal politics. He had enormous resources of money and influence, but we had youth, the passion of the war and a blind ignorance of the downsides, the last of which always helps. We had about six weeks to enlist any Democrat from the district willing to attend Concord-Carlisle High School on a Saturday in February to participate in a party caucus. We had to get the word out—an open invitation to all activists—it was a gigantic organizational task. The energy was electric. It was fun and ridiculously, but excitingly, quixotic.

I jumped right in, attending Democratic committee meetings whenever and wherever I could. When we could find even a few Democrats gathered together, we tried to persuade them to help us end the war in Vietnam. We assembled a small group of friends who loyally jumped in feetfirst. It was liberating. The fact that I was targeting a guy who supported the war with every old cliché and factless slogan was invigorating. I felt finally that I was doing something to bring the war closer to its end. My argument was straightforward. Freshly back from Vietnam, with war experience under my belt, I argued that I had a better chance than any other candidate of holding Philbin accountable. I was self-confident enough to think that when Philbin said, "Support the troops," I could look right back at him and say, "Congressman, we are the troops." I wondered whether Father Drinan, incredibly articulate and qualified as he was, would have a harder time as a priest convincing hard-core folks in parts of the district that he should be in Congress. On many issues, there was no difference between us, but we went at it in a pitched battle of Massachusetts activists all aiming to end the war.

The question many asked was: Who was this upstart who just parachuted in to upset the regular order? For others, there was an excitement over having someone who had been to Vietnam and checked off several normal boxes of politics to challenge a long-term, recalcitrant incumbent.

On February 22, 1970, I made my first speech to an election audience. It was freezing outside, but the auditorium was sweat warm, every seat jammed with the most ardent end-the-war activists Massachusetts could find. It was citizens' activism at its best and most exciting. I had worked hard on my speech, sitting on the floor of our temporary apartment with my brother, David Thorne, George Butler and Chester "Chet" Atkins, who would later become a congressman. We read it through, edited and read it through again, and now it was time to deliver.

Father Drinan had given his speech. Near the end of his comments, he had visibly paused, taken a deep drink from a glass of water on the podium and then finished up. When I took the podium, you could feel the tension. Who was this young intruder who was taking on the powerful core of the district's liberal base? For many of the attendees, it was their first introduction to me. I looked out at the tense room of activists, reached for the glass, drank and said, "See, it can't be that bad. We're all drinking out of the same glass."

The laughter and applause that followed broke the ice. The audience listened. I delivered my vision of the choices before the country and how we could win in November. At the end, whether they were with Drinan or me, people were on their feet. The vote was going to be close. It was not going to be the favorite crushing the upstart. There was, notwithstanding the liberal machine's turnout of people brought to vote for Drinan, great curiosity about the two very different candidates.

The caucus broke into sub-caucuses so candidates could be questioned. Then there was a first-ballot vote that winnowed the field, followed by another, which was split nearly evenly, with a slight edge to Drinan. The question was, What now? Did this caucus mean anything? Was it just the springboard for a Kerry candidacy, or would it unite the progressive, anti-war wing and go after Philbin? The outcome depended on my decision. I could argue that the caucus was an arbitrary, completely ad hoc, tiny representation of the party and the people deserved a choice. I could take my case to the people in a primary and risk reelecting the war hawk, or I could throw my support to Bob Drinan and help defeat Congressman Philbin.

My small team and I retired to a room while those at the caucus waited. I didn't agonize over the decision. Drinan had won more votes than I had. I wasn't running just to go to Congress. I was running to end the war and change the politics of the Congress and country. Since we would all be running in the primary, winning there was tantamount to election. It was better for this nascent, anti-war citizens' effort to come out united rather than split the vote so that Philbin would win again. Certainly there was the option of calling the hand of Drinan (and Grossman) by stubbornly staying in and forcing him to think about whether I ultimately had the better chance. That path seemed completely antithetical to what we were trying to achieve. It flew in the face of the moment and made the whole thing about me and not about the war. The moment needed resolution and it called for the power of unity—for a message that this citizens' effort had succeeded and this new grassroots energy was to be reckoned with. So I withdrew, throwing my support to Bob Drinan. The grassroots group had produced unity. The concept of the citizens' caucus was vindicated. Everyone could leave Concord-Carlisle High School with a genuine sense of excitement for the campaign ahead.

I became part of the leadership of the campaign. I helped to win the race that saw the first Catholic priest ever elected to the U.S. Congress.

Most important, some of the best friends I've made throughout my career came from that campaign, which shaped Massachusetts politics for years to come. Bob Drinan became an important voice in Congress, serving on the Judiciary Committee and helping to craft the impeachment of President Nixon. He and I became friends. I will always look back on that election as a victory of aspiration over ambition.

I did face a practical reality, however. I had mustered out of the Navy early in order to run. Six weeks later I had ceded that option to someone else, so what was I going to do next? I was already an ardent environmentalist. My childhood nature walks in the woods of Massachusetts with my mother had always stuck with me—her somewhat hokey but earnest exhortation to stand silently among the trees, close your eyes and "just listen." My mother could identify birds by their call.

Later, Rachel Carson awakened all of us with her book *Silent Spring*. Friends were already busy organizing the first Earth Day in Massachusetts, so I did some events with them, trying to build on the awareness that came through the caucus, including speaking at the Earth Day events in Massachusetts. Again, there was a feeling of belonging, of possibilities. Twenty million Americans rocked the nation that first Earth Day on April 22, 1970. Merely by coming out and making a powerful statement of personal concern about the environment, they gave birth to a political movement that turned the environment into a voting issue. They forced Nixon to take note of a powerful new constituency; he even signed the Environmental Protection Agency into law. Before then, it had been okay to vote against the environment. What had been deemed acceptable was now taboo. It was a sea change, a lasting lesson for me of what can happen when important issues become voting issues. Accountability works, but individual citizens must make it work. Only those who decide to work their asses off end up holding public officials accountable.

May 23, 1970, Julia and I were married at her family's Long Island home looking out on Great South Bay. The ceremony was both traditional and modern; for her dress, Julia chose a family heirloom passed down from generation to generation for close to two hundred years, but in a nod to the times, we chose "witnesses" from among our closest friends and family, not traditional attendants. Before we were whisked away by helicopter for our wedding night in the city, my college friends threw me into the pond. When we arrived back at our apartment, I discovered my new father-in-law had sent us some surprise guests: large brown fish were swimming in our bathtub. Julia wasn't quite as amused by her father's idea of a practical joke. The next day we set off for Jamaica, a honeymoon trip with David Thorne and his wife, Rose, and our friends George Butler and his wife. It was an innocent, quirky time.

I'd come up short in my long-shot race for the House, but I was hooked by grassroots politics. Out of uniform, my hair was growing a little longer. A whole generation was transformed. David Thorne and I had gone from short-haired freshmen at Yale to Beatles impressionists. Just out of uniform, we now appeared as shaggy-haired, gangly twenty-six-year-olds, feeling we'd weathered a lot of living in just over a quarter century. But we weren't alone. Since David and I had met as college freshmen, Bob Dylan had gone electric. The Beach Boys and the Beatles had traveled an electric journey of their own. The Beatles moved fast from "I Want to Hold Your Hand" to "Revolution." Their journeys were helped along by marijuana, acid and Eastern influences; ours by a war and a whole lot of disillusionment, but everything was converging in 1970.

Amid the chaos and constant flurry of life at that moment, I still had to pick my next battle. Only a few months out of the Navy and hearing regularly from my friends still in Vietnam as well as those who'd returned, everything kept coming back to the war, the war, the war. The effort to persuade people during the lead-up to the caucus had underscored the power of our personal testimony about Vietnam. Most Americans didn't know the reality. They had heard Walter Cronkite turn against the war, but they hadn't heard from veterans themselves.

Early opposition to the war had seemed relegated to the fringes. The early demonstrations seemed out of sync, the war itself completely distant. However, with the Gulf of Tonkin Resolution, which ultimately led to Lyndon Johnson's call for five hundred thousand troops in Vietnam, the scope and depth of the protests began to grow. In 1967 the first March on the Pentagon jolted the country. Draft-card burnings became more frequent. America took notice of blood being dumped on the steps of the Pentagon. The shock value of creative, radical protest increased the polarization of the country. Families were torn apart over the war. Life decisions about marriage, possibly going to jail, leaving the country, all reached the heartland. The war shattered a traditional passing of responsibility from one generation to another. It began to change the nation and, for many, made it unrecognizable. Language, music, dance, dress, people at all levels of society—the entire culture of America—were in turmoil, dragged, sometimes willingly and sometimes kicking and screaming, through turbulent upheaval.

I could relate to upheaval because I'd lived it. My decision to go into the Navy shortly after President Johnson's call for more troops now felt as though it had taken place in another world and time. But by 1970 the change was sweeping and profound. There was no center, and if there was, it clearly couldn't hold.

There was an infectious certainty in the air that we were onto something transformative. We believed we were defining a new world and thinking bigger than we even had at the dawn of the Kennedy administration. Indeed, it was a different Kennedy—Bobby—whose challenge to Lyndon Johnson seemed revolutionary, even in the bold title of his campaign book, *To Seek a Newer World*. It was a fitting phrase for our mission now.

I needed to join this parade of activism. Because of my visible anti-war stand at the caucus, I began to be asked to speak at various events, particularly those involving veterans. I noticed an advertisement in *Life* magazine for Vietnam Veterans Against the War (VVAW). The ad featured an image of a rifle with a fixed bayonet on it, planted in the ground with a helmet hanging on top. It was a powerfully evocative symbol. It meant there were a lot of other guys out there who felt as I did. It may have been Peggy who suggested I check out VVAW at the group's Labor Day events, including a march to Valley Forge, Pennsylvania, where George Washington and his troops had spent a famous winter after a string of setbacks.

Looking at the flyers for the event, I thought immediately of the powerful link between the Vietnam veterans marching in 1970 and the original revolutionary patriots whose endurance was essential to the survival of a democratic experiment in its infancy. Both the men in uniform in 1777–1778 and those in 1970 who'd served or were serving still were all trying to put their country on course.

I signed up as a speaker. I was not particularly enthusiastic to join other parts of what was a weekend-long, eighty-six-mile demonstration of sorts. Operation Rapid American Withdrawal, or RAW, as it was called, included guerrilla theater to convey the brutality of war. I thought that would just scare people off. Part of me flashed back to the reaction of passengers on that flight home to New York. It made me think about the need to know our audience and to communicate who we were, not who they might fear we were. At the same time, I realized, even then, that if I was going to have any say about what this group did, I had to be willing to sign up and help organize. In many ways, the culture of the VVAW was still a military one: I would have to prove myself to those men already on the front lines of the anti-war movement, the same way I did when I inherited my crews on Swift boats who had been fighting long before I showed up. The vets felt abused by the politicians who had sent them off to this war. Some were in terrible shape, physically and emotionally. Many carried a story they were burning to tell, a story that could spill out in tears and cries of pain, but also with remarkable eloquence. Many had never known the welcome home I had received, the tenderness of a family and a fiancée who perhaps didn't understand everything we all went through but embraced us—especially me—with open arms. For many veterans and even their families, protest was therapy and catharsis.

While, on reflection, I almost certainly did return with some PTSD, I was lucky to get immersed immediately in efforts to help other veterans. I think that helped me as I saw so many guys seriously messed up. Perhaps I was also conditioned—a product of a buttoned-up education and family where I was taught as a kid to keep a "stiff upper lip." But I had to tell my story. So I spoke at Valley Forge, expressed the anger I felt for the incompetence and stubborn myopia that I had witnessed, expressed the outrage of all veterans against the war who heard politicians tell us it wasn't patriotic to oppose it, when in fact better men than they had spent a winter at Valley Forge to win for all Americans exactly that right.

And we had earned the right to speak our mind and to set our country back on course. It was liberating. Valley Forge reinforced in me just how important it was for our voices to be heard. I couldn't yet speak about Don Droz or Persh or my other friends who were in graves, gone far too soon for a war gone wrong. I just couldn't speak their names. It was still too raw, but I found purpose in saying to anyone there who was listening that it was immoral to send thousands upon thousands of men to die for a mistake.

I started to throw myself more into the life of a full-time activist. The invitations to speak at local gatherings piled up. As I spoke publicly about the war, I became more effective at articulating the combination of anger and facts that wove a compelling argument. I had to tread carefully. There was the war itself, about which we were unanimous, and then there were other issues—injustice, rank discrimination against African Americans and Hispanics, the inequities of the draft among them—that were intertwined with the war but on which there was no unanimity. We all felt a level of alienation from our government. That was ironic for me. Eight years earlier I'd sailed with a president of the United States, and now I was dedicating my time to protesting a policy that had been escalated by his own vice president and that was being expanded even further by a new president, the man he'd defeated in 1960.

We veterans were particularly turned off by the bromides of politicians who talked about supporting the troops but forgot us by the time we came home. I heard story after story about VA hospitals in New York and elsewhere where the care was an insult—unsanitary conditions, suicides, a parade of horrors. I was lucky. You always tell yourself, "There but for the grace of God go I," but there were guys in VVAW in wheelchairs, their spines severed by bullets; guys missing eyes and limbs; men looking troubled and vacant, with wounds that weren't so visible. All too often we found that if it wasn't you yourself, you had a friend who couldn't adjust to being home. There was a lot of self-medication. In all this agony of transitioning out of war and into civilian life, few of us felt as if the government was on our side. Many vets could no longer relate to their father's generation at the Veterans of Foreign Wars or the American Legion. Thus, without a singular moment of decision, without debate, we coalesced into a new fighting force determined to do battle for the veterans—for our own agenda, not just against the war.

We connected with a leading, innovative therapist, Dr. Robert Lifton at Yale University, and together we helped veterans build their own support groups, pioneering "rap sessions," where vets could share their painful stories with other vets. It was part of the healing process, and it was part of the process that probably previous generations—the "stiff upper lip" generation—couldn't relate to, but it was saving lives. We started raising money for this kind of therapy. We even worked to raise money to support a rehabilitation farm for veterans who were really struggling, horribly haunted by the experience of combat. There were times when I wasn't certain of the approach, but I came to understand we all heal in different ways. My healing required activism. What was critical to me was, as it has always been, the act of just getting up in the morning and pressing forward, but different people are motivated differently. And, in fairness, different branches of the service saw different wars. It is in many ways remarkable that as many veterans from different units, in different parts of Vietnam, carrying out different missions, all saw the war as similarly as they did.

And no matter how one saw the war, I thought it was essential we give a damn about each other, because the government wasn't living up to fundamental promises. We were losing vets at home—to alcohol, narcotics, depression, PTSD, unemployment, inadequate benefits and, perhaps mostly, a complete indifference across the nation—if not hostility—to our service. In the end, we lost more returning vets to these curses than there are names on the Wall of those lost in Vietnam. Rather than addressing these concerns, our "leaders" were playing to the divisions, to the lowest common denominator of politics. Right out front was Vice President Spiro Agnew blasting away, trying to define who was American and who wasn't. The administration's rhetoric became more and more frantic, more divisive. We knew there were many ways to be patriotic. Telling the truth was prime among them. In the end, Agnew neither told the truth nor lived up to his own rhetoric. He resigned as a confirmed crook, having betrayed his office and his nation.

Almost to a member, VVAW consisted of men who hated the war but still loved their country.

I was invited to attend the next big VVAW gathering, Operation Winter Soldier, set for January 1971 in Detroit, Michigan. I was told the Midwest had been chosen as the venue in order to try to reach people—voters—in the heartland, perhaps a chance for veterans to give their "testimony" about the war they'd seen and to appeal to those who might be receptive to their message. I went as a kind of observer. All attendees were instructed to bring their discharge papers—DD-214s—as proof of their service. What I heard and saw in Detroit was disturbing, raw and human. Grown men breaking down in anguish, describing terrible, terrible things that they'd seen and done, actions they said had robbed them of their youth and their innocence. It was painful to listen. It wasn't what we'd seen on the Swift boats, though we had our share of haunting memories and sorrow—for example, machine-gun fire aimed into an oncoming Vietnamese fishing junk that had failed to heed our command to stop, only to discover that a woman or a child was caught in the cross fire. Free-fire zones, harassment and interdiction, burning thatched huts and villages in VC areas despite knowing that the VC would rebuild and indoctrinate an angrier population—that was the war many of us resented. That's certainly the war I brought home and could speak to. But these men in Detroit were speaking to something different and even more horrifying: throwing one prisoner out of an airplane in the hope of making his terrified comrade confess, a necklace of VC ears worn around the neck like a trophy. Much was written about the My Lai Massacre and the Phoenix Program and other places where the war went wrong. These weren't examples of what the average veteran experienced, but they weren't complete outliers either. We all knew horrible things had happened. My heart hurt for these broken young vets, many of whom had gone abroad for the first time to a country they didn't understand to kill an enemy they didn't know for a cause that seemed dubious or out of reach. So many were fresh out of high school, off a farm or out of a small town in the Midwest or South.

Some have speculated as to whether everyone there was telling the truth. I don't know. PTSD, nightmares, catatonia—I can't tell you if everyone there was sharing his own experience or some amalgamation of what he had experienced, heard or seen. We wondered even at the time whether there were Nixon plants and moles inside the group to discredit and disrupt the meeting, something Nixon advisor Chuck Colson would one day confess to me was true.

I thought the depths of pain released during those three days, coupled with the continuity between testimonies, all documented by each person's official papers certifying his service in Vietnam and corroborated in many cases by others from the same units, all combined to provide a remarkable validation of what they were saying. As with any testimony in any situation of proving something, witnesses are judged in the totality of their presentation. Anyone legitimately there to listen and learn could not see young men bare their souls so painfully, with such obvious grief and guilt, without being profoundly concerned about what they were saying.

Veterans would break down, leave the room to smoke or come back drunk or high. None of it appeared contrived. But I did wonder whether there was any possibility the country could "hear" and "digest" the rawness of what the veterans were saying.

Activism is about one thing and one thing only—a goal. The stated goal was to persuade Americans about the war. I couldn't see how this would really help end the war. The media response confirmed my reaction. There was close to total silence. It angered me that such obviously searing testimony couldn't be processed. I think the media just didn't know what to do with it. I didn't believe everything I heard, but there was more than enough corroboration, more than enough linkage to incidents we had heard about and more than enough veracity in the presentations for the veterans to be taken seriously. These veterans deserved to be heard. But most of the media apparently thought otherwise. Someone from the press shared with my friend that for reporters to come, "you need more amputees." Appalling. When veterans couldn't be heard because of what they looked like, something was wrong.

I proposed to VVAW that we try something new. It was a risk, in part because it ran against the instinct of many who genuinely and justifiably felt alienated from Washington and had given up on the government. But I argued we should take the fight directly to Washington and make Congress hear us, go door-to-door in the Senate and House, demand meetings, march on D.C. the way the Bonus Army had once marched. After some debate, everyone agreed to give it a shot. VVAW being VVAW, it was given a name—Operation Dewey Canyon—after the last major Marine offensive mission in Vietnam. It was planned for the third week of April 1971.

We had to rush like hell to pull the damn thing together. The organization was unalterably democratic—except when it wasn't. Everything seemed to be put to a vote—except when it wasn't. I learned quickly that we were in a financial hole and was slightly irritated to find out that something like $100,000 had been blown on a series of print ads without appropriate authorization. So it was a mad scramble to raise the money to bring the veterans to Washington, to "bivouac" on the Mall.

A dignified march into Washington through Virginia, past Arlington National Cemetery, joined by Gold-Star wives like Judy Droz was agreed to with unanimity. Some fights weren't winnable: the guerrilla theater and the painted "ghost faces" of some activists, which I thought scared folks, were going to be a part of the days in Washington whether I liked it or not. A demonstration to reach the hearts and minds of the country by "returning" our decorations from Vietnam was a particularly fraught debate. I agreed with the idea of "returning" our decorations. I thought it captured our anguish. But what bothered me was I couldn't look at a Silver Star, a Purple Heart—whatever decoration—without thinking of Persh, or Don Droz, or families of other deceased for whom the medal they had was their final connection to their loved one. It was all that was left of some people. Return it, yes, I thought, but return it the way the military returns a flag to a war widow: with dignity, with solemnity. I proposed having a table covered by a white tablecloth, with each veteran approaching solemnly to lay his medals down, and then we could collect them to be officially delivered to the Pentagon. I was outvoted. Instead, the other vets wanted to leave them on the steps of the Capitol.

I was aware always that I was one of thousands, speaking and acting not just as an individual with individual opinions, but for a group. We pressed on. The whole enterprise almost crumbled when I was informed that we still didn't have the money to pay for buses. Unless we found $75,000 quickly, the buses wouldn't roll. I had to make a last-minute trip to New York to see if we could find this emergency infusion. We had no credit, but thanks to good friends and strong opponents of the war, Adam Walinsky, Seagrams CEO Edgar Bronfman Sr. and Jerry Grossman all helped us raise the money to pull it off.

Once we arrived in Washington, it sometimes seemed as though everything that could go wrong did go wrong. The National Park Service refused to issue us permits to camp on the Mall. The sense of indignity was profound and made a lot of the veterans angry. President Nixon's Department of Justice actually sought an injunction to prevent us from camping. The court ruled we could stay, but not remain overnight. We counted down anxiously as the sky darkened and night crept in. At midnight, an alarm clock went off loudly, to cheers. We stood our ground, pitched tents and laid out sleeping bags. We gave the police a choice: arrest us or let us be. The police never moved in.

As we met during the day with members of Congress, we told them of our precarious situation on the Mall. To this day, I remember how some pulled closer to us while others backed away. Some no doubt worried about being associated with so-called shaggy-haired rabble-rousers, while others bought into rumors of drugs or worse being used in our encampment. Still others thought that the occupation of the National Mall could turn violent. There are many ways to measure character. Even as the police threatened to arrest us, I saw Senator Ted Kennedy come down to the Mall. I was impressed. He spent an hour among the veterans, listening, learning and cheering us on. His commitment to the cause was bigger than politics. I was at a VVAW fund-raiser at Senator Phil Hart's house in Georgetown one night—keeping the lights on and paying our bills was never far from our minds—when, unbeknownst to me, someone from Foreign Relations Committee chairman William Fulbright's staff heard me speak. Fulbright was courageous, an opponent of the war even though his home state of Arkansas was conservative. Not soon after, I was asked to take a phone call: Would I be willing to come to the committee to testify the next day?

My answer was yes. Now I just had to encapsulate in brief testimony not just everything I felt, but everything the men of VVAW felt. I holed up in the temporary VVAW office in northwest Washington, pulled out my sheaf of papers from the last year and a half, from the "Letter to America" I'd shared with Pete Hamill to my notes from speeches, and I started writing. The sun was coming up over Washington when I finished. I showered, shaved, went to the encampment to check signals and touch base and then headed toward the Dirksen Senate Office Building. I was locked and loaded when I passed the Supreme Court and saw a few VVAW vets in an argument with the police. It looked as if they were being arrested. It was the one occurrence we'd managed to avoid thus far. I walked up to them and tried to calm the situation. The police were nice guys. They had a job to do, but the last thing they wanted to do was handcuff a bunch of young veterans who could have been their kids. In the end, we worked it out, but now I was late.

To my right was a cub reporter for the *Boston Globe*, Tom Oliphant, a kid about my age straight out of Harvard. "Let's run," I said to him. I entered the hearing room breathless and sweating. It was packed. Senators stood behind the dais talking. Apparently, they were waiting for me, as, unbeknown to me, I was the only witness. I apologized for being a few minutes late and sat down at the witness table. I'd had no idea what I was walking into. Adrenaline took over. I spread my notes out in front of me and described why we were there and what we hoped to accomplish.

At the end, I summarized, at one point posing a question:

How do you ask a man to be the last man to die in Vietnam? How do you ask a man to be the last man to die for a mistake?

We are also here to ask, and we are here to ask vehemently, where are the leaders of our country? Where is the leadership? We are here to ask where are McNamara, Rostow, Bundy, Gilpatric and so many others. Where are they now that we, the men whom they sent off to war, have returned? These are commanders who have deserted their troops, and there is no more serious crime in the law of war. The Army says they never leave their wounded. The Marines say they never leave even their dead. These men have left all the casualties and retreated behind a pious shield of public rectitude. They have left the real stuff of their reputation bleaching behind them in the sun in this country.

Finally, this administration has done us the ultimate dishonor. They have attempted to disown us and the sacrifice we made for this country. In their blindness and fear they have tried to deny that we are veterans or that we served in 'Nam. We do not need their testimony. Our own scars and stumps of limbs are witnesses enough for others and for ourselves. We wish that a merciful God could wipe away our own memories of that service as easily as this administration has wiped their memories of us.

But all that they have done and all that they can do by this denial is to make more clear than ever our own determination to undertake one last mission, to search out and destroy the last vestige of this barbarous war, to pacify our own hearts, to conquer the hate and the fear that have driven this country these last ten years and more and so when, in thirty years from now, our brothers go down the street without a leg, without an arm or a face, and small boys ask why, we will be able to say "Vietnam" and not mean a desert, not a filthy obscene memory, but mean instead the place where America finally turned and where soldiers like us helped it in the turning.

CHAPTER 6

Finding My Way

"ARE YOU THE one who testified against the war?"

It was an innocent question, but when strangers approached me with a glint in their eyes, I never knew what to expect. I learned quickly to steel myself for the possibility of what might come next.

It was strange to walk down the street, get on a plane or sit down at a restaurant and be recognized. Generally, people were nice, often emotional: the veteran who said he wished he could have been there in Washington for the protests, or the sister of a fallen soldier, or, especially, the African Americans I met who put it right out there that the war was still going on because they were the ones being drafted, while the sons of the "elected and connected" found a way out.

Occasionally someone would unleash a torrent of abuse. Didn't I know good men were fighting in Vietnam? Well, yes, I sure did, sir. That's why I was protesting, so they'd come home alive sooner, instead of letting Nixon keep sending young men to die for his still unrevealed secret plan for peace. The people who would sometimes shout "support the troops" as we vets walked by were the most vexing: We *were* the troops. We had done our duty and earned the right to speak our minds. When I was on the receiving end of a tirade, I realized the critics didn't distinguish between us and the hordes of hippies piled into VW buses headed for the Haight. But whatever the reaction, it was clear that our week in Washington in April 1971 had struck a chord. My testimony had received three or four minutes of direct coverage on the evening news of all three television networks. It was a different era in media. Morley Safer interviewed me soon after for *60 Minutes*. He even asked a question that seemed preposterously removed from the activism that had motivated me: he asked whether I would run for president someday. Black-and-white posters with my photo appeared—origins unknown—and I was asked for autographs. We didn't have this word then, but Dewey Canyon had gone viral and I'd gone viral with it. Seemingly without warning, at twenty-seven, I was a public figure with a public purpose but without a public position from which to lead.

For a number of months after the Washington protests, I gave speeches around the country, drawing a small salary and donating money raised from the speeches to VVAW. I was booked for speaking engagements as far from home as Norman, Oklahoma, to standing-room-only crowds. As the fall of 1971 turned toward the winter, I began to pull back a bit. I had been going nonstop since I had come home from the war. VVAW had become more fractious. I was inspired by all the men and women who had poured their pain into our movement, many of whom became friends for a lifetime, brothers and sisters I know would be at my front door in ten minutes tomorrow if I asked them. But within VVAW, there were suddenly too many different agendas competing for priority—some of them controversial. Mirroring the national mind-set of the times, VVAW was divided over issues of class, between those doing drugs and those who weren't, between opposition to the war in Vietnam and opposition to all wars, between those who believed America could be put back together and those who thought the whole system was rotten to the core. I was decidedly in the camp that wanted to set the country right.

Julia and I sought a measure of peace and refuge at our home in Waltham. We settled down for a tranquil Christmas in a rented cottage on Squam Lake in New Hampshire, together with Julia's brother David and his wife, Rosie. George and Victoria Butler were nearby at George's family property, True Farm. It was a cozy time, with long snowshoe and cross-country ski expeditions across the frozen lake, incredible silence, gray skies and early dark, warm fires and hearty meals. Nearly a half century later I can still feel the peacefulness. Then, in early 1972, word leaked out that Congressman Brad Morse, who represented my hometown of Groton, together with a large swath of Middlesex County, was leaving Congress.

I was nearly two years out from the Concord-Carlisle citizens' caucus. Father Drinan had gone to the House, and the war was still raging. Nixon was still president. I wanted to go to Washington, to join Drinan and do all I could to end the war. And I believed I could do far more as a member of Congress than as a professional activist.

I knew I would be criticized for jumping into the race. But the district included my hometown where we had lived since my father returned from the Foreign Service in 1962.

I decided to go for it. We campaigned our hearts out. It was exciting, fun and brutally hard work. First, I had to contend with a crowded Democratic primary against nine other candidates. Conventional wisdom argued that the winner would have the wind at his or her back for the general election. Coming out of movement, activist politics, I had strengths and weaknesses.

The strengths were clear. I had a singular passion to end the war. I had a national fund-raising base that set me apart from the other candidates, whose base of support was entirely local. I brought home with me a group of the most creative and talented political organizers who were changing the way campaigns were run in the early 1970s, guys like the strategist John Marttila, the pollster Tom Kiley, Frank O'Brien, and David Thorne, who was now a budding political consultant.

We had idealism on our side. The campaign was a family affair. Peggy was calling every friend she'd ever met as an activist, begging for help for her kid brother. Cam took off time from Harvard to be my loyal lieutenant. My mother became the biggest and best booster of all. She proudly wore a button that proclaimed "I'm John's Mom," a button I have to this day, tucked away in a safe place. Despite her formal upbringing, my mother discovered her activist genes and never looked back. I still double over in laughter remembering the lengths to which she went to see me speak at an anti-war rally at the Capitol in Washington, D.C., during Dewey Canyon. She drove down from Massachusetts and found herself a place on the Mall to watch the speeches. As the crowd filled in, her view of the far-off podium became obstructed by the sea of onlookers. Near some picnicking hippies, Mom climbed a tree and watched the rally from her own personal balcony. That evening, Julia, David, Peggy, Cam and I went out for dinner. My mother was supposed to meet us there. She was late. Finally, we saw her car pull up. She parked it in the middle of the street with the lights on and the engine running, hopped out and came into the restaurant. "Mama—are you okay?" I asked. Her pupils were enormous. It turned out that for hours as Mom sat in the tree watching the speeches, the hippies sitting below her were smoking joint upon joint. To our amazement and eternal amusement, Rosemary Forbes Kerry had showed up to dinner secondhand stoned.

Collectively, our campaign was like nothing the district had experienced before. That was precisely part of the problem that we didn't realize was developing. To many in the district, I was appearing out of nowhere, crushing the ambitions of favorite sons, without local ties that mattered to most of the district. Despite what I told myself, my roots were not tangible to voters who lived there. I didn't have a mentor who advised me to tread lightly or think harder about the local sensitivities. There were culturally conservative neighborhoods in the district, people who had voted Democratic for decades but were feeling unsettled by the cultural changes of the era—including the anti-war movement. Furthermore, the most powerful news outlet in the district, the *Lowell Sun*, boasted an editorial page run by a famously colorful, eccentric John Birch Society zealot, Clem Costello, who set out to turn me into a caricature.

Sunday night before the primary, around one in the morning, Cam and my field director, Tom Vallely, were in our headquarters. They were planning the details of a massive primary day operation. Tom had received a warning that people might mess with our phone lines in order to disrupt our activities on primary day. We had developed a state-of-the-art political operation to turn out the vote. It depended on more than one hundred phone lines to turn out record numbers of voters. Cam and Tommy were spooked. Everything Tommy had seen in VVAW taught him, and me, that dirty tricks actually happened in politics.

They went downstairs to check the phone trunks terminating in the vacant building between our office and that of a primary rival, Tony DiFruscia. Tommy kicked open the door, walked down to the basement, and within minutes, they were met by the Lowell police force, which appeared on cue to arrest them for breaking and entering. I was awoken by my first-ever 3:00 a.m. phone call in politics: Cam and Tommy were in jail. The next afternoon, the *Sun*'s blaring headline announced "Kerry Brother Arrested in Lowell 'Watergate,' Breaking into the Headquarters of an Opponent."

I won the primary anyway, but it was an omen of things to come, including a persistent barrage by the *Sun*. I started the general election considerably ahead of my relatively unknown and underfunded Republican opponent, Paul Cronin. But what Cronin was unable to do for himself, the *Lowell Sun* did for him.

Rumors swirled that the Nixon White House—en route to a landslide reelection—was fixated on my campaign. Years later, the Nixon tapes would reveal the president himself had talked to his closest aides about me when I was protesting in Washington. But in 1972, even absent audio evidence, we feared he and his henchmen would do everything they could to deny me a seat in Congress. The race was tightening. Suddenly, a week before the election, the third candidate in the race, an independent named Roger Durkin, pulled out, threw his support to my opponent and then disappeared, mysteriously unavailable to answer questions about his withdrawal. We suspected the fix was in.

I could feel the race slipping away. It wasn't Kerry versus Cronin. It was the *Lowell Sun* versus Kerry, and the *Sun* made it Kerry versus Kerry—their distortions and my war. On election night, I lost convincingly.

I stood at the podium in a subdued hotel ballroom for a painful concession speech and, gritting my teeth, made one thing clear to the *Lowell Sun* and challenged the newspaper to print it: if I had to do it all over again, I would still stand with the veterans in Washington, D.C.

I learned decades later that even after his landslide reelection was secured, Richard Nixon waited to go to bed until he got confirmation of my defeat.

IT WAS CRUSHING. We'd been way ahead in the polls and had missed an undercurrent pulling me away from the voters. As a candidate, I was left with a lot of scar tissue.

It was over. The world moved on, but it took me a little longer. I didn't have a job, let alone a profession. I was unsure of what I would do—unsure by that time of what I even wanted to do. Public service seemed out of reach. I felt more than a little sorry for myself. If VVAW had been a balm for my pain about the war, this personal rejection opened up every wound. Nixon had carried forty-nine states—and it seemed as if the worst kind of politics was being rewarded.

Thanksgiving and the late fall of 1972 were dreary. I lost myself for hours in making a model ship and helicopter that could actually fly. Nixon was still there, lying to the American people and manipulating Vietnam. That Christmas he unleashed a massive bombing attack on North Vietnam, "to force the North Vietnamese to accept the concessions we had made," according to veteran diplomat John Negroponte. Nixon was trying to surrender without saying it, to bring the troops home, and hoping there would be enough of an interval between their return and the fall of South Vietnam that Americans wouldn't notice or care. In early January 1973, talks resumed. Within a few weeks, the Paris Peace Accords were signed. The end of the war as we knew it had arrived.

I took a small measure of pride in the fact that those of us who put our reputations on the line had helped force Nixon to bring the war to a close. But we'd paid a price for our activism. Nixon had manipulated divisions skillfully: he and his vice president wanted the country divided, wanted veterans divided, and wanted to reap the political dividends of the culture war they abetted.

I felt like political roadkill myself, but for others the wounds were immeasurable. The warriors of this war had been confused with the war. Many veterans melted into the background. Too many were lost to the streets, abused their bodies with drugs and alcohol, or never quite got back on track. Some slipped quietly into careers, others became hugely successful, but almost none talked about the war. The nation as a whole consigned Vietnam to the recesses of memory. I felt the awful weight of this era.

The only good news that could snap me out of my funk was the best news of all. In January, life changed for us on the home front: Julia told me she was pregnant. We rejoiced in the news. It was a new beginning that brought the joy of our first addition to the family and brought me instant clarity about the future. There was no time to feel sorry for myself. I resolved then and there that never again would I get sidetracked by self-pity. I was the luckiest guy in the world. I was alive. Unlike Dick Pershing and so many others, I was about to be blessed with fatherhood. My sense of gratitude was profound.

This jolt of renewed purpose restored my confidence about other things in life. I had plenty of time to do the things I wanted to do. I suddenly saw the campaign in a more positive light. We had tried. We had given it our all. We had fought for the right things, and while it didn't work out, it also hadn't brought the end of the world. Sometimes you have to pick yourself up off the mat and just keep moving ahead. But most of all, I was going to be a father, and I was determined to live fully in every minute of that fatherhood.

Julia and I bought a house in Lowell. We wanted to stay there and prove the skeptics wrong. I wanted to buckle down and go to law school, to give myself income-earning capacity so that never again would I be adrift even if I wasn't in public service.

Sometime in the late spring, Paul Tsongas, a former Lowell city councilor, visited me. Paul had supported me in my race for Congress. It was an unselfish thing for him to do. He was a lifelong resident of Lowell who had every reason to see me as an interloper and competitor, but he went all out and even said that if I decided to run again in two years, he would support me. But I was educated by my loss. I thought another round against Paul Cronin would just be the same race all over again. I thought Paul Tsongas had a better chance of winning. It was perhaps the demarcation of a new maturity. I told Paul he should run and urged all my supporters to vote for him.

By the time I had settled with certainty on law school, as Julia felt ever more pregnant by the day, it was summer. I had to move fast. I hadn't even applied to law school. I visited the deans at Harvard, Boston University and Boston College to ask if I could apply late. Harvard and BU gave me the same answer: "We can't open it up now. Why don't you take the year and apply next fall?" BC alone at least asked to look at my transcript. Within days the admissions office called to say I had been accepted.

The night before my first law school class, as Julia and I sat at home enjoying the stillness before the push and pull of studying began, the tranquillity was interrupted. Julia's water broke. It was surreal. We had read all the popular books about childbirth. None prepared us for the suddenness of the moment: after nine months of waiting, just like that, the baby was actually coming. I packed a suitcase, searched for the car keys, nursed Julia into the car, wondering if our child would be introduced to life in the back seat of an automobile. We rushed to Emerson Hospital in Concord, where my fears of imminent birth were immediately dispelled. Julia began a long labor.

We had been through all the Lamaze lessons. I dutifully breathed away with her as the contractions increased in force and tempo. It dawned on me just how ancillary fathers are to this miraculous process. I was there to hold a hand, bring Dixie cups filled with ice chips and call our parents with the news that we were at the hospital. But as every dad learns watching his wife in pain, pushing away, nothing prepares anyone for the full awareness of motherhood that comes with labor. Eventually, Julia was wheeled into the delivery room. I stood by in my surgical gown, trying to be of some use. Twenty minutes ticked by. And then, finally, a baby appeared: long, dark-haired, wet and limp, held up by the doctor. Adrenaline coursed through my body: I thought for a moment she was dead, but suddenly she jerked to life and began a healthy wail. "You have a baby girl," said the doctor, amid the tears flowing from Julia and me. It was surreal that one moment ago, we were a family of two, and suddenly and forever we had this new light in our life—Alexandra Forbes Kerry. It was a miracle. I had never in my life felt such pure joy and amazement.

Later that day, after basking in the afterglow of new fatherhood, Julia reminded me: you have to be at law school. It hit me: I was a new father—and if I didn't hurry up, I was about to be a prodigal law student. I drove to Chestnut Hill. It was a dizzying and auspicious day.

The next months were all like *Groundhog Day* with the same routine—changing diapers, feeding in the night, studying law wherever I could and fighting the traffic commuting from Lowell to Chestnut Hill and back every day. We were at the height of the 1973 OPEC oil embargo, and I read contract, property and tort law in long lines just waiting to get gas. The next three years were a blur spent in the law library, in the Middlesex district attorney's office, where I was a student intern, and at home loving the baby who had entered our lives, watching her turn into a little girl who could walk and talk and bedazzle her parents.

I threw myself into law school in a way I never had in my undergraduate years. Together with my superb partner Ronna Schneider, I took on the moot court event. We won the school competition, went on to win the regionals and then went to New York City for the national finals. There we thought we clobbered the Duke Law School team in oral argument. We waited hours for the decision. The judges had wanted to award the victory to us, but the Duke team had slightly bested us in the brief, which counted for more than 50 percent. The judges were locked in battle trying to find a way to award us the victory. They couldn't bend the rule, so we lost. It was the last time in the National Moot Court Competition that the brief outweighed the oral argument. The rule was subsequently changed.

I credit law school with teaching me how to think. I enjoyed the give-and-take of Socratic dialogue at a Jesuit law school. I was part of a terrific study group, five classmates who met frequently to dissect the cases we had been assigned. The fights we had over the meaning of one word taught me to be far more critical, far more demanding, in my own thinking.

As a student, I was permitted under Massachusetts law to try misdemeanor cases. I could even appear before a six-person jury. I was mesmerized by the art of trying a jury trial and spent hours upon hours watching the full-fledged assistant district attorneys prosecute rape, armed robbery or murder cases. I couldn't wait to get a real felony trial.

On the first day that I reported for duty as a student prosecutor, I walked into the District Court of Cambridge and was assigned a drunk driving case. The assistant DA handed me the papers twenty minutes before the trial, saying, "There's no better way to start than to start." He disappeared and left me alone to face the judge. "All rise"—I stood up. I stumbled through the story, which was set out in the police report, and called the officer and put him on the stand. I asked far more questions than necessary. I could see the judge was half-amused, half-annoyed, tolerating my rookie performance. I actually placed into evidence the empty bottles the police had collected in the car. The judge was almost audibly chuckling. I didn't know that these cases were typically concluded in rapid-fire fashion. There were too many not to. I was treating this one like a murder trial. But I got the conviction and, stupid as I felt, I had tried a case.

In the spring of 1976 I graduated and prepared to take the bar exam with a heightened sense of urgency: I was promised a job as an assistant district attorney as soon as I passed the bar. I was excited about the chance to become a full-time prosecutor, but I was also eager to get the job for another reason: I needed the income. Julia and I had stumbled across a perfect home for our family on Chestnut Hill, near Boston College. We had stayed in Lowell for three years. But with a baby at home and a job in Cambridge, the commute didn't make sense anymore. The distance from friends and work had also taken a toll on Julia. It was important to both of us to try to lead a more normal life.

The house, with its slight Italian flavor, appealed to our romantic impulses and Julia's nostalgia for Italy. Perhaps the stucco with the terra-cotta tile roof drew us in. A wonderful brick wall enveloped a garden—our own secret garden. Ample bedrooms were ready for a larger family, and the closing on the house came just in time: Julia was pregnant with our second child, due sometime in late December or early January. It was a great feeling to think of this new home, to know I had a job I wanted, to have the dreaded bar exam behind me. We were at peace as we moved in and were greeted by the most thoughtful of surprises: a friend left a lobster and champagne dinner in the front hall on our first night in our new home.

Happily, in the late fall, we learned that each member of our study group had passed the bar exam. The same day I was sworn into the bar, I took on my responsibilities as an assistant district attorney. I was immediately assigned to prosecute a rape case, squaring off against a well-known defense attorney, Bill Homans. I felt a genuine sense of accomplishment putting a rapist behind bars. Shortly thereafter, on New Year's Eve, before the page turned to 1977, we returned to Emerson Hospital as seasoned veterans for the arrival of our second daughter, Vanessa Bradford Kerry. The beginning of the new year was a good time. We were blessed—new house, new job, healthy newborn.

I buckled down to work in the office of the Middlesex district attorney. John Droney, the boss, was an old-school, crafty politician. He had followed my ill-fated run for Congress and respected my service in the military. We spent a fair amount of time talking politics. He would also regale me with stories of some of his great prosecutions. He had put a number of infamous criminals behind bars, including the Boston Strangler. Sadly, John had fallen ill with a nerve or motor disease, which he tried to keep out of the public eye. He would allow no discussion of how he was doing or any other deviation from the work of the office and the certainty of his reelection.

The problem, of course, was that his reelection wasn't certain at all. John thought he could run an old-fashioned race, stay under the radar, rely on name recognition and let city and ethnic politics do the rest—but politics was changing. A very capable former assistant attorney general, Scott Harshbarger, was planning to run against John as a reform candidate. He represented a formidable challenge in the new environment. Moreover, the office had fallen behind the times. In New York, District Attorney Robert "Bob" Morgenthau was setting new standards for prosecutors. In Massachusetts, Bill Delahunt was doing the same in Norfolk County. Washington was making grant money available to prosecutors to modernize. John Droney didn't have one grant, let alone any plan for modernization. There was a backlog of thousands of pending cases, each on an index card in a floating file box. There was no computerized system. Crime was rising. Justice was delayed. John one day asked me what I would do to change the office. I told him. The next day, he shocked me: he appointed me first assistant district attorney, reporting only to him and with full authority to get done what needed to be done. He called a meeting of all the office. People jammed into his office to hear what he had to say. He announced my new role.

I was both dumbfounded and excited: never in my wildest imagination did I expect to be running one of the largest district attorney offices in the country only months out of law school. I knew that knives would be out. Change doesn't come easily anywhere. But I had a chance to turn the office around, and I was eager and anxious to earn my spurs.

With young reformers recruited for the effort, we established accountability in the assignment and flow of cases, created a Victim Witness Assistance Program, set up a rape counseling unit and a white-collar crime unit to specialize in complicated financial crimes and installed a new computer system.

By the time John Droney's 1978 election came around, the office was humming, but John was reticent about advertising our accomplishments in a modern campaign style. I was finally able to persuade him to let us run one full-page advertisement in the *Boston Globe*: ten reasons John Droney should be reelected—a stark, quick narrative of each brutal crime he had cracked that made the county safer. John won the election, and I went back to trying cases.

One case in particular stands out. Austen Griffin, a decorated veteran and a member of one of the local American Legion posts, walked into my office on the second floor of the courthouse. He told me he was being strong-armed by Howie Winter, the number two organized crime figure in New England, who was pushing to force slot machines into the post. Austen wanted none of it. He was outraged by Howie's tactics and wasn't going to be bullied. Howie and his Winter Hill Gang had earned their reputation as head-smashers the hard way: in blood. Bodies piled up wherever they went. There were dead bookies washing up on the shores of the Mystic River. There were small-time thugs who regularly disappeared. Winter was in cahoots with James "Whitey" Bulger and some of the most notorious killers of their time. None of it could scare Austen Griffin.

Going after Howie Winter was a challenge. But here was this citizen whose credibility was beyond reproach, expecting us to take action. I called the state police, who worked with us day to day. We provided protection to the witnesses. Austen never wavered. We won a grand jury indictment, and I asked the brilliant prosecutor Bill Codinha to take the case on full-time.

He was our best trial attorney and there was no way I could run the office and take on a case of that length and importance. In a superb prosecutorial coup, Bill brought home a conviction. For the first time, a huge dent was put in the Winter Hill Gang and organized crime. We had done at the county level what neither state nor federal government had been able to do—and all because of a gutsy citizen with values and nerves of steel who was willing to stand up for his rights and unwilling to bend to evil.

I stayed with the office until 1980, when I felt my presence was cramping John Droney. He never said anything to me, but he did begin to reassert himself on a few personnel decisions, and I sensed that it was time for me to move on. Droney had been a mentor, something I'd lacked in Massachusetts. His personal example battling a terrible affliction, which turned out to be Lou Gehrig's disease, and the opportunity he gave me were both life-shaping.

But it was now time for me to start a new chapter.

It was 1980. Ronald Reagan had swept the country, including Massachusetts. I began practicing law privately in a boutique law firm I had set up with another assistant district attorney from Middlesex County, Roanne Sragow. We were working on medical malpractice cases that were eye-opening. A local doctor had become mixed up with a company that provided hair transplants using rug fibers as plugs—the ultimate harebrained scheme. The photos of heads infected by these carcinogenic fibers would make any stomach turn. Roanne and I just needed to find the right jury to nauseate! The insurance companies were unwilling to settle. Accordingly, we went to trial. We succeeded in getting the carcinogenic qualities of the rug fibers entered into evidence. Winning that trial convinced the insurance companies we knew how to try a case and uncorked a flow of settlements.

Taking on these cases was interesting, but I found the practice too predictable. From the moment a client walked in, I could guesstimate fairly quickly what the outcome would be. But one case was an exception. Roanne had taken on a court appointment to represent an indigent prison inmate, George Reissfelder, who insisted that he was innocent of murder. Both Roanne and I initially took his claim with a grain of salt because we had learned as prosecutors that "they're all innocent," as the saying goes. Prosecuting can breed some measure of cynicism into the practice of criminal law, but having represented one court appointment for a defendant in a murder, I knew that so can defending.

George Reissfelder confounded our cynicism. Roanne first, and then I, came to believe he really was innocent. He was in prison for a murder he hadn't committed—he was a criminal, yes, but not a killer. Roanne put extraordinary hours and sweat equity into the case, and I undertook specific assignments on her behalf to ease the load. We thought we could prove it, but there were key hurdles we had to get over, including getting a priest released from his vows of confidentiality in order to help exonerate George. We also needed to secure a release from lawyer-client protection to make admissible exonerating information from George's codefendant, who was now deceased. Unbelievably, George's accomplice told his own lawyer George didn't kill anyone, but the lawyer, in protecting his client, allowed George to be convicted. Finally the truth could come out, provided the lawyer was free to testify. Long before the days of DNA testing, the case was a reminder that it was possible for someone who wasn't guilty to end up behind bars, and it hardened my opposition to the death penalty.

By 1981, I had been back in Massachusetts for almost ten years, ever since the loss in the Fifth Congressional District. I was starting to miss politics again. Michael Dukakis was gearing up to run for governor—but he first had to challenge the incumbent Democrat, Ed King. It seemed like a good time to try to reenter electoral politics. I thought serving as lieutenant governor would be a good way to contribute and also to learn the ropes the right way—paying dues, not rushing in as I had before.

Shortly after I started to nose around, using the law office as my base of operations, a red-haired young kid from Dorchester walked into my office and told me he wanted to work for me. This young self-starter, who knew exactly what he wanted to do, when and for whom, was named Michael Whouley. Little did I know that politics would bring us back together over a lifetime, and that he would become one of the great organizers of a generation.

The race for lieutenant governor shaped up to be a tough, hard-fought primary with several candidates. Normally, the job of lieutenant governor could be written off. I sometimes told the story of Calvin Coolidge, the thirtieth president of the United States, who had earlier been the lieutenant governor of Massachusetts. He was at a dinner party when the woman sitting next to him asked what he did. "I'm lieutenant governor of the state," he said in the dry clip that characterized his speech. She responded, "Oh, that's wonderful! Tell me all about the job." He didn't miss a beat and replied, "I just did." But to be number two in Massachusetts was still enticing, especially under Dukakis.

In Massachusetts, politics is a passion fed by ideology and idealism. It's serious business: intense, demanding and nonstop. Each of the candidates in the donnybrook for lieutenant governor went all out. I barely made the 15 percent at the state convention required to get my name on the primary ballot, but once I did, it was a sprint to primary day in September.

The year 1981 was consumed by the campaign. It was also consumed by a growing tension in my marriage. Julia and I had been on cruise control for a while. The experience of total immersion in the anti-war effort, then the race for Congress, then law school, then the move, then a new job, then more political decision-making—all combined to make us drift apart. I take the lion's share of blame for this and always have. No matter where the discussions led—and there were lots of discussions, including with professional intervention—the damage was done. Julia was suffering from depression and I was, at first, sadly oblivious. She told me about it, but things got worse before I really understood. She had changed. She had come to detest public life, with its perceptible insincerities and incessant demands. There was no way to find happiness sharing her life and family with politics. In the end, this wonderful relationship—which had started at Yale and carried through Vietnam and the journey of twelve years of marriage—was broken. In mid-summer of 1982, we agreed to separate after the election was over.

It was an agonizing decision. I knew our marriage was in trouble. Still, I hated beyond hate the idea of not tucking my kids into bed and being with them at home, no matter how much public life could get in the way of that ideal. I also hated the thought of missing Christmas or sharing it in some lawyer-agreed-upon schedule. I was filled with a sense of failure. It was harder than hell to get out of bed, go out and campaign, put a smile on, when you had just finished a deeply emotional, tugging argument. There were times when I felt like crawling into the fetal position and going into a great sleep like the reporter in *All the King's Men.* The great sleep— sometimes I thought maybe I'd wake up out of the nightmare to find the great sleep resulted in the great repair. Not to be. So I entered this strange, dual world—one I lived in, campaigning on automatic, and only half lived in at home. It required all the focus I could summon.

I won the September primary, and on November 2, 1982, Michael Dukakis and I were elected together. I walked into his office shortly thereafter and told him Julia and I were separating. It was the kind of conversation I never anticipated having with the governor as his new lieutenant.

We were inaugurated in January 1983. It didn't take long for me to conclude that Michael was probably going to run for president in due time. It wasn't that he told me, but certain decisions he made about which duties would be performed by whom made it abundantly clear—or so I thought. One of the ideas I had put forward in the primary was the creation of a crime council that would unite all the law enforcement agencies by holding frequent meetings to coordinate our anti-crime efforts. After I won the primary, Michael agreed that I would chair the crime council, which is what I wanted to do; but very soon after the inauguration, I was called upstairs to meet with him and learned that he had decided to chair the council. When he told me and I reminded him of our earlier discussion, he acknowledged the change, but then said, "I need to do this." Whether justified, I immediately interpreted the "need" to be the imperative to build a strong law enforcement profile. This was entirely his right and it was understandable why he would do it, but I left that meeting with a great lesson in the nature of lieutenant governors. You don't live on your own politically in that job—not if you wish to have any job to do. You live with the blessing, or lack thereof, of the governor and his or her team. In principle, I knew that getting into the race, but the reality had an altogether different—and personal—impact.

In fact, Michael was a terrific governor and a great person to work with. He treated me throughout with decency and friendship. He brought intellect and integrity to the job and had a sense of public responsibility as deep as anyone I have ever met. My own father, who had never been involved at the grassroots level in politics, without even talking with me, had been one of Michael's early delegates to his first state conventions.

As competent as Michael was, at times he could frustrate everyone with his insistence on doing something strictly by the book. He would never bend and everyone knew it. On one occasion, we were headed up to Concord, New Hampshire, for the funeral of Governor Hugh Gallen. By this time Michael's presidential ambitions were publicly known. He had been asked to deliver one of the eulogies at the statehouse service. It was to be nationally televised—therefore an important moment for Michael on the national stage.

Michael and Kitty, the state's First Lady, rode up with me to New Hampshire. They were in the back seat of my station wagon. We started out late, but within minutes of hitting Interstate 93 from Boston to Concord, Michael issued an edict to my driver, Chris Greeley: "Not over 60 mph. . . ." Chris and I looked at each other and knew we were never going to have the governor there on time. The minutes were ticking away, and every time Chris would inch above 60 mph, Michael would remind him: "Not over 60." Finally, as we neared the New Hampshire border, when it was obvious we were dangerously late, I turned to Michael and basically said I was calling the New Hampshire State Police to get an escort or he would miss the funeral. Michael didn't say anything. Meanwhile, Kitty was lighting yet another cigarette and seemed to be on my side. The New Hampshire State Police picked us up at the tollbooths, and we started following them at breakneck speed, pushing our Buick diesel engine to the absolute limit. I looked back to see Michael clearly unhappy but at least no longer fixated on the speed limit. We arrived at the statehouse, engine smoking, late but not so late that the governor missed speaking.

Michael very graciously asked his colleague governors if they would mind his lieutenant governor chairing a subcommittee of the National Governors Association. Governor John Sununu of New Hampshire and Governor Dick Celeste of Ohio agreed. I may well be the only lieutenant governor who has done so, but thanks to Michael's delegated authority, I chaired the NGA's committee on acid rain. John Sununu and Dick Celeste became key partners in developing an approach resulting in a market-based cap-and-trade system to deal with sulfur—the major emission of coal-burning power plants killing our lakes and streams. Here was this market-based method of reining in damaging emissions, dreamed up in several conservative think tanks, which we adopted and which later became federal law. It successfully eliminated the problem of acid rain.

My work on acid rain soon led me into a race for the U.S. Senate long before I might have considered it. In early 1983, I was on a fact-finding mission about atmospheric pollution for the NGA. I traveled first to Norway and Sweden to witness and try to understand what was happening to the lakes and rivers of Scandinavia. There I saw evidence of extraordinary damage from the high concentrations of sulfur in the rain. Lakes that had once teemed with fish were now completely dead. From the Scandinavian countries, I traveled to Germany's famous Black Forest. It was beautiful but shocking. The ranger who escorted me into the forest pointed out frightening levels of disease in the trees.

That night I was sound asleep in my hotel when the phone rang. It was my second 3:00 a.m. phone call in politics. The voice at the other end belonged to Ron Rosenblith, one of my closest, most valued political advisors. He said, "Are you sitting down?" I laughed and said, "No—I'm lying down. I was sound asleep." He apologized for waking me but immediately explained the reason for the call: Paul Tsongas had just announced he was not going to run for reelection to the U.S. Senate because he had cancer. I was stunned. He was only a few years older than me and he was in his first term. We had been through my battle and his in Lowell. Ron went on to say that two congressmen, Ed Markey and Jimmy Shannon, as well as Speaker of the Massachusetts House David Bartley had already announced they were in. Ron said I had about forty-eight hours to decide whether I was going to contest for this seat. I was floored but wide-awake.

There was no way I was going to decide in forty-eight hours. To the frustration of my team and those who wanted me to run, I said I would complete the trip and we would sit down when I got back to make a rational decision. Moreover, I clearly had a first stop—with the governor. I had been lieutenant governor for only one year, and if I ran, I'd need to start running full-time. I had to get a handle on my own feelings, then determine the politics.

Immediately on my return to Boston I was inundated with advice. The principal tension was the short span of time I had served as lieutenant governor versus my lifelong concern with issues of war and peace, as well as global environmental matters. I had always known what I wanted to do but I was chastened by my own impatience in 1972. I knew that if I ran and failed now, that would essentially be it for elective office. It was gut-check time. No one could make this decision for me.

I spent time with myself—just stood back, prayed for guidance and tried to plumb for what would make me comfortable with my decision. In the end, I was more than ready to go. It was 1983. Ronald Reagan was president. The war in Central America was raging. Drugs were rampant. President Reagan had come to office with a determination to significantly increase the defense budget during difficult economic times in the United States. Russia and the United States had absurd numbers of nuclear weapons pointed at each other.

In the first years of the administration there had been considerable rhetoric about potential use of nuclear weapons. At one point, Secretary of State Alexander Haig actually talked about the possibility of firing a "nuclear warning shot" in Europe. One of Reagan's National Security Council team members asserted that there was a 40 percent chance of nuclear war, and the president himself had said at an October 1981 press conference that it was his opinion tactical nuclear weapons could be employed on certain battlefields without leading to an all-out nuclear war. There was talk and concern about the direction of the administration at that moment. Cold War proxy battles in El Salvador and neighboring Nicaragua, which had undergone a left-wing coup, flashed warning signs that the Reagan administration could take us into another quagmire.

Issues of war and peace were very much back on the front burner, the issues that had brought me into politics more than a decade before. I just couldn't stomach sitting on the sidelines of a race that could potentially put me in a position to help decide such important issues. I also knew that this might be the only chance in my generation to run for the Senate, because it was sure as hell certain Ted Kennedy wasn't going to vacate his seat. Something told me to run. Was I brimming with confidence that I would win no matter what? Absolutely not. Was I brimming with confidence at my ability to make this work because it was the right thing to do? Undeniably. I had to take the leap if I wanted to be involved with the issues that most motivated me. Suddenly, I was back out there asking the voters of Massachusetts to send me to Washington.

The fight for the nomination would be tough. Ed Markey and Jim Shannon were especially able competitors. But Markey, who is very smart, never found his stride and decided to run for reelection to the House instead. Shannon and I dueled to differentiate ourselves from each other. Our policy positions were almost inseparable. But in a debate late in the campaign, days before the primary, Jim inadvertently highlighted a real difference between us. I had brought up Jim's change of heart on one of Reagan's proposed military increases. Jim shot back—oddly—that people can change their mind and said that, for example, by the standard I'd set out, if I'd really been opposed to Vietnam, I shouldn't have gone to the war. It was strange. I didn't think much of it in the moment. But our campaign phones started ringing off the hook. Veterans were calling in from all over the state, angry that, to their ears, Shannon had called them stupid: they felt he had questioned their character by impugning the right of veterans to speak their conscience, right or wrong. I fired back at Shannon over the issue in the very next debate and demanded he apologize. "John, that dog won't hunt," he replied. Veterans booed Jim, and a group of vets followed him everywhere he went the next few days, drowning out his message. They called themselves "the Doghunters." I won the primary, thanks to hard work and thanks to each of them. It was on to the general election.

My opponent was a self-funded businessman named Ray Shamie—a former John Birch Society conservative who lost to Ted Kennedy in 1982 and then won the Republican nomination against the more moderate Rockefeller Republican Elliot Richardson at the state convention. Shamie was out of touch with Massachusetts, but I took nothing for granted. I remembered the lesson of Lowell in 1972; I knew that certain social conservatives could play the wedge issues and ignite their bases of support. Reagan was cruising to a landslide reelection, and he was pulling Massachusetts into the Republican column again. I was not about to repeat what had happened the last time I'd been on the under ticket of a presidential ballot. A freshman congressman named John S. McCain parachuted into the state for a day to rally veterans for Shamie. He campaigned in South Boston. I didn't meet him or know him—but I knew that this former POW could draw a crowd. I worked harder to organize veterans on our side, to make sure that the state knew me, not a cardboard cutout. It worked. On election night, I defied the Reagan tide that swept Massachusetts. Running as a "warrior for peace," I was going to be a U.S. senator.

CHAPTER 7

The Old Senate

"GEORGE BUSH COULDN'T sell pussy on a troop train!"

These were the first words of senatorial conversation I heard on the floor of the world's greatest deliberative body on January 3, 1985. I don't think it was a quote from the *Federalist Papers*.

It happened just after Ted Kennedy walked me onto the floor for the first time and introduced me to three or four colleagues engrossed in conversation about something the Reagan administration was trying to push through Congress. I'm not sure what I expected, but it certainly wasn't what I heard.

Much about becoming a U.S. senator tended toward the surreal. Here I was, just forty-one years old, ninety-ninth in seniority—I would have been hundredth (dead last) had Paul Tsongas not generously offered to resign a day early so Governor Dukakis could swear me in before I departed Boston, thereby giving me the tiniest edge in an institution built on longevity. I had big shoes to fill. Cancer had cut Paul's Senate service short, but in just six years he'd built a reputation for a willingness to break with liberal orthodoxy on occasion and as a smart and creative wonk on issues from entitlements to deficits.

Before Paul Tsongas from Lowell had served, there had been Ed Brooke, one of the last remaining African American Republicans from New England, a liberal, the first in his party to demand Nixon's resignation in 1973. Stretching back before both Paul and Ed (and now me) was a veritable anthology of names seemingly ripped from the membership directory of the Daughters of the American Revolution or the Mayflower Society: Federalists and Whigs, then Republicans and the occasional Democrat, with names like Strong, Sedgwick, Dexter, Foster, Pickering, Rockwell, Hoar, Crane, Coolidge, Lodge and Saltonstall. I suppose, with my patchwork of heritage, I had a foot in both worlds, not entirely the product of either.

I happily accepted some small measure of weight from the history preceding me. It reflected the real story of America. I was proud to now share in it. I'd previously read a great story about then freshman senator Harry S. Truman sitting in the back of the Senate, ninety-ninth in seniority, same as me, writing letters home to his mother in Missouri. He described how he sat there one night and listened to the great debates of the day. He wrote that he could almost hear the voices of giants like Daniel Webster, and being impressed, he would look at his colleagues, pinch himself and ask, "How the hell did I get here?" Months went by. Again, he wrote to his mother: "It's late at night in the Senate and once again I can hear the voices of the Senate giants from years past. I look out at my colleagues and I pinch myself and ask, 'How the hell did they get here?'" I always laugh at that story, but there's some hidden wisdom in it too, because it sums up the hypothetical expectations and real-life contradictions in the Senate, as well as the lessons you can learn from both of them.

In a tradition that's both quaint and grand, Ted Kennedy—now my senior senator, but long ago the thirty-year-old candidate I'd interned for in 1962 and spent time with on the Mall in Washington in 1971 with the veterans—walked me down the aisle of the Senate like the father of a bride. In the well of the Senate I was ceremoniously sworn in as the twenty-eighth man to hold my seat, just the sixty-fifth citizen overall to hold the title "United States Senator from Massachusetts."

The person dutifully performing the honors of swearing me in was the vice president of the United States, George H. W. Bush, Yale class of 1948. His father, Prescott Bush, was serving as the Republican senator from Connecticut the day I walked onto campus in New Haven. I shook Vice President Bush's hand, reminded him of the kindness he had shown my eight-year-old daughter, Vanessa, that past July, sharing his popcorn with her at Harvard Stadium during the Chile versus Norway Olympic qualifying soccer game. Back then Vice President Bush had not allowed the politics of the Massachusetts Senate race to get in the way of relating to my family; little did either of us know then that a political collision awaited us.

I liked Bush very much. Aside from the ugly nature of his 1988 campaign against Michael Dukakis, I always found him decent and thoughtful, straight dealing in his interactions. I never doubted whether he was in politics for the right reasons. He loved the Navy as I did, and we talked about that at the soccer game at some length.

Minutes after I was sworn in, Teddy steered me around the Senate floor to meet my new colleagues. It was as we approached a huddle of veteran senators that I heard Alabama's senior senator, Howell Heflin, cast the Republican vice president in a decidedly colorful light. So much for Senate formality. I can still hear Heflin's courtly accent emphasizing each and every word before the group broke out in laughter. And so it was that I met my new colleagues. Senator Heflin was then the chairman of the Ethics Committee, a Marine awarded the Silver Star for service in the thick of the fighting in the Pacific in World War II, the onetime chief justice of the Alabama Supreme Court. Back then the Senate was stocked with memorable characters. Majority Whip Alan Simpson from Wyoming was an Army veteran with a quick wit, a great debater who could cut you to pieces when he wasn't promising to "stick it right in the old bazoo." Russell Long from Louisiana, the Senate's leading expert on the tax code, bore a striking resemblance to his famous father, the legendary Kingfish, Huey Long, who had inspired Robert Penn Warren's masterpiece *All the King's Men*. I'd read that book by flashlight under the covers at St. Paul's, when I was only vaguely aware of the icon on whom the book was based, the real-life, flesh-and-blood Huey Long, who was assassinated when Russell was just sixteen. What I knew of Huey Long came from black-and-white newsreel footage that occasionally flashed across a television screen. By the time I met Russell, the senator was, amazingly, in his final term, winding down thirty-eight years in the Senate. It was the only job he'd ever had since being elected at age twenty-nine, two days and two months before he met the thirty-year-old eligibility requirement of the Constitution. He'd outlasted Lyndon Johnson and Hubert Humphrey, both of whom came to the Senate the same year—1948. Now he was enjoying his last years, still pulling the strings back home in Louisiana.

Another larger-than-life senator was Fritz Hollings, the former governor of South Carolina who courageously presided over the integration of the University of South Carolina. He had served in the Senate since 1966, the most senior junior senator in history, paired with the nonagenarian Strom Thurmond.

Fritz was a hoot. "I don't want to rust out, I'd rather wear out," he used to say. He possessed one of the great repertoires of colorful phrases. Diplomats, for example, were "striped-pants cookie pushers." I never knew him to hold back, even when talking in less appetizing terms: "Letting y'all regulate yourselves is like delivering lettuce by way of a rabbit." Fritz was a longtime friend of the Kennedys going back to President Kennedy's campaign. Teddy once described Fritz as "the first non-English-speaking candidate for President," but once I figured out how to translate Hollings's deep, rich Charleston accent, we became close friends. He became a great mentor to me on the Commerce Committee and in the Senate. On one occasion he shared a surprisingly personal but invaluable piece of advice. It benefited me in those early days: when I was in hot pursuit of appropriations to bring home some money to Massachusetts and needed to make the case in person—to kiss some rings, in other words—Fritz was pretty clear to me which senators I shouldn't go see after about 4:30 in the afternoon. His comment needed little explanation but nonetheless he added one with a sly smile: "Either the meetin' won't go well or, hell, he won't remember it the next day. Either way, I'd go ask to see Orrin Hatch at that hour instead. Orrin's a teetotaler and a deacon in the Mormon Temple."

I had arrived at a Senate in transition, much as I had arrived twenty-three years earlier on a campus in transition.

Howell Heflin's off-color language with his colleagues wasn't unusual back in 1985. The Senate then was an institution that at times sounded a lot more like a bar or a locker room. There was a fair amount of drinking, and the aroma of cigars crept out of many of the senior members' hideaway offices in the Capitol.

You didn't have to look far to understand why that might have been the case: I had as many daughters as there were women in the U.S. Senate. Only two of my colleagues were women, Nancy Landon Kassebaum, the junior senator from Kansas, and Paula Hawkins, a Republican from Florida who would soon be defeated by my friend Bob Graham in 1986. We were working in what at times felt like a hermetically sealed vault—a time capsule that had not kept up with social progress.

Years later, Teresa would tell me about her experience as the wife of a Republican senator, hosting a gathering for the National Republican Senatorial Campaign Committee, which her husband, Jack Heinz, a senator from Pennsylvania, was chairing. As the evening wound down, she spotted Strom Thurmond charmingly filling his pockets with chicken wings and cookies to take home with him. She laughed and made him a little plate to take on his way. Strom then was a mere eighty-three. He was dapper in his own peculiar, very senior way: his orange hair was not a color found in nature, and he wore the heavy scent of his favorite cologne, which he stockpiled when he learned the company was going out of business. He thanked Teresa for the goody bag and gave her a hug. She suddenly found ol' Strom's hands digging into her sides: "Still maaghty firm, my dear, maaghty firm!" he bellowed. Some old dogs were not changing with the times. He was to cause some consternation a few years later when he similarly greeted Senator Patty Murray of Washington in an elevator and tried to excuse his behavior by explaining that he thought she was an intern.

It was a Senate overwhelmingly old and white and male, something I was reminded of on days when the eighty-four-year-old senior senator from Mississippi, the legendary John C. Stennis, who the year before had a leg amputated due to cancer, rolled by me in his wheelchair. Here he was, a man who had come to the Senate in 1947 when I was not quite four years old. When I was raising money at Yale to help support the Mississippi Voter Registration Project, Stennis had two good strong legs under him as he joined the Southern Caucus's filibuster of the 1964 Civil Rights Act. But you learn in the Senate that no matter the history, every vote still counts, and as long as people in a state have sent their choice to the Senate, you have to work together to get anything accomplished.

And Stennis had changed with the times, supporting voting rights legislation a couple years before I showed up in the Senate, a vote he once told Joe Biden had "cleansed his soul." A year after that he'd campaigned for Mike Espy, the Mississippi Democrat who would become the first African American to represent the Magnolia State in Congress since Reconstruction. Stennis was nonetheless a voice from a distant era, a name I had probably first heard in 1971 when he was chairman of the Armed Services Committee, a pro–Vietnam War southern stalwart whom angry anti-war activists made a target of their anger. Now he was my colleague, an old man who had lived almost immeasurable amounts of American history, who described his legislative motto as "stay flexible" and who now surely knew, as Bob Dylan would write (an artist Stennis most likely had never listened to), "it's not dark yet, but it's getting there." He was hanging on for dear life—literally.

Stennis wasn't alone. The Arizona icon Barry Goldwater was in his last term in the Senate, the father of modern conservatism whose libertarian ways were chafing against the rising social conservatism of a new Republican Party, a sea change fast transforming his movement. Tom Eagleton of Missouri was in his last term as well. He was a gentle soul whom I had gotten to know in those intense days of the anti-war movement, a proudly liberal colleague who always looked out for me as a freshman senator. Tom took me under his wing and graciously ceded his seniority to me on the Foreign Relations Committee so I could lead a subcommittee, moving up one place from dead last on the dais. He personified collegiality.

For all the ways the Senate I entered was too homogeneous, it did have a certain, wonderful heterogeneity that has, tragically, been lost in recent decades in ways that have made governing in the United States infinitely more difficult. There was ideological diversity within the parties. Liberal Republicans who cared about the environment as passionately as many of us on the other side of the aisle still existed and still had clout: Jack Heinz from Pennsylvania, John Chafee from Rhode Island and Lowell Weicker from Connecticut were prime examples. There was also geographic diversity among the parties: two Democrats from Alabama, one from Missis-sippi, one from South Carolina, one from Arizona and two from Georgia. On the other side were two moderate Republicans from Pennsylvania, one from California and several from the Pacific Northwest. There were liberal Republicans further to the left of conservative Democrats, and vice versa.

The rightward turn of the Republican Party and the way in which the Deep South would become almost a wall of near-automatic Republican Senate seats pressured Democrats to do all we could to make sure that reliably blue states elected Democratic senators. Never recognized in the battle for Senate control was the downside of Democrats having to win Senate seats in places like Connecticut and Rhode Island: liberal Republicans were gone forever from those states and, with them, their often constructive voices in their caucus.

I lived through plenty of those early moments Harry Truman talked about: "How did I get here?" I was tempted to pinch myself when I looked to my right and realized that the soft-spoken, unassuming man sitting next to me in our weekly Democratic caucus luncheon was none other than John Glenn of Ohio, the legendary astronaut I had watched on a tiny black-and-white television set at St. Paul's as America welcomed him home with a ticker tape parade in New York City after orbiting Earth three times. "Godspeed, John Glenn." The words still gave me goose bumps, the memory was so indelible. Yet here he was. I knew little about him then beyond the heroism and plainspoken determination he had shown the world at NASA. The love of John's life was his wife, Annie, as kind a person as I had ever met. She was quiet, almost shy, something that stemmed from her battle to conquer a lifelong stutter, but she was inseparable from John and lit up when you asked her a question. We often sat next to each other at Senate functions. She was especially nice—without even having to say a word—about pulling me into a conversation, since she realized I was in a slightly awkward position: separated from Julia, I didn't have a spouse with me, where most senators did. My friendship with John Glenn deepened. He was my colleague on the Foreign Relations Committee, and as he opened up, we talked about everything from John's enduring friendship with his wingman from Korea, the baseball legend Ted Williams, to family and kids and our shared love of flying. Imagine, me, a private pilot, talking flying with John Glenn.

John let me in on a little secret he counted on for good luck: he told me that before every mission, in the Marines and at NASA, before he'd go into harm's way, he relied on a good luck charm he had picked up in Korea, a wooden "fat" Buddha. He'd give its round belly a rub for good luck before flying. It had never let him down. One day, after we made a journey to Vietnam together on the POW/MIA Committee, a gift from John arrived unexpectedly in my office: a wooden Buddha of my own, a gift from one pilot, one veteran, to another. I wasn't going into space, but I rubbed that Buddha's belly before a heavy or hard decision in the Senate.

Surrounded by these men who seemed like giants, many of them legends of a great generation, a nagging question kept recurring for me and my generation of senators: How would we make our mark in the Senate? Where did we fit?

The Senate runs on seniority. At number ninety-nine, I didn't have to excel at math to know that I wasn't going to be a committee chairman anytime soon. I had asked Minority Leader Robert Byrd for that seat on the Foreign Relations Committee and Byrd hadn't hesitated; but in front of me in seniority were twenty senators. The same was true on the Commerce Committee. The only committee I might chair within a decade was the Senate Small Business Committee, which sounded more comprehensive than it was. Its jurisdiction was limited to oversight of the Small Business Administration, and it specifically was prohibited from touching the issue small business owners cared about most—taxes.

There were a handful of senators in their prime years who had the blessing of seniority. Joe Biden, having been elected at twenty-nine, was in his early forties wielding the gavel of the powerful Judiciary Committee, and he was right behind the aging Claiborne Pell on the Foreign Relations Committee. Ted Kennedy, just fifty-three, was the most senior Democrat on the Armed Services, the Judiciary and the Labor and Health committees.

Of course, both of my predecessors, Paul Tsongas and Ed Brooke, had gently warned me about Teddy. He was a subject they tap-danced around carefully. He was fun, charming, engaging, but he cast a big shadow. I never really worried about that because I grew up admiring the Kennedys enormously, from my speech at St. Paul's on behalf of JFK, to my internship with Teddy's Senate campaign, to the sad, wistful, shock-filled weekend in Long Beach knowing we had lost Robert Kennedy to yet another assassin's bullet. But Ted was the Kennedy I had known in a different way—more personal and immediate and even intimate. He was the senator who campaigned for me in 1972 in Lowell and Lawrence, touching the heartstrings of the blue-collar Democratic voters who didn't know me in the district where I'd planted my flag. I liked him. I imagined a big brother and mentor would await me in the Senate. Shortly after I was sworn in, Teddy sent me a black-and-white photo of the two of us at the corner of Constitution and Delaware Avenues on my first day as a senator headed to my first vote. On it, he had scribbled, "Like Humphrey Bogart said, here's to the start of a beautiful friendship."

Teddy was the master of the personal gesture, acts that came to him instinctively. He knew I was running back and forth on weekends to Boston, trying to be there for soccer games and time with my daughters, and that I was doing all I could to be in the places I wanted to be as well as the places I had to be. He could see it all took a toll, and one day that fall Ted noticed a hacking, deep, rattling cough was getting the best of me. The girls were away with their mom for the upcoming weekend. "John, you're going down to Palm Beach this weekend to get well," Teddy ordered. It wasn't an invitation; it was a command. So I found myself for a Friday through Sunday not freezing up in Boston alone, but in the warmth and sun of Florida, staying in what had been President Kennedy's Winter White House, which was a special home for the Kennedy family. It was a generous, personal gesture.

Ted was also great fun to be around. In the cloakroom sometimes, the roars of laughter were so loud they could be heard out on the Senate floor. One night, Teddy was holding forth behind the doors in the cloakroom and the presiding officer in the Senate chamber pounded the gavel and demanded, "There will be order in the Senate—and in the cloakroom." Even his pranks were works of art and brilliant calculation. After a long series of night votes had pushed senators past time to catch commercial flights home to the Northeast, our colleague from New Jersey Frank Lautenberg, another World War II veteran and a self-made millionaire, arranged for a private plane to get to Massachusetts. It turned out that a number of senators needed to travel in that direction, and when Frank learned of it, he kindly offered a ride to Claiborne Pell, Ted and me. There was no discussion of sharing the cost. Everyone thought Frank was being very generous, but the next week, all of us were on the Senate floor for a vote when official-looking envelopes were delivered to us under Lautenberg's signature, with exorbitant bills for the flight. Claiborne was a soft-spoken, genteel, flinty New Englander, as Brahmin as they came with his Newport accent and his sometimes threadbare, timeless suits; Claiborne never threw anything away. This evening, though, Clairborne Pell absolutely roared down the aisle, brandishing the bill. The sight of Claiborne roaring anywhere was itself notable. Back in Rhode Island when he first ran for office, the press nicknamed him "Stillborn Pell." But this was the scene; something was afoot. Senator Lautenberg was red-faced, protesting he knew nothing about it, when out of the corner of my eye I spied Ted by his desk—Cheshire Cat grin—so pleased with himself. Mystery solved: Ted had commandeered a few sheets of Lautenberg's stationery and sent false bills to each of us. I give him credit: he knew how to make even the monotony of a late-night Senate vote-a-rama a hell of a lot of fun.

This was my dilemma: I couldn't imagine a rivalry or a tension-filled relationship with Ted, but I also couldn't imagine quietly waiting and waiting and waiting until I was in my sixties to have a voice in the U.S. Senate. I had arrived in the Senate among a special class, at least as we saw it. In our own way, we thought of ourselves as agents of change. We all thought we were going to change the world—Tom Harkin, Al Gore, Jay Rockefeller, Paul Simon and a lone Republican from Kentucky named Mitch McConnell, who was the first of his party elected to the Senate from that state since Reconstruction. Tom Harkin had been in the House and, before that, a Hill staffer himself. Al Gore was the son of southern political royalty. Jay Rockefeller, in addition to having served as one of the youngest governors in the country before he had turned forty, had first come to West Virginia as a VISTA volunteer and fallen in love with Appalachia. He carried all the weight of being born with the name "John D. Rockefeller IV." None of us intended to be seen and not heard. Moreover, in an age of competitive and increasingly expensive Senate races, of special interest groups issuing more and more scorecards of votes and legislation, and with C-SPAN cameras set to be installed covering the Senate floor a year after we arrived, our constituents would not allow us the liberty of waiting as quiet understudies, deferring any effort to make a mark. There was a pressure to produce now. Somehow, I had to make my moves, to breathe fresh air into my ideas, even in a Senate that rewards longevity, not new ideas, and with Ted Kennedy as my partner, not my rival. I had to find my own way.

ONE OF THE first Senate road maps I was offered came amid a rookie senator rite of passage: an audience with the Democratic leader and Senate minority leader, the legendary Robert C. Byrd. I didn't know much then about this now venerated figure from West Virginia, other than that in 1971—just a few months before I'd testified against the war—he had seemingly come out of nowhere to unseat Ted Kennedy as the Senate Democratic whip, the number two position in leadership behind then Majority Leader Mike Mansfield of Montana. He was well to the right of Kennedy and had cut a decidedly different profile on issues like civil rights that animated my generation; but the whip job was a nuts-and-bolts position requiring many hours just manning the Senate floor and the cloakroom, understanding all the nooks and crannies of Senate procedure and the sweeteners potentially required to win enough votes to turn bills and resolutions into laws.

Robert Byrd had mastered all the institutional minutiae of the Senate—much of it no doubt learned at the right hand of two mentors: his first, Speaker of the House Sam Rayburn, and Rayburn's disciple, whom Byrd backed for president in 1960, then Senate majority leader Lyndon Johnson. Senator Byrd skillfully parlayed his tutorials into the next step up the ladder. By 1984, at sixty-seven, he was the top Democrat in the Senate and an able foil to the Republican majority leader, Bob Dole.

We met in the leader's ornate office in the Capitol. Still to this day, I remember Byrd well, his full head of perfectly coiffed hair, not yet completely white as it would turn over the next quarter century. He was resplendent in a robin's-egg-blue suit and a tie a smidge wider than the narrower cut that was becoming popular at the time, as if he had no interest or intention of changing along with popular tastes. He had the big smile and courtly manner I'd expected, but I knew it belied a sophistication and a cunning that was by then already legendary among my colleagues.

We sat facing each other in upholstered wing chairs, not far from a framed copy of an album recorded several years before, *Mountain Fiddler*, a collection of his favorite tunes played on a fiddle and even sung by none other than Robert C. Byrd. Leaning in, pronouncing every word with his distinct baritone, Byrd was patient and solicitous of me as a freshman senator. He told me about his friendship with Ted Kennedy and his warm relationship with the Speaker of the House of Representatives, Tip O'Neill, a Massachusetts icon preparing one final hurrah in Congress.

From the moment we sat down, though, I sensed Byrd also had an agenda beyond the pleasantries: he was well known as a defender of the Senate's institutions and traditions, but surely, he also understood that this class of freshman senators was determined to make a mark, and I think he wanted to meet us all halfway, to encourage us to spread our wings a bit, but to do so within the confines of the institution. He probably also wanted to ensure he had our backing in two years when he'd be running for reelection as leader—next time, perhaps, for majority and not minority leader.

When Tom Harkin, Al Gore and I compared notes on our initial individual meetings with Byrd, we all noted that he'd sprinkled in the same piece of wisdom he no doubt had shared with incoming senators for a long time: "A big man can make a small job important." None of us had signed up for a small job, but Byrd hadn't just thrown out a morsel of homespun wisdom; his words meant something much more interesting, much more compelling, and they got my attention. He explained to me that if you persistently worked an issue that your colleagues knew was critical for you, particularly if it mattered to you back home, or if it reflected your expertise, that if you exhausted the remedies available to you, mastered the procedures of the Senate and really took the time to understand the Senate's rhythms, you could achieve something beyond your own seniority. "The rhythms of the Senate" became a magical phrase to me and others. What he meant was common sense. For example: as a Thursday late afternoon turned to Thursday evening and colleagues rushed to make flights so they could get home to campaign or meet with constituents, if there was "must-pass" legislation on the calendar, then, done correctly, within the system, applying the right amount of pressure at the right time might well open up accomplishments outstripping the power that mere seniority offered.

It was the first time I'd heard how procedure, working the process, could be the great equalizer among senators. A senator at one of these moments might call on the leader to be recognized, to offer an amendment or demand a recorded vote, to exercise a senator's prerogatives, and that was a source of leverage. Maybe you wouldn't get your amendment accepted right there and then, but you might unlock a guarantee of a hearing, or a vote on the next debate, or some important concession. Byrd offered a warning, though: it was a break-the-glass option to be held in reserve, after all the normal channels had been worked. It was a currency best spent cautiously and sparingly.

The rules were open to all senators to pursue to maximum effect, but the Senate ran on relationships and on an unspoken code of conduct that frowned on show horses and shortcuts. You didn't surprise your colleagues—at least those in your caucus—at the eleventh hour.

I tucked these lessons away in the back of my mind. This man of the Senate, who had taught himself to read by candlelight growing up in coal country and carried a copy of the Constitution with him at all times, was sharing with me the rules that weren't written down but were nonetheless essential to making progress in the Senate.

Byrd also shared with me two other lessons that hit home for different reasons. Perhaps not knowing that, while not yet divorced, I remained separated from Julia, he told me that one essential building block of being a good senator was maintaining a happy home. It came from the most personal place of all for Leader Byrd: orphaned at age one after his mother died, he'd been married to Erma Byrd since 1937—six years before I'd even come into this world. Byrd could count on two hands the number of nights he'd been away from home in the Virginia (not West Virginia) suburbs, even as he had been the Democratic leader, with all the demands of fund-raising and politics. Unspoken was the fact that he'd seen colleagues come and go, many succumbing to the long hours and lost weekends, too many who had come to the Senate with families, lost that connection to their wives and kids, and ended up unhappy in life or even ineffective as senators.

The leader couldn't have imagined the juggling act I was engaged in, racing to be back in Massachusetts for the weekends, Julia and I trading off our time, the holidays no longer spent as a family under one roof, the lonely feeling when I came home to my empty Capitol Hill row house.

Although I wasn't about to share with Senator Byrd the challenges and complications of my life at that time, I took his words to heart, knowing they were genuine, even if they stung more than a little bit and even if I didn't have any good answers or remedies for the difficulties of the present moment.

The second lesson from our meeting came shortly after the now familiar buzzer sounded announcing a quorum call. As I shook Leader Byrd's hand, preparing to let him get back to the pressing business of minority leader, he said, in his classic West Virginia drawl, "Wait. Before you go I have some pic monay for ya." He walked over to his beautifully carved desk and reached into an elegant bowl.

Pic monay? I thought. *What on earth is pic monay?*

Byrd held an envelope toward me. "It is a crahm how expensive campaigns are getting, and I know yo'ah reelection begins faave minutes after yo'ah swoan in," he said warmly, as he reached out and put the envelope in my hand.

It suddenly dawned on me that he was saying "PAC money." He was giving me a check from his political action committee to help with my re-election. Byrd had no reason to know that I had run for the Senate by refusing PAC money of any kind and trying to make campaign finance reform an issue. An awkward moment ensued, at least on my end, as I mulled my options. Did I just pocket the check? Return it to one of the leader's aides later? The clerk for the Senate Foreign Relations Committee had briefed those of us new to the committee about the best way to navigate uncomfortable situations when traveling overseas and being offered traditional gifts by foreign leaders: we could accept them graciously, bring them to the Foreign Relations Committee upon our return, along with official paperwork denoting "accepted gift to avoid diplomatic offense," and then have the gifts whisked away to some dusty Senate archive, never to be seen again, without ever insulting a gracious foreign minister or head of state.

There was no such office of protocol in the Senate to handle awkward moments like these between colleagues. "Mr. Leader," I said, "that's very generous of you, but you know I actually ran for the Senate without accepting any PAC money, and . . ." My voice trailed off a bit as I searched for an easy way to slide out of a tricky moment while still acknowledging the leader's intended gift. I tried a smile. "Well, I don't think the first thing I should do now that I'm elected is, um . . ." The moment felt like it lasted an eternity.

Senator Byrd let me off the hook: he looked at me quizzically, touched me on the shoulder and walked me to the door. He insisted that he himself hoped to see real campaign finance reform in the next Congress, and sure enough, just three years later as majority leader, he would allow the Senate to be all but shut down through a fifty-three-hour filibuster that revealed the Republicans' determination not to enact anything resembling reform.

That day, however, my lesson had to do with the extent to which one's best efforts to stake out a position in any campaign can look and feel quite different when faced with actual governing and the reality of relationships. I'd been sincere about refusing PAC money, and I was proud of the race I'd run and won without it. But now, here I was, face-to-face with the Senate minority leader, with whom I agreed on probably 90 percent of the issues, and I couldn't accept his PAC check to help my reelection; but just fifteen feet outside his office, walking the halls, were paid lobbyists who could write a check to me as individuals. I wondered: Where's the appropriate line to draw to make anything more than a rhetorical point?

The absurdity hit me: in earnestly trying to take a stand, I'd actually created an artificial distance between me and my new colleagues over a minimal difference. I realized the Senate would never be free of the impact of money—the truly corrosive kind, the kind that disconnected people from their government—until we actually insisted on greater public financing of campaigns and made the whole system fairer. The obstacle to making that happen wasn't a campaign contribution from the Senate leader.

Instead we were trapped in a broken system. Ronald Reagan was president; we Democrats were in the minority; and it was time to let the distinguished minority leader get back to his real job, which didn't include a long harangue on "pic monay." Byrd put the envelope back in the bowl.

"Wait, I have something else for you," he said. Since I'd already found a way to screw up the first gesture of goodwill between me and the minority leader, I wondered what it could possibly be. He reached into a drawer in his desk and pulled out a book. His favorite analysis of the Constitution? I wondered. A treatise on the Senate? Either of these seemed likely from a man who was the institution's resident historian. He placed the book in my hand, its plastic binding immediately recognizable, and tapped my hand: "Something for Mrs. Kerry," he said with a smile. It was a copy of the Robert C. Byrd West Virginia cookbook.

My reelection might cost $10 million, but now at least I had a recipe book and a priceless tutorial on both senatorial courtesy and the Senate itself.

IF KENNEDY AND Byrd had helped me understand a new environment, something else was pulling me back toward the place I'd come from and probably still felt most comfortable: activism on issues of war and peace.

On Thursday, April 18, 1985, three months after we were sworn in as freshman senators, Iowa's Tom Harkin and I boarded a plane to Managua, Nicaragua.

We were flying on TACA Airlines. We joked that with its safety record it probably stood for "Take A Chance Airlines," but, politically, that's also what we were doing. Tom and I were the most freshman of freshmen senators, but we both came to the Senate animated by our concern for American involvement in the wars in Central America. We wanted to see and understand for ourselves a Cold War proxy battle right in our own hemisphere that had echoes of the war that defined our formative years. President Reagan was seeking congressional approval to provide military assistance to the rebels fighting Nicaragua's Marxist government. His secretary of state, George Shultz, had even written to Congress inviting all members to go to Nicaragua and see what was happening for themselves. This was invitation enough for Tom and me.

We came from different backgrounds. Tom had grown up in a small Iowa town built by Catholic immigrants. Years later, I would travel there as a presidential candidate and see for myself that the community's pride in Tom still ran deep. It was similar to places in Massachusetts where whole neighborhoods stay forever connected, the kind of connection I'd missed out on because of my father's nomadic diplomatic lifestyle. Tom didn't have it easy. He lost his mother at age ten and watched the struggles of an older brother who was deaf in the days before America fully understood its responsibility to provide equal access to those of different abilities. An ROTC scholarship sent Tom to Iowa State, and he became a skilled Navy pilot.

In 1969, just as I was coming home from combat in Vietnam, Tom's real confrontation with the war began. He was working for one of Iowa's congressmen, Neal Smith. Tom traveled to Southeast Asia with other congressional staff to Con Son Island on a fact-finding mission. He was horrified to see the way our ally was brutally holding enemy prisoners captive in tiger cages. It was a moment of conscience. He saw in the South Vietnamese military a brutality not dissimilar from that of the Viet Cong. Tom took a series of photos and leaked them to *Life* magazine. He wanted the country to see what was happening. It could have cost Tom his job; instead, it created a groundswell of activism and helped Tom win a seat in Congress a few years later among the Watergate class of 1974. Ten years later, he was a senator.

Given the parallel paths we'd traveled, the different journeys we'd taken to similar conclusions, it made sense for our paths to converge. We both knew from experience the importance of not automatically swallowing official Washington's version of events. We wanted to see for ourselves what was actually happening in a conflict tearing Nicaragua apart. We needed to better understand the ways in which the United States might get involved.

Some of the parallels to Vietnam were obvious. The United States had supported the Somoza government for decades as a bulwark against communism in our neighborhood. We had looked the other way as its paramilitary forces violated human rights with impunity. Within a large portion of the country, those forces were corrupt and unpopular, but so too were the insurgents who had sprung up and deposed them. Known as the Sandinistas and led by Daniel Ortega, they clearly modeled themselves on the Castros and any number of Marxist leaders of the era. As the Sandinistas forced their will on the Nicaraguan people, a counterrevolution grew in response. The opposition, known as the Contras, and including many former Somoza regime dead-enders, had launched a guerrilla war in an attempt to regain control. The Soviets, of course, were thrilled to have a client state—another one—right in our hemisphere.

From my vantage point, it was far from a simple black-and-white battle of good versus evil. Even then it felt much more like a classic choice between shades of gray. Were the Contras fighting the communists? Yes. On the other hand, many credible reports surfaced that the Contras had been committing violent human rights abuses. I worried that they were the kind of ally that would become a real liability in the long run. President Reagan argued the case in terms that hit a little too close to home, talking of a "domino theory" in our own hemisphere. It was the same talk that had led us down a tragic path before. Both Tom and I knew too many close friends whose names were on the granite Wall in Washington as a result of that thinking. Given the road we had both traveled, it was difficult, if not impossible, to accept anyone else's word about what was really happening. We felt compelled to engage in our own reconnaissance and due diligence.

Our goal was not only to inform our vote, but also to explore whether there was a better policy to put in place. Rather than a false choice of either backing the Contras all out or doing nothing, there might be a different approach that could actually benefit Nicaragua and the hemisphere. Peace talks had been stalled for months. Could they resume?

Our first night in Managua, we attended a working dinner at Foreign Minister Miguel d'Escoto's home. We suspected he was launching a charm offensive. As we discussed steps that could be taken to lay the groundwork for negotiation, I couldn't help but notice the opulence with which the minister surrounded himself. I remember thinking, *This guy is supposed to be leading a people's revolution?*

The next day we asked to meet with as many people as possible on both sides of the conflict. We engaged in dozens of conversations, many of which seemed to confirm our suspicion that the Contras had committed shocking atrocities. I will never forget meeting with a woman named Zoila Rosa Domínguez Espinoza. She was probably in her early fifties, I doubt even ten years older than I was. Fighting tears, she described how, three months earlier, the Contras had ambushed a civilian Jeep, murdering her daughter and three other young professors. She carried her daughter's graduation picture in her hand, begging us to do anything we could to make the war stop. It reinforced the sense that Washington and Moscow were seeing this civil war purely through an ideological lens. It was just another proxy fight. Instead of listening to people on the ground who, first and foremost, wanted to live their lives without violence, both capitals were content to "proxy" onward.

The night before we returned to Washington, we had a five-hour dinner meeting with senior Sandinista officials, including, finally, President Daniel Ortega. He outlined his theory of a potential peace. For several hours, we kicked ideas back and forth, with Tom and me listening carefully for any hint of an approach that could actually fly in the United States. Late at night, Ortega determined he wanted us to take an idea back to President Reagan.

The next morning before we boarded our flight, we were handed a document at the airport that represented his formal proposal for negotiations. I was comfortable taking it to the administration. It was two and a half pages and basically boiled down to this: Ortega said he was prepared to enter into a cease-fire with the Contras, rein in his police state and kick out the Soviet and Cuban military advisors working with his military, hold elections and embrace a peace agreement, if, in return, the United States would drop its matériel support for the rebels.

I couldn't vouch for the Sandinistas' readiness to live by their own proposal, but given the steady descent of the region into greater violence, I thought the United States had a responsibility to test whether they were serious. I believed that unless you want to go to war, you don't lose by trying for peace. If it leads to progress, that's terrific, and if it doesn't, then you've earned greater credibility with allies and neighbors. I thought the Reagan administration should treat this proposal as a first volley and at least make a counterproposal. But Tom and I weren't negotiators. All we could do was convey Ortega's message. Little did we know there was no appetite for that kind of diplomacy in the White House. Before Tom and I were even back in Washington, the State Department's assistant secretary for the region, Elliott Abrams, was already calling around to Capitol Hill to pour cold water on the entire idea.

The day after we got back, the White House convened a meeting with Senate leaders to discuss the issue. Tom and I were told only one of us could have a spot in the meeting, so we flipped a coin. I won the coin toss, or maybe I lost, depending on what was to follow.

Sitting at the White House as a freshman senator was one of those moments you imagine will be important. I argued the case for exploring renewed peace talks. The Reagan administration officials followed with their case, which boiled down to one argument: it was naive to believe anything Ortega said. They saw no reason to talk to the regime at all. This was my introduction to some of the neoconservatives who would bring us the war in Iraq. They refused to accept what I believed, that negotiation isn't based on trust; it's a way of probing to find out if advances can be made. They didn't want to stop the war; they wanted to widen it. The meeting was just window dressing. Minds were already made up. We were a couple of years away from President Reagan making "trust but verify" his mantra in dealing with the Soviets; but I wondered why on earth the United States could negotiate with the Soviet Union, the same power that had invaded Afghanistan and had nuclear warheads pointed at us, but couldn't even explore talks with a tiny country in our neighborhood.

Days later, Speaker Tip O'Neill and the House of Representatives voted down a Reagan Contra aid proposal. I hoped that that vote might mean the administration would come back to the Senate with a new approach on peace talks and put Ortega to the test.

Instead, I learned a very different Washington lesson, a lesson about bare-knuckle politics in our nation's capital. It was also a harbinger of a different kind of politics that would break the city itself as the years went by.

It started with Senator Barry Goldwater—someone I knew mainly by historical reputation for his 1964 hostile takeover of the Republican Party, which began the exile of the moderate Rockefeller Republicans. Goldwater had been my colleague for just a handful of months. We exchanged pleasantries but had never had a real conversation. He didn't know me, and I didn't know him.

Ted Kennedy had schooled me in Senate norms of civility, in which colleagues spoke privately to each other before they took aim at each other in the media. Two words I heard often from Leader Byrd were "senatorial courtesy."

Clearly there was another rule book with which I wasn't familiar. Without warning, Senator Goldwater blasted Tom Harkin and me to the media, accusing us of violating the Logan Act, an obscure federal law from the late eighteenth century that makes it a crime to negotiate with a foreign government without prior authorization.

Goldwater didn't know us, but that didn't stop him from employing an often-used tactic of the Far Right, accusing us of being traitors. We were two senators who had traveled through the auspices of the Foreign Relations Committee, abiding by all the regular protocols and procedures, doing what senators are supposed to do before they vote on issues of national security: we were gathering facts. The legislative branch is a coequal branch of government to the executive—something I'd have thought a veteran U.S. senator like Goldwater would have wanted to protect as an institutional prerogative.

The accusation was ludicrous. We had never entered into any negotiation, and Goldwater knew it. Leader Byrd told me not to take it seriously. The intention wasn't to engage the legal system but to silence us. It was the political equivalent of a brushback. It created a media firestorm. Conservative pundits pounced. Washington had two newspapers—the *Washington Post*, which was serious and fair, and the *Washington Times*, a right-wing broadsheet not known for being "fair and balanced." The *Times* wasn't what we call a "paper of record," but it could drive television coverage with its exaggerated headlines, and it surely did this time.

Tom and I were on the defensive. We huddled with Ted Kennedy and Chris Dodd on the Senate floor. Chris slapped me on the back, smiling as he said, "Looks like you scared somebody." Teddy was his usual upbeat self. "Never explain," he warned us, repeating his mantra that in politics if you're explaining, you're losing. He didn't believe in getting into a defensive crouch, and his own thick skin, developed over years of being a punching bag for the Right, had numbed him to their theatrics. There wasn't a Republican flyer or direct-mail fund-raising letter in conservative politics that didn't mention Ted. He had come to revel in being their bête noire. I wasn't there yet.

In fact, I was seething. It felt as though facts didn't matter. Senators who had taken dozens of overseas trips just like mine didn't say a word in defense of the Senate's prerogatives, let alone of two of their colleagues. The media reaction was just as Ted had predicted: rather than focusing on the absurdity of Goldwater's attack, rather than noting its lack of substance, the reporting was about the political process and the atmospherics. The story was "Kerry on the Defensive."

I kept asking myself: If this was all it took in Washington to torpedo debate about a serious issue, how were we ever going to get anything done? The right wing had a narrative and a playbook, and they were effective. We had facts and logic, and those two assets didn't feed the political beast.

Within a couple of days, the right wing was handed a new talking point, courtesy of Ortega himself, who boarded a plane to Moscow to collect another $200 million from his Soviet sponsors. Ortega's dance with the Soviets didn't surprise me that much. He was a Marxist, and the Reagan administration hadn't been interested in talking with him. But it was another kick in the teeth for Tom Harkin and me. The right wing could argue Ortega had proven that we were naive.

It was clear to me that the Senate was not going to break new ground on the war in Nicaragua. Most Democrats were content opposing a growing role for America in the war, and most Republicans were content doing the opposite. A diplomatic third way wasn't going to be embraced in Washington. Other countries in the hemisphere were still looking for diplomacy, so I sent my foreign policy staffer, Dick McCall, to meet with Costa Rica's president, Oscar Arias Sánchez, and advise him on the conversations Tom Harkin and I had shared on our trip. I wound up lending Dick to President Arias to work on the peace process. I suspected that in the right hands—not American or Russian—a peace plan that put hemispheric negotiations at the local level had a real chance for success. Arias was the right person for the job—so much so that he was awarded the Nobel Peace Prize in 1987 for being the principal force behind a regional peace plan signed by five Central American countries. Meanwhile, Washington was headed for an entirely different drama when it came to the Contras.

IF MY EXPERIENCE on the receiving end of a Washington partisan attack had chastened me about the limits of Senate collegiality, an unexpected experience renewed my faith that the institution really was special. Orientation for freshman senators teaches you the basics—how to hire a staff, how to manage an office budget, the parliamentary fundamentals—but just as Robert Byrd and Ted Kennedy had shown me in the lessons and reflections they shared, the really important rules aren't written down, nor do the most meaningful locations necessarily show up on a map.

As it turned out, there were two places in the Senate where politics really was put aside: the Senate gym and the private, weekly Senate Prayer Breakfast.

The gym was a place for senators to get away from the phones, the confrontational debates on the floor, the deluge of meetings and fund-raisers. Former senators had privileges at the gym for life, and some who had stayed in Washington after defeat or retirement would still come back, ostensibly to work out but more likely because they missed the camaraderie and sense of purpose. The man who had held my Senate seat before Paul Tsongas, Ed Brooke, was one of them. When we ended up together in the gym, he always asked how I was enjoying the Senate. He was wistful about a career interrupted by defeat in 1978. But by 1985, he was a man without a party and a senator without a seat. The gym was his refuge, much as it was for those still serving. Some senators chatted away an hour each day while restoring flexibility to tired old legs in the Jacuzzi; others went for a massage to stretch out muscles sore from long flights and long days. Some, like Ted Kennedy, who was haunted by a broken back from a 1965 plane crash, depended on those massages just to stand straight, although Teddy never complained. A few hit the showers to wash away hangovers from the night before. Some even exercised.

The weekly prayer breakfast, on the other hand, was a chance to exercise different muscles. At 7:00 a.m. every Wednesday, senators put aside policy and party and gathered in Room S-15 in the Capitol, under the quiet guidance of the Senate chaplain, to reflect on their journeys of faith.

I had grown up with the Latin Mass and the formality of the Catholic Church in the days before Vatican II aimed to create a more personal relationship between Catholics and their God. I spent a lot of time mastering my Latin responses and becoming the fastest reciter of the Our Father (Paternoster) in my class, but no one encouraged us to analyze the Bible. There was no wrestling with doctrinal texts.

So the prayer breakfast was new and different, and I began with a bit of reserve. It certainly wasn't like anything I had experienced at home. Neither my Protestant mother nor my Catholic father was demonstrative about faith. They were believers, but they shared an abundance of New England restraint—private in their religious views. My mother dutifully accepted that her children would be raised Catholic and made sure we attended catechism class regularly, even as we shuttled between boarding schools. But we never had dinnertime conversations about the Bible, and the churches where I served as an altar boy were formal. No after-hours Bible study awaited adults, just children receiving Sunday school lessons—and I do mean "receiving." These teachings were always one-way, with no back-and-forth, no examination of our hopes, fears and beliefs.

The Senate Prayer Breakfast gently challenged those traditions. It was focused on Scripture and charged senators with exploring the Bible itself to find meaning. The Senate chaplain was present, but the group was really led by two senators, one Democrat and one Republican, acting as conveners. Each week we would hear from senators or former senators, usually describing how a relationship with God helped them navigate the trials life had thrown their way. It was a view of my new colleagues that defied stereotypes, caricatures and the straitjacket of party labels. It was where I heard the Republican leader, Bob Dole, describe the ways in which his family's church in Russell, Kansas, rallied around him after he came home from World War II in a full body cast with a withered arm, underscoring the virtue of Christian charity. I heard my classmate Mitch McConnell, 1984's lone Republican freshman senator, talk about how his Baptist faith helped him overcome childhood polio and how he had come to believe that God had a plan for him. It was where I first heard from senators about missions they'd taken to Africa and Central America to share their faith and serve the poor.

It was, I realize now, the first and only place where I heard Ted Kennedy speak to the way faith had helped him overcome the death of his beloved family members. The world knew Ted as a keeper of Camelot and the champion of liberal ideals. I had gotten to know him as a colleague and a mentor, but until that moment I'd never known him as a quiet devotee of his Catholic faith who had found solace in our religion at his lowest moments.

Those of my generation remembered where we were the day President Kennedy was killed, and we remembered Ted's eulogy to Bobby in St. Patrick's Cathedral in 1968. Those memories represented indelible tragic tributes to icons lost rather than empathy with the brother who remained. Never had I heard Teddy talk in personal terms about the two brothers stolen from him by assassins' bullets, or about his eldest brother, Joe, lost in a war, or his beloved sister, Kathleen, who died in a plane crash in her twenties.

Here in the privacy of a quiet room in the Capitol, as the sun came up slowly over Washington, I heard Ted talk about a knock on the door from a Navy chaplain with news that Joe's plane had exploded over the Atlantic Ocean, and the way his mother poured her pain into the recitation of the

Rosary. He talked about finding grace in the teachings of the Church. After that day, I thought differently about the pain Teddy carried with him, the suffering hidden behind that twinkle in his eyes.

For a long time, I felt far from ready to speak up much at the prayer breakfast. I had come to the Senate "in a hurry" in many ways. Whereas Ted Kennedy had waited more than a year to give his first Senate floor speech, just a couple of months into my tenure, I used my maiden speech to address military spending and the MX missile. I approached the prayer breakfast the opposite way. I was immediately fascinated by the Scripture lessons, intellectually engaged, but I wasn't ready to use the Bible as a vehicle to talk about my own journey. In fact, in a room where many colleagues seemed to have such certainty about their faith, such deep conviction, I began to wrestle privately with nagging doubts that had followed me ever since the Navy.

My faith had experienced highs and lows, times of engagement and times when I pulled back or seemed to let it all go on autopilot. I'd felt deeply connected to the Church as an altar boy and even in high school at St. Paul's, where through my relationship with Reverend Walker I felt a connection to the values side of religion, to the lessons of living out the Golden Rule.

By the time I went to Vietnam, though, I was the average parishioner, showing up for major days of obligation but going to church when it suited me. In between, especially in college, there had been a lot of Sundays when I slept in after a Saturday night spent chasing a different kind of salvation. The most urgent prayer usually was for God to make my head stop pounding.

I would rise and fall in my zeal—faithful, but not "faith full." In combat, I wore a St. Christopher medal around my neck and asked God to protect me, but some of that was transactional and superficial. It translated to a plea of "Please, God, get me through this, and I promise I'll be good." But it wasn't long before doubt crept in and I got angry at what I was seeing and doing. All the questions asked a million times by millions of people before came to mind—none brilliant or original, but all earnest, heartfelt and genuine. Some words of chaplains and priests rang hollow, especially when they were applied to the loss of my close friends. How can there be a merciful God who allows this carnage to take place? How does God choose between one child and the other as to who lives or dies or is maimed? Did they not pray enough? Did only the good die young? Were they heathens? Were they godless communists? Did they somehow deserve to die? The questions and the doubts became pointed and personal. I refused to believe that it was

God's will that Dick Pershing never made it home alive from the war to marry or that it was God's will that Don Droz would never see his infant daughter grow up.

I thought back to my father's anger over his father's absence, his sister's polio and, later, her cancer. I didn't want to let my bitterness linger the way his had. But still, I was haunted by the killing I'd seen, and the losses I'd experienced had unsettled my own faith. When I came home from Vietnam, I lived with gratitude that every day was extra. I was thankful for surviving, but all the words about God's will working in strange ways fell on deaf ears for me. Instead, I channeled my energy into service and activism and left much unreconciled about the foundations of my beliefs. I wanted my daughters raised Catholic because I was Catholic; but if they had asked me, I would have struggled to share with them much more than that. I hadn't found satisfactory resolution to the biggest questions about what my faith really meant beyond the power of the sacraments and the comfort of the rituals.

The prayer breakfast implicitly pushed me to work through those unresolved questions. No one asked me to do it, but the weekly hold on my calendar was a reminder in itself. With Chaplain Halverson's suggestions and my own memory of Sacred Studies at St. Paul's, I began to read or reread Paul Tillich, Reinhold Niebuhr, Billy Graham, St. Augustine and Thomas Aquinas on just and unjust war, and Pope John XXIII's *Mater et Magistra* and *Pacem in Terris.* I started listening more carefully to the personal journeys of different senators and how they might inform my own.

That's when I met and became friendly with a lay minister named Doug Coe. Doug was an evangelical Christian, not a Catholic, and his work was focused on the life of Jesus. He was a counselor to many of the Senate chaplains, which is how I was introduced to him, and he led the nonpartisan National Prayer Breakfast. Doug was close to sixty years old, and a group he led, the Fellowship, had long brought together policy makers and faith leaders in Washington. Because Doug had little appetite for publicity, some conspiracy theories easily attached themselves to his ministry and to the Cedars, an old mansion in Arlington that the Fellowship maintained for prayer groups and sometimes even off-the-grid diplomacy.

I was struck by Doug's quiet, thoughtful presence. We shared a common belief that many organized religions spent far too much time and energy chewing over the interpretations of one faith or another, when the real essence of faith was the life and teachings of Jesus. Doug understood that Jesus's ministry of just three years, culminating with his death on the cross, was the central teaching and meaning of Christianity. He started sending me articles and excerpts from Scripture to supplement what I was reading on my own.

The hardest and highest barrier for me to get over in reconciling my faith with my experiences remained the issue of human suffering. The shorthand about "God's plan" didn't sit well with me. If I watched a day of college football and listened to the postgame interviews, I heard again and again that God had a "plan" to help certain quarterbacks win upset victories. By the time the evening news rolled around, was I supposed to believe that God had no plan for kids starving in Ethiopia, children suffering with distended bellies, covered in flies? Or worse, was this God's will? Sometimes in our rush to have God take sides in trivial things, we miss entirely the places where God might really be seen, or the reasons we might not see Him present at all. In my mind's eye, I came back again and again to the faces of Persh and Don Droz, and I just refused to see God's hand in their deaths.

What brought me a certain kind of peace about my faith finally arrived after reading and rereading, underlining entire paragraphs and scribbling notes in the margins of Pope John Paul II's Apostolic Letter, which helps the faithful understand the concept of "salvific suffering." It spoke to me, reminding me of the words of St. Paul, which I had heard so many times in catechism: "In my flesh I complete what is lacking in Christ's afflictions for the sake of his Body, that is, the Church." John Paul II was remarkable: the pontiff had stood up to the Soviet Union, embraced children everywhere, survived a would-be assassin's bullet and forgave the unstable shooter who had caused him so much suffering. In his letter to the faithful, *Salvifici Doloris*—the meaning of Christian suffering—written just three years after he was shot four times; his words brought clarity to issues that had caused me abundant confusion. Evil in the world was the cause of suffering, not God's will. Evil was why innocents suffered, why people who desperately wanted children couldn't have them, why there was illness and famine here on earth. His Holiness pointed to the Old Testament, where Job's suffering was God's punishment, and he contrasted that with the New Testament, where God didn't save his only son from suffering but gave him eternal life to end the suffering, all in return for Jesus overcoming his doubts and putting his faith in the Father.

After multiple readings, it made a certain kind of sense. Something clicked in a way that hadn't before. God didn't make us suffer. Evil was what had taken Dick and Don. God hadn't fired those rocket launchers into pilothouses on the Mekong Delta, and God wasn't directing Tet when rocket fire stopped twenty-four-year-old Lieutenant Dick Pershing from searching for a fallen comrade. However, God had been there to bring Dick and Don home, to "deliver them from evil," to bring their suffering to an end, as He had for His only son, whom He had given to the flesh.

I did pause and ask myself, If my daughters were suffering, could I be so understanding? Could I still imagine that in suffering there is the gift of being closer to Christ, who suffered on that cross? I hoped I'd never be tested in that way.

But at least now I had an intellectual, spiritual course correction: suffering brought us closer to understanding what Jesus himself endured on the cross, how extraordinary it was that even as he was slowly tortured to death, he prayed for his captors. Evil was all around us and it brought suffering, but rather than inflict it, God relieved suffering through eternal life, the mystery of which was the basis of faith itself.

I was ready to speak up at the Senate Prayer Breakfast. I brought my notes of writing and reflection and talked not about my certainty, but about my doubts, and about how I'd drawn closer to an understanding of something unknowable than I'd ever thought possible. I talked about my journey, one more meaningful to me because the path had been anything but straight.

Afterward, Alaska's sometimes acerbic senator Ted Stevens, a Republican who wore Incredible Hulk neckties as an inside joke about his own volcanic temper, came up to me in the hallway. He'd been in the Senate since 1968, a champion of Arctic drilling, which Paul Tsongas and I had both vehemently opposed. Stevens and I were on different ends of the ideological spectrum. He touched my elbow and told me about his journey. He and his wife, Ann, had five children and lives filled with joy. But just ten years after he came to the Senate, it was all turned upside down. They were in a plane crash, and Ann suffered and died right there next to him. There was nothing he could do. He had spent years asking why God would have done this or let this happen. He told me he wished that someone had shared with him then what I had just talked about at breakfast.

I was speechless.

Ted Stevens, a private, buttoned-down older man who embodied Greatest Generation stoicism, had just opened up in ways I couldn't have imagined doing with a near stranger. "Thank you," he said, tapping me on the shoulder again and disappearing down the hall.

It was one of those moments I never would have predicted when I came to the Senate, or when I reluctantly came to my first prayer breakfast, but it was a lesson about life that stuck: to find the truth in people, sometimes you had to open up to the truth inside yourself. I never looked at Ted Stevens in the same way after that day. No matter which side of a debate we'd be on—and frequently it was the opposite side—because of the common ground we'd found together that morning, Ted was no longer just one of the Republican senators. He was a friend. My eyes saw a human being who loved and suffered, searched for meaning and was willing to share it. That's a gift the Senate made possible, the gift of an unlikely moment with an unlikely friend.

I was beginning to feel more comfortable with my personal exploration of faith. But I was still wrestling. I was still looking for rational, linear answers to all my questions, questions asked for centuries. It was one thing for the actions of people to be cast as the struggle between good and evil. But where was God's hand in a tsunami in Japan or a volcanic eruption in Hawaii? How could those horrors occur if a benevolent God was both omniscient and omnipotent? It was a debate between my mind and my heart—and everything in between. I kept looking for the rational exposé of truth when this truth wasn't rational at all. That's why we call it "a leap of faith."

A couple of years later, I awoke from a vivid dream. It wasn't like the nightmares that could still awaken me back then—my heart pounding, adrenaline coursing through my body, back on the rivers of the Mekong Delta. It was the opposite of that. I awoke feeling profound emotion and calm.

In the dream, I was walking in the mountains with a priest, listening to him. I knew him well, although I couldn't figure out exactly who he was. He told me he was going to die. He had terminal cancer and only months to live, so he was putting his affairs in order.

I was completely undone. I couldn't bear the thought of saying goodbye to this friend, and I couldn't see the justice in this young man of God dying when he had so much to share with all of us, when he had given his life to God already. Where was the righteousness or common sense in that? I said to him, "How can God do this when you have so much more to give to all of us, to share and teach? This is so unfair."

With amazing grace, and a calm acceptance in his voice, he turned to me and reassuringly said, "No, that is not the way to understand this. By accepting God's design for me, by using this moment to share with you and my friends the faith I have in Him, I am teaching you and leaving you far more than I could in any other way. I accept this because I believe, and believing is my strength."

"It's hard to have faith in God when God is taking you from us," I said.

"No, it's precisely why you should have faith. My suffering opens the door for me to understand God's will and share in the suffering of others, which is the greatest manifestation of love there is. This moment between us could not happen without my dying. That is His gift and, through me, my gift to you. Faith!"

From that moment forward I was clear: Faith is putting yourself totally into God's hands without waiting for evidence sufficient to convince you. Faith is believing not because of a completely rational line of thought, or presuming to know God's will in this life, but because your heart and your whole self—your being—is comfortable and contented believing. That revelation forever changed my relationship with my faith.

So many books have been written about why God would allow so much evil in a world He had total control over. None of them provides a completely convincing answer. The only answer in the end is faith.

I STARTED TO find my footing in the Senate working in the areas where Ted Kennedy's presence was less outsized, places where a good idea and patience—rather than seniority—might make the difference. Foreign policy was a logical place to start, and it mattered to me. My father sparked my interest in foreign policy, and his life in the Foreign Service had been my first window into a world shaped largely by the United States. Now that I was in the Senate, Pa still loomed large—including by occasionally sending faxes to my office, written in all caps, warning of the tendency of some policy makers to see the world almost entirely through the lens of our own policies and our own interests, casting aside the history of other peoples. Pa's instruction that you had to study the other side if you were going to make good foreign policy had an impact on me. Inside the Senate, I was from a generation in a hurry, a generation disinclined to wait on protocol and tradition before speaking up, but overseas I wanted to listen and learn before I jumped to conclusions. As in so many chapters of my life, another branch of my family history had a funny way of colliding with the present. My grandfather's cousin William Cameron Forbes had served a tour of duty as a diplomat. President Teddy Roosevelt had sent him to serve in the Philippines before he was even thirty-five. President Taft appointed him governor-general of the colony, and years later another Republican president—Harding—sent him back to the Philippines to help the United States decide whether the time had come for independence. When Cousin Cam, as we called him, first boarded a steamer for Asia, not long after the United States was handed the Philippines among the spoils of the Spanish-American War, I'm sure he couldn't have imagined a more exciting destination than Manila.

When I met Cousin Cam as a kid, he was getting on in years, and struck this young kid as a little serious and formal. I was impressed that he had traveled the world and lived in the Philippines. But what I most remember was a photo of him—much younger, but only slightly less bald—alongside Teddy Roosevelt, with TR's unmistakable bushy mustache much more memorable than my cousin. I was captivated by his tokens and trophies of service in a far-away place: he'd come home from the Philippines with a seemingly endless supply of beautiful mahogany wood baskets and cabinets, mottled, beeswing, and curly. Some found their way into the homes of family. We grew up with these exotic artifacts, and I would say to myself, "Wow, what an amazing place that must be. I want to go there someday."

Cousin Cam died just shy of ninety and just a couple of weeks after I turned sixteen. He was a sepia-colored memory by the time it was my turn to go to Asia eight years later.

I wish I'd been old enough to ask Cousin Cam about that history back when I had the chance. Although his views weren't as retrograde as the imperial-minded senators of his day, like Albert Beveridge, who saw the Filipinos as a lesser people permanently incapable of self-government, or President Roosevelt's secretary of state, Elihu Root, who described them as "children," Cousin Cam had helped cement these paternalistic attitudes. In 1921, the commission Warren Harding appointed him to lead determined the people of the Philippines were not ready for what they'd fought for against the Spanish and what they demanded under the United States: a democracy to call their own.

Sixty years later, not enough had changed. President Truman finally granted the island its independence on the auspicious date of July 4, 1946. But the Filipino people were hardly living out the benefits of democracy or freedom. President Ferdinand Marcos was a brutal but reliable Cold War ally—a strongman who had run the country for twenty years before I showed up in the Senate. Most of that time Marcos ruled under martial law. As was the case with Suharto in Indonesia and the revolving door of governments in South Vietnam, we tolerated a long litany of abuses that violated our ideals and hurt our credibility. Marcos was a central-casting tinhorn strongman. Incredible amounts of money, much of it siphoned off from American aid, lined his pockets while the country suffered in poverty. He was constantly held up by the human rights community as an exemplar of thugs wrongly supported in the name of Cold War realpolitik.

I doubt the human rights activists in Massachusetts had ever heard of my distant cousin Cameron. They just knew me as their new senator on the Foreign Relations Committee, and figured I might be sympathetic about the betrayal of American ideals under Marcos. Cory Aquino, the opposition leader in the Philippines whose husband, Benigno "Ninoy" Aquino, had been assassinated by Marcos for speaking out, had spent years living in exile in Newton, Massachusetts, so there was a beachhead of anti-Marcos activism back home. I was horrified by the photos the activists shared with me of dead bodies stacked like cordwood, victims of torture in Marcos's police state, and stories of a free press silenced from reporting on a regime enriching itself while children suffered from malnutrition. The flashbacks to the South Vietnamese government were unmistakable: Marcos seemed at best like a cagier, savvier version of Ngo Dinh Diem. How could we export and encourage democracy around the world and urge it as an alternative to the Soviets when we looked the other way in a place like the Philippines?

I decided that my first trip to Asia as a member of the Foreign Relations Committee would be to the Philippines, to determine whether Marcos would change his behavior if he at least knew that Congress was watching.

I was determined to approach the trip armed with facts and with an open, if skeptical, mind. I didn't want to rely merely on the reports from the human rights community. I wanted State Department briefings, intel community briefings, and even though I had been critical of Reagan policy in my campaign, Secretary of State George Shultz was always responsive to the Senate. He arranged a long phone call for me with our ambassador to Manila, Steve Bosworth. Bosworth was a terrific briefer. I asked him rapid-fire questions, and he pulled no punches. Was Marcos as brutal as the human rights community described? The answer was, more or less, yes. Was Marcos as corrupt as rumored? Certainly he lived a lifestyle beyond any other explanation, but, no, the administration didn't have a smoking gun, and over the years there were arrangements with the CIA that had feathered Marcos's nest. He warned me that I might want to be careful going down that rabbit hole. How would Marcos defend his hesitancy to hold elections? He'd describe all the opposition as communist revolutionaries doing the bidding of the Soviet Union. Were they communist? For the most part, no. Were they pro-American? For the most part, yes.

It would take about twenty hours to fly from Dulles International Airport to Manila. I couldn't help but think of the incongruity of leaving an airport named after John Foster Dulles, father of the Southeast Asia Treaty Organization that hardened Cold War alliances in the region, even if it meant looking the other way on democracy. Dulles, along with his brother, Allen, who was CIA director in that same era, had reversed the revolution in Iran and reinstalled the shah and toppled a democratically elected government in Guatemala. And here I was: forty-two, having been part of the tip of the spear in the failed extension of that philosophy in Vietnam, now an elected senator off to the Philippines to tangle with exactly the kind of autocrat whom Dulles would have found quite useful. History is funny that way: I was taking my trip by air, but it was Cousin Cam who had taken the trip by ship and who would have likely found a soul mate in Dulles, though I know his conscience would have never tolerated Marcos.

I landed at Manila International Airport, the location where Ninoy Aquino had been assassinated less than three years before upon his return from exile. Dictators love to mark their territory with an exclamation point. Now, every visiting dignitary taking the ride to the Malacañang Palace would begin that transit disembarking from the place where Marcos had dispatched his leading political opponent once and for all.

Ambassador Bosworth greeted me at the gate. We rode together in an embassy car to my visit with Marcos, whose office had already informed the embassy he was running an hour late—a tactic I've since learned is somewhat comically relied on by autocrats around the world to shape the power dynamic. They love to stick it to you in little ways, like keeping you waiting, to remind you who is holding the cards in the relationship. We made our way down Lacson Avenue while Bosworth told me about its history. The road used to be called Governor Forbes Street.

If the onetime name of the road weren't enough to evoke family history, the site of my meeting with President Marcos would have done it. Adobe on the outside, narra wood floor throughout on the inside, mahogany paneling everywhere—Cousin Cameron's ghost could well have sauntered through the halls of the presidential palace.

As prepared as I was for the meeting, Marcos had hosted enough American delegations over the years to know what lines of argument would be effective. He complimented my family history in the Philippines, our friendship to his country dating back nearly a century, and expounded on the importance of the relationship with the United States, our close collaboration in the fight against communism. I looked down at my watch: Marcos had opened with a nearly forty-minute-long discourse on the progress the country was making and the importance of the Subic Bay Naval Base, which stood, he argued, as a symbol that Southeast Asia remained a bright beacon of hope against communism. Marcos even invoked his own service in World War II, fighting alongside the Americans—something Ambassador Bosworth would later tell me was fiction. It dawned on me: Why litigate a list of complaints that Marcos would deny when, instead, I could play to his false sense of strength?

Marcos was arguing that he alone reflected the will of the Filipino people. He said some in the population were like "children," uneducated and easily transfixed by communist sympathizers like the Aquinos, but that in the end he—Marcos—was the real father of the country. I stressed that it would help the United States in the Cold War if he demonstrated progress on democracy. If he was so popular, couldn't he embrace elections by a specific date? Marcos was condescending. He said he had nothing to fear from elections but that he knew his country best. He would never lecture me about Massachusetts, he intoned, so why should I suggest I knew what was best for Manila? I suspect he believed that if he outtalked me, I'd simply give up.

He was wrong.

After five hours alone with Ferdinand Marcos in the Malacañang Palace, I was convinced that the United States needed to change its policy toward the Philippines. So, on the long flight back to Washington, it wasn't Cousin Cam on my mind, but Senator Robert C. Byrd. I remembered our conversation more than a year before: have an idea, be an expert, work your colleagues, work the process, and find your opening. That's exactly what I set out to do.

I went to see Claiborne Pell, who was now chairman on the Foreign Relations Committee, and the senior Republican on the panel, Indiana's Richard Lugar. I then met with the assistant secretary for Far Eastern affairs at the State Department. I spoke to some of my fellow concerned senators who were on the Appropriations Committee, not just Robert Byrd but Vermont's Pat Leahy, who believed that in the name of Cold War realism, we had too often ignored American values. I reported to them that President Reagan's own ambassador didn't dispute Marcos's corruption. Word about my activities quickly reached the Marcos lobbyists, who were paid handsome retainers from stolen funds. Paul Manafort and Roger Stone regularly trotted out a gold-plated playbook on the Hill: Marcos was our resolute ally who must not be abandoned in the fight against the communists. But this time, the lobbyists were too late. I had done my homework and worked the process. The result was victory: the first amendment I ever passed as a freshman senator conditioned American foreign aid to the Philippines on free elections.

In Manila, Marcos figured he was going to show this young whippersnapper who was boss. He called a snap election in order to relegitimize himself, obviously believing that he would be reelected. Because I'd been so active on the issue, President Reagan had no choice but to put me on the official election-monitoring delegation from the United States, paired with Dick Lugar, who had kindly been my partner on the amendment. I will never forget arriving in Manila and seeing this unbelievable flood of people in the streets all decked out in their canary-yellow shirts and carrying banners of pro-democracy protest. Some of us knew at that time there were allegations of fraud. Initially, I was sent down to the southernmost island of Mindanao to observe the morning votes and then came back to Manila. I was sitting in the hotel there when a woman came up to me crying and said, "Senator, you must come with me to the cathedral. There are women there who fear for their lives. They have asked for you." Thirteen courageous women had walked out of the computer center where votes were being tabulated and taken refuge in a church. I met with them at the cathedral, and they told the story of how they were putting into the computers legitimate and correct vote counts that gave Cory Aquino the victory, but coming out on the tote board were completely fictitious numbers showing votes for Marcos. These women blew the whistle on the dictator.

I knew the best way to protect these women and the results was for them to tell this story publicly as soon as possible. I gathered our team and the international media at the cathedral. The women stood by the altar, the klieg lights giving them the soft glow of a halo, and one by one they told the world that Marcos was cheating. Their courage and the courage of the Filipino people lit a spark that traveled around the world. It was hard to believe that just months after my insulting meeting with a smug Marcos, the very people in his own country, those he had sneered at and compared to children, had exposed the fraudulent election.

Marcos wouldn't concede, but the handwriting was on the wall. Senator Lugar and I joined the rest of the election-monitoring delegation back in Washington for a meeting at the White House. Secretary Shultz presided, and soon White House chief of staff James Baker entered the room to announce that President Reagan himself would be joining us. It was a "pinch yourself" moment. Reagan, his hair ever dark brown even into his seventies, came in and sat down. He insisted that his administration stood on the side of freedom, even if he wasn't crystal clear which side that was. He said they were deeply concerned about the election irregularities. A few minutes later, he slid a note to James Baker that read, in his elegant handwriting, "Can I leave now?"

Reagan was a savvy reader of international opinion. He had a natural flair for drama. Baker was a natural diplomatic poker player. The administration was not going to be dragged down with Marcos now that he'd been exposed as a fraud. Reagan sent his friend Senator Paul Laxalt to Manila to deliver the message to Marcos, who was quickly gone, living in exile in Hawaii. God only knows how much gold bullion and cash he had accumulated for his exile.

I was gratified and energized. Perhaps for the first time since I'd come to the Senate, I felt like I'd made a difference by taking what I knew (foreign policy) and the best of what I was learning (process, people and protocol) to set something in motion. More than that, I felt as if I had tapped into a synergy bigger than any one senator: when you can use the Senate to send a message, when you can point the United States toward its true north and when our values align with people who actually share them all over the world, you can make something happen. Just three years after her husband had died fighting for democracy, Cory Aquino defied the odds and rose to the presidency atop a wave of people. William Cameron Forbes could only have wished for such a development, and Robert C. Byrd didn't have it in mind when he gave me a recipe for action, a PAC check and some great lessons about the Senate, but finally I was finding my way.

CHAPTER 8

Holding Washington Accountable

"My brother says the government is sending arms to the Contras illegally."

My legislative director received a call from a constituent recommending we talk to her brother, Jack Mattes, a public defender in Florida. His client claimed to have firsthand knowledge of a secret network with ties to the U.S. government that was illegally supplying the Contras with military aid. If what Mattes was describing was true, the administration was engaging in an illegal war. Perhaps this is why some in the Reagan administration had seemed so determined to stop my early interest in the war in Nicaragua.

Particularly after my dustup with Senator Goldwater, I was determined to get the truth and I wasn't going to let anyone put me on the defensive again. The irony wasn't lost on me: I had followed the law but in the purest of politics been sandbagged by Republicans for something I hadn't done. Now I was looking at evidence that suggested some element of the Reagan administration had overtly broken the law by doing something Congress had specifically forbidden it from doing, which was to aid the Contras.

We quietly began to dig into these allegations. Falling back on everything I'd learned as a prosecutor, we wanted to make sure their research was done precisely and meticulously, almost as if we were going to trial.

All in all, members of our small but energetic team conducted more than fifty interviews over the course of 1986, even traveling to Costa Rica to speak with people who allegedly worked in a U.S.-funded supply network. What we began to uncover was hard to comprehend: mercenaries, drug smuggling, even a fanciful scheme to assassinate a U.S. ambassador and blame it on the Sandinistas.

I encouraged the Senate Foreign Relations Committee to launch a more formal investigation. I also pressed the Department of Justice to launch an investigation based on the evidence that the CIA and others may have been deliberately circumventing the congressional ban on Contra aid.

At first, neither did much with my request. Nonetheless, our team, undaunted, continued to work. Through a fascinating set of connections involving modern-day buccaneers, a group of coconspirators who reeked of unreliability, we learned that the trafficking of cocaine into the United States was a primary source of funding for the Contras. The hypocrisy was offensive. As a prosecutor, I'd seen drugs rip apart communities. Nancy Reagan was promoting her "Just Say No" effort. But the trail we were uncovering suggested that the federal government was supporting rebels funded by the same drugs that were killing kids on the streets of New Bedford. You couldn't say no to drugs but say yes to the Contras and look the other way. I knew that the senator I had to go see was the hard-line conservative senior Republican on the Foreign Relations Committee, Jesse Helms of North Carolina. It shocked my staff. Jesse and I were worlds apart ideologically. Jesse regularly referred to gay men as "perverts" and sodomites, while I had picked up where Paul Tsongas had left off, authoring a bill to outlaw workplace discrimination against gays and lesbians. My staff argued Jesse was an extremist who would likely reprise Senator Goldwater's smears against me. They were wrong. I went to see Jesse one-on-one. He listened as I went through the evidence piece by piece. Jesse hated drugs as fervently as he hated communists. He made it clear that his Republican colleague on the relevant subcommittee, Hank Brown from Colorado, could join me in going wherever the facts led us. Jesse Helms was genuine and consistent in his beliefs. I had learned from Ted Kennedy and others that often in the Senate you must compartmentalize to move forward. Jesse and I saw civil rights issues differently, but on drugs, we could find common ground.

As my team continued to interview people who worked with the Contras, we heard about a network of secret bank accounts, the use of remote airstrips and unmarked planes, and, perhaps most important, the involvement of government officials, including Lieutenant Colonel Oliver North, a senior staff member of President Reagan's National Security Council.

I knew of Oliver North. We were the same generation and had both fought in Vietnam. He had come home from the war a decorated combat vet, with a Silver Star, a Bronze Star, and two Purple Hearts. I didn't know what his politics were, but I respected his service and his courage. I wondered how someone with his credentials could be led down a path of illegality. The Marines live by a code. If what we were hearing was true, a Marine should have been horrified.

It was becoming clear that our inquiry wouldn't be the end of the story. I thought that a full-fledged Senate investigation was warranted, one that would allow for formal depositions and subpoenaed documents, but my recommendations continued to be shrugged off.

That changed suddenly on October 5, 1986. A plane was shot down over southern Nicaragua. Two Americans were killed; one American was captured. The plane was filled with military arms, including seventy AK-47s and about one hundred thousand rounds of ammunition.

When President Reagan quickly denied any connection between the plane and the U.S. government, my team and I rushed to release a full report of our findings. We had collected credible evidence that Oliver North and other former military officers had set up a network to ship weapons and ancillary military equipment to the Contras. There was no way the downed plane was a coincidence.

Later that month, both the Senate and the Justice Department announced investigations into whether and how Americans were assisting the Contras with military aid.

In November, thanks to a Lebanese news report, we learned that the Contra scandal was even more complicated. The United States was involved in arms sales to Iran, which was at war with Iraq. Before long, administration officials acknowledged that some of the money from the Iran arms sales had been diverted to support the Contras—under the direction of none other than Lieutenant Colonel North.

Suddenly, seven or eight different committees in Congress wanted to investigate. An orphaned investigation had several fathers claiming paternity. A possible constitutional crisis was on the horizon. The leadership of Congress agreed a special committee would have to be created.

I learned an unmistakable lesson about seniority in the Senate. I had done the digging and laid the foundation for the inquiry—and taken plenty of criticism for it from the Republicans—but was left on the sidelines while the investigation was handed to a series of more senior Democrats. They were distinguished senators: Chairman Daniel Inouye of Hawaii, a World War II veteran who had given his arm in battle; George Mitchell, next in line to serve as majority leader; Sam Nunn, the centrist Democrat from Georgia whose relationships with the Pentagon ran deep; Paul Sarbanes, a liberal who had served in the Senate for twenty years, and one of the most respected members of the Foreign Relations Committee; David Boren, a centrist from Oklahoma; and Howell Heflin, a respected judge from Alabama.

I didn't take it personally since there wasn't a freshman Democrat on the select committee. It also occurred to me that with the buzzed-about inevitability of a Dukakis presidential bid just a year away, no one was going to appoint his former lieutenant governor to a post where the likely Republican nominee, Vice President Bush, might be under the microscope. But the decision still left me feeling I had poured energy into a fight only to be kept out of its final round.

I learned another lesson. When you're the first one to pop your head out of a foxhole, you're in the crosshairs. I had become a lightning rod on the Iran-Contra issue. The Republicans had spent a year arguing that my investigation was a wasteful conspiracy theory. They couldn't now explain why the House and Senate were convening blue-ribbon joint hearings if I was on a fool's errand. They would have loved to use me as a convenient whipping boy. By leaving me off the committee, Byrd didn't give them that chance.

There was an even bigger truth at play, however. Senate Democrats suspected the investigation was unlikely to end in the impeachment of President Reagan. That's because the institutionalists were in charge.

Chairman Dan Inouye made that clear to me in a private conversation. Dan had led a life of courage. He was the kind of patriot we should all hope to be. Dan had signed up to serve his country despite the internment of his fellow Japanese Americans at home. In battle, he suffered a grievous injury. After prying a live grenade out of his nearly severed right arm, Dan lobbed it into a German bunker, saving the lives of his brothers-in-arms. He was subsequently shot again in the leg, falling to the ground. When he woke up, his men were hovering over him, and he instructed them: "The war's not over. Get back to your positions."

During his recovery back in the States, he met a young vet named Bob Dole at the Percy Jones Army Hospital in Battle Creek, Michigan, and they became fast friends. In the Senate, you could see and feel the connection between them.

Dan had been in the Senate for decades. He had lived and made a lot of history. He confided in me his reaction to living through the Nixon impeachment saga and the resignation of a president. As a member of the Senate committee that investigated Watergate, he had seen the scandal rock the country and fray the national fabric. We might disagree about whether the real source of those divisions was Nixon's illegality and lies, as opposed to the process charged with addressing them, but those were mere debating points. The bottom line was Inouye had lived through Watergate, and he wasn't eager to invite a repeat performance.

Nor was Majority Leader Byrd. He and Dan were institutionalists who were unwilling to see an entire Congress and the next election consumed by the impeachment of a president finishing the final years of a second term.

While I wasn't contemplating let alone cheering for impeachment, my prosecutor and activist instincts told me the full story had to be told. The World War II generation was quietly pushing back. My generation was shaped by a very different war, one that taught us that governments can lie and break laws, and when they do, sunshine and accountability are the required disinfectants.

I felt torn. I'd spent capital standing up for my principles, and if I hadn't, Congress might not have been forced to take the issue seriously. But I was seeing that my activist intensity could also unsettle an institution and its custodians, a valuable lesson in a place that runs on relationships. Ultimately, to shape events in the Senate, I had to find new ways to advance issues while staying true to my core.

Not being stuck in the most junior position on the select committee did present an unexpected opportunity for an investigation of my own. Dan Inouye told me specifically that the Iran-Contra Select Committee would not dig into the rumors that the Contras were awash in illegal drug money. I could take on that issue and see where it led. Some charged that the CIA was purposefully bringing cocaine to the inner cities of the United States to fund the right-wing Contras in Nicaragua. I didn't believe that. I believed that the United States was simply looking away from the obvious connections between the Contras and drugs. I had little tolerance for right-wing paramilitary groups dealing in drug trafficking and just as little patience for left-wing rebels, like the FARC in Colombia, doing the same.

I built a team of staffers committed to uncovering the truth, whatever it looked like. They were a great band of idealists and truth-seekers, though there were a few times when I wondered if perhaps we were too zealous. My chief investigator was a dyed-in-the-wool liberal crusader named Jack Blum. Jack was idealistic. He saw the world in black and white. He tugged mightily at the end of the Senate leash. He was joined by David McKean, a brilliant young lawyer educated at Harvard, Duke and Fletcher, a gifted writer with a contagious sense of humor who became invaluable. Jonathan Winer was dogged. He was a whip-smart investigator I'd first met during my 1972 campaign, when he was the earnest seventeen-year-old editor of his high school newspaper and had grilled me. I joked that I hadn't been able to shake him since. He was highly intelligent and capable. One day I spotted my receptionist nervously standing in the hallway talking to my executive assistant. I asked what was wrong. "Senator, um, why don't you walk by the reception area? Someone's, um . . . one of your investigators' next meeting is there and it's, uh, making the, uh, tour group from Leominster nervous."

I walked by the open office door and glanced inside. I could see why the Ladies Auxiliary was getting uncomfortable. On the couch next to the tour group sat a uniformed Bureau of Prisons official accompanying a manacled federal convict in an orange jumpsuit, apparently a potential witness with whom my staff was soon meeting. I made a mental note to tell the team to move some of these meetings to a different Senate building pronto.

Despite such moments, our investigation was all too serious. The drug trail led to something eye-opening. I wasn't surprised that the Contras were up to their eyeballs in drugs, but I was astonished by just how easily they laundered their illicit gains through supposedly legitimate financial institutions. We discovered a shady and unsavory bank with an innocuous acronym: BCCI. It stood for the Bank of Commerce and Credit International. BCCI was a dream for criminals and money launderers, and it was hiding in plain sight. We discovered that Panamanian dictator Manuel Noriega, a longtime Cold War ally installed by the United States, was personally involved in drug trafficking, and he used BCCI to ship his ill-gotten money out of the country. The prosecutor in me was intrigued.

The next months were almost a redux of the DA's office: reviewing evidence, taking depositions, examining testimony. BCCI was a $20 billion banking empire. At the time of our investigation, it had branches in more than seventy countries and boasted nearly a million depositors. I sought subpoenas, but the Department of Justice delayed my requests. Someone was protecting something or someone.

By the spring of 1989, it was apparent that my inquiry had rubbed more than just DOJ officials the wrong way. BCCI, I would find out, had friends in high places. The chairman of the Foreign Relations Committee, my friend Claiborne Pell, was hearing that our investigation was cracking, if not breaking, considerable pottery along the way. He didn't ask me to stop, but he encouraged me to bring it to completion. The message that became abundantly clear: people were uncomfortable.

It was impossible, let alone wrong, to sweep what we'd discovered under the rug. The Department of Justice didn't care, so we brought our evidence to New York district attorney Robert Morgenthau. Morgenthau shared our alarm and succeeded in convincing a grand jury to indict the bank on fraud and bribery charges. We learned that the CIA had prepared hundreds of reports outlining the criminal connections of BCCI. Thankfully, the Department of Justice soon had a new head of its criminal division: my St. Paul's classmate, a Vietnam veteran and a diligent law enforcement professional named Bob Mueller. Our subcommittee's two staffers had exposed the perfidy of BCCI, and I felt vindicated when Mueller assigned thirty-seven prosecutors to the case. By July 1991, regulators had seized the bank. BCCI was dead.

There was a reason the law enforcement and intelligence communities had started to call BCCI the "Bank of Crooks and Criminals." As one U.S. indictment put it, money laundering was the bank's "corporate strategy." If you needed to move money quietly, BCCI was the one who moved it for you. The BCCI client list was a who's who of bad guys: Noriega, Saddam Hussein, Abu Nidal and even, as we'd find out, the early leadership of al-Qaeda, which was dealt a huge blow and had to abandon its base in Sudan when BCCI was shuttered.

Why was it so important to me to pursue it? Because if you start backsliding and trimming on the rule of law, you contribute to the inexorable deterioration of democracy. Corruption is cumulative. I believed the rule of law has to mean something in the United States. If we knowingly turn a blind eye on the rich and powerful, enabling them to escape accountability while two-bit criminals go to jail for years, we create a tiered system of justice. That is no justice at all. Drug money leads to illicit arms sales, human trafficking and money laundering. Terrorists love banks that operate in the shade. For a long time, BCCI was successful in concealing its dirty work from the public in part because, as our investigation helped to uncover, an astonishing number of prominent people seemed to have ties of varying degrees to its operations. It was former defense secretary Clark Clifford whose connections to BCCI brought me the most awkward interactions. He was a legend who had walked the halls of power since the days of Harry Truman. More than one of my Democratic colleagues asked me why I was going after one of their friends. I even received calls from former First Lady Jacqueline Kennedy Onassis and Pamela Harriman, a prominent Democratic fund-raiser and the widow of New York governor Averell Harriman, asking what I was doing to their good friend Clark Clifford.

I tried my best to explain we weren't targeting him or anyone else. We were surprised ourselves by what we were finding, but we couldn't back off. Clark Clifford was pulling out all the stops to obstruct the inquiry, if not end it. Most of my colleagues knew not to push me, but I knew I was once again an outsider in an insider's city.

In the fall of 1991, Clark Clifford testified before our subcommittee. By that point eighty-four years old, frail and hard of hearing, Clifford claimed that he had never realized that the owners of his bank weren't who they said they were. He had been fooled. When I questioned him on the details, he essentially repeated several versions of the same point: he couldn't remember.

My staff lit into me during a break at the hearing, telling me I was pulling too many punches. "He's an old man," I told them. "I'm not going to humiliate an old man."

I was looking for truth, not a trophy. We had gotten all the testimony we needed. Viewers would draw their own conclusions about Clifford, who candidly acknowledged at the hearing that the facts had left him with "the choice of seeming either venal or stupid." At the same time, I was drawing a conclusion of my own about how I would operate in the Senate. I wasn't going to let anyone—no matter how powerful—prevent me from doing what was right and seeking the truth. However, I resolved that never would I lose my own sense of decency. There's a right way and a wrong way to operate. I didn't care if people called me a crusader, but never was I going to give anyone a reason to call me a bully.

I had learned a great deal as an investigator, both in Iran-Contra and in BCCI. I'd been reminded that when you push hard for truth, people who are invested in lies or in convenient avoidance resist, and they retaliate. But truth is worth fighting for; truth is the American bottom line. On Iran-Contra, while President Reagan finished his term and George H. W. Bush became president in 1989 despite questions about what he had known, justice was carried out. People like Oliver North who had broken the law were convicted in the justice system. Pardons and commutations followed for many, but the courts had validated the truth. On BCCI, despite the enemies I had made, the bank was shut down, and a light shone on a network of illegal and illicit efforts that funded drugs, terror and murder. I was getting things done as a U.S. senator. I was paying a price, but this was why I had come to Washington.

CHAPTER 9

Making Peace

JOHN MCCAIN AND I sat somewhat stiffly opposite each other on the Boeing 757 with "United States of America" emblazoned on its side. It was a late February evening in 1991, after a long day in the Senate. We were part of a fairly large delegation led by Senators Strom Thurmond and Daniel Patrick Moynihan, heading to Kuwait City immediately after its liberation in Operation Desert Storm. All senators were assigned seats on the basis of seniority, and so it was that two Vietnam veterans who had lived very different stories regarding the same war found themselves face-to-face on a long flight. We were part of a foursome at a table, John facing backward and me forward, and for a while we exchanged light pleasantries about the Senate and politics.

As the night wore on, neither John nor I had fallen asleep. I began to ask John about flying, his experience in the Navy and at the Academy in Annapolis, his family's long and distinguished military history, and then, finally, Vietnam itself and being a POW. John had his own questions. We listened to each other and shared honest observations about our different journeys.

The importance and uniqueness of this conversation probably escaped both of us at the time. Though there had not been animosity between us, there was certainly suspicion and mistrust of the other in both of us. When John was suffering incomprehensible abuse and indignity at the hands of his North Vietnamese captors, I was first traversing the rivers of the Mekong Delta in the brown-water navy—an altogether different kind of hardship and danger—and later traveling America, speaking out against the war. John had parachuted out over Hanoi in October 1967. He wasn't released until late 1973. For him, every impression of the war and the politics back home basically froze on the day he was captured. In contrast, October 1967 was the first March on the Pentagon. It was before Tet, before the moratorium, before the assassinations of Martin Luther King Jr. and Bobby Kennedy, before Nixon's promise of a secret plan for peace. John would have seen Henry Kissinger as a diplomat who helped him, in John's words, "keep his honor" by rebuffing North Vietnam's offer to set Admiral McCain's son free ahead of other POWs who had been captured earlier, whereas for the anti-war movement Kissinger became a symbol of the war's continuation.

For John to survive as a prisoner of war, I imagined it was essential to hold on to the core values that he had brought with him to the Hanoi Hilton—the fight for freedom, the stopping of communism, "keeping faith with our fathers." I knew at the time that those of us opposing the war could not possibly be well received or understood by these patriots. I didn't expect it. Being a target was part of the price we paid for choosing to speak out. It was a price I will pay every day of my life in some quarters.

What John didn't and couldn't know then was how difficult the journey to being against the war was for so many of us. I joined the military for most of the same reasons he did—my father's example, a heightened sense of duty to serve my country, the strong and embedded belief that "to those whom much is given, much is expected," the awareness of the unacceptable inequity that far too many of those who were bearing the brunt of the draft were people of color and low income. I knew I was not ready to go to graduate school—and certainly would not have gone as a means of avoiding service—but I also knew that service in the military, with leadership responsibility, would be a graduate school of a quite different kind. There was much I had loved about the Navy. My journey from patriotic, young, newly minted ensign to equally patriotic veteran and anti-war protester was driven by a fury over what I had seen the war do to the young men who served, over the neglect and even rejection of returning warriors, over the deception, the outright lies that had been told for years by government officials and top military brass about the war itself, about the tactics and strategy—if they could be called that—which resulted in unnecessary dying and killing in Vietnam for more years than anyone anticipated—and for what?

There was in all of us who went through this difficult transformation a profound sense of loss and betrayal. John and those who supported the war no doubt felt betrayed by us. We, on the other hand, felt betrayed by our leaders, a few military but mostly civilian.

Here we were, eighteen years later, two U.S. senators, both of whom believed deeply in the strength of our Constitution and the importance and value of public service, both of whom shared hard, lived-out definitions of patriotism. We had both learned the importance of respecting other people's views—no matter how intensely we may have disagreed—and we both had learned enough about life to understand that as senators, it didn't pay to burn bridges. There was always another vote and another day, and even if you couldn't support someone on one day, the next dawn might bring an issue of shared passion and importance.

John had also studied and confronted enough history, talked to a full share of military experts, processed and analyzed what he'd seen and heard over the intervening years, and he had come to understand the mistakes, to detest the deception and to even become fast friends with people who had opposed the war. Although he had traveled to Massachusetts to campaign for my opponent in my first Senate race, he didn't attack me personally. I would have preferred he hadn't shown up at all, but I understood the game. We didn't know each other yet and I could not have expected otherwise. But all of this backdrop swirled in my head as I sat three feet from him sharing our experiences.

What became obvious to both of us in this meandering but wonderful—and memorable—conversation was a shared sense that the divisiveness of the war was still with us as it was with the country, and it needed to be purged. We agreed that America had for too long been at war with itself. The war at home was not and could not ever be over as long as the specter of prisoners being held or unaccounted for hung over the nation. While deep down John felt the issue was being cynically exploited by politicians fanning a conspiracy, we both understood that the nation could never move beyond the war and genuinely make peace with itself without resolving doubts and recognizing realities. We could never make real peace with the Vietnamese as long as people questioned their compliance with the agreement to return all prisoners, not while the image of Rambo saving American boys from tiger cages in Southeast Asia was drawing millions to the box office.

For John, this notion that people might have been left behind alive was more than personal. Based on his own horrendous experience, which shockingly some zealots were willing to challenge and even dismiss, he was convinced the so-called evidence of live Americans was wrong, for he and his fellow prisoners had developed a code by which they communicated and memorized the names of every prisoner captured. He believed that those who perpetuated the POW myth exploited the families of the missing in a cruel way and did America a disservice.

The plane droned on flying east. The cabin was darkened. Most senators were sleeping. We too needed to grab some shut-eye. When, finally, we had exhausted this time of honest talk, we also agreed not to let the moment be forgotten. We agreed right then and there to find ways to work together to bring peace to Vietnam and America. It was the beginning of a new friendship and a new opportunity. It was one of the most significant and valued moments for me in my entire time as a U.S. senator.

When I returned to my office and related to my staff that John and I were willing to tackle Vietnam, they thought we were crazy, especially me. To a person they saw the POW/MIA issue as the domain of zealots, charlatans and ideologues. Everyone thought it would be a gargantuan waste of time. But when a *Newsweek* magazine cover showed a picture of American POWs with the headline "Are They Still Alive?" it was clear to me America could never make peace, could never be at peace with itself, without resolving this issue. The families too deserved answers. The country had to live up to its code of never abandoning those who serve. How could any of us talk about honor and duty if we did not complete this mission?

With the mounting pressure from the families of those missing and still unaccounted for and in the face of stories like the one in *Newsweek*, the issue was taking on a larger and larger life. No matter how improbable one thought the odds that POWs had been left behind, it would be impossible to ever have a conversation about Vietnam in the future without being confronted about the accusations of betrayal and abandonment. And in truth we had not yet turned over every stone, followed every lead, and we owed it to ourselves and future generations to do exactly that.

After gathering the signatures of a number of Republican senators, Bob Smith of New Hampshire sent a letter to Majority Leader George Mitchell requesting a select committee to find the answers. I talked with John McCain to see if he would join me in trying to get those answers and begin a process (I hoped) of putting the Vietnam War behind us. He said yes, so I went to George and, against the unanimous advice of my staff, I took on the role of chairman of the Senate Select Committee on POW and MIA Affairs. Thankfully, on the Democratic side, George assigned a terrific group of senators who gave the committee the gravitas it needed to deal with such a thorny issue: Vietnam veterans Bob Kerrey, Chuck Robb and Tom Daschle, along with Harry Reid and Herb Kohl. On the Republican side, Bob Dole picked Bob Smith as vice chair, a position that John McCain had turned down, but McCain joined the committee, together with Vietnam veteran Hank Brown, Nancy Kassebaum, Jesse Helms and Chuck Grassley. I hoped we had the credibility to work through the minefields that lay ahead, domestically and abroad.

For years, slivers of information had been collected by all of America's intelligence agencies, particularly the Defense Intelligence Agency and the CIA, alleging sightings of an American still in captivity. On flagpoles all across America, the black POW/MIA flag still flew right under or beside Old Glory as a reminder to all Americans of a duty not to forget.

The right wing of American politics was deeply suspicious of our intelligence gathering on this subject. Many of the strongest advocates believed that at least the CIA and DIA had been engaged in a cover-up ever since the agreement of 1973 in order to protect the decisions made by Richard Nixon and Henry Kissinger in their haste to be done with Vietnam. Secretary of State Kissinger never negotiated for those who were last known alive or missing in and over Laos and Cambodia.

The reason my staff was so concerned about my taking this on was the difficulty of disproving a negative. Twenty to twenty-five years later, it would be a near impossible task to satisfactorily disprove a "last seen alive" report of as many years ago. But John and I believed that with an exhaustive inquiry, one that delved into the traditional oral history maintained in provincial "history houses" in Vietnam, interviewed old soldiers, followed through on the last reports, dug up supposed burial sites—if we did all that was humanly possible, we could persuade the majority of people of our conclusion and provide the basis for proving to the families the good faith efforts of their government. Clearly that was the only way to bring some measure of closure to individual families and to America.

• We began a series of hearings, some very straightforward, some controversial. All the bases needed to be covered. To convince those who believed in a conspiracy to cover up the knowing, willful abandonment of live captives, it was critical that we bring in players who had made key decisions during that period of time. Just getting agreement on witnesses was difficult. Every decision was second-guessed by the outside advocacy groups who were perfectly prepared to label the committee a continuation of the cover-up. Many of these groups were led by sincere families of the missing, families whose lives had been frozen in amber since the war. But other groups were schemers and charlatans profiting from the perception that Americans might still be alive. They were glorified direct-mail fundraising operations filling their pockets at the POW/MIA families' expense. Ted Sampley was a self-appointed POW activist who sold T-shirts, flags and newsletters on the Mall, a stone's throw from the Vietnam Veterans Memorial. He profited grossly from the myth that prisoners were still being held in tiger cages in Vietnam. As McCain and I worked painstakingly to bring the facts and the truth to families who had waited twenty years for any word, Sampley was at work ignoring the evidence and purposely promoting lies. After all, the truth would cut into his business. He launched a campaign to label John McCain the "Manchurian candidate." He publicly accused John of having been brainwashed into betraying his fellow POWs. I'd watch the veins in John's neck bulge every time Sampley would interrupt one of our hearings. I'd reach over and tap his forearm before I banged my gavel and asked for order in the hearing room. Once, John's chief of staff, Mark Salter, got into a fistfight with Sampley and clipped him pretty good. Sampley went to jail for assault. I liked Mark before that but even more afterward.

John McCain and I bent over backward to be exhaustive in the witnesses as well as in the evaluation of the paper trail going back to the war. Thousands of documents from the DIA and the CIA were declassified. In one single day we released the largest dump of classified documents at one time ever. We felt we needed to overwhelm people with transparency and we did. It was difficult for anyone to assert we were hiding something, which was exactly what we wanted.

My committee assignment was cause for my first-ever trip to Moscow. It was the period after the fall of the Berlin Wall and the disintegration of the Soviet Union itself. Things had not yet sorted out. I arrived in the dead of winter to the bitter cold of a Moscow in disarray. My mission was to pursue the evidence regarding rumors of American pilots having been transferred from Vietnam to Moscow for interrogation during the Vietnam War. Fortunately for us, perestroika worked in our favor, breaking some of the barriers to the exchange of information. I was following up on specific reports we had of these interrogations.

I visited Russia's equivalent of the State Department. I was brought to a large, currently vacant office to wait for my meeting. Seven phones sat on one desk. I thought, *whoever works here must be someone very important.* I asked our ambassador why there were so many phones. The answer stunned me: Soviet technology couldn't link all the lines into one phone. And these were the guys who were going to march across Europe?

Along with a minder and a bureaucrat from the office, I made my way down into the bowels of KGB headquarters underneath Lubyanka Square, the former site of the famous statue of KGB founder Felix Dzerzhinsky. In August 1991, when the citizens of Moscow fought back against the counterrevolution and won, perhaps twenty thousand people gathered to celebrate their freedom by removing Dzerzhinsky's statue. One of their labor leaders said, "We are cleaning away the waste from our lives." It was fascinating to visit this site where people had courageously stood up against a vastly superior force to reassert their thirst for freedom.

I may have been the first American ever to walk down into the deep recesses of the KGB records. There were endless long corridors with wire mesh screening protecting reams of files sitting on shelves and desks, collecting dust. I wondered about each individual file and the person or persons it represented. How many moments of horror—sheer terror—were collected in those files? I wished I had a hundred researchers and permission to go through them all. I was also surprised by how haphazard and antiquated it all appeared—no visible order or system, just piles of "stuff" representing some of the worst of human behavior stuck away in a dustbin of history.

The next day I was informed I would be met by a car that would take me to meet with Yevgeny Primakov. He had previously been an advisor on Mikhail Gorbachev's Presidential Council and was tapped to transform the KGB into the new intelligence service called the Foreign Intelligence Service, or SVR, which it remains today. In truth, he preserved most of the existing KGB apparatus. That drive was harrowing. The early Moscow night had descended on us. We were careening along the narrow roads outside Moscow, going to some compound in the country. It was snowing like crazy. I had visions of us barreling off the road, crashing into trees or sliding into a river.

Eventually, we arrived at the imposing gate of a secluded compound. I had no idea which direction we had driven or where we had wound up. The gates opened. We drove in, passed some random dachas and arrived finally at one where the car stopped in front of a door. I got out, walked up to the door as it opened, and Primakov stood there to welcome me. I said hello, walked in and quickly asked him, "Have any Americans ever been out here before?" Without missing a beat, he said, "Not voluntarily!"

That was precisely what I had come to talk about, but his answer was merely humorous. We talked at length about the Soviet Union's support for the Vietnamese and their intelligence gathering at the time. Clearly this was a conversation that was inconceivable only months earlier. I had no reason to expect revelations or confessions, but I did want to see if we could establish a process where some of the files I had viewed cursorily at the headquarters could actually be examined. Our committee also possessed documents from that period that we wanted to discuss with them to help resolve some issues. He agreed, and we worked together quite constructively going forward. For a Cold War kid, what a long, strange trip that was.

We also began a series of visits to Vietnam that were essential to achieving our goal. A lot of the higher-ups in Vietnam thought we were either crazy or trumping up the POW/MIA issue in order to delay lifting the embargo and avoid the thorny issue of normalization. The Vietnamese themselves had well over a million men and women unaccounted for or missing.

Our perceived obsession with allegedly alive or unaccounted for American captives seemed contrived to them, particularly when measured against their losses. My job was to build trust, to persuade them of the authenticity of this issue. Over more than twenty trips to Vietnam, through several foreign ministers, party chairmen, presidents and prime ministers of Vietnam, I built up a reputation as an honest broker. I believe I managed to convince Vietnamese officials of the sincerity of our inquiry and the importance of this inquiry to the task of changing the perception of Vietnam, which of course was essential to changing the policy.

Nguyen Co Thach, the first foreign minister I dealt with, and the father of Vietnam's current foreign minister, believed in this initiative. He made a huge difference in helping us build credibility. He understood America. More than that, he was sensitive himself to the deeply held concern of American families. His early intervention was a key step forward in this endeavor, as was the commitment of the president, prime minister and chairman of the Communist Party. These leaders all put their reputations on the line to push reluctant soldiers, jailers, government officials, historians and citizens to embrace the task. On one occasion, when I was talking with Party chairman Doi Moi, himself a veteran of the war, trying to emphasize the importance of putting this issue to rest, as if to convince me of the sincerity of his commitment, he stood up, pulled up his shirt and showed me several massive scars he bore from wounds in the war. He said to me, "We both have great losses and have suffered greatly. We will get this done and we are committed to help make it happen." I was impressed and taken aback at the same time. I never expected to be standing in the reception hall of the Presidential Palace with the powerful chairman of the party and have him bare his stomach and back to show me the price he paid in the war. It was a dramatic, moving, spontaneous moment.

As chairman of the select committee, I traveled alone to Vietnam many times to advance the inquiry. On a number of occasions, many of my colleagues joined me. Always these trips were complicated but fascinating. In many ways it's hard to describe the range of emotions I went through. On the first visits it was naturally bizarre for me to be reliving the smells, the sounds of motorbikes, the bustle of the markets, the joy and enthusiasm of the children, the sight of sampans plying the muddy brown rivers, the earthen scars on battlefields, the still-damaged buildings and the bomb craters that had grown over with new green but unmistakably reflected the shapes of the bombs themselves. It is hard to convey how weird it was to be in Hanoi, sitting in the presidential reception hall under a giant bust of Ho Chi Minh, with the president of Vietnam or chairman of the Communist

Party, trying to persuade him that we needed to talk with his top generals, enter his history houses, fly helicopters into hamlets and possibly, without prior notice, drop from the sky to determine if Americans were secretly being held in one village or another. But that's exactly what we did.

The Vietnamese deserve enormous credit for letting us do all that we did. Helicopters make an unmistakable sound with the whirr of the rotors. It defined air cover, medevac, mail, lift into battle, lift home. It was the sound of the war, but not just for us. For the Vietnamese, that sound was reminiscent of the war not so many years in the past. It had so often been the sound of impending death and destruction. It had so often signaled the arrival of a search and destroy mission, the imminent deployment of troops who would descend into a village to seek out the enemy. Sometimes, with luck, it brought help or safety, but it was the unmistakable and distinctive sound of the Vietnam War. Now we were asking the government of Vietnam to allow us again to descend in helicopters, without notice, into hamlets where the memories of these machines were fresh and raw with emotion. It was a lot to ask, but it was the only way to convince doubters that the search was real, that we were following up on a live sighting report without letting the Vietnamese know ahead of time where we were going so they could "move the prisoner."

On one occasion, I was going to a prison that was the subject of supposed sightings. A crew from ABC television and a reporter from the *New York Times* were with us to observe the spontaneity of the spot check. This occurred toward the end of the committee's work. A lot hung on the ability to conduct a spontaneous spot check on a number of prisons. This was one of the most notorious. We arrived at the gate only to be refused entrance. I was shocked because we had been told we would be cleared at whatever prison we went to when we notified the headquarters we were there. Apparently, the district commander had not yet given the instructions to let us in. I could envision the headlines in the *Times* and the story on TV— "Vietnamese Refuse POW/MIA Committee Entrance at Suspect Prison." It would confirm the worst suspicions. It could undo months of painstaking work. I stepped away from the group to call the foreign minister. In no uncertain terms, I told him that unless we got immediate access to this prison he and the government risked blowing up months of work. Five minutes later the commander of the prison politely let us in and apologized that he hadn't been instructed earlier to do so. Despite a moment when I had feared that our mission would be frustrated, that day could not have worked out better, because this incident proved that the visits were unannounced and spontaneous. The fact that the commander did not know we were coming was positive evidence of no collusion on anyone's part. We walked through the whole prison, inspecting walls for scratched messages as well as interviewing prisoners. We found nothing indicating foreigners had been held there at all.

This kind of drama played out several times, but none more surreal than at the very end of the committee's work, when Senator Bob Smith insisted that we had to chase down allegations that there were tunnels in which Americans were being held under the tomb of Ho Chi Minh. Imagine—we, the United States of America, were going to tell the Vietnamese leaders we had to inspect Ho Chi Minh's tomb because we had information there might be prisoners held there. Only the "we" in this case was me. I was going to have to tell them this. As fanciful as it sounds, this rumor persisted in the United States. It had been circulated among the most passionate of the believers, so it had to be dealt with in order to secure the sign-off of all senators on our report.

To make this happen I knew would take every ounce of credibility and persuasion I could summon. I arranged to meet with the president of Vietnam and the chairman of the party. They were the only two people who could possibly make an inspection of the underground beneath Ho's final resting place available to the prying eyes of Americans. I departed the Senate on a Thursday night, flew commercially to Bangkok, picked up a military flight to Hanoi, where I met with the president and chairman separately. I explained how this was really the last hurdle in a long journey. All of us had invested so much in trying to resolve the POW/MIA issue so we could move on and change the relationship between our countries. I told them we would not say anything about the visit publicly until perhaps years in the future, but certainly in no way would they be embarrassed by an early public disclosure. I also told them that, as difficult as this decision was for them, without it they would inadvertently give credence to the allegation that they were hiding something. I was personally squirming at having to ask for this but I knew it was critical to completing our task.

I was on the ground in Hanoi for less than twelve hours before I headed back to Washington. At the end of the weekend I was back in the Senate, where I related to Bob that he and I would be going under Ho's tomb together to complete the mission. We returned to Vietnam for the inspection. At four in the morning or so, with minimal possibility of exposure, well out of sight of the prying eyes of onlookers, we met a couple of uniformed guards who took us down a set of stairs on the edge of the square dedicated to the tomb. We walked through a long corridor, then came to the spaces below the square where Ho Chi Minh's remains lay in state encased in a glass viewing casket. There we were, two U.S. senators, walking around amid a mass of tubes, compressors and pumps, with weird, pulsating, gurgling sounds reverberating through the lower bowels of the tomb. Bob was opening various doors to look behind them and make sure there were no hidden passageways or chambers. I was pinching myself to make sure this was really happening. True to our word, Bob and I have never said much about this underground journey in Hanoi. It put an exclamation point on the lengths the Vietnamese went to, to help us dispel rumors and conspiracy theories. It was also, I think, an immense credit to our committee for seeing the job through and to Bob Smith for being true to his beliefs and loyal to those who counted on him. In the end, our committee did what so many predicted was impossible: we arrived at a unanimous conclusion, supported by all twelve senators, bringing much-needed closure to so many families who had gone decades living with nothing but question marks.

Over the next years, many who had served on our committee, Republican and Democratic administrations, the Pentagon, the intelligence agencies, forensic experts, on-the-ground American military personnel and the Vietnamese, all coordinated and worked, sometimes at risk of life, to get answers to any lingering questions. No country in history, in all of warfare, has ever done as much to implement an exhaustive accounting of all the missing and captured in a war. The American people can be proud of what our teams accomplished and continue to accomplish in this endeavor. Most Americans are simply unaware that even today, we have American military personnel who continue the search in Vietnam. We still dig up the crash sites of a C-130 or Phantom jet. We still climb to remote mountaintops and excavate the earth in a rice paddy or village. On one visit to Vietnam, I was taken out to a lush green field near a small farm. There, a complex scaffold of wood had been built leading down a ramp into the excavated area of a downed C-130 that had crashed and never been recovered. I walked into the area and had an eerie feeling that I was literally walking into the crew's resting place, their grave. God had buried them in the very place they had died, but we were going to finally bring them home. I wondered about the circumstances of their loss, whether they were killed before impact or whether there was time for terror or panic as they plummeted to earth. Had anyone survived for a while? Did the plane hit with such impact that it drove itself twenty feet below the surface we were walking on? Inside the excavation, the troops working painstakingly to sift the earth and scrape away time, explaining to me how they managed their own emotions and performed the difficult task of recovering the fragments of what was once a vibrant, determined team of young Americans at war.

I was amazed by the meticulous archaeological methodology of finding scraps of clothing, a tooth, a fragment of a bone, and then undertaking the extraordinary forensic investigation in our labs in Hawaii to make a positive identification. This enormous commitment to keep faith with American military values has produced a remarkable record: the remains of more than seven hundred service members, brought home to still-mourning families who all deserved answers.

This work was one of those rare chances you get in public life to actually bring people something they'd waited for, for more than two decades: peace. The peace that comes with closure. But for me, and for John McCain, that wasn't the only reward: in our new friendship, and in the work we did, we were ending the war about the war. If a protester and a prisoner of war can find common ground on the most divisive of issues, finding common ground on almost anything else didn't seem so hard after all.

CHAPTER 10

A Time of Transition

"Senator, before I got here, I never had anyone say 'I love you.' I never had anybody care where I was at night." He was a big, brawny kid whose size belied the baby face beneath the hard hat. He told me he had dropped out of high school before his junior year and been in trouble with the law more than once. A judge offered him a better deal than going to jail again for a longer sentence: he could go back to school to earn his GED at night, come to this job site every day on time, learn a trade and in eighteen months he would be the proud owner of a work card to be a union electrician, coupled with a high school equivalency degree.

His words haunted me: he was seventeen or eighteen years old. Never until now had anyone looked him in the eyes and said "I love you." He'd raised himself, or the streets had raised him, and he had been on a one-way journey to jail until someone made all the difference. That someone was Dorothy Stoneman, a natural-born evangelizer for a program she called YouthBuild. A mutual friend had urged me to visit Dorothy's program in East Harlem the next time I was in New York, and I'd chosen this sweltering day in July. In the middle of a run-down block, vacant houses boarded up left and right, a construction crew was working to restore an old brownstone. The city had donated the condemned building, and with some funding from philanthropic foundations, union craftsmen were teaching teenagers and twentysomethings a trade. Every one of their students had been plucked out of juvenile corrections facilities or court diversion programs. A few sought entrance off the street. All of them were turning urban blight into affordable housing. They were also, for the first time, turning themselves into full citizens with a stake in the future, with an unfamiliar dignity and self-esteem in their lives.

Dorothy beamed as her army of young people shared their stories. I asked Dorothy how she had invented this effort. She told me she had once asked a group of teenagers how they would improve their community if they had some support to do it. Their answer came through fast and clear: "Rebuild houses in our neighborhoods. We'd take empty buildings back from drug dealers and fix them up and eliminate crime." And that's exactly what they were doing.

My political antennae went up: Why couldn't this be a national program?

I knew what I was up against. Ronald Reagan had been elected in 1980 and again in 1984—comfortably—on the credo that "government is not the solution to our problem; government *is* the problem." Eight years of Reagan talking government down took a hefty toll. The Republicans had played the politics of division with considerable intelligence and intensity, dog whistles and all. But cities were hurting for real reasons, not just politically contrived ones. The public had grown weary of many Great Society social spending programs. I heard from police and firefighters in Massachusetts who had moved out of the neighborhoods where they'd grown up because crime was soaring, drugs were everywhere and the public schools weren't safe. They dutifully paid their taxes but increasingly perceived that the system was working against them.

Something wasn't working; in fact, lots of things weren't working. Relentless campaign promises to get tougher on crime—with minimum mandatory sentences, especially for drug crimes, being imposed—were creating a vicious cycle in the justice system. Young men were going to prison and coming out unemployable. Kids were left behind, fatherless and growing up on the streets. The death penalty was wildly popular. In 1990, Massachusetts elected a Republican governor, Bill Weld, a former prosecutor who pledged to get tough on crime and said he would restore the death penalty and put convicts in chain gangs "breaking rocks."

The former prosecutor in me hated where the dialogue had ended up. I opposed the death penalty in large part because as a prosecutor I had seen justice delivered unevenly. In court in Middlesex County, I sometimes saw wealthy people commit crimes, lawyer up with impunity and walk out of court with a second or third chance, while poor people got caught up in a vicious cycle of drugs, crime and violence. Their lives were in the hands of overburdened legal counsel paid for by the state. George Reissfelder's struggle to overturn the life sentence for a murder he didn't commit reminded me that had he been wrongly convicted of a capital crime in a different state, he might well have left prison as a corpse, not a free man. I'd met a group of young men in their late teens in Roxbury. Jobs were scarce. I asked them how quickly they could find a gun, if they wanted one. Without hesitating, they answered "five seconds." But if I turned on talk radio in my car, I heard callers describing young African American men as predators, with the familiar refrains to get tough on crime and welfare. It was a call-and-response of disgust and disapproval. A trial in New York City for the so-called Central Park Five was in the news: young men of color convicted of raping an investment banker jogging through Central Park. A million-aire real estate tycoon from New York had taken out full-page ads in all the newspapers urging New York to bring back the death penalty. His name was Donald Trump. It took a long time before we learned that the five young men were innocent.

Fear was becoming the currency of the political debate, but my hope was that YouthBuild might be a new alternative to a debate that left all of us unsatisfied.

I returned to Washington and began working on legislation to make it possible for YouthBuild to receive federal funding. In 1991, my legislation passed with broad bipartisan support, but the funding itself was held up in the appropriations process. The money might not move through the legis-lative pipeline, and even if it did, it would certainly not move as quickly as we'd hoped.

For these kids, an IOU from Congress wouldn't amount to anything but a broken promise. I brought the legislation to a different committee, the subcommittee that appropriated funding for housing.

Dorothy Stoneman told me about a conversation she had with a man named Bruce Katz, the general counsel for the subcommittee we were tar-geting. He told her he liked YouthBuild but federal housing money wasn't going to new federal programs. He concluded, "Unless John Kerry cares about this bill more than any senator almost ever cares about anything af-fecting poor people, you don't have a chance."

As it turned out, I did. I called him and pushed him. He realized Dorothy and I were not going away easily.

National YouthBuild funding was mandated by law, and as the money flowed, the program expanded to nearly all fifty states. Each year, I'd walk around the floor of the Senate during appropriations season and round up signatures on a letter urging the committees to increase the funding levels for the program. Democrats and Republicans bought in, and support grew in each state.

The kids themselves were their own best advocates. I met a young woman named Dorothy, who had spent more than a year in jail for sell-ing crack and was on welfare when she found YouthBuild. Now she had a job as a construction supervisor with a major contractor. Loss had defined their lives, until now. They all craved community, and they were finding it, but they were the ones doing the hard work of rebuilding lives—their own and many others. Certainly one of the most fulfilling moments I enjoyed as a policy maker was when Dorothy Stoneman called me "the Senator from YouthBuild."

We got something done the old-fashioned way—vote by vote, person by person, but to this day I wonder: in Washington's gridlock, and in today's polarized politics, how many good people like Dorothy Stoneman, with good ideas to save lives, are stuck on the outside looking in?

I FIRST MET Teresa in 1990, when I was briefly introduced to her by her husband, Jack Heinz, as he and I were both waiting to speak at the twentieth anniversary of Earth Day in front of the Capitol. I had heard from colleagues that Jack's wife was hugely engaging, smart and a lot of fun, but that day, other than saying hello, we barely had a chance for any conversation in the push and shove of the crowd.

The next time I was to see her was at Jack's funeral in 1991. Well more than half the Senate flew in two Air Force planes to Pittsburgh to attend the services in the Heinz Chapel near the Carnegie Mellon campus. Buses took us right past the park near where the Monongahela River joins the Allegheny River to meld into the Ohio, the famous starting point of the Lewis and Clark expedition. In the packed chapel, I sat in the section of pews set aside for the Senate. It was a stunningly intimate space, graceful and beautiful. The music was powerful. My mind wandered to the day Jack had died, April 4. The Senate was on spring recess. I was in Massachusetts traveling around the state, staying in touch with constituents through listening tours, town halls and various meetings. I was in my car heading to another meeting in the Merrimack Valley, not far from the New Hampshire border. The news station interrupted the normal flow to announce that a senator from Pennsylvania, Jack Heinz, had been killed in a small plane crash near Philadelphia. It was stunning for many reasons—a brilliant, gifted senator, someone everyone thought might well run for president; an extraordinary storied family in Pennsylvania; three boys suddenly without a father and a state without its favorite son. I felt the loss particularly because just before the Easter break, Jack had sat in my office for an hour as we discussed how we would collaborate on banking reform. Now he was gone.

The unfairness of his death underscored the shock, and for every senator there was a huge "there but for the grace of God go I" moment, because we all flew in small planes when we "had to get there at all costs."

When I heard the news on the radio my first impulse was to think of going straight to St. Paul's School, which wasn't far from our location, because I knew that Jack's youngest son, Chris, was there, and I thought as a senator and friend of Jack's, I might be able to offer some comfort. I quickly thought better of it since I didn't know Chris, and I felt that my or anyone's presence would have imposed on him in his grieving. He didn't need to cope with an unknown senator, but I couldn't help but think of my father and the impact the violent loss of his father had on him for a lifetime.

As I thought about what had happened, the service began. I saw Teresa come into the chapel, but in reality, I didn't see her. I saw a bundle of four people moving in a tight huddle, each holding on to the other, their arms entangled in a gliding, slow-moving embrace. Each lost in his or her grief and holding on to each other for dear life in order to get through the next hour. I was incredibly touched by the intimacy and the total lack of self-consciousness. They were there for and lost in one another, which is how it should have been.

I saw Teresa briefly in the receiving line at her home in Washington after the memorial service at the National Cathedral, and then I didn't see her again for more than a year, until we were both in Rio de Janeiro for the Earth Summit in April 1992. It wasn't until Rio that I actually had a real conversation with her and began to get to know the person I was to marry three years later.

We were seated next to each other at a dinner for the delegation to the Earth Summit. Senators Frank Lautenberg, Chris Dodd, John Warner and Larry Pressler were all part of the delegation that had joined up at a restaurant in downtown Rio, where we debated and laughed our way through a very entertaining dinner. Teresa was funny, sassy, quick-witted and engaging. She had a wonderful way of communicating with her eyes, talking with a sparkle that reflected a range of moods and emotions. We somehow wound up quietly trading observations about our companions in French. For both of us I think the evening was the opening of a door—but it was a door to a complicated journey on the other side. We didn't see each other for quite some time after that. I think both of us were shy and both had reasons to move slowly.

With Jack's death, Teresa had become the head of the family, and much more. Her two older sons, John and Andre, were both in college, and Chris was about to head to Yale, Jack's alma mater. Teresa felt the need to be there for them, independent as they were. She had assumed Jack's role as head of the Heinz philanthropies, a huge and daunting task. She was sought after for countless conferences and events, representing the family in the exercise of enormous public responsibility. There had been talk of her accepting the appointment to the Senate and then running in her own right in the subsequent special election. The seat was hers for the taking, as had happened many times in history when a widow stepped into the job. But Teresa decided that she could do more outside the Senate than within. That realization, together with her responsibilities at home, shaped her choices ahead.

For my part, as a divorced father, I was single parenting with one daughter in high school and one about to go. I was still commuting to Boston from Washington. Literally, for eighteen years as a senator, I never spent a weekend in Washington except for rare occasions when the Senate was in session. If I wasn't fund-raising somewhere or traveling on business, I would always get back to the state, even for a day or a few hours. In fact, for the full twenty-eight years I was privileged to serve in the Senate, while I didn't always get back to Massachusetts, it was rare that I would remain in Washington on the weekend.

When I was elected in 1984, I had found a fixer-upper on Third Street NE, one block from my office, which I loved because there was no commute. I had a lot of fun playing frustrated architect and redid the whole house. I created what I thought would be the perfect room for the girls and envisioned being in Washington with them as Julia and I shared parenting responsibility—a completely wacky miscalculation with my daughters. I think the girls made it down twice at the most! Little had I considered or understood the social schedule of teenage girls. The idea of their traveling to be with Dad without their friends was unheard of. So I sold the house to my Senate colleague Bob Graham of Florida and bought an apartment in Boston.

As a result, even as I started seeing Teresa, I was constantly returning to Boston and performing the duties of a senator. For Teresa this was something new, because Pittsburgh was closer, and since Jack's family had been living with him in Washington, his schedule could work out more effectively. As a result, there was some initial tension in our developing relationship because it was hard to work the logistics and meet everyone's expectations—Teresa's, my daughters', both families'—and my own political demands and personal wants. One thing politics does is put enormous pressure on time and therefore on families. Somehow, we all stumbled through it, but I can't say it wasn't without cost to almost everyone. I could never have done what I've been able to do in public life without the extraordinary support and understanding of every member of my family. Not only have they poured their hearts into the endeavor, but they have all patiently sacrificed some part of themselves.

It's something that I don't think the public knows well enough—the burdens put on the families of those who go into public life. From the unfair, unasked for criticism that comes their way, which can be cruel and scarring, to the lost time, none of us in public life could make it if our families weren't willing to endure the hardships that come along with our public calling. Those of us who are the principals never feel it as much as our families because it is what we have chosen to do.

Only four years earlier, in 1988, I had received my final divorce decree after a tortured journey through separation, semi-reunion and another, more final separation. In the end, the guillotine descended on a marriage that at one time had seemed so natural and ordained.

Divorce is horrible, no matter how necessary or how much brighter it might one day be on the other side. I know there are people who, having come to the conclusion they made a terrible mistake, can't wait to get divorced. Some move quickly, as if they were taking off one coat and putting on another. Even though I knew Julia's and my marriage was troubled and we were on separate tracks, I still found divorce the most wrenching, sad and brutal emotional process I have ever gone through. When you have young children, it is even worse. When I knew the marriage was over, I was still heartbroken—partly, I'm sure, for the loss of some powerful sense of what it was meant to be, all that idealism, imagination and hope that is part of marriage. I couldn't shake a significant sense of just plain failure.

There was another reason things were not easy as Teresa and I developed our relationship. She had had a love affair of twenty-seven-plus years violently terminated by a senseless accident. By definition any accident is senseless; some are more senseless than others. When it truly comes out of the blue, is totally avoidable, it seems unthinkable, and it is even harder to come to terms with the aftermath. Even though two years had passed, I certainly felt the weight of Teresa's loss. And I was only a few years beyond the final divorce decree, had been seeing another woman off and on, and was uncertain about a new, serious relationship.

Whatever wounds or baggage we both carried, time began to work its will. More and more we wanted to be together and made sure we were. We slipped into sharing our lives on a regular basis and, as we did, it began to change both of our outlooks. She more than me initially, but we could both feel a healing and a new set of possibilities emerge.

We began to grow closer as we shared different aspects of our lives. Teresa had boys. I had girls. We found pleasure in exploring the not-so-obvious differences. We found a common bond in our interests—appreciation for travel, for exploring different cultures; for cooking and enjoying a great meal with great wine; for architecture and music; for politics and the environment. Teresa, who was born in Mozambique of Portuguese ancestry, was Mediterranean and African at the same time—full of curiosity, passionate and caring.

One September we traveled to Europe. We stopped in London before we went to Paris, rented a car and drove to Brittany so I could introduce her to Les Essarts. It was the best of early fall, trees just beginning to color, still warm, still long evenings. On the way, I diverted to take her to the beaches of Normandy. She had never been there. I wanted her to see the staggering beauty and have her feel and share the same awe I felt every time I visited.

Because it was September, there weren't that many people. The setting is always breathtaking. And when you are walking almost by yourselves amid the crosses and Stars of David, noting the dates of death and the names engraved on the headstones, the emotional and historical sweep of the place overwhelms you. We went all the way down to a near-deserted part of the beach where troops had broken through on D-Day. There we sat on some rocks at the edge of the beach. The tide was rising and we measured each wave as it reached closer and closer to the rocks.

The entire time we were there, mesmerized by the stillness and the beauty, an older gentleman and, we presumed, his wife were sitting together in an embrace, looking out at the water, not moving, lost in thought. I am certain he was a returned veteran, someone who survived that extraordinary landing, someone who had come back to find peace and perhaps remember the friends he had lost at that very place. Quietly, but deliberately, he stood up. He took off his clothes piece by piece. Then, completely naked, with a squeeze of his wife's hand he walked straight out into the water. Unabashed. Unembarrassed. Without awareness of anybody watching, lost in his memories and the moment. He seemed to be performing a ritual purification, allowing the waves to carry him in and out as they had once washed soldiers' bodies back and forth until the dead were finally recovered after the fighting on the beach.

Teresa and I, holding hands, watched in silence. We were frozen in that spot on the beach as if for an eternity. To this day it is one of the most touching, beautiful moments we have ever witnessed together. It was mystical and a gift.

Not long afterward, back home in Boston, Teresa and I started a conversation about our lives together. Without a formal proposal, it just became self-evident: this was our life—we were going to be together. There was no "if." Over Memorial Day weekend, on May 26, 1995, with our families and friends present at her house on Nantucket, we were married. It was an outdoor ceremony on a cool, windy day. We chose Nantucket because it was a place with special meaning for both of us. Teresa and Jack had brought their kids to the island from the earliest days of their lives together. They started out as renters, then poured their hearts into the rebuilding of their own home. Their boys had grown up enjoying Nantucket long before it became more popular and populated. I had sailed in many times with my father and, through the years, had enjoyed many weekends with friends there. The Cape and islands were in my blood from my youngest days. For both of us, the day packed emotions well beyond the joy of marriage. It was a melding of past, present and future.

Johnny, Andre and Chris sang a wonderful German song in honor of their Heinz heritage. Alexandra and Vanessa read poems and Scripture. Teresa and I had written our vows, and once exchanged, we enjoyed a spectacular meal in Siasconset. The next day we took off for Napa Valley for the five days we could get away before returning to Washington.

TERESA AND I were getting settled as a newly married couple, blending our two families, learning how to split our lives between Boston, Washington and Pittsburgh.

We were working on our new home together in Massachusetts. I wanted her and her sons to feel perfectly at home in my city, and I was well aware that Boston can be a tough place for new people. Remodeling the brick town house we'd purchased together focused our energies on something we both enjoyed doing. It brought out the hidden architect in me. It was a special time, but also a period of adjustment. Teresa had a better sense of priorities than those I'd been living as a bachelor. Our early days together incorporated a new balance of expectations about work, family and time off from politics.

Through all of it, Teresa and I made sure we were preserving time for each other. Sometimes it was a weekend at her farm in Pittsburgh or a casual dinner near the Senate. On warm summer evenings, when I would be voting late into the night on Capitol Hill, Teresa would join me, and as soon as there was a window before the inevitable vote-a-rama, we'd sneak off. I'd put the top down on my well-worn silver Dodge convertible, and we'd drive over to Barracks Row for a quick dinner at a hole-in-the-wall Salvadoran place that I'd discovered as a freshman senator. These simple escapes were enjoyable for both of us, but maybe especially for me since, separated and then single with my kids, closest friends and family in Boston, Washington had always felt transient. It was a headquarters city, a business place where you were always on, always subject to being lobbied when out to dinner or at a show. I found there was no off switch in Washington. Teresa managed to soften that. It became more of a home and, with her, I felt more grounded there.

But that time was cut short, with a jolt: a rumor started to spread that Governor Bill Weld might be gearing up to challenge me for reelection to the Senate in 1996.

Suddenly, talk of "work-life balance" sounded like a distant aspiration.

If I wanted to keep my job serving Massachusetts, I had my work cut out for me. It would be a very different 24/7 balance, juggling fund-raising, campaigning, work in Washington and the need to be in Massachusetts every possible moment to translate that work back home.

Politics in Massachusetts is a celebrated tradition. The Kennedy family wrote many of those chapters, but they have good company. It's no coincidence that the state has counted among its leading exports myriad presidential candidates from both parties, Speakers of the House and cabinet secretaries; Massachusetts tests and teaches those who tackle public life.

Among the national myths about Massachusetts is that it's the bluest of blue states, a Democratic mainstay. Many assume that the state that gave America the Kennedys and elected Michael Dukakis must be impenetrably Democratic. But seven of our last ten governors have been Republicans. We were the second state in the nation to live through the property tax revolt—Proposition 2½—and Ronald Reagan carried the state twice.

Enter Governor Bill Weld—central casting for a Bay State Republican chief executive.

William Floyd Weld's family pedigree preceded him. Two buildings at Harvard were named after the Welds. After an audacious race for attorney general in Massachusetts, Bill joined the Reagan administration as a tough-on-crime federal prosecutor rooting out public corruption. Reagan promoted him to a job at the Justice Department, where, coincidentally, our careers, if not our paths, intersected.

While I was a sophomore senator pushing for the United States to sever ties with a corrupt, narcotics-tainted Manuel Noriega in Panama, it was Weld who would ultimately be charged with handling the law enforcement elements of Noriega's prosecution. Weld later joined other senior Justice Department officials in quitting in protest of Attorney General Edwin Meese's financial misdeeds. It was an act of political courage. The glowing headlines earned Weld a hero's return to Massachusetts as a candidate again, this time as an outsider gunning for the governor's office.

The irony about Weld was that for all the blue-chip pedigree, his calling card was a disarming, devil-may-care demeanor. He was quirky in ways the media and the local pols found endearing. It's almost as if there was "William F. Weld, United States Attorney," and his alter ego, aptly nicknamed "Pink Floyd" by one of the local columnists. That other Bill Weld listened to the Grateful Dead, wrote fiction, played poker late into the night and happily copped to smoking weed in college. He had a head of shaggy red hair that almost passed for Irish. He didn't care if a reporter had reason to wonder if he was hungover after a night of, in a famous Weld-ism, "enjoying amber-colored liquids." He gave off an aura of charming flakiness. In 1990, an outsider's year, I was running for reelection and Weld was the Republican nominee for governor. Weld was disciplined and stuck to a script of tax cuts, fiscal responsibility, welfare reform and crime fighting. On election night, voters split their tickets: I won convincingly with almost 55 percent of the vote, while Weld slipped by the Democratic nominee.

Weld and I had an immediate and easy rapport. We were the same generation and both former prosecutors, and we listened to the same music and spoke the same language. Our daughters were even in the same class at college. Shortly after he was elected, I asked Weld to join me in hosting a bipartisan economic summit on the state's fiscal crisis. We put politics aside, dug into the issues, and it helped contribute to the goodwill Bill would enjoy with the Democratic legislature.

But four years later, Bill and I would see our political careers intersect again, only this time I was in his political crosshairs. He was reelected as governor in the Republican wave of 1994 with 71 percent of the vote, even as Massachusetts split its ticket: Ted Kennedy defeated a guy named Mitt Romney that same year by almost 20 points. Bill's landslide victory made him a big national star in the Republican constellation. The Republican takeover of the House and Senate that year put Bill's trademark issues front and center on the congressional agenda, and he started telling people that he wanted to go to Washington and join that Republican Revolution.

We were on a collision course.

From the start, it was going to be the country's most closely watched Senate race. The day Bill announced in November 1995, any semblance of our past cooperation was erased. He said I "couldn't have a worse voting record" and launched into a litany of votes he said demonstrated I "disagree with the people of Massachusetts" on the "most important questions of the day." Just listening, my competitive instincts perked up.

I had been standing up to be counted again and again on issues I knew mattered to Massachusetts, speaking out when it wasn't easy or popular, from the first speech I gave in 1970 at Concord-Carlisle High School in opposition to the Vietnam War. As a senator for eleven years, I'd been a lonely voice standing up for my convictions. I welcomed a debate about who was really in step with the conscience of Massachusetts.

But it was guaranteed to be a slog, and Weld had a daily home-field advantage. He was in Massachusetts every day, whereas I had to spend most of my time during the week in D.C., held hostage to a voting schedule I couldn't control and to committee hearings and legislative mark-ups where important work was happening, but in ways that couldn't always connect to voters. I had to remind myself that the language of the Senate—"legislate-ese"—holds little meaning to the people who send us there. Campaigns are by definition an effort to translate issues into people's lives.

That's part of why running against a governor is a steep climb for a legislator. He could sign legislation in the morning in front of the television cameras, give a speech or hold a fund-raiser at lunch, and meet with mayors and local elected officials in the afternoon in time for ample coverage on the 6:00 p.m. newscast. I might be slugging it out in a legislative markup on the Commerce Committee, offering amendments to bring home federal dollars for the cleanup of our polluted waterways, while, in front of the television cameras, Weld jumped into the Charles River to demonstrate that the water was now clean. You can guess which narrative the media ate up.

But my competitive instincts took over. After the last vote on a weekday, I'd race to catch the last US Airways shuttle to Logan Airport, sometimes arriving with moments to spare to drop by a union hall or walk into the Channel 5 newsroom and speak about the work I was doing in Washington and why it mattered. Then, first thing the next morning, I'd try to swing by a workplace, a jobs site, a community center or a school, before racing again for the shuttle back to Washington. After a time, the National Republican Senatorial Committee caught on to the midweek sprint between Boston and Washington, and the pressure grew on Majority Leader Trent Lott to schedule more frequent "bed-check votes" to make it harder for Democrats in competitive races to shuttle between D.C. and their home state.

In unexpected ways, running against a governor like Bill Weld turned out to be a gift. It helped me relearn some of the lessons of politics that I'd taken for granted, lessons that didn't come as naturally to me as they did to those who worked long apprenticeships in local politics before being elected to the Senate.

Before 1996, I thought the work spoke for itself. It was an activist's instinct; all that mattered was the issue. For too many years, I would win on an amendment, succeed in securing an appropriation, and the staff would send out a press release. I assumed people knew what I was doing for them.

But a bitter lesson retaught me a corollary to Tip O'Neill's old adage that "all politics is local." In Massachusetts, all politics is personal.

Bill Weld had a gift for the personal. He might cut the revenue going to cities and towns, but he knew to drop by the state senator's birthday party, to show up at the Elks Lodge for the mayor's campaign kickoff. I'd spent years racing for that first flight home on a Friday to be there, as a single dad, for Vanessa's and Alex's soccer games and plays at school. My years of being a policy shark—get it done, move on to the next challenge—caught up with me when Democratic mayors from Quincy and North Adams endorsed Weld. Why? Because they could see him, he was present. It was a reminder that ten-point plans and legislation get you only so far; if people can't feel a connection to that politician on the other end of the line, all the work in the world can too easily be forgotten. I would never again underestimate the value of personal relationships.

But not everything in the campaign was a lesson learned the hard way; in fact, a certain set of personal relationships came roaring back to remind me of the blessings of a life fought in the activist trenches. Friends started showing up by the dozens to stand with me: friends from college, from the environmental movement, from anti-war days and from the Navy.

Chris Greeley had been with me since he drove me around the state on the 1982 campaign for lieutenant governor, and he could talk hockey and politics for hours. Chris was street-smart and funny. As he had been in 1972 and all the races before, John Marttila was back and I could always turn to him for candor. There was Ray Dooley, a Pied Piper political operative and chain-smoking ball of determination who approached campaigns like a field marshal. He dropped everything and came to my defense.

Ron Rosenblith was by my side, reminding me in the shorthand we shared from so many campaigns together just exactly what the fight was about: "It's not just policy. People want someone who will stand up and fight for what makes a difference to them. It's the stand-up guy test. That's you." Ron was the ultimate stand-up guy himself, the same guy with the same moral compass I'd known since long before anyone would have thought I'd make it to the Senate.

Tommy Vallely, the Newton-born, straight-talking Marine who had spent hours driving in the car with me in 1972, showed up again—Infantryman Thomas J. Vallely. He had been a state representative before leaving politics to start the Vietnam Program at Harvard, where he would contribute enormously to the effort to change the relationship between our countries and really make peace. But Tom was putting all that on hold for this campaign, because Marines are forever loyal.

Ted Kennedy also sent reinforcements. He had been friends with Bob Shrum since he served as his press secretary in the Senate. Ted revered Bob as a writer and debater. The former collegiate debate star from Georgetown joined the team.

This team had an ability to distill politics down to big choices. They helped me suspend some senatorial habits. In the Senate, you succeed by mastering detail. Watch a good debate on the floor of the Senate, and you'll see seasoned legislators discussing the minutiae of an issue. It's how you get things done in an institution that can only function with consensus: you exhaust the ability of the other side to ask questions. I'd been a legislator for more than a decade. I was more removed from my prosecutorial days than Weld, whose rapid-fire, staccato attacks left you fighting for time to respond point by point. I was reminded that voters needed a reason to understand why I would be the better senator for them than Bill Weld. Rather than a pinprick at the capillary, we had to go for the jugular.

We decided to make this a race about what a senator would do for Massachusetts. At the height of the Republican Revolution, I'd be fighting with Ted Kennedy to raise the minimum wage, while Bill Weld, who had once called Newt Gingrich his "ideological soul mate," would be fighting against Ted. The story was the same on student loans for middle-class kids to go to college, Medicare for senior citizens and the environmental fights that defined me. Weld was a genuine environmentalist in Massachusetts, but the reality was his first vote as senator would be to elect a majority leader who was gutting the Clean Water Act and the Clean Air Act.

Late one morning, I spotted a ten-year-old reporter for a school newspaper eagerly waiting for me as I was leaving a campaign event to race for my flight. I stopped and bent down to say hello.

"Why should my parents vote for you and not Mr. Weld?" he asked earnestly, a tiny spiral notebook and pencil at the ready to record my answer. I told him, "Well, I'm fighting in Washington to pay for schools, and Bill Weld's cutting schools in Massachusetts, and I'm fighting to raise the minimum wage so when you are in high school, you can make more money to save for college. My opponent is against those things. And I'm fighting for student loans so you won't come out of college with too much debt. And that's what this is about."

I was locked in the conversation with the kid, as if it were just the two of us. I didn't notice the swarm of cameras that had gathered around us. You didn't have to be Robert Byrd to understand what a senator's job was; you just had to remind yourself that the common denominator is people. Weld and I had our similarities and our differences, but at the end of the day, we had completely different philosophies about how you fight for a kid like the one who asked me the bedrock question. I'd found my footing.

It's a funny thing in politics. When you get that rush of adrenaline, when it makes sense, you see straight ahead. The next event, the next fight, the next moment—there's a clarity.

The clarity had arrived just in time. Billy Bulger's St. Patrick's Day Breakfast in South Boston is the Madison Square Garden of Massachusetts political theater, and Bill Weld and I had a date there on March 14, 1996. The breakfast in its heyday was less of a roast and more of a bonfire upon which plenty of political carcasses were thrown over the years. Florian Hall in Dorchester was the location, a command performance if you're on the ballot—and especially if you don't want to be on the menu.

Weld had an advantage. As a Republican making the pilgrimage to Dorchester among the Democrats, he got points just for showing up. For me, the bar would be set higher.

Politics in Boston is not for the faint of heart. I have had colleagues from many states where politics isn't part of the culture; instead, their campaigns are mostly television ads and a few weeks of politicking after Labor Day.

Not so in Massachusetts.

No ritual was more iconic than Billy Bulger's St. Patrick's Day Breakfast at its peak. Bulger defined the breakfast's place in political folklore. Bulger was fascinating. He was a self-made scholar—a "Triple Eagle" graduate of Boston College High, Boston College and Boston College Law School. He'd grown up in South Boston during the Depression and ruled as state senate president for nearly twenty years, a record which will never be broken.

Bulger's wit was a powerful weapon. He could cut you to pieces with a one-liner, and he had a gift for limericks crafted for the occasion. Many of his best lines still left a mark.

"John F. Kerry. JFK. It stands for 'Just. For. Kerry.' "

"The junior senator arrived late. But it wasn't his fault. He got stuck on his way—in front of a mirror."

"John Kerry was campaigning in the other part of his district—the Philippines."

The crowd ate it up. Ridicule could be a great tool in American politics, and nowhere was it more skillfully deployed than in Florian Hall.

But it was an unusual event, quirky and tribal. There's a great scene in *The Departed* where Frank Costello's enforcer announces, "I'm the guy who tells you there are guys you can hit, and there's guys you can't hit." It was that way at the Bulger Breakfast too. There were unwritten rules: there were things you could joke about and things that were off-limits.

Billy Bulger's brother was one of the taboo subjects. James "Whitey" Bulger was the unrecognized elephant in the room of Billy's life and political career. Whitey Bulger had done time in Alcatraz, come home to Southie and picked up where he had left off. He and his crew terrorized Boston. I had prosecuted members of the Winter Hill Gang and put Whitey's cohort, Howie Winter, behind bars. In 1994, after he got a tip that he was about to be arrested, Whitey fled Boston. He would be on the lam for sixteen years.

There would be no jokes about South Boston's most wanted fugitive as long as Billy ran the breakfast.

But in a business of big personalities and often even bigger egos, you could win over Billy's crowd if you were willing to laugh the hardest at one person above all: yourself.

This time, however, I needed a partner.

The glare of the Senate campaign had been tough on Teresa, in part because it was so different from the kind of politics she'd known in Pittsburgh. In Pennsylvania, the Heinz name was synonymous with philanthropy and service. During Jack Heinz's first reelection, when a broken leg kept him off the campaign trail, Teresa filled in for him and found people thoughtful and engaging. She was revered in Pittsburgh. In her life, she'd never experienced skeptical, let alone critical, press.

Not so in Boston, where gossip columns fixated on everything—her wealth, her accent, her last name, her partisan affiliation, our courtship.

I had a thick skin when it came to the little potshots. After all, I was the one who had chosen a life in politics. But I hated seeing Teresa receive the digs from the tabloids just because she had fallen in love with a senator from Massachusetts.

Some of it was astonishing. Boston was a city built by immigrants, yet the tabloids loved to poke fun at Teresa's Portuguese accent. It was a state where women's rights had long been championed, and yet the gossip columns obsessed over Teresa's decision not to change her last name, the name that she had used for a quarter century since she was twenty-eight, the last name of her three sons. Wealthy lineages from Lodges to Kennedys were accepted without dwelling on their bank accounts, but somehow there was never a column that didn't conspicuously describe Teresa as a "ketchup heiress" instead of portraying a person, let alone a warm, nurturing wife and mother. She could walk into a Portuguese bakery in Taunton and greet the cook behind the counter in their mutual language or talk fluently in wonkish detail with environmentalists and health care advocates, but somehow that never seemed to be the story.

A bruising Senate race is no way to introduce someone to a new state, let alone a marriage.

I was reminded that in campaigns, small things become big things. Teresa and I had moved to our new neighborhood on Beacon Hill and realized that with the occasional news trucks parked out front, we would soon be driving our neighbors crazy on a parking-deprived cobbled street. A fire hydrant smack in front of our house blocked a logical parking spot, so we decided to go through the city process to relocate the hydrant several feet away to the corner. Given the choice between annoying the neighbors and enduring the bureaucratic process, we opted for the latter. But someone immediately called the tabloids. It became a front-page story and a round of television coverage followed, with live shots filmed right in front of the house. So much for preserving peace in the neighborhood.

The St. Patrick's Day breakfast was our chance to turn the tables.

When my turn came to speak, I wasn't alone. Out from behind the curtain came Teresa—a surprise guest walking into Billy Bulger's lion's den. Under her arm, Teresa carried a big plastic fire hydrant.

The crowd was laughing and clapping in spite of themselves.

When the laughter died down, I turned to Teresa and, in our best George Burns and Gracie Allen imitation, I asked her whether she was happy to be living in Massachusetts.

"Oh yes, I love Massachusetts," she deadpanned to the audience. "How much is it?"

The crowd exploded in laughter.

That was the morning Teresa won over the doubters. A laugh can go a long, long way.

But I still had miles to go in the Senate race.

Both Bill Weld and I had reasons to be worried about the potential impact of money in the race. Our race would be one of the most watched in the nation, with every expectation that it would be decided in the closing weeks. That would make it a magnet for donors and outside interest group spending. I was concerned that outside Republican groups might perceive a rare opportunity to defeat an incumbent Democrat in Massachusetts. Bill Weld, on the other hand, worried my campaign would spend Teresa's money.

Weld and I were both independent-minded enough to wonder whether there might be a way to protect our interests and ensure that, even in a contentious, high-profile race, money didn't win. We could keep circling each other warily—Bill challenging me to keep the Heinz family money off-limits, me challenging Bill to eschew third-party advertising. Could we do something really radical and reason together?

That's exactly what we did. I don't remember who called whom first, but soon we started to talk, and after a few conversations, I invited him to our home in Beacon Hill. Together, in my living room, we hammered out a deal on campaign spending. We agreed to cap our total spending at $6.9 million each, with no more than $5 million going toward TV and newspaper ad buys. Importantly, we both agreed to refrain from using third-party money. We asked the press not to carry campaign ads on our behalf from outside groups. If, notwithstanding our request, an independent organization put out a negative ad, we pledged that the candidate whom the ad supported would deduct the cost of that ad from our agreed-upon budget; this served as incentive for us to do all we could to prevent outside parties from jumping into the fight.

It was the first time in modern political history that two candidates for statewide office voluntarily came to such an arrangement—and, for the most part, it worked. Sure, we traded combative press releases at various points and fought over the fine print. But at the end of the day, it made our race different.

Of course, our agreement didn't cover the quality or content of the advertising. We reached the spending agreement in early August. Bill started bulking up his TV ad buys shortly thereafter, filling the airwaves with blistering attacks on me. I remember that they always seemed to picture me with a five o'clock shadow, a little seedy. By mid-August, Bill was ahead in a public poll for the first time.

Nowhere else in the country that year was there a Senate race pitting two well-known, popular and politically capable candidates against each other—candidates with similar strengths and unusual backgrounds.

Both of our campaigns believed we had an interest in getting in front of as many statewide audiences as possible and slugging it out. It was a contrast to many campaigns today, where candidates let the ads speak for them.

Not us.

I needed to puncture the bubble of personality around Bill that insulated him from the baggage of Newt Gingrich and the Republican Party nationally.

Weld clearly believed that he could corner me—relentlessly—on issues like the death penalty, welfare reform and taxes. He thought that if he did that, then his likability would give voters license to continue to forget that he was a Republican.

The battlefield we agreed upon would be unlike any in the thirty-four Senate races held that year. We shook hands on a series of eight statewide televised Lincoln-Douglas-style debates, where the moderators would actually encourage us to engage each other directly.

I tried to carve out time to prepare for the debates, but it was a daily struggle between campaigning around the state, working in Washington and traveling to fund-raise. Debate prep became a series of phone calls, falling asleep with a briefing book on my chest. Bob Shrum and I found we often got the most done away from the noise, including one memorable Sunday boat ride, after I'd put in a full morning of campaigning on the Cape.

But in the end, no matter how you prepare, when the bell rings, it's two competitors facing off, and you have to trust your head and your heart to execute.

Debates rise and fall on big moments. But it's the unexpected ones that can make the difference. For a debate's moderator, it is a chance to put him- or herself at the center of the story.

A debate question from left field caught both Weld and me by surprise. It wasn't about a political issue at all. It struck at the heart of the kind of question someone watching at home must have thought plenty of times: How can these two guys relate to me? The moderator summarized our uncannily similar résumés—the boarding schools, the Ivy League educations, law school, prosecutors, elected office—and added a twist: So what would you say was your greatest failure?

Bill chose to answer with a joke and then bounced around through a series of bills the state house refused to pass.

I saw Alexandra and Vanessa sitting right in the front row, next to Teresa. I was proud of who they were growing up to be, Vanessa with her fascination with science and medicine, Alex always gravitating toward the arts and drama. I felt lucky that they were smart, determined, good people. Both Julia and I had worked very hard to give them the kind of childhood we had both missed in different ways. Julia wanted to raise strong, independent women with lives of their own, a contrast to the expectation of her parents' generation that young women's identity would be found solely in marriage and their husbands. Mission accomplished—both of our girls had dreams and destinies of their own. I wanted them to feel rooted, with the security that comes from knowing where home is and growing up with a set of friends from elementary school through high school. I had been determined to be a connected dad, without the formality or distance I'd sometimes struggled with in my childhood relationship with Pa. When my daughters and I were together, we made the most of our time. We crammed a lot in. I had a closeness and a candor with them that my parents could never have imagined.

But I couldn't help but feel a twinge of guilt about the way they'd grown up, shuttling between homes, a dad back from Washington on the weekends, a mom who ultimately found peace in the West, away from the politics of Boston. It was a long distance from the life either of us had imagined when we held them as babies in our arms those first times in 1973 and 1976.

Even after our divorce, Julia and I always made parenting the priority. Still, I hated that in any divorce, the kids pay the real price for the failings of the adults.

That thought brought me full circle to the moderator's question. I spoke from the heart. I said that I had a marriage that failed, and it was as personal a setback as I'd ever known—harder to lose a relationship than to lose any campaign. I said it was hard because the children paid the price, and that Julia and I worried about making sure they always knew that both their parents loved them and that, despite the breakup of the marriage, Mom and Dad were always going to be there.

After the words escaped my mouth, I hoped for a minute that it didn't sound as if I was on *Oprah*. But suddenly the slow-building crescendo of applause took over. Something had struck a nerve. On the car ride back home after the debate, Teresa summed it up: "Honesty. It's real, people can touch it. They know when it's not there too." She was right. I'd come to the debate to contrast my positions with Bill, but ended up revealing something that's not contained in briefing books.

But the race wasn't just a clash of personalities. Issues were at the heart of our eight debates. The differences that emerged scraped away the veneer of surface similarities between us, exposing different beliefs about issues and values.

The tension was high at Faneuil Hall as we faced off in front of a packed house. Despite the moderator's insistence that our supporters and cheering sections should hold their applause, the give-and-take elicited competing cheers and groans.

Bill Weld scripted a dramatic moment designed to catch me flat-footed and separate me from the voters I relied on to get reelected.

The death penalty was a definitive wedge issue. It was probably 80 percent for, 20 percent against at that time. Weld had hammered at it over and over again. It was pure bread and butter for him.

My convictions on the death penalty run deep, going back to George Reissfelder and connecting to my faith and a plain old sense of right and wrong. I'd also studied the issue from a public policy standpoint. It wasn't a deterrent to crime. The death penalty was even one of the reasons the United States had a difficult time winning the extradition of criminals and killers to the United States from other countries.

But Weld knew the issue was emotionally powerful. His team believed they had a winning issue and a debate ambush from a familiar playbook.

Any Democrat who watched the 1988 presidential debate between Vice President George Bush and Governor Michael Dukakis knew we would lose in November. It was the iconic moment when CNN's Bernard Shaw asked Dukakis, a death penalty opponent, whether he would still oppose the death penalty if his wife, Kitty, were raped and murdered. Mike Dukakis is one of the most decent men I've ever known. He loves Kitty with every fiber of his being. After fifty-five years of marriage, Michael still calls Kitty "my bride." Together, they waged her battles with depression and addiction, and through it all they loved each other more and more. You'd think Mike would have reacted passionately to Shaw's question. Instead, he gave an intellectual, policy response, a cold answer on an emotionally hot issue. I have no doubt the Weld folks thought I'd do the same when they hatched a scheme to hold my position on capital punishment up to the light of public passion.

The moment unfolded in an instant. Weld banged away on my votes against expanding the federal death penalty. Then he gestured toward a woman in the audience. Her son was a police officer killed in the line of duty. Bill said I had to defend my position not to him or to the voters, but to her. "Tell her why the life of the man who murdered her son is worth more than the life of a police officer," he said.

I swallowed hard. I looked at her. Weld's debating ploy was obvious, but the mother's pain was real. She had suffered. I thought of Alex and Vanessa. I flashed on the phone calls I'd made to the families of fallen police officers and firefighters killed in the line of duty, the pain I'd heard in so many voices, the children left behind, the funerals I'd gone to, the wail of bagpipes.

Then I answered the only way I knew how. It wasn't something I'd learned at Yale in hours of debate competition or on the Senate floor. Bill Weld was just a few feet away from me, but for a moment it was just me, alone with a mother who had lost her child violently, inexplicably. Her longing for retribution was justified. The room was silent. Her son's killer's life wasn't worth more, it wasn't worth anything, I said to her. The killer was scum who should be sent to prison for the rest of his life. But I wasn't going to lie to her, and I wasn't going to duck the issue at hand. Weld was right about one thing: she deserved an honest answer. I continued: "The fact is, yes, I've been opposed to the death penalty. I know something about killing. I don't like killing. I don't think a state honors life by turning around and sanctioning killing."

I hadn't planned it that way. None of the academic studies I'd seen on the futility of the death penalty as deterrent was remotely relevant to the pain of a deceased police officer's mother. All I could tell her was what I felt deeply: I'd seen killing up close in ways that I could never forget, and nothing in that searing experience told me that's who we wanted to become as a society.

Weld wouldn't repeat a question like that one again. He'd opened up my voting record to scrutiny, but in so doing, he'd also forced me to open up a part of myself that I didn't share lightly or easily.

My experience in war wound up playing a more significant role in the campaign than I ever would have imagined, and this time I don't think it was Weld's doing, but the strange and unexpected intervention of one unlikely columnist at the paper of record in Massachusetts, the *Boston Globe*.

Nine days out from Election Day, a column appeared in the *Globe* by a business columnist, David Warsh, speculating whether, rather than having been properly awarded the Silver Star in 1969, I was actually a war criminal who had shot and killed a defenseless, wounded Viet Cong out of view of everyone else who had been ambushed that day.

I remember picking up my morning stack of newspapers off the front stoop and bringing them up to my kitchen table, where I'd take notes on a long legal pad, make phone calls and get ready for the day. I made it through the *Globe* and was preparing to push myself through the daily ritual of reading the conservative tabloid *Boston Herald*, to learn the Weld campaign's version of the day. Then the phone rang.

"Senator, have you seen the *Globe*?" It was Michael Meehan, my communications director. Michael had been with me since he was a college intern, a big Irish guy with an even bigger handshake and a love of hockey that rivaled my own.

"Yeah, I read the *Globe*, Mikey," I said.

There was a long pause on the speakerphone.

"The Warsh column is a problem," he said.

Warsh? I'd read the columnists. Tom Oliphant had a good piece on the campaign. I opened the op-ed page again. Nothing by Warsh.

"In the business section," said Michael.

I flipped through the newspaper. I wondered how a finance and business columnist buried in the back section of the newspaper could be creating a problem for us. Michael must have been overreacting, but something in his tone sounded uneasy.

I found the column, and my blood pressure began to rise.

Warsh had taken out of context some comments by the forward gunner on PCF-94 who had been closest to me in the decades after Vietnam, Tommy Belodeau of Chelmsford. Tommy mentioned that he had shot the Viet Cong guerrilla who had ambushed us before I had pursued the man behind a hootch and killed him.

To this day, I'm not sure whether Warsh, who had covered the war after graduating from Harvard, was trying to start a political fight or whether he just wanted to speculate on the fog of war.

I knew his reputation was that of a conservative at the *Globe* and that he had graduated in Bill Weld's class at Harvard. But the accusation he printed wasn't something I could swallow regardless of background or credential: he speculated, in print, whether, out of sight of my crewmates, I'd actually committed a war crime, a coup de grâce. He dared to ask whether I had shot in the back a defenseless, mortally wounded Viet Cong, not a dangerous soldier with a live B-40 rocket launcher who was running to regroup and could have killed us all with one pull of the trigger.

"What happened behind the hootch?" Warsh asked his readers.

I was apoplectic. Tommy Belodeau was beside himself. Tommy had been there for me through it all. He was a proud, quiet, loyal friend who had worked hard to put the war behind him. Tommy was shy, particularly about his days in Vietnam. He couldn't believe that one of the few times he'd ever talked to a reporter had resulted in his words being turned into a political weapon.

"I'm starting to get a lot of calls about this," said Michael Meehan.

It was stunning that at the eleventh hour of the campaign, an event from twenty-seven years ago was being distorted so casually, a bolt from the blue.

I was confused. *Globe* staffers had spent hours upon hours writing carefully researched profiles of me and Weld. They'd asked us for military records, which we had provided in a responsive way, and yet a business columnist who wasn't covering the campaign was suddenly allowed to speculate in print that I might be a war criminal. It was beyond irresponsible, let alone inflammatory.

I didn't care about the campaign schedule—I wanted a press conference scheduled right away to respond to this smear, and I was calling in reinforcements. Tommy Vallely understood that this was a character test. I called Admiral Elmo Zumwalt and faxed him the column from the newspaper. He was outraged.

Admiral Zumwalt was loyal to the men who served under him, but he was also loyal to a bigger institution: He believed in the Navy. He believed that the Navy's decisions had to mean something and had to transcend politics or party labels. He believed that all those who served deserved to have the truth known about their service.

Zumwalt was bringing the firepower of his chain of command to Massachusetts.

The very next day, there we all were, assembled together at the Charleston Navy Yard, the place where USS *Constitution* stands as a reminder of our country's naval origins. Zumwalt brought with him Captain George Elliott, my commanding officer, and Commander Adrian Lonsdale (ret.), who had overseen shoreline operations.

Tommy Belodeau spoke, and my crewmates from PCF-94, from around the country, joined in person or by telephone. Their testimony was unimpeachable. Tommy Belodeau said it best: "This man was not lying on the ground. He was more than capable of destroying that boat and everybody on it." Captain Elliott took to the microphone and defended my taking the initiative in combat. He understood what it meant. He said, "The fact that he chased armed enemies down is not something to be looked down upon." His words brought back those life-or-death, flee-or-fight instinctual decisions that you can understand only if you've been there. Admiral Zumwalt could not have been clearer: "It is a disgrace to the United States Navy that there's any inference that the process was anything other than totally honest." He even surprised all of us when he announced that day that he had wanted to award me the Navy Cross for my actions but awarded me the Silver Star because it could happen on a more expedited basis.

I felt vindicated. Truth can be the first casualty of political campaigns. Truth carried the day, and it was the men I'd served under and those I'd served beside who made it clear that facts were facts, twenty-seven years before and in 1996. If only politics had never gotten in the way. If only Admiral Zumwalt had lived to be there in 2004.

Within a week, Warsh expressed regret for the language he used.

I was angry that the column had found its way into the *Globe*. For the time being, however, the vile lies were effectively debunked.

A week and one final, rip-roaring debate later, Election Day finally arrived. The results were clear by nine o'clock that night: I won reelection by 8 percentage points.

It had been a long slog. Weld was an uncommonly talented politician. In the process, I'd learned a lot about myself as a public person.

I'd been reminded that politics is personal and that I had to fight to connect my work to the people I worked for, but that when I did, politics is still the process by which average people get to have their say.

But I also learned that my own compass was pretty damn good. Bill Weld was as smart as they come. I was happy though that when I'd been tested in the campaign on a human level, I'd done just fine. In Massachusetts, even in the company of legends like Ted Kennedy and Billy Bulger, I had my own brand of politics, and I was comfortable in my own skin.

On election night, after my victory speech, I invited the men I had served with in Vietnam over to my house. We stayed up till 3:00 a.m., reliving various moments from our time together in the brown-water Navy and the decades since. There was laughter, and some misty-eyed moments remembering Don Droz and those others who hadn't made it home.

Some of my crew had met with struggle after they'd come home. Drugs, alcohol, a hard time finding a job, wives or girlfriends who couldn't relate to what the men had seen in Vietnam. Every line in their faces had been earned the hard way. Others had just gone quietly home to the field or the factory and started life over, lucky to be alive. I'd had my own journey. But how incredible, what a rare moment, that politics—which had long divided America—brought us all back together twenty-seven years later. I was so lucky to have the chance to say to each of them, "Thank you." Thank God we'd kept each other alive when it could have gone the other way.

The campaign focused my mind in a way I hadn't felt in months, if not years.

In the morning, when I woke up, Michael Meehan brought me the *New York Times* and some of the other stories from around the country. The coverage made clear that between me and Bill Weld, whoever won was having his ticket punched for a national stage in 2000. "I don't want to hear it," I said. "Today we're driving to Worcester and Springfield to thank the people who just reelected me."

A few nights later, Bill Weld and I met for a beer at McGann's in the North End to mark the end of a tough, hard-fought election.

As I raised a glass in my opponent's honor, I remembered how, when it became clear that he would challenge me that year, so much was made of our similar backgrounds: the prep schools, the Ivy League degrees, the experience we had as former prosecutors. The campaign had brought out our differences, but in the best way. It was never personal between us. I owed him. Having a competitor like Weld taught me as much about politics as anyone ever had.

We hugged, and off we went into the night, home again.

Months later, with some wise advocacy from the First Lady of the United States (she and Weld had worked together under the House Judiciary Committee during the Watergate scandal) and with some quiet assurances from me and Teddy, President Clinton appointed Weld as ambassador to Mexico. His own party in the Senate derailed his nomination and sent such a promising career into an unpredictable direction. Weld had resigned as governor to fight for his nomination, then left Massachusetts for New York and tried to run for governor there. It was a strange twist for a career that had held such promise and for such a colorful, capable character the likes of which I haven't seen since. For me, I had promises to keep and work to do in the Senate—and soon the politics there as well would pass through the looking glass into a strange world.

THE YEARS FOLLOWING my reelection to the Senate in 1996 were filled with stark reminders of the breakdown of American politics. No sector of public life seemed spared.

I had returned to the Senate from the '96 campaign energized. The race against Weld forced me to concentrate on many things. I synthesized my thinking. I minimized my legislative-ese. I was more focused on the fight. I came back determined to apply the important lessons of the campaign trail to my work in the Senate.

During the campaign, I spent a lot of time in the state with mayors and kids in youth centers and schools. I also spent a lot of time with graduates of YouthBuild. These visits reminded me of the spectacular job so many local programs were doing to give at-risk children the opportunity for a life of hope. Some were run by churches, others by public-private partnerships. The mayors depended on them. They were desperate for support to replicate the successes and meet the demand.

Teresa had long been a primary mover behind early child interventions like these across Allegheny County and Pittsburgh. We talked often about the incredible promise she was seeing in those efforts. We traded newspaper articles, and Teresa in particular, ever the daughter of a doctor with an interest in science and medicine, got me hooked on learning more about the science of brain development. It was jarring to read study after study that documented the difference in brain development when babies and small children are read to and nurtured versus the consequences of never having those things in their lives. The disadvantages of neglect were staggering and depressing. I didn't care whether the answers were labeled liberal or conservative, I just wanted to know that we were reaching more kids with greater impact before we lost a generation to neglect.

An idea began to crystallize in my mind: Why not, without creating any new federal bureaucracy, use some federal dollars for grants to local organizations with proven track records? I could envision a grand bargain where

Democrats got the money needed to bolster early childhood efforts, as well as after-school initiatives, but Republicans won their cherished local control, and money could flow to institutions both sides trusted to get the job done.

Everyone could find something to buy into: money could flow to secular groups like YouthBuild or to local churches, which often provided schooling and childcare, to open their doors earlier and stay open later. In many cases faith-based groups were the most effective deliverers of services. Those services had nothing to do with proselytizing. They had everything to do with humanitarian initiatives. We needed to harness that energy for our kids and our country.

I started working with my Republican colleague Kit Bond from Missouri on legislation. The Senate, I thought, was created for partnerships that break the partisan mold. A Democrat and a Republican working together for children seemed like something that could find its way into law.

But soon I had the feeling Kit and I were in the right place at exactly the wrong time. Democrats were still in the minority, and the center of gravity for policy was still the Clinton White House. I thought that perhaps after the partisanship of the last years, perhaps there would be a new window to get the country's business done again. But from the minute Clinton was elected president, the Republicans wanted to delegitimize his presidency. They spent most of his first term doing so. Now that Clinton was the first Democrat reelected to the presidency since Franklin Roosevelt, I hoped the witch hunts and obstruction might give way to regular order and collaboration.

But that wasn't meant to be. It was the last Congress for people like John Glenn, who embodied a Greatest Generation spirit of possibility. I was troubled that, by and large, when big people left, smaller figures seemed to replace them. Senator Howell Heflin retired and was replaced by Senator Jeff Sessions, a hard-edge Republican with a chip on his shoulder because in the 1980s he'd been denied a judgeship over his civil rights record. Sessions didn't work with Democrats.

David Boren of Oklahoma—thoughtful, centrist, an expert on national security—retired and was replaced by Jim Inhofe, a climate-change denier.

One of my mentors, Fritz Hollings of South Carolina, had privately decided that if he were reelected in 1998, this would be his last term as well. Wendell Ford of Kentucky was retiring.

We were losing people willing to use the rules of the Senate to deliberate and legislate and replacing them with people who wanted to posture and pontificate. The Senate was starting to feel more and more like the House: a daily shouting match, theater. Not collaboration. Certainly not the "world's greatest deliberative body."

Bipartisan partnerships were still forged—besides working with Kit Bond, I was also working across the aisle on education reform with a new Republican senator, Gordon Smith of Oregon—but the institution didn't respond the way it once had.

Instead, loud, coarse rhetoric, conducted in the style of cable news, became the dominant new presence in Washington. But the worst was still to come—much worse.

January 17, 1998.

I was at home in Boston working on a speech to be delivered in a Roxbury church on Martin Luther King Day. I planned to talk about children and education as the new battle in the civil rights movement. The phone rang. It was my communications director, Jim Jones.

"You need to know because you might be asked by reporters: the *Drudge Report* says that Ken Starr's investigating Clinton having an affair with an intern."

"The *Drudge Report*? What the hell is that?"

"It's this guy who posts stuff, news articles and gossip."

If I sounded puzzled, it's because I was. "He's a reporter?" I asked.

"Not exactly. No. He's just a guy who posts stuff on the internet."

How did "a guy" with his own website know what Ken Starr was or wasn't investigating before Congress knew?

I turned on CNN. The speculation was everywhere. Television reporters seemed to be trying just as hopelessly as my aide to explain what the *Drudge Report* was and what this alleged scoop meant.

I wasn't a stranger to the tabloidization of public life. In the Senate over my first twelve years, I'd seen a change in the media. Foreign bureaus were shut down first because of costs, then the number of news bureaus in Washington started to shrink. Cable news was transforming news cycles from daily to hourly, changing the definition of deadlines for reporters and creating a rush to be first to report a story. Then cable news entities started to fill the day with opinion programming, televised partisan bickering, beginning with CNN's *Crossfire*, a far cry from the long-debate format I'd first encountered jousting with William F. Buckley on *Firing Line* in 1970. It created a swirl of noise where news and opinion bled into each other.

Now the internet was the new catalyst added into that volatile crucible. Bottom line: whoever Matt Drudge was, and wherever he had come from, after January 17, 1998, he would never again be just "some guy on the internet."

We were about to enter a bizarre period in American political life.

All my instincts about politics and prosecutors told me we were headed toward a very dangerous place. Sure, it sounded like a cheap paperback thriller: the president of the United States, an intern, a new phase of Special Prosecutor Ken Starr's ongoing investigation. But as surreal as it sounded, unless it was a complete fabrication, as a former prosecutor, I knew that Starr wouldn't be going down that road if he didn't have some credible evidence of an affair, evidence he believed would give him leverage in his investigation.

While it struck many as a strange Republican fixation, Starr's investigation was deeply entwined with the overall delegitimization strategy.

It began in the spring of 1994, almost four years before the *Drudge Report* popped its salacious headline. Initially it was a simple investigation into an Arkansas land deal known as Whitewater, dating back to 1979. At the Clintons' request, after the First Lady held a news conference stating they had nothing to hide about Whitewater, Attorney General Janet Reno appointed a special prosecutor to investigate. Months after that, his work was curtailed after the independent counsel law allowed the appointment of a new special prosecutor, one who hadn't been appointed by Clinton's attorney general. A three-judge panel chose Judge Kenneth Starr to play that role, and he had been investigating, and investigating, and investigating since the summer of 1994.

Now, closing in on the four-year anniversary of the Starr investigation, Washington was igniting in scandal.

I was relieved when, nine days later, President Clinton angrily looked into a bevy of television cameras and denied the allegations emphatically. The words are now indelible in everyone's memory: "I did not have sexual relations with that woman, Miss Lewinsky."

Less remembered is how the president concluded his statement: he said he had to "go back to work for the American people."

But that wasn't going to be easy. There was already a feeding frenzy at our end of Pennsylvania Avenue.

Reporters were chasing all of us about one topic and one topic only. Inside the caucus meeting, the overwhelming sentiment was clear: there was near unanimity that the Starr investigation had gone on for almost four years without any finding of any wrongdoing and it was becoming abusive. But there was equally powerful concern that the president had better be telling the truth regarding the intern.

I looked around our caucus. I saw the faces of the frustrated: colleagues who knew well that the Republicans had been out to bring down the president from day one, but colleagues who also knew that whatever the cause, it wasn't fulfilling to be trapped in hyperpartisanship. No one had come to Washington for this.

There's always a tension between a president and his colleagues down the road in Congress, even those of the same party.

I'd had a good, constructive relationship with the Clinton White House. I didn't know the president that well on a personal level. I wasn't among his friends from home who would join him at the White House to swap Arkansas stories. But I liked him. When he vacationed on Martha's Vineyard, he and his family came over to Naushon for a day of quiet. The president and I enjoyed a long horseback ride, just the two of us, with a lone Secret Service agent trailing two hundred yards behind us. It was a rare moment of genuine privacy. The president had a great gift for storytelling and a unique instinct and talent for communication. When President Clinton and the First Lady campaigned for me in 1996, it made a difference. I was lucky to have their help.

But I also understood the frustration of my colleagues. Ted Kennedy felt health care reform had been botched badly, and he lamented that the White House had insisted on its own approach, instead of joining with Bob Dole in 1993 on something that would have actually looked much more like Obamacare.

But it wasn't just Teddy who had been frustrated. Many of us who were of the president's generation had been burned when, in the first term, he listened to the insiders and "old bulls" and punted on tackling serious campaign finance reform. Joe Biden, Bill Bradley and I had been leaders in the campaign finance reform efforts in the Senate. We had crafted a thoughtful approach based on a combination of public and private contributions with limitations that would have greatly reduced the power of money to set the agenda in American politics. The three of us requested and received a private meeting with the president in the Oval Office. Each of us made the strongest pitch we could to him. He listened intently. We told the president that he could restore and reinvigorate our democracy by safeguarding the ability of average folks to be heard. If the grassroots had more ability to set the agenda in Washington, we would all do better.

We also expressed our view that the stranglehold of money would stand in his way of achieving health care reform as well as other parts of his reform agenda. The president expressed his appreciation and support for our efforts. He said he would give it thought. We left there encouraged, believing we had a real shot to win.

In the following days the president was importuned by powerful chairmen in the House as well as some senators and some members of the leadership for whom the current system of fund-raising was a power base. They liked raising money in large sums without doing a lot of travel and organizing. It was simpler and it allowed them to be "helpful," which most likely could translate into a favor to be collected someday in the future. The system had a pretty powerful vertical structure; it was not about to transform easily, and the leadership had little appetite to upset it. Regrettably, the president felt he needed those old bulls to help him carry the day on health care. Many told him he wouldn't get health care if he did finance reform. In the end, the president got neither.

It's part of why Bill Bradley, David Boren and some others I had worked with stepped away and retired. The money chase sickened them. Ironically, a number of the key committee chairmen and members of the leadership who counseled Clinton against reform wound up losing their seats in the '94 elections at the same time the president also lost the majority in both houses of Congress. Most significantly, we lost a unique moment to get the money out of politics, which many believe might well have changed our politics and saved Congress from itself.

But we were where we were. I thought President Clinton had done a good job with a very tough hand. There's not enough appreciation for how difficult it was to be a Democratic president in the 1990s or, frankly, a Democrat in Congress.

Still, it didn't excite me to think that I'd gone through the bruising re-election battle with Weld, accumulating almost $3 million in campaign debt, only to find that the Washington I'd fought to return to would be consumed by a sex scandal.

So, like my colleagues, I came back to that one thought: *He better be telling the truth.* This was affecting our ability to do our job too.

For months, the drip-drip of leaks continued: tapes, a dress, DNA evidence.

Then, in mid-August, while Congress was in recess and I was back in Massachusetts working in the state, the dam broke. Bob Shrum was summoned to the White House to help on a presidential address to the nation. Bob told me he was arguing for an apologetic, remorseful tone. What the president ended up delivering was much more heated and confrontational after an initial apology. Clinton explained that his previous answers had been "legally accurate," but that he and Monica Lewinsky did have a relationship after all. But he flashed palpable anger, ripping into a partisan effort to undermine his presidency and attempting to take back his private life for himself and his family.

It was one of those moments in politics that makes you angry at everyone. What the president had done was wrong. Just hearing about it made you wonder what on earth he was possibly thinking. I was furious that a president who knew how much the Republicans were out to destroy him had given them a weapon to use. I was angry that he'd lied about it to people who then defended him. Tom Daschle was on the ceiling about it. He felt he had put his caucus on the hook for a lie. I felt terrible for Al Gore, who had personally vouched for the president and would inherit the baggage if he were the next Democratic nominee.

But I was also furious at the Republicans who had spent all these years pursuing conspiracy theories about everything from Whitewater to Vince Foster's suicide until finally they found some piece of truth with which to beat the president over the head. If they'd discovered some illegal business venture or bribes or corruption unrelated to Whitewater but in the same ballpark, fine. My prosecutorial background would have made me perfectly comfortable with that kind of investigatory connection. But this felt like a sordid journey no one wanted to share.

But the issue wasn't going away. A few days later, President Clinton ordered cruise missile strikes in Sudan and Afghanistan in response to al-Qaeda's attack earlier that summer on our embassies in Kenya and Tanzania. A congressman from Nevada made headlines comparing the strike to the movie *Wag the Dog*, in which a president starts a war to distract from a sex scandal. The partisan line of attack was an insult to the American troops flying that bombing mission.

Still, we were all stuck waiting for Starr to conclude his investigation.

President Clinton was vacationing on Martha's Vineyard, trying to stay out of sight. I can't imagine what a painful trip it was for his family. But on August 27, the president broke off from vacation and headed to Worcester for a public event on crime prevention and youth violence.

These were issues I'd worked on closely with the administration. Despite my anger and frustration, I knew I needed to join him for this event. If I stayed away, it would be a public signal that I didn't want to be anywhere near the president. It might even have signaled I would end up in the camp calling for him to resign. I couldn't allow the president's mistake and the Republican effort to make it the lone issue in politics keep me away from an event in my state on an issue important to me. I thought it was important to be there.

Ted Kennedy, Congressman Jim McGovern and I rode with the president in his limo for the six-mile ride to the event. It felt like a sixty-mile ride.

The president wasn't getting any sleep. I thought he was pretty raw. He was very open about where he found himself. It was the most vulnerable I had ever seen him. He wondered if he needed to apologize more. He knew he had created a mess for himself, for friends, for his party, but mostly I sensed he was in genuine agony over the impact on Hillary and Chelsea. I wondered what it was like for him to look out the window of the limo and see the signs waving in support or opposition, with the occasional personally insulting placard about the most personal, private failing of all.

I was glad I went. But I cringed at the media circus. They were measuring how close we stood to the president, how many supporters were crowded outside versus how many detractors. Meanwhile, the educators, who had hoped this might be a chance to reach the public about school violence and rescuing kids before their lives spiral out of control, could only have been sorely disappointed about the feeding frenzy that drowned out their concerns.

A couple of weeks later, Starr submitted his three-thousand-plus page report to Congress. It was seedy. I thumbed through it, and as much as I was upset at the president, I found the forensic detail in which the scandal was recorded to be troubling. It struck me that there were a lot of people in Washington and in government who wouldn't want their life put under that microscope. There was a creepiness to partisans foaming at the mouth on cable about every sordid detail. The calls for impeachment and resignation grew.

I wondered whether there might be a chance to create closure. The longer the scandal was drawn out, the longer Capitol Hill would remain paralyzed. I couldn't imagine that most Republicans really wanted this issue to consume Washington interminably. I also knew that the longer their chief partisans kept the issue center stage, the more their own private lives would be fair game to the press. Already rumors were swirling about the Republican Speaker of the House.

Did they really want this to be the dominant issue? Fritz Hollings and I rode together on the Senate subway to a vote. "Woo-wee, you impeach a president about an affair, you'd have a whole lot of impeached presidents," he said, and laughed.

I also knew that like anything in politics, there was an issue of morality and there was an issue of math. The GOP controlled both houses of Congress. Winning an impeachment vote in the House with a simple majority was achievable, but it would endanger some of the moderate Republicans from tough districts.

But an impeachment trial would have to happen in the Senate, and it would take two-thirds of senators voting to convict on "high crimes and misdemeanors." That's a tall order. You'd need every Republican—including liberal Republicans from Maine, Vermont and Pennsylvania—plus twelve Democrats to remove the president from office. That math was improbable at best. I remembered something Harry Reid used to joke about when he was the Democratic whip: "They don't elect me to talk, they elect me to count." Anyone who could count votes knew there was never going to be enough votes in the Senate to remove the president from office.

I came up with a path forward that might bring the issue to an end while satisfying everyone. It was an expedited, rip-off-the-Band-Aid strategy. The weekend after the Starr report was released, I went on a few of the Sunday news shows and proposed that the president should testify before the House Judiciary Committee, answer any questions and explain his decision to mislead the nation. In return, Congress would commit to an expedited vote to censure the president. I believe it could have passed the Senate 100–0, a strong rebuke, the first time since 1834 that a president would have been censured. A punishment doled out only once every 150 years seemed an adequate statement. Dianne Feinstein and others were supportive. It would be swift justice in weeks, not a yearlong political circus.

The White House didn't shoot down the trial balloon, but the GOP did. They were in no hurry. They thought it was a winning issue.

A month later, Larry Flynt, the publisher of *Hustler*, printed a challenge: cash for trash—he'd pay for stories of Republicans who backed impeachment but were cheating on their spouses. Washington was really in the gutter.

In the midterm elections, the big Republican wave Newt Gingrich had promised would be the result of the Clinton scandal didn't materialize: balance remained the same in the Senate and a talented outsider named John Edwards scored an upset in North Carolina; in the House, we actually picked up five seats. Newt Gingrich was toast. His party made it clear it would no longer tolerate him as Speaker.

Still, the House Republicans seemed determined to plunge forward with Gingrich's impeachment plan.

In mid-December, President Clinton ordered air strikes to compel Iraq's Saddam Hussein to allow arms inspectors back in the country. Many of us in Congress had been urging the president to increase the pressure on Hussein. The air strikes should have been applauded in Congress loud enough to be heard in Baghdad. But instead it was another moment of division: the usually courtly majority leader Trent Lott called the timing "suspect."

Just three days later, the House of Representatives voted to impeach

President Clinton on charges of perjury and obstruction of justice. The trial would begin in the Senate the following month. What a sour Christmas break it would be.

When we returned, for five weeks the Senate met as a courtroom, with all one hundred senators serving as jurors.

I can't tell you how strange it was to see the chief justice of the Supreme Court, William Rehnquist, descend the marble steps of the highest court in the land, cross First Street NE and trudge two hundred yards up to the Capitol to preside over the makeshift court that was the Senate floor. Rehnquist was eccentric in the way that only those with a lifetime appointment can be: a couple of years before, he had added four gold stripes to the sleeves of his otherwise nondescript black robes in an unspoken tribute to his favorite character—Lord Chancellor—in a Gilbert and Sullivan musical.

It was surreal, sitting at my desk and listening to a debate not about legislation, but about the removal of the president of the United States.

Like any jury, we would deliberate in private.

I remember thinking how helpful it would have been at the time for Americans to have a window into the closed-door deliberations. It was a stark contrast from the rancorous back-and-forth that had filled the airwaves for months.

Senators took those deliberations seriously. I stayed up late the night before in my office sketching out my rationale, what I would say when my turn arrived in the old Senate chamber. My memory flashed back to my early Catholic education, and I pulled out my dictionary to double-check the difference between the words "venal" and "venial"; the difference between a sin that is mortal and one that doesn't rise to that level given its circumstances. It seemed an apt comparison.

No matter what side of the issue a senator was on, the tone of the conversation in the chamber after the cameras departed was respectful and constructive. Perhaps we recognized partisan politics had gone too far. Perhaps we were simply exhausted. But I think it was something else. The president wasn't the only one on trial: the Senate was too, and most senators knew that was the case.

In the end, there were only forty-five votes to convict the president of perjury, just fifty on obstruction of justice. The president hadn't come anywhere near being removed from office, but a year had been wasted nonetheless.

I wondered whether the Republicans who had been so quick to insist on this fight would, in retrospect, have rather accepted my proposal for a bipartisan censure. I wondered even more when the heir apparent Speaker of the

House had to resign when his own affair was exposed by Larry Flynt later that month. House Republicans scrambled to find a suitable replacement. They landed on Denny Hastert, a little-known former high school coach who eighteen years later would go to prison after being exposed as a child molester. What a strange Washington journey.

Later that year, I was on my way to Myanmar to meet with Aung San Suu Kyi. She was becoming a global symbol of democracy, one woman's resistance against repression and brutality. She dressed entirely in white to identify with the suffragettes, as did her supporters. She had seen her own father assassinated and had been under house arrest for years, fighting to force her country's ruling military junta to allow free elections. I saw how hard some people struggled to try to get what many took for granted in the United States: democracy. I wondered whether there was any way to restore some sanity to the institutions we had made work for hundreds of years, some way to make the system work before you arrived at an impeachment vote. I'd be asking those questions a long, long time.

I was in Bangkok waiting for my flight to Myanmar. My phone rang. There had been a tragic fire in Worcester, Massachusetts: six firefighters were dead in the old abandoned Cold Storage and Warehouse Company on Franklin Street. The insulation of the building had turned it into a fire-trapping furnace. The brave men who had run into danger were dead.

I immediately canceled the trip to Myanmar and booked the next flight to Boston. I needed to fly twenty-seven hours back to the other side of the world because I wanted to be there to stand in solidarity with the families of the fallen. In a job too often consumed by political theater, the tragedy of real life and the courage of real-life uncelebrated heroes hit home again. As the bagpipes wailed at the memorial service, as Democrats and Republicans stood side by side in prayer, I was reminded again not just how fleeting life can be, but how these first responders got up that morning, kissed their wives and kids goodbye, and hours later ran into a burning building for the very last time. They did the right thing, instinctively, without fanfare, and gave their lives for it.

How wasteful it seemed that we were all spending so many of our extra days in the pointless noise machine that had become Washington. It was an insult to those firefighters, to everyone who depended on their leaders acting like adults.

BACK IN WASHINGTON, the presidential campaign to succeed President Clinton was soon in full swing. I had some hope that after the division of the last years maybe, just maybe, an opportunity to turn the page might finally be at hand. The country hungered for a different kind of politics, and that spirit evinced itself in different ways. While he didn't have the president's natural political gifts, Al Gore could claim the mantle of being Bill Clinton without the personal scandals. He was smart and capable, and I believed he would be the first Vietnam veteran elected president if a Republican friend of mine didn't beat him to it: John McCain was mounting an insurgent challenge in the GOP field and was striking a chord in New Hampshire's first-in-the-nation primary.

I agreed on most issues with Al Gore, and I particularly respected him for the work we'd done together on global warming long before it was a household term. But John's campaign on the Republican side was much more compelling viewing. He was tapping into an enthusiasm in the country for something different: a selflessness about country and a determination to shake up Washington that was refreshing. But his well-funded opponent, Texas governor George W. Bush, wasn't going down without a fight. Bush had bet his campaign on claiming the outsider lane as well, running as a champion of change from far outside Washington, an impressive claim given that his father had been president and his grandfather a U.S. senator. After McCain trounced Bush in New Hampshire, the two dueled in South Carolina. I was watching CNN when I caught a glimpse of a familiar face from the distant past standing behind Bush in Sumter, South Carolina, at a rally with veterans: J. Thomas Burch. I turned up the volume on my television. Burch accused John McCain of abandoning veterans. To the average viewer, Burch was described as head of a veterans' organization, but I remembered something else: he'd been among those who had accused John McCain and me of betraying Vietnam veterans. His crowd was the very crowd that had smeared John McCain as the "Manchurian candidate" and opposed us every step of the way on the POW/MIA investigation. He was a charlatan. He'd blasted Presidents Reagan and Bush along with John and me for finding the truth. Yet Bush was basking in Burch's endorsement in a primary where veterans' votes could be the difference.

I called my friends among the Senate's Vietnam veterans: Bob Kerrey, Chuck Hagel, Chuck Robb and Max Cleland. We had to defend John. We had to set the record straight. In half an hour, we'd banged out a letter to Governor Bush defending John's honor. We faxed it to each other for signatures and off it went. It was a rare moment of genuine bipartisanship; the broken Senate couldn't legislate, but the five of us weren't going to let party label stand in the way of sticking by our Republican friend. Service was bigger than party. I will never forget John's response when he heard what his band of brothers from the Senate had done in his defense: he said our collective bond was "all the honor he needed in his life." We all felt the same.

But the attacks on John as a veteran, in hindsight, were just a preview of what the Bush campaign had in store for him. Robocalls and anonymous phone calls alleged that John had fathered a baby with an African American prostitute, even as photos were passed around South Carolina suggesting that John's daughter—adopted from Bangladesh—was the alleged child. It was despicable. Sadly, the Bush campaign's offensive made the difference in the South Carolina primary, and John McCain's captivating campaign soon ended. It would be a presidential race between a Bush and a Gore— political dynasties doing battle, and I didn't need to think twice to know which side I was on.

As the summer began, former secretary of state Warren Christopher called and asked to meet with me. He was heading Al Gore's team searching for a vice presidential running mate. The campaign wanted to consider me. I agreed to be vetted. I had never thought of myself as a second-in-command in the political arena, but Michael Whouley argued that my political assets—combat veteran, former prosecutor, Catholic, seasoned debater—would all advantage the ticket in the course of a close campaign.

The vetting came at a difficult time for my family. Pa's cancer was back, and it was in his bones this time. He had decided not to fight it anymore. On the weekends, I had a new reason to get home to Boston whenever possible: I didn't know if each time would be the last I'd spend visiting him at the hospital.

The Gore campaign was prolific in its leaks to the media about the vice presidential sweepstakes. As headlines blared the rumors that I was one of three finalists for Gore—along with my Senate colleagues Joe Lieberman and John Edwards—it became increasingly hard to visit my Pa with the privacy he deserved and expected. Anytime I was seen heading anywhere— including to the hospital—the *Boston Globe* tried to read some hidden meaning into it. The paper assigned a reporter to watch my front door in Washington and Boston for any comings or goings. On the one hand, the vetting process kept me busy and at times was a helpful distraction from Pa's illness. On the other hand, there were many times I just wanted to visit his bedside anonymously or slip away for a long bike ride to take my mind off the inevitable for an hour. No matter how long a parent has been sick or how expected the outcome is, you're never prepared to say goodbye, and while my Pa was always stoic, his choices and passions in life—including foreign policy, flying and sailing—had been passed down to me, his oldest son. This was not going to be an easy demarcation point in life.

Dad drifted off and died July 29 in Boston. Cam, my sisters and I planned a quiet, private memorial service for family that befitted a man who never enjoyed public attention. Our attention turned to our mother, who had steeled herself for this day but who was now without her partner of sixty years. Teresa and I spent a weekend on Nantucket, where she alternated between encouraging me to talk about my father's passing and doing anything to lighten the mood.

On a bright Sunday morning, there was a knock on the door. It was Ted Kennedy. He had sailed over from Hyannisport to visit. I wondered how many times in his life Teddy had performed such thoughtful gestures with such uncalculated spontaneity. It was more than just Irish even in the best of ways; it was the act of someone who had endured loss and appreciated the unspoken comfort that came from being with friends at life's lowest milestones.

Eight days after my father passed away, I was back in Washington. The Senate was soon to recess for the party conventions. On August 8, I woke up to the news on television that Joe Lieberman was Al Gore's choice. The Gore campaign had leaked the decision but had yet to announce it publicly. The stage was set for an afternoon rally at Veterans Plaza in Nashville. Cameras surrounded our home and reporters melted under the hot August sun. They needed a comment from me before their newspapers would allow them to file their stories back at their air-conditioned offices. The only problem was I hadn't spoken to the vice president. A busy campaign had not yet called to pass along the news and thus liberate me to make a public comment and escape my media-imposed house arrest. It was comical, to a point. Finally, Gore's campaign chairman, Bill Daley, called to thank me for having been vetted and officially convey the now well-publicized news. I stepped outside, congratulated my old friend Joe Lieberman, and we were free to go back to our lives.

I did my best to help Al's campaign: I attended the first debate in Boston, and the last week of the race crisscrossed the country as a surrogate at Michael Whouley's direction. Michael had me puddle-jumping state to state wherever the race was tight, from Wisconsin to Pennsylvania, Nevada to Oregon, and dipping down into California for a quick stop. Vice presidential nominee Dick Cheney had parachuted into conservative Orange County to try to steal a blue state, and Whouley wanted the Gore campaign to counter with a high-profile surrogate. At the Orange County fairgrounds, I held a press conference just a few hundred feet from where Cheney would speak. I presented Cheney's Far Right voting record as a congressman to put the lie to the ticket's claims of compassionate conservatism. A crowd carrying Bush-Cheney signs ran after my van as we pulled away, their angry faces screaming all sorts of epithets as they held up a number of one-fingered salutes. I gave them a big thumbs-up and had a good laugh. It was great fun.

On the evening of November 2, 2000, I was back in Boston. Teddy was reelected that evening to his seventh term, scraping by with a mere 73 percent of the vote. Ted's win had been expected, but I expected the race at the top of the ticket to be tense. I was backstage with Teddy at his victory party when we heard a roar from the partygoers gathered in the ballroom on the other side of the curtains. Ted's nephew, who was managing his race, yelled across the way: "NBC called Florida for Gore." It wasn't even eight o'clock, and I wondered optimistically if maybe, just maybe, it wouldn't be such a late night after all. Gore's big bet on winning Florida, the state where Bush's younger brother was governor, had paid off. I thought Al would win.

About an hour later, Ohio went for Bush, and Al's home state, Tennessee, also settled in the Bush column. It had to sting for Al to have lost the state he'd represented, the state where his dad had served as senator. But Ted joked, "It'll hurt a lot less when he's sitting in the Oval Office."

Teddy wisely wanted to address his own crowd while everything looked promising for Al. He delivered his speech and shook hands with his volunteers from the campaign trail, many of whom were veterans of Kennedy campaigns back to Ted's first race in 1962, including me.

As the hour approached 10:00 p.m., a different murmur, peppered by a few boos, rumbled through the reception area: NBC's Tim Russert announced they were moving Florida back to "too close to call."

I invited a couple of friends and staffers back to my home to watch the results come in. The hours ticked by as the electoral map became increasingly red, then a bit more blue when West Coast states went for Gore.

At 2:17, Florida was declared a Bush victory by the Associated Press. A second Bush presidency. I sent everyone home, climbed into bed and tried to sleep. It was futile. I tossed and turned. A couple of hours later, I gave up, went back downstairs, turned on the television and learned that ninety minutes before, the networks had signaled Florida was again too close to call. I texted Michael Whouley in Nashville. "Recount," he wrote back.

Weeks later, after the recount wound its way through the court system, I sat at the Supreme Court to watch opening arguments in *Bush v. Gore*. As a citizen, I was riveted. This was history unfolding. I was outraged that so many Americans had been disenfranchised and troubled even more that the recount was covered by the media as an extension of the political horse race rather than a test of our democracy.

Gore lost in the Supreme Court. I was absolutely confident that Al had won the election but was denied the presidency on a technicality. Once more, I would be serving in the Democratic minority under a Republican president.

I thought the newly inaugurated President Bush had a responsibility to unify a divided country. But he proceeded as if he had a partisan mandate. Many of his nominees, like former senator John Ashcroft for attorney general, represented the hard right wing.

The president announced a massive tax cut disproportionately benefiting the wealthiest Americans. I opposed it as a matter of fundamental fairness. I didn't believe that Teresa and I needed a tax cut more than kids needed decent schools or cities needed help repairing crumbling infrastructure.

Bush announced he wanted to open Alaska's pristine Arctic National Wildlife Refuge to oil drilling, a pointless political decision to destroy some of the last pure wilderness in our country over oil that would be difficult to bring to market. The oil leases themselves would create a scramble of exploratory drilling that would forever mar the unspoiled tundra. I filibustered to stop them. I was whipping votes and keeping a close count on an issue where we had to hold on to Democrats from oil-producing states. A couple of Republican senators from the fast-disappearing Teddy Roosevelt wing of the Republican Party, including John McCain, joined me. We won. It was a good feeling.

But I was also frustrated. I was fifty-eight years old and felt like the best I could do as a senator was stop bad things from happening.

I was opening myself up more and more to the idea of running for president in 2004. I began traveling weekends trying to help elect Democrats up and down the ballot. I got to know people and places where I hadn't spent much time before. I enjoyed the process and I enjoyed getting to know the rhythm of each state—accents, food and people. I hadn't traveled the country this way since I was working full-time for the veterans in the early 1970s. I liked getting to know local reporters with encyclopedic knowledge of the politics of their states, and I was lucky to have my own political team, led by a tough-talking, savvy southerner named Jim Jordan, who was building a national political operation.

That summer, a few potential 2004 Democratic candidates were invited to Columbia, South Carolina, for the state party convention. The Democratic governor Jim Hodges kindly invited us to stay the night at the governor's mansion. Late Saturday night, after attending Congressman James Clyburn's annual fish fry, surrounded by a canopy of old elms, oaks and magnolias, I drove up to the mansion. Under the warm glow of the porch lights, in rocking chairs, sat the governor and my Senate colleague John Edwards, who had been born in Seneca, South Carolina. We sat up together swapping stories and drinking sweet tea with mint. So began a low-key, friendly rivalry.

On September 10, Boston's World Affairs Council honored John McCain and me for our partnership to make peace with Vietnam. It was a special evening made more so because John had only a couple of weeks before endured surgery. I wasn't sure he'd be able to travel at all. But with the help of a chartered flight, we made it up to Boston. We both spoke that night about the importance of always finding common ground. John was hurting on the flight back. We landed around 1:00 a.m., said goodbye and each headed home.

I was back in my office in the Russell Building seven hours later. There wasn't a cloud in the sky. It was one of those beautiful, bright, blue-sky September days you wish would last forever; it was still summer, but the humidity had disappeared. I had to head over to the Capitol shortly for Leader Daschle's Tuesday morning leadership team meeting. I had the news blaring on the television set next to my desk, the syndicated *Imus in the Morning* show on which I was a frequent guest. At ten minutes before 9:00, my ears perked up as I heard Imus's news anchor say that they would be switching to live footage from the World Trade Center, where a plane had flown straight into a building. As a pilot, I was filled with questions. Was the weather in New York bad? A glance at the television footage quickly showed New York's weather that morning was as placid as it was in Washington. Had the pilot had a heart attack? Was it a suicide? My longtime assistant Tricia, a native New Yorker, rushed in to make sure I'd seen the news. Something felt strange to both of us. It didn't feel like an accident.

I headed to the Capitol for the leadership meeting. Senator Barbara Boxer of California and I were chatting about the news that was now being broadcast live on all the networks. I was talking about it from a pilot's perspective when we saw, on live television, United Airlines Flight 175 fly straight into the South Tower. This was no accident. Jay Rockefeller, the Democratic assistant floor leader Dick Durbin, Barbara and I were transfixed. "That's terrorism," I said. Jay Rockefeller was chairman of the Senate Intelligence Committee. He knew right away that this was an attack. We wondered if it was Hezbollah or Hamas.

Tom Daschle was in and out of the conference room taking phone calls, trying to find out the latest. Jay went to call his office. Something suddenly clicked in my mind: Alex. My daughter, a young actor and filmmaker, was living in New York in an apartment on West 22nd Street, between Seventh and Eighth Avenues, a few miles from the World Trade Center. Plenty of her friends from college worked on Wall Street. Where was she this morning? I called my office and they couldn't reach her. Finally, she called me from a phone booth. I was relieved to hear her voice. Her cell phone wasn't working but she'd jammed enough dimes into the phone and eventually reached an operator who connected her to the Senate. Rumors were spreading on her block that Washington was under attack. She feared I was dead. I assured her I was fine, but that she should head to her friend's house, away from the chaos. We were all going to be all right, but at that moment I knew that she had every reason to be terrified: her adopted city was under attack and her father was in another city she feared was being targeted. Then I heard the sound I will never forget: a boom, followed by billows of smoke over the Washington Mall. It was 9:40. "The Pentagon has been hit," someone said. I hung up with Alex, and all of us who were meeting in Tom Daschle's office huddled, watching out the window.

The night before, I'd been honored for making peace. This morning, we were at war. The Capitol was being evacuated. I was filled with anger. I wanted to go fight someone. I certainly didn't want to be driven out of my own workplace by terrorists. I hated that they were interrupting the work of America.

I hustled back to the Russell Building to make sure everyone was getting out of the office as ordered. Capitol Police instructed us to leave our computers on, to just get out. I stood in my empty office seething as the South Tower of the World Trade Center collapsed in Manhattan. I couldn't believe what was happening. I was sick thinking of the people trapped inside, let alone those who had been trapped in those planes.

Amid the rush of hundreds of staff and senators, I headed down the stairwell leading toward Delaware Avenue, where my Dodge was parked. On the second-floor landing, I ran into Joe Biden. We talked for a few seconds. "They think there's a plane headed for the Capitol," Joe said. He was chairman of the Foreign Relations Committee and as a result was receiving information from the FBI in real time. "This has to be some form of Islamic jihad," he said. We were both furious.

I had to get home. Cell phones across the city were jammed. It took me ninety minutes to get back to Georgetown. When I got there, Teresa was upset, sitting in front of the television. Plane crashes of any kind brought back the hardest memories; 9/11 evoked a different kind of horror. "John, the planes were from Boston," she said. I called my state director in Boston. Washington was in chaos, but Boston was numb. "Sonia Puopolo was on Flight 11," he said solemnly. Sonia was a beloved philanthropist and diehard Democrat. We'd often see her and her husband on Nantucket. She was flying to Los Angeles to visit her son when terror and tragedy intervened. Recovery workers would find her hand amid the rubble, her wedding band returned to her grieving family.

I wanted to be in New York helping in some way. Firefighters, cops and rescue workers were caravanning to New York to pitch in, but the People's House was closed for business. Flights were still grounded, so I couldn't even get home to Boston to comfort those who had lost loved ones. The country had come to a halt. I hated the feeling of helplessness, shut out of our offices, stuck at home to do little but follow the news and work the phones. Members of Congress gathered on the steps of a deserted Capitol to sing "God Bless America." It was a moment of unity, but I hoped we were about to summon a moment of action.

In the days and weeks ahead, there was a burst of long overdue legislative activity. The events of 9/11 brought progress on decisions Congress had previously found reasons to defer or delay. We passed new tools for the FBI, the intelligence community and law enforcement to prosecute the fight against al-Qaeda. In the Patriot Act, Congress finally passed anti–money laundering legislation I'd written and been urging since my investigation of BCCI. Banking interests had stood in the way. They couldn't any longer. I knew too well that it was too easy for terrorists and global criminals to move illegal money through legal means, and now at last we were clamping down. When my investigation and Robert Mueller's prosecution shut down BCCI, it cut off Osama bin Laden's foothold in Sudan; now we needed to go after the entire dirty financial network that operated in the shadows.

We also had to take the fight to al-Qaeda directly, on the battlefield. I supported military action to take out the Taliban in Afghanistan, the government that had harbored bin Laden and offered him a staging ground. A broad NATO coalition joined us. It was the right way to go to war.

But something soon changed in the way the Bush administration argued its foreign policy case. Bush's campaign against Vice President Gore had focused almost exclusively on domestic issues. In years of peace and prosperity, that's to be expected. I don't think Bush came to the job with much of a foreign policy philosophy. He had not been focused on terrorism. In the summer weeks before 9/11, I appeared on *Meet the Press* opposite Secretary of Defense Donald Rumsfeld to debate the administration's number one national security priority: billions of dollars to expand missile defense installations in Europe. After 9/11, the world was united by our side to fight extremism. Even the streets of Iran had been filled with young people marching in solidarity with the United States; it was moving to see Iranians waving our flag instead of burning it. I thought Bush could seize this moment to galvanize our allies and create new ones. Bush's one major foreign policy speech of the 2000 campaign had intriguingly promised a "humble" foreign policy. It reflected his father's sensibilities. Now was a time for that kind of diplomatic outreach.

But in the months after 9/11, the White House approach to the world was anything but humble. On January 29, 2002, the president used his first State of the Union address to excoriate an "axis of evil" linking three dangerous regimes that hardly behaved as an axis: Iraq, Iran and North Korea. It was strange. Those countries were vastly different. The rhetoric hinted at regime change in all three countries. Afghanistan and the immediate war against al-Qaeda seemed downgraded as priorities.

The next month, as I was coming out of the Russell Building, I bumped into a four-star general whose expertise I respected. I knew him from his private briefings to Congress. He was assigned to the Pentagon. We struck up a brief conversation. Newspaper reports had suggested that, months earlier, at the battle of Tora Bora in Afghanistan, the United States' intelligence community had radio intercepts providing certainty that Osama bin Laden was pinned down and could be captured. Somehow, he had gotten away. I asked the general what had happened. "Senator," he said, "we are fighting a risk-averse operation in Afghanistan." The world's most wanted terrorist had escaped because we had relied on Afghan warlords, who months before had been fighting on the other side, rather than rely on U.S. Special Forces. We were screwing up the war we had to win, as Washington's gaze drifted elsewhere.

Later that year, the administration began to ramp up its arguments against Saddam Hussein and Iraq. There were plenty of legitimate reasons to be concerned about Hussein. Hindsight sometimes obscures that reality. Ever since the Gulf War, Hussein had remained a challenge. He'd obstructed the international arms inspections that had been the condition by which the coalition left him in power after his invasion of Kuwait. He had promised unfettered access to inspectors, but had kept them out since the late 1990s. He had a history of using chemical weapons against his own people and a documented history of pursuing nuclear weapons and other weapons of mass destruction. He had been a master of miscalculation, especially miscalculating what turned out to be a seven-year-long Iran-Iraq war, which almost bankrupted his country, and underestimating the effects of the invasion of Kuwait and the world's response. The intelligence community believed Hussein had kicked out international arms inspectors to pursue a weapons program. All his history would suggest this was the case.

I thought Saddam Hussein was betting that the United Nations wouldn't do a damn thing to enforce its own restrictions on his regime. On the Foreign Relations Committee, Joe Biden, Chris Dodd and I, along with Dick Lugar, spent years digging into Iraq and concluded that the Clinton administration didn't have the leverage it needed to press the United Nations to get the inspectors back in Iraq. We passed committee resolutions. We ratcheted up pressure as the Clinton administration reached its end.

Now we had a new president, and 9/11 changed the national security debate in the United States. Saddam Hussein still wasn't cooperating with inspectors. The Bush administration seemed determined to deal with Hussein unilaterally. I feared it was a dangerous miscalculation. It was the wrong way to deal with the right question.

I never doubted that Hussein was pursuing weapons of mass destruction. That had been his history. I went to the Pentagon and saw the photos and maps indicating the regime's latest efforts. Had I known that a dubious source like Ahmed Chalabi was behind much of the new "evidence," I would have seen what they were showing us in a very different light. But the lion's share of my time was spent worrying not about whether Hussein was a threat, but about how we would address it.

A Washington parlor game ensued, one I ultimately learned a lesson from. Friends inside the administration like Colin Powell believed unilateral action would be a disaster. Washington was filled with whispers that wise voices around former president George H. W. Bush were campaigning to set the policy right. Brent Scowcroft and James Baker wrote brilliant analysis columns aimed at an audience of one: the forty-third president of the United States. I wrote an op-ed in the *New York Times* arguing that if we ever had to take military action, it was imperative to exhaust the UN process, build legitimacy and a coalition and isolate Hussein instead of letting him isolate us. By the fall of 2002, it seemed that the more moderate and deliberate school of thought was winning. President Bush in Cincinnati gave a speech laying out a multilateral case to disarm Hussein with allies by our side and to go to war only as a last resort.

The United Nations, however, remained skeptical. Pressure built in Congress for some mechanism to demonstrate that the United States was united and that the United Nations could no longer ignore the issue. The White House wanted Congress to vote on an authorization of military force to back up our policy.

I went to New York and met privately with the permanent representatives of the UN Security Council. I wanted to hear from them whether it would be possible to build consensus about arms inspectors, or whether the

United States was off on its own. What I heard from them confirmed that if the United States worked the multilateral process and exhausted it to build legitimacy, we could either unite the Security Council to force arms inspectors back into Iraq and avoid war, or as a last resort build a broad coalition to disarm Hussein militarily. Either option would take time. The ambassadors were skeptical whether the United States was serious. I came to believe that we needed a credible threat of force to get our allies moving.

Several senators—Biden, Dodd, Bob Kerrey and me—were uncertain whether we could trust President Bush to approach the process the way he had pledged in Cincinnati. Colin Powell reassured us that we could. Colin had lived the Vietnam War from the perspective of an infantryman. He wasn't Dick Cheney with his five deferments. Colin knew what happened to a country when troops die for a policy that's ill-conceived.

I was persuaded that the reasonable foreign policy crowd was winning the internal White House struggle for an Iraq policy. Maybe I was convincing myself of what I wanted to be true.

Joe Biden and Dick Lugar were negotiating a bipartisan resolution that could unite the Senate. It would give President Bush the authority to use force—the key to unlocking leverage at the UN—but required a second vote before Bush took military action. It gave Bush the tools he needed for effective diplomacy while leaving Congress ways to hold Bush accountable if he went off the rails.

Administration officials didn't like it. We might have been able to force them to live with it, but the Democratic minority leader in the House announced he supported the White House's request for broad authority to use force. I was surprised by his unilateral announcement, which eviscerated our leverage to negotiate with the White House.

There was nothing left to negotiate. In the Senate, we had to either vote yes and hope Bush was telling us the truth about how he would proceed or vote no.

I thought of it as the first presidential decision I would make as a likely candidate. If I were president, I would have wanted that authority. If I were commander in chief one day, how could I ask Congress to grant me the same authority I'd refused to give another president who was promising to behave responsibly?

On October 2, I went to the floor of the Senate and announced that I would be voting yes, based on the steps the president had promised he would take before going to war. I read that speech today, and I wish I could go back in time and tell myself, "Change your vote; the administration isn't going to do what they promised." I used my speech that day to lay out the right way to deal with Iraq; looking back, we now know the administration was intent on going to war in Iraq in the worst way imaginable: alone, based on a lie. I've said it many times: My vote was the single biggest mistake I made in twenty-eight years as a senator. It wasn't rash. It wasn't political. It wasn't for lack of doing my homework. But it was a mistake nonetheless.

That October day before history took its course, after my long speech on the Senate floor, I rode the Senate subway back to the Russell Building with the junior senator from New York, Hillary Clinton. She was sympathetic to the difficulties of being a legislator having to vote based on a prediction of how the executive branch would behave. She had seen both sides of that equation. She kidded me about my speech, saying it reminded her of that oft-quoted saying "If I'd had more time, I'd have written a shorter letter." Iraq didn't lend itself to short, simple explanations.

We spent the next months hoping the president meant what he said and praying Colin Powell was right. But he wasn't. And I wasn't.

In the short term, our vote had exactly the effect I'd hoped for: less than a month later, the UN Security Council voted unanimously on Resolution 1441 to give Saddam Hussein a final opportunity to disarm. Even countries like Syria voted in favor. It was precisely the outcome we had hoped for. But that moment of unity was short-lived.

I bet wrong on who would win the struggle for President Bush's heart and mind, if he had ever been undecided at all. It wasn't my friends Scowcroft, Baker or Powell. It was the neocons. President Bush seemed determined to go forward with military action by whatever means necessary. I'd never thought harder about the policy implications of a vote and the diplomatic leverage it presented, only to get it wrong because I'd failed to adequately measure the most important variable of all: the president of the United States. Bush was going to do what he wanted to do. He had abandoned his "humble" foreign policy. It was a humbling lesson for me, and it would become a core issue at the center of the 2004 campaign for the presidency.

Cancer and Comebacks

I WAS FINISHING MY Christmas shopping, felt the phone vibrating in my pocket, and I picked up as soon as I saw the caller ID flash "Massachusetts General Hospital." I assumed it was the nurse calling to relay routine results. When I heard Dr. Doyle's voice, I knew immediately that something was wrong.

"The results came back positive."

It was prostate cancer, the kind that had killed my father. Six of the twelve plugs extracted for a biopsy were positive.

Not just cancer at Christmas, but cancer sixteen days after I'd announced I was running for president of the United States.

My head was spinning. It had begun with the usually uneventful annual blood test. Teresa had noticed a jump in my PSA levels, nothing I would have thought twice about—all still within the range of normal, but a jump nonetheless. She had pushed me to get tested.

It turned out her cause for concern was justified.

Every possible feeling imaginable now raced through me—shock, disbelief, numbness, a sense of dread as I realized I would soon have to share the diagnosis over Christmas with Teresa, Vanessa, Alex and the family.

I needed to digest the news. I sat on it for a couple of days and planned to keep it to myself until after Christmas, but Teresa sensed something was going on. I told only her at first. She wrote me a beautiful note and placed it in my Christmas stocking. Her support was selfless and more than reassuring, a reminder that, after I'd fought a number of life's battles in a solitary way, I wasn't alone anymore. We agreed we'd get through it together.

First, though, I had to get through the holidays. Our annual New Year's Eve open house was surreal. It should have been a high point. Friends rushed up to me to share their excitement about the nascent campaign, pulled Teresa and me aside to talk about people they knew in California or New York who wanted to host a fund-raiser or to engage in impassioned buttonholing about issues they hoped I'd raise on the campaign trail. All the while, as I tried to stay focused on the conversation, I knew that I had this secret hidden deep inside, always lurking in the background.

A couple of days later, I woke up mad, not at the unfairness or the unfortunate timing, but at the cancer itself. I was determined to stay on course with the campaign and to fight to get this invader out of my body. I wanted to find the closest thing to a guarantee and know that the disease was gone. I also knew that to be elected president, the press, the public and the process wouldn't let me up for air. If, as the doctors suspected, it was at the earliest stage, then I'd be able to press forward with my life. I was not going to be deterred.

Each day, I was doing homework on surgeons and statistics. Friends led me to the best surgeon in the business—Dr. Patrick Walsh of Johns Hopkins Hospital. After a long talk with him, with a plan to meet as soon as I was back in Washington, the doctor penciled in a date for surgery. This next phase was becoming real. He asked me to talk with his secretary, who would take some insurance information for routine paperwork. It struck me how for so many would-be patients, this would have been the least routine part of all. Members of Congress have the best health care, and I was additionally blessed that paying extra for extraordinary care at Johns Hopkins wouldn't be a question either. For all the moments of frustration I was feeling, there was absolutely no reason for self-pity. How many thousands of men each year got the same diagnosis but didn't have the option of searching for the best surgeon at one of the best hospitals in the world? How many died because they never got the diagnosis early enough or couldn't afford to see a doctor at all?

The first days of the new calendar year—those days when everyone is still saying "Happy New Year"—made me impatient and anxious. I just wanted to get on with it. But I had to get back to Washington, back to share the news with a newly hired campaign team that had never contemplated a campaign punctuated in its earliest days by the word no one is ever ready to hear: "cancer."

Then I had to tell the press. We went to the Senate radio and television gallery for a hastily arranged appearance that, fittingly, my communications director warned would be a "proctologic" experience, as it indeed was. I made the announcement, encouraged men to get tested because it had saved my life and joked that I'd soon have my "aloof" gland removed. The Band-Aid had been ripped off.

Over Presidents' Day weekend 2003, at the crack of dawn, wearing my talismanic St. Christopher medal, I headed to Johns Hopkins to go under the knife. Teresa squeezed my hand and said goodbye as they wheeled me on a gurney into the operating room, where they put me under.

When I woke from the anesthesia, groggy and disoriented, I didn't feel much. As the room came into focus, I saw Dr. Walsh and Teresa together. Their caring smiles said it all; they gave me the best news imaginable: everything looked great, we were "clean at the margins," and I would need no further treatment. I started to feel like I'd been hit by a train, but at least I hadn't been derailed. The campaign would continue and, most important, I was going to be healthy. Teresa, who had lost a husband in an instant once before, had tears in her eyes knowing that this time, at least, good luck had arrived.

"Go slow, don't rush," Dr. Walsh urged me. Teresa's instincts as the daughter of a doctor—Dr. T, some called her—all kicked in, but I didn't have the luxury of going slow. A presidential campaign waits for nobody. Someone who might have erred on the wrong side of omission let me know that as I lay in the hospital, the governor from Vermont, Howard Dean, was holding a fund-raiser for his presidential campaign in my hometown of Boston. My campaign aides thought it was insulting. Dick Gephardt had sent our staff pizza; other candidates had called with well wishes, but here was a candidate on my home turf, raking in contributions before the anesthesia had even worn off. The chutzpah of life—and certainly of a presidential campaign—made me smile. Politics wasn't a genteel game for the weak and the faint of heart. You have to put the personal aside, focus intensely on your goal—care about what you can control and learn how to control what you care about. What I could control at that particular moment was getting out of the hospital, getting home and getting my strength back.

Two days later, two of my close communications aides, on this day a not-so-dynamic duo, stood outside my hospital room as I prepared to go home. The color was completely gone from their faces. After encountering patients walking the halls carrying catheter bags, they had almost passed out. "I can't make a fist," said one. "I see stars and spots," said the other, as he sweated through his suit. I couldn't help but laugh, even though laughing hurt like hell. This was the rescue committee?

"Let's get the hell out of here," I said to the two of them. The Baltimore air was crisp and cold as they escorted me to a waiting van, which I hoped was blocking any television cameras across from the protected pickup area for patient discharge. The cold air had deflated the foil balloons the campaign had sent as a get-well gift. Gallows humor abounded. "Don't even go there, guys," I said with a smile, relatively jocular with the gift of pain medication and freedom from the hospital.

At home resting and recovering, I was frustrated being off the campaign trail. All my synapses were firing, every instinct told me I should be out there fighting for votes, talking to the activists who in less than a year would vote in Iowa and New Hampshire and set the course of the Democratic race. In politics, a lot of people think the finite resource is money. It's not. Momentum can create money overnight. Time is the one resource that's never renewable. Every minute, every hour, every day, it's the one thing you never get back, and I was losing days flat on my back because sitting up hurt too much.

Teresa was incredible, doting on me, pushing back against my determination to pick up the pace and instead telling me to focus on feeling strong again. My doctor gave me every warning about the importance of giving myself time to heal so that when I got back out there I'd feel like myself. I was completely cured, but I'd been through a brutal surgery. Even the anesthesia itself took a while to work its way out of my body.

About a week after I got out of the hospital, what would have been a big command performance in Washington was the talk of the town and a magnet for the political media: the Democratic National Committee's winter weekend cattle call—a big gathering where every presidential candidate would be granted seven minutes to introduce himself. Rumors spread that I'd make a surprise appearance. I think some on my campaign team may have inadvertently fanned the rumors. I was soon getting texts and emails from friends who had heard I'd be "the Democratic Willis Reed," an allusion to the unforgettable Game 7 of the 1970 NBA finals when the gutsy, gritty Knick, down and out with a torn muscle from Game 6, surprised everyone by walking onto the floor of Madison Square Garden, limping but lethal. The Knicks went on to beat the Los Angeles Lakers for the championship. But my doctors—both actual and those vicarious doctors like Teresa—were adamant: I couldn't go. Getting out of bed to deliver a stem-winder of a speech was the last thing my recovery needed. This time, despite every other instinct, I couldn't head out to the floor to join my team. The news from the DNC meeting in Washington didn't take long to make its way to me. Governor Dean had dispensed with the usual niceties and fired up the crowd with a barn burner of a speech, opening by saying, "What I want to know is why in the world the Democratic Party leadership is supporting the president's unilateral attack on Iraq." Jill Alper, my deputy campaign manager, told me the crowd had eaten it up.

I can't say that I didn't see it coming. I did. In fact, as someone who had been a full-time activist before a full-time politician, my antennae had always been tuned to understand just how quickly a grassroots prairie fire could spread around an issue like Iraq.

Looking back, I know I was not yet properly calibrated regarding the disconnect between a senator's head and an activist's heart. I was still seeing Iraq as a policy issue, an intellectual issue, not a "feeling" issue, which required gut reaction. I remember reading the Dean speech and thinking, *There is no unilateral attack on Iraq—the Democratic Party leadership isn't advocating that there be one.* Indeed, here we were, February 21, 2003, and no bombs had been dropped on Iraq. There was no war. No one I knew in the Democratic caucus, except for possibly Joe Lieberman, wanted there to be a unilateral attack if there was going to be a war at all. What was Dean talking about? I thought.

That, of course, was exactly the problem. Where you sit is where you stand—and I'd been sitting in the Senate, not in Iowa. I wasn't looking at Iraq through the same lens as Howard Dean or the activists in Washington.

That was ironic given the road I'd traveled. On December 2, 2002, the *Meet the Press* studio was cold as a meat locker. No bunting, no band, no crowd. I was there to announce my campaign for president of the United States. When I had first appeared on the show, I was wearing fatigues, not a suit. I was twenty-seven, a shaggy-haired leader of Vietnam Veterans Against the War—and the idea that I'd ever be back would have been laughed at, most of all by me. American politics had never been kind to war protesters. But there I was. The studio was hushed, then the familiar theme song played, the camera light switched to red and we went live. In response to Tim Russert's very first question, I leaned forward and made the news he was waiting to hear: I announced that I intended to run for president.

I never had the chance to exhale. Now, two months and one major surgery later, my campaign was on the defensive, because life had come full circle: I'd gotten into public life to end a war, and now I was being accused of helping George W. Bush prepare to start a new one. Worse, I was lying in bed at home, unable to do anything about it. I knew there was an opening for Dean to get a jump attacking other Democrats for a war that had not yet begun, a war we only contemplated as a last resort, not a first one. My friend the columnist Joe Klein said to me that Dean "got Iraq right" because he was the one guy running who had never had an intelligence briefing. That may be correct, and it's possible that some of us had spent too much time in the weeds over too many years on the issue. We might have come to different conclusions if we too didn't have to cast a vote or answer all the follow-up questions that come with being a policy maker. It was a reminder of the burden of being a senator who has to vote yes or no on complicated issues when you have next to no control over the outcome. My brother, Cam, called them "yes-but" and "no-but" votes. They were another reason to want to be commander in chief: not just to vote based on a prediction of a president's behavior, but to be able to shape the decision from the Situation Room, to turn sound judgment into appropriate action. But the life lesson is simple: When you vote, you own it. There are no asterisks in the *Congressional Record.*

In March, President Bush defied the promises he and his administration made to many of us about giving diplomacy time and building a big coalition: bombs began dropping on Iraq, and quickly Saddam Hussein was vanquished, as all of us knew he would be if it ever came to war. The progressive base was enraged. I was naive and overly optimistic to think that the activists would judge my record since 1971—including the peace movement, the nuclear freeze, work to try to stop Reagan's illegal war in Central America—and stick by me rather than get behind someone who had never bled with them. Iraq was suddenly the issue underlying every other issue. It was the litmus test of whether you had stood up to President Bush, and the formerly centrist governor of Vermont was the poster boy. I needed to get back on the campaign trail—pain or no pain.

The spring and summer of 2003 were a slog. There were votes in the Senate tying me up in Washington while some of the other candidates were practically living in Iowa and New Hampshire. My hometown newspaper, the *Boston Globe*, more than surprised me with two pieces of news presented to me in an interview. Not only had reporters discovered the gruesome story (which I'd never heard) of the circumstances of my grandfather's suicide in the Copley Plaza, a hotel where I'd attended hundreds of events, but they'd also meticulously researched long-lost genealogy and discovered that both my grandparents Frederic and Ida Kerry had been Jewish, that my grandfather had changed the family name from Kohn to Kerry and had immigrated, inventing a new life in America. It was a strange feeling to learn such intimate information from a reporter, with a handheld tape recorder running. To have it all happen in the heat of a presidential campaign was a doubly disturbing way to process information. However, in this age well before Ancestry.com, it made my family more like millions of other families with immigrant stories and all kinds of gaps in the past, histories sometimes hinted at and others hidden away. But in a campaign, there's never a moment to process any of that, and talking about it risked seeming exploitative.

Of course, to the wise guys of Boston, it was a buffet of new material, just in time for the annual South Boston St. Patrick's Day political rite of passage.

This year, I'd be on the menu—not boiled, but roasted Kerry.

My phone rang.

The voice was unmistakably Boston and Irish: Chuck Campion, a political operative and beloved longtime friend. "Hey, buddy, how you feeling? You going to South Boston for the St. Patrick's Day Breakfast?"

"Chuck, I just had my prostate removed. I'm in bed. I think they'll understand that I'm not there."

Indeed, many of my national campaign staffers who were not steeped in Massachusetts political lore had turned down the invitation when we announced my surgery. They were putting doctor's orders ahead of the order of the local chapter of Hibernians.

But Chuck knew better. There was a long pause on the other end of the telephone. "Buddy, they're gonna kill you there. If you don't show up, you're gonna feel like somebody just put your prostate back in."

Chuck, as always, had a point. But, fortunately, he also had a plan. He negotiated my secret, surprise appearance. The morning of the breakfast, I covertly sat in the parking lot outside Florian Hall—"Halitosis Hall," as the right-wing *Boston Herald* columnist Howie Carr called it—listening to the breakfast program over the car radio. The state's new Republican governor, Mitt Romney, quickly pounced on my absence. "If he were here, he'd be eating his corned beef on a bagel," said the governor.

"Everyone is Irish on St. Patrick's Day . . . except for John Kerry," guffawed the event's emcee.

Chuck snuck me in the back. I came in through the green curtains. The crowd was surprised. I got to the microphone and delivered a knockout punch: "Who said I didn't have the matzo balls to be here?"

We had turned the tables on Romney and the Republicans.

I counterpunched once more. "You might've heard I recently had some work done on my shillelagh."

Again, a hit. And that was that. It reaffirmed two lessons that you learn in politics only by experience: you won't get far if you can't laugh at yourself, and part of winning means learning how to take a punch and keep jabbing.

We would have plenty of cause for both in the period ahead.

In late March, we went to California for the state party convention—an important cattle call for all the Democratic candidates. The flight to San Francisco was long and painful. Every part of me still ached from the surgery. I ran into the veteran *Washington Post* political reporter David Broder shortly after I got on the ground. He could see that I was dragging a little. He pulled me close and asked me if I was pushing too hard. He confided that years before he'd gone through the same surgery and didn't feel like himself for a year. It was a completely genuine, kind moment from a reporter who was speaking not to a candidate he was covering, but to another human being he was concerned about. I assured him I was just fine. Meanwhile, after slogging through the receptions and the photo lines and the events, on my feet for hours and hours after sitting uncomfortably for the five-hour commercial flight, I was wrecked. I gave my speech, went back to the hold room and stretched out on a long conference table, my hands clasped together on my chest, my eyes closed. I looked like I was lying in state. It was the strangest damn thing. I was just fifty-nine, fit, a clean bill of health from my doctors, strong from head to toe, in better shape than most of my campaign team, and I still felt the fatigue pulling at me. Getting rest wasn't an option. I was heading off for Easter with my wife and I had a lot to be thankful for. I was cancer-free. I had great health care. I was running for president and I was in the thick of the hunt, but damn, I was tired. This wasn't going to be easy. But at least I was alive.

By the late summer, I was feeling like myself again, but the campaign wasn't feeling like the campaign I'd envisioned. There were too many disconnects. The summer had belonged to Howard Dean. He was raising money on the internet in ways that were exciting and that motivated traditional fund-raisers to want to be a part of his movement. I still remember reading a story about a Dean rally in Bryant Park in New York, with thousands of people in attendance. The organizers brought in Wi-Fi (in 2003 an innovation itself) so that people could contribute $10, $15, $25 online—right there and then. Some on my staff sort of sneered at it. One even used to imitate the Dean staffers as shut-ins pecking away on a keyboard to the tune from the famous *Star Wars* bar scene. But it struck me as the kind of campaign I'd envisioned running—a big grassroots campaign of movement politics, the kind where I'd cut my teeth as a twenty-seven-year-old kid. Bryant Park to me was the place where I'd introduced John Lennon in 1971 to an anti-war crowd of thousands and had seen people my age or younger passing the hat and pitching in to fund the Vietnam Moratorium and end a war. It bothered me just how much I had lost control of the narrative and how hard it was to seize it back.

We were yesterday's story. But I felt that people had turned the page on us too quickly.

There really were two campaigns. There was the national campaign, in which day by day, week by week, I was less and less of a factor. All the big endorsements were flowing to the Dean campaign, from unions to elected officials to activists. It was a self-sustaining, momentum-creating, ever-unfolding event.

That was the national campaign. But ignored was the fact that (if I wasn't deluding myself) something very different was happening on the ground in Iowa and New Hampshire, the two states where a universe of 280,000 citizens would cast the first votes of 2004 on January 19 and on January 27, respectively.

Make no mistake, in both Iowa and New Hampshire, Howard Dean was becoming the dominant front-runner. He was sucking up significant oxygen. As August turned into September and into October, his campaign was soaring in the polls in both states, racing past me in New Hampshire and blowing past Dick Gephardt in Iowa (the formerly prohibitive front-runner had won the caucuses in 1988).

But people in Iowa and New Hampshire were courting, not committing. There was a lot of runway left before those two states decided which candidate they wanted to send flying out into the next round of states with a head of steam. Iowans were taking their time to get to know me, not a caricature. John Norris, my Iowa campaign manager, was a great student of the caucuses. He had gotten to know one of my crewmates from Vietnam, Gene Thorson, who lived in Ames, and John pretty quickly figured out that Gene—shy, earnest, unassuming—was a secret weapon. If Gene liked me and I liked Gene, then maybe Iowans could connect with a guy from Massachusetts after all. John was also quick to understand that actually organizing veterans might be the best secret weapon our campaign could imagine. Veterans had never been a force in the Iowa caucuses on the Democratic side before, but every four years, the single biggest difference a campaign could make was to change the profile of the caucus turnout. In some of the tiny towns in rural parts of the state, bringing five or ten or fifteen new voters to a caucus could turn that entire precinct. Long before our campaign began to slide, John Norris had made a brilliant investment: he bought the registrar of voters' complete list of ninety thousand Iowa veterans. If we could reach even one in ten of those ninety thousand vets and bring them to the caucuses, we could change the contours of the electorate. Seemingly everywhere, there was a veteran who welcomed us into his home or his VFW hall. Life felt like it was coming full circle: here I was thirty-three years after I left the Navy, back in the company of those who served.

New Hampshire was just as much of an adventure—an active one, no matter what the polls said. I started out with a romanticized view of the primary. For me, the nostalgia of the New Hampshire primary went back to 1968. As a twenty-four-year-old, I was stationed on the other side of the Earth, where radio broadcasts and weeks-old newspapers in a mail pouch gave me my idealized introduction to the phenomenon of this primary. Just forty days after the North Vietnamese had shockingly launched the Tet Offensive and just three weeks after Persh had been killed in combat, New Hampshire was no longer just the place where I'd gone to high school, the tucked-away, quintessentially New England place where I'd first taken my cuts playing hockey on the black ice of Turkey Pond. Now, suddenly, New Hampshire was someplace else entirely, the place where legions of kids my age—the peanut butter and jelly brigade—were carrying pamphlets (while I was carrying guns thousands of miles away) and knocking on doors, proving themselves powerful enough to send a message all over the world that Lyndon Johnson couldn't be president anymore. It was an earthquake, a palpable awakening. It was a grassroots prairie fire and a lifelong lesson for me in people-powered politics.

Thirty-six years later, New Hampshire taught me another lesson or two, and sometimes the best lessons were those learned and earned the hard way, on icy roads marked by frost heaves and at town hall meetings where the air crackled with skepticism. This time it was New Hampshire as a crucible. In the fall of 2003, I was written off as political roadkill. A reporter wrote that I looked like the Granite State's fabled "Old Man of the Mountain," and then that rocky edifice crumbled days later. The wise guys laughed at the metaphor.

One gray and misty day, we held an event on the banks of the Merrimack River, a short hike down through the trees off the main road, and not more than twenty feet away I could hear the Boston television wiseacre recording his promo for what would be the latest political obituary: "Live from Manchester—Howard Dean surging in the polls—and we're lost in the woods with John Kerry." So it was that New Hampshire taught me that no matter what polls and pundits say, no matter how often I was written off, as long as I believed in what I was doing and I just kept my formidable chin up, I could push through the noise and power through what was right in front of me and come out stronger for the experience.

There was something special about the intimate primary process that I didn't fully realize in 1968 when New Hampshire tapped into my activist heart. Back then, it reinforced in me that people who believe in a cause, an issue—especially a single moral issue—and who act on that conviction really can move a whole country. Vietnam was just that way. Whichever side one was on, there was a right and a wrong. But in that activism, it's the issue, always the issue first and the issue last. It's easy to overlook the people of character who give the cause its energy. As a candidate a few decades later, I realized it wasn't all about issues, let alone the issue. It was fiercely personal.

Truth be told, I can't remember the finest policy distinctions between me and most of the group of Democratic rivals (opponents, not enemies) I got to know that year. Basically, we were all reliable Democrats. I remember as if it were yesterday the people I got to know, the friends I depended on because I couldn't get wherever I was headed on my own. It's the firefighters who opened up their firehouses for chili feed after chili feed because, no matter how low I sank in the polls, firefighters were loyal. They played those bagpipes outside every debate and stood outside in the snow holding those signs, pundits be damned. Loyalty doesn't fit in an activist's ten-point plan, but it turns out it's worth a lot more than tomorrow's white paper.

Manchester mayor Bob Baines had promised privately to endorse me months before his own reelection, keeping that promise all those months later when my campaign was lagging. "A promise is a promise," said Bob, and he kept his.

The volunteers were awe-inspiring. The kids in wheelchairs and the woman who had just beaten breast cancer and the Vietnam veterans, some of whom had never volunteered for a campaign before, were in those headquarters night after night because some bonds are a lot stronger than the day's headlines.

That was New Hampshire. Gene McCarthy talked in 1968 about how lonely he had been those months before the New Hampshire primary. That's activism. You believe in the cause and you work for it. For me, this fight was activism. It was issues, for sure, but the great lesson I took away from New Hampshire was that the strangers I met who became friends and family were the ones who gave meaning to our activism. In New Hampshire, I was never alone.

But that's not to say it was easy.

THE LATE SUMMER and fall of 2003 were filled with tough choices and two near collisions that could have altered the course of the campaign.

First, I could tell that Joe Biden was thinking of running for president. I could tell because Joe told me. He's candid to a fault, if you consider honesty a fault. Joe had a great gift of easily connecting with people. I'd gotten to know his boys, Beau and Hunter, who would often be with him around the Senate during summer vacations or spring breaks. We had sat and talked a few times about politics and presidential fortunes, and I especially remember one conversation on Nantucket at the end of a dock where we both concluded that if either of us was ever president, he'd want the other on the team.

Now he could potentially be my rival. I didn't particularly relish running against someone who was genuinely my friend, a colleague of twenty years, same generation, same values. I also worried that if Joe jumped in the race this late, we would lose more time overwhelmed by a big new story in the media. Every week that went by without a positive development for my campaign was great for Howard Dean. I asked Joe to come to Boston to meet and talk, just us, no staff. The meeting would stay a secret. He agreed. There was only one problem: Joe was being secretly ferried to my house by a Senate volunteer, I was running an hour behind in New Hampshire, fielding question after question from voters who had come to look me over, some of whom no doubt were there as a favor to our flailing campaign. I couldn't rush out of there. I also couldn't be late for Joe.

As soon as the town hall meeting ended, it was back into the minivan, where the driver and my staff had no idea about the meeting I had secretly arranged. After a white-knuckled 90 mph adventure down the Mass Pike into Boston, I raced up the steps of my house, and there in the living room sat my friend the senior Democrat on the Senate Foreign Relations Committee.

We fell easily into conversation, talking about where we were in life. I shared with him what I was seeing out on the hustings, and we turned to an exchange about where my campaign stood. I sensed that he was ambivalent about the whole idea of joining the fray. Running as a late entrant no doubt would be complicated, but potentially giving up what could have been a last shot at the nomination must have also seemed difficult. Who knew if the conversation made any difference, but I was relieved when a couple of weeks later, Joe announced he wasn't running this time. His decision avoided a collision with a friend.

Second, a near collision that wasn't fatal occurred when General (ret.) Wes Clark jumped into the presidential campaign in late September after months of rampant rumors. My struggles and Dean's rise had clearly created an opening for a political consultant's dream: a decorated military leader's biography contrasted nicely with Howard Dean's opposition to the war. No one knew where Wes stood on many issues, or even whether he was really a Democrat, since he was known to have voted for Nixon and Reagan and had spoken at a few local Republican events. None of it mattered. His entry into the race quickly caught fire and instant polls had him overnight at the top of the heap.

We had big worries about Clark. Our campaign's gasping hopes at this point depended on making a big splash in Iowa to alter the race's dynamic. We needed a big bounce there. Now, suddenly, there was another Vietnam veteran with national security credentials running, a fresh new face and an outsider who wasn't weighed down by a voting record. Clark could suck up all the momentum there at a time when we couldn't afford another person contesting Iowa for the unique swath of voters we were betting on converting. Luckily, Clark announced he was opting out of Iowa and rolling the dice on New Hampshire as a springboard to bring him into South Carolina strong, where presumably he would plan to finish off Howard Dean.

It was the first time in months a ball had bounced our way. With Clark out of the mix in the caucuses, we were working on a different theory— that if we could steam out of Iowa, we'd be the alternative to Dean in New Hampshire.

Next, it was tough decision time. We were big underdogs, and every day there was a drumbeat of news that only reaffirmed that Howard Dean was poised to run away with the nomination. First, it was the two biggest unions endorsing Dean just as I was hitting bottom. That these rival unions made the endorsement together underscored how the ground had shifted: people were racing to get on the Dean bandwagon. A couple of weeks later, while in the parking lot of a Mexican restaurant near Stanford, my phone and all the phones around us in our cramped campaign van started to vibrate with rumors: Vice President Al Gore was poised to endorse Dean. It was a shock. We had been classmates in the Senate, he'd considered me for vice president, I'd campaigned hard for him around the country. Would he do this without even a courtesy conversation? I called Al right away and asked if it was true. I asked him whether he had made a final decision and if we could meet. Then the line went dead. I checked the battery—it was full. I had four bars on my phone, reception was fine. I called back, and it went straight to voice mail. Four consecutive times. It was too late.

I had to put this news out of my mind. It did no good to dwell on these setbacks. But each week between October and the middle of December, there seemed to be some announcement. Momentum is a hard thing to stop once it starts snowballing.

I sat down with my traveling staff—by then typically whittled down to a hearty band of three plus a local campaign volunteer picking us up when we landed somewhere—and tried to clear the air. I suppose I was really trying to reinforce the message to myself. I remember emphasizing that we couldn't lose ourselves in the things that we couldn't decide. Besides, we had enough hard decisions regarding actions we could control.

I had a very hard decision to make, one that was a big gamble. Howard

Dean had opted to skip the public financing of his presidential campaign, to reject the public matching funds and instead raise his campaign coffers in traditional contributions. It's what George W. Bush had done in 2000, and it was a coup at the time. Now Bush was sitting on $85 million to attack the Democrats during the primary season, but no Democratic candidate had ever gone in this direction. Dean, however, had built a grassroots fund-raising network on the internet that was awe-inspiring.

Our money was hard to come by, while Dean was taking off exponentially. We had no shot of turning anything around if we were unilaterally disarming, summarily choosing to limit how much we could spend in Iowa and New Hampshire, where the federal funding came with strict limits on television spending. No, if we couldn't be on the air when it counted, competing with Dean dollar for dollar, we should forget the race and pack it in now. I grudgingly declared that Dean had broken the system and I would join in pursuing private funding for the primaries. I had spent so many decades defending the public finance system, but I didn't believe in unilateral disarmament, and at this stage both Bush and Dean had doomed the system.

Even as I announced I was turning down the federal money, there was a much harder bullet I'd have to bite. We were running low on money, worrying about laying off staff at the holidays. I knew we couldn't raise enough money to compete without some major intervening change to the dynamic. I had only one option: I had to mortgage my home to loan the campaign the money to get through Iowa. I signed the papers without flinching, but inside I wondered if I was doing the right thing for my daughters. If I lost, the debt was going to be monstrous, and some presidential campaigns went decades without ever paying off their debt. Raising money for a campaign that's already lost is a miserable slog. If I went back to the Senate, I would have to retire that debt in thousand-dollar increments, missing family on weekends trying to raise the money. This was my kids' inheritance, but my running for president was also about their future. Vanessa encouraged me to do it. She believed in what we were fighting for. So it was that on Christmas Eve 2003, we finally publicly put out the news I'd been keeping to myself: the stakes were high, and I was betting my house that there was still time to turn around the campaign and win Iowa.

I hoped I was betting right.

There was something liberating about being out of the national spotlight. As fall turned to winter, as the rich and colorful autumn foliage turned to bare gray and brown branches, the time we spent in New Hampshire was less and less, but I had to keep the fires alive there. We had to leave our organizers and our team with the hope that after Iowa, we really would return with a reinvigorated campaign—that if they could keep fighting there, we'd be back. Not Douglas MacArthur "I Shall Return" kind of stuff, but close enough.

I was still current on my pilot's license, so I would take the left seat in the cockpit of a rented twin Cessna, copiloted by a friend, and we would land late at night at tiny New Hampshire airports, sometimes little more than landing strips with little picturesque shingled houses for flight facilities. I remember one late night as we headed up to the North Country, our New Hampshire political director, Theo Yedinsky, sitting in the back nervously, not entirely sold on my piloting skills. He was crammed back there, in this very small plane with a number of six-footers. A warning light and warning sound came on, requiring a simple adjustment, but to Theo it must have sounded as if we were heading into a tailspin. He turned white as a sheet. "I can see the headline: 'Theo Yedinsky Gone at the Senseless Age of 32,'" he joked. The gallows humor was infectious. "You might be in the subheadline, Theo," I shot back. "'More Turbulence in the Kerry Campaign; Unknown Aides Lost in New Hampshire Snows.'"

I put the tiny plane down on the runway, and we hopped out into a brutal winter wind whipping across the dark tarmac. There were no airport support personnel to be seen anywhere, only my advance guy from Boston, standing at the door of the solitary building on the edge of the tarmac. He explained that the flight support manager wanted to go home and trusted him to lock up after we landed. Only in New Hampshire.

We carried on.

I loved the intimacy of the process. It wasn't easy—in fact, it was demanding as hell—but it was genuine. Some people criticize the outsized role of the early caucus and primary states in our political system. To my core, though, I think there's nothing like the test they provide, the close inspection of each candidate, the way they push you. They can spot a phony a mile away.

The process was making me a better candidate. My speeches were getting crisper, my answers shorter, but more than that, after a year on the trail to the presidency, the issues I'd been talking about somehow seemed to jump off the pages of a speech and become more real.

Life became more real as well, intervening from afar. I received a call from Julia, who told me she had been diagnosed with transitional cell carcinoma. Thunderclap! In the span of a few months our kids were facing the prospect of both their parents battling cancer and one running for president. The more I think about what they put up with through no choice of their own, the more in awe I am of their resilience and strength of character. Julia began treatments in Boston. The girls kept me abreast, and I visited with her and the kids when I was in town between stops on the trail. In many ways it was a sweet, soft time. The tensions of divorce and whatever issues always exist in the aftermath seemed to melt away in the face of our mutual vulnerabilities. That and the at first unspoken and then well-discussed imperative to make sure the girls were okay. Julia and I had worked incredibly hard to make sure that whatever our issues were, they would not belong to the kids. Nor would the kids be used as pawns in the process. I am convinced we succeeded. Julia wanted me to stay focused on the campaign even as she fought her own battle.

The Iowa Jefferson-Jackson Day dinner was the seminal event of the political season and the official kickoff on the sprint to the finish line, the hardest weeks ahead, lasting from Thanksgiving through Martin Luther King Day, when the caucuses were held. Our campaign was out in force. We entered the hall with a drill and drum corps of young people—the Isiserettes—and an army of firefighters wearing their emblematic black and gold colors. There was energy in the Veterans Memorial Arena in Des Moines—the music, the air horns, the adrenaline flowing for all of us. The event also came with a built-in warning: after six minutes of a candidate speaking, the mics would be cut off, with brevity regulated and enforced. Strict time limits on speeches were a gift that forced discipline and drove me to try to crystallize my thoughts about why I was running, what the race was about, and the kind of leadership I believed the country deserved, as well as the fight it would require for the Democrats to win back the White House.

When I got my chance, I took direct aim at President Bush in a shot that implicitly underscored the national security credentials that separated me from some of the other candidates in the field: "I know something about aircraft carriers for real, and I have three words for George W. Bush that I know he understands: Bring. It. On."

The crowd's response that night was raucous, and not just because our campaign had packed our section of the arena to the rafters. No, something was happening. For all the talk about the race being over, or even for the pundits' obsession with the idea of some white knight swooping in and rescuing the Democratic Party from Howard Dean, this felt like a horse race. The *Des Moines Register* poll showed the numbers: Gephardt—27 percent; Dean—20 percent; me at 15 percent; and John Edwards not far behind, inching up toward 10 percent.

The next morning, I ran into my friend and long-ago campaign traveling partner the *Time* magazine columnist Joe Klein. "Great speech," he said. "But it's too late, it's just too late." I pushed onward.

The weeks before the caucus, it was lock and load time. It was also a time for loyalty. My traveling press secretary kept a mental list of who was there when you needed them and who wasn't. He was frighteningly Irish in that respect. There were certainly a few people who starred on the "not being there" list, such as the much-courted congressman who had signed on with an honorific title when I was the supposed front-runner in January 2003, then professed to have a terrible cold in January 2004 when we needed him in Iowa, and then made a miraculous recovery before the ink was dry on the headlines of our comeback. Funny how that works, but I always took the long view—never burn bridges, because tomorrow is always a new day.

So much about Iowa was about new friends and old friends coming through in ways that were extraordinary.

Max Cleland became the patron saint of our campaign—a triple-amputee Vietnam veteran and former senator from Georgia who had been drummed out of the Senate when Republicans questioned his commitment to the war on terror, showing him in the same frame as bin Laden and Saddam Hussein. Max, a hero who endured hours of a grueling routine each morning just getting ready to go out of the house, had voted with Bush in line with Georgia. Max found a new lease on life in the campaign, though. He went everywhere to talk to anyone he possibly could. Every time I saw him, he said the same thing: "Brother, give me a hug." I still choke up to this day thinking of how hard he worked for us and how badly I wanted to win for Max.

Ted Kennedy was omnipresent. Despite his aching back, he traveled the state with me from rally to rally, up and down the Mississippi River. He packed the crowds. Just two weeks before the caucuses, his voice boomed out to the overflow crowd in Davenport: "You voted for my brother! You voted for my *other* brother! You *didn't* vote for me!" As the crowd roared with laughter, Ted bellowed, "But we're back here for John Kerry. And if you vote for John Kerry, I'll forgive you! You can have three out of four . . . and I'm going to love Iowa. I'm going to love you." And they loved him!

Teddy's wit was always sharp. He'd open an event saying, "I will never forget 1971 and walking down to meet the Vietnam Veterans Against the War camped down on the Mall. There stood a bold, handsome, intelligent leader, a man who should not only be president, but should end up on Mount Rushmore, tall, thin, handsome. But enough talk about me. Let's talk about John." The crowds ate it up, and I did too: when Teddy was laughing, no hill felt too steep. Our campaign bus—dubbed the *Real Deal Express*—was a rolling petri dish of every manner of germ imaginable. But it came with a

Pied Piper whose name was Peter Yarrow. Life was coming full circle. I'd first heard Peter, Paul and Mary sing at Woolsey Hall when I was at Yale, then I'd actually met them and we became great friends in those long-ago days of the peace movement. Peter was older and grayer now, more than three decades on from 1971, his once-thinning dark hair gone on top but still boyishly long on the sides and back, and he remained a liberal to the core. He showed up with his guitar case and offered to pack any living room in Iowa as my opening act. One January night, late on the road, rolling down dark highways set against frozen, barren fields that just months before had been green and alive with rows of corn, the *Washington Post*'s Ceci Connolly convinced Peter to come to the far reaches of the creaky old tour bus and play a song or two for the reporters. I came back with him. After serenading them with a couple of everyone's favorites, including "Leaving on a Jet Plane," which always brought back those memories of arrivals and departures and young people who didn't always make it home, Peter dedicated a song to me, "Sweet Survivor." The words, sung quietly and caringly by an old friend who had been through the same struggles, hit home:

Carry on my sweet survivor, carry on my lonely friend
Don't give up on the dream, and don't you let it end.

I'D FOUND MY voice again in the people I'd met and the adversity we'd faced, and in the simple act of getting written off and writing myself back in because I believed I was fighting for something much bigger than me. I didn't want Iowa to end, and I was determined not to let my campaign end there either. The lump in my throat grew increasingly large as I hung on the refrain's last line: *"For everything that matters carry on."*

If Peter Yarrow brought with him old-fashioned inspiration, Michael Whouley was a jolt of black coffee. "Where can we find a fuckin' helicopta?" he'd bark. The Dorchester accent was unmistakable, a discordant note in a symphony of flat midwestern niceties. Whouley always got straight to the point. We were surging in Iowa, especially in the Catholic communities along the Mississippi River, but there weren't enough hours in the day to catch Howard Dean unless we could add more events to the calendar. But how? Michael had an idea he had first pioneered in the final days of my 1984 showdown Senate primary: charter a helicopter to get me around Iowa faster and cover more ground. An added bonus was that the helicopter landing in each little town was a media event in itself, something that grabbed people's attention and underscored just how much we were fighting for every single vote. As a pilot, I liked it, and as a candidate,

I loved it. It captured the fun, the energy, the excitement of the closing days of a campaign—that amazing sound of the helicopter rotor blades spinning, watching from the sky as we popped down over a little field or ballpark, the wind from the rotors blowing grass and debris everywhere. Then down, out we'd jump, into the van, and head off to an exhilarating event.

Two days before the Iowa caucuses, fate seemed to intervene in a way I never could have predicted—and it came in the form of a voice mail left at our headquarters in Washington, D.C., from a far-away voice in California. He said I had saved his life on the Mekong Delta.

A volunteer jotted it down and linked the man up with our veterans' co-ordinator, John Hurley, who immediately called him in California to check out his story.

His name was Jim Rassmann.

Thirty-five years before, I never knew how to spell his last name, nor had I even known his first name—and when a historian had searched for him, he'd assumed his last name was spelled "Rassman." But the story made sense.

Jim was now a retired Los Angeles sheriff's deputy living in Florence, Oregon. He was earnest, sober, determined—a registered Republican. He just wanted to do his part and suggested he might volunteer in Oregon. John Hurley had other ideas: How soon can you be in Iowa? he asked.

Jim was outward bound on the next flight.

Without my knowledge, a press conference was hastily arranged in Des Moines, where every bigfoot media personality in American politics was camping out to cover the caucuses.

There was only one problem: I was supposed to be in Dubuque for a rally.

With a series of phone calls, the schedule was shifted. I finished the event in Dubuque, got on the bus, and shortly after we started rolling, a staffer crouched down by my seat and explained to me that there had been a change: we were heading to Des Moines. Something was clearly afoot.

Partly to pressure test the authenticity of Rassmann's story, he asked me what I remembered about the man I had pulled from the Bay Hap River in 1969. I told him about a tall, rail-thin Green Beret with reddish hair. The aide swallowed hard, looked at me and said, "Well, he's on his way to Iowa and he wants to endorse you. We're about to have a reunion."

There are few truly spontaneous moments left in American politics, let alone those that happen in front of a mass of television cameras, beamed live into living rooms around the country.

This was one of them.

I walked into the event, and already standing there near a podium was Jim Rassmann. Neither of us could speak. I just walked up to him and we hugged. Words wouldn't have done it any justice anyway. It was the best of a brotherhood and a bond that had endured—without mention—for thirty-five years.

Jim said I had saved his life once—and, hell, maybe now he was back to save my political life. Politics, not unlike sports or life or combat, can be a series of near misses, with its moments that look insignificant but end up monumental.

What if the volunteer in Washington had deleted Jim Rassmann's voice mail? But he had done his job, and Jim Rassmann had given me an extraordinary gift. We headed into the final forty-eight hours of the campaign with a story about real life, not politics.

On caucus day, I finished an eight-event sprint, visiting caucus sites to shake hands, go inside and make my final pitch to the crowd before the voting began. When the doors shut, I was back outside standing on the asphalt, and I realized it was all now completely out of my hands. Thirteen months of all-out work—$20 million raised, fifty counties visited, thousands of miles traveled by bus—plus cancer surgery, bouts of laryngitis, holes in my shoes, a ballooning mortgage on my house, but there were no more hands to shake, no more questions to answer, no more Iowans to ask for their trust. All I could do was wait.

Just as you're firing on all cylinders, just as you're going a million miles an hour, flat out, full bore—all adrenaline and aspiration—it stops. Just like that.

The *Real Deal Express* headed to Des Moines. In the back of the bus, in the area the embeds had nicknamed the "Champagne Lounge," my spokesperson was talking with the reporters. As the lights of Des Moines showed on the horizon, with about twenty minutes left in our ride, I could hear some rumbling back there. The press secretary handed Bob Shrum someone's BlackBerry, and even Shrum, about as superstitious as I was, chastened by the memory of unpredictable election nights (including Florida in 2000), broke into a roar, declaring, "The exit polls look good!" Being superstitious and full well knowing the importance of that old adage of not counting any chickens before they've hatched, I didn't want to hear it.

Up in the presidential suite of the historic Hotel Fort Des Moines, which the ever-competitive John Norris had booked months ago less out of optimism and more out of a determination not to let a different campaign secure the reservation, the scene quickly became a family reunion as we waited for official results. In the big suite, Teresa, my daughters, Alex and Vanessa, and soon Chris and Andre Heinz joined my political family. There was the predictable pacing, the hovering around television sets, cable news blaring everywhere. I decided to take a shower, and through the steam, as I shaved, I heard Teresa announcing the words that prognosticators had once said were a pipe dream: "John, hurry. CNN says you've won!"

What startled even us was that it wasn't even close. I carried Iowa with almost 38 percent of the vote, about 20 points in front of Howard Dean. John Edwards had a late surge himself and trailed me by only 7 points. The media reaction was hysterical, with everyone digging in, trying to explain what had happened to the front-runner who had been on the cover of every magazine, who had secured so many powerful endorsements. To this day, I can only tell you that we'd believed in ourselves. I'd put my campaign of loyal operatives, veterans and firefighters, and faithful friends from Massachusetts up against anyone anywhere. A week later, we won in New Hampshire by a whopping 12 points. The race was effectively over. Everything afterward became a sprint to the finish line of the nominating process, through fun and fatigue, through pain and promise. The energy and expectations after Iowa reset the entire campaign: in the rest of the primaries we amassed a win-loss record of 46–4.

On March 2, I carried nine out of ten states on Super Tuesday, and President Bush called me with his congratulations: I was the presumptive Democratic nominee.

My call that evening with the president was short and cordial, but it belied the long slog to come that would be anything but gentlemanly. The incumbent wartime president was sitting on $85 million to spend that spring through the summer. Before we could catch our breath, the fight was coming at us.

I NEEDED TO get on the road and raise money to fund our first television advertising blitz. We needed to introduce me to a swath of voters who hadn't been tuned in during the primaries, but even as I traveled to fund-raise, we also needed to make news and remind voters what the race was about. On April 9, the morning after the Illinois primary, both of those goals brought me to Chicago, for an economic event at the Greater West Town Training Partnership. It was a chance to talk about investing in workers, cutting taxes for the middle class and restoring fiscal sanity. I was to be joined at the event by the newly minted Democratic nominee for U.S. Senate from Illinois, a tall, lanky, young state senator whom my finance chairman, Lou Sussman, gushed about. His name was Barack Hussein Obama.

I met Barack offstage in a little holding area as the two of us were mic'd up for the event. The first thing I noticed was one of the best smiles I'd ever seen in politics. Joking with his staff, his whole face lit up. His eyes sparkled. But more than that, he also exuded confidence. Sometimes, when you're the nominee for president, down-ballot candidates show up with their families and ask for photos. Or they come overly prepared with well-rehearsed lines to try to steal the show. Not Obama. There was no effort to impress with something witty or political or catchy. Onstage together, he stood back and relied on "less is more," a tactic that a lot of folks in public life would do well to adopt. He was clearly taking me in, deciding what kind of person I was and what kind of nominee I was going to be. We have never talked about that moment. But I liked him instantly. He had a future, I could feel it. Lou said the same and wondered whether he'd be doing something nationally in ten years. I suggested we find a way for him to shine in this campaign. I never suspected how fast that moment would come.

A couple weeks later, Mary Beth Cahill and my convention manager, Jack Corrigan, gave me a list of potential keynote speakers for my convention. One of the names was Barack Obama. We quickly settled on him. It was an easy decision—a clean slate, someone fresh who could articulate a new vision, someone who was unexpected. I wouldn't see him again until the night I was formally nominated in Boston.

Before you're even officially the nominee, choosing a vice president is the first significant, always fraught presidential decision you make. It's an inherently subjective decision, influenced by myriad intangibles. Who would make a good partner in the campaign? In the West Wing? Who would complement your strengths and help fill out the profile of the ticket? Most of all, who would be a good president of the United States if you weren't able to fill out the term the voters had granted you?

I asked my friend Jim Johnson to manage the process while I campaigned. Jim had worked for Vice President Walter Mondale. He had experience and savvy. He assembled an extremely qualified team of lawyers to help with vetting, including Jeff Liss, who had vetted me four years before. Jim was discreet and careful and preferred to operate out of the limelight. So discreet was Jim that we even managed a couple of times to sneak him on the campaign plane without the press knowing, so the two of us could confer during long flights. But beneath Jim's businesslike approach was a progressive, passionate, committed citizen; we had both come of age in the activism surrounding the peace movement. I knew Jim would have my best interests at heart throughout the process.

After 2000, when he looked back at Vice President Gore's selection, my friend Michael Whouley told me, "We ended up with Mr. August, not Mr. October." It was Michael's view that Gore had made an excellent choice to help with the campaign's narrative at the convention and in the weeks that followed. But, he thought, in the fall, in the course of the debates and the final, definitional skirmishes between the two campaigns, Lieberman had not been as effective in prosecuting the case for Gore and defending the nominee.

I thought hard about Michael's colorful formulation: Mr. August, Mr. October. The perfect candidate for vice president probably doesn't exist. You have to make a bet on who can fill the different roles best. But I did want to try to find someone who would be the "Mr." or "Ms." not just for two seasons, but three: August, October and January, when governing would become issue number one.

The list quickly narrows when you're thinking hard about the vice presidency. You might think that there's a big universe to consider. But you realize what a distinct slot you're trying to fill. Who meets the threshold qualification? Who can survive the scrutiny? Who can perform on day one? Who is actually comfortable dealing with the media glare? Who fills gaps and brings additive qualities to the ticket? Who is really willing to play a number two role not just for four months, but for eight years? There are candidates with great profiles who don't pass a vetting. There are people you admire and like who don't have the comfort level with campaigning and politics, which is a different beast from success in the world of business or the military, for example. There are people who might make good presidents but wouldn't ever feel comfortable wearing the mantle of vice president. It is a unique formula.

I did try to think broadly and cast a wide net. I thought of leaders from the business world and former military leaders. But I came back to people I thought could help govern on day one, people who had a broad understanding of government, politics and the issues.

There was one idea I considered but knew would become impossible if it ever leaked to the media, so I kept it quiet. At the highest level of my campaign we had been approached by one of the people closest to John McCain. He suggested that John might be open to joining me. It was at least interesting—super-complicated, but interesting. I thought it shouldn't be dismissed out of hand. John and I had successfully navigated turbulent periods as copilots before; the scrutiny we faced on the Vietnam POW/MIA investigation had been politically intense, and the emotions swirling around the issue demanded a certain level of judgment and maturity.

In that experience, I had seen that John and I made a great team when we shared a sense of purpose. I thought his ability to be the maverick, his independence, could be a critical ingredient for a country that was increasingly suspicious of government. He had helped define the insidious impact of money in politics. We shared a passion for reform.

I knew John felt, viscerally, that President Bush had squandered the unity of 9/11 and was dividing the country in ways that were simply wrong. On a number of issues, from campaign finance reform to climate change to standing up to HMOs on behalf of patients, John McCain had very publicly broken with the White House. There was a point where John's independence and annoyance was so palpable that Tom Daschle believed John might leave the Republican Party and join our caucus as an independent.

Politically, 2004 is an eternity ago. John went in some very different political directions over the years after my race with President Bush. But back then, in that campaign, there were compelling reasons a Kerry-McCain ticket might have been powerful and at least merited examination. It would certainly have underscored unity when the country needed it. While obviously we had differences on some social issues, including choice, I knew those weren't issues that animated John McCain's political journey. Of course, we would have had to reach an understanding there. But I knew John was committed to moving the Senate, to making institutions of government work, to restoring people's faith that government could put the average person's interest ahead of big money. And I knew he had no patience for the lies about my military service. In fact, he had already defended me against the first attacks in the late spring, before the GOP made "Swift Boating" a big strategy and put huge money behind it. John could potentially have changed the electoral map, I believe, putting Arizona and Colorado in play. He was tested. He was tough. There were people around John who thought he would want the job, and they pressed me to consider him, in a way that made me think John was very interested.

But in the end, despite the two of us sitting together a couple of times one-on-one and "talking about it without talking about it," John couldn't get over the hurdle of tearing up what had for him been a bumpy but lifetime association with the Republican Party. In essence, we flirted but we never went on a date.

In the end, all the what-ifs and what-may-have-beens in the world are largely a waste of time when you're in the thick of a campaign and you have to make a decision.

There were three to four leading choices to consider, good ones our entire senior campaign staff and senior party figures all agreed could make sense for August, October and January as well. No matter how much I looked out of the box at various unconventional possibilities, the list narrowed down to Dick Gephardt, Bob Graham and John Edwards.

DICK GEPHARDT CAME with a wealth of experience. He was steady and popular with organized labor. Many people have suggested he could have made the difference in Ohio and they may well have been right.

Bob Graham had been governor of Florida. He had chaired the Intelligence Committee, brought southern credentials to the table as well as a commonsense approach to public life. He and his wife, Adele, had become good friends of Teresa's and mine.

John Edwards was the potential choice who campaigned hardest for the job and who had captured the excitement of the party. John had both fans and detractors in the Senate. Ted Kennedy had worked with him on health care and thought he was gifted. Something about Edwards reminded him of his brother Bobby. Other senators, though, warned me there was something about John that didn't quite add up. They thought he was too ambitious, in too much of a hurry, and several expressed concerns he couldn't be counted on to be a team player under the heat of governing.

I had gotten to know John pretty well in the lead-up to the primaries. I liked him. I had seen him campaign effectively, with discipline, and I watched as he gained some traction in the final weeks before the caucuses in Iowa, around the same time my campaign was taking off. John had not been able to stop my momentum anywhere except in the state where he had been born, South Carolina, but I'd come away impressed by his ability. He had run a good race, and we had never clashed on any big issues.

Teresa and I had always been impressed by John's wife. Elizabeth Edwards was smart and funny and had gone through hell to have two beautiful children late in life, after their son Wade had been tragically killed.

John, Teresa and I had first gotten together for dinner in 2000 after we had both gone through the crucible of Gore's vice presidential vetting. After talking about the Senate, politics, raising kids and our collective journeys, John and Elizabeth talked about why they had gotten into public service. Losing their son had changed their lives. John spoke movingly about getting that phone call every parent dreads and learning that their beloved son had been killed. He described something he said they hadn't talked about before: the horror of seeing his son's lifeless body and of holding him in his arms. They'd been through so much and somehow come out stronger for it as a family, with a sense of public purpose, a sense that they were together, living for their son Wade. It struck a chord. I heard John tell that story at the Senate Prayer Breakfast afterward, and I could see just how much he and Elizabeth had wrestled with their loss and its place in their lives.

As I considered John as my running mate, I did wonder about his ambition. I wondered whether he could remain committed to a joint venture if everything got hard, as politics and governing always, inevitably does. I thought back to Bill Clinton's first couple years of the presidency. After losing Congress in the 1994 midterm elections, Clinton had been at an all-time low. Gore's loyalty at that moment was critical. Could I count on the same from John Edwards? Something made me uncertain whether I could count on him for an eight-year partnership, which, in turn, would set him up for a presidency of his own.

I think in an effort to reassure me, John recounted a story he told me he hadn't shared with anyone before. It was the story of Wade's death and that moment alone with his body. Something unsettled me. It seemed too familiar. It was the exact same memory he had shared four years before at dinner.

I slept on the decision. I thought about how people find all kinds of ways to deal with grief; perhaps John recounted that same story the same way because it was the only way he could get through the pain of the memory. I wasn't going to judge or put myself in his shoes when, thank God, I'd never lost a child.

I asked to meet with him again. We talked about the kind of partnership I was looking for in a running mate. John assured me he would never run against me. We would be a team for the long run. He used the word "family."

I offered him the place on the ticket. Our families shared a wonderful cookout at the farm in Pittsburgh and stayed up late talking about the future. Teresa and I instantly took to their kids, Jack and Emma Claire, and their elder daughter, Cate. Cate was my daughters' age, and the three of them clicked instantly. It felt good. The next morning, at a big rally in downtown Pittsburgh, I introduced John Edwards to America as my running mate.

Just as I had completed the vice presidential selection, I had another dramatic decision to wrestle with, one with far-reaching implications that would end up looming larger even than choosing Edwards.

In a presidential campaign, some of the biggest tactical decisions about money and resources wholly alter strategy, because they can so easily restrain a candidate's freedom of action.

After Watergate, with the best intentions of ridding presidential campaigns of the possibility that powerful donors could decide elections, Congress passed a law establishing the public finance system. The idea was simple: after each political party selects a nominee at its convention, the nominees would receive a check from the federal government to last through Election Day. The goal was parity between the campaigns, so elections would be decided by issues, policies and political skill, not money.

As campaigns grew more expensive and people found creative ways to dump more money into the system, the presidential public finance structure sprang leaks. The political parties' national committees—the DNC and the RNC—could accept large-dollar contributions to spend on what were supposed to be "party-building activities." The spirit of the law was meant to protect grassroots activity—getting out the vote. Skillful campaign lawyers on both sides reinterpreted that provision to include issues advertising. It grew into a huge loophole. So long as the television and radio advertisements didn't say "Vote for president," and so long as the advertising spending hadn't been ordered by the candidates, ads were allowed. Finally, we passed the McCain-Feingold campaign finance legislation to close the "soft-money loophole." Unfortunately, the bill would do nothing to stop shadowy groups funded by anonymous individuals from bankrolling advertising.

Still, as we planned our campaign, I had to conclude that, despite hiccups here and there, overall the public financing of general elections was better than the alternative. Since 1976, Democratic and Republican nominees had spent essentially the same amount of resources for the general election. The big decisions were centered on how to spend those roughly equal resources in the three-month slog from convention to Election Day.

Many on my team had been through the Gore campaign. They remembered bitterly how in October, just a month before the election, Gore confronted a dreadful choice about resources: Should he go all out in Ohio or in Florida? He couldn't do both. No Republican has ever been elected president without winning Ohio. No Democrat who has won Florida has ever been denied the presidency. Gore didn't have enough money left to fight in both states, so Al bet the house on Florida, where I am convinced he would have been declared the victor if all the votes had been counted.

Making a choice like that is a lousy situation to be stuck in when you're talking about finding paths to winning the presidency. The electoral map in 2000 and 2004 wasn't especially kind to a Democrat. There was little room for error. If you have only one path to victory and your opponent has many, that's a tough hand to play.

I knew from the very start of my campaign that, come October, we did not want to be in the position Gore had found himself in. We wanted to be able to compete in both Ohio and Florida and, with John Edwards on the ticket, possibly make a run in North Carolina. Edwards promised to deliver his home state.

I knew that as soon as I said the words "I accept the nomination," my campaign would be wired $75 million for the general election—money that had to last through Election Day.

But years before, Karl Rove figured out something just novel enough to roll a tactical hand grenade into the 2004 election. Rove is smart. The party in control of the White House chooses its nominating convention date after the other party announces its selection. For fifty years, the conventions were held roughly a week apart, sometimes two. Rove saw an opportunity to do something that had never been done before. He turned convention scheduling into a political IED. After Chairman Terry McAuliffe announced that our convention would be held from July 26 to July 29, the Republican National Committee announced its convention would happen five weeks later, during the week before Labor Day weekend.

I can't blame Rove. After all, if the trigger to receive public financing is pulled the moment a candidate becomes the nominee, and you're an incumbent Republican president awash in private campaign donations, why not schedule your convention much later in the summer? Why not force your Democratic opponent to spend every dime on a thirteen-week general election, while you could spend the same amount of money over just nine weeks?

That's exactly what Rove and the Republicans did.

The overwhelming conclusion inside our campaign was that there was little we could do about it. Most everyone argued for conserving resources in August, so that after Labor Day, as we entered into the next season, we would be well positioned to compete with the Bush campaign down to the wire.

A few of my closest friends had a bold idea. They believed we did have an appropriate response to what the Republicans had done to weaponize the political calendar. David Thorne and Ron Rosenblith argued that with the unprecedented amount of money I was raising on the internet, we could opt out of the public finance system and control our own destiny in the general election.

After Iowa, I'd raised close to $180 million and I had about two million Americans signed up at JohnKerry.com. At the time, it was the largest email list in progressive politics. Our small-dollar fund-raising had soared in scale far beyond anything even Howard Dean's netroots campaign had achieved. Now, millions more Americans were just about to tune in to the campaign. What if they were asked to fund a grassroots campaign?

Looking at it today the answer seems simple. But in the summer of 2004, it was an idea full of risks and unknowns. What if we hit a rough patch and raising money got harder? What if the grassroots donations slowed, as they had a long time ago for Howard Dean when his campaign cooled off? What if we ended up flat broke in October? What if a national tragedy— an earthquake, hurricane or, God forbid, a terrorist event—made political fund-raising unseemly and untenable one week or month when we were dependent on bringing in donations? What if this meant I had to take time away from places like Ohio, Wisconsin and Michigan to go fund-raise in blue bastions like New York and California?

Besides, in politics, as in science, every action has an equal and opposite reaction. What if I stayed inside the public finance system but Bush opted out of it? It was the same dilemma I'd faced against Howard Dean, only worse: Dean had jumped first, opting out of public finance, making my de- cision easier. On the flip side, what if I opted out and Bush followed suit, which he almost certainly would have?

After four years in the White House, the Bush campaign had mastered data mining and direct small-donor fund-raising. Bush had about six mil- lion email addresses. We believed that grassroots momentum was with us—the agent of change running against the incumbent—but that was an awfully big bet to make. If Bush could match our small-donor, low-dollar fund-raising, then we were better off staying within the system.

The biggest hurdle for me, however, was that campaign finance reform was part of my DNA, and I had spent decades advocating for the public fi- nancing of campaigns. I knew that everything Rove and Bush were doing to tilt the calendar in their favor violated the spirit of campaign finance re- form, but I also knew that everything I had fought for on the issue would be twisted if I were the first candidate to reject public financing for a gen- eral election. I faced a lousy choice between staying inside a broken cam- paign finance system to prove a point of principle or breaking out of that system and being attacked as a flip-flopper. The irony of Rove and the Re- publicans possibly attacking me on campaign finance reform was rich. It would have been the ultimate example of the arsonist riding a fire truck to the scene of the very house they had set ablaze. They had broken the sys- tem, but they stood ready to blame me. That's politics. Furthermore, I was already being attacked for flip-flopping where I hadn't, which prevented me from flip-flopping where I should have, because then I could have answered the charges effectively. Damned if you do, damned if you don't.

I decided it just wasn't the right environment to make a big, complicated bet like this one. We didn't need another distraction. I owned the decision. I was going to accept the nomination in Boston, stay within the campaign finance system and conserve our money in August.

The first night of the Democratic convention in Boston, I was in Philadelphia. The irony is, when you're the nominee, you're barely at your own convention: you are on the hustings, campaigning in swing states, taking advantage of the added voter and media interest that the convention attracts. I raced through a picturesque rally, speaking from the famous "Rocky steps" outside the Philadelphia Museum of Art. It was a magical rally at dusk, with crowds reaching far back into the setting sun. I remember seeing fireflies in the air. But we had to hurry: I wanted to be back at the hotel in time to watch on television as Teresa addressed the convention. I caught her by phone in my motorcade to wish her luck. It was strange to hear in the background the convention buzz in my hometown, when I was hundreds of miles away.

Back at the Hyatt, I leaned forward as the convention programming continued. The skinny state senator I had met in April took to the podium, keynote speaker Barack Obama. The speech absolutely soared. I was feeling the moment. Halfway through it, I walked quickly across the hallway into Marvin Nicholson's room to share in the moment. I pushed open the door and stepped into a haze: Marvin had blocked the smoke alarm and was smoking in the hotel. I had to laugh at him. But despite the smoke, I stayed there, and together we watched the emergence of a political shooting star: Barack Obama had blown the roof off the Boston Garden.

SOON IT WAS my turn to get home to my own party.

"*Ker-ry!*"

"*Ker-ry!*"

"*Ker-ry!*"

The sounds echoed in my hold room, and I thought just how different it was from the usual chants in Boston Garden of "De-fense! De-fense!" I'd been stowed away in a converted executive office usually filled with Celtics or Bruins season ticket holders devouring hot dogs between periods. The new "Boston Garden," initially named the Fleet Center and today called TD Garden, was teeming to the rafters with delegates, donors, organizers, foreign dignitaries anxious to view the American political process, everyone waiting to participate in one of the great pageants of American life. How many times had I been there for a Bruins game or Bean Pot Tournament? Never had I imagined I'd be there for this occasion: not many nominees for president get to accept the nomination in their home city.

In my lap was the acceptance speech I was about to deliver, long before loaded into the teleprompter—there was no more time for edits. I tried to stay focused on the task ahead but couldn't help but reflect on the long road from cancer surgery at Johns Hopkins to the acceptance of the nomination of my party to be president. On the television set anchored to the wall, my entire focus was suddenly consumed not by the long journey of a campaign, but by the journey of life itself: Vanessa and Alex came out onstage to begin the introductions. I was proud beyond words. They were two incredibly articulate, accomplished young women talking about their dad. Tears came to my eyes, and the only thing that kept them there was knowing they would ruin the makeup plastered on my face for the television cameras. It was time to go out. I walked through a sea of people up to the stage, greeting so many who had been part of my life. The emotions were overwhelming until I got to the podium and it was time to speak.

But for a moment, all I could think was just how improbable it was that a kid who had stood outside the old Boston Garden hoping to catch a glimpse of soon-to-be president Kennedy would, forty-four years later, be at the new arena following his own path to the same goal.

How improbable. How lucky. How rare.

It was a joyful moment, a feeling so few ever experience. As I stood on the stage after the speech and the balloons slowly dropped, my arms were filled with family—with Teresa, Vanessa, Alex and the Heinz boys— and with political family—the Kennedys, the Edwardses and Michelle and Barack Obama. For one night in July, it all seemed to be on the right track.

Little did I know the guns of August were about to be trained on me and the men I'd risked my life with thirty-five years before.

CHAPTER 12

Within a Whisper

"WAREIUHSSS."

I summoned my best internal Rosetta Stone to translate what the Ragin'
Cajun James Carville had just said, but it failed me. My perplexed stare
might have been revealing, so he said it again, the intonation slightly different this time.

"Weshissuhs."

"Wedge issues," Paul Begala translated, and only then did it click. I was
having dinner at the Palm with the two veteran political strategists. They
were describing the holy trinity of how Republicans usually won the presidency: "guns, gays and God."

I thought I had the credentials to insulate me from the social issues
the Republicans used to drive a wedge between Democrats and the voters whose economic interests—jobs, affordable health care, a fair tax code,
sensible trade deals—were exactly what I'd always fought for in public life.
I wanted to make sure voters saw me for who I was.

Guns? I'd fired more guns in my life—in the Navy and as a hunter from
a young age on Uncle Fred's farm—than George W. Bush ever had. As a
kid, I had even been a junior member of the National Rifle Association
(NRA) long before it became a right-wing cult. I was a gun owner. I just
didn't believe that weapons of war belonged on American streets, so I'd
voted for the assault weapons ban. Law-abiding citizens had nothing to fear
from a background check. Neither one threatened the Second Amendment,
and the police agreed.

Gay rights? I hate discrimination. I believed that even on then-divisive
issues such as gay marriage, leadership meant finding common ground, and
presidential leadership meant reminding people that we were all Americans,
not trying to divide us. A church shouldn't and wouldn't ever be forced to
violate its tenets and perform a gay marriage, but surely we could find civil

legal protections so that people who loved each other could be together. Even Dick Cheney seemed to favor the civil unions I supported.

And God? I had been an altar boy. As a senator, I had spoken in churches and humbly taken my seat at the Senate Prayer Breakfast. In 1993, after I was invited to address the National Prayer Breakfast, Charles Colson, who had tried to destroy me on behalf of Richard Nixon in 1971, wrote me a moving letter. He had found God after going to prison for Watergate-related crimes and began a prison ministry that would define real service to Christ. In the letter, he wrote, "Some years ago, you and I were on opposite sides . . . but I must tell you we certainly are not today. In the twenty or so years that I have been attending the National Prayer Breakfast, I have never heard a more articulate, unequivocal presentation of the Gospel than your scripture reading. . . . I suppose we all have to live with our stereotypes; I certainly have. But whatever stereotype I have of you is totally changed. I write this letter asking your forgiveness for any ways in which I hurt you in the past."

I was deeply touched. I wasn't ready yet to forgive everything that happened in 1971, when I was a twenty-seven-year-old veteran being spied on by the same government that had sent me to war, but I thanked Colson, and I thought hard about what he'd written. Politics did create destructive stereotypes, but it could also break them down. I thought I had learned an important lesson: by giving people (even those on the opposite side) a chance to know the real me, I might defy the caricature adversaries had concocted. I thought of my personal journey as private, but I wasn't going to allow any politician to belittle my devotion. I didn't think that was the turf on which the first presidential campaign after 9/11 should or would be fought.

Paul and James warned that the Republican playbook had nothing to do with reality and reminded me that Karl Rove's political roots were in the direct-mail business, scaring people with stereotypes.

As a presidential candidate, I would see firsthand that the stereotypes the other side used to divide America remained potent. They'd get plenty of help from some powerful interests anxious to promote their false choices. We would have to fight back.

When it came to guns, I knew the GOP believed it had a surefire winner. In 2000, George W. Bush said he supported the gun control laws that were on the books, so it was hard for the Republicans to run against the reality of what the Clinton administration had done.

Instead, the NRA announced that if Al Gore were elected president, he would lead "a war on guns." They painted him as an elitist who didn't believe in the Second Amendment. The gun issue cut strongly against Gore in a down-to-the-wire election. Michael Whouley called me and asked if I could go to Wisconsin and Pennsylvania to speak to union voters about guns on Al's behalf. I headed immediately to a union hall in Eau Claire.

These voters, who probably just wanted to relax over a beer at the end of their shifts, had been subjected to a barrage of television ads and leaflets eviscerating Gore's fidelity to the Second Amendment. It was deer hunting country. I talked about hunting, but I also asked how many of them had ever killed a deer with an AK-47? They laughed. The phoniness of the NRA's appeals could be punctured by a lifelong hunter. Al would hold on to Wisconsin narrowly, but Bush pulled a couple of hunting states into the Republican column, including New Hampshire. I applied those lessons to my own campaign. I was determined to show up often and just be myself.

I didn't think any candidate could win by ignoring an issue like guns or by trying to be Republican-lite and pandering to the NRA. Some argued that Democrats had to take this issue off the table. That view was rooted in the scar tissue left not just from Gore's loss, but from the memory of dozens of incumbent Democrats losing their seats in 1994 over the gun issue. I just didn't buy it. I'd tangled with Howard Dean in the primaries over guns when he touted his A rating from the NRA as governor of Vermont. I didn't want to be the candidate of the NRA then, and I didn't think the NRA would sit out an election cycle if we abandoned our principles.

The NRA did nothing to disabuse me of my suspicions and had plenty of help from Republican leadership in Congress willing to use the Senate floor as a stage for election-year theater. Just as I was squaring up against Bush, the Republicans suddenly scheduled a series of gun control votes on an otherwise unrelated piece of legislation. The Senate Republican majority leader, Bill Frist from Tennessee, was a friend of mine and had been a legislative partner. Bill was a genteel medical doctor who ran for the Senate, a scion of a respected Nashville family and a humanitarian who traveled to Africa over Senate recesses to care for those living in extreme poverty. Bill and I had joined together in 1999 to write landmark legislation to make medicines available to combat AIDS and malaria in Africa. It was the foundation of U.S. efforts on AIDS and ultimately was wrapped into a program that has helped roll back the pandemic of AIDS once ravaging sub-Saharan Africa. I liked Bill. He'd been willing to work on an issue that was, at the time, still controversial in his party.

As majority leader, however, Bill crossed some lines that hadn't been crossed before. That surprised me. Years before, back in the Senate of Byrd and Dole, the majority leader and minority leader refused to campaign against each other, but Bill was already working this year to defeat his Democratic counterpart, Tom Daschle. Bringing the 2004 presidential race to the Senate floor would be no different: Bill seemed compelled, I assume, to march in lockstep with the Bush White House.

With the 1994 military assault weapons ban expiring in September, after Bush and his Republican Congress had done nothing to reauthorize it in four years, suddenly we were going to have a vote. There was no chance the House could pass it even if the Senate did. It was a transparent trick to put guns front and center in the presidential campaign.

Some on the campaign argued I should skip the vote. "It's theatrics, it's politics," one person argued. "You're giving them what they want by going back to Washington to vote." But we'd probably give them more by not going back. Everyone could have attacked a candidate's failure to take a position. Several of my senior campaign teammates were haunted by memories of the way Vice President Gore's tie-breaking Senate vote in favor of gun background checks had been weaponized against him in the presidential race. "Win the race and then you can do something about guns," said one of those who had traveled hundreds of thousands of miles with Gore and knew the price he had paid on guns.

It wasn't crazy political analysis. But I was convinced you pay a bigger price for hiding from your own position on an issue.

"We're going back to Washington," I announced. "If you can't defend keeping the weapons of war off the streets of America, you don't deserve to be president."

I had voted thousands of times in the Senate. But this was my first time back there as a presidential candidate. The motorcade pulled up under the covered area in front of the Capitol. Dozens of reporters swarmed toward us, cameras flashing. It was chaotic. The elevator doors opened to shouted questions from gaggles of reporters five people deep. I was glad to make it to the cloakroom and onto the Senate floor—away from the crush of the crowd. My Secret Service detail remained in the cloakroom: the only attacks on the Senate floor would be partisan.

Looking up, I saw the gallery was filled with both reporters and activists, an unusual sight usually reserved for swearing-in ceremonies or impeachment. "Aye," I told the clerk at the desk with a big thumbs-up. I cast my vote to extend the assault weapons ban. After the vote was tallied, I sought recognition to speak on the Senate floor, as was my right. I said the Second Amendment protected rights, but "there is no right to place military-style assault weapons into the hands of terrorists and/or criminals who wish to cause American families harm. There is no right to have access to the weapons of war in the streets of America. For those who want to wield those weapons, we have a place for them. It is the U.S. military. And we welcome them."

I pointed to the assault weapons ban's accomplishments over ten years, and I repeated a story I heard while hunting the previous fall in Iowa with a local sheriff and his deputies. "As we walked through a field with the dogs, hunting pheasant, he pointed out a house behind me, a house they had raided only a few weeks earlier, where meth and crack were being sold. On the morning when they went in to arrest this alleged criminal, there was an assault weapon on the floor lying beside that individual. That sheriff and others across this country do not believe we should be selling these weapons or allowing them to be more easily available to criminals in our country."

I also felt compelled to call attention to the Republican ploy in staging the vote in the first place. I continued: "Let's be honest about what we are facing today. The opposition to this commonsense gun safety law is being driven by the powerful NRA special interest leadership and by lobbyists in Washington. I don't believe this is the voice of responsible gun owners across America. Gun owners in America want to defend their families, while the NRA leadership is defending the indefensible. There is a gap between America's *Field & Stream* gun owners and the NRA's *Soldier of Fortune* leaders."

This is a fight worth having, I thought as I walked back into the Democratic cloakroom. I ran into Dick Durbin, the Democratic whip. "It's going to be a long campaign, John," he said warily. "I don't know where the Bush campaign ends and the Senate begins."

Dick had a good nose for politics.

After the vote, I walked off the Senate floor with Ted Kennedy and Dianne Feinstein, the senior senator from California. Dianne had been the first senator besides Teddy to back my campaign. She was a trailblazer who had helped break the glass ceiling in California Democratic politics.

The *click-click-click* of the cameras almost drowned out what Dianne was saying to us as we walked along. I got back into the motorcade to head to the airport, so we could get back to the campaign trail.

I turned to my traveling chief of staff, David Morehouse, who was next to me in the car, and asked him what he was hearing. "Ron Fournier [of the Associated Press] says the Republicans are giddy. They got the photo they wanted."

"The photo?"

"Yeah," Morehouse replied, "liberal John Kerry, gooey Californian Dianne Feinstein, and their bogeyman Ted Kennedy huddling about guns. A gift to the NRA."

I stared ahead as the cars pulled into Dulles Airport. I thought about the meaning of a single photograph and the craven politics being played in the world's greatest deliberative body. I still believed this was a fight we needed to have.

Ted Kennedy had thirteen nieces and nephews without fathers because twice guns had been used to murder his brothers. He had been there at Andrews Air Force Base in 1963 to embrace Jackie when she was still covered in President Kennedy's blood. Five years later he had rushed to Los Angeles as his lone surviving brother lay dying, shot at point-blank range. In 1978, Dianne Feinstein was president of the San Francisco Board of Supervisors when a deranged colleague assassinated Mayor George Moscone and Harvey Milk, the gay rights leader elected to the board. Dianne heard the gunshots and found Milk's body lying lifeless in his office. With Milk's blood on her clothes, in the lobby of city hall, Dianne had to announce to her city and the world that her colleagues had been gunned down.

To me, the alleged Republican giddiness was a sign of how insulting our politics had become and how empty the new Republican Party was becoming. Power rather than good governance. A surrender to the lowest common denominator. I thought, *I'm happy to be counted with Ted and Dianne on that issue. I'll debate that vote anywhere in America.*

The NRA and the GOP ran that photo in flyers and pamphlets and television ads. The media, which too often covers the political horse race and not the substance, never seemed to point out that Ted and Dianne had seen the cost of gun violence up close in ways that the NRA's CEO, Wayne LaPierre, never had. Most revealing, no one seemed to point out how the NRA's attack was all propaganda. No serious person in either party ever talks about taking away people's guns. They talk about responsible ownership and keeping guns of war in the hands of uniformed warriors in the military or law enforcement.

The NRA put its public campaign, totaling $20 million, squarely behind George Bush's candidacy. I saw the ridiculous ads in newspapers across the Midwest: "If John Kerry wins, hunters lose." They had their fun too. President Bush even mocked my hunting, saying of my F rating from the NRA, "He can run—he can even run in camo—but he cannot hide." I didn't need hunting lessons from a president whose running mate accidentally shot his hunting partner, and my history in camo dated back before my campaign.

It was an authentic American hero, John Glenn, who reminded me of the disconnect between the symbolism of NRA politics and reality. One day we joined Congressman Ted Strickland and went trapshooting in Ohio, not far from where John had grown up. The photos would be a nice counterpoint to the Republican mythology that we were taking away anyone's guns. John blasted the clay traps out of the sky. On the bus afterward, I asked him how often he still fired a gun. "Not since Korea."

When you stop and think about the priorities in communities across America—dealing with the opioid crisis, making our schools safe, building our infrastructure—it is deeply disturbing that increasingly our choices are defined by images alone. In a firefight of any kind—political or real—I'd want John Glenn to have my back, even at eighty-three, not some baby-faced NRA lobbyist. I spent the campaign comfortable with who I was: a hunter who knew no one needs an AK-47 to hunt geese, a believer in the Second Amendment who knew that weapons of war are for hunting people. Reinforced by events of the last several years, I can look back and know I was right to call out the NRA for its ugly, corrosive politics. We carried Wisconsin, Michigan and Minnesota and brought New Hampshire back into the Democratic column despite the NRA's lies. Most important, I didn't lie awake wondering how I'd justify my voting record to a mother whose child was killed by an automatic weapon.

Politics is tough, and I'm okay with tough politics. But the gun issue was just the beginning, a mere preview of the political weapon the Republicans would create on the issue of gay marriage. The contrast between what I was seeing and hearing from people as I campaigned and the debate the Republicans were trying to ignite was stunning.

The Republicans were up-front about their reasoning. Someone told me a long time ago that a gaffe is a moment when a politician tells the truth. The Senate Republican conference chairman, Rick Santorum from Pennsylvania, committed one of those gaffes. He explained to the press why they suddenly planned to schedule so many Senate votes on social issues like guns and gay rights. He said that my campaign "loved to talk about education and health care." Implicit in his statement was the fact that his political party wanted to create an entirely different, parallel conversation.

I didn't need a pollster to tell me Santorum's political gambit was far removed from the issues most Americans worried about. I had the best focus group in America, free of charge, at least three times daily: the people, most of whom had never stepped foot in Washington, D.C., along the rope lines at rallies.

If you've ever let C-SPAN take you behind the scenes of a campaign rally, you know that today a rope line is a place where a candidate is greeted by a phalanx of smartphones, people reaching out to snap a selfie or record a frantic three-second video.

The 2004 campaign was the last presidential campaign of a more personal era. Back then, you could still have a conversation with someone in the rope line, even amid the sea of arms reaching out for an autograph.

The Secret Service erected heavy-duty iron Jersey barriers for protection. They warned me of the many possible scenarios where what appeared to be innocent might not be so harmless. The baseball someone was handing you with a pen for an autograph could be an improvised explosive device that would leave you without hands. The cell phone someone was trying to pass you to say hi to their elderly mother? That too could be a bomb, they warned.

But I felt the input from talking to people was important. In many ways it was my only real daily contact with the folks who would be making the decision on Election Day. Nothing in the faces I saw up close along those rope lines indicated anything but warmth. Sometimes I would spot the flicker in someone's eye, or the creases in a worried forehead, indicating they had something to get off their chest.

When they shared their stories, the common theme was almost always struggle. Someone at home was sick, and insurance wasn't keeping up with the medical bills. A mother would lift her young son with Down syndrome and tell me that special education wasn't getting the money needed for the attention her son deserved. A father worried about his son headed off to Iraq after a tour of duty in Afghanistan. "My boy, this is my boy," he'd say, passing me a dog-eared snapshot. I would flash back to that moment thirty-six years before when I bid farewell to my father at the service station as I headed off to war. I won't ever forget that look in his eyes, and now that very same look was on the face of someone else's father.

Many stories were about jobs. It wasn't just that over a million jobs had disappeared under President Bush, or that we'd lost 2.7 million manufacturing jobs in places like Pennsylvania, Ohio and Michigan. What I heard was more basic. A man a few years younger than I, but weathered by a lifetime of working outside, or a burly fellow with a walrus mustache and two noticeable hearing aids, the aftereffects of decades manning a loud machine in a factory. They would lean across the barricade and put their face close to my ear to make sure I could hear what they were saying: they were working harder, working two jobs, or out of work entirely, or their pensions had disappeared, or their kids were moving away because the jobs didn't exist anymore at home. They were unburdening themselves. These were proud people who had always counted on the dignity that came with working hard, raising their kids and knowing that one day they'd retire with their grandkids nearby to enjoy the reward of a hard-earned pension and Social Security. It wasn't too much to ask after years of backbreaking work, but that way of life was disappearing.

The people I met stuck with me: the faces, the intensity, the emotion. Not once did anyone come up to me and say, "Please, John, whatever you do, stop gay people from getting married in Massachusetts," although that was exactly what the Republican Party seemed determined to talk about. Rick Santorum, a true believer when it came to this issue, was probably the most honest about his views. With Rick, it wasn't an act. He had granted an interview with the Associated Press and let loose with his worries, speculating that if gay marriage could stand anywhere in America, you'd wind up with men marrying children and even dogs. He meant every word.

One day on the campaign in Milwaukee, when the staff was so bold as to let me have some fun and break the monotony of three rallies a day, I went for a motorcycle ride with a group of firefighters and cops. Most of them were active in their local union. Afterward, we sat down for a beer. They were candid about the race.

"Open the mail from the Republicans, pick up the phone at night, and it's another robocall. It's all we hear about. If it's not guns, it's gays," they said.

The resident wiseass in the group fired off a quick one-liner. "I've been married for thirty-five years. If these gays want to be miserable too, who am I to stop them?"

I smiled. "Guys, do you know anyone who actually is worried their marriage is going to fall apart because two men or two women somewhere want to spend their lives together?"

In my mind, that was the craziest part of the GOP hysteria, the insinuation that suddenly our heterosexual marriages would be undermined if a state chose to allow civil unions or gay marriage. It was all built on the premise that being gay was a choice, with more than a hint that it was contagious.

I'd heard it all before and not just from Republicans. Back in the early 1990s, I'd testified in front of Strom Thurmond's Armed Services Committee in favor of letting gay people serve openly in the U.S. military. West Point had an honor code that forbade lying, but if patriotic gay Americans were willing to lay down their lives for our country, they had to break that oath every day. Who were we kidding? Did anyone really believe that of the 416,800 Americans killed in World War II, none of them was gay? Did none of the 59,000 names on the Vietnam Wall belong to a gay American?

One night soon after I'd come to the Senate, I went for a long walk near the congressional cemetery. Lo and behold, I came across a tombstone with a surprisingly defiant inscription: "A Gay Veteran: They gave me a medal for killing a man and a dishonorable discharge for loving one."

All of this was a big fight in the Senate as the Armed Services Committee deliberated. I still remember a history lesson from Senator Byrd about how the Roman Empire perished when homosexuality could flourish and a strange, meandering line of questioning before the Senate Armed Services Committee from Senator Thurmond about sodomy.

People had every right to believe what they wanted to believe. I'd been raised to believe marriage was a sacrament, the union of a man and a woman, but not everyone had to believe that. No government was ordering my church to perform a gay marriage. What on earth was the problem with trying to lower the temperature and find a legal way to protect gay people so that partners could pass on property or custody of children, or make health care decisions for each other? It felt like a parallel universe when Santorum and the Right declared a culture war.

The big question was how far the Bush-Cheney campaign was willing to go to put the issue front and center in the 2004 campaign. Would they leave it to the Christian Coalition and Jerry Falwell, or would they weaponize it themselves?

The president and First Lady had gay friends. There were senior people in their White House and in their campaign who were gay, including the vice president's daughter. I don't believe that either President Bush or Laura Bush has a bigoted bone in their body. They regretted that the first President Bush's renominating convention in Houston in 1992 wasn't a Texas homecoming but a parade of Pat Buchanan clones playing social issues like a poorly tuned fiddle. At that ugly convention, RNC chairman Richard Bond declared, "We are America, they are not America."

We'd occasionally hear from one of my gay campaign staffers that a Republican counterpart on the Bush campaign—living in the closet—was fighting to keep that issue on the backburner. President Bush was a competitive person, but he was uncomfortable with social issues defining his campaign. Left to his own devices, he would've been very happy to be reelected on the strength of wartime incumbency and post-9/11 unity. But there weren't enough votes there. I had made the race tight. With the math turning against them, Karl Rove successfully sold the campaign on a path of division.

Rove knew the power of social wedge issues. Thirty-eight states had already enacted some measure to define marriage as being between a man and a woman. It ginned up Republican turnout and galvanized the kind of conservative evangelical voters who had lagged in turnout in Bush's down-to-the-wire battle with Al Gore.

The Bush campaign doubled down on elevating gay marriage in the campaign, siding with Karl Rove over their own campaign manager, Ken Mehlman, who had not yet publicly announced that he was gay.

President Bush dedicated an entire presidential radio address to the case for amending the U.S. Constitution to ban gay marriage. I remember listening to Bush's words that Sunday morning. Bush sounded like he was reading a hostage statement prepared by his captors, the words foreign sounding, but each calculated to give the social conservatives just what they needed to motivate their voters and drive a wedge between us and them.

The radio address was transparently political. Even if you believed gay marriage was a federal issue, it would require sixty-seven votes in the Senate and two-thirds of the House to amend the Constitution. Nowhere near those majorities existed. Congress had no vote scheduled. The president of the United States was using a radio address to the country to focus on this single issue in the middle of two wars, with no congressional action scheduled and its hypothetical outcome a foregone conclusion. We'd come a long way from Franklin Roosevelt using the radio address to tell us "we have nothing to fear but fear itself."

The line I still remember from the president's message was a soft nod to civility, while he pried the lid off Pandora's box. "We should also conduct this difficult debate in a manner worthy of our country, without bitterness or anger."

Give me a break, I thought. Civility was never going to be the hallmark of an issue fueled by division.

In 2004, eleven states had already put banning gay marriage on the ballot for November, driven by the conservative movement. Among the measures was so-called Issue 1 in Ohio, also known as Amendment 1, which stipulated that the only marriage that would be valid and recognized in the state was one between a man and a woman. This was the lone ballot initiative that the Buckeye State's voters were asked to weigh in on in the state that could determine which party controlled the presidency. Ohio's Republican governor, Bob Taft, didn't want it on the ballot. He feared it would

drive businesses from investing in his state. Neither did his Republican attorney general. They missed the memo that its entire purpose was to spark
conservative turnout and cost Democrats votes.

Issue 1 had the Bush campaign's fingerprints all over it. Ohio's secretary
of state, Ken Blackwell, responsible for ballot initiatives from certifying
signatures to rubber-stamping language, was cochair of the Bush campaign
and a hard right, social issues zealot.

Blackwell traveled the state campaigning for Issue 1 in crude, unmistakably anti-gay language. He obviously missed the president's words about
conducting the debate with civility. He said gay relationships "even defy
barnyard logic . . . the barnyard knows better." It was a not-so-subtle way of
describing some of his fellow Americans as less than human, less even than
animals.

The irony wasn't lost on me that for all the Republican attacks on me
as a flip-flopper, or the way they sneered at the word "nuance," Bush's use
of the gay marriage issue was a master class in having it every which way.
He had run in 2000 as a compassionate conservative, but his Ohio chairman
was belittling Americans because of who God made them. In 2000, Bush
had said he supported civil unions, but his campaign supported this ballot initiative, which would make it illegal for Ohio even to recognize civil
unions. Until Bush jumped on the federal constitutional amendment bandwagon, we had the same position: we believed marriage was between a man
and a woman but supported civil unions. Now his campaign said we were
on opposite sides of a gulf they wanted to widen. So much for President
Bush's promises in 2000 to be "a uniter, not a divider." That's what bothered me the most. Presidential campaigns are tinderboxes, and social issues
are rarely thoughtfully discussed in an environment where hundreds of millions of dollars are being spent on ads and interest groups are constantly
trying to turn even small differences into big ones.

I had no qualms opposing amending the Constitution of the United
States over this issue. I don't believe in playing around with the Constitu-
tion except when it's the only means to right wrongs or protect freedoms.
That's what I'd call being an actual conservative.

Affirming the humanity and citizenship of freed slaves was a reason to
amend the Constitution. Giving women the right to vote was a reason to
amend the Constitution. In the Senate, I regularly opposed efforts to change
the Constitution to do something we didn't have to do or that Congress
could do on its own. I used to go down to the floor of the Senate and speak
out against the predictable effort every Congress made to pass a constitutional amendment banning flag burning. I'd remind my colleagues that the

countries that had banned flag burning included Nazi Germany and Saddam Hussein's Iraq. I had no qualms reminding anyone that while I detested the act of anyone burning an American flag, I'd fought in a war for freedom, and that included someone else's right to be stupid or even unpatriotic.

Here we were, though, debating another trumped-up constitutional amendment, another politically rigged fight, but this time the disagreement and disputes were unleashing ugliness, vulgarity, viciousness and vitriol in America that politics and our country's leaders should seek to avoid at all costs.

The people whom Ken Blackwell was trivializing were all someone's sons and daughters. I've never forgotten meeting Matthew Shepard's mother in 1999 on the steps of the Senate when she came to lobby for a national hate crimes law. Her son was beaten, tortured and left to die on a barbed wire fence in Wyoming the year before for the "crime" of being gay. Her eyes were hollowed out, deep circles underneath them. I couldn't begin to imagine the sadness, the horror, of wondering what was going through her son's mind as he hung there dying. Where did hate come from that could allow such a thing to happen?

In the immediate heat of the campaign, we had to guard against the issue's political potency. Social issues were working against us in some places where the Bush campaign was banging that drum the loudest. Arkansas and Kentucky, which had been long shots all along, pulled out of reach. A flyer appeared all over West Virginia showing two men holding hands and promising that if John Edwards and I were elected, men would be free to marry each other. Our poll numbers were dropping in the Midwest, in areas where voters were socially conservative and in counties where the biggest job losses of the Bush presidency—the issue we wanted to debate—had occurred.

What could we do? It came down to two choices. We could dial up our appeals on economic issues, or we could try to blunt the appeal of the Bush-Cheney social issues agenda. I wanted to drag the race back to economic issues. But there were places in American politics that I just wasn't comfortable going. When you're in political trouble, it's not a bad idea to check out old playbooks from the past. You can usually find some wisdom. President Clinton was the first Democrat reelected since President Roosevelt. I respected his political skill, and to this day I think many of his critics conveniently forget just how hard it was for a Democrat to win in 1992 and 1996. But when some veterans of those campaigns began to push me to take the gay rights issue "off the table" by appearing at an event in favor of Ohio's Issue 1, or by voting for the constitutional amendment, I recoiled.

I understood their point. Clinton in 1996 had signed the so-called Defense of Marriage Act into federal law, guarding against gay marriage, and ran radio ads in rural America celebrating it. It denied Bob Dole a wedge issue.

The bill became law—but without my vote. In fact, I'd been the only senator running for reelection to vote against it. I could not now in good conscience endorse a ballot initiative in Ohio that would make it impossible for Ohio to ever have civil unions. That was just plain wrong.

We were going to have to win this race the harder way—by redefining the race around the real issues.

The collision of faith and politics in the presidential campaign was a bolt from the blue, but certainly not from the heavens. It was a sad reminder that the modern, bare-knuckle political season doesn't shed light on life's most personal, difficult and thorny issues, it only distorts them. Back when I was fighting my way to the nomination, winning primaries and consolidating support, the archbishop of St. Louis, Raymond Leo Burke (who would years later be demoted and benched by Pope Francis), inserted his personal politics into the campaign by unilaterally announcing that because I supported a woman's right to choose, I would not receive Communion in his archdiocese. A couple of other conservative bishops would go on to join him. Burke had been a controversial figure in the Church for a long time, issuing similar edicts when he was ministering to the faithful in Wisconsin.

The private reaction among many in the Church, including many of his fellow bishops, was that Burke was out of bounds, inviting a dangerous politicization of the tabernacle. The U.S. Conference of Catholic Bishops issued statements that individual bishops could tend to their flocks, a subtle but clear message: it meant Burke spoke for himself, not for the Church and not for the Vatican. Regrettably, like most retractions in newspapers, the position of the bishops did not get broad dissemination.

The Church has its own way of sending messages about politics, and in an election year, the bishops produce a voting guide for the faithful. In 2004, the voting guide was based on ten questions for every Catholic voter to wrestle with, ranging from how, after September 11, we might build "not only a safer world, but a better world," to how we might best "protect the weakest in our midst—innocent unborn children," to "how we can keep our nation from turning to violence to solve some of its most difficult problems—abortion to deal with difficult pregnancies; the death penalty to combat crime; euthanasia and assisted suicide to deal with the burdens of age, illness, and disability; and war to address international disputes." The list went on identifying challenges that struck deeply at convictions of

Catholic faith: children dying of hunger, inequality in America, access to health care, the environment, nuclear nonproliferation and peace.

I know my position on a few of these issues differed from that of the Church. I'd long wrestled with the issue of abortion. I wasn't alone. Fellow Catholic senators—Dick Durbin, Joe Biden, Barbara Mikulski, Chris Dodd—also grappled with these issues to try to reconcile their views about life and the articles of our faith with the fact that we didn't just represent our fellow Catholics. These weren't easy matters. I would flash back to a conversation I once had with an archbishop about abortion. I shared with him the difficulty of legislating in a Senate of one hundred different opinions, representing fifty different states and myriad Americans of different beliefs and convictions, keeping in mind the role of the courts, the fact that individual senators don't control what comes to the floor or which amendments they must vote on, and the ability of special interest groups on both sides to keep us polarized. I also pointed out that while I am allowed in public life to have personal beliefs as a matter of faith, and I can advocate for them, I can't impose an article of faith on someone who doesn't believe what I do, who doesn't share a similar article of faith.

"The Church can take a position," I recall saying to the archbishop, "but we have to vote on a policy. That's a very different thing." He didn't disagree. I think that's why the voting guide from the Conference of Bishops implicitly acknowledged the challenges and instead asked each parishioner to wrestle with the moral challenges rather than instructing him or her to be a single-issue, hot-button voter.

One afternoon, as my campaign staff and I flew across the country on a long flight to California, I tried to explain all this to them as we debated how to respond and what to do. I set out on the table in front of us a printed list of the issues the bishops had defined for critical thinking.

Our conversation got heated. "Guys, hold on here. Has anyone in the press asked Archbishop Burke about the issues? The Church opposes the death penalty. I'm against the death penalty. George Bush electrocuted record numbers of people when he was governor in Texas. The Church is opposed to the war. I fought to end a war. Bush started a war of choice. The Church is against the growing inequality in society. I oppose tax cuts for the rich; my opponent campaigns on them. The Church calls on all of us to protect God's creation—Earth. I'm one of the strongest environmentalists in the Senate, and he's gutting environmental protections. Why isn't he on the defensive? Why isn't Burke concerned about my opponent's position on issues of life and death, fairness and justice, which often mean life and death?"

"Burke says this only applies to Catholics," explained the campaign's policy director. In other words, if my faithful Episcopalian mother had told my agnostic father that she wasn't going to raise the Kerry kids Catholic as he wished, I wouldn't be having this fight.

We were stuck in a dynamic that promised nothing but a political food fight about the most difficult and divisive issues in the country, let alone about the meaning of Catholicism and being a person of faith. What we Catholics called "the whole cloth of Catholic teaching" was supposed to be the basis for discussions about policy and public life, but one archbishop in one archdiocese had taken the entire conversation hostage with the encouragement and support of folks who were pursuing policies completely alien to Catholic teaching.

Catholics of my generation had grown up in a Church that never would have wanted this fight, this rank politics. We had very different expectations about the Church's role in politics, and politics' role in religion. Catholics had been proud when America elected its first Catholic president in 1960, but mindful of what President Kennedy said before his election: "I am not the Catholic candidate for president. I am the Democratic Party's candidate for president, who happens also to be a Catholic. I do not speak for my church on public matters, and the church does not speak for me. . . ."

How ironic that Kennedy had to prove he wasn't "too Catholic" to be president, while now one archbishop had created a different litmus test entirely: Was I Catholic enough?

Growing up I seemed to remember being taught in church by the priests that true faith is private and personal. The Church we grew up with looked inward. It reveled in the authenticity of its separation from the modern world, from the Latin Mass to the rituals. More than that, we were taught to be pious, but remain private. I remember going to Mass during the Lenten season and hearing our priest at Our Lady of Blessed Sacrament read from Matthew 6:5: "And when you pray, do not be like the hypocrites, for they love to pray . . . on the street corners to be seen by others. Truly I tell you, they have received their reward in full." I was taught not to boast about piety.

If you truly have faith and your faith informs your life, it is hard to reconcile separate worlds of political ideology and religious theology. I believe the most important teaching of the Gospels is, at least for Christians, that it is not enough to say one believes in Jesus. Believing in Jesus requires action, a bona fide effort, a commitment to live the example of Jesus. Jesus himself commands that: in Mark 8:34–35, he says, "Whoever wishes to come after me must deny himself, take up his cross, and follow me. For whoever wishes to save his life will lose it, but whoever loses his life for my sake and that of the gospel will save it."

So, as the Senate's chaplain Barry Black likes to say, you can "separate church from state, but not faith from state." The question is how you judge what acts make faith real. Belief in Jesus requires action to "keep his commandments." Jesus's words can't be much clearer than that.

The media didn't help. Every president or presidential candidate since Ronald Reagan has been followed by what is called a "protective pool" of reporters. Anytime I, the candidate, was out in public, I was followed by a handful of reporters who documented everything in astonishingly minute detail—what I wore, what I ate, who was with me, wherever I went.

They followed me to church every Sunday and began what the media feasted on in 2004, thanks to Archbishop Burke's attacks—the "wafer watch."

The press turned it into a Sunday-to-Sunday spectacular: If I went to Catholic Mass in a city, would I take Communion? If I were instead a guest at an African American Protestant church, was it because I feared the Catholic archdiocese would have turned me away when I came up to the altar rail for the Eucharist? The foolish feeding frenzy distracted from the intimacy of actual faith.

In 2004, I was home in Boston for one of the most special days on the Christian calendar, Easter Sunday, a day for family and a day to reflect on Jesus's resurrection from the dead after the sadness of Good Friday. I looked forward to attending Mass down the street from our home at our church on Park Street, the Paulist Center. Social justice, economic justice, fighting for the underdog, caring for the sick and the poor were all at the forefront of the center's work. Gay and straight were welcome, and all were at the heart of this inclusive Catholic community. The Mass was often celebrated in multiple languages on the projection screens behind the altar.

As much as I had grown up in the formality of the old Catholic Church and sometimes missed the High Mass and the beauty of the Latin, I appreciated the determination of this parish to break down barriers. The Mass on this Easter was beautiful, and it was especially meaningful to have my church pray for me before I went back out on the campaign trail. How many people ever get to experience that kind of spiritual embrace?

After Mass, I walked outside holding Teresa's hand. I could hear in the background a television anchor broadcasting live across the street: "And on Easter Sunday, live from Boston, our reporters inside tell us that Dem-

ocratic nominee John Kerry did successfully receive Communion today."
He could have just as easily been broadcasting a sporting event. It missed
the entire meaning of Easter Sunday, or the point of what we believe—
and why.

Not once in 2004 was I refused Communion, but anyone watching at
home could be forgiven if they believed otherwise. In the end, only 3 bishops out of 180 expressed support for Burke's position. But this tiny minority got the headlines.

To me, the real tragedy was that the debate never happened—the one
about what it really means to live the teachings of Jesus. That debate
doesn't fit into thirty-second sound bites, and it certainly isn't won or lost
by a "wafer watch."

I KNEW FROM my experience in 1972 that my opposition to the war in Vietnam was a big target for the political Right. I never doubted that a presidential campaign would raise the stakes even higher.

When I protested in 1971, I lost a few friends forever. Vietnam was a
divisive war, fought in a divided country by men from an increasingly divided country. Many politicians wanted to keep us divided, so they attacked
those who were telling the truth. My activism was distorted to hurt me in
1972, the only campaign I'd ever lost.

I knew then what I still know now—I did the right thing by speaking out
against the war. It saved lives, and when I go to meet my Maker, I'll do so
with a clear conscience about everything I said and did at the time. I made
enemies by telling the truth to save lives. Others hid the truth to protect their
political fortunes, at the cost of tens of thousands of names on the Wall in
Washington.

In 2004, in the cauldron of a country still fresh from 9/11, just one year
into the war in Iraq and two years into the war in Afghanistan, the benefit
of the doubt was going to go to the commander in chief. In the first presidential election after 9/11, the Republicans' playbook was to pit my 1971
position against the commander in chief card.

Republicans had previewed that playbook in the 2002 election cycle,
when they ran a fear and smear campaign in Georgia against my pal Max
Cleland, a decorated Vietnam veteran and triple amputee, to elect a senator
who got out of the war with five student deferments.

Politics is a tough game. The Bush team had proven itself as skilled as
the Kennedys and as hard-assed as LBJ. No one should have been fooled by
the "what, me worry?" look on the face of George Walker Bush.

I knew they'd throw the kitchen sink at me, and it was logical that in a time of war, when commander in chief credentials were at stake, they would try to tarnish my legitimacy. Indeed, as it became clearer that I'd be the Democratic nominee, the shape of the attack started to unfold. The Bush campaign and the RNC distorted my voting record, while simultaneously the more unsavory elements of the right-wing machine—removed just far enough from the official Bush-Cheney apparatus—teed off on my patriotism.

Enter Ted Sampley from stage right. Ted was one of the most deceptive human beings I'd ever encountered. Ted pushed the limits of my Christian belief that all could be redeemed.

I'd first seen him in action when John McCain and I were investigating the fate of the Americans unaccounted for in Vietnam.

My campaign brought Sampley out of the woodwork again, hawking T-shirts proclaiming me "Hanoi John." Armed with a website titled "Vietnam Vets Against John Kerry," Sampley was back in business. He and those like him proffered what they called new material: an old photo depicting me standing next to Jane Fonda at an anti-war rally. Guilt by association. But it was a fake. Just as the photo was going viral, spreading across the internet and appearing in newspapers nationwide, two photographers stepped forward. Owen Franken had been a photographer and writer for decades. He recognized the photo of Fonda. Another photographer, Kenneth Light, recognized the photo of me from an assignment he had in 1971 covering the VVAW. The photographers confirmed the two images had been photoshopped into one. It was, literally, fake news.

Sampley was exposed for the exploitative liar he was. We won the initial battle in the media by punching back. We made sure that in real time, the media knew who Ted Sampley was, and we made his vile record the issue.

This episode, however, was the canary in the coal mine, an early warning of what would lie ahead. I believed that the antidote to the inevitable lies would surely be the complete story of who I was. I also believed we could tell that story during the campaign.

I knew that the most compelling testimony would come from the men who knew me best, who had already weighed in and wanted to be deployed everywhere and anywhere all over the country: my crewmates from Vietnam. They weren't politicians. Many weren't even Democrats. They were proud of our service together, and they'd long ago made peace about whatever differences we had over the war. When they spoke, crowds got quiet. They were effective because they were genuine. They defied whatever caricature of me the Republicans or the likes of Ted Sampley were trying to paint. Their friendship is the record that endures.

I believed the truth would carry the day—that is, until the day I began to hear that Admiral Roy Hoffmann was making calls to veterans, stirring up opposition to me. Hoffmann, whom I'd known as Captain Hoffmann, was a tough old bird. Skip Barker blamed him for Don Droz's death in an ambush, and as I've mentioned, it was Skip's eloquent, contemporaneous letter describing Hoffmann's decisions that day which pushed me into anti-war activism. Ironically, I had enjoyed several positive interactions with Admiral Hoffmann over the years. I'd seen him at Swift boat reunions, and I'd seen him in 1995 at the Washington Navy Yard, when the last Swift boat was officially decommissioned and dozens of us reunited. I was surprised by his sudden about-face in this campaign, so I picked up the phone and called him. I said I had heard he was working the phones against me.

He said he didn't like the way the historian Douglas Brinkley had portrayed him in the book *Tour of Duty*, which covered my service in the Navy, my protest years and my work with John McCain to make peace and come to terms with the torment and troubles over the MIAs and POWs. I first pointed out that his complaint was with Brinkley—not me—but if there was anything inaccurate in the book, I was happy to put him in touch with the author and the publisher, or to be in touch myself to rectify any inaccuracy. It became patently clear, though, that this wasn't at all a question of inaccuracies. He just lit into me about everything I'd said when I came home from Vietnam. He said we always had to support the troops. I told him that I had supported the troops by speaking out. He said he was voting for Bush, no surprise there. It was clear he didn't want to have a conversation.

If Admiral Hoffmann wanted a referendum on whether the Vietnam War was right or wrong, or on whether I had a right to oppose it, that was fine by me. He had a right to his opinion.

On May 4, 2004, Admiral Hoffmann and a group of former Swift boat officers held a press conference in Washington to announce their opposition to my campaign because of my position on the war.

The only person there who had served on my first boat—the PCF-44—was Steve Gardner, who had resurfaced in March in the pages of *Time* magazine, announcing that he was a Rush Limbaugh–listening right-winger and warning that I'd be another Bill Clinton in the White House. Steve was the only one of my crewmates on either boat who seemed partisan. His feelings surprised the rest of the crew of PCF-44. Steve was not with me or on my crew in any of the later actions for which I was decorated. He knew nothing firsthand about any of those missions.

The assembled group called for me to release my military records, which didn't make any sense because we had already posted them online weeks before, which the press knew well. My crewmates held a press conference immediately afterward to respond to Hoffmann and company. They hit back hard and quickly. The media barely covered either of these events.

The morning of July 30, at the crack of dawn, we set out for a postconvention cross-country tour by bus, boat and train to build on the momentum of the convention in Boston. We were taking the campaign through the swing states. Bill Clinton had started the postconvention trip tradition in 1992, traveling by bus and seizing a chance to reach small towns too often bypassed. People get a chance to hear and see the candidate. I'd been looking forward to this moment of retail politics. On day one of our bus trip from Boston to Scranton, Pennsylvania, with multiple stops along the way ending with a big evening rally in Harrisburg, the politics of national security intervened. The federal government announced a surprise increase in the color-coded terror threat alert. There's been a lot of debate about the real motivation and timing of these alerts. It immediately dragged the campaign away from our positive convention and the issues we wanted to put to the country. Five years later, Homeland Security secretary Tom Ridge would say that he'd felt pressured to raise the terror alerts for reasons that made him wonder whether it was about security or politics. Our campaign strongly suspected that we knew the answer, but we couldn't say so at the time.

More surprises were on the way. A few days later, on August 5, as we were caravanning through the country with spotty cell phone reception and limited internet connectivity, the Swift Boat Veterans for Truth (SBVT) came back with a television advertisement accusing me of lying about everything I had lived through in the war.

The words in the ad were stark. "John Kerry has not been honest about what happened in Vietnam." "He is lying about his record." "I know John Kerry is lying about his first Purple Heart because I treated him for that injury." "John Kerry lied to get his Bronze Star. . . . I know, I was there, I saw what happened." "John Kerry has not been honest." "John Kerry is no war hero." "John Kerry betrayed the men and women he served with in Vietnam."

All of this was hard enough to hear and rebut, but the floodgates opened when a book appeared to accompany the ad, authored by none other than John O'Neill, an operative from 1971 whom Chuck Colson and the Nixon White House recruited to debate the VVAW, and Jerome Corsi, a conspiracy theorist who would later go on to accuse Hillary Clinton of being a lesbian and Barack Obama of being a closeted Muslim. We heard that the book, published by a conservative imprint and leveraged by the right-wing network, would debut at number one on the *New York Times* bestseller list.

Money, lies and television—and more money—are a toxic combination.

As our bus rumbled through the countryside, we sensed a new danger building. Our opponents had created an entirely new medium—dozens of outright lies adding up to one big lie, all footnoted and backed by signed affidavits to strike the pose of being meticulously researched.

I remember standing with our press secretary behind the reception desk at a tiny motel. Page by page, a faxed version of the book, titled *Unfit for Command*, was coming in to us.

I'd pull each page off the fax machine before it cascaded into the paper tray. The book was filled with lies. The primary author, John O'Neill, implied to have known me from Swift boats; in fact, he had appeared on the scene long after I'd left. Nothing about his reappearance was a coincidence.

People who weren't there were polluting the airwaves with lies, trying to undermine the service of every one of us who was. I was seething. I called my campaign manager. She believed that the advertising buy was minimal, but we were tracking it. John Edwards said the Republicans were just trying to get us to "chase a rabbit."

None of this reassured me. I had lived through too much during the Nixon years to forget what Mark Twain said: "A lie can make it halfway around the world before the truth pulls its boots on." But the campaign made sure the truth started to kick back. The so-called affidavits from SBVT members began to fall apart when the press questioned them. Incredibly, the only member of the SBVT who was there on February 28, 1969, testified the exact opposite of what they alleged. Larry Lee, a crewman on PCF-23, told a reporter, "I have no problems with [Kerry] getting the Silver Star."

And yet the ads stayed on the air.

Bill Rood, a Republican and a reporter for the *Chicago Tribune* for decades, was the skipper of PCF-23. He was awarded the Bronze Star with a "V" device to wear with the medal, recognizing his valor in combat and for his leadership that day. Each member of his crew won the Navy Commendation Medal. For years, Bill had stayed out of politics, but he felt compelled to write down exactly what happened that day and rebut the smears. It ran as a front-page story.

But the ads stayed on the air.

The Republican smear book alleged that the only enemy combatant that day was a kid in a loincloth, but when investigative reporters looked at the official Navy after-action report, based on the debriefing of all present, submitted by the senior officer on the Coast Guard cutter, they discovered proof that there was "heavy small arms fire" and three confirmed enemy dead even before the troops were landed and the enemy was overrun.

But the lies continued.

Confronted by the media, the SBVT's stories changed. If the Navy records contradicted the lies of their book, they'd say I must have written the records. When confronted by our superior officer's signature on the records, they'd say it must have been forged. When reporters confronted members of SBVT who themselves had received military decorations for events they now claimed never happened, they'd just go to ground and stop returning phone calls. John McCain denounced them, but they continued.

And still the ads stayed on the air.

Admiral Zumwalt, commander of all naval forces in Vietnam, had stated that what happened that day in 1969 "stood out among heroes as acts of total heroism." But Admiral Zumwalt, who had defended me in 1996, was dead. Now these men were discrediting his words and his legacy. The investigative journalists did a brilliant job of pushing the truth to the surface.

But the ads continued.

Then the ultimate debunking: the media discovered Captain Hoffmann's 1969 message that went up and down the chain of command praising me and my crew, stating,

> 1. The extremely successful raid and land sweep conducted along the Rach Dong Cung which demonstrated superb coordination and aggressive tactics stands as a shining example of completely overwhelming the enemy. 2. The tactic of attack and assault thoroughly surprised the enemy in his spider holes and proved to be immensely effective in rousting him into the open. This devastating application of the firepower of the Swifts may be the most efficacious method of dealing with small numbers of ambushers. . . . 3. This operation did unrepairable [*sic*] damage to the enemy in this area. Well done.

Imagine that—a contemporaneous "attaboy" from the man who was now conspiring with the Republicans to destroy me and my reputation.

It was extraordinary. They were lying about me, lying about themselves, lying about history—a history they knew was documented, in some cases by themselves, but always by the Navy they purported to love and respect.

But *still* the lies continued.

We kept fighting back with the facts in the national newspapers. The

New York Times, *Washington Post*, *Chicago Tribune*, *Boston Globe*, *Los Angeles Times*, *Miami Herald*, *Wall Street Journal* and others all ran front-page stories laying out Navy documents, service records, medical records and more. Every member of my crew who had engaged in any of the actions contradicted the reports about the attacks.

While the investigative journalists told the truth on the front pages, the pundits on cable ran everything through the prism of politics. They debated whether it had been a campaign blunder to tout my military service as a qualification for the presidency. Had we brought this on ourselves? It was absurd. It was a little bit like saying that because voters in 2000 respected John McCain's years as a POW, it was okay for smear tactics to be used in South Carolina insinuating that he was the "Manchurian candidate." Didn't the truth matter?

Voters in August were watching the news, looking at the ads, seeing this book with its scary title, *Unfit for Command*, on the bookshelves and in storefront windows, and their conclusion was "I'm uneasy about this guy."

Winning the argument didn't matter much. This was a fight for public hearts and minds—and guts. The SBVT disgraced themselves, were exposed as liars, but they were creating a question mark for voters. The presidency is about character. These lies had created a question about mine.

I was champing at the bit to answer the lies on television. Everything in my gut told me that when a lie is being repeatedly exploited on TV, it must be refuted on TV. But one plain and simple fact was that because we were operating within campaign finance reform limits, we had limited money. If we spent it in August, we wouldn't have enough money to run a national campaign for president in October—if we made it that far. Spend it now and we might have to pull out of Ohio or Florida.

Once I decided to stay within the finance system, I was always going to be fighting with one arm tied behind my back, especially when I faced a calculated attack machine of the combined Republican apparatus and right wing.

Within the leadership of the campaign there was a strong view that the lies had been exposed. Some argued that there was no need to "waste" money on ads regarding something the public wasn't concerned about. "It's not showing up in the polling data" was a phrase I heard several times when I called in to ask why we weren't on the air.

One night in a hotel late in the campaign, I couldn't sleep. We were in Ohio, and I was restless. I turned on the television and there was the Swift boat ad blatantly lying about me. If I were a citizen watching that ad, if that was my principal frame of reference, I wouldn't vote for me.

I called our headquarters and again made my argument. Again, I was told we needed that money. "It would be dangerous for the campaign and irresponsible to waste it now" was the sentiment. Some of the things going through my mind were admonitions I had received early in the lead-up to the campaign. "Don't be your own campaign manager," people warned me. "You've got to trust the professionals."

"You need to think about this in a cold-blooded way," I was told by a very well-intentioned campaign staffer. He didn't like that I was raising my voice about it.

"I lived this—if I can't get hot about this, what the hell can I get mad about?" I barked back.

"The press doesn't believe the lies, they know this is about 1971," my press aide told me.

I sighed. I knew, of course, that a lot of guys came home from Vietnam and hated the anti-war movement. No parades, no thank-you for their service—it all had become one big feeling of having been mistreated. The irony is that I understood that undercurrent of resentment. Much of what brought VVAW together was that feeling of alienation. It's just that we blamed the politicians and the war, not our fellow veterans. But no resentment of protests gave anyone fair license to lie about me and to lie even about themselves.

No matter what the campaign's polling was showing, I was sure the lies were having an effect. I'd pull into a campaign rally and see "Hanoi John" signs lining the motorcade path. Something ugly had been unleashed. We talked about sending John Edwards out to defend me, but somehow it seemed that the speech would be diluted by the vice presidential candidate himself and delivered without passion or conviction. My team started to ask whether Edwards was capable of carrying only a positive message. My communications director, Stephanie Cutter, wanted me to fight back myself, as did the staff there who knew me best.

In the end, when I look back, I have no one to get mad at but myself—and I've kicked myself many times. It was my campaign. These experts gave me their best judgment as to what they thought I should do. In the final analysis it was my decision—no one else's—to overrule them or not.

What I should have done was stop the campaign, stand up with my crew and answer every lie in detail and create and air ads to run in every market where theirs ran.

I should have delivered a thoughtful, personal speech about the war, taken people back to that period, put the war into context as Barack Obama had with his personalized speech about the Reverend Wright controversy in 2008.

But even as I write these words, a part of me wonders if the speech would have been anything but cathartic. The year 2004 was a time of division and confusion, and I wonder if such a speech could have been digested in that time after 9/11, with troops in the field fighting two wars, one of which seemed at times eerily like Vietnam.

I can still hear Ted Kennedy's old saying that "if you're explaining, you're losing," but the better part of me still feels I should have given that speech. I should have put it all in context, not just to win the campaign, but to try to end the war over the war.

Time is the one resource you can never get back. It's truly finite. No one takes sick days in presidential races. Sleep is allowed only after the election, and you sleep a whole lot more soundly if you've just won. It's also true that if you're not hammering away at your message, if you're spinning your wheels explaining why the other side's message isn't accurate, well, then you're on the defensive, and defense isn't how you win a race. There's a reason both of those axioms apply approximately 99 percent of the time. This was the 1 percent of the time when they didn't.

It turns out that sometimes you can lose by not explaining, and sometimes, like it or not, you have to address something that's too big and too important to become just another firefight between campaigns.

Bill Clinton told me that no one wants to hear about a war thirty years ago. I understood what he was saying. He was looking at the same polling we were, that voters said they wanted to know more about the economy and wanted less bickering between the campaigns. But it was easy for Clinton to say. This issue wasn't seminal to who he was, but it was personal to me and hit all the raw nerves in my body.

At its core, it was a matter of honor. The friendship of the men I'd served with on PCF-44 and PCF-94 told the truth, but I didn't want anyone anywhere to doubt that the truth really *was* the truth. It came back to what my mother had told me before I'd begun the journey of the campaign and before she'd passed away: integrity.

I couldn't rationalize how good men could make things up about another veteran when they knew the truth. Shortly before August turned into September, I called one of them, Bob Brandt. I'd seen his name on the list of the SBVT. Bob was a character, a big, burly man whose call sign in Vietnam was "Friar Tuck." I liked him. He served his whole career in the Navy until he hung up his spurs as a commander. I'd seen him in 2003 at our Swift boat veterans' reunion in Norfolk, Virginia, not long after my cancer surgery. We had hugged and laughed together. There was a warmth in the room, as we had all just watched the film that Don Droz's daughter, Tracy, had made about her search for her father's story—the father she had known only as an infant, the little girl Don had told to "be good, smile pretty." So it was a punch to the gut when I saw Bob Brandt's name on the list of vets discrediting my service, and I called him from my living room in Boston late one night.

The booming voice at the other end of the line was instantly familiar. "Is that Friar Tuck?" I said. He realized right away it was me. I told him I'd heard he might be getting involved with the SBVT and that I wanted to call him and talk to him because he knew that what they were saying wasn't true. Bob cut to the chase: he told me he had been mad at me for thirty years over what I said about the war. It wasn't a long conversation. I asked him to separate how we felt about the war from how we felt about each other, about Swift boats and about our service. I offered to get together, man-to-man— privately. I could tell he wanted to get off the line. About an hour later, my campaign called me because the *Drudge Report* had flashed one of its tantalizing headlines, saying that I was calling around pressuring veterans to change their stories about the SBVT. It posted an inflammatory mischaracterization of our conversation. How quickly word of a private conversation had made its way to the big Republican news megaphone at *Drudge*. The smear machine was in full throttle, and it wasn't going to stop.

There's a lot that revolted and angered me about the SBVT smears and their effect on my campaign. What still sticks in my craw is the way these men who served on Swift boats themselves turned the words "Swift boat" into a pejorative. It is an insult to the 3,600 men—3,000 enlisted and 600 officers—who served as Swifties.

After the campaign, I started hearing political operatives use "Swift boat" as shorthand for smears and lies about someone's core character. It rankled me, because to all who served with distinction on those rivers, who risked their lives every day, and for the families of men like Don Droz who died on those rivers, it was horrific to think of their units and their divisions becoming a synonym for "to lie."

The unavoidable fact was that August had knocked us on our butts. It began with the Swift boat assault and ended with the Republican convention. I needed to get off the mat and back into the fight.

"YOU CAN ASK a focus group whether they'd vote for a candidate who farts in public, and they'll say no. It may stink, but it sure is effective at clearing the room. What voters tell a focus group they want and what works aren't always the same thing."

It was an observation from former president Clinton at his folksy best. He'd asked what the campaign's polling showed about our best options fighting back against President Bush. The research showed that voters said they were turned off by negative campaigning and it would backfire. Only President Clinton could reduce that nonsense to one colorful expression. Howell Heflin, eat your heart out.

President Clinton was lying in bed in a New York hospital room, awaiting heart surgery to clear a blockage. I was lying on a hotel bed a thousand miles away looking for ways to clear what had become a blockage in my path to the presidency.

I'd called Clinton earlier in the day to wish him well as he entered the hospital, and we'd quickly ended up talking about the campaign. His love of politics was visceral. He generously offered to connect again later that night and even invited some of my campaign team to dial in as well and compare notes.

The polls confirmed what Clinton had said, not that we needed much reminder at this point. We were all wearing the scars of an August in which the airwaves and cable television had been chockablock full of lies about my military record, a month when the Republican convention crowds thought it was clever to wear purple camouflage Band-Aids on their cheeks to mock the severity of the wounds I received in Vietnam. It was amazing how low their party stooped. I had volunteered to go to Vietnam. Bush didn't. Cheney didn't. I didn't control who shot when or where and what kind of wound I received. The same shrapnel that went into an arm or leg of any number of our crew could just as easily have penetrated the brain or an eye. It was stunning to see a party of a war of choice in Iraq mocking the consequences of combat. Politics had clearly entered a dark, new chapter.

The bottom was falling out in several states that had been competitive coming out of the Democratic convention. August had badly damaged our campaign. All the numbers were down. States like Missouri and Virginia, which we had fought so hard to make newly competitive, were falling fast, possibly irreparably. But most alarmingly, we were hemorrhaging in Ohio, Florida and places we needed to win the presidency.

Press, pundits and nervous Democrats were calling for a campaign purge. My staff had been loyal and committed. The bed-wetting and hand-wringing by the pundits weren't fair to them.

I was as furious as anyone, more so than anyone, about the damage that had been done to us. Blowing up the campaign wasn't going to fix it. The calls for resignations and firings were sophomoric. Weren't the people they said I should now fire the same people who had been hailed as heroes when we were winning Iowa and New Hampshire against all odds? Weren't the new geniuses in the Bush operation the same ones who had overseen a drop in the incumbent president's approval ratings from historic post-9/11 highs to trailing me after my convention in July? What an unproductive and unforgiving ride in the barrel it can be for staff who work long hours with little reward.

We were headed into Labor Day and President Clinton knew as well as anyone that people were starting to write off our campaign. After forty-five minutes or so, I hung up the phone with President Clinton. His advice had been freewheeling and candid. Some resonated, some didn't. I was touched that the night before a serious heart procedure, he cared enough to talk at all.

I knew I had to get back on offense in this race or I was finished. I called an old friend from politics: Ron Rosenblith. Ron was always there when times were difficult. He had believed in my potential political resurgence after I'd lost in 1972. He saw that I could win in 1982 and 1984, saddled up again in 1996, and was back now for a campaign that had hit turbulence.

Ron was matter-of-fact in his analysis of the race. "You have to change the dynamic, and you've got fifty-four days to change the dynamic," he said. "You need to turn the boat into the shore." Ron's shorthand reflected the words of someone who really knew me and my history.

There would be no bigger or more consequential opportunity to do that than in the presidential and vice presidential debates less than one month away, the few opportunities a country ever gets, without the filter of the media, to measure the candidates side by side.

September 30 at the University of Miami became our campaign's shot at redemption: I had to win the first debate and win it handily.

I was itching for that moment to stand on a stage on live television, in front of tens of millions of Americans, and speak for myself directly to the country.

But first I had to prepare.

In campaigns, you're always fighting the drawing down of daylight, you never get back the time you lose. The pressure to schedule every minute becomes intense in the last weeks of a race. But you can easily lose track of the big picture that way too. We simply needed to invest time in preparing for the debates, even as we kept up a grueling pace in September. The time was costly, but I could never get back the ninety minutes of each debate: it was do-or-die. I was not going to sacrifice preparation for squeezing in one or two extra stops on the trail.

On the campaign plane for two weeks, I held debate prep sessions, straining to hear over the hum of the engines. Ron Klain managed the prep process, Bob Shrum provided expert advice on the back-and-forth. But I knew the real work would come when we stopped the campaign for five full days of preparation off the trail.

A week before the debate in Florida, we set off for Spring Green, Wisconsin, and a tucked-away treasure of a retreat site amid the green hills forty miles outside Madison: the House on the Rock resort, a vacation destination that was largely vacant after Labor Day.

The air was turning a little cooler, but the leaves weren't yet changing colors. It felt like what I'd known at home in Massachusetts: political weather, campaign weather.

The campaign headquarters had cleverly chosen to schedule our debate camp in a swing state, so we'd benefit from daily media coverage in a relevant media market. Whatever I did—a quick press conference, or even heading into town for ice cream—was treated as a news event.

But the real event was happening far away from any cameras. Just a few years before the campaign, Brad Pitt had starred in the movie *Fight Club*, which made famous a line that my young campaign team often quoted: "the first rule of fight club is never talk about fight club." I felt the same way about debate preparation. I had no tolerance for the temptation of some political operatives to leak debate strategy. Tipping your hand to your opponent isn't just undisciplined; it's a great way to lose before you've even shown up. It also turns off voters—if everything's a game, if it's all theater, no wonder people think politicians offer precious little relevant to their lives.

So we practiced each day, bright and early, beneath the tin roof and iron beams of an air-conditioned barn in a secluded corner of the property, where a perfect copy of the actual presidential debate set had been assembled, replete with matching insignia and exact replicas of the podiums President Bush and I would be using in Florida.

If the practice stage had been painfully replicated, the debate format had been meticulously negotiated. Debate negotiations are informed by each candidate's idiosyncrasies, but also by immediate history. Legend had it that four years before, when Al Gore had been the nominee, the Gore team came in with a long list of demands, everything from the temperature of the studio (they feared a Nixon-Kennedy 1960 moment of sweaty contrast) to the length of the segments and the division among topics. The Bush team, represented by former secretary of state James Baker, had just three demands, but they were committed to fighting for them. It ended up an easy trade: Baker happily gave Gore his dozen-plus demands in return for the three that really mattered to Bush.

Come 2004, we knew that the format was important, but the most critical issue for us was more fundamental: We wanted three debates. President Bush's team wanted just one. He was an incumbent wartime president and they wanted him to bask in the glow of the office instead of looking like a candidate. They also knew that the more often Bush was exposed to questions, the more room there was for error. They weren't going to let me back into the race; I'd have to maximize my opportunity.

The tables were turned from 2000. The White House team came in with a long list of demands. Remembering the way Al Gore had invaded then governor Bush's personal space in the 2000 debate in Boston, the Bush team requested that neither one of us could step out from behind our lectern. Remembering my history in the eight Lincoln-Douglas-style Kerry-Weld debates, they requested that we be able to ask only rhetorical questions, not questions explicitly directed to the other candidate. They had specific demands about how far apart the podiums would be. They had specific camera angles they deemed acceptable and unacceptable. Most of all, in a tactic designed to take advantage of any senatorial tendencies toward long-windedness, they requested strict time limits: one-minute answers, thirty-second follow-ups, and if we spoke for too long, a light would start flashing and a buzzer would sound for all to hear.

I was represented in debate negotiations by the Washington lawyer Vernon Jordan, a legendary figure in the Democratic Party. Vernon stared across the table at the Bush team, looked down at their long list of demands. The representatives from the presidential debate commission suggested that the two sides take a week to review each other's offers and make counterproposals. Vernon seized the initiative: "No need for counterproposals, we can strike a deal today—we're fine with the Bush campaign's many requests as long as we have three debates." The White House team was stunned. They had no choice but to accept the terms.

I had to chuckle hearing the details. I had no intention of invading Bush's personal space. That was hardly a concession. I didn't care how far apart our podiums would be. I didn't think asking questions of an incumbent president was likely to make me look good; in fact I thought it could come across as petulant or arrogant. So that wasn't a concession either.

As for the flashing red lights and the buzzers? Well, that's why God made debate prep.

Debate camp in rural Wisconsin felt comically similar: we were away from the glare of the media and the crowds. A crisp uphill hike to the barn each morning got my blood flowing, and then I went straight to work through drill after drill: lightning rounds, practice sessions, mastering the lights and the buzzers so my answers stayed short.

Ron Klain and Bob Shrum captained the prep process. Shrum sat in the front row taking notes, chomping on nicotine gum that he'd stick to the top of his coffee cup when he was done, his foot nervously tapping on the floor. Ron was calm and orderly. He kept meticulous notes, demanded real-time research from a gaggle of staffers who seemed to rush in and out by his desk constantly, anticipated any curveballs, and as mock moderator he kept the process moving.

Each night, at the exact hour at which the real debate would occur, we would dim the lights of the barn and rehearse a mock debate, start to finish, as if it were the real deal.

My sparring partner onstage was Greg Craig, my friend, a longtime Kennedy staffer and a Washington lawyer, who dutifully played President Bush. Greg had memorized every Bushism he could find, ripped from transcripts of the president's rallies and interviews.

As the last day of prep ended and we sat on the edge of the stage drinking ice-cold Leinenkugel's beers, Greg looked at me wearily and asked how he had done as Bush.

"I don't like you very much right now," I said. "So I guess that means you did a hell of a job."

It was a four-and-a-half-hour flight from Madison to Miami. We arrived in time to get a good night's sleep.

Debate days are among the quietest the candidate ever experiences, eerily so. Almost all the staff disappears early in the morning to do television and radio interviews all day long at the debate site, anything to help fill in the blocks of cable coverage. There's a surreal location set up by the media called "Spin Alley," where political operatives from both parties swing through like celebrities and offer their canned predictions and deliver their side of the story. Largely it's a game of managing expectations, puffing up the other side's debate skill while lowering expectations on your side. The Bush people were famous for doing this, shameless even. In 2000, they'd convinced the media that if Governor Bush managed to utter a coherent phrase against Vice President Gore, the master debater, then it was a big victory. It's hucksterism at its finest, and you just have to laugh. Of course, it's all covered breathlessly by cable news, as if there was anything unexpected that either campaign would say on a day like that.

As for me, after a leisurely morning with Teresa, and generous calls from my brother and sisters wishing me luck, I made the mistake of turning on the television. CNN's chyron announced, "Bush campaign to go for kill shot in first debate."

My competitive instincts didn't need much of a jolt, but this would certainly do. The Bush campaign had demanded that the national security debate lead off the trio of debates. It was the topic they considered the president's strong suit. Now, with the incumbent pulling away in the polls, someone on their team had apparently gotten cocky and defied the usual expectations game. "We'll see, gentlemen," I said as I sat down to play a few hands of Hearts with Marvin Nicholson and Setti Warren at the hotel.

The motorcade moved quickly to the University of Miami campus in Coral Gables, past cheering Kerry-Edwards supporters waving signs and booing Bush-Cheney supporters delivering one-fingered salutes. Secret Service whisked me, Teresa and Alexandra to my hold room. We were together as a family in a moment few get to experience, an unlikely moment. Vanessa joined by phone: "Kick his butt, Dad," Nessie encouraged. But soon I was standing there in the green room alone: the families were seated in the audience. In the solitude, I whispered a prayer, not for victory, but for the hope that I would keep faith with who I was and with what had brought me to this unlikely point in my life.

As I fidgeted with my tie, Cam Kerry and David Thorne popped into the room. It seemed only fitting. We'd traveled a lot of miles together. Cam had been through every campaign with me since 1970. "Have fun out there," he said. David and I had been through it all: college, Vietnam, the anti-war movement, my years in the political wilderness before statewide office beckoned again, the loss of friends and parents. David was the rarest kind of friend on this planet: How many people are still as close as brothers with a former brother-in-law?

"How ya feeling, Johnny?"

"We'll know soon, Davey." I smiled.

"You'll get him. You know these guys. You know how to do this, man."

There was a knock on the door. It was time to go.

An advance staffer led me down a series of hallways to the wings of a stage, curtained off. Across the way, on the opposite wing of the stage, looking straight ahead, was President George W. Bush. We were doing the exact same exercise at the exact same time. We were like two bulls waiting for the wranglers to pull the chute.

It dawned on me that except for a couple of group Senate meetings here and there, and an occasional handshake in passing at the State of the Union, the next ninety minutes would be far and away the most time I'd ever spent in close proximity to Bush.

What a strange phenomenon in our democracy that two people who went to the same college a couple of years apart can end up running against each other for the highest office in the country, campaign for almost a full year, and not really know each other. Friends insisted I'd had an impassioned conversation with Bush about civil rights in the dining hall my senior year, but I had no memory of it, and I don't think Bush did either.

But now it was time to live in the moment instead of trying to remember an elusive one. The lights flashed. It was time to debate.

Ninety minutes rushed by like ninety seconds.

The president and I agreed on a big question for the most powerful country on earth: that the single greatest danger we faced was the risk that nuclear weapons could fall into the hands of extremists. It was a rare but important moment of common ground on an issue that should unite serious people across the ideological spectrum.

But the evening was defined by differences and disagreements. If the Bush campaign believed national security would be the blade on which they cut me to pieces that night, they were sorely mistaken.

I don't think the president was ready to debate someone who challenged him on issues where he was used to hearing only applause and agreement. His smile turned to a smirk and soon a scowl when I went straight at the heart of his entire case for reelection: that he'd been strong in waging the war on terror.

Wrong, I argued: the president had squandered the goodwill that had come to us after 9/11, pushed away our allies and actually botched the war on terror. Osama bin Laden had murdered thousands of Americans. He'd killed friends of mine from Boston. He should have been rotting in a grave or in a solitary prison cell. I took the fight right at the president.

"Unfortunately, he escaped in the mountains of Tora Bora. We had him surrounded. But we didn't use American forces—the best trained in the world—to go kill him. The president relied on Afghan warlords—and he outsourced that job too. That's wrong." Bush scowled. The president was very effective at going on the attack. He had an easy manner coupled with a lighthearted delivery that allowed him to cut you without seeming mean. Bush went after my position on Iraq hard, mocking my now well-recorded comment about voting on the $87 billion supplemental funding bill. But I was ready.

"I made a mistake in how I talked about the war," I said. "But the president made a mistake in invading Iraq." I paused for a beat. "Which is worse?" I knew I got him when I saw the unmistakable grimace on his face as he reached for his pen and frantically took notes.

President Bush looked stunned and perturbed, and he appealed to the moderator, Jim Lehrer, in exasperation. "But the enemy attacked us, Jim," he said, and continued to defend the decision to go to war almost alone in Iraq before finishing the job in Afghanistan. I wondered if I'd heard him correctly: Had he really conflated Osama bin Laden and Saddam Hussein?

I pounced: "The president just said something extraordinarily revealing, and frankly very important in this debate . . . he just said the enemy attacked us. Saddam Hussein didn't attack us. Osama bin Laden attacked us. Al-Qaeda attacked us."

Bush frowned. "I know who attacked us," he replied.

It was amazing just how much of what Greg Craig had rehearsed actually came out of President Bush's mouth and how many of his answers were either too short or went right through the buzzers his own team had insisted on installing.

I walked off the stage confident, but I didn't know if my performance could resuscitate our campaign. The instant polls that night and the next morning made it clear we had earned our second chance in this contest. I'd won the debate convincingly. Meanwhile, chatter began to focus on a curious bulge in the president's suit jacket, as commentators speculated that he had hidden a transmitter back there to convey tips and lines to use in the debate. "If that's the case, we hope he wears a radio next time too!" quipped Bob Shrum.

The morning after the debate, we were bleary-eyed but feeling good. I told Shrum and Klain we had to be just as sharp in the next two debates as we had been last night. I assured them that Bush would raise his game as well. Teresa was off to campaign for me in Pennsylvania. Everyone was heading their separate ways, returning to the campaign trail: I was off to another stop in Florida before heading to the Midwest, all the more important to capitalize on the momentum of the night before. David Thorne was to join me on the flight.

As we walked out of the hotel to the motorcade, out of the corner of my eye I spotted someone waving, and clearly concerned—just outside the security perimeter. But it wasn't just "someone": it was my daughter Alex. Something was wrong. You never forget that look on your child's face, whether she's three years old or thirty. After I told my detail, Alex was able to run up to me and her uncle David. She had to talk. She climbed in the limo with us and revealed a terrible secret: Vanessa had just called her with the news that Julia's cancer had come back in full force throughout her body. The early sense of her personal victory over this curse, as a result of the first round of treatment, was instantly wiped away and replaced by a sense of dread. My God. Alex looked so much like her mother. In the privacy of the limo, as it sped toward the airport, the three of us shared our pain and shock.

I called Vanessa, who, it turned out, had learned the news herself just a day before, ten minutes before she'd had to stand onstage and represent the campaign at a rally of energetic college students. Vanessa had kept this sad knowledge to herself until after the debate. I was both touched and pained that Vanessa and Julia had protected me at that horrible moment. They did not even tell Alex for fear that her body language would give away that something was wrong. They wanted me to be able to concentrate completely on the debate—a selfless choice. I thought of the road ahead measured against the debate of the night before and the stakes of the next few weeks.

It all seemed small and distant from the prospect that Julia was in a battle for her life and that my children could soon lose their mother. As we arrived at the airport, I didn't want to let go of Alex. I asked her to join us, but she couldn't. She had to get back home, she said. We stood on the tarmac and hugged a long, long time, as she tried to put on a brave face. Twice she pulled away, and I pulled her back, and ultimately walked her to the terminal, where one of the Miami staff agreed to arrange her transportation to commercial aviation. I walked back to the campaign plane completely numb. It was a gorgeous Florida morning. The sun was shining. But I felt a chill throughout my body.

As I climbed the steps of the plane and stepped inside, Stephanie Cutter handed me the printout of a magazine story and cover that would be on newsstands the next day. The story said, "Debates don't always shake up a presidential race, but this one did." The cover, with a smiling picture of me from the debate, simply read "Off the Ropes." My feelings were all over the place. It was now October, and while Julia battled for her life, we were in the sprint of our political lives. Life always comes at you in ways you least predict; the challenge is to just keep going forward.

After a return to the stump, I parachuted into Denver on October 5 for a truncated version of debate camp. We headed to another out-of-season, half-empty hotel complex in Englewood, outside Denver. The solitude and the mountain air had the feel of the Overlook Hotel in *The Shining* (filmed at the real-life Stanley Hotel in Colorado), missing of course any haunted history of mass murders. I called John Edwards to wish him luck: he was debating Vice President Cheney that night, and we were hopeful that the momentum from the first debate would keep going after what I expected would be a strong performance from John. He'd been a trial lawyer for decades, one of the most skilled in front of a jury. Cheney would be a terrific contrast for John, we suspected. But when I caught him on the phone, he sounded uneasy.

"John, what do you do about your nerves on days like these?" he asked.

I was startled. Of all the people who seemed ready for his close-up, it was Edwards. I called both Bob Shrum and Bob Barnett, who had been brought in to play Cheney in Edwards's debate prep: Edwards would be fine, they said, but they acknowledged it had been very difficult to get him to focus on his prep materials. If they had concerns, they didn't let on. I wondered if Edwards was more of a gut-instinct performer, but I started to worry: I knew Cheney loved to lower expectations and then come in with an avuncular but muscular performance. He'd beaten Joe Lieberman in 2000.

I settled in with the road team to watch the Edwards-Cheney debate, and I thought back to all the promises John had made in his aggressive campaign to be the vice presidential nominee. I'd been assured he'd be tough, loyal and hardworking. But he'd watered down the talking points defending me against the Swift Boat Veterans for Truth. I'd been promised he'd be a team player. But there was a growing buzz of gossip that he was rejecting speech input from headquarters and gravitating back to the stump speech he'd delivered in the primaries when he was selling himself as a candidate. I'd been promised he'd be tough. But he'd been hesitant to take on Bush in a frontal way, and now I'd heard that he didn't take debate prep seriously enough. It worried me. He didn't do a bad job against Cheney that night, but he also didn't do a great job. Some said Cheney won by a nose; others called it a draw. But what I knew was I hadn't seen the Mr. October I'd been promised.

Days later, I'd have to meet the president again on a stage in St. Louis: another debate, another opportunity to define the differences between us. The format was a town hall debate, one many presumed was to the amiable incumbent's advantage. The format has almost grown too predictable since the famous debate in 1992 when Bush's father was spotted checking his watch, as if counting the minutes before he could stop taking audience questions and go home. I didn't wear a watch to ensure I never looked down and provided pundits such an easy opportunity to write a column that could almost write itself.

This night, most of the action was between the candidates, rather than with the audience.

Bush attacked me, and I parried: "This president didn't find weapons of mass destruction in Iraq, so he has really turned his campaign into a weapon of mass deception."

But I also found myself wanting a more honest interaction. As the night wound down, a question from a woman in the audience about taxpayer funding of abortion spoke to me. I told her about my thinking and my journey on an issue of conscience, about the fact that I'd decided long ago that I couldn't "take what is an article of faith for me and legislate it for someone who doesn't share that article of faith, whether they be agnostic, atheist, Jew or Protestant," but that I wanted as president to help find common ground. Common ground on prevention. Common ground on adoption. Common ground on family planning. It was an honest combination of heart and head.

And standing there ready to respond to it was President Bush, whose own grandfather had been treasurer of Planned Parenthood. He jabbed back, with his smirk: "I'm trying to decipher that. My answer is, we're not going to spend taxpayers' money on abortion." It struck me as a highly calculated response to an issue that deserved greater honesty, but a good reminder nonetheless of ways in which campaigns can too often be efforts merely to charge a partisan base.

Polls again showed that I got the better of Bush in the second debate, and we headed into the last twenty-five days neck and neck, but with momentum on my side. There'd be one more debate—October 13, in Tempe, Arizona. In nearby Santa Fe, New Mexico, where I put in a couple days of debate prep, I watched the Red Sox lose Game 1 of the American League Championship Series to the hated Yankees. Game 2 was the night of the debate, which made me certain that win or lose, the debate wouldn't make a difference in the swing state of New Hampshire: every television set would be tuned to the playoffs. Politics may be a competitive sport in New England, but real sports come first.

The last debate was to be focused on domestic issues, but what became immediately evident was there's no such thing as "foreign" policy—what happens "over there" matters here, whether it was the president's unilateral war in Iraq that was putting us deeper in debt, or the way multiple deployments overseas were breaking our military.

I look back on that debate and what stands out is that we fought over issues, real issues, serious choices. The president argued that tomorrow's workers should have the right to invest their Social Security in the stock market. I argued that would be a disaster, because it meant one economic downturn could destroy the retirement future of millions. I'd grown up around people who remembered the Great Depression. I knew a great recession was always a possibility and I wasn't going to return to the days when so many senior citizens lived in poverty. It was an honest difference.

So too was our difference over the question that would drive most of the debate conversation on the news in the days that followed. The moderator, Bob Schieffer, asked us whether we believed homosexuals choose their orientation. I was surprised by President Bush's answer: "You know, Bob, I don't know." I knew that he didn't believe it. The president then pivoted into a hard-liner statement about gay marriage. He seemed determined to force a message home for his political base. "I think it's very important that we protect marriage as an institution . . . the surest way to protect marriage between a man and woman is to amend the Constitution."

When I had my chance at the question, I wanted to restore some sense of humanity to the conversation. Marriage wasn't under assault. That was malarkey. But real people—people's sons and daughters—were under assault from what mere politicians were stirring up in the country. I spoke honestly. "We're all God's children, Bob, and I think if you were to talk to Dick Cheney's daughter, who is a lesbian, she would tell you that she's being who she was, she's being who she was born to be. It's not a choice."

Afterward, the response from the Right was furious. Lynne Cheney said I was "not a good man." It was surreal. I'd defended the character and humanity of her daughter, who was proudly out of the closet and open about who God had made her. Yet *I* was branded by Mrs. Cheney as the problem, not her husband's campaign or the politics of 2004 that had made gay Americans a political football in the first place. It was a strange exclamation point on the politics of division.

But now the debates were behind us. We were even, and our campaign's polling showed the momentum was with us. The race would be decided by the way we ran through the tape.

Then, on October 29, news set off every pager and cell phone on the plane. We had just landed in Florida. There were rumors: Osama bin Laden's first video appearance since 9/11 was about to shake the campaign with just four days to go.

We heard that American intelligence was poring over the tape and had asked for time to analyze it, but Al Jazeera refused. An al-Qaeda propaganda tape by the world's most wanted terrorist was going to be wall-to-wall news the last eighty-six hours of the closest presidential election since Gore and Bush dueled in Florida. The news set the right-wing media into overdrive.

On Fox, a Republican guest said, "It looks like an endorsement by Osama bin Laden of John Kerry."

The anchor Neil Cavuto replied, "He's all but doing that. I thought I saw a button."

I had a sinking feeling. We'd been cresting and climbing in the polls. We had been pummeling Bush over a mismanaged war in Iraq and leaked plans to privatize Social Security—both of which were sadly prescient. But now Bush was back on his favorite footing: 9/11.

Mark Mellman, my pollster, is a deeply religious, observant Jew. He doesn't drive or work or use electronics on the Sabbath. Saturday morning, the overnight polls were hand-delivered to him by his assistant. We had dropped a point in every battleground state. Mark was so panicked, he walked all the way from his home in Georgetown three miles to the campaign headquarters to share the data in person.

In Ashwaubenon, Wisconsin, that afternoon, President Bush said, "In less than seventy-two hours, the American people will be voting, and the decision comes down to, who do you trust? I offer leadership and results for a time of threat and a time of challenge."

I had a more difficult challenge. I had to call for unity but remind people that President Bush's approach to the war on terror was the reason bin Laden was still alive at all.

But momentum had shifted. I just prayed it hadn't shifted irreparably.

Election Day was its own jolt of adrenaline, a burst of anxious energy. We had arrived in Wisconsin around 3:30 in the morning, hours after our final big event in Ohio: a raucous, hopeful concert in Cleveland where once again Bruce Springsteen lent his poetry and troubadour gifts to the campaign. Bruce was accompanied by his wife, Patti, and their kids, and I thanked him for stepping into the political fires for me, always a risk for a celebrity. He gave me a memento to keep with me: the guitar pic he had used on all our stops together, another treasured talismanic object for the pocket of my navy blazer, company for the four-leaf clover, Ohio buckeye and St. Christopher medal that I kept with me at all times. It was emotional hearing Bruce—with his harmonica, his guitar and his unique sound—play our campaign's adopted ballad one last time, his song that had come to mean so much to me: "No Surrender."

I believed we were going to win.

Over the last weeks I could feel the momentum growing. The bin Laden tape four days before the election had stopped our growth, panicked our pollsters and given Bush a bounce, but my gut told me we were going to make it over the finish line on Election Day.

We had one more event: a brief stop by a local polling place and a chance to cheer on our volunteers in a must-win state. My closing words in Wisconsin would be replayed over and over throughout the day on all the local networks, a reminder to everyone of the difference their vote could make in what would be one of the most fiercely contested, down-to-the-wire contests Wisconsin had ever known.

And then it was back onto the plane and home to Boston.

The emotion on the flight was palpable, from the crew and the attendants, who asked for photos, to the road team, who had racked up hundreds of thousands of miles in pursuit of this moment. They all knew that no matter what happened, this was going to be the last flight like this one: everything afterward would be different.

I gathered the team in the cabin one last time before we would all scatter into our different roles in Boston: I wanted to say thank you for all we'd gone through together. Some, like John Sasso and Mike McCurry, had walked away from lucrative businesses to be in the fight again by my side, bringing great maturity to our team. Others, like my young speechwriter Josh Gottheimer, had started out with another candidate but plunged into my campaign with zeal (and, in Josh's case, even a grudging willingness— as the plane's lone Yankees fan—to follow my entreaties and wear a Red Sox cap as the Sox roared all the way back from three games down to beat the Yankees, sweep the Cardinals and take their first World Series victory in eighty-six years, something I believed was an omen of another Massachusetts losing streak soon to be snapped). Stephanie Cutter was tenacious and determined, smart as hell, and she'd transferred her loyalty to Teddy Kennedy to me when she signed up in the bad old days of November 2003. David Morehouse was a former boilermaker from Pittsburgh who had become one of Al Gore's most loyal soldiers, the man who had stopped Gore from conceding in Nashville four years earlier, and he had been just as tough and faithful on my campaign. And then there were the three amigos—body guy, trip director and traveling press secretary—who had been with me from the very start, by then as close as brothers, always my traveling companions in good times and bad.

I wanted the mood to stay light, not maudlin as sometimes can happen when the weight of a moment hits you. I look back and wish I'd said more— reminisced more, opened up more—but we had more fights ahead—and besides, we were going to win.

I handed out inscribed silver mementos to the staff and fleece jackets to the traveling press.

Our leased 757 touched down at Hanscom Air Force Base in Bedford, just outside Boston, nestled between Concord and Lexington. For a moment, as the motorcade chugged toward the city on an overcast day about to turn rainy, I indulged my nostalgia.

Thirty-four years before, I'd given my first political speech at the citizens' caucus at Concord-Carlisle High School, speaking from my heart and my gut in opposition to the war in which I'd fought, and one year after that while in VVAW, I'd been arrested a few miles down the road, on the town green in Lexington, in an act of civil disobedience, an act of dissent.

And now here I was in a motorcade, speeding along those same roads on my way to cast a vote for myself for president of the United States.

It hit me that I was marking the end of one of the greatest journeys anyone can take anywhere in the world—the race for the presidency of the United States.

Every nation in the world watches closely what we do. Their hopes and fears are integrally tied to ours. So many foreigners say to me, "I wish we could vote for your president—it matters as much to us what happens."

I could feel both that weight and the excitement of the day as we climbed up the hill on Mt. Vernon Street to the Old State House, where I would finally, improbably, see my name on the ballot and cast my vote.

My polling place for Ward 5, Precinct 3, was in the basement of the building where I had been sworn in as lieutenant governor twenty-two years earlier, the golden-domed Old State House that had been pastureland where John Hancock's cows grazed more than two hundred years before.

As she had for thirty-five years, Teresa was voting in Pittsburgh. She'd be flying home to Boston, but Alexandra and Vanessa were by my side to vote with me. Just looking at them, I could see my mom and dad in their faces, in their eyes and their expressions. For a misty moment my mind flashed back to my visit with my mom in 2002, just weeks before she passed away, to tell her about the campaign journey I was about to begin. Her four-word reminder of the one resource in public life that is never renewable sticks with me always: "Integrity, John, remember—integrity."

I put on my reading glasses and leaned down to be sure to darken each circle of my ballot.

My moment of introspection was interrupted by the flash of the cameras and, of course, the obligatory "Who did you vote for?" question barked out by the herd of reporters waiting to see what clever or stupid answer I might give.

It was off to the Union Oyster House to continue my superstitious Election Day tradition of eating at the old counter where Daniel Webster had long, long ago devoured platefuls of oysters and countless pints of lager. I had first been introduced to the Oyster House by my father, who had sat at that same counter as a young practicing attorney, and as a kid I used to marvel at the mechanical dumbwaiter still ferrying plates of baked scrod and fried fish from the kitchen up two floors to the dining room above. Dad had taken me there many times. But ever since 1982, I came each Election Day and had the same meal: a dozen cherrystone clams, a bowl of chowder and a dark beer. Each time, it had done the trick.

I sat at the bar with my longtime friend Chris Greeley, who had been my driver and body man when I ran for lieutenant governor and went on to be my chief of staff in Massachusetts, always a quick wit and a diehard hockey fan. Chris had become good friends with my dad, breaking through Pa's reserve. Chris and I talked about the early beginnings of our political journey—and how if just a handful of votes at the state party convention in 1982 had gone a different way, we might be sitting at this bar as spectators to a presidential election, not protagonists. We enjoyed a wistful moment.

At a booth not far away, little did I know that when they weren't enjoying a well-deserved beer of their own, Mike McCurry and company were transfixed by their BlackBerrys. The first wave of exit polls was pouring in, and the news was exhilarating: I was comfortably ahead in big battleground states, including Michigan, Wisconsin, Pennsylvania and New Hampshire, with a 3-point cushion ahead of Bush in Ohio and Florida, which would decide the presidency. There was a debate, I was later told, about whether to pass me a cocktail napkin with the results. I'm glad they didn't. A San Francisco Giants die-hard, McCurry compared it to the old baseball tradition: you don't ever talk to the pitcher in the middle of a no-hitter.

Besides, we had work to do.

A large crowd had gathered outside the restaurant. I walked out to the encouraging cheers and shouts of folks who wondered like I did what history would come out of this day.

It was off to the Westin hotel complex near Copley Square, which had been transformed into a kind of political tent city: an enormous stage with massive television screens, miles of Jersey barriers to separate the citizens from the media, who were broadcasting live—a presidential Brigadoon of sorts, a spectacular site that would last for a day only to be broken down within thirty-six hours as if it had never happened.

For the next five hours, I was holed up in the Westin, confined to a chair and pouring my remaining energy—and my tired voice—into the one and only useful activity of a candidate on Election Day: I bounced from one remote satellite television interview to another, crisscrossing the nation with three- to four-minute live interviews, cajoling and exhorting the deciding voters to get to the polls.

It was a marathon sprint: a tour through the battleground states in thirty-seven different interviews, each a short, clipped message touching on key issues—jobs, health care, the war on terror, the way the middle class was getting squeezed.

We were punch-drunk by the time it was over. I wanted to go home, shower and shave, and get upstairs to my study and work on my election night speech.

By six o'clock, there was no point in anyone hiding information from me: the final exit polls were in—and they were every bit as encouraging: tied in Iowa, ahead from New Mexico to Florida and Ohio.

I flashed Stephanie Cutter a quick salute and a wink, motioned to Marvin to head downstairs, and was about to depart into the elevator when Bob Shrum uttered the words I know he immediately wished he could take back: "May I be the first to call you, Mr. President."

I immediately replied, "No"—not just because I was superstitious, but because I knew too much could happen between the exit polls and the counting. I refused myself any premature celebration, though the polls did raise my hopes.

Shrum had heard through a press contact at the White House that President George H. W. Bush had been in the Oval Office and prepared his son for the possibility that he had lost. It was accompanied by Secret Service chatter that a presidential movement to the Reagan Building had been scheduled for not too long after the polls closed.

I wouldn't and couldn't invest in any of it, but it gave added urgency to the work of buttoning down a speech for the evening.

I arrived home and disappeared upstairs to finish some work on my potential victory statement. At that point, it was the only speech I was working on. The polls closed at 8:00 p.m. in most places. Of course, even as they closed on the East Coast and started to report, the heartland and the West continued to vote for one, two and three hours. During that time, states began to tally much as we had expected. I won key states I had to win—Wisconsin, Michigan, Pennsylvania, New Hampshire. I lost a couple that I had hoped to win. But not long after the polls closed my boiler-room team detected hints of trouble. The exit polls were either wildly off or something strange was happening.

I'm not sure when I realized things were not playing out as predicted, but at some point, it became clear that we needed more votes to close out Ohio and win the presidency.

It was going to come down to the wire.

I thought about some of the issues we were hearing that I feared would become the backdrop of a long night.

Election days are always chaotic. But in the first presidential campaign after the Florida recount, we were especially sensitive to protecting the vote.

Our campaign headquarters had received frantic calls from our poll watchers in Ohio that some people said they were pushing the electronic machines for Kerry, but the vote was coming up Bush. Our lawyers immediately went to work. We had machines taken out of precincts where that had been reported.

Moreover, our team on the ground in some states was reporting huge lines outside the Democratic precincts because too few machines had been allocated to those voting areas but no lines in front of Republican precinct doors. Republicans breezed through. Democrats waited for hours.

To make matters worse, Ohio suffered monumental downpours from thunderstorms. In key Kerry strongholds we heard that if the long lines didn't drive people home, the rain might.

Some on the team were bothered by the fact that many voting machines came from a private company, Diebold, owned by two Nebraska brothers who were the chairs of the Bush campaign for president.

I wonder how many countries have elections in which the machines are privately owned and controlled, where the coding for the tallying cannot be inspected or verified because it is "proprietary information."

It was a major problem of voting in the United States of America—and one that is rarely given enough attention except when elections are too close to call. In anticipation of problems, we had built an army of lawyers—four thousand on the ground in Ohio on Election Day, an unprecedented operation.

It was no secret that Republicans have worked hard in many states to suppress the vote. They regularly come up with legislation in states to make it harder for folks who are anticipated not to vote Republican not to be able to vote at all. The party of Abraham Lincoln is unrecognizable.

I'd hoped we wouldn't have to think about these variables on election night. I had hoped for a clear outcome.

But in many parts of Ohio we were hearing about the difficulties people were having voting. In America, each state's voting process is managed by the secretary of state for that state. Even the election for the president of the United States is managed by the state voting system. And so it was that in Ohio, early in the year, we began to lay the groundwork for a fair election. Alarm bells had been sounded for months because we were dealing with a highly partisan Republican secretary of state.

As the evening wore on I was receiving more calls from Mary Beth Cahill and the team working the boiler room. At 3:00 in the morning, I consulted the team in Ohio. The problems in Ohio and even elsewhere made it clear we would not really understand the situation—particularly the provisional ballots in Ohio—until some dust had settled. It meant that once again America had to go to bed not knowing for certain who the president was. I was wrestling with the reports of chicanery in several states but particularly Ohio. It was the only state still in play—the state that would decide the presidency. We sent John Edwards out to the Copley Plaza crowd to deliver a holding-action message. I decided to get a few hours of sleep before tackling the question of options.

When I woke up early, it felt like a bad dream. The evening before hadn't really happened. I had to shake my head and register consciously that votes had been counted. The election had turned razor-thin. We were still waiting for word from Ohio. All the energy, all the action, had shifted to a near-slow-motion, hazy heaviness. I was now wrestling with the reality of losing. The last word from Ohio was that the provisional ballots were not of a sufficient number and representation that they would close the tallied gap between Bush and me. The problem was we didn't know whether we could trust the count itself.

I had a new appreciation for what Al Gore must have gone through in 2000. For the duration of the morning we examined the options.

I gathered a small group in my kitchen. Ted and Vicki Kennedy were all there when I convened a conference call with our lawyers on the ground in Ohio. We sat at the kitchen table and listened to their analysis. I was furious about the voting system, the extraordinary discrepancy between the ease of Republicans voting and the purposeful hurdles placed in front of Democrats by a partisan secretary of state. I wondered if a due process or equal protection under the law constitutional challenge would be legitimate.

A challenge could tie up the country in litigation for three months.

I consulted with the team on the ground in Ohio, my brother among them. I discussed the situation with John Edwards, who thought we should challenge. But setting aside the emotion and anger over the way our voters were treated, I had to also consider how my decision would affect the country. I was deeply concerned about a nation at war, with the world looking at us, coming out of a second consecutive election where we would be sitting in limbo, wondering for the next six weeks or more who the president would be.

The concerns of others in the room and on the phone were the same. We might win in a district court, we might win on an appeal that was sure to come, but ultimately this was going to be decided the same way *Bush v. Gore* was. It would be a 5–4 decision in the Supreme Court.

We would lose and we would tie the country up in the spectacle of the world waiting for the United States to untangle itself from another messed-up election. No one at the table or on the phone thought we could be successful.

The decision was mine. I didn't want to put the country through that again. It would be selfish and irresponsible. I knew some would be angry. People had a right to know that their votes were counted properly. They were correct to be incensed. But I decided I would continue that fight in a way that didn't put our nation into banana republic status. We weren't going to close the gap of provisional ballots and, with this court, we wouldn't overturn the election on constitutional grounds no matter how legitimately rights had been violated.

So, with just six of us sitting in the kitchen in the early afternoon of Wednesday I decided the right thing to do was concede, no matter how much it rankled.

I instructed the campaign to place a call to President Bush, who I was told was waiting with his family in the Oval Office. A few minutes later, he came to the phone. I said, "Congratulations, Mr. President—it was a close race but now we have to put it behind us." He said, "You're a tough competitor. That was a hell of a race and I appreciate your comments." I then said something to the effect of "Mr. President, this has been a really divisive period. The nation needs healing and I hope that you and I can find a way of actually working together to turn things around and show the world the best face of our country." It was not a long call.

I was resigned—and pissed. I had given it my all but there were things that had happened and things that didn't happen, any one of which could have changed the outcome of an election as close as this one.

There would be plenty of time for the postmortem.

Right now, I needed to go out fast and speak to our supporters and the nation. I needed to do my part to bring a divided country together. We collected our belongings and our wits as the motorcade formed up for the short journey to Faneuil Hall.

As we walked down the stairs from the kitchen, Teresa slipped on a step, taking a nasty tumble, twisting her ankle badly. We waited a few minutes for the pain to subside, got some ice and then helped her limp to the car. She had been there at the very beginning and throughout, and she was not going to not be there at the end. Teddy and Vicki rode with us. At Faneuil Hall, we met up with John and Elizabeth Edwards. Hugs and handshakes and commiserations all around, and then up the back stairs of the hall where I'd spoken at an announcement rally, now to speak at a very different conclusion.

John Edwards was given the job of introducing me. He delivered what most of us interpreted as the first campaign speech of his 2008 campaign for president. It was a sour coda to his troubled performance as the VP candidate.

When I stepped out on the stage to a prolonged standing ovation from friends who had been with me through thick and thin, people who had marched every step of this difficult, incredible journey, it hit me. The faces were drawn. Eyes were red or puffy. There were no smiles. A dour, heavy mood had settled over everyone because we had traveled up and down the full scale of the emotional ladder in just the last twenty-four hours. The stakes had been so high. The impact of the loss was weighing them down.

In the best spirit of my campaign—the campaign that was meant to lift and unite Americans, the campaign that aimed to show new respect and create new opportunity for people who had been left out and left behind, the campaign that tried to speak to the world about decency and leadership based on universal values—I tried to speak to all Americans.

I spoke about "the danger of division in our country and the need, the desperate need, for unity for finding the common ground, coming together," and said, "Today I hope that we can begin the healing."

I thought of all the work that remained to be done, and to the 59 million Americans who had voted for me I said, "Don't lose faith; what you did made a difference. And building on itself, we go on to make a difference another day. I promise you: That time will come; the time will come; the election will come when your work and your ballots will change the world. And it's worth fighting for."

I ended where my campaign had begun—both literally and metaphorically. I reminded all those in Boston and all those watching at home that "in an American election, there are no losers. Because whether or not our candidates are successful, the next morning, we all wake up as Americans. And that—that is the greatest privilege and the most remarkable good fortune that can come to us on Earth. With that gift also comes obligation. We are required now to work together for the good of our country. In the days ahead, we must find common cause. We must join in common effort without remorse or recrimination, without anger or rancor. America is in need of unity and longing for a larger measure of compassion. . . . So here—so with a grateful heart, I leave this campaign with a prayer that has even greater meaning to me now that I have come to know our vast country so much better thanks to all of you. And what a privilege it has been to do so. And that prayer is very simple: God bless America."

When the speech was over we descended the stairs in the back of the hall.

A different drama had been unfolding over the course of the last weekend of the campaign. Elizabeth Edwards had discovered a lump in her breast. Teresa connected her to the best diagnosticians we knew in Boston. Elizabeth had seen them, but now, right after the concession, she needed to report for tests and evaluations. It was a very difficult, personal transition from the heights of a presidential campaign to the most fundamental human frailty of facing disease. We wished them well and said goodbye at Faneuil Hall.

The motorcade dropped us off at home. It was over—just like that.

CHAPTER 13

Dusting Myself Off

I STEPPED ONTO MY front stoop in Boston on a cold gray late-November morning to pick up the morning newspaper. Tucked between two bright orange pumpkins marking the season peeked an envelope addressed to me and Teresa. I picked it up. There was no return address. Overnight, someone had quietly, anonymously stopped by and, without knocking on the door, without disturbing us, left a handwritten message: they were thinking of me and Teresa, still praying for health care for their child.

The scene repeated itself more than once that fall. A note from a kid who said she was still fighting for a clean environment, or a letter from a veteran who said he still prayed for a sane foreign policy.

Not since 1972 had I been knocked on my ass in an election—and this had been no ordinary election. Sometimes amid all the cynicism about politics, most of it justified today, people and pundits forget that most of us who run for office are in it because we believe in what we're fighting for. It's not an act. There are exceptions; frauds and charlatans have always dotted the political landscape. But most of us who put our reputations on the line and expose our families to the ugliness of modern campaigns do it because we believe in our ability to make a difference and we believe the issues at stake are enormous.

When you believe deeply and you lose, it hurts like hell.

The first presidential candidate I ever worked for, Mo Udall, said that after his campaign ended, he "slept like a baby"—every three hours he woke up and cried. I didn't cry. But I felt a galloping sense of frustration, disappointment, anger and sadness, often all at once.

When I least suspected it, the campaign would come rushing back to me: on my dresser in a little leather tray, I'd spy the lucky Ohio buckeye, or the four-leaf clover, or any of the talismanic objects I'd accumulated on the campaign trail and carried with me to its bitter end. Even the contents of my emptied pockets reconnected me to the extraordinary supporters who invested their hopes in the campaign. On my wrist, I'd look down and see the yellow "Livestrong" bracelet I'd received in a rope line from a man battling cancer. I wondered whether he'd made it through to the other side of his fight. Bruce Springsteen brought me the guitar picks he had used when playing my campaign appearances, and I kept them close by, a reminder of his loyalty even when the sun wasn't shining, and of the song that had become our campaign anthem: "No Surrender."

I especially derived disappointment and determination from the young people who came up to me and said they'd cast their first presidential vote for me. I hated to feel as though I'd let them down. They'd yell, "Keep fighting!" and all I could say was "We all need to keep fighting."

The campaign's abrupt end was at odds with what I felt inside. I had to figure out how to keep acting on my beliefs, even as I tried to process the loss itself.

Friends were putting on a brave face. Often after expressing their sorrow or shock about the end of it all, or when they didn't know what to say, they'd blurt out, "But you look good!" They sounded just a little too much like they were standing a few feet away from the casket at an Irish wake.

I didn't want anyone to feel sorry for me or pull their punches, and I worked hard at not feeling sorry for myself. I'd gather friends for dinner or the New England Patriots game, and I'd eventually push them to open up about the campaign. What mistakes did I make? How could it have worked out differently? Where do we go from here?

I relied on a close group of friends who weren't afraid to be candid: Tommy and Tory Vallely were especially direct, and David Thorne unflinchingly honest but protective. David McKean, who had been staffing the potential transition for a Kerry administration just a month before, faithfully continued as chief of staff.

By contrast, it was hard not to miss media commentary by those who positioned themselves as wise, even prescient, as they looked forward to a future political landscape that didn't include me. Initial exit polls had chalked up the outcome to cultural issues like guns and gay marriage, on which I was supposedly on the wrong side. Not coincidentally, a story appeared in which it was revealed that John Edwards regretted that the campaign didn't allow him to talk more about his personal values. Funny, I had never heard John say that in the campaign. Another analysis suggested I'd failed to heed President Clinton's advice to take gay marriage off the table by endorsing state ballot initiatives that were discriminatory. Candidates already jockeying for 2008 suggested I need to "go away." That's politics: after a tough loss, you have to move forward, trust your own compass and separate constructive advice from expedient positioning.

Teresa and I went to London over Thanksgiving just to be together and escape cable television, to again walk down a street without a press pool or Secret Service for the first time in almost a year. It marked our first holiday in a long time where the destination wasn't dictated by the campaign, and we looked back nostalgically at New Year's Eve 2003, which we had spent together in Sioux City, Iowa—dinner with our adopted family of reporters and campaign staff, including a magnum of red wine that Teresa had brought as a surprise for all of them. Dinner had been followed by dancing at a community center with a hundred volunteers and guests. I give Teresa enormous credit: she had an instinctive wariness of politics and the bruising nature of campaigns, but she'd committed. She had been "all in" all the way through. Now our memories flashed back to the parts of the campaign that were filled with good humor and even better friends.

In London, after dinner one night, we stepped outside onto the cobblestone sidewalk and, as snowflakes fell against the darkness, noticed a crowd had gathered. They burst into applause. We hadn't escaped the remnants of a campaign the world had followed closely, but it buoyed our spirits, even as we pondered what could have been.

Senate votes called me back to Washington briefly before the holidays. It was wind-down time, a lame-duck session of little consequence. The Republicans would have a bigger majority in the next Congress to work their advantage, so the votes would be predictable and perfunctory.

Despite that, I never thought about skipping out on the votes. It just wasn't who I was. I was determined not to skulk off, retire from the Senate or just sit on a beach somewhere. The fight still animated me, as it had defined me since I left the Navy. Massachusetts had given me a job to do in the Senate, even if I'd fallen short in reaching for a promotion to the other end of Pennsylvania Avenue.

I came back quietly, voted, but I found out quickly that there's a certain kind of ritualistic damned-if-you-do, damned-if-you-don't melodrama to the year after you lose a presidential election. If I attended the Democratic caucus meeting, I was written about anonymously as a "distraction" to those looking toward the future. If I didn't attend, apparently it was evidence that I thought I was still the nominee for president and not just one of a hundred.

At lunchtime, I would still pop down from my office in the Russell Building and head for the Dirksen cafeteria, as I had for nineteen years as a senator. Pundits wrote that it was awkward for onlookers to see me filling my tray at the salad bar or standing in line just like everyone else. What would they have preferred I do? Sequester myself in my office wearing a smoking jacket and an ascot, waiting for a valet to lay out my lunch on a white tablecloth with cloth napkins? Marvin Nicholson, who had graciously come back to the Senate staff, joked, "We should've brought the press here when you were running if that's all it takes to show you're such a man of the people." The Marv had a gift for lightening the mood.

There was nothing I could do about gossipy news stories except press onward. Al Gore had been a target after the 2000 election for going away, and I was a target for sticking around, but both of us had something in common. We had a lot of political life left in us, and I had a job to do for my state.

On Thursday, December 2, I headed to Arlington National Cemetery for the graveside service for a young Marine from Haverhill, Massachusetts, Lance Corporal Dimitrios Gavriel.

The date was exactly one month after the presidential election and two years to the day that I'd announced for president on *Meet the Press*, but amid the headstones, I could not have felt further from those milestones.

The day was bitter and cold, with gun-barrel-gray skies overhead and a strong wind blowing. Gavriel was a Marine—I should say "is" because in life or death, you're forever a Marine. He had graduated from Brown University the same year as Alex. A high school wrestler, after 9/11 Gavriel walked away from Wall Street and signed up for the Marines. Before his thirtieth birthday, an insurgent's grenade ended his life in Anbar Province. His parents were stoic, holding on to each other with all they had, holding on as a close-knit Greek family doing all they could not to be devoured by grief for the young man they loved so deeply.

Someone passed me a prayer card. On it were words pulled not from the Bible but from a poem written by the fallen Marine himself:

Hope lives among so few,
Yet strong it is I know,
For I am still a dreamer,
Along the track I go.

Finding peace and understanding in good men dying young remains a question that only God can answer, as I'd felt since Vietnam shook my faith. Thirty-five years later, the familiar feeling of premature loss surrounded me again. Gavriel was a young man I'd never met, but I felt I knew him because I'd known so many good, young idealists, all gone too soon.

Taps blew hauntingly, and a three-volley salute pierced the dry late autumn air. I knew the ritual too well.

After the funeral ended, I drove over to Persh's grave. Thirty-six years had passed since he'd been stolen from us at Tet, at just twenty-five years old. He'd never gotten to marry his fiancée or have children, let alone grandchildren, or see his hair turn gray. I have lived all those gifts, which had been taken now from the young Marine America had just buried. I was alive and healthy with a voice I could use any way I wanted. I had nothing to wallow about. I had a battle to rejoin. Wallowing now would have been an insult to the memory of all those whose graves surrounded me.

Yes, I'd lost an election I should have won. Others lose far more and summon incredible dignity. I didn't need to take a poll or hire a bunch of consultants to reevaluate my life or my next steps. I was who I was. I needed to use all my extra days in a way that valued the gift they really were.

To my surprise, in a Senate that at times had seemed foreign to me—clubby in ways where I'd once been more reserved; competitive when I'd wished it could be more collegial—I was reminded that there are extraordinary friends you can count on when you need them, even when you least expect it.

Senator Tom Harkin asked to see me one-on-one. Some on the staff were skeptical. They predicted that Tom planned to ask me to donate my remaining campaign account to fund the Iowa Democratic Party. They were still bitter that Tom had endorsed Howard Dean one week before the Iowa caucuses. But Tom was my classmate in the Senate's class of 1984. We'd traveled together to Central America as freshmen. We respected and liked each other. Of course, I'd meet him.

Tom walked straight into my personal office. We sprawled out in two big wing chairs. After exchanging pleasantries, Tom cut to the chase. "John, this will just take a minute," he said, and leaned in to look me straight in the eye. "I just want you to know how proud I am that you were our nominee and you did a hell of a job." I choked up. We talked for a bit, then in a flash he was gone, off to a hearing. I will never forget it. It was the nicest meeting I'd experienced in nineteen years in the Senate. Tom's simple act of going out of his way—privately, quietly, and without fanfare—meant everything. One of my aides popped his head into my office.

"How much did you commit to the Iowa Democratic Party?" he asked.

"Go away," I said, and smiled.

Teddy Kennedy, of course, had a sixth sense for moments like these. Joe Biden told me about a saying in his family: "If you have to ask, it's too late." Teddy never had to ask if you needed company, he just showed up. I

wasn't especially looking forward to President Bush's inauguration ceremony and the prospect of sitting there wondering (and knowing I wasn't
alone in wondering) what it would have been like if sixty-five thousand
votes had switched sides in Ohio. Not attending wasn't ever an option. I
managed a big smile when the jumbotron exposed me to a crowd of Republicans stretching down the Mall, who booed and jeered in unison. To the
victors go the spoils.

Shortly after the ceremony, Ted came up to me and all but announced
that he and Vicki were coming over to our house for dinner that evening.
Oh, and Chris Dodd was coming with his wife, Jackie, as well. It was a
transparent but endearing conspiracy Teddy had probably hatched with
Vicki long in advance. He'd kept the plan a secret because he knew neither
Teresa nor I wanted a pity party on a night that could have been very, very
different. He probably suspected we might try to wriggle out of it if he gave
us much advance notice.

That night, we cooked a feast of spaghetti and meatballs, drank far too
much red wine and listened as Teddy shared outrageous stories about colleagues past and present. It was all the more entertaining thanks to Ted's
gift of mimicry, and even funnier when he'd break character and, in an instant, his best Strom Thurmond impression would be punctuated by that unmistakable Boston accent.

As the night faded and not long before Teresa and I walked everyone to
the door, we were reminded of a different time in our history together.

In 1995, after the 1994 Republican Revolution cost us control of the
Senate, I was thrown into a tense choice I hadn't seen coming. We knew a
full year before that there would be a contest for Senate Democratic leader.
Tennessee's Jim Sasser was likely to win, but Tom Daschle, a sophomore
senator, was poised to give Sasser a run for his money. Tom was appealing to senators like me who weren't committee chairmen but hoped for a
greater voice in the caucus. It was old bulls on one side, young bucks on the
other. I signed up to help Tom. Teddy was signed up with Sasser, and Sasser
was a strong favorite.

On election night, though, Sasser was unexpectedly defeated. The race
for Democratic leader was wide open. In jumped Ted's best friend, Connecticut's Chris Dodd. Chris was my friend too, but to Teddy he was the
younger brother Ted had never had. Uncomfortably, I was committed to
Chris's opponent. I couldn't switch sides. If I did, my word wouldn't have
meant anything. It was awkward on the Senate floor, in the cloakroom, even
in my hideaway when I explained to both Chris and Ted that I couldn't
abandon Tom. It grew ever more awkward after Tom beat Chris by a single

vote. A frosty time followed. I'd see Ted and Chris sitting together at their desks on the Senate floor, laughing, and I knew it was better not to wander over and intrude. Now, Tom Daschle didn't have a Senate job to return to the way I had. On election night, he'd lost in South Dakota, and suddenly he'd gone from being the Democratic leader to needing to start over after a lifetime on Capitol Hill. His Republican successor had been sworn in earlier that day.

Ten years later, we were together on a tough night, as if the vote that had divided us in 1995 had never happened. Now we were just three friends, three senators, three guys leaning on one another on a night that hadn't turned out the way any of us had hoped for. Teddy was that galvanizing force making sure no one spent the evening alone. It was a great quality of Ted's, but a bigger reminder that the Senate runs on relationships, without which it can't run at all. I emailed Tom Daschle to get together for dinner, and I was reminded that I was lucky to have a role to return to, while Tom had to start life all over again.

I threw myself back into the work of the Senate. It wasn't always easy. I was in the minority, and the only committee on which I was even the senior Democrat was the Small Business Committee. It's culture shock to go from being introduced everywhere as "the next president of the United States" to speaking to half-empty hearing rooms about legislation to reduce paperwork at the Small Business Administration.

I felt most empowered and most at home on the Foreign Relations Committee. Joe Biden, Chris Dodd, Nebraska Republican and fellow veteran Chuck Hagel and I were all good friends who cared about America's role in the world. We were joined by a new member, one whose arrival on the committee brought with it a trail of television cameras: Illinois's junior senator, Barack Obama. Barack had an automatic platform in the Senate thanks to his performance at the convention in Boston, a freshman celebrity like none we'd witnessed since Hillary Clinton had come to the Senate after eight years as First Lady.

Every one of us was consumed by what we were watching unfold in Iraq. As a candidate, I'd described Iraq as "the wrong war, in the wrong place, at the wrong time." It had been a controversial statement back then. In the eyes of many, the war was going pretty well, even though all the ingredients were in place for full-blown disaster: a slow-growing insurgency, sectarian division and a weak government in Baghdad. Now, as President Bush began his second term, it was as if lighter fluid had been poured on those glowing embers. The insurgency became a full-fledged civil war. Anbar Province was exploding in violence.

Reading the comments of the Bush administration and listening to their witnesses testifying in front of the Foreign Relations Committee, I had a powerful sense of déjà vu. It could have been 1971. The hearing room hadn't changed in thirty-four years, and neither had the arguments. Another administration was in denial. Their witnesses would say we were three months or six months away from compromises among Iraqis that would alleviate the sectarian tensions. I asked my staff to check and, sure enough, those same witnesses had made those same predictions three or six months before. Once again, there was always "light at the end of the tunnel." Once again, we were being told that America was about to turn the page.

The Bush administration's policies had made Iraq into what it wasn't before the war: a breeding ground for jihadis—sixteen to twenty thousand jihadis and growing. Someone had to tell the truth to the American people. Happy talk about the insurgency being in its "last throes" led to frustrated expectations at home. Every day that we stumbled along, our troops were at greater risk, casualties were rising, costs were going up, the patience of the American people wore thin, and the specter of a quagmire stared us in the face.

I felt compelled to speak out. We couldn't turn back the clock and reverse the decisions that had brought us to this point in Iraq. Neither could we achieve the clear and simple victory the administration promised so often even as the conditions in Iraq grew worse and worse.

I wanted Congress at least to force the Bush administration to stop denying reality and together find an exit strategy that preserved our core interests in Iraq, in the region and throughout the world.

I believed I had a particular responsibility to push the policy in a realistic direction. As someone who made the mistake of voting for the resolution that gave the president the authority to go to war, I also felt a personal responsibility to act and to help create political cover for others who had made the same error. It was okay to admit you'd made a mistake. If Vietnam taught us anything, it was that for too long, too many stayed silent for fear of admitting they'd been wrong. Half the names on the Vietnam Veterans Memorial Wall represent young Americans killed after our leaders realized the policy was doomed to failure.

I began sitting down one by one with colleagues and talking about Iraq.

Some, like Chuck Hagel, were as disturbed as I was. Others, like John McCain, were deeply angry about the Bush policy but believed the answer was more American troops and infinite presence.

But there was also a mood among many in the Democratic caucus to hang back and let the president own the mess he had made in the Middle East, to continue with calls for Bush to find a strategy but never to offer one of our own. This would have been politically palatable if it weren't morally wrong.

Americans were dying. This was, by definition, America's problem, no matter who had created it.

In the late summer, I headed to the Middle East with a number of senators. I needed to go to Iraq again and evaluate for myself the situation on the ground. After a day and a half on the ground for round after round of meetings and briefings, I departed from Mosul.

Three senators and staff were gathered in the forward part of a C-130. In the middle of the cavernous cargo hold was a simple aluminum coffin with a small American flag draped over it. We were bringing another American soldier, just killed, home to his family and final resting place. The starkness of his coffin in the center of the hold, the silence except for the din of the engines, was a real-time cold reminder of the consequences of decisions for which we senators share responsibility. As we arrived in Kuwait, a larger flag was transferred to fully cover his coffin, and we joined graves registration personnel in giving him an honor guard as he was ceremoniously carried from the plane to a waiting truck. When the doors clanked shut, I wondered why all of America would not be allowed to see him arrive at Dover Air Force Base. Why hide him from a nation that deserves to mourn together in truth and in the light of day? His lonely journey should have been enough to compel all of us to come to grips with our choices in Iraq.

More than two thousand brave Americans had given their lives. Iraq had become a breeding ground for homegrown terrorists and a magnet for foreign ones.

I thought we had an obligation to talk about that and offer answers. The country and the Congress were misled into war. There was, as Robert Kennedy once said, "enough blame to go around," and I accepted my share of the responsibility. But the mistakes of the past, no matter who made them, are no justification for marching ahead into a future of miscalculations and misjudgments and the loss of American lives with no end in sight. We each had a responsibility to our country and our conscience to be honest about where we should go from here.

That's what I tried to do. I laid out a plan to set a deadline for Iraq to get its political house in order and deadlines to bring American combat troops home. I believed that saying to the Iraqis "We will stay as long as it takes" was an excuse for them to take as long as they wanted. That wasn't acceptable when Americans were coming home in caskets. By the end of the year, my position would become the Democrats' position and the mainstream foreign policy argument. I was glad I'd spoken out.

I was also glad that I did something that was long overdue. April 22, 2006, marked the thirty-fifth anniversary of my testimony against the war in Vietnam. So many who hadn't served at all had smeared that testimony for political gain. I was determined to speak up about the real meaning of patriotism. I thought the country needed to hear it. America was embroiled in a war over the war in Iraq, and too often the flag was invoked to shut people down instead of empowering them to speak up. It all felt so familiar. Too many had made it an art form to wield contrived appeals to patriotism as a means to turn our troops or our flag into the property of a political party. That was wrong. That was un-American. I gave a speech at Faneuil Hall in Boston thirty-five years to the day from when I had appeared in front of the Foreign Relations Committee. The old hall, meeting place of the original patriots and the "cradle of liberty," held great meaning.

On this bright April morning, it was packed to the rafters with old friends and new activists who had come to hear not about a war from a distant past, but about values at stake today, about how "fighting for your country overseas and fighting for your country's ideals at home are not contradictory or even separate duties. They are, in fact, two sides of the very same patriotic coin." I concluded with words I stand by to this day, just as I stand by what I said and did in 1971: "The most important way to support the troops is to tell the truth and to ensure we do not ask young Americans to die in a cause that falls short of the ideals of this country. When we protested the war in Vietnam, some would weigh in against us, saying, 'My country, right or wrong.' Our response was simple: 'Yes, my country, right or wrong. When right, keep it right, and when wrong, make it right.' And that's what we must do again today."

I was completing the unfinished business of 2004. I threw myself into the work of electing a Congress that would make a difference in the country. I helped recruit decorated veterans to run for office, and when they were attacked and when their military records were smeared, I defended them. I applied a lesson learned the hard way in 2004: keep hitting back until the truth is understood.

But it was a lesson about life's fragility—one in which I needed no refresher course—that punctuated the spring of 2006. In April, Vanessa suggested I call her mom right away. I had a sinking feeling of the reason behind the urgency. Julia was in Texas at MD Anderson Cancer Center, where doctors were valiantly trying all the latest approaches to save her life. It had been a long year and a half against a horrible adversary. She was quite weak after all the treatments. Julia knew she was in her final days and wanted to come back to Massachusetts to die.

We immediately made arrangements to have her flown back to Boston in a private plane. When she arrived, she went to Brigham and Women's Hospital for a week. When I went to the hospital to visit, only Alexandra and Vanessa were present. Julia shot me her resigned smile. I walked up to the bed, leaned over, and we both wrapped each other in a quiet, intense hug that seemed to last forever. We just hung on to each other as all the differences over the years melted away. Out of the corner of my eye, I saw the girls slide out of the room sobbing.

Julia didn't want to pass away in the hospital. She wanted somewhere that was more personal, more connected to her life. She settled on the guesthouse of a great friend in Concord, on a farm where she could open a window to see and smell spring in her final days and spend time with those closest to her.

For the next days, her husband, her children and I—her ex-husband—hung on to precious time as she faded away. On April 27, in the morning, Julia died. Relationships change, and some of the very best of them bend and even break as people grow in different directions. The sadness of our divorce, the sense of failure, clouded our relationship for many years. I was lucky that we both found love again, and that we made peace with each other, and that before it was too late, we had the chance to say goodbye the way we did, to remember the sweetness of early times and to share the gift that endured: our daughters. I will always be reminded of Julia in my memories and in the faces and laughter of Alex and Vanessa.

IN THE FALL of 2006, the tide was turning in the country. We won back the House and the Senate. President Bush was officially a lame duck.

I had decisions to make. I had sought the presidency in 2004 to lead us on a different course. Now the country was voting for the kind of change I'd proposed during a difficult, divided period.

There were powerful reasons to want to continue that fight now. Many of my most loyal friends were urging me to run again. They felt that my 2004 race had been so close and so affected by illegitimate factors that in an open year with no incumbent, I had grown enough as a candidate that I should give it a second shot. After all, they argued, Nixon and Reagan had both done so successfully—Nixon even after running for governor of California and losing.

But I felt viscerally that the country needed a different narrative. The year 2004 was just too close in time, and the current demand for someone new would be too strong, in my judgment, to overcome.

I decided it was time to put my energy to work as part of the majority in the Senate to do all I could to end the war and strengthen our security and our ability to fight the real war on terror. In January 2007, on the Senate floor, as I gave a speech about Iraq, I made it very clear: I would not be a candidate for president. I wanted people to trust that the issues I was talking about were grounded in purpose, not politics.

Ted Kennedy was sitting a few feet away. He rose and spoke about how close we had come in 2004 and how much good remained to be done. Afterward, he brought a bottle of Chivas to my hideaway office in the Capitol. He reminded me that it was after he turned down the chance to run for president again in 1984 that his legislative career really blossomed.

I had work to do. I wanted not just to end the war, but to help rebuild congressional momentum on the environment and climate change so that the next president could actually do something about it.

And I wanted perhaps to have a role in selecting that person. I started quietly considering whether there was someone running in 2008 whom I might help be that kind of president, the transformative, unifying kind the country so desperately needed.

I had Senate friends running—Chris Dodd and Joe Biden. But the strongest campaigns were mounted by two others—Hillary Clinton and Barack Obama.

We didn't see a lot of Barack after the campaign began. I would have a brief conversation with him if he came back to the Senate to vote, but most of my contact was with the campaign through friends who were on the trail, particularly in Iowa and New Hampshire.

Initially, I thought hard about endorsing Hillary. We had been colleagues in the Senate longer than I'd served with Barack. I sat down with her to listen to her thoughts about her campaign and offer a few observations from my own. Hillary had always been warm and welcoming to my children and me. I respected and liked her. She was smart and genuinely passionate. I felt she got a bum rap from many in the media. If you were having a casual conversation in the cloakroom, joking around in a caucus meeting or just sitting down for a personal conversation, she was real, present, funny and caring. But I felt powerfully, having run against Bush and lost, and having a pretty good feeling at that point for national politics, and having examined and found wanting the potential of my own repeat candidacy, that the country might want a unifying politics. For some of the same and some different reasons that I thought I shouldn't run, I felt her campaign would have a hard time.

I felt strongly, as a matter of gut politics, that Barack Obama could provide that narrative. Barack and I had dinner in Washington in the fall, one-on-one. We talked about growing up overseas. We talked and laughed about the ironies and indignities of life on the campaign trail in those early days of a campaign. I liked him. I liked that he didn't feel the need to sell you on his campaign or his candidacy. Back home there was a generational divide: my sister Peggy, the longtime activist, was firmly for Hillary; Barack was the candidate my daughters were most excited about.

After Thanksgiving, I flew to Bali for the UN Climate Change Conference. I was struck that everywhere I went, countries were so excited that hope was on the way in the United States, no matter who won. But Barack was the candidate they asked me about most often.

I had to decide whether to get involved in the race. Teresa believed I had earned the right to speak my mind. My heart and my gut told me to endorse Barack. Ted Kennedy urged me not to endorse early. He thought it was too big a risk for me, and pressed me to wait until the nomination process was largely settled and help bring the party back together. Many on my staff were nervous, and not without reason. Al Gore had endorsed Howard Dean four years before and been derided when Dean's candidacy imploded. I didn't want to blow my credibility as a former nominee on a pyrrhic endorsement.

I was also friends with Joe Biden and Chris Dodd, whose campaigns were stuck, but who were still going to be my friends after they came back to the Senate.

John Edwards was in the race, and he was betting the farm on Iowa. While we had not spoken in months, and no one expected me to be with Edwards, I didn't want my checkered history with John to be seen as the reason I was endorsing someone else. I wanted to make a statement about the future, not the past.

In December, talks with the Obama campaign about making an endorsement in Iowa right before the caucuses intensified.

We went back and forth. There was a comfort level settling into the campaign that they would win Iowa and it would be better to save my endorsement for a more strategic moment.

Their big win in Iowa on January 3 was a political thunderbolt. They were on their way.

Then a week later came a solid loss in New Hampshire.

Suddenly, the Clinton comeback was the big story.

Around midnight that night, I got a call at home in Boston: "You still with me?" It was Barack. He had delivered his concession speech in Manchester.

I laughed and said, "Yes—for sure. I told you I'm with you and I'm with you. When do you want to do it?"

"Let's do it this week in South Carolina," he said, and that was it.

Two days later, I was headed to Charleston, where I'd begun my own presidential announcement tour in 2003 at Patriots Point, only this time it was to help choose a new standard-bearer.

One of the hardest calls I ever made in politics was to Hillary Clinton that morning. I wanted her to hear from me personally that I was going in a different direction. She is a professional. The call was cordial. But I could tell that this was a moment in party lore, like Carter versus Kennedy in 1980: everyone would remember who supported whom in the race between Clinton and Obama.

We landed in balmy, beautiful weather in Charleston. Barack's campaign plane was across the tarmac. I climbed into his waiting Suburban and together we drove to the College of Charleston. He looked thin, run down by the miles on the road and the hectic pace. But he was calm, as always. He never seemed to get too high or too low. He was a profile in contrasts. He was just a bit beyond two years in the Senate, running for president, and it struck me that even as he had extraordinary political talent, he was also a somewhat shy person. He seemed intellectual enough that some of the requisites of campaigning—perhaps even public life—didn't necessarily sit well with him. He could be naturally gregarious, exuding that big, warm, flashy smile, but he didn't seem to exult in the give-and-take or love the process. It became tedious and mechanical faster than it might have for other candidates. But he was disciplined; clearly, he kept churning through so many events with such great talent, even when his body or his mind wanted to do something else.

At the college, I spoke first. I talked about choosing a president who could offer America a transformation. I was glad to be part of the journey. Obama bounded down the steps, basked in the applause of the crowd, thanked me, made his obligatory recognitions of the assembled political world, delivered his speech and disappeared.

I flew back to Washington to resume work in the Senate. When I landed, my cell phone was buzzing: eight voice mails. There was one from Teddy, congratulating me on my decision. But there were seven from friends of mine who were raising money for Hillary—messages of profound disappointment. One was even explicit: "Don't come near my boat on Nantucket this summer, asshole."

Politics is a tough business—and nothing rubs emotions rawer than being in the foxhole of a presidential campaign.

Over the spring and summer, I campaigned hard for Barack. It was exhilarating. I'm competitive to begin with, but I was reminded how much fun it is to walk into a town hall meeting, community center, church or VFW hall and be an advocate for a cause you are excited about. At the convention in Denver, I took on my friend John McCain, the Republican nominee, on foreign policy and made as strong a case as I could that Barack Obama was the best person to lead America in these difficult times. It was tough to criticize McCain. We'd lived a lot of history together. We fought and loved each other like brothers. But in a political party that demanded ideological purity to win a nomination, I was disappointed that candidate McCain wasn't able to speak what the real John McCain means to America.

I was in Boston on Election Day for my own celebration: despite having earlier faced a spoiler primary opponent in my Senate reelection campaign who had been put on the ballot in part to punish me for endorsing Barack, I was reelected to a fifth term in the Senate, with 66 percent of the vote. Later that night, Teresa and I sat together and watched one of the great tableaux of all my time in politics—that extraordinary moment when President-elect Barack Hussein Obama walked out on the giant stage in Grant Park, Chicago, hand in hand with his family. The young president-elect, the first African American president in our history, was now making himself history. The tears of joy were profound.

CHAPTER 14

New President, Broken Senate

On JANUARY 5, 2009, Ted Kennedy once again walked me down the aisle of the Senate to be sworn in for a fifth term—a wonderful tradition, but particularly bittersweet this time since we both knew it was the last time. I flashed back to 1985, the first time I was sworn in. That first day Ted took me around the Senate floor and pulled me into the huddle of his seasoned colleagues as if it were a fraternity mixer. It was a different Senate now, of course, and we were both living different seasons of our lives. We had each put countless miles on our odometers since that first day, each added a lot of gray hair. More important, our relationship had developed into a genuinely deep friendship over the intervening years, tested by campaigns and cancer, and strengthened by shared issues to tackle and ideologies to lean on, reinforced by faith and fun. It was quite a journey together.

We were the longest-serving senior-junior senator combination since old Strom Thurmond and Fritz Hollings. My God, how did that happen? Where did those years go, and how did they fly by so quickly? Today, Ted seemed to be doing well, despite his terminal cancer, walking with a cane and husbanding his energy for the times he really needed it. Maybe he was leaning a little more on me as we made it down into the well of the Senate, but he was still very much Teddy, very much present. It was one of those moments Ted just wouldn't miss being a part of.

"Vice President Cheney, are you ready to swear in the five-term junior sena-tah from Massachusetts?" Teddy bellowed theatrically, and that big, broad smile was back for a flash, the deep, unmistakable belly laugh. He slapped the back of President Bush's famously dour vice president. I'm not sure I'd ever seen Cheney crack a smile before, but he did for Ted.

There was a surreal symmetry to being sworn in by Vice President Cheney, who had represented so much of the last eight years that I'd spoken out against, while just feet away stood the vice president–elect, Joe Biden, whom Cheney had sworn in just moments before to Joe's seventh term representing Delaware, just weeks before Joe would resign his Senate seat to succeed Cheney.

Chapters were closing and others beginning at the same time. None of us knew quite where the stories would end up. There was a bittersweet sense of comings and goings—big changes in Washington, some hopeful and others much less encouraging—as I was about to begin another term in the U.S. Senate. Once again in my life, I felt as though I was standing in a moment of multiple transitions, some literal, some figurative.

Today, though, wasn't a day to dwell on the changes. We had work to do, and I had a couple hundred friends from Massachusetts and beyond in town to celebrate my swearing-in. The crowd in the Dirksen Building was boisterous and full of fun. Gathered together were the stalwarts, friends from the campaigns in Massachusetts from 1972 on, people who had stuck it out in Iowa and New Hampshire when things didn't look so promising, alumni and friends and family. At the center of it all was Max Cleland, ever the happy warrior, his special loyalty on display. Max faced a daily barrage of medical hurdles—it's rare that triple amputees from the Vietnam era live well into their sixties as Max so bravely had. Never did he let on to anyone that he faced such a daily struggle. That wasn't Max. He kept it all inside. He just showed up for his band of brothers. I asked Max and Ted to say a few words, and what a pair they made at the podium. The room was still and quiet as everyone leaned in to listen to these two men who had been central figures in so many of the political battles we'd fought together over the last years.

Max was excited. "And John Kerry is still my commander in chief!" he yelled, as the crowd applauded.

And then, to even more clapping, Teddy shouted out, "And he's my secretary of state!"

"Ted," I said as I touched his arm, trying to stop him.

"No, no, noooo," Teddy bellowed with his signature laugh and a theatrical line: "I can say it!"

More applause followed his emphatic rejoinder. It was classic Max and even more classic Teddy, a remark of unspoken solidarity that broke the ice in a room where the subject was taboo, a subject about which there was no doubt some chatter in the perpetual conversation of who's up, who's down, who's coming, and who's going in Washington parlor games.

The unspoken elephant in the room, which only Ted was plucky and audacious enough to mention, was a swirl of media speculation about the president-elect's pick to head the State Department, which had peaked before Thanksgiving. Unbeknownst to anyone in that room besides Ted and

Vicki, just a few days after the election, the president-elect had flown me out to Chicago to meet one-on-one and talk about the possibility of a role in his cabinet. Alyssa Mastromonaco, who had headed the scheduling operation for my campaign in 2004, was by now a trusted jack-of-all-trades for Barack Obama, and she worked with my team to make sure the meeting stayed a secret to protect the equities of everyone involved.

As the private plane touched down in Chicago, I was reminded just how quickly the days grow shorter in November, the midwestern air crisp but not yet cold. With the skies darkening, we drove into Carl Sandburg's "City of the Big Shoulders." The incredible skyline approached as the sun set softly and swiftly.

Chicago had always been one of those cities that marked memorable milestones on my journey, from Harvey Bundy's wedding on the eve of Officer Candidate School, to the newsreel footage of violence in the streets at the bloody convention in 1968, to all the stops in the decades to come for one political event or another. Little could I have ever predicted just how much my future would intersect with the Senate candidate I'd met on the South Side of Chicago in the spring of 2004, a man whose campaign I'd endorsed during a tough primary season and who was now the president-elect of the United States.

An office building in Chicago had been transformed overnight into a temporary transition headquarters until the president-elect and his team picked up stakes and moved the whole operation to Washington, D.C. There was a buzz on the streets around the site of so much planning for a new administration in which many had invested such extraordinary hope for renewal. As the office building approached, and we spotted the steel Jersey barriers assembled to keep the gathered press at bay, I ducked down and pressed myself flat on the seat so no reporter would see me entering the garage. I wanted to avoid press speculation. Having once planned for a transition of my own, I knew how unhelpful leaks and leakers were, and I didn't want to take any risk of contributing to a swirl.

Fittingly, the first face to greet me upstairs was Marvin Nicholson, a familiar and friendly presence, self-effacing as ever. Marvin had by now traveled hundreds of thousands of miles on back-to-back presidential campaigns, one ending in disappointment, one ending in a remarkable victory that, at least for now, had created a sense of unity and purpose in the country unlike anything I'd seen in my political lifetime. We hugged. I'd kept up with Marvin through texts and emails during this last campaign and we'd remained close friends. He'd been a confidant, a mischief-maker and a mood-lightener extraordinaire during the highs, lows and in-betweens of the race in 2004, and I couldn't have been happier for him that all those weeks and months spent cramming his six-foot-seven frame into tiny vans and little planes had landed him here where he belonged, next to a president-elect.

Barack Obama came out of his office and welcomed me inside. A non-descript General Services Administration suite of offices had been whipped into a working transition space, and in the office reserved for the president-elect there was a small couch, a couple of chairs and, on a wall, a television set tuned to a football game in action on the screen. The look and feel of the office was utilitarian, temporary and efficient.

One of Obama's great gifts is his calm demeanor, always perfectly self-contained. We sat down and began to talk informally. When I referred to him as "Mr. President-elect," he stopped me and said that when we were in private I should call him Barack. He asked about Teresa and reminded me that so much of my political family had helped form his earliest staff, from the speechwriter Jon Favreau to Alyssa, Marvin and his heads of domestic policy. He was chewing what by now I knew was Nicorette gum, a valiant effort to keep his smoking habit at bay, but he was loose and relaxed for a man who now had the weight of the world on his shoulders. He thanked me for my contributions to the campaign and began talking about all the work that lay ahead, starting with the economy. He'd had his first briefings on the economy, all of which had confirmed for him that things weren't as bad as he'd argued during the campaign—they were actually a whole lot worse—but he was moving quickly and efficiently to build a government. He'd immediately announced Rahm Emanuel as his chief of staff, and Rahm popped his head into the meeting to say hello. I'd known Rahm going all the way back to his staff job running point on NAFTA for President Clinton. He was certainly a good choice.

Our meeting was friendly and polite. Obama asked me about my interest in serving as secretary of state. I told him that I knew from having run in 2004 that these are personal decisions that only the principal can make, but that I believed in the promise of his administration and wanted to be helpful in whatever way I could. I'd just been reelected and wasn't grasping for an exit strategy from the Senate. We talked a bit about the job itself, a handful of big challenges from Iran to Afghanistan, and he emphasized how much the years ahead would be consumed with domestic challenges as the first order of business. He said he would come back to me, that he had some politics to figure out, chairs to arrange, and that perhaps we should talk more soon.

I walked out with a clear feeling that he had a very specific person in mind for the State Department and that it wasn't me. Soon we would learn that it was my colleague Senator Clinton, a bold decision to bring inside the administration his chief political rival. Many wondered whether it could work, remembering what a friction point foreign policy had been during the primary season and how much they'd clashed. Some of the bad blood between the Obama team and the Clinton team had no doubt lingered, something I knew from my own experience in 2008 dealing with the hurt feelings of Massachusetts's Clinton backers who were angry that I'd backed Obama. For the activists and insiders, whichever side you were on in this campaign had become a dividing line, not as indelible as Carter/Kennedy in 1980, but sometimes not far off either.

Stepping back, however, and taking in the view from a higher elevation, I knew it could work if the two principals wanted to try. On Obama's part, I thought it was a bold move, one that reinforced his campaign's narrative about bringing people together and one that also conveniently ensured that if the first couple years of the administration went poorly, he wouldn't have a chief Democratic rival waiting in the Senate. When I met with my own transition team in 2004, we'd actually talked very specifically about uniting the party that way, finding ways to bring not just allies but former opponents into an administration. I believed that Hillary and Barack could make it work, and I thought it would be well received globally, a message about unity and governance.

While it would have been great to start out as President Obama's first secretary of state, the quick resolution of whether I was staying inside the Senate or being drafted into the administration gave me certainty about my role in the Senate and my focus. Certainly, when friends had laid out the case—doing foreign policy full-time in an administration I believed in, surrounded by friends—it had been attractive. I'd always said, even when I was running for president, that secretary of state seemed like the best job in the world—no fund-raising, no politics, just focusing every day on making the world a better place. It would have been an extraordinary opportunity— but there was also an element of relief about the choice I wasn't facing. I'd just been reelected with 66 percent of the vote in Massachusetts. I'd worked for years to earn that trust. I'd gone through very tough campaigns to get to the Senate and to stay there, including running against America's most popular governor in 1996, William Weld. Now I had a big mandate from Massachusetts, and Teddy was sick, which meant, inevitably, that Massachusetts would be contemplating life without a giant who had been a rock of responsive government since 1962. This was not the ideal time for me to be leaving Massachusetts or the institution.

Stepping back, I felt as if I was in a new and different space and place than any in my Senate career, with seniority I'd never dreamed of in 1985 when I was number ninety-nine out of one hundred. Now I had a seat on the Senate Finance Committee, where senators like Russell Long and Daniel Patrick Moynihan had passed some of the most important legislation in generations, shaping social policy through the tax code, and I knew we would be working to pass health care reform, which I'd always hoped would become a reality. My perch on three different committees—Finance, Commerce and Foreign Relations—gave me a chance to help shape policy in a whole array of issues I cared about, from technology, trade and globalization to climate change. There was a lot to do, and I was especially excited about what we might be able to get done in the first years of this administration, with a big majority in the House of Representatives and fifty-nine—soon to be sixty—Democratic seats in the Senate. I'd never been around (with seniority) for a moment like this, and neither had most of my colleagues. For someone like me, who had read about the New Deal, the Lyndon Johnson–era Senate, and then the Great Society, but had never witnessed an era of extraordinary progressive legislating, it promised to be a great time to be a U.S. senator.

Everything on Inauguration Day 2009 only bolstered that sense of possibility and that burst of idealism. History seemed to be shining its brightest light on Washington that day, the inauguration of our first African American president serendipitously falling the day after Martin Luther King Day. It was bitter cold but the sun was shining. Our children and their families gathered at home early that morning and bundled up together, along with my sisters and Cam, for the trek to the Capitol through the toughest traffic and largest crowds I'd ever seen in Washington (and, yes, larger by far than the Trump inaugural). Teresa particularly had been captivated by the presidential campaign. She'd even headed home to campaign in Pittsburgh with Michelle Obama, introducing the future First Lady at a boisterous rally at Carnegie Mellon. Teresa and Michelle, of course, were filled with an idealism that was infectious.

It's hard to adequately describe the excitement of the moment. I'd been to many inaugurations, from Eisenhower's, sitting on my dad's shoulders, trying to sneak a peek at the far-off scene playing out on the east steps of the Capitol, to those I'd attended closer up as a senator for four other presidents, three Republicans and just one Democrat. This was different. It must have felt the way it did when President Kennedy was inaugurated, the palpable sense of energy and purpose.

Down the length of the Mall, the mass of people stretched on and on, and the signs and the faces in the crowd spoke to the powerful connection so many African Americans were sharing in this moment. For me, who had been inspired in college by Allard Lowenstein's exhortation to march for civil rights, and then that next spring had been horrified by the "White Only" and "Colored" signs David Thorne and I had seen in rest stops when we drove through the South, this moment was a long time coming in America. President Obama's inauguration proved more powerfully than any speech or piece of legislation ever could that we really could be the country we aspired to be.

The inauguration was also personally touching. These were two colleagues of mine being sworn in as president and vice president. I'd sat on the Foreign Relations Committee for twenty-four years with Joe and for four with Barack. Our staffs, advisors and political families intersected in so many ways, and both Teddy and I had thrown ourselves into the campaign with gusto. Now, up here on the steps of the west front of the Capitol, we felt that hope had found a home in this sea of human hearts.

The transformative power of an inauguration is remarkable. I watched as Joe Biden became Vice President Biden and as Senator Barack Obama became simply "the President." Together with their families, they moved from the crisp air of the steps of the Capitol into the rotunda. They accepted congratulations and warm wishes from all gathered inside. When I stood there with the new president and offered my best, and said the words "Mr. President," he arched his eyebrows slightly, as if to say, "What a crazy world this is." The president scribbled a note on the program I intended to keep as a souvenir: "I'm here because of you." Of course, I didn't think that was true. Barack Obama was president because of his skill and determination, and because with remarkable confidence he had judged the political moment correctly and zigged when others zagged. Nonetheless, his note was a reminder of the funny way our lives and careers had intersected. *What if . . . ?* I had to wonder—life is full of so many what-ifs. What if we hadn't tacked on a jobs event on the South Side of Chicago in 2004 and I hadn't met him again in the campaign? What if a different name had risen to the top of the list as Mary Beth Cahill, Jack Corrigan and I mulled our options for the keynote speaker at the Democratic convention later that summer? What if? History is history when it happens, but there are so many little moments along the way that could have altered its course, but here we were in this present moment that would be ensconced in future history books, and it all felt real and right.

For me, however, the excitement and anticipation of that moment weren't to be savored much longer. At the traditional, bipartisan celebratory luncheon after the ceremony in the beautiful rooms of the Capitol, as the new president mingled with the group, a murmur and a gasp rippled through the crowd: Ted Kennedy had collapsed. Ted had no doubt saved up a lot of strength for this day he had worked so hard to see, but the room was hot after so much time out in the cold earlier. A seizure had interrupted the day that was so important to this seventy-six-year-old man who was loved by so many of us in that room. *Oh God, don't let this happen today*, I prayed, as a rush of adrenaline raced through my body. I stood by Teddy, trying to block the view from the cameras as we worked through the beginning of the seizure. Chris Dodd, Orrin Hatch and I helped get Ted out of the luncheon into an adjoining room. There we stretched him out on the carpet as the seizure continued to lock his body. A doctor appeared, but both Vicki and I were struck by how little he contributed to resolving the episode. Then Capitol medical technicians arrived, and after they got things stabilized a bit, we accompanied Ted to a waiting ambulance. Not wanting to distract from the festive day, he urged us to go back inside. By the time I did get back, I learned that shortly after Ted's medical episode, Robert Byrd, my first Senate Democratic leader, now a white-haired, wheelchair-bound ninety-one-year-old, had also become ill and disoriented, upset by what he'd seen happen to the man he had defeated for whip in 1979.

Later that day, I headed over to the hospital to see Teddy. He was laughing, feeling much better, mad as hell about what had happened. Vicki was a rock through it all, a protector and a comforter, but it was a crystallizing moment, a reminder for all of us that even lives lived at the center of history don't last forever. The clock was ticking.

I tried to apply that lesson quietly to my work in the Senate. Early in the year, I sat down with my senior Senate team. I wanted to talk about the next two years, and I wanted to set the tone right from the start. "Everyone may expect us to carry the load on foreign policy, but I want each of you to hear and know this from me: I care about a whole lot more than that and I've waited for a moment like this a long time, with a Democratic president and a Democratic Congress and a chance to get a lot done, and we're going to do more than foreign policy."

The domestic policy staff was thrilled. I'd seen in the Senate how too often assumptions can become reality if you let them. I cared deeply about foreign policy, but it wasn't all I cared about, not by a long shot, and it wasn't all I was now well positioned to help shape. I'd seen Ted step out from his core issues to be an important voice on issues like Iraq and seen the great appropriator Robert Byrd do the same. Foreign policy was an asset for us, but I wanted to be a senator who made a difference on more than one issue, and I knew we could. We were going to have a very full agenda. At the top of the list were three causes that had animated me for a long time: providing affordable health care for everybody, protecting the environment and preventing war.

Health care had been the cause of Ted Kennedy's career, but it was also a personal passion of mine. I had cared about health care as a policy issue for decades. When I ran for president, health care was one of the first proposals I put in front of the country because I believed it was the right thing to do for moral reasons and also the smart thing to do for the economy. Skyrocketing health care costs were hurting the competitiveness of our businesses. But it had become personal to me and my family. My daughter Vanessa was practicing medicine in Boston. She saw a system that was separate and unequal in every way. There had been so many times through my cancer diagnosis and surgery when I had to remind myself how blessed I was that I had the best insurance in the world and money out of pocket if I wanted to create new options. I'd been able to put my care first, not the bills. Forty-four million Americans weren't so lucky. They had no insurance. Millions upon millions more had lousy insurance or had health risks that drove up the costs of their policies so much that they were choosing between their insurance and paying for their kids' college. That shouldn't happen in the richest country on the planet.

One of the reasons I had been so personally invested supporting Barack Obama's campaign and worked so hard to help elect big majorities in Congress was that I thought we could finally pass health reform in the new president's first term.

My seat on the Senate Finance Committee put me in the center of the debate. Ted Kennedy, Chris Dodd and Tom Harkin were the stalwart liberal champions on the Health, Education, Labor and Pensions Committee (HELP), but the Finance Committee had jurisdiction over tax revenue, Medicare and Medicaid. Our role would be critical to passing a bill. We had the job of finding the money and the savings to pay for reform, and we could shape its contours.

I started out with optimism about the process. The chairman, Max Baucus of Montana, had been smart to hold the first public listening sessions on health care in 2008, a year in advance of the legislative process. He wanted senators to start going on record with proposals. He wanted to build the public record. He wanted everyone on both sides of the aisle to feel they had been given time to have input.

The Finance Committee has usually been a collegial place. In past years, Republicans like Orrin Hatch had worked closely with the Democrats on health care. There was ample reason to believe the policies could be bipartisan. After all, Republicans for years had supported measures like the individual mandate, the idea that every American had a responsibility to buy health insurance the same way every driver has to buy car insurance. It was the basis of the reform Mitt Romney supported as governor in Massachusetts. We were willing to move toward that proposal. Suddenly, Romney himself disavowed it, disavowed his own bill! He was gearing up to run for president in 2012, and he wouldn't stand a chance if he looked "too bipartisan."

There were warning signs inside the Senate from the start. Max Baucus reached out and met repeatedly with Republican senator Mike Enzi of Wyoming, a key vote on the committee. Max wanted to partner with him on a bipartisan agreement. Enzi committed to work with him but wanted to keep their meetings private. There's nothing wrong with that as long as you're working in good faith. But not only did the process drag on and on with nothing to show for it, but Republicans began attacking health reform with an effective talking point: It was being done "behind closed doors." It was a "backroom deal," they said. We had essentially created a news blackout at their request, but now they were filling the vacuum with lies about the process. Worse, they took the public vacuum of not having a bill and began making wild allegations about what might be in Democratic health reform. The very Republicans who for years had tried to cut money out of Medicare began filling the airwaves with accusations that we were cutting Medicare to pay for socialized medicine. The irony, of course, was that we were spending time trying to persuade Republicans to join us on health reforms they had once championed, only to have them excoriate us for advocating to do something about those policies. They attacked from every direction.

We knew Teddy didn't have much time left. He was no longer as present in the Senate. When there was a critical vote on health care, however, Ted made a superhuman effort to be there. I remember coordinating with Vicki to make sure we could get him in and out as easily as possible. Just the trip down from Hyannis was dangerous because of his weakened immune system and the threat of infection, not to mention fatigue.

I will never forget that day in April 2009, when the familiar van pulled up to the ramp on the east side of the Senate building. The door slid open and

I was greeted by this great, warm Kennedy smile. As difficult as the journey was, it was evident Ted was thrilled to return to the Senate. I wheeled him up the ramp with Vicki and a coterie of Senate police. We came in the back door, took the elevator up to the rear hallway of the Senate chamber, then wheeled him to the door. Once at the door, Ted wanted to get out of the chair and walk onto the Senate floor under his own power. When he appeared, the Senate erupted in prolonged, emotional applause. Many of us had tears in our eyes. Except for a few of us, no one had expected him to be there for the vote on this particular day. In fact, the minute the Republicans saw him enter the chamber, they knew they were going to lose the vote. Those senators who did not want a recorded vote against Medicare immediately switched their votes now that the victory was predetermined. We on the Democratic side of the aisle knew that Ted's difficult trip was worth the effort. Senators crowded around to shake his hand and welcome him back.

Chris Dodd and I sat in the back row beside his desk and listened to Teddy regale us with an imitation of his efforts to practice throwing out the ball at the Red Sox season opener on April 7, ninety-seven years after his grandfather Boston mayor John "Honey Fitz" Fitzgerald had done it in 1912, at the first major league game played at Fenway. Ted laughed and poked fun at how reluctant his hand and muscles were to obey his commands. I was in awe of this moment of humility and self-deprecating humor in the face of a frustrating reality. As Teddy so often said over the years, we have to take issues seriously but never take ourselves too seriously. He was a master of that too.

Because I had been in regular contact with Vicki over the weeks and months since Ted had taken a turn for the worse, I knew that he had only a limited amount of time left. At the end of July or early August, I arranged with her that I would come for a visit at their house in Hyannis. As I drove by the famous dock where hundreds of pictures must have been taken of Teddy walking toward the sea for an afternoon sail, surrounded by grandkids and nephews and nieces, the Pied Piper of an afternoon on Nantucket Sound on his beloved schooner, *Maya*, a sweep of memories overwhelmed me as I approached the compound.

I walked up to the porch of the house he grew up in, the famous house of his parents, Joe and Rose, where so many extraordinary moments of history had played out. I knew this was most likely a goodbye visit, and since I hate goodbyes, I wasn't sure how to get through this one. We sat on the porch looking out at the stunning view of the sound, at the waters that Teddy and Jack and Bobby had sailed on all their lives. We talked about the good times sailing, about the Senate, about what was happening in politics. Ted seemed incredibly peaceful. I wondered if there was some Dylan Thomas inside him to "rage against the dying of the light," but he gave no hint of anger or rebellion against his fate. I could feel the closeness of his relationship with Vicki, who had been heroic in managing Ted's life from the moment of his diagnosis and before.

When I felt I had stayed long enough and run the limits of his stamina, I said I thought I should get back to Boston. We got up. I went over to Teddy and hugged him. In all the years I had known Ted Kennedy, I had never hugged him, not even after my election victories or his. Our partings had always ended with a boisterous celebration, a hearty handshake, a great thump on the back. This time I hugged him close and held on for a moment, as did he.

Knowing how much Ted lived life to the fullest, I had earlier wondered whether he had gone through a stage of anger or even bitterness about his condition. Vicki had told me that he never felt any bitterness, not only because he had lived through the loss of all his brothers and two sisters, but particularly because two of his children had fought cancer. He felt lucky looking back on his life.

Ted thought that perhaps his treatment and journey could help other people, maybe even save some lives. He consciously came to a spiritual, peaceful place believing it was important for him to help show people how to die. He did that by living to the end. He sailed until just two weeks before he died, when he couldn't pursue this particular passion any longer. Until the very last night, he sat at the dinner table as head of the family. Vicki later said he didn't go quietly. On the contrary, from the day of his diagnosis, Teddy and Vicki shared a concentrated time of purpose, one that they both came to describe as joyous. Certainly it was filled with challenges—pulling off a speech at Obama's convention in Denver, preparing to receive an honorary degree from Harvard, finishing his inspirational memoir, *True Compass* (although he didn't live to see it published the month after he died), continuing to fight for health care, attending sessions of the Senate until May 2009—all the while being treated for the tumor that was eating away at his life. He passed away on the evening of August 26. I looked out at the ocean, where gray sky met gray water, with no evident horizon. The sky almost seemed to be in mourning. It was not a time for sailing. The next afternoon, however, as I sat at his home, I looked out at a perfect Nantucket Sound and thought with certainty that he was on a schooner now, smiling and sailing. At Ted's memorial service in Boston, when I was introduced to speak by Paul Kirk, the man who would be appointed to temporarily fill the Senate seat, the introduction left me speechless for a moment: "the senior senator from Massachusetts, John Kerry." I'd never thought about those words referring to me because I'd never imagined the Senate or Massachusetts without Ted. But when I heard them, I felt a weight that was different from before. There was an immediacy to what I had to do as a senator at this moment: we had to finish the job on health care.

WHEN I HEADED back to the Senate after Ted's burial, I remembered one of the conversations we had had as spring turned to summer. I had told Ted that I feared we were getting stuck on health care, that the Republicans were playing rope-a-dope. Ted was following the process closely through his staff in Washington and through Vicki, herself a health care expert. I told him that Majority Leader Harry Reid thought that in the end we might need to pass a bill just with Democratic votes. Teddy's eyes lit up. He had been down this road so many times. He knew these historic opportunities were in short supply.

In our Democratic caucus meeting, I argued that we needed to pass a bill, period. What we were trying to do was not easy. It wasn't easy for Franklin Roosevelt when he tried, it wasn't easy for Harry Truman when he tried, it wasn't easy for Bill Clinton when he tried. But you don't sound the retreat, and you don't make the perfect the enemy of the good. I told the story I thought Ted would have told if he were there. Ted Kennedy always said his biggest political mistake was turning down a health care deal with Richard Nixon in 1971 that would have required all companies to provide a health plan for their employees, with federal subsidies for low-income workers. Teddy backed away from it under heavy pressure from Democrats who wanted to hold out for a single-payer system once the party recaptured the White House. Thirty-eight years had passed and single-payer still wasn't a reality. Here we were in 2009, fighting to get less than what we could have had in 1971! The lesson Teddy taught me, I said to the caucus, was that when it comes to historic breakthroughs in America, you make the best deal you can, then immediately start pushing for ways to improve it. We wouldn't have sixty Democratic votes forever. We wouldn't always have a Democratic president. Now was the time. We couldn't allow ourselves to get bogged down in internecine fights. Those who wanted what was called a "public option" were right. It should be law. I supported it. It deserved a vote. I'd support it as I always had. But I wasn't going to lose the chance to pass reform just because I couldn't get everything I wanted.

We began a public process in the Finance Committee to move legislation to the Senate floor. We weren't waiting for the Republicans any longer. I came up with a plan to raise significant revenue to pay for reform: an excise tax on the so-called Cadillac health plans provided by some companies. It was not a tax on individuals, but on big corporations that could afford it. My colleagues embraced it. I also convinced the committee to adopt a central plank of the health plan I had proposed as a presidential candidate: lowering health care costs for people with catastrophic medical expenses by creating a pool of money to pay for those costs. It was called "reinsurance." I thought of the people I'd met on those rope lines in 2004, people with rare cancers, or kids with chronic diseases that required lifelong care. They should be able to get insurance that was affordable. I also managed to include in our committee's legislation a package of tax cuts to make health insurance affordable for small businesses. These were not minor things. These were things we had been striving for for decades, certainly in the twenty-five years I had been in the Senate.

That fall, health care became personal again, unexpectedly. In our family, we endearingly call Teresa "Dr. T." Her father was a doctor in Mozambique. As a young girl, she had followed him into the bush to watch him care for the indigenous population. She was always fascinated by medicine and, later in life, almost certainly knew more about it than most senators and even some doctors. I would frequently hear her on the phone giving advice to friends who inevitably called her to get "second opinions" about one thing or another. She was uncanny in her ability to sense or interpret one symptom or another. That fall, she forced an exam that resulted in a diagnosis of breast cancer. She had surgery to have the cancer removed and then went through radiation to get a clean bill of health. Exhausted and a little scared, but in the hands of great doctors and nurses, she was doing all this at the same time that Congress was dithering and delaying. More time was being spent on television talking about Sarah Palin's made-up "death panels" than about a real-life lifesaving medical system that was denied to millions of women. While Congress delayed, how many women weren't getting the mammograms that had saved Teresa's life?

Teddy's death had left a void in the Senate that in many ways is still felt today. But it also left a void in the votes needed to pass reform. Ted would have loved to stand in the well of the Senate one last time and be the sixtieth vote for the reform for which he'd fought since age thirty. But his passing triggered a special election in Massachusetts that jeopardized the prospects for its passage at all. Massachusetts is not immune to the national mood. Republicans had spent a year blocking progress and then blaming President Obama for lack of progress. It was disgraceful. But it was effective. The Tea Party was at its peak. In January 2010, a little-known Republican state senator from Wrentham, Scott Brown, was elected to replace

Ted. Scott was a good campaigner riding a big red wave. Health reform was in jeopardy.

I thought we needed to put health care to a vote, and soon. I was proud of what we were doing. But more important, we were putting Republicans on record: They had a chance to propose amendments. They had a chance to be constructive. If they just wanted to say no, the country would see them do it.

No one could credibly claim that he or she did not get a chance to have input on this bill. The Finance and Health Committees of the Senate spent months negotiating and passed bills including more than one hundred amendments by the minority. The Republicans still wouldn't vote for them.

The question was whether we would fold—or fight. There were people in the White House urging President Obama to back down. They knew the risks to his presidency if he lost a legislative fight after the midterm shellacking. He made the courageous decision to demand a vote. And vote we did: using the budget reconciliation process, we passed health care reform without a single Republican vote in support of ideas they had to campaign on for decades. The Tea Party had taken over the Republican Party, but more Americans were getting health care.

I had once wanted to name the bill after Teddy, but it took on a name of its own: Obamacare. I knew Ted Kennedy would've liked that just as much. Ted was up there smiling that big Irish smile.

THE ENVIRONMENT WAS both a passion and a fascination since I was a kid, and particularly since I became involved in that first Earth Day in 1970, after my return home from the service.

Maybe it was the lessons my mom taught me—as her community's first recycling pioneer, or in the nature walks she took us on as little kids trailing behind her in the woods. Perhaps it was also that early excitement of watching the first Earth Day channel grassroots energy into a political movement that could actually defeat members of Congress who voted against the environment; at a time when so much was going wrong in Richard Nixon's America, average citizens had done something powerfully right in making the environment a voting issue.

But whatever the reason, with the exception of issues of war and peace, I'd probably worked on the environment more steadily than any other issue my entire career, as a citizen, as lieutenant governor, and through the Senate years, including as a candidate for president in 2004.

My commitment had certainly been tested. Some even on my own political staff tried to convince me it wasn't a winning issue—a "political landmine," they argued. They were furious when, in the run-up to the presidential campaign, I teamed up with John McCain to try to pass legislation to increase vehicle emissions standards: "It can't pass, why introduce a bill and screw yourself with every Democrat who votes in the Michigan primary?" I understood their concern for my politics, but I was not going to give up who I was and what I believed in. I don't think you win that way. You win by fighting for something—the test Ron Rosenblith used to call the "stand-up guy test." Sometimes the national headquarters would cut climate change remarks out of my speeches; I'd add them right back in. I believed there were a lot of Democrats in Michigan—veterans, environmentalists, union workers—who thought it was a pretty great idea to build fuel-efficient cars so no one's son or daughter had to go die in the Middle East for oil. That's exactly how we went out and won Michigan twice—in the primary season and again in the general election. I made my case face-to-face with voters, persuaded almost 2.5 million Michiganders we cared about their jobs and their clean air, and denied Karl Rove his high hope of turning Michigan red.

By 2009, I thought we could turn those years of working on climate change into an effort that might finally break the gridlock of Congress on one of the truly existential issues for our planet.

I'd spent a lot of years stopping bad things from happening on the environment—filibustering Bob Dole's efforts to gut the Clean Air and Clean Water Acts in the 1990s and leading filibusters again and again to stop drilling in the Arctic National Wildlife Refuge. I loved those fights. But as I began my fifth term, with President Obama in the White House and sixty Democrats in the Senate, I thought we finally had a chance to do more than stop bad things from happening. I thought we could actually make climate change a governing issue. I thought that the legislative environment might be right.

President Obama had campaigned with a promise to address climate change. He now had the big working majorities needed to advance an agenda. Plenty of Republicans had voted in the past in support of legislation acknowledging that climate change is real. They had embraced market-based solutions to address it. Now, with the choice of either passing legislation that included incentives to help businesses pay the costs of cutting carbon pollution, or just having the executive branch institute regulations, I thought senators would feel empowered to legislate.

We needed to "put a price on carbon," which is to say, make it in the interests of the market to pursue low-carbon energy solutions, and create millions of jobs in the process.

But the Senate is a tough place for climate change legislation. You can't just look at a list of Democrats and Republicans. You have a lot of senators from the Midwest who represent heavy industrial manufacturing counties. You had to help them persuade their states that this legislation wouldn't be a job-killer, that in fact the turbines and rotors necessary for low-carbon energy could be manufactured in Ohio and Missouri too. You had to be able to speak to an audience that wasn't already converted.

A couple years before, after we'd seen the environmental movement demoralized and caricatured as "elitist," Teresa and I had written a book called *This Moment on Earth.* We'd talked to ranchers, farmers and union laborers who didn't think of themselves as environmentalists but who depended on clean air and clean water for their livelihoods. These folks were losing out because climate change was bringing droughts to the West. Some farmers had even made money turning their fields into solar installations providing electricity. I was convinced climate change was—and should be marketed as—a kitchen-table, middle-class issue. I believed that was the case that had to be made in the Senate, and I thought we could do it.

The House passed a climate change bill but the Senate was a different story. We needed sixty votes. That meant we needed to think about everything that might be problematic for senators serving in states like West Virginia and Ohio and Pennsylvania and, yes, Michigan.

We had to address up front the full array of concerns about cost to the taxpayers in those states and how all their industries might be impacted. It was imperative we do whatever we could to get not just Democrats but also Republicans on board.

I needed a Republican as my partner.

Enter Lindsey Olin Graham, Republican from South Carolina. Lindsey is out of central casting for the old Senate I'd known in 1985: he's smart as they come, funny, always a great conversationalist, strong-willed and opinionated, but always determined to find a way to achieve something. Our voting scorecards do not match. Lindsey is a very proud conservative. But we had gotten to know each other well during the 2008 election, when he and I were often booked together as surrogates for John McCain and Barack Obama, respectively. Lindsey joked that we faced off on every television station except the Food Channel. After our appearances, when we'd be wiping off the pancake makeup from the television studio, Lindsey would, always smiling, lament my full-throated defense of the Democratic nominee, as he opened what would often be his second or third bottle of Coke Zero. He had grown very close to John McCain, and we had in common our affection for John, even if we were on opposite sides of the campaign that year.

I had had Lindsey over a few times with other colleagues and guests for dinners centered on a certain topic. One night, Lindsey discovered Teresa's schnauzer Clousseau under his chair. Fortunately, Lindsey is both a dog lover and a big fan of Peter Sellers. He and Teresa bonded quickly. Lindsey also came to a dinner on climate change and national security, and the gears in both our heads started spinning. We had a few conversations about a market-based climate plan that might entice Republicans to sign on to legislation.

In October 2009, Lindsey came to my office and told me he had thought about it, and he was in. I was thrilled. Fifteen minutes later, we were pecking away on my computer, writing a joint op-ed for the weekend's papers to frame a new approach to a persistent issue.

I felt like the Senate was working the way it was supposed to. You studied an issue, you did your homework, you took the time to invest in personal relationships and to listen to other perspectives, and you learned to see an issue through other people's eyes. That's what Lindsey and I had done, and we thought we might just have a formula that could attract people from both parties who wanted to be part of the Congress that addressed climate change and started an energy transformation.

Our bipartisan effort became tripartisan when independent Joe Lieberman, who was a veteran of climate change policy for as long as I had been, joined us.

Joe had been a friend for a long time. He had been a young, progressive state senator from New Haven—a Yale law school student named Bill Clinton volunteered on Joe's first race in 1970—before serving as state attorney general. In 1987, I had helped recruit Joe to challenge Lowell Weicker for U.S. Senate. Later, he got crosswise with our party over the Iraq War and ran for reelection as an independent in 2006. It had been a very difficult time for him and hard for many of us who didn't like Joe's position on the war but liked him personally. I was looking forward to working with him again, to rekindling our friendship in the context of an issue where the two of us had always stood shoulder to shoulder.

Lindsey, Joe and I had hopes of adding John McCain to our merry band. John had earned some of his old maverick bona fides on climate change years ago, working with Joe on a bill. When he saw the opportunity to be the Republican nominee in 2008, he stopped emphasizing that environmental credential, but even during the campaign, he continued to acknowledge that climate change was real.

When I flew to Bali for the UN Climate Change Conference in December 2007, I'd told the crowds there that with McCain, Obama or Clinton atop the tickets in 2008, we would have consensus on doing something about climate change.

But John's running mate in 2008, Governor Sarah Palin, had been ahead of her time: the Tea Party was coming. In 2009, John McCain was a marked man—marked for a primary challenge. He avoided working with Democrats, even Joe Lieberman and me, his longtime friends. We understood. But we still held out hope that John would dodge a primary challenge and come join our effort. We would talk to him about it on the Senate floor. It wasn't a happy time for John, but Lindsey could always make him smile. Joe started calling our recruitment campaign Operation Sidney, a tip of the hat to John's middle name. I even had T-shirts printed. Sadly, they're still in a box somewhere in storage—the pressure on John, a proud and principled man, that entire election cycle of 2010 was too immense.

John McCain's primary wasn't the only issue getting in our way.

For one thing, we were still knee-deep in the health care debate. Not only was that taking up all the oxygen in the Capitol, but a number of moderate Democrats made it clear there were only so many difficult votes they could bear. When I heard the news that a midwestern Democrat wasn't running again for reelection, I thought we had a good chance to get him more engaged in a climate bill. The prospect of not having his name on the ballot might be liberating.

I asked my team to go meet with his team. The response was jarring "The senator will want a poll done to know if he will want to play a role." He became a lobbyist and a cable pundit after he left the Senate—interesting choices for someone who said he was leaving government because politics was broken.

We were also finding ourselves far down the pecking order of White House priorities, and Lindsey Graham knew it. The White House was focused on health care and did not seem prepared to help us whip up the votes. They leaned on Lindsey to help them with another issue, immigration. Lindsey started to believe he was more committed to climate legislation than the White House was, and he got discouraged.

But we thought we had one winning argument for the insiders of the Capitol: the House had cast a risky vote in vain if we didn't get our act together.

Barbara Boxer, who held the chairmanship of the Environment and Public Works Committee, and I had been allies on climate issues for years. We started convening a group of senators for lunch on Tuesdays in the Capitol's Senate Foreign Relations Committee conference room to strategize on climate change. Our staffers called it our "climate club." Every week, we'd bring in a guest speaker to talk about how climate change affected his or her line of work and what solutions might make a difference. We didn't just invite the traditional climate crowd to meet with us; we'd also bring in CEOs like Jeff Immelt from GE, who had real concerns about the impact of climate change on their businesses, and military brass like Admiral Michael Mullen, who worried about the national security implications of climate change. Barbara and I believed that the only way cap-and-trade legislation would make it through the Senate would be with significant support from all the sectors and stakeholders we had been talking to and more.

Even with health care on the front burner and immigration taking up attention as well, Lindsey, Joe and I were meeting with folks one-on-one to try to convince them we had a plan worth getting behind.

We also spent ample time trying to get industry support. We met with the CEOs of the big oil companies, including the man who would later succeed me at the State Department, Exxon CEO Rex Tillerson.

At one point, Joe Lieberman's staff mentioned how valuable the support of Texas oil baron T. Boone Pickens could be. Almost as soon as they'd said it, they remembered that Pickens had bankrolled the Swift Boat Veterans for Truth against me to the tune of millions of dollars out of his own pocket.

I broke the ice. It was worth reaching out to an old adversary.

"Get him on the line," I said. In minutes, I was talking to the man who had helped put those ads on television. The next week Pickens flew in from Oklahoma. We talked about what it would take for him to publicly embrace the bill. We shook hands and agreed to continue working together. He would endorse our approach.

We were weeks away from a historic announcement: for the first time ever, we had lined up major oil companies to endorse a cap-and-trade bill. Shell was in the vanguard, but most enthusiastic was British Petroleum (BP), who penciled in a date in the calendar to join us for a press conference and endorse the bill. Three days before the announcement, which would have been attended by all the major oil companies, a BP oil rig exploded in the Gulf of Mexico, killing ten people and releasing millions of barrels of oil into the waters off Louisiana and Mississippi. Because of the BP disaster, the press conference had to be postponed. Timing is everything in politics—and life.

But the biggest blow was still to come.

It became clear that the Senate would vote on immigration before climate change. It put Lindsey Graham, an immigration moderate, in the crosshairs of the Right. The Tea Party had emerged as a real threat to "establishment" Republicans like him, and he was facing the prospect of a tough primary challenge. The pressure was intense. I remembered something Lindsey's chief of staff had once told me about his boss: "Lindsey sometimes gets ahead of his supply lines."

I know Lindsey wanted to work on immigration and climate change, and on issues like the detainees in Guantánamo, which spoke to him as a military lawyer. But all those IOUs were coming due. On a Friday afternoon, a call came in. Lindsey asked to speak to me and Joe. We had scheduled a press conference for the following Monday to unveil our planned legislation, with all the stakeholders slated to join us.

In almost thirty years in the Senate, I had never heard one of my colleagues as distraught as Lindsey was that day on the phone. He was back in South Carolina and realized how bad the political backlash had become. Local Tea Party members were calling in to talk radio and savaging him. Coal companies were spending huge sums to tarnish Lindsey's reputation at home.

"They're all calling it 'Grahamnesty' for illegals," I remember him shouting to us, breathless. "This is too much. I just can't do this too. It's too much."

Joe and I tried to break in and reassure him about how much support we had.

"You don't understand! This is it."

The line went dead.

The best we could do was convince Lindsey not to poison the effort with a public statement pulling back, so that the two of us could try to pass something without him, and maybe if things cooled off at home, he could rejoin us.

But the next day, Lindsey put out a statement blaming immigration for cratering climate and energy legislation. He was in a tough spot. It was a Saturday, and I had to call Joe on Shabbat to break the news to him, interrupting a day he observed faithfully.

Joe and I kept the event on the books, even without Lindsey. We tried to soldier on with what we both viewed as a necessary and innovative piece of legislation, but the effort slowly died.

When Democrats lost the House in the 2010 midterms—and about two dozen members who voted for the Waxman-Markey cap-and-trade climate bill were replaced with Republicans—we knew it would be a long time before we could attempt to pass anything similar.

It was the beginning of climate change denial going mainstream. Primaries were used to torture good people and hold them hostage to ideology and special interests.

Working across the aisle was becoming apostasy.

As Mitch McConnell famously said at the time, the Republican caucus's top priority was "to make sure Obama was a one-term president."

The Senate wasn't the Senate anymore—and that was a sad reality for capable people like Lindsey Graham. The Senate now seemed paralyzed by the politics of gridlock and empty division. Solving problems would have to wait. I started to believe that for the sake of the issues I cared about most, the most important thing any of us could do was help reelect Barack Obama. Otherwise, Washington was going to destroy itself—and take the planet down with it.

IF THE SENATE was broken, there were at least other parts of life that we could make right. Several months before Julia had passed away in 2006, blessedly, she met Vanessa's boyfriend, Brian. She told me she knew they were going to get married and it gave her enormous pleasure to know that she had met the husband-to-be of one of her daughters, knowing that she would not be at the wedding herself. Her knowledge of this and her ability to talk about it, despite the obvious pain, was striking.

Indeed, a year later Brian called to make an appointment to meet me at my house in Boston. When you get a call from your daughter's boyfriend asking to meet, it is kind of a tip-off. I already liked him, and knowing that Julia had approved, the visit was easy. I was excited to hear the words "I'd like to marry Vanessa," and with tears in my eyes I gave Brian a big hug.

Brian and Vanessa finally set a date: October 10, 2009. Planning the wedding was one of my great parenting experiences. I was the wedding planner. As a veteran of many campaigns and many fund-raising concerts through the years, I was confident I could produce a pretty good checklist, particularly if I used Steve Martin's example from *Father of the Bride*.

Together, Vanessa, Brian and I did it all until essentially "the day of." I even booked the band and thought about critical decisions like whether to have a parquet floor to keep women's heels from being destroyed by the grass at the outdoor wedding. I assessed flowers, booked security and, in a completely new experience, helped design lighting. At the last minute, I arranged for heaters to stave off an October chill we hadn't anticipated. As we waited for the ceremony to begin, the sun sank slowly behind the trees and a cold fall night descended on the guests. Everyone except my strapless-gowned daughter and the groom, who were lost in their moment, was shivering in the rapidly dropping temperature. There was a scurry to the tent the instant the ceremony ended.

It was a memorable event that many of Vanessa's friends labeled the best wedding they had been to—the ultimate compliment, whether it was sincere or not, for a part-time wedding planner who was doing his best to make up for his daughter's lack of her mom. It was a reminder of how blessed we all were with family, those present and those present only in our hearts.

CHAPTER 15

Mr. Chairman

In 2009, a synergy I had never experienced in the Senate finally materialized: a partnership with a president and vice president whom I knew well and, in Joe Biden's case, had worked with closely for years; the chairmanship of the Foreign Relations Committee, a critical committee with impact; and a role and relationships in my caucus and across the aisle that allowed me to engage meaningfully on a whole set of issues that had long animated me.

I had reason to doubt whether I'd ever experience the Senate in that way. Basic math predicted otherwise. I loved the Foreign Relations Committee, but ahead of me in seniority were two friends and contemporaries: Chris Dodd, a year younger than I was, who had been elected in 1980 to take Abe Ribicoff's seat, and Joe Biden, sixty-seven, who had been elected at twenty-nine in 1972 (sworn in only after he turned thirty, per the constitutional requirement) and would always outpace any of us in seniority. The three of us enjoyed and respected the committee, its history and its potential impact. I never imagined the Senate without Joe or Chris, and I certainly never dreamed either of them would give up the committee's gavel voluntarily. Meanwhile, I was behind Max Baucus—with whom I shared a birthday— and Jay Rockefeller on the Senate Finance Committee, and Jay was ahead of me on the Commerce Committee as well. In other words, I had phenomenal committee assignments for me and for Massachusetts, but I had zero expectation of being a chairman of any one of them. It would take an act of God for me to chair any committee besides the Small Business Committee.

God may well have intervened. Suddenly, Joe was Barack Obama's vice president. Chris, who was next in line for the chairmanship of the Foreign Relations Committee, felt that at least for the 111th Congress, with Connecticut's economy reeling from the financial meltdown, he had to take the helm of the Banking Committee to oversee financial regulatory reform and focus on the economic recovery.

Living in Washington, D.C., a Cub Scout and aspiring outfielder for the Washington Senators, circa 1950.

Sitting with my beloved Cairn puppy, Sandy, in Pa's easy chair at 3806 Jennifer Street in Washington, D.C., circa 1953.

My dad, Richard J. Kerry, in 1954 in front of the American Mission Berlin, where he served as legal advisor to the high commissioner of Germany, James Conant.

My mother, Rosemary Isabel Forbes, after she came to the United States in 1940 to marry my father. It was the beginning of World War II and she had escaped Paris on a bicycle ahead of the German invasion, eventually boarding a ship in Portugal for the United States.

5

Our family gathered at the captain's dinner aboard the SS *America* traveling from New York Harbor to Le Havre, France, as Dad headed off to another posting in the Foreign Service. From left to right: me, Diana (who clearly didn't want her picture taken), Peggy, Mom and young Cam in his sailor suit.

My brother and sisters. Left to right: Cameron, Diana, me and Peggy after returning from Berlin in 1956.

My War Department identification card, age thirteen, in 1956. My parents probably thought the clerk forgot to type the letters "In" in front of "Dependent Son," especially after I had ridden my bike unattended into Cold-War East Berlin.

Probably my first Forrest Gump moment, as Roger Simon used to call them: sailing with President Kennedy in Narragansett Bay in the summer of 1962. Jackie's mother, Janet Lee Bouvier Auchincloss, is in the foreground.

The 1965 Yale soccer team. First row from the left: David Thorne and yours truly. First row, third from the right: Dick Pershing.

Admiral Zumwalt and Captain Hoffman flew from Saigon to decorate the crews of PCF-94, PCF-23 and PCF-43. Front row kneeling left to right: Rear Gunner Mike Medeiros, Ltjg. John Kerry, Ltjg. Don Droz. Back row, standing, left to right: third from left, Radarman Seaman Tommy Belodeau; fourth from left, Gunner's Mate Fred Short; Engineman Gene Thorson; ninth from left, Chief Petty Officer Del Sandusky (in glasses); far right, Ltjg. Bill Rood.

PCF-94 leading an exposed line of Swift boats up a small river in the Cà Mau Peninsula to insert troops near Năm Can in early 1969. Ltjg. Bill Rood's PCF-23 is in the foreground.

On a Sealords mission, PCF-43 and her crew, led by my friend Ltjg. Don Droz, who was later killed in action on April 12, 1969, in a nearby river where their Swift boat was destroyed by a B-40 rocket.

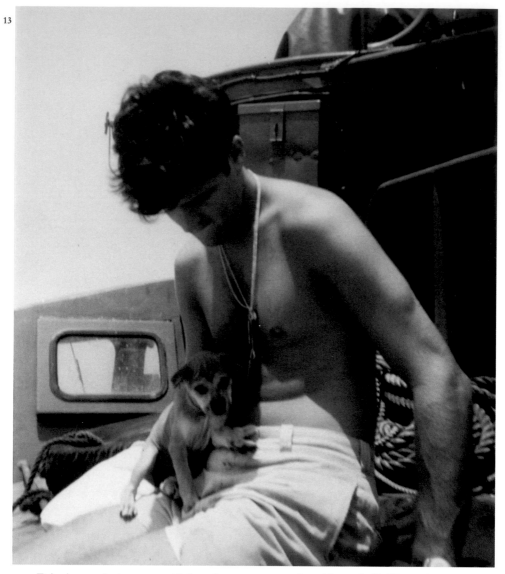

Enjoying a relaxing moment below the gun turret on the cabin roof of PCF-94 with our boat's mascot, VC, who yapped his way through several firefights.

Aboard PCF-43 after the ambush, beached in the mangrove alongside PCF-94, where we overran the enemy. Left to right: Ltjg. Bill Rood, OINC of 23 boat; Ltjg. Don Droz, OINC of 43 boat; BM2 Wayne Langhofer; Engineman Lloyd Jones and me. In the tank in the very front is Radarman Michael Modansky; in the big gun tub in the upper rear is Gunner's Mate Bob Harnsburger.

My boss and a gentleman, Admiral Walter F. Schleck, commander of military sea transport, pinning the Bronze Star with Combat "V" on me, his personal aide and Flag Lieutenant, at the Brooklyn Navy Yard in the fall of 1969.

Testifying before the Senate Committee on Foreign Relations on April 21, 1971. I was to spend twenty-eight years on the other side of the dais on a committee I loved. In this photo, my older sister, Peggy, a stalwart activist who introduced me to many of the vets I was to work with, is right behind me, supportive as always.

I was then and remain a Beatles fanatic and suddenly found myself in a pinch-me moment with John Lennon, before introducing him at an anti-war rally in New York's Bryant Park, in April of 1972. The Nixon administration was debating whether to deport Lennon for his anti-war activism.

Addressing the rally in Bryant Park in April of 1972 before introducing John Lennon.

Seated: Middlesex District Attorney John J. Droney, with Senate candidate Paul Tsongas and me, first assistant district attorney, in the DA's office during Droney's reelection campaign in 1978. I loved my time as a prosecutor in Middlesex County—it was one of the best jobs I've ever had. We took on organized crime and modernized the office.

With Ted Kennedy, prior to being sworn in to the Senate for the first time on January 2, 1985. My friend and senior colleague inscribed it: "To John—as Humphrey Bogart would have said, 'this is the beginning of a beautiful friendship.' Day 1, 1985."

On a summer's day ride with my daughters on Naushon Island. Vanessa riding with me, and Alexandra following.

In the Speaker's office with Teddy Kennedy and the legendary Speaker of the House Tip O'Neill on Tip's last day as Speaker.

Serving as Chairman of the POW/MIA Select Committee, seated with John McCain during a hearing on December 1, 1992. John and I were working to make peace with Vietnam after we made peace with each other.

Teresa and I relaxing in Pittsburgh during a quiet weekend off the campaign trail.

On stage after accepting the Democratic nomination for president at home in Boston.

Teresa and I at a massive rally in Portland, Oregon, in the final months of the campaign for president, on August 13, 2004.

Playing hockey in the then–Verizon Center in Washington, D.C., at the annual Lawmakers vs. the Lobbyists charity game on March 15, 2009.

My grown-up, accomplished, always inspiring daughters Vanessa (left) and Alexandra (right), with me at the wedding of a family friend in the summer of 2011.

Conducting "Stars and Stripes Forever" with the Boston Pops at Symphony Hall in Boston during a celebration of my twenty-five years in the Senate and forty-five years in public service. Conductor Keith Lockhart didn't have to worry about his day job.

President Barack Obama and I "sparring" after our final mock debate in 2012. The President had asked me to play the role of Mitt Romney.

My first morning at Foggy Bottom as secretary of state: delivering welcoming remarks in the C Street lobby of the State Department's Harry S Truman Building. It was February 4, 2013, and I'm holding up my first-ever diplomatic passport, issued in 1954. Life came full circle; I was thinking of Dad that day and the around-the-world journey he set me on, literally and figuratively.

Six days after being privately sworn in as the nation's sixty-eighth secretary of state by Supreme Court Justice Elena Kagan, I was publicly sworn in by my friend Vice President Joe Biden in the Benjamin Franklin Room of the U.S. Department of State on February 6, 2013.

With my Russian counterpart, Sergei Lavrov, at the Department of State on August 9, 2013. Sergei is among the smartest diplomats, a tough interlocutor and a fanatical soccer fan.

Meeting with Russian President Vladimir Putin at the Kremlin in Moscow, Russia, on July 14, 2016. Ukraine and Syria were on the agenda.

Meeting with King Salman (right) of Saudi Arabia at the Royal Court in Jeddah on May 15, 2016.

I probably spent more time as secretary with Israeli Prime Minister Benjamin "Bibi" Netanyahu than I did with any other world leader. Here we were meeting in New York City on September 23, 2016, during my last United Nations General Assembly as secretary.

Negotiations with Javad Zarif and the Iranian delegation on January 16, 2016, at the Palais Coburg hotel in Vienna, Austria. Zarif sits directly opposite me.

Checking my speech with Ben the Diplomutt on the eighth-floor balcony of the State Department overlooking the Lincoln Memorial.

Catching up on some calls while kicking around the well-traveled soccer ball during a re-fueling stop in Sal Island, Cape Verde, on May 5, 2014. Dad jeans courtesy of The Gap.

In November of 2016, I became the highest-ranking United States government official ever to visit Antarctica, where I met with scientists from all over the world to learn more about climate change. The scientific evidence presented was compelling, and it dramatically increased my sense of urgency about the problem.

Signing the historic UN Paris Agreement on Climate Change at the United Nations Assembly Hall in New York City on April 22, 2016, with my two-year-old granddaughter, Isabelle, in my lap.

Visiting the State Department initiative to preserve the Mekong Delta. Back on the Bay Hap River in the Năm Can and Cái Nước Districts of Vietnam with Yale classmate, fellow veteran and Senior Advisor David Thorne during my last visit to Vietnam as secretary on January 14, 2017. As I said to David that day, "this is strange, getting even stranger."

43

More than four decades after PCF-94 was attacked by Vo Ban Tam and his team on February 28, 1969, I shook hands with a former adversary at the Năm Boat and Bus Station in Năm Can, Vietnam. It's hard to believe that almost forty-eight years ago, our job was to try to kill each other.

Meeting with President Obama and Pope Francis in the White House. Pope Francis had just grabbed the president's arm and said, "This is the Ambassador of Peace." He overwhelmed me with that compliment and said that he prayed for me during my journeys.

The last minutes of my last day: in my packed-up seventh-floor office, one final review of my farewell remarks with my daughter Vanessa on January 19, 2017. Stripping the office bare turned out to be a prelude to what was to follow after my departure.

So there I was, against a lot of odds: chairman of the same committee before which I had testified at the invitation of Chairman William Fulbright in 1971. This was a committee rich in history—a committee where future presidents, from Jack Kennedy to Barack Obama; future vice presidents, from Hubert Humphrey to Joe Biden; and legends of the Senate, from Henry Clay to Arthur Vandenberg, had all served.

My chairmanship meant a lot to me. I had invested years to get there. Most of all, I was excited for what we might be able to accomplish. I knew from my own experience in 1971, admittedly in a very different era, that the committee could make a difference and its chairman had a responsibility to try.

I knew that the new administration, by necessity, would be focused first on rescuing the U.S. economy. That meant there would be ample opportunity for our committee to take on some off-the-grid challenges. I started out with a solid relationship with the president, who had been a member of the committee, and especially with his then deputy national security advisor Tom Donilon, who was as clear-eyed about the challenges as he was competent in harnessing the bureaucratic process.

I knew there might be opportunities, if not for collaboration, at least for cross-pollination with the new administration, but I was nevertheless determined to protect the committee as its own independent entity, with prerogatives separate from any administration, something Dick Lugar had tried to do during Republican administrations. I also wanted to restore the committee's investigative capacity, which had atrophied over the years. Remembering how important that work had been in the 1980s and '90s, I recruited Doug Frantz, the lead investigative journalist for the *Los Angeles Times*, to come to the committee and build his own cell of investigators. Indeed, there was a lot to do, and I was eager to put my shoulder to the wheel.

EVEN A BRIEF glance at the world beyond our borders indicated that Afghanistan was especially critical for many reasons. As the administration was getting its sea legs, it was clear a new chapter with Iraq was in the offing. The unwillingness of the Iraqi government to provide a workable status of forces agreement to keep a substantial number of American troops in the country seemed to force the administration's hand. The last American troops would be leaving Iraq.

As a result, all eyes were shifting from Baghdad to Kabul—back to the war in Afghanistan, which many of us argued had lost its focus the minute the United States, voluntarily and unilaterally, plunged into what I had called the "grand diversion" of the war in Iraq. The Iraq War came at enormous cost to our interests and influence, and Afghanistan in particular paid a huge price for this misadventure in the Middle East.

As I took on the chairmanship, I remained especially anxious about Afghanistan for a number of reasons. Its history as the "graveyard of empires" was instructive. Afghanistan was the country where Great Britain and Russia had suffered enormous losses. Even knowing that historical background, I still believed that history is not destiny. However, there were some (if not many) people—including some of my staff on the committee—who argued that Afghanistan was destined to be a quagmire because it had been a quagmire for other countries. I thought we owed ourselves a more rigorous intellectual examination. I wanted to know if we had clear goals, with clear limitations and understanding about what we were there to do. I wanted Afghans to understand that we were not there to stay or conquer, with hopes we could avoid the traps that had befallen others. Could discipline and clarity of purpose make a difference for us? I was always mindful that unlike the British and the Russians, we didn't go into Afghanistan with imperial aims.

But there were many key questions: Did we have a clear plan and a coherent strategy? Did we know why we were there and when the country would be stable enough to leave?

When I chaired Hillary Clinton's confirmation hearing for secretary of state, I tried to probe these questions, not so much for the benefit of the nominee, who was smart and capable and didn't need a lecture, but for the entire committee, for all of us involved in foreign policy making. Where were we going in Afghanistan?

The rationale that had earned one hundred votes to go to Afghanistan was a direct response to an act of war—the most egregious, spontaneous attack on the United States since Pearl Harbor. We went in to get Osama bin Laden, and we kicked the Taliban out of Afghanistan because they had harbored al-Qaeda and provided it a platform for terror. Most critically, they refused to retract their support when given ample opportunity to do so.

Now, in 2009, almost eight years after 9/11, the impunity with which drug traffickers operated, coupled with stories of rampant corruption undermining the faith of Afghans in their new government and ours, had become significant problems. It seemed we were assuming full responsibility for solving them. I reminded the committee that we had not intended for Afghanistan to become our fifty-first state, a statement that rankled some of the neoconservative media outlets, who thought I was dumbing down our goals in Afghanistan. I was simply stating what I thought was obvious and in this case important: our goal there was stability, an Afghanistan that could hold together on its own, even if it wasn't going to be a model of Jeffersonian democracy. Looking back, it is amazing to think that was a controversial statement at all. To the contrary, almost a decade later it looks more like an optimistic one.

The administration was wrestling with this issue as well. There was no consensus. My friend Richard Holbrooke, whom Secretary Clinton had brought on to lead the State Department's diplomatic effort, ran into a dual buzz saw. He didn't click with President Obama, and more problematically for Richard, Hamid Karzai decided that Holbrooke was plotting against him, which limited his room to maneuver diplomatically. I'd heard from Vice President Biden that the Pentagon—General David Petraeus and General Stanley McChrystal both—seemed to be pushing the president into a corner about an additional surge of troops, after he had already begun his term by sending thirty thousand more troops than had been promised initially. The president worried that the military's requests for more troops would be infinite, no matter what the actual conditions on the ground.

I worried that the debate in Congress and the public seemed to focus almost exclusively on absolute numbers—how many U.S. and allied troops were required, how many Afghan soldiers and police we needed to train, how many more billions we needed to invest at a moment of enormous need at home.

What we weren't talking about nearly enough was whether any amount of money, any rise in troop levels or any clever metrics would make a difference if the basic mission was ill-conceived. We needed to expand the discussion to wrestle with fundamental questions and examine core assumptions. We had to agree on a clear definition of the mission and decide what was an achievable and acceptable goal for Afghanistan and for the United States. We also needed to know the size of the footprint that goal demanded and to weigh the probabilities and costs of getting there.

At the same time, we had to assess and evaluate some intangibles, including whether we were looking at Afghanistan and our presence there through the same set of eyes as the Afghans themselves. On my first trip to Afghanistan as chairman, I looked out the window of the armored Humvee as we drove through the dusty streets of Kabul. A little girl was playing with some toys on the side of the road. My mind immediately flashed back to Vietnam and the kids who often lined the canals or streets, staring at us with a "what are you doing here?" look. Right away I thought, *What do we look like to that young girl?* I might as well be from another planet. I was driving around in a massive armored vehicle with General Petraeus, a brilliant military leader who literally wrote the book on counterinsurgency strategy in Iraq and Afghanistan. We both knew that winning hearts and minds was the centerpiece of any counterinsurgency effort and operations, but one look in that girl's eyes told me that we faced an uphill battle. I had strong misgivings that even with the best of efforts, we wouldn't be able to persuade many ordinary Afghans that any foreign military presence on their soil represented a force that could possibly be on their side. We did have vital national security interests at stake and couldn't walk away precipitously, but I wanted to make sure we weren't setting ourselves up to wear out our welcome either.

Afghanistan's disastrous elections in August 2009 almost left the United States with no choice but to reconsider staying at all. It pulled me into the country's challenging politics and personalities in ways I wouldn't have predicted.

I had long planned to go to Afghanistan and Pakistan over the Senate's Columbus Day break. It made sense to take five or six days, get out and see for myself what was happening in the country. I managed to get to Helmand Province, the region in Afghanistan they call the "snake's head"—lush with vegetation—where the surge of new U.S. troops was helping turn Taliban territory back into the hands of the central government and allied troops.

As it turned out, the real combat I witnessed was political and right in Kabul.

The tension was palpable. Ambassador Karl Eikenberry, a retired general and former commander of our forces in Afghanistan, briefed me and was candid about his level of concern. The August 20 first round of elections had been denounced by many—from the way Karzai had announced the date in the spring (leaving the opposition little time to organize), to the lack of security and turnout, to wide allegations of fraud. After votes were thrown out as fraudulent, neither Karzai nor his leading opponent, Abdullah Abdullah, was over the 50 percent needed to avoid a second-round runoff. Karzai refused to accept that he hadn't been reelected outright, and he refused to agree to a runoff. Governance was gridlocked with the prospect of the entire government collapsing.

From the outside, after the disputed election of the late summer, the dysfunction was evident to the entire country. But on the inside, Eikenberry told me it was even worse. Karzai was clashing with Americans and believed that the United States had conspired against him and that the international election observers had disenfranchised his Pashtun voters. He saw the UN monitors' disqualification of around 250,000 votes from Pashtun areas as an international conspiracy.

It seemed entirely possible that a constitutional crisis was unfolding, and if some way forward wasn't devised, then Karzai was going to risk having the NATO coalition fall apart. Clearly, European countries suffering from Afghanistan fatigue weren't going to stick it out on the ground if the country's government was imploding. I got the strong sense that the United States wouldn't be long for the battle either if Karzai transformed himself into an autocrat dismissing the political will of perhaps half of his own population.

Ambassador Eikenberry hoped I could at least engage Karzai a bit more and see if he was willing to listen to the American perspective. I was happy to try, and certainly I could convey just how much the Congress was watching and listening carefully to the standoff in his country. I suspected that half the value I could bring wouldn't be in what I said but in what I heard. Listening is critical coin in diplomacy, too often devalued and dismissed. I liked President Karzai. I had a good rapport with him in part because I respected his patriotism and the courage of his journey to get where he was. He seemed to know that intuitively. He knew that I listened to him, and frankly, I had a pretty high tolerance for his rants, something I'd learned in the Senate dealing with some colleagues who often needed to vent before you could have a productive conversation with them.

I came to the table with Karzai able to relate to him on a level that was important: a political level. Most diplomatic issues for the United States were also someone else's domestic political problem. I'm always a little bit surprised how, in the Senate or in the media, we often chalk up a colleague's actions to the politics of their base or their complicated standing with voters, but we forget that political leaders of other countries answer to a constituency as well. I was mindful that I could relate to Karzai as one politician to another. I hoped this common ground might help open up avenues for solving problems that otherwise were not apparent.

Clearly, though, nothing was going to be easy.

At the time, there was a popular book out about Afghanistan and Pakistan titled *Three Cups of Tea*, a reference to the old saying that "the first time you share tea, you are a stranger. The second time you take tea, you are an honored guest. The third time, you become family." I'd soon be joking that my marathon sessions with Karzai were more like three thousand cups of tea. Hours went by, sometimes four, five or six hours at a time. I tried to listen to all his concerns about his country, not just those that were on my agenda. But when we got into the nitty-gritty of the election, the intensity picked up palpably.

We were sitting in a palace with giant rooms and dark oak paneling straight out of *The Addams Family*. At one point Karzai looked me dead in the eye and said, "John, I cannot disenfranchise 250,000 Pashtun voters. I will not survive." He walked out of the room to take a phone call, but I think he intended to let his words sink in and collect himself for his next volley.

I turned to our deputy ambassador to Afghanistan at the time, Frank Ricciardone, a terrific Foreign Service officer from Medford, Massachusetts. He was always a straight shooter. "Frank, were there actually 250,000 Pashtun voters who were disenfranchised?" I asked. Frank smiled as he replied, "No, it's more like 25 Pashtun voters, each of them filling out 10,000 ballots."

We took breaks over two days to let the tension recede a bit. We spoke about our families and Afghanistan's history, about his father's assassination and his own journey home from Pakistan, his aspirations for his country and his concerns about the U.S.-Afghan relationship. He voiced his worry that Afghan Pashtuns were being treated unfairly and complained how no one appreciated the weight of the decisions being foisted upon him. I told Karzai that I thought I had some idea of what he was going through and took him back to the 2004 election, to the years I'd spent building a presidential campaign, the debates with President Bush, the Swift boat smears, and the feeling of elation on election night when I believed we had won. I also talked about the debate I'd had over whether to concede or whether to take Bush to court over Ohio's provisional ballots and the voter suppression allegations and irregularities with the voting machines. I ended this digression by saying that in the cold light of morning, I had come to the conclusion that it wasn't good for my country to see two consecutive presidential elections litigated in the Supreme Court when the legitimacy of our democracy was so important. Karzai opened up in a way that he hadn't before, and I believed he was getting close to accepting that he had to embrace a second-round runoff.

I now began to feel some pressure on our travel clock. I had to get to Pakistan for a preplanned stop that I simply couldn't cancel. I was reasonably confident that President Karzai was moving to a more reasonable position. Unfortunately, by the time I was wrapping up my stop in Islamabad and aiming to get back to Washington in time for votes, I got a call from Ambassador Eikenberry to the effect that all hell was breaking loose. Karzai had told him there would be no runoff. Eikenberry asked if I could return.

I called Washington to find out the vote schedule. I asked Leader Harry Reid if there was any way he could delay the votes by one more day. Let's just say that Harry doesn't pull punches or waste his time with small talk, and on the best of days, he never ends a phone call even by saying goodbye. Harry was not pleased, to say the least. Before I could explain the details of just how tenuous things were in Kabul, he said, "Absolutely not," and *click*, that call was over. I told Eikenberry I didn't see a way for this to work. He had Secretary Clinton call me. She had been terrific throughout the trip, both in welcoming me as an ad hoc additional member of the team and never making me feel as if I were treading on Richard Holbrooke's turf. She put the arm on me to give Kabul one more shot. I agreed on one condition: she had to call Harry Reid. She laughed.

I got back to Kabul around dinnertime, and by the end of what was now my third night with Karzai, I thought we had a deal. When we got to the palace the next morning, it was clear something had changed—and not in the right direction. That's the nature of diplomacy. You're dealing with human beings. Sometimes when they sleep on things and talk to different people, they wake up with a different point of view. In this case, I felt as if the political considerations we'd spent so much time working through with Karzai had reasserted themselves. I really was out of time. I had to go back to Washington, and it wasn't clear if I would be able to return to Kabul anytime soon given the Senate schedule.

I decided to try to separate Karzai from his advisors, to make it a one-on-one Hail Mary conversation. In my experience over the years, I've learned that sometimes it's essential to isolate the decision-maker from any external influence so that, in effect, you can have the last word. As the day wound down, I still couldn't get Karzai over the hump. Finally, when we were two or three hours away from my wheels-up time, I decided we needed a little fresh air. Atmospherics matter. I wanted to shift his focus. The grounds around the palace ensured that I could be alone with him. We walked down a long path. I put my arm around him and said, "Mr. President, we're going to find a way to make this work for both of our countries."

As we walked, we went back over the ground we'd covered the past four days. Most leaders like to think of themselves in a historical context. I talked to President Karzai about the historical context of this moment. He could go down in history as the founding father of the new Afghanistan, or he could be a failed petty politician. I painted a picture for him of two different paths—one in which he was respected as a statesman and the first democratic leader of Afghanistan, and another where he undermined the democratic process and helped lead his country down a dark path toward war and dictatorship. I told him that I hoped he would pick the right path, but that I needed to know his answer. Karzai said simply, "Okay, I'll do it, but I cannot accept the invalidation of 250,000 Pashtun voters." I told him that as long as he was on board with the runoff, we were heading in the right direction.

As Karzai and I took the stage to announce that he had agreed to a runoff, one of his aides passed my team a note: Karzai's final vote tally. I opened it and read: "The final number—49.7 percent." I flashed my palms very subtly toward the sky and shot my team a look. Sometimes diplomacy isn't pretty, but in the end, we achieved the right outcome.

Secretary Clinton was a person of her word. She did call Reid and thanked him for allowing me to screw up the best-laid Senate plans for votes. Harry—whom I really liked as a colleague for many reasons but most of all because he was a straight shooter, although you never wanted him mad at you—made one of the most gracious and entirely unnecessary gestures I'd seen in twenty-five years as a senator. In a speech on the floor of the Senate, he described our uncomfortable phone conversation and acknowledged he had been angry, but he said that he was proud to see that a member of the Senate—a chairman of one of his committees—had made a difference in solving an international crisis. It was vintage Harry Reid, totally unexpected, and the moment smacked of the old Senate, the Senate of 1985 that I'd known and revered and, sadly, seen fade away—sure, a place where tempers might flare, but where, in the end, a strong sense of shared purpose prevailed.

For me, it was back to the work of democracy at home—and a sense of satisfaction knowing that at least in Kabul, a democracy that the sacrifice of American troops and our diplomats had helped create had dodged yet another bullet. President Karzai and Dr. Abdullah's decision to agree to a runoff election showed that both men were willing to put their country ahead of politics. It wasn't our mission to determine the political realities of Afghanistan, and it shouldn't be. That job belongs to the Afghans themselves. Now at least we knew that they still had a democracy to hold on to and that they'd live to fight another day.

None of the work we were doing in Afghanistan during the Obama years had much of a shot at long-term success if we couldn't improve cooperation with Pakistan. The odds against us were long and complicated. In 2008, Joe Biden, Chuck Hagel and I had sat in Pakistani president General Pervez Musharraf's office the morning after the vote tally showed he had lost an election. We'd visited some polling stations with election monitors the day before, which is an interesting proposition in Pakistan. I think the number of armed Pakistani escorts along with the three of us outnumbered actual voters by about a hundred to one. The security situation was challenging, but the elections turned out to be free and fair. As we were sitting in Musharraf's office the next morning, the only question was whether he'd accept the results. He had been a military man in a country that had a long history of military coups, which was famously how he had arrived on the scene. We were concerned that he'd find a pretext to invalidate the election and continue as a military ruler.

None of us knew what would happen. There was a palpable sense of uncertainty in the air. The second Musharraf walked into the room, I tried to read his facial expression. He lingered for a moment, then sat down and barely said any of the customary diplomatic pleasantries, but cut straight to the chase: "I know why you all are here. I'm going to respect the results of the election because it's the right thing to do for my country, but I'm not going to do the other things you want." He had incarcerated a supreme court justice and we'd made clear our interest in seeing him released from prison. Musharraf turned toward us again. "Let me say to you very clearly, be careful what you wish for. Pakistan is an incredibly difficult country to govern. If we're not careful, it could be overrun by extremists." It was a chilling reminder that while we had made it over one hurdle in Pakistan, there were always more to follow—and Pakistan's direction would matter enormously to Afghanistan.

Now, more than a year after that trip, I was chairman of the Foreign Relations Committee and the new administration was trying to think of its Afghanistan strategy in a broader context that included Pakistan. We wanted to make a big move to secure greater coordination and cooperation from Pakistan. Everyone, administration and Congress, understood that our relationship with Pakistan was messy. There's a long history in Pakistan and the region of these governments hedging their bets. We were concerned they were playing a double game with us, supporting the United States on the one hand and the Taliban and the Haqqani Network, an Afghan guerrilla group, on the other. I still remembered Daniel Patrick Moynihan describing to me what he saw as the difference between Pakistan and Afghanistan: "Pakistan is a government without a country, Afghanistan is a country without a government." It was a sad statement but a wry insight: Pakistan's security apparatus had endured and thrived in a very tough neighborhood for a very long time precisely through shifting allegiances. Its survival was our confusion. As a result, we were never certain how much we could trust the Pakistani government. One thing we were certain of was that we needed to change our relationship with the Pakistani people. If the people of Pakistan had a better sense of the United States as their partner, then regional cooperation and reconciliation could be made easier.

For decades, the United States had sought the cooperation of Pakistani decision-makers through military aid, while paying scant attention to the aspirations of the broader population. This arrangement was rapidly disintegrating: we were paying too much and getting too little, although most Pakistanis believed exactly the opposite. As a result, an alarming percentage of the Pakistani population saw America as a greater threat than al-Qaeda. Until that changed, I knew there was little chance of ending tolerance for terrorist groups or persuading any Pakistani government to devote the political capital necessary to deny such groups sanctuary and covert material support.

During our trip to monitor the elections, Chairman Biden, Senator Hagel and I joined in promoting a major aid program to Pakistan to try to change the relationship for the better. Now, as the new chairman, I continued to shape this concept. The theory was simple: a major commitment of civilian aid might change the nature of our relationship. We wanted to empower those Pakistanis who were trying to steer the world's second-largest Muslim country onto a path of moderation, stability and regional cooperation. That was the goal of the bill I introduced with the critical partnership and support of Senator Dick Lugar.

By then, Dick's Nunn-Lugar efforts on nonproliferation had become shorthand for bipartisanship in foreign policy. We'd worked closely together in the 1980s to help bring about free and fair elections in the Philippines. He was the right partner for this effort to jam major foreign aid funding through a Senate still reeling from the way issues such as foreign aid had been demagogued to death and turned into surefire negative applause lines. With our economy and a whole lot of people still hurting from the Great Recession, it was not the ideal time to ask Americans to send money to a country where we weren't popular.

I believed in this new approach to Pakistan because I'd seen it work firsthand. Following the 2005 Kashmir earthquake, the United States had spent nearly $1 billion on relief efforts. Having visited places like Mansehra and Muzaffarabad in the earthquake's aftermath, I knew the awesome power of the operation we launched. I'll never forget flying by helicopter to the northwestern part of Pakistan, not far from the big Himalayas, and landing in a small spot by the river. I met kids in a tent city. It was the first time they had ever come out of the mountains and the first time they had ever gone to school. It was extraordinary to see American servicemen and -women saving the lives of Pakistani citizens. Frankly, it was invaluable in changing the perceptions of America in Pakistan.

In the wake of natural disaster, we weren't the only ones to recognize the need for public diplomacy based in deeds rather than words: the front group for the terrorist organization Lashkar-e-Taiba (Army of the Good) had set up a string of professional relief camps throughout the region. Our effort, however, was far more effective, and the permanent gift of the U.S. Army's last mobile Army surgical hospital helped seal the deal. For a brief period, America was going toe-to-toe with extremists in a true battle of hearts and minds and actually winning.

I knew it was up to us to re-create this success on a broader scale, without waiting for a natural or even a man-made disaster. The question was: How could we most effectively demonstrate the true friendship of the American people for the Pakistani people?

The aid bill was an important first step. It was a prime example of "smart power," because it used both economic and military aid to achieve an overall effect greater than the sum of its parts. Nonmilitary aid was increased— both in actual dollars and for a longer time frame. These funds would build schools, roads and clinics. In other words, they aimed to do on a regular basis what we briefly achieved with our earthquake relief, but this money would do a great deal more than good deeds. It would empower the fledgling civilian government to show that it could deliver the citizens of Pakistan a better life. It might embolden the moderates, giving them something concrete to put forward as evidence that friendship with America brings rewards as well as perils. It could also encourage the vast majority of Pakistanis who rejected the terrifying vision of al-Qaeda and the Taliban but were angered and frustrated by the perception that their own leaders and America's leaders didn't care about their daily struggle.

To do this right, I knew that we needed to make a long-term commitment. Most Pakistanis felt that America had used and abandoned their country in the past—most notably, after the jihad against the Soviets in Afghanistan. They feared we would desert them again the moment that the threat from al-Qaeda subsided. It was this history and this fear that caused Pakistan to hedge its bets. If we ever expected the country to break decisively with the Taliban and other extremist groups, I knew we would have to provide firm assurance that we were not merely foul-weather friends. This bill offered just such an assurance.

On the security side, the bill placed conditions on military aid that would ensure that the money was used for the intended purposes. For Pakistan to receive any military assistance, it had to meet an annual certification that its army and spy services were genuine partners. Just as important as the economic and military components of the bill were how those elements fit and worked together. Making this unequivocal commitment to the Pakistani people enabled us to calibrate our military assistance more effectively. In any given year, we could choose to increase or decrease it, or leave it unchanged. For too long, the Pakistani military had felt we were bluffing when we threatened to cut funding for a particular weapons system or expensive piece of hardware. If our economic aid was tripled to $1.5 billion, we could afford to end this game. We'd finally be able to make this choice on the basis of our national interests, rather than the institutional interests of the Pakistani security forces.

When the bill passed on October 16, 2009, we were confident that the Pakistanis would be appreciative. Instead, I got a real-life reminder of the danger of what can happen inadvertently when certain compromises are necessitated in order to get a bill passed. Dick Lugar and I had passed a straightforward bill through the Senate. The House, on the other hand, had larded up their near-identical bill with a lot of language that the activist community had recommended, most of it boilerplate about civilian control of the military, conditioning the money on reform inside Pakistan, and insisting on a rather cumbersome process of showing how the money was being spent. Most of it was perfectly reasonable thinking from the American policy perspective, but I worried how it would play in Pakistan. Still, because my priority was getting a bill passed into law, and this bill didn't actually change anything in practice, we swallowed the House's language. The bills were combined and the final act was titled the Enhanced Partnership of Pakistan Act, but became known as the Kerry-Lugar-Berman Act.

Unfortunately, in Pakistan, the bill was initially reported not as a new day in the relationship between our people, but as an infringement on their sovereignty, an act of neocolonialism. It was obvious it was necessary for me to return to Pakistan. I had envisioned my trip as a rollout in-country of our bill, an opportunity to talk about its benefits and make clear that the United States cared about the Pakistani people. Instead, I wound up spending most of my time just trying to keep Pakistani stakeholders on board and explaining to them that we respected their sovereignty. The whole trip had a no-good-deed-goes-unpunished quality about it. Any politician who thinks a town hall meeting in the United States is confrontational ought to try one in Pakistan. We'd worked hard to get support for the Pakistani people, despite real misgivings in the Congress and among the American public. Now here I was in Pakistan, trying to convince the leaders and the public that the United States was not violating their sovereignty. Why didn't I just pack up and say, "To hell with all of you"? Because like it or not, it was in the United States' interests to help enable success in Afghanistan and stronger regional security, and you couldn't do that if you weren't willing to endure a frustrating exercise in public diplomacy in Pakistan.

The trip and this entire period was a big reminder that so much of what we try to do here at home depends on how things are messaged and framed overseas. No matter what we do, we have a responsibility to explain it properly, taking into full account how the effort will be seen by a public that can't possibly be expected to understand and isn't much interested in our domestic politics. At the same time, we have a right to hold a country accountable for its politicians playing politics with the generous intentions of American taxpayers. I made a mental note to myself of a lesson learned, that when we decide that doing something is in our country's interests, we have to overcome the instinct in Congress to act in a way that scores points and makes people feel good but might contribute to undermining our goals along the way. All the extra language in that bill did nothing to advance our actual goals, but it sure got in the way of communicating our intentions to the people we aimed to help.

Then the floods came. Weeks after the legislation was signed into law and the initial media firestorm had dissipated, in the summer of 2010 raging floodwaters killed more than 1,600 people and left great swaths of Pakistan devastated. I detoured from another trip to return there to observe the American aid effort. I had to helicopter out to the hardest-hit areas. It was important to show how the dollars from the act just passed by our Congress would be used to address immediate humanitarian needs. As we were choosing our landing sites, it dawned on me that it was all well and good for me to go there to make the case that the United States was on the side of the Pakistani people, but what about the president of Pakistan? I called President Asif Zardari and asked him to tour with me. He was out of the country at the time, so I suggested he get back to Pakistan right away and join me. He agreed, but once he was added to the mix, the number of places we could visit diminished by orders of magnitude. There were few areas in the country where President Zardari was welcome. When we cross-referenced those places with the areas where our security detail could land, we were down to two or three.

When we finally landed at our first site, we were shepherded over to a corner of a soccer field, where we were briefed on relief efforts by President Zardari's military people. Thousands of Pakistanis had gathered around the soccer field, but none of them could see what we were doing. The entire purpose of the visit was defeated. We had wanted to share the visual of a president actively working to help his people in distress, accompanied by my speaking directly to Pakistanis about America's efforts to address their humanitarian needs. Instead, the event turned into a briefing on a soccer field with a security perimeter of a hundred yards in every direction. The Pakistani people were blocked from seeing what we were doing. It was a microcosm of the frustrations I experienced when we passed the bill in the first place, only to be forced to convince the Pakistanis that we weren't violating their sovereignty. I was concerned that this recent episode would only increase the sense of alienation that the Pakistani people felt for the United States. Watching from hundreds of yards away as military helicopters landed in a soccer field seemed to exacerbate rather than alleviate the problems. I wondered whether there would ever be a way to truly communicate the good we were doing in a country where mistrust and paranoia had clouded our relationship for a long, long time.

On a personal level, my extracurricular efforts resulted in my becoming a trusted interlocutor with the Pakistani government. I was known to be fair and legitimately concerned about U.S.-Pakistan relations. However, there would soon be another crisis requiring some quiet intervention, a crisis that fell squarely into the no-good-deed-goes-unpunished category that was much in evidence throughout this entire effort. It became known as a four-word phrase that made it all seem more mysterious than it really was—"the Ray Davis affair."

At the end of January 2011, on the streets of Lahore, which is a pretty tough area and the world's largest Punjabi city, there was a shoot-out that had left two Pakistani civilians dead. The shooter was an American citizen working for a private security firm, an Army veteran named Ray Davis who was a federal contractor. It quickly became what in diplomatic terms is most unartfully referred to as a shit sandwich. Davis said he was the victim of an attempted robbery, but with two dead Pakistanis and crowds growing apoplectic, police threw him in jail and charged him with murder. Our consulate's appropriate efforts to secure his release based on diplomatic immunity weren't working.

There was plenty of public attention in Pakistan, along with a lot of conspiracy theory–type rumors about the CIA that inflamed suspicions about the too many armed Americans to begin with in a country sensitive to our presence—and the streets of Lahore had been seething. Worry abounded on both sides, but we Americans were constantly concerned about how much anyone was really in control in Pakistan—something we all had reason to question again later that spring after Osama bin Laden was found and killed in Abbottabad. We were all aware too of how quickly any spark could set off a powder keg. Sometimes, of course, members of the government in Pakistan played off that dynamic as an excuse not to do things we asked for, but other times it was real. This was one of those times when the complications were real. The local government in Lahore was led by the political opposition to the central government, and it saw a chance to thumb its nose at Islamabad. The crisis metastasized when a local court ruled that Davis didn't have diplomatic immunity. The Taliban leaped into the fray, promising retribution against any lawyer or judge who set Davis free.

Now we had a real mess on our hands. Tom Donilon, then the national security advisor, thought that a third-party mediator might be helpful—someone who wasn't part of the administration, someone who knew the Pakistanis and, unlike our capable ambassador, someone who wouldn't have to operate on a daily basis with the Pakistani government.

Back in Washington, I asked the Pakistani ambassador to come over to my house so we could talk and try to see if we could defuse the situation. We needed a release valve in Pakistan, some expression of remorse. On the Pakistani street, there was speculation about who Ray Davis was, what he was really doing and why, and how many more people like him were in their country. With a situation like this, the public dialogue is never about just one issue. Rather, issues get conflated. This was fast becoming a debate about armed Americans on the streets of a Muslim country, a debate about the CIA, a controversy about everything including drone attacks that were reported on the front pages of newspapers around the world.

Ambassador Husain Haqqani thought that I could help. We wondered if I should meet with the families of the men who had been killed, but that seemed likely to inflame the situation. We discussed whether, by making some kind of statement of remorse in Pakistan, I might defuse some of the public tension. Haqqani had an interesting if unconventional proposal to deploy Islamic tradition that allowed for the payment of "blood money" in return for a life lost—a way to settle a dispute that had resulted in death, a settlement of sorts. First, though, someone had to calm the waters.

My staff wasn't pleased, but I was headed back to Pakistan to play the good cop in a bad situation. The Obama administration's public statements were calibrated to emphasize why the international, well-enshrined legal concept of diplomatic immunity is so important and just how much was at risk—including American support for Pakistan—if an American diplomat was left languishing in a Lahore prison cell. Beneath the surface, we all knew that this wasn't going to get settled through interpretations of international law. It was going to get done through politics.

I met first with some officials in the central government in Islamabad.

Prime Minister Gilani and I shared a public message about the importance of all the issues between our two countries, including economic aid and cooperation on counterterrorism. Then, without much announcement to minimize the security risk, I traveled to the eastern part of the country—into Lahore, the belly of the beast. I wanted to make a public statement that would hopefully be heard differently by the public: as a friend of Pakistan, as the author of legislation that aimed to begin a new era of mutual cooperation with the people of Pakistan, I wanted to see this tragic situation resolved. I emphasized that the United States would have our Justice Department investigate what had happened, just as Pakistani justice would be appropriate for Pakistani citizens. It was a tense visit. I went back home, however, confident in our belief that the situation was successfully on a glide path to resolution. A little steam had been let out of the system, hopefully creating enough room for the Pakistani government to work with the families on an agreement for blood money so the whole episode could be put behind us.

When I got back to Washington, jet-lagged but glad the trip was behind me, a staffer had printed out a photo from the wires in Pakistan: a charming image of street protests in Lahore, crowds surrounding a stuffed dummy hanged in effigy with a sign pinned to it that read "John Kerry and Obama." Lovely. "That's a keeper," joked my communications director.

I knew the protest and photo were part of the necessary stagecraft for local politics. A couple of weeks later, the gambit bore fruit: the blood money was agreed to, the families let the local courts know, and Ray Davis was released and whisked home efficiently and quietly. What a process. . . .

Six weeks later, Hillary Clinton called to let me know that American Special Forces had killed Osama bin Laden—not in a cave in Afghanistan or hidden in the mountains of the ungoverned tribal areas of Pakistan but living quite comfortably in a gated compound not far from the Military Academy in picturesque Abbottabad. I congratulated her and the administration. The news was quickly made public.

No one should underestimate how gutsy it was for the president to decide to go into Pakistani territory without advance warning to get Osama bin Laden, not knowing with certainty whether the mission would succeed, whether Americans would be killed or it was certain bin Laden was even there. The what-ifs were almost too many to count: What if Pakistan had shot down an American helicopter? What if bin Laden hadn't been there? What if our members of Special Forces had been killed? What if it turned out we'd entered a compound of alarmed innocent civilians and in the fog of the moment had to shoot? I thought of President Carter's downed helicopters in the desert in 1980 in a failed mission to free American hostages in Iran and how it may have cost him the presidency. President Obama put his presidency on the line to bring Osama bin Laden to justice. Thank God this had worked, I thought, and thank God for the great training and extraordinary capacity of our military and especially our Special Forces—all of them.

After we hung up and I processed it all, another thought crossed my mind—another what-if. What if Ray Davis had still been in jail? When I made my uncomfortable trip to Islamabad and Lahore, little did I know that the intelligence community and the military were already working to plan and execute the raid that killed bin Laden. No wonder there had been so much urgency to get Davis home. All our arguments about diplomatic immunity and sovereignty and the relationship between the two countries would have been out the window if the United States had had to execute the bin Laden raid with Davis sitting there in a jail cell. It hit me just how much Tom Donilon and Hillary, let alone the president, had on their collective desks at once, just how many complicated and interconnected equities were at stake affecting one decision, one deadline, one issue—and how little latitude they had to explain or even discuss these problems.

Later that month, the administration asked me to take one more trip to Pakistan. It came at a moment of enormous and understandable tension on both sides of the relationship. The Pakistanis were furious that their sovereignty had been violated without any advance warning by the United States. Their feelings were inflamed by the explanations given by American officials that they feared coordination could have tipped off bin Laden and doomed the mission. It was one of those cases where saying what was true and obvious was far from helpful diplomatically.

There were voices in Congress calling for an end to American aid for Pakistan. There was also a detail important to the American military: one of the Black Hawk helicopters from the bin Laden raid had been disabled on the grounds of the compound, blown up by our forces as they pulled out, but the wreckage, including its intact tail, remained in the Abbottabad compound. The Pakistanis had threatened to share it with China. It was a distraction that served no one's real interests, but at the time the Pakistanis were not thinking about the long term. I hoped that with so much unresolved in Afghanistan, let alone across another border with India, I could secure a promise from Pakistan to return the remains of the helicopter and see if, once again, there was any way to return this bilateral discussion to real strategic interests.

After stopping in Afghanistan, I flew back to Islamabad. I was traveling with two of my Foreign Relations Committee staff members, Doug Frantz and Fatema Sumar. As a reporter, Doug had covered a large part of the Afghan war, and we talked on the flight about a great what-if that fascinated us both: What if the United States had killed bin Laden at the Battle of Tora Bora at the start of the war?

We could have and we should have. I'd argued since 2002 that it had been an enormous mistake to rely on Afghan warlords at Tora Bora—people who had previously fought on the other side instead of sending in Special Forces to go up the mountain and kill bin Laden.

Now, almost ten years after the 9/11 attacks, we were deeply entangled in a complicated but necessary set of relationships with Pakistan and its security services, with mercurial leaders across the border in Afghanistan, and with the Shia government in Iraq. How different, Doug asked, would it have been had the United States put an end to bin Laden in the first days of Afghanistan?

Then Doug asked another question. If bin Laden had been apprehended at Tora Bora, there would have been no bin Laden tape on the eve of the 2004 presidential election, no last-minute boost in the polls for Bush-Cheney: Would I be the president now? My reply: "If I were, Doug, trust me we'd have a nicer plane." It was an intriguing historical question, but after conceding the race I have never allowed myself to get lost in hypothetical mazes. It's a waste of time and energy, especially when there's so much to do to keep me pointed forward. At two in the morning on a runway in Islamabad, we just put one foot in front of the other and moved forward. We had marathon meetings to undertake that would no doubt exhaust our collective patience.

We went directly to the army enclave in Rawalpindi, where we met for two hours in a smoke-filled room with the Chief of Army Staff General Ashfaq Kayani and General Ahmad Pasha, the head of Pakistan's powerful intelligence service, Inter-Services Intelligence.

The military leaders are very powerful in Pakistan, far more powerful than those in the United States. Civilian control of the military is sacrosanct for us, so I was always mindful of the optics, but reality dictated that I talk with the people who had the authority to give us what we wanted, and that wasn't going to be Pakistan's elected leadership, not on this issue. When it came time for the public press conference, I would insist that it be with Pakistan's civilian leadership so as not to create a problematic public misimpression, but the hardest conversation had to be with Kayani and Pasha.

It was a tough slog, which didn't surprise me but certainly tested my patience. We had found bin Laden living it up in the backyard of the Pakistan

Military Academy, and yet we were the ones on the defensive? Nonetheless, the generals were outraged. The raid had occurred and they hadn't known anything about it beforehand. They considered it a violation of their sovereign territory, and I had to work hard to convince them that total secrecy had been imperative. I emphasized that it wasn't mistrust but operational security so tight that even I was not aware of the raid until after it happened. I think that opened their eyes. I asked them what they would have done if they'd been in our shoes. What if they had located their number one most wanted terrorist enemy in Afghanistan? Would they have called Karzai ahead of time? They smiled. I let them vent, but I always came back to core interests. Both sides had a lot at stake.

At the end of the meeting, we drafted a statement. I had Doug look it over and he said, "If you want to say nothing, this is perfect." That was precisely what we wanted. What I said publicly mattered far less than what was committed to privately—in fact, at this stage any public statement might only have erased the progress made privately.

The next day, I met with President Asif Zardari, Prime Minister Yousaf Gilani and Pakistan's ambassador to the United States, Husain Haqqani. They wanted a written statement to assure the Pakistani people that the United States was not going to invade their country and grab their nuclear weapons. It was a curious concern at a moment like this. We negotiated the statement word by word. At one point, someone from the Pakistani side tried to insert a line that read, "I, John Kerry, swear on a blood oath." That was never going to fly, but it did reveal two things: first, how urgent this issue was to them; and second, that my relationships with Pakistan's leaders had become personal. I gathered from their suggested language that they judged that I had a reservoir of credibility to help put the relationship on a stronger footing.

The Pakistanis announced that they would be returning our helicopter tail and would renew engagement in other areas of cooperation. The internal challenges of Pakistan, coupled with their own complicated domestic politics, preordained that this was never going to be an easy relationship. As it had been for decades, it would continue to be marked by mistrust, highs and lows, moments of confrontation and openings for occasional breakthroughs. For every member of Congress back home who thought we should just write off the relationship, I always thought, *What's your alternative?* Walk away from Afghanistan? We did that in 1979 and we know how well that worked. Cede a relationship with Pakistan to China or Saudi Arabia? Lose our leverage to get involved as a broker on both sides when India's tensions with Pakistan would inevitably flare up? Shut down our channels of communication with a nuclear power in the world's most dangerous region, surrounded by pockets of extremists? Good luck with all that.

As we flew home, Doug joked to me, "Senator, will you swear a blood oath that we never have to go back to Pakistan?"

DESPITE THE OBAMA administration's early interest in a pivot to Asia, which to many in the Middle East sounded like a receding of interest in their region, there was a full plate of issues that would inevitably draw any administration back into what some derisively called "the sandbox"—Iraq, Iran, Lebanon and other Middle East countries where there were myriad issues to be addressed, each of which had a common thread running through the tapestry: Syria. A new round of peace negotiations was being started by the president's special envoy, George Mitchell.

In the years preceding the Obama administration, Syria had been engaged in peace talks with Israel brokered by Turkey. The country had also been a key transit point for weapons and fighters into Iraq. It remained Iran's last ally in the region, played a destabilizing role in Lebanon, and was a chief sponsor of Hamas and Hezbollah—a series of actions and behaviors that quite appropriately kept Syria on a list of the state sponsors of terror.

The Bush administration's approach had been a policy of nonengagement. They saw meetings and diplomacy as a reward. President Obama viewed diplomacy as a means to an end and believed that a meeting was a tool, not a gift. This was common sense and Diplomacy 101. You would always be careful about how you choreograph engagement. Sometimes it's smart to start with a quiet back channel that doesn't raise public expectations or complicate existing relationships, and certainly you don't roll out the red carpet and lavish public praise on a bad actor. In my mind, however, meeting, talking, listening and exchanging arguments and ideas are the only ways you can test whether there's a potential avenue for progress.

You can't be afraid to have a conversation, and my experience has always been that even if the conversation goes nowhere, there has at least been a signal or demonstration that you've tried. This can help bring allies and partners to your side in the event that you have to build support for sanctions or military force. Of course, when it came to Syria, it made sense to try to engage diplomatically to change Syrian behavior on any number of issues, because the alternatives were always imperfect. The country—75 percent Sunni, 12 percent Shia—was a demographic powder keg that would be hard ever to put back together again if it broke apart, and that process could be very ugly for Syria, for its neighbors and for the world.

It was worth an attempt to see if engagement could lead somewhere. Many regional issues ran through Damascus, as mentioned, and there was a case to be made that Syria's actual interests were not advanced by being entirely aligned with Iran. Bashar al-Assad, the relatively new head of state, had demographic pressure to deliver something resembling economic opportunity for his population. On the surface, it didn't seem unfathomable that the regime might soften its approach in some areas in return for relief from sanctions and a new relationship with the West and with Israel. After all, that kind of reconciliation has been known to happen in the Middle East from time to time: Jordan and Egypt were once Israel's leading enemies, before, with American backing, they negotiated peace agreements that have endured for a long time now. The entire story of the region is marked by shifting allegiances—alliances always in transition—and ongoing assessments of interests. With Syria, there had even been what looked like occasional instructive moments: after Iraq invaded Kuwait in 1991, President George H. W. Bush did the improbable and convinced then Syrian president Hafez al-Assad to join an American-led coalition against a fellow Baathist regime. Secretary of State James Baker made more than a dozen trips to Syria before Operation Desert Storm, and the first President Assad's price was simple: U.S. support for Syrian dialogue with Israel. The ultimate challenge—moving Syria away from its marriage of convenience with Iran and into a different relationship with Israel—wouldn't be easy, but why shouldn't we at least try?

I was intrigued by the prospect and knew that the Obama administration was interested in exploring the possibilities, so I thought the committee could dip a toe into those waters. The president encouraged me to reach out to the regime. I did so without knowing Bashar al-Assad well. I'd met his father, who was brutal and devious, but I didn't have much of a relationship or history with Assad the younger beyond a short stop I had made in Damascus in 2005. Nobody in the White House, and certainly not I, placed any trust in him, but I believed that if he had his own self-interest at heart, then he would be interested in a frank conversation.

In 2009, I had my first long meetings with Assad, which left me with two important takeaways: the strange predicament he faced in managing his country and that I couldn't take anything he said at face value: it all had to be tested.

In our first meeting, I confronted him about a Syrian nuclear power plant that Israel had famously bombed and that the International Atomic Energy Agency (IAEA) now wanted to inspect. The fact that this was a nuclear facility had been well established publicly. It was beyond dispute. "If you want to show the world that you're prepared to move in a new direction, let the IAEA in," I argued to him. Assad looked me in the eye and told me it wasn't a nuclear facility, with exactly the same affect and intonation with which he said everything else. It was a stupid lie, utterly disprovable, but he lied without any hesitation. The next time we met, I had been briefed by the White House on the smuggling of weapons across the border to arm Hezbollah. Again, the evidence was incontrovertible. Again, when confronted, Assad denied it. I asked for everyone to leave the room besides the two of us. "Mr. President, this isn't a debate. I've seen the evidence. It is happening and we know it's happening," I said, and let the words hang in the air to gauge his reaction. "Everything is to be negotiated," he replied, and stared ahead. It was a purposeful non sequitur from an immature autocrat caught in a bald-faced lie. It was a revealing moment that would come in handy years later when I was secretary of state and had to face the Syria conundrum from a different perch. A man who can lie to your face four feet away from you can just as easily lie to the world after he has gassed his own people to death.

Assad's interest in a three-way peace negotiation with Israel and the United States was an area where he leaned forward. Israel and Syria had had several negotiations over the years, dating back to the Clinton era. Most recently, the Turks, under Recep Tayyip Erdoğan, had engaged with Assad and then prime minister Ehud Olmert of Israel to see if they could agree on the baseline for resuming negotiations. That effort was interrupted by the Gaza War in 2009, which was the beginning of the deterioration of Israel's relationship with Turkey. The Obama administration was interested in renewing the Israel-Syria negotiations.

Assad asked me what it would take to enter into serious peace negotiations, in the hope of securing return of the Golan Heights, which Syria had lost to Israel in 1967. I told him that if he were serious, he should make a private proposal. He asked what it would look like. I shared my thoughts. He instructed his top aide to draft a letter from Assad to President Obama asking for American support of peace talks with Israel, stating Syria's willingness to take a number of steps in exchange for the return of the Golan from Israel. His father had tried and failed to get the Golan back, so he was willing to do a lot in return. The next day, I flew to Israel, where I sat down with Prime Minister Bibi Netanyahu and showed him Assad's letter. He was surprised that Assad was willing to go that far, significantly further than he'd been willing to go with the Turks. I took the letter back to Washington. I gave it to Secretary of State Hillary Clinton and also to Dennis Ross at the

National Security Council. Subsequently it became part of the State Department's effort on the Israel-Syria negotiations.

I continued to work with Assad to test him on what would have been small confidence-building measures—areas where he could demonstrate some good faith—and made clear that anything the United States could ever consider doing for him would be contingent on verification that he had followed through on his end. In coordination with the White House, I made several requests, ranging from easy ones, such as working on the transfer of land for the American embassy in Damascus and the opening of an American cultural center, to difficult and trickier issues, like border assistance with respect to Iraq and a visit to Iraq by the foreign minister, reconciliation with Bahrain, and dispatching an ambassador to Lebanon to send a message before the elections that Syria would stay out of Lebanon's election process. All of these were largely done and delivered.

Everything Assad did always had to be verified. He would tighten up on some misdeeds for a couple weeks or so by limiting the transit of weapons or saying the right things about engaging with Israel, but words were easy, while sustained actions told a different story. A few weeks later, I remember hearing that Assad was continuing with exactly the kind of behavior on Hezbollah that we told him needed to stop. It was disappointing but unsurprising. I once asked a leader of one of our close allies in the Middle East why Assad chose Iran over a different kind of future for his country. He told me, "When Assad goes to Iran, they offer him a sumptuous feast with a buffet stretching as far as the eye can see. When you guys see him, you offer him some raisins and dates." I answered bluntly, "Well, we aren't going to offer him anything if he continues to behave like this."

For all his lies, there were times when Assad could seemingly acknowledge his predicament and lay out a candid rationale for moving in a different direction. He made clear that he was most concerned about providing jobs for a young population beginning to enter the workforce. He told me he had hundreds of thousands of people joining the workforce every year, and that he needed to loosen the economic restrictions and spur private sector investment. I made very clear that if there was any chance that that was going to happen, we had a long list of things he would have to do, none of which was going to be easy. Assad said he was interested in having that conversation because the pressure grew every year: the promise of a secular state, even the authoritarian police state his father had built, demanded a population believing that their quality of life was better than it would be with the alternative.

The alternative he feared was the Islamist movements his father had crushed decades ago. As the oil dried up and Syria became a net oil importer and as the youth population boomed, it was more apparent than ever that in an overwhelmingly Sunni country, Assad was a leader from an Alawite sect, in effect a minority within a minority. He talked with nostalgia about a different, more secular time in Syria and once showed me a picture of his mother going to the Umayyad Mosque in a midlength skirt, her head uncovered. At one point, his foreign minister said, "If we don't find a way to get more jobs for our people, you'll come back in ten years and he'll be Mullah Assad!" Assad laughed. "I will be Bashar with a beard." His message was unmistakable: one way or another, he was bent on regime survival, even if it meant posing as a theocrat, but the easiest path was by moving his country in a new direction.

Assad wasn't alone in that challenge. King Abdullah had faced similar demographic challenges in Jordan, but Abdullah was strong and smart, the son of a brilliant, revered military icon turned peacemaker. By contrast, Assad had always been underestimated. His ruthless father had never envisioned him leading the country, so he'd been buried in the line of succession behind his uncle and brother, but fate and a funeral had placed him at the front of the line. He was long and lanky with a head that sat atop a very long neck out of proportion to his body. He had a quality that sometimes made you wonder if he wished he'd still been an ophthalmologist living out of the political limelight in London, enjoying the regime's ill-gotten wealth and chasing his glamorous, cosmopolitan wife all over Europe. I wondered how he would react if he faced a real crisis at home. Would this young, unlikely head of state cut an independent, modern path, or would he try to one-up his father and turn even more brutal to try to hold on to power?

We were at a standstill when the Arab Spring came to Syria in the form of protests in Deir al-Zour and then spread around the country. I made very clear to the Syrian ambassador that if Assad killed innocent civilians, it would be the end of direct engagement with me. Period. He told me that Assad intended to address the country soon and engage in a reconciliation process for a reform agenda. I told him the United States would be listening very carefully. The next Friday, after prayers, more protesters were killed. I never spoke to the ambassador or Assad again.

Not long after, Assad delivered the first of what would become a running series of increasingly surreal addresses on Syrian state-run television. He announced that the opposition were terrorists trying to destroy the state and stop his experiment in reform to benefit the Syrian people. Some speculated that Assad had ceded control to his mother's family, while others suggested that he had simply fallen back on his father's old playbook. What became increasingly clear as he twisted the screws tighter and tighter was that he was transforming himself into the very magnet for religious extremism and jihadi intervention he had professed to fear the most. His actions were making Syria a beacon for regional conflagration. I soon argued that he would never be able to lead a united Syria and, like many other autocrats of the Arab Awakening, he should go. Not long afterward, in August 2011, President Obama also said he should give up power. After that, the president drew a famous red line about the potential use of chemical weapons.

About two years later, all these issues would find me again at the State Department, and they haunt all of us to this day. We'll never know what would have happened if the Arab Spring hadn't intervened and if we could have fully put to the test what Assad said he was willing to do to change his economy. It's impossible to go back and replay the many directions history might have taken. In the end, all you can do is make your best judgment at the time. Assad's horrific, sadistic series of judgments have brought ruin to his country and infamy to his reputation.

If diplomatic overtures overseas were an interesting study in mercurial personalities, broken and byzantine politics, and dysfunctional democracy punctuated by occasional breakthroughs, it turned out I didn't have to travel far to find similar challenges. All I needed was to get on the US Air shuttle from Boston to Washington.

Foreign policy in the Senate could be riveting and at times deeply frustrating. When I talk about it, I hope I don't sound as if I'm channeling Everett Dirksen or Mike Mansfield, guardians of a bygone era. The Senate I knew was never perfectly functional or efficient. It rarely behaved as imagined in the *Federalist Papers*. In 1985, I had arrived in a Washington on the cusp of sweeping, disruptive change. I witnessed a big shift in the first ten years that I was in national office, and then my presidential campaign unfolded at the dawn of an even bigger change in how America communicates. It's gotten only more complicated since then.

I point this out because when I became chairman of the Foreign Relations Committee in 2009, I wasn't an idealist nostalgic for a time long gone. I never expected everyone to sing "Kumbaya," nor did I expect the seas to part in Congress allowing the entire Obama foreign policy to advance unimpeded, but I couldn't have predicted just how corrosive the atmosphere would be and how broken the Senate would become, all of it standing in the way of doing things that in previous Congresses would have been automatic. Inside the Senate during the first four years of the Obama administration, even on foreign policy issues which not long ago had been the least partisan, the level of dysfunction, terror about primaries, raw politics, rancor and excuses for inaction became a way of life.

The fate of three treaties are as good an illustration as any of the way the Senate, sadly, became compromised. By 2009, I'd debated enough treaties to know both the Senate's traditions and its travails. Even across the five terms I'd been there, for the most part the Senate had largely kept intact a bipartisan tradition when it came to nuclear nonproliferation treaties. From John F. Kennedy to George W. Bush, nuclear treaties worked their way through the Senate typically with eye-popping margins that affirmed the national security community's commitment to reduce the nuclear threat. Votes that tallied 99–0 or 93–1 were more common than not.

Still, I knew that "treaty" had become a dirty word that the conservative think tanks criticized in every voting scorecard and endorsement questionnaire. There were Republican colleagues who handed me examples of the direct-mail letters that were sent to their constituents soliciting ten-, fifteen- and twenty-dollar contributions to stop a "one world government," inveighing against treaties that were supposedly designed to strip America of its sovereignty and put average citizens in jeopardy of being told what they could and couldn't do by the United Nations. These were fact-free scare tactics, but they worked.

One Republican brought me an example of the way the language of these appeals would permeate the letters his office received from his constituents, parroting the conspiracy theories word for word. Facts didn't matter. The pressure on my Republican colleagues was real, although that didn't excuse them from doing the right thing, but it put an onus on me as chairman to try to be mindful of their politics at home. It was important to run a process that would, I hoped, help them disprove the false statements point by point so that they could go back home and credibly demonstrate that they'd taken their base's concerns seriously and voted yes only after getting the needed answers. One of my early lessons learned in the Senate is never tell other senators that you know their politics better than they do. Instead, where possible, just help them see how they can overcome those challenges.

I thought that getting over that hurdle would be most surmountable on a modest nuclear nonproliferation treaty. I wish I could say I'd been right. Our nuclear treaty with Russia expired in December 2009. That meant the United States was losing its day-to-day visibility into the Russian nuclear arsenal. Under ordinary circumstances, this would have created a sense of urgency to quickly put in place a new accord. The administration sent one to the Hill—the Strategic Arms Reduction Treaty, called New START, which cut by nearly a third the maximum number of deployed strategic warheads, instituted a verification regime and kept us on the path toward reducing our reliance on nuclear weapons. At the time, a number of former secretaries of defense and state had made a splash arguing that the United States should be moving toward an aggressive goal of zero nuclear weapons. By that measure this modest Obama approach seemed almost incremental.

Enter Sarah Palin.

The half-term governor whose expertise on Russia seemed to begin and end with its proximity to Alaska had become a Tea Party heroine before many even knew what the Tea Party was. She appeared on Facebook and Fox News to attack the treaty in a fact-free frenzy. I knew the committee would hear differences of opinion on treaty specifics, from missile defense to telemetry, but I didn't think anyone would have predicted we'd be sitting in the ornate committee meeting room in the Senate parsing Palin's open letter to Republican freshmen on FoxNews.com.

It was never too early for presidential politics, so former Massachusetts governor Mitt Romney joined her in a footrace to the right, attacking the treaty as possibly "Obama's worst foreign policy mistake." The early 2012 presidential field joined in, from Gingrich down the line.

On the Foreign Relations Committee, we had our own version of the Tea Party on the committee's roster, Senator Jim DeMint of South Carolina—the "Palmetto Palin," as David McKean called him. Jim was a freshman senator of outsized influence. He had won my friend Fritz Hollings's seat in 2004, an example of the transition happening to the Senate in many ways and coming from the South in particular. Fritz had been a groundbreaking governor before he came to the Senate, a liberal who prided himself on working across the aisle and partnering with his senior senator, Strom Thurmond, on issues affecting South Carolina. By contrast, DeMint was an ideologue, a proponent of term limits who had been elected president of his freshman class in the House before he moved to the Senate a few years later.

Jim set out to break a lot of china—and he did. While other freshman senators were dutifully learning the institution, he penned a book titled *Saving Freedom: We Can Stop America's Slide into Socialism.* Most unusual was Jim's approach to his Republican colleagues. He took the extraordinary step of founding a political action committee of his own dedicated to electing Tea Party–style candidates, including those running against his Republican Senate colleagues. For example, he backed Lisa Murkowski's primary opponent, helped a self-described former witch win the Republican nod for the Senate seat previously held by Joe Biden, and defied his own leader,

Mitch McConnell, by endorsing Rand Paul in the Kentucky primary for Senate after Mitch had convinced the popular Republican secretary of state Trey Grayson to get into the race. (Grayson lost in the primary.)

Jim was hard to get to know because he didn't have a lot of interest in getting to know anyone on the other side of the aisle. He'd slip into a hearing, ask a question that was a polemic thinly disguised as an inquiry, and then he'd leave. His arrival on our committee was punctuated by his vote—one of just two in the entire Senate—against Hillary Clinton's nomination for secretary of state.

Not surprisingly, Jim DeMint was hell-bent on defeating anything with the word "treaty" attached to it. Indeed, he was out to paint treaties of any stripe as an assault on American sovereignty, something that had been a rallying cry when DeMint's endorsed primary challenger to Utah Republican Robert Bennett shocked the country in early 2010 with a convention victory against a conservative who had been an icon of Utah's Mormon political establishment.

We had a steeper hill to climb than logic would have predicted. The right-wing strategy was clear: those in DeMint's camp were opposed to all treaties and dead set against anything that had Obama's name associated with it—Obama, Obama, Obama!

Above all else, we had to take the rhetoric out of the debate if we were to have a chance to win, and in particular I needed to help change the dialogue about the nuclear treaty. It couldn't be about the president, otherwise we would never win enough Republicans to our side. I worked very closely with Secretary Clinton on a validator strategy: to put front and center as many trusted Republican names endorsing the treaty as possible. Hillary was terrific, really digging in to help. She called on her predecessors at State and helped draw out each Republican to weigh in on a treaty some assumed would be an easy lay-up. It made a difference to have former Republican secretaries of state Kissinger, Rice, Baker, Shultz and Powell publicly counterbalancing Palin and Romney, but I wondered why that was even a close fight. On the one side were people who had advised Republican commanders in chief from Nixon to Reagan and both Bushes, and yet Sarah Palin's voice was the one ringing the clearest (and loudest) in the conservative echo chamber.

Still, I knew guiding this treaty over the line was going to take time and tenacity. I made it a point to meet with Republicans even though they might never be in play as votes for the treaty, because any approach to their party could demonstrate to their caucus that our side was taking the process seriously.

If they asked for more time to review the treaty, I tried to give it to them, even if they gave me nothing in return. If they asked for another hearing or to include a particular witness, I tried to accommodate them, again because it would demonstrate good faith in the process.

The whole effort was tedious, but I wanted at the end of the trail to be sure that no one could credibly claim a question hadn't been vetted or they hadn't been given time to consider their position. After months of both open and classified hearings and hundreds of questions for the record, it was time to vote in committee.

Dick Lugar was with us from the start, but the Republican caucus had moved far right and almost marginalized him in a way that pained me to watch. Senator Bob Corker of Tennessee was the key vote for us. If we won over Corker, then we had a conservative Republican on board, which might give us a shot at another conservative, Johnny Isakson of Georgia, a kind, gentle man who taught Sunday school and had been in both the House and Senate of the Georgia legislature before he'd come to Washington.

I got along well with Bob Corker when we were colleagues on the committee, in part because Bob was eager to make a contribution and, especially in 2009 and 2010, he wasn't afraid of being in the fray. Having Bob interested in the treaty was worth an investment of time, even if it delayed getting the treaty to the Senate floor.

Bob wanted the White House to agree on a commitment to spend billions on nuclear modernization, which was important to Tennessee, where the Oak Ridge National Laboratory was based. I suspect that he figured it would help him demonstrate that he had persuaded the administration to move on an issue. I thought Bob was critical to the vote so I backed him up. But Bob and Johnny made a difficult ask of me as well. They suggested that Republicans felt rushed and opposed having the vote in committee in the summer before they headed home to campaign. They said I could have a more successful committee vote if I waited until after recess.

Frankly, I thought timing could be argued either way. If we voted in July, Republican senators might get beat up at home in August during recess. On the other hand, postponing didn't necessarily avoid that outcome—and might make them less likely to vote yes in September. I came down on the side of giving Bob the benefit of the doubt and, in my mind, building up a balance in the bank of political goodwill with a key Republican ally. I postponed the committee vote. The White House wasn't so sure I was making the right decision.

In September, when we held the vote, the gamble paid off. Our committee approved the treaty 14–4, with three Republican supporters. The Senate

was headed into recess before the November elections, and we had to finish the job when we returned in November. A committee staffer popped a
bottle of champagne in the conference room, wishful thinking or youthful
optimism.

That vote turned out to be only a momentary victory. When Republicans
crushed Democrats in the midterm elections, Sarah Palin and the hard right
wing of the party piled on. Their message was clear and simple: no lame-
duck votes on treaties.

Never mind that we had taken the entirety of the 111th Congress to do
the deliberation the right way under immense public scrutiny—we had held
twenty hearings. Never mind that the Joint Chiefs had briefed the Senate.
Never mind that we had not yet brought the treaty up for a floor vote precisely because senators had asked for extra time to do their homework.

Now, Palin, the neocon former UN ambassador John Bolton, the conservative machine and the fringe were arguing that dealing with a treaty like
this one was the job of a brand-new Congress, including freshmen who had
never even once been briefed on the details.

I could envision *Groundhog Day* if we caved to their requests. In January, we'd be right where we had started, with senators demanding a new
year and a half of briefings and hearings to get up to speed. I dug in and said
no. Republicans who had been leaning toward voting yes started coming
up to me and saying, "I can't be with you because of lame duck." Alterna-
tively, I also got a lot of "John, I hear Obama's going to force us to repeal
'don't ask, don't tell' in lame duck, so I can't be for New START." The non
sequiturs piled up, one thrown on top of another. I wondered what possible
connection there was between voting on letting gay people serve openly
in the military and whether you could vote that same month to reduce the
number of nuclear weapons pointed at the United States. The excuses were
astounding.

I remembered the lesson I'd learned in law school: if you don't have the
law on your side, argue the facts; if you don't have the facts on your side,
argue the law; if you don't have either, just argue. In this case, with the merits pushed to the side, Republicans were arguing and inventing all kinds of
process reasons for why they couldn't do something now even after they'd
asked me for additional time so they *could* do it now.

To say the least, this was all very frustrating. I sat down in the Democratic cloakroom with my team and laid out the options. We could go forward and lose, which would mean the first Senate defeat of a treaty since
the Comprehensive Nuclear Test-Ban Treaty went down in 1999 (itself the
first time a security-related treaty fell since the Treaty of Versailles). That

had been an ugly moment that had cost the United States globally. For years afterward as I traveled, I'd heard complaints from foreign ministers. Other countries began to wonder then whether the United States could be a dependable partner at the negotiating table if the Senate could just quash the work of multiple administrations. I didn't want to repeat that kind of sorry, sad episode.

At the same time, I didn't want to lose the investment of so many months of work and careful analysis to bring the treaty this far. It deserved a vote. Dick Lugar and his team were uncertain whether it was a good idea to go forward. Dick's argument was that a poor vote would "damage" the treaty irreparably. I didn't disagree about that risk, but I also asked whether the treaty wasn't damaged already if after a year and a half of effort we couldn't even bring it up for a vote. How feckless is that?

A lot hung in the balance. What worried me was the underlying political dynamic: thoughtful, serious members of the Senate Republican caucus were all running scared of the Tea Party. They were desperate to duck "tough votes." Others couldn't see past any opportunity to stick their finger in President Obama's eye. It wasn't exactly an atmosphere that summoned statesmanship.

In the end, it was the math that I found most persuasive—cold, hard numbers. We had fifty-nine Democratic votes for the treaty, and I knew I could count on Lugar. Corker was committed; the two moderate Republicans from Maine were going to vote yes. I could see my way clearly to about sixty-five of the sixty-seven votes we needed for victory. I thought, *Waiting on the next Congress means never.* It wasn't just that we'd have to start fresh in a new Congress, but that the Democratic margin had shrunk by seven in the Senate. The year 2011 would mark the start of an election cycle where Democrats would have some tough seats to defend, and every time that happens, the demand from those senators to the Senate leadership is for plenty of time at home to campaign and fund-raise and for plenty of bread-and-butter issues on the Senate floor, especially those that matter most to their constituents.

In my own caucus there would be little appetite for legislating on foreign policy unless it could be done quickly, easily and with certain victory. On the other side, in addition to the promise of more Tea Party primaries to scare the hell out of Republican incumbents, we would be into a presidential election cycle. If 2010 had been a year when many wanted to deny a Democratic president victories, heading into 2012 that sentiment would be nearly unanimous. I was not optimistic about our odds in the next Congress. In fact, I hated them.

I called Pete Rouse, President Obama's right-hand man, who had been Tom Daschle's chief of staff and was as smart a Senate whisperer as anyone in Washington. There were risks here for the president too—a loss in the lame-duck session on a critical treaty a month after what the president himself had called a "shellacking" in the midterm elections wouldn't just be a bad story, it could hurt him in foreign policy making going forward. Pete was famously steady. Like Obama, he never gets too high or too low. He didn't like our chances now, but he liked them better now than in January. Secretary Clinton agreed and reiterated her willingness to do anything required to win. She was indefatigable. It was fourth down, and we decided to go for it.

If Jim DeMint represented the bomb-throwing agitator extraordinaire in opposition to all treaties, then Senator Jon Kyl of Arizona was both his twin and his opposite. Jon was an insider's insider, the son of a congressman, and was the Republican whip. He was competitive, smart and ideological about issues like this one. He did his homework on the minutiae of New START, which made him a very agile debater. We had often squared off against each other on television. He was a wily opponent, respected and feared even inside his caucus. Just as it was on our side, where people like Bob Byrd and Harry Reid rode the whip position all the way to majority leader, Jon had enormous influence in his caucus. He took the position that he opposed the treaty but wished the administration was willing to wait and work with him to answer his questions and address his concerns. The White House and my staff saw that as a cynical ploy. Surely any legitimate concerns about this treaty should have been taken care of in the course of the past year.

My reaction was that it didn't matter what we thought. Because Jon was important in his caucus, how we played our hand in response to him would matter. We had to demonstrate that we were exhausting the process of trying to get Jon to yes, even if it was impossible. At least then other Republicans would see we were operating in good faith and they would feel permitted to vote their conscience. I started going over to the Republican cloakroom to meet with Jon one-on-one. The bonus of meeting that way was that every one of our Republican colleagues saw us talking respectfully.

After some time, it became clear that Jon Kyl's strategy was to play for time and move the goalposts with no intention of ever supporting the treaty. I hate to admit this, but it was a compliment to Jon's mastery of the Senate and his knowledge of the secret Bob Byrd and Ted Kennedy had shared with me in 1985: time matters. Jon was very cagily using the clock to achieve his objective. Nothing can make senators want to get out of Washington more than the clarion call of the Christmas holiday break. He knew that in a December when senators were already tired from a busy legislative session, when many had just gone through a dispiriting election, when there was a lot already on the agenda, he could just stall the bill into the next Congress.

I think it is safe to say that Jon figured we Democrats might fold when his side made it clear that they were going to use the entire ten days of floor time that had been allotted under the rules to consider New START. If they were going to try to wear us out, I'd accommodate them. I sat at my desk on the Senate floor for many of those days while little happened. A few times, when the Senate looked especially like a ghost town, I would turn to the cameras and say, "I know some of our colleagues have said repeatedly that they have questions about this treaty, and I want to answer them. I'd urge them to come on down." A few hours later, I'd say again, "Colleagues, we are here, we will stay here, we are ready to debate anytime." Then we would repeat the arguments over and over. Occasionally, a Republican would come down and read a short statement, and we'd have a brief exchange. Then he would leave and I'd spend the next hour responding to the arguments he and many others made.

If we lost, it would have meant that I had misread the Senate tea leaves. But at that point, I was willing to take the risk. The alternative was just walking away from the certain death of the treaty. I heartily endorsed John McCain's favorite expression, "a fight not joined is a fight not enjoyed."

It was time to vote.

All fifty-nine Democrats voted yes—including Oregon's Ron Wyden, who got out of his sickbed just a few days after prostate cancer surgery to register his vote. I knew those early days weren't pleasant, particularly when just walking the steps to the Senate floor is painful. But that's Ron Wyden, a stand-up guy. I watched the tally in the well of the Senate like a scoreboard, counting down the final minutes of a tight game: Corker, Lugar, Collins, Snowe. . . .

Scott Brown, my new colleague from Massachusetts whose surprise election had signaled the rise of the Tea Party, voted in step with Massachusetts. We were up to sixty-four votes and needed three more.

That's when the dam broke. Republicans whom I had met with for hours and hours came to the floor of the Senate and voted aye, including a former governor of Nebraska, Mike Johanns, who had come to the Senate in 2009. Former governors seemed to have less tolerance for the antics of the ideologues because they knew they could never have run a state that way. Neither Judd Gregg from New Hampshire nor George Voinovich of Ohio (both were retiring that year) was going to go out playing a political game. Lamar Alexander, whom I'd spent hours with going through the treaty, was a serious person who had been a successful governor. He was going to vote his conscience and at the same time stick by Bob Corker, his colleague from Tennessee.

We hit the magic number, and then something wonderful happened. Robert Bennett and Lisa Murkowski, both of whom had lost Tea Party primaries to Jim DeMint's ideologues, put up their thumbs and voted aye, but it was a different digit they were really signaling with to DeMint and company.

Three days before Christmas, and we'd won.

On the way home, I talked with Vice President Biden. It had been an intense first year and a half for the administration, and on the personal front, Joe's son Beau, Delaware's attorney general, had come home safely from a yearlong deployment in Iraq and made the decision not to run for the seat Joe had held for thirty-seven years. Joe and I had shared a lot of history in the Senate, and at least on this night the outcome suggested that there was a little bit left in the tank for the institution we revered.

However, we both saw the storm clouds on the horizon. Treaties used to pass 99–0. If 71 was the new 99, then what would be the fate of bills that used to pass with 51 votes? Gridlock was predestined.

I thought about what the Tea Party and the hyperpartisanship were doing to the institution. Of those twelve Republican senators who supported the treaty, three were retiring either by choice, from fatigue or in defeat. Senator Murkowski would be back, but to earn her next term, she had to overcome a primary defeat and win as a write-in candidate. Scott Brown was worried about biting the Tea Party hand that had first fed him, so he wouldn't cast many more votes in line with Massachusetts. The others? Most would either soon retire in frustration or face brutal primaries. The years 2011 and 2012 weren't going to be easy, and the Republican ranking member on the Foreign Relations Committee, Dick Lugar, would soon succumb to the Tea Party's ammunition.

I didn't want to give in automatically to the pessimism that says "don't try, it can't happen." It seemed premature to think that the Senate was shut down for any further foreign policy debates, and I hoped that perhaps the Tea Party wave had crested and there might be a return to some degree of normalcy.

Ted Kennedy always said that good issues and good ideas find their moment, and you want to have laid the groundwork to be able to seize that moment when it comes. There were two good ideas sitting in front of us that the Foreign Relations Committee had a responsibility to try to put into action. Unfortunately, they both had the words "United Nations" attached to them: the UN Convention on the Law of the Sea and the UN Convention on the Rights of Persons with Disabilities. There was certainly a case to be made that both were reasonably achievable. The Law of the Sea Treaty was being urged on us by the U.S. Navy because freedom of navigation was gospel to them. They wanted the United States to be a party to the treaty because we lived by its rules anyway, and joining gave us a seat at the table.

Hillary Clinton and I were both huge believers in the treaty for geostrategic reasons. While we sat on the sidelines, Russia and other countries were carving up the Arctic and laying claim to the oil and gas riches in that region, but we couldn't take them to task because we were outside the treaty body that provided international legitimacy for Arctic claims. China controlled the production of rare earth minerals—90 percent of the world's supply—and the world relied on that supply for cell phones, computers and weapons systems. Yet we weren't a party to the treaty vital to determining the rules to secure these minerals from the deep ocean seabed.

I wanted to make an effort to move the treaty forward. Dick Lugar supported the treaty, but he was facing a primary from an extremist who had made Dick's residency in Indiana an explosive issue. Dick asked me to wait until his primary was over to push full throttle and not to force a vote. I agreed. Dick had earned that much and more over his thirty-six years in the Senate, and I'd never forgotten his collegiality with me when I was a freshman senator partnering with him on the Philippines.

Hillary and I became a tag team gently pushing the issue. She helped me pull off a public hearing in the committee that brought together America's top diplomat, top defense official and top military officer. Secretary Clinton, Defense Secretary Robert Gates and Joint Chiefs chairman Admiral Michael Mullen all testified in support of the Law of the Sea. I took the campaign in another direction to try to persuade Republicans to give the treaty a look. Reasoning that many Republicans might not want to believe John Kerry and Hillary Clinton, but couldn't ignore the oil industry and the single biggest, most powerful interest group of the conservative movement, I brought in the head of the American Petroleum Institute and the Chamber of Commerce to testify in favor.

But write it off is exactly what the Republicans did. The Tea Party froze the Senate. Dick Lugar lost his primary. The message to the Republicans was clear: work with Democrats and you're toast. After an extensive round of hearings and debate, two swing senators—Kelly Ayotte and Rob Portman—apropos of nothing, signed on to a letter drafted with the rhetoric of the Heritage Foundation: "No international organization owns the seas."

The treaty was dead in the water before it ever had a chance to sail.

Thirty-four senators announced "no" votes, so we didn't even bring it up for a vote. I liked Rob Portman a lot. He was a substantive guy, but he saw the writing on the wall. He was enough of a moderate to be a Tea Party target, and in Ohio he wasn't going to risk his job for a treaty covering the oceans. He and Senator Ayotte together sent a letter to Majority Leader Harry Reid, citing what they called "significant concerns" with the treaty and expressing opposition to ratification. Portman's press release on the letter was proudly headlined "Senators Portman and Ayotte Sink Law of the Sea Treaty." Rob knew better than this. It was just all part of the spectacle and circus the Senate was becoming.

I asked John McCain what had happened. John was unhappy, which might have contributed to his candid response. Jim DeMint was torturing John's wingman, Lindsey Graham, on a daily basis. John told me about the discussion in his caucus about the Law of the Sea Treaty. He told me that DeMint had passed a letter around for signatures opposing it. John had argued against that gamesmanship. He said DeMint had asserted loudly—and John said the words with a roll of his eyes—"we had to be a warrior party, this was war." "A warrior party," John grumbled, adding something to the effect of "most of these guys who want to be warriors have never had a single shot fired at them in their lives."

It wasn't John's caucus anymore, and that was a tragedy. John McCain could be stubborn, ideological and cantankerous as hell. He was no moderate. Admittedly against his own better judgment, to try to win his party's nomination, John had filled out those same silly special interest group questionnaires, but he thought they were bullshit and told me so. He was in public life to do things, not to bow to the false populism of the Tea Party. John was made for the Senate, but made for a Senate that actually worked. Now he saw a Republican caucus that he barely recognized. He and I were determined to make one last fight of the Congress together, as partners once again. We were going to try to force the Senate to pass the Disabilities Treaty.

For John, it was very personal. Bob Dole was one of John's heroes. Bob was minority leader when John and I were freshman senators. Bob had worked every day to stand and walk and use his arms after his injuries in World War II. In the 1970s, as the Vietnam War raged, Senator Dole wore a bracelet with the name of POW John McCain etched on it. When John came to the Senate in 1986, his bond with Bob Dole was unbreakable. When Bob was the Republican nominee for president in 1996, John traveled with him across the country. Now Bob was in a wheelchair, in and out of Walter Reed hospital, in his late eighties. His proudest legislative achievement had been passing the Americans with Disabilities Act. Now Bob asked his protégé John McCain to pass the Convention on the Rights of Persons with Disabilities and make America's legacy on disability rights universal. John and I were a team again, trying to make it happen.

To me, there was nothing controversial about the Disabilities Treaty. It just says you can't discriminate against the disabled. It asks other countries to do what we did twenty-two years ago when we set the example for the world and passed the Americans with Disabilities Act. In four simple words, it says to other countries that don't respect the rights of the disabled, "Be more like us." It didn't require any changes to American law, but it would require other countries to improve their record on disability rights— in effect, taking our gold standard here at home and extending it to the rest of the world.

The Tea Party, however, had a bucket of excuses and conspiracy theories. In 2006, Rick Santorum had been drubbed out of the Senate by eighteen points. Unfortunately, Rick became a lobbyist. Now he was working against the Disabilities Treaty, whipping the grass roots into a frenzy by promising that the treaty would replace parents of disabled children with UN bureaucrats. It was absurd, but it seemed to be working.

We needed sixty-seven votes. We had on our side two former presidential nominees of the Republican Party, Dole and McCain. America's veterans' groups endorsed the treaty, and dozens of veterans in wheelchairs went door-to-door in the Senate for weeks, pleading with Republican senators to do the right thing.

The veterans made a powerful statement, but no statement was more powerful than what I witnessed the day of the vote. In the nearly thirty years that I'd been there, I had never once seen a former majority leader come to the Senate floor for a vote, but eighty-nine-year-old Bob Dole was wheeled into the chamber by his wife, former senator Elizabeth Dole from North Carolina. Bob Dole wasn't on the Senate floor that day to support the United Nations, under whose auspices and convention this human rights treaty had been written, and certainly not to undermine the sovereignty he'd nearly given his life for in World War II. He was there because he wanted other countries to treat people with disabilities the way we do. He was there because he wanted to ensure that when American veterans with disabilities— our wounded warriors—traveled overseas, they would be treated with the same dignity and respect that they received at home.

In the end, only sixty-one senators had the guts to agree with him, that the rest of the world should live by the standard of decency the United States had set in 1990 with its Americans with Disabilities Act.

In 2012, however, this was one of those votes that leaves an indelible mark. Senators who told John McCain and me in private that they wanted to vote for the treaty had folded when it mattered. Fear was driving the Senate, so much so that senators could shake Bob Dole's hand and then send his dream to die. It was a disgrace.

Something is deeply wrong with politics in America when the Senate can't do the things it was created to do. I wondered why some of my colleagues even wanted to be there if they couldn't vote the way their hearts and minds told them. I headed back to my office. The staff had opened a bottle of Scotch that Teddy had given me in 2007, two years before he passed away, with a note: "For use after good votes and bad votes, too." Today marked a little of both. We'd fought a very good fight with a very bad outcome.

A COUPLE OF days after the Disabilities Treaty met its demise on the floor of the Senate, the White House called to say President Obama needed to reach me. I sat behind my desk in the Russell Building, looking out on Constitution Avenue, which was almost pitch dark, illuminated only by the occasional headlights of cars, the glowing lampposts and, there in the distance, the lights on the Capitol dome. God, the days were growing shorter, and I wondered whether my time in the Senate was growing shorter as well. My frustration was building with a Senate that seemed to be a shell of its former self, an institution unable to step up even when the same tried-and-true tactics that had worked for previous generations were applied and appropriate. That gnawed at me: I had learned the lessons of how to unlock the Senate, but the institution had changed. Three tokens of that celebrated Senate history sat on my desk: the framed photo from Teddy on our first day together as colleagues in 1985, with its promise of a "beautiful relationship"; John Glenn's carved wooden Buddha, the lacquer on its well-worn belly rubbed off from so many entreaties for good luck; and the sailor's compass that John Warner left me the day I moved into his old office.

My internal compass left me no doubt whatsoever that I needed to find new ways of working on and fighting for the issues that had defined my life ever since I'd come home from Vietnam, and possibly find a new place for that fight if the Senate wasn't going to be the Senate anymore. I expected the president's phone call might give me some clarity about where my own compass would soon be pointing. I leaned forward in my chair as I waited for President Obama to come on the line. I waited and waited until the now familiar voice said my name emphatically: "John!" Barack Obama doesn't beat around the bush. He's not fond of small talk and gets to the point quickly. The White House would have to complete their intensive vetting of me, but he asked me to serve as his secretary of state.

Two months later, John McCain and Hillary Clinton would join together with Elizabeth Warren to introduce me on an unfamiliar side of the dais at the Foreign Relations Committee for my confirmation hearing—a place I hadn't sat in since 1971. Two days later, I'd be confirmed by the Senate 94–3. Supreme Court justice Elena Kagan, my friend since the days she had served in the White House in the 1990s, came across the street to the Capitol to swear me in right where so much of my public service had occurred—in the historic Foreign Relations Committee room in the U.S. Capitol.

I made a bittersweet peace with leaving the Senate and was ready for my new chapter.

CHAPTER 16

Diplomacy in a Dangerous World

"I AM PROUD TO take on this job because I want to work for peace."

Vice President Biden had graciously come to the State Department to publicly swear me in as the sixty-eighth secretary of state, five days after my private swearing-in made me official. The ornate Benjamin Franklin Room on the eighth floor of the State Department was packed with hundreds of my friends and family from the journey of my life, from the soccer fields in high school, including a former Marine who now ran the FBI, to the debate team in college, brothers from the Navy, friends from Massachusetts and the campaigns from 1972 through 2004 and 2008, colleagues from the Senate, and my staff alumni from over twenty-eight years. It was one of those "this is your life" moments. But it was also a moment of great clarity. My time as secretary of state would fly by, and I wanted to make every day count.

Two days before, I had stood in the lobby of the Harry S Truman Building and spoken to a sea of my new colleagues—a tradition at the department for every incoming secretary. I told them that the Senate was in my blood, but the Foreign Service was in my genes. I held up my first diplomatic passport: Number 2927—and its faded black-and-white picture of eleven-year-old John Kerry, "Height: 4-foot-3, Hair: Brown." The first stamp in it was from 1954 in Le Havre.

Fifty-nine years had passed—my hair was far from brown—but at its best, the work of the State Department in 2013 was still what it had been during that very different era. Good people, too many whose names never make it into the newspapers, get up every day and do their best to advance our country's interests and live up to our values.

I wanted to convey to the department the kind of secretary I hoped to be. I had connected with all my available predecessors to talk about the job. They were generous with their time; it was a welcoming, close-knit club of people who had done a tough job and genuinely wanted to help their successors of either political party. Their advice was as invaluable as it was incongruous. James Baker told me that you have to run the department instead of letting the department run you. He said that your value comes from traveling and doing hands-on diplomacy. Colin Powell said the opposite: don't travel, stay in Washington, your most important job is to manage the department. George Shultz was somewhere in the middle of those two poles, as were Hillary Clinton and Madeleine Albright. Henry Kissinger stressed the importance of staying close to the national security advisor, wise words from a man who had served in both positions and written the book (literally) on diplomacy from both perspectives.

The diversity of opinion also extended to the small details. Condi Rice stressed big goals like the importance of reforming international assistance and development programs for a modern world while Colin Powell wisely, practically pointed out the importance of tangible accomplishments like fixing the department's email and bringing it out of a distant technological era. Some said it was important to rely on special envoys, others said a glut of envoys had "remuddled" the diplomatic architecture. All agreed there were some diplomatic efforts only a secretary could bring to reality, and all agreed that quality time to get work done is much shorter than it looks on a calendar.

I found truth in everything they said. But like every secretary before me, I had to make the job my own. I sent an email to the entire department—in Washington and overseas—in which I recalled a previous chapter in my life. When I inherited PCF-94, I was assigned to be skipper of a crew that had been on the rivers, in grueling combat, a lot longer than I had. I had to earn my credibility with them, not the other way around. I was secretary of state, assigned the "S" on a flowchart consisting of an alphabet soup of dozens of dizzying acronyms from "D" to "DMR" to "S Specials" and more. I sat atop the organization, but I was its newest addition: I had much to learn from those who were already there, and I wanted to listen closely to their perspectives.

I did bring to this enterprise some insight I'd gleaned many years before. My dad had sometimes found life in the Foreign Service consumed too much by bureaucracy, by a culture that could discourage creative problem-solving. Young officers I met with had a different spin on that same experience: they said that the culture was sometimes "risk-averse," that the incentives didn't always empower those who might fail greatly while trying to achieve greatly. Ambassador Tom Shannon, the department's diplomatic dean on all issues Latin America, said the best way to empower smart risk-taking was for the secretary to model it himself. I took that to heart. I wanted everyone to know it was best to "get caught trying" rather than merely, as Bill Burns warned, "admiring a problem."

I was lucky also to have a mix of State Department veterans and my own Kerry Senate family close by to help me in the mission ahead. David McKean returned as my head of policy and planning, a position made famous by George Kennan. David was as insightful as ever and never hesitated to disagree when I needed a different point of view. Heather Higginbottom, who had been my legislative director, left a Senate-confirmed position at the Office of Management and Budget to serve as deputy secretary and lead a modernization effort for the State Department and USAID. U.S. Ambassador to France Charlie Rivkin, an old friend, and Ambassador to Italy David Thorne, the oldest of friends, joined me in Washington, as did Drew O'Brien, my Massachusetts state director. I poached a *Boston Globe* reporter, Glen Johnson, who would accompany me for each of the 1,417,576 miles I would travel through ninety-one countries. It was a good team of old and new, career and political, and I felt confident about our ability to get the job done.

No matter how hard you plan in advance what you want to do as secretary of state, no matter how many interagency meetings are held in windowless rooms trying to anticipate every contingency and create policy guardrails and metrics to define whether as an administration you're doing what you set out to do (and we held more meetings than I can count), diplomacy isn't a science. It involves human decisions, imperfect actors around the globe and impossible-to-predict crises.

At any time, a call from an embassy, a cable on your desk or a crisis wake-up alarm in the middle of the night demands a rapid decision whether and how to engage. Usually, what's not an option is doing nothing. Wishing the problem away or saying "Well, that's not what we planned to do" doesn't work. The United States needs to lead.

By the same token, even as I focused on major strategic priorities, and even as I confronted crises coming at us from unlikely places, sometimes there are opportunities in problems that couldn't be solved but could be prevented from getting worse, or in some cases falling apart or imploding. I learned that just by dint of our engagement, good things could happen, and if we didn't move, usually no one else would.

I took to heart two lessons shared with me by a couple of experienced hands—my former majority leader George Mitchell and his boss President

Bill Clinton while they were working on the Northern Ireland peace process. Mitchell described it as "seven hundred days of failure and one day of success." Likewise, Clinton made the same point: "If I'm working on a problem, at least I know it's not getting worse." It was great advice. If I could do something that was better than staying on the sidelines, it was worth the additional jet lag.

The world we live in today doesn't leave you much choice anyway. It's vastly more complicated because change comes at us faster than ever before. It's more crowded, more interdependent, less hierarchical, more influenced by nonstate actors, and filled with connections between economic issues and social, political and security concerns. Technology has brought the world closer together, while also empowering anyone and everyone to spread messages of hate far and wide with the click of a button.

Conflicts are fought using an eclectic mix of weapons and often by combatants who wear no uniforms and have no permanent address. The world is more prosperous than it has ever been, but the overall picture matters little to those left outside the prosperity: the debate over income inequality is overdue and rages in almost every country. Each day, there are more people in the world, putting additional pressure on limited natural resources. Big chunks of the Middle East, Central America and Africa are torn by violence, creating a record flow of refugees. The age-old problems of nationalist ambition and religious extremism are testing the resilience of the rule of law. And the devil's marriage of technology and terror means thirteenth-century battles are fought with twenty-first-century weapons.

My inbox was always full. The world wouldn't wait just because we were busy with one negotiation or another. Managing the agenda required a fast-moving, skilled team. Diplomacy done right—whether it's strategic or crisis-driven—requires groundwork: research, briefings, the right talking points, the appropriate coordination of messages and actions—from the sequencing of first interventions by ambassadors and trips by assistant secretaries all the way through the call or visit by a secretary of state.

The administration put all hands on deck to tackle simultaneously an extraordinary number of problems: whether it was Ebola ravaging Africa, counterterrorism in the Horn of Africa, holding reluctant feet to the fire on free and fair elections from Nigeria to Sri Lanka or talking to an African president about the dangers of his appeals to anti-gay bigotry, there was always some intervention needed. If a country didn't hear it from the secretary of state, they could dismiss it as a lower-order priority—a pet issue of someone, somewhere, rather than the government of the United States.

So I'd find myself on the phone at two in the morning from Europe asking China's foreign minister to consider contributing more—to fight Ebola. As my colleague from Canada, the conservative foreign minister John Baird, once told me: "If the United States doesn't lead on this, no one will."

Christmas 2013 was supposed to be a break after a year of intense travel and hands-on diplomacy. I delayed and delayed joining my family, but finally met up with them on Christmas Eve morning—and proceeded to spend the next seven days largely working out of the shed behind my house that Diplomatic Security had equipped with state-of-the-art, secure video technology. The State Department's mobile communications technology paid off: a security crisis was reaching a boiling point in South Sudan, and we would need to spend our holidays deciding whether it was safe to keep our embassy open or whether we had to evacuate to protect our people.

South Sudan was a profound disappointment. I had invested hundreds of hours as chairman of the Foreign Relations Committee trying to help the country become independent and secure. I'd missed my chief of staff's wedding on a November 2010 emergency trip to deliver a private letter from President Obama to the stakeholders. Despite all the United States had done to prepare the way for a peaceful, successful referendum on independence, and after all the world had done to invest in this new democracy, within two years it was hanging on for dear life. After the referendum in 2011, I had received a text from George Clooney, who was passionate about South Sudan: "So, now the hard part begins." He was right. South Sudan was showing the world that one vote doesn't make a country.

President Salva Kiir, whom I had gotten to know well, appeared distracted from his duties. The politics of South Sudan had become more and more tribal—a different kind of sectarianism. Kiir dismissed his vice president, Riek Machar. Neither man evinced the slightest quality of statesmanship. As Christmas 2013 approached, violence was breaking out—all because of petty squabbles among politicians. At the State Department, we had cobbled together temporary agreements and broader efforts to at least provide a framework for a political reconciliation, but not every young democracy has a Thomas Jefferson or Alexander Hamilton—people who may disagree vehemently but are patriots above all.

So here we were at Christmas: every couple of hours, I was talking to our embassy in Juba and the White House as we tracked militias and fighters we worried were advancing on the capital city. If they reached Juba, and if the fighting devolved into chaos, we would have to evacuate, with tragic consequences. When the United States pulls out of a country, others follow. The country could descend into civil war. We did not want to leave unless we absolutely had to, but neither were we going to put American lives in jeopardy if South Sudan's politicians weren't willing or able to protect their own capital. It was touch-and-go. I pressed both Kiir and Machar in phone call after phone call to understand that if things went to hell over their squabbling, we would hold them each responsible. On Christmas morning, I called to reach Kiir and was told he was unavailable, busy celebrating the holiday. I was incredulous. "If I'm working on Christmas because of his security situation, he better be working too," I said, and asked that the message be passed on. He called back—grudgingly—and insisted there was nothing to fear. We made it through the holiday week with only a few more scares in Juba. Insurgencies don't pause for Christmas and they don't pop champagne corks on New Year's Eve, but we woke up in 2014 knowing a major crisis had been averted and, for now, this country we had helped midwife into existence would not have to be abandoned in its cradle. There were moments that week when I was tempted to call certain members of Congress who had attacked us over Benghazi and ask whether they too were working on South Sudan. The entire State Department was forgoing the holidays to do the work of protecting America's diplomatic family.

There was no time to waste complaining. Our jobs were a privilege. The work mattered to millions of people. When I look back at the diplomacy that didn't always occupy center stage, from Bogotá to Kiev, I know our work saved lives in a complicated, fractious, troubled world. I know that we used every minute we had, exhausted every option available to us.

AS I'VE SAID, the roller-coaster ride of high public office demands a lot from families. It's hard to wall off family life from a global crisis. But on Fourth of July weekend 2013, it wasn't a crisis on the other end of the world—it was a far more personal and frightening close call in our house on a quiet afternoon.

After months of nonstop travel, our family had looked forward to celebrating Independence Day together in rare quiet on Nantucket. It was the place where Teresa and I had been married, and always provides a picturesque getaway on Independence Day when the fireworks illuminate the harbor. My grandson Alexander would be joining me for his first sail, a rite of passage especially anticipated given how much I had been away from home.

Instead, I spent most of my time on the phone. Egypt under President Mohamed Morsi was coming apart at the seams. Tahrir Square was filled once more with thousands of frustrated Egyptians, teeming crowds, just as it had been two years earlier under Hosni Mubarak. I was working the phones, pressing my counterparts in the Gulf and teaming with the United States embassy in Cairo to do what we could to mitigate a slow-motion disaster still unfolding and at least avoid a bloodbath. I feared Morsi could be killed, or that the capital could descend into chaos. We were trying to keep a lid on the situation, while countries opposed to Morsi and those who supported him pushed their own agendas, jockeying for influence. We were working feverishly to try to keep our finger in the dike. By July 3, Morsi was in military custody.

Too quickly, Vanessa and her family went home to Boston. The time had raced by. Teresa was upstairs. I was on the phone, again, when I heard a panicked voice.

"Mr. Secretary—can you come up quickly. Your wife is very sick."

I raced upstairs to our bedroom. Teresa was writhing in the throes of a massive seizure. Our aide called Diplomatic Security and 911. I jumped on the bed, grabbed Teresa's arms to keep her from hurting herself. She was straining for breath. For a moment, I was really scared she had stopped breathing altogether.

I whispered to her "Hang in there—stay with us," as she seemed to drift further and further away. It was a matter of minutes, but it felt like hours before the convulsing stopped. She lay still, barely conscious. The medics arrived, and soon we were riding to the hospital by ambulance—a cavalcade of state police cars, local police, Diplomatic Security and ambulance as we raced through the tiny streets of Nantucket to Cottage Hospital.

The hospital attendants did a terrific job of getting Teresa stabilized. Dr. Timothy Lepore, who knew most of the members of our family through a tick bite or fever or other malady, supervised. He decided we needed to get her to Massachusetts General Hospital in Boston. We hastily made arrangements for a plane to leave immediately.

When we finally arrived in an ambulance at MGH, where Vanessa and her husband were practicing physicians, we had a team of experts ready to evaluate Teresa's condition. We began a long road of tests, rehabilitation, diagnosis, more tests and more evaluations and varied medications.

The afternoon felt eerily, ominously like it did five summers before, rushing back from western Massachusetts to see Vicki Kennedy right after she had received the worst possible diagnosis about Teddy. Thank God, the doctors quickly eliminated the potential of Teresa having a tumor or a stroke. Those were our most immediate fears. How blessed we were and how unfair life is for so many.

The doctors told us it was just too early to draw many conclusions about

Teresa's long-term prognosis. While there was no sign of brain damage, there was an impact on her balance and the speed with which she could process things. It would take time before one could ascertain how it would all settle out.

There was no explanation for what caused the seizure, but life was not the same as it had been. As I sat holding Teresa's hand, my mind drifted back to our lunch with Secretary George Shultz months before, during the time I was awaiting Senate confirmation. Teresa knew George well from the Reagan years. She left our lunch excited for the possibilities of traveling with me during my years as secretary, as George's late wife, Obie, had done on many of George's diplomatic missions. Obie was to this day revered inside the State Department, remembered for her dedication not just to her husband but to the institution. For Teresa, who spoke five languages and had studied to be a translator at the United Nations, it had been a hopeful time. She was invested in the work ahead. Now, that aspiration would be deferred.

While we were in the hospital, an aide showed me an article online. Glenn Beck speculated that Teresa's "illness" had been staged—a "Wag the Dog" moment to distract from what was happening in Egypt. I wanted for a moment to have him sitting there watching a worried family grasping for answers. Even at life's most private, difficult moments, some always seemed to find room for the vilest of politics. But we didn't have time to dwell on Glenn Beck. The compassion of the doctors and nurses, and the supportive messages and calls from our administration family—President Obama, Michelle, Joe and Jill Biden, Chuck and Lilibet Hagel—were what really mattered, and what buoyed our spirits. That kind of human reaction was a complete contrast to the filth circulating in the fever swamps of the right-wing blogosphere.

For the time being, the seizure changed life for Teresa. For the duration of my time as secretary, she was not able to travel with me. In the beginning, she had someone around her twenty-four hours a day to help prevent falls. For the next four years Teresa underwent her own aggressive physical exercise and rehab efforts. She took anti-seizure medication despite the side effects, which would slow anyone down. She stayed at it and finally, just last fall, she got off the anti-seizure pills altogether, which has made a huge difference. Our whole family remains in awe of her discipline, her pluck, her determination not to throw in the towel but to fight back. Through it all she has shown great good humor and courage, and through it all she encouraged me to press on, cheering me on from afar in a way that is always tender and touching. It wasn't the life she'd planned, but determination to overcome it and her strong spirit helped her navigate the road ahead as she did so many of life's sad, sudden turns.

WHEN I ARRIVED at Foggy Bottom, it was logical that I'd end up being the principal interlocutor for Afghanistan, to use a terrible piece of diplo-speak jargon. It's also safe to say that no one was especially jealous that the assignment was headed my way!

I had a strong relationship with Hamid Karzai, particularly after the role I'd played as chairman of the Senate Foreign Relations Committee resolving the 2009 election crisis. I also had strong relationships on the other side of the border in Pakistan.

Afghanistan presented tricky choices for President Obama's second term. The Bush administration had turned its attention to Iraq to the exclusion of implementing or even developing a strategy for success in Afghanistan. In 2008, then candidate Obama had run pledging to put Afghanistan back on course and win what many came to call "the good war," in contrast to the disastrous war of choice in Iraq. The first term had marked both a surge of troops and a surge of diplomacy to jump-start the progress, some of it successful, some notably less so. My friend Richard Holbrooke had died trying to break the political gridlock, trying to get somewhere, somehow—his big heart literally just gave out.

By 2013, to many Americans, Afghanistan had simply become the "endless" war. Every year as we moved further and further away from fresh memories of September 11, it was easier for citizens and for members of Congress themselves to wonder whether it was worthwhile to be there at all. I wouldn't be candid if I didn't acknowledge that many war-weary members of the president's national security team had the same sense about Afghanistan: they were increasingly tired of the emotional ups and downs of life with Karzai. Furthermore, twelve years after we'd invaded and overthrown the Taliban, we were still spending unbelievable amounts of money—and still losing lives. We were doing so in a country where our strategic interest was principally eliminating a platform for terrorism, not building a Jeffersonian democracy. We were spending infinitely more than we were in countries where our interests were more urgent.

All of this was true, but it didn't change the fact that in Afghanistan we had a big presence—diplomatically and militarily—and that the last time we wound down our commitment to Afghanistan too quickly, too precipitously, we ended up with the Taliban and al-Qaeda training camps and sanctuary for the world's worst terrorists. My view coming into the administration was that, yes, we had to transition in Afghanistan from a war foot-ing and a permanent dependency to a country and a government that could stand on their own. That would demand more work at the State Department, not less, with less leverage than in the days when Afghanistan was a cause uniting the world.

I plunged into the work on Afghanistan right away. One of my first calls was to President Karzai in February 2013. My experience with Karzai taught me that it was important to call and listen even when you didn't have something specific to ask of him. By turns charming, volatile and emotional, Karzai had previously made the point to me that too many Americans sim-ply dictate terms and lecture. He was sometimes maddening to deal with, but he was a patriot first and foremost. He wanted his country to remain to-gether as a country—something seared into him by his father's assassina-tion and his own exile and journey home from Pakistan, as well as his work with the Afghan Northern Alliance. We started talking right away about the hard work it would require to see another successful democratic tran-sition in Afghanistan. I found that if I stayed in close touch with him, that helped modulate the public comments he'd make, which were sometimes quite unhelpful. More important, I knew that even as Karzai accepted that Afghanistan's 2014 elections would mark his exit as president, he was still going to be a player in the country with influence both behind the scenes and publicly.

Karzai warned me: 2013 wasn't going to be an easy year. Negotiations were gridlocked over joint status of forces agreements to allow the United States to keep troops on Afghan soil, having become particularly volatile after some incidents where civilians had been killed. Karzai was always convinced (and, frankly, not without some justification) that whatever trou-ble he faced was the work of Pakistan and its intelligence services.

I decided to make a surprise trip to Kabul less than a month after I was sworn in. I wanted to try to finesse some of those issues one-on-one with Karzai and also lay the groundwork for a more collaborative relationship in the run-up to the 2014 Afghan presidential election.

I landed in Kabul aboard a C-130, having come straight from Jordan and, before that, Baghdad. I was greeted by Ambassador Jim Cunningham and the bright twenty-five-year-old diplomat Jim had assigned to be my control officer—the tour guide for matters both substantive and mundane who shepherded me through the entire visit. She was idealistic, outgoing and energetic. Her name was Anne Smedinghoff. She had grown up in the suburbs of Chicago. After Johns Hopkins, she'd joined the Foreign Service. She was just four months from her next assignment and was working hard on her Arabic. She reminded me of my own daughters. I was struck by her curiosity about the country in which she was serving and could tell that, even while serving in a country where security was a constant challenge, she was immersing herself in Afghan life and culture—always a sign of a promising diplomat. Two weeks later, Anne was killed delivering books to schoolchildren in Zabul Province, a victim of a suicide vest blast detonated by a Taliban terrorist. Three soldiers, their interpreter and Anne were lost in the blast—and another State Department diplomat was terribly injured and medevacked out of Afghanistan. I got the news early that Saturday morning as I prepared to leave for Asia, and was sick that someone I'd met and been so impressed by was suddenly gone. I flashed back to the calls I'd placed to families in Massachusetts as a senator when they'd lost a son or daughter in Iraq or Afghanistan. Here we were at Andrews Air Force Base, ready to fly to Japan, and yet our hearts were back in Afghanistan. I asked for the phone number to connect with Anne's family. The State Department Operations Center—our central clearinghouse for all kinds of information—swung into action and an alert appeared on my senior staff's BlackBerrys: "S is Connected on NOK Call." NOK—next of kin.

I picked up the phone to tell Anne's parents the terrible, almost unfathomable news that no parent should ever have to hear. There aren't words that could ever meet the test of such a horrific moment. I thought of Anne and the meaning of her loss every time I heard an Afghan politician dismiss the contributions and sacrifices the United States had made for his country, and I thought of her every time an American—congressmen or pundits mostly—hastily announced we should just leave Afghanistan and let the country fall apart. It mattered to me how we transitioned, and it mattered to the United States whether we left Afghanistan as a country—or in chaos. I believed we could choose an outcome worth the sacrifice.

But it wouldn't be easy. Karzai was shrewd and calculating. He was going to make the next Afghan government own the status of forces agreement for NATO and American troops, even as he engaged with me on negotiating the framework that would give us what we needed to stay in Afghanistan at all as a security partner. But Karzai's punt to the next government made the outcome of the 2014 elections all the more important.

The stakes couldn't have been bigger. There was a very real concern that the Afghan state was at risk of fracturing from internal divisions if the elections didn't lead to a government capable of providing cohesion. It didn't take a great leap of imagination to think that civil war was just around the corner.

The first round of voting in June went pretty smoothly. The process of getting a wide spectrum of candidates to run was successful, and international engagement was coordinated and constant. Dr. Ashraf Ghani and Dr. Abdullah Abdullah emerged as the two front-runners. They were a study in contrasts.

Ghani was a pro-Western Pashtun nationalist with a flair for technocratic jargon. Having spent much of his career at the World Bank in the United States, Ghani had a difficult time connecting with some of the local politicians. He had a brilliant mind but was an inexperienced politician. Sometimes he was prone to overreacton. He was also an intensely private man who had a tendency toward micromanagement that hadn't always served him well.

Abdullah, by contrast, was cool, calm, studious and soft-spoken. He didn't have Ghani's vision or technocratic expertise, but he always had a sense of the moment. He was an effective coalition builder and knew how to work behind the scenes. He was a good pol.

The view from those who had been working the Afghanistan desk was that either Ghani or Abdullah could be a big improvement over Karzai, if they could get their foothold. Both looked to the West for a partner and wanted a relationship with the United States. Both were well known to us and good leaders in different ways: Abdullah was the natural politician; Ghani was the cerebral policy wonk with a PowerPoint for every occasion.

The problem was that the second round of Afghanistan's presidential election in June was a debacle. We thought that, regardless of how you examined the results, the outcome would be a Ghani win. But charges of fraud and other irregularities cast a pall over what should have been a triumphant moment for the Afghan people.

It was not up to the United States to determine who would lead Afghanistan—nor should it have been. And we supported no individual candidates throughout the process. But it soon became clear that breaking this impasse and restoring the legitimacy and credibility of the electoral process required Afghan electoral institutions to address serious and extensive allegations, including voting irregularities in provinces like Paktika and Khost.

Coming out of a hotly contested presidential election, each candidate honestly thought and continued to believe he had won. For Abdullah, it was déjà vu—he believed he had won in 2009 and he believed that he had put country over ambition back then. He wasn't about to do so again without a fight. Abdullah tried to manage his constituency, but it was clear that his people were growing restless. In July, one of Abdullah's key supporters threatened to form a parallel government of twelve to fourteen breakaway provinces. One of my deputies warned me that he thought secession and even civil war were real possibilities; our ambassador in Kabul argued that the risk of a coup was real. I asked my team what the implications would be if we cut off all assistance. The answer I got was pretty sobering: the Afghan army would disband; the police would stop being paid and attrition would grind away most of the gains we'd made; clinics and schools would close, leaving millions of boys and girls without a future. In short, the country would go back to the turmoil of the 1990s, when the civil war flared.

We had to take control of the situation before it imploded, because we were in real jeopardy of losing everything and because the costs of ignoring this problem were growing by the day. I also knew that Congress was at a breaking point. Karzai had poisoned the bilateral relationship and American casualties were mounting. If we couldn't get two qualified, pro-Western candidates to form a government and prevent another civil war after all that investment in blood and treasure, what were we fighting for? Many members of Congress were ready to wash their hands of Afghanistan.

The situation was so dire that some people were urging me not to get caught in the middle of it. "Don't diminish your currency," they warned. "Don't own Afghanistan—you saved it before, everyone knows it's a mess, don't touch it."

I thought the concern was pointless: the United States wasn't going to sit on the sidelines while Afghanistan burned. In diplomacy, showing up is half the battle. We still had a chance to avoid a terrible outcome. And I thought that if I made a visit, that could create breathing room for diplomacy—which, at this point, meant at least giving Abdullah a lifeline so he could calm his followers.

I told Ghani and Abdullah that I was headed to Kabul and appealed to them to give my trip a shot. Abdullah could dissuade his constituents against any rash actions on the pretext that he needed to see what we'd accomplish during my seventy-two-hour visit.

My approach was to listen and learn. I had my team put together a list of the key power brokers and proposals. Our goal was to work through the election irregularities and find a way forward on the political track. In any negotiation, you need to know what you want and you need to understand both the substance of the disagreement and the politics. Abdullah wanted an audit of the voting in four or five key provinces, which were mostly Pashtun areas that he claimed had voted in some cases five times higher than in previous elections and a hundred to one in favor of Ghani. His team wanted to throw out the votes from those provinces altogether. I was very clear that that approach wouldn't fly. Ghani's people were adamant they had had a brilliant mobilization plan for getting out Pashtun voters who would otherwise be attracted to the Taliban. To challenge the fact of their participation, they argued, was to threaten the stability of the country. In their view, any questioning of the results should be on an equal basis. So we spent a lot of time deliberating and debating what role the UN would play and how to guarantee the integrity of the process.

On July 2, the situation looked bleak. The way I saw it, we had two options: make the process work and try to conciliate Abdullah, or promote some sort of power-sharing arrangement.

We were nearing a critical moment in the negotiations when, in a surprise move, Ghani picked up on the idea of forming a unity government. I always suspected he knew this idea was popular among some factions of the Northern Alliance. Maybe he was just saying what Abdullah wanted to hear. Maybe he was searching for a reasonable compromise between two extremes. Either way, the proposal for power sharing bought us some breathing space. I worked closely with our special representative for Afghanistan and Pakistan, Dan Feldman, whom I'd known and liked since he was on my foreign policy team in the 2004 campaign, and we built an engagement strategy. Dan had worked as a deputy to Richard Holbrooke. He proved himself to be an extremely hard worker, dogged like his mentor. Dan and I stayed in constant touch with both sides and met with them virtually nonstop over those seventy-two hours.

That's when we had a breakthrough.

We were debating the finer points of the recount in four or five contested provinces when Ghani looked me dead in the eye and said, "Let's just audit everything." I immediately embraced the idea. Ghani knew this was a smart move. It would increase his moral authority without conceding any foul play during the elections. He didn't believe that his campaign had done anything to encourage fraud, but his campaign had benefited from fraudulent votes.

The audit wasn't a silver bullet. But I knew we needed a clear and verifiable process that would make certain that the numbers added up.

Convincing both sides to move forward required some doing. After one particularly long discussion, I invited both candidates and their teams into the ambassador's residence at our embassy. I met with them separately, but I delivered the same message.

I told them that the United States of America and dozens of other countries had invested for more than a decade in Afghanistan—thousands of our soldiers had died and spilled blood on their behalf, and for the rest of my life, I had to be able to look Anne Smedinghoff's parents in the eyes and tell them that the men running Afghanistan were worthy of Anne's sacrifice. Countries had made long-term commitments to Afghanistan's future—but if that future was stolen because two men who wanted to be president of Afghanistan couldn't work out their differences, the responsibility of what happened would be theirs. Leaders have to lead and put personal feelings aside. I told them that they were running the risk of civil war, of complete and total implosion.

I then turned to Ghani, put my hand on his shoulder and said, "Ashraf, you're going to be president. Abdullah will help you implement a common agenda. But you have to be willing to transfer real power to him and give him the opportunity to share in governance, because it is in the interest of the country."

After about forty-five minutes, the candidates and their teams went on the patio for *iftar* prayers against an amber sky, just as the sun was setting. When they came back, they agreed to the audit and the need to form a national unity government. Abdullah said to me later that this was a turning point. Ashraf told me that both sides were on track to replay the events that had led to the civil war and that their agreement saved "between one hundred and one million lives."

In my press conference at the UN mission in Kabul, I laid out the concrete steps and commitments that, if implemented, would move Afghanistan closer to the vision of a sovereign, stable and unified democracy.

After the press conference, Ghani said he needed time to engage his constituents before he could sign the agreement. Back in Washington, the reports I was getting weren't good. The monitoring and auditing process wasn't going well. The teams of both candidates were at odds over how the new CEO position for Abdullah would operate, whether he would chair the Council of Ministers, and who would have power over appointments.

We knew that Ghani was always going to have a hard time navigating the transition from a winner-take-all election to a power-sharing accord. The ink on the agreement wasn't even dry and yet the agreement was on life support. Even as we were working to get the political negotiations back on track, we had to wrestle with problem after problem on the audit. I made another trip to Kabul in August. We identified several outstanding issues and tried to get Ghani and Abdullah to resolve them. On September 3, I spoke with both men by phone. I talked about the importance of an agreed description of the outcome that would bring legitimacy to the result and confer it on the elected president and how the statement should also acknowledge real problems in the electoral process. Ghani focused much more on the need to vindicate the outcome and the presidency, but he did acknowledge that the audit had turned up fraud, which I said would need to be part of a common narrative describing the election. I encouraged Ghani to attend the NATO summit in Cardiff with Abdullah in order to iron out their political agreement.

My conversations with Abdullah were focused more on the impasses in the draft political agreement, especially but not exclusively the issue of the CEO chairing weekly cabinet meetings. I noted on several occasions the extensiveness of Ghani's proposal of delegated powers to the CEO in the draft text. I argued that the agreement needed to close and that Abdullah couldn't afford to walk away, forcing us and the UN into a position of defending the audit without a political agreement or an agreed narrative about the election.

On September 17, Abdullah convened a tribal *shura* to build support for the unity government. Special Representative Dan Feldman, Ambassador Jim Cunningham, UN Special Representative Jan Kubis and some seventy of Abdullah's worthies were in the crowd. In total, they talked for six hours, until about 2:00 a.m. Kabul time. The *shura* got off to an inauspicious start. Many doubted that Abdullah had achieved a good deal for them. His team reached out to me and asked if I'd talk to them on speakerphone. So here I was, half a world away, attempting to persuade a tentful of tribal elders that their interests lay with the unity government, not against it. I talked to them about the definition of "country"—not as a sectarian institution or a spoils system—but as a nation with a common purpose. I told them that Abdullah represented them well and how persuasively he argued for the sharing of power. In an election, I argued, often there are discrepancies and challenges, but you have to move forward. I said that "compromise" was the watchword, and that the United States was supportive, but that both sides were running the risk of losing that support.

I concluded by saying, "If you fail to reach agreement, many people will ask themselves why Afghanistan still deserves so much international funding and other support. We outsiders can't want political stability in Afghanistan more than you do—we can't want to create a chance for a better future more than you do. The draft agreement may not have everything you wanted; no agreement in circumstances like this could. But it is a good agreement. It is a fair agreement, and it will give your team real power and influence in the next government."

The tide shifted. A majority backed Abdullah and we were back on track. I talked to Abdullah again later that week by phone. He thanked me for my intervention and said that without the U.S. commitment, the negotiation would have never reached this moment. He said that it had been an exhausting process. He told me that he saw no alternative to the unity government. Both sides had to live up to their responsibilities. Before we got off the phone, he said simply, "Time spent on negotiations with Ghani is time spent on investing in the unity government." I believed we were on the right path.

On September 18, my team hosted hours of proximity talks because the candidates didn't want to be in the same room until there was final agreement on language. It was tough work, but we made progress. In the course of the discussions we actually had to invent a new Dari word that meant "equitable" because no such word existed in that language. The secret to diplomacy in a dangerous world? Speak softly and carry a Dari dictionary.

On September 21, Ghani and Abdullah officially signed the agreement for the unity government. It was a joyful moment. It is easy today to underestimate the measure of courage and leadership that that agreement demanded and that these men continue to show. Yes, there were many high-wire moments when it seemed just as likely that Afghanistan's political future could lurch in dangerous directions. But in the end, statesmanship and compromise triumphed.

Tough decisions still lie ahead. Afghanistan today faces huge economic and security challenges, but it has a chance of being known as a country, not just a war. It was worth the diplomacy it took to get to this point. I have hope for Afghanistan because I know there's a generation to come that doesn't want to fall backward into the terror and travails their parents and grandparents knew. Once, my staff handed me a letter from a young Afghan girl who had earned a scholarship from the State Department to study at the American University of Afghanistan. One line stood out to me. She wrote about the importance of education and women role models and how her goal is not just to help herself, but to lift her community, her society and her country. She said very simply, "I want to be one of them." Think about that. She feels ownership over the future that she is creating in Afghanistan, and that's not something that her sisters or her mother could say even a decade ago. But girls all over Afghanistan are saying it today, girls who can grow up to be Afghanistan's own Anne Smedinghoffs. That's a reason to be hopeful that Afghanistan can break the cycle of chaos and tragedy that defined the country for decades. That's reason enough to be glad we stayed at it—to give Afghans not a guarantee, but a chance to succeed on their own.

SCOTT GILBERT DIDN'T pull any punches: it was June 2014, and as Alan Gross headed into his fifth year stuck in a dank Havana prison cell, his ninety-two-year-old mother, Evelyn, lay dying of cancer 1,100 miles away in Plano, Texas. Scott didn't think Alan could hold on any longer.

Alan Gross had been jailed on trumped-up charges, held as a bargaining chip for the Cuban regime, which was determined to secure the release of the so-called Miami Five, Cuban spies imprisoned in the United States. Alan had wasted away in prison, separated from the love of his life, Judy.

But now Scott worried: If Alan wasn't able to say goodbye to his mother, would he be able to hold on with no end in sight?

Scott was not your typical Washington lawyer. He had quit a big white-shoe law firm to start his own practice. He didn't wear suits but he did wear a single diamond stud earring. He rode a Harley-Davidson, loved good wine. He cared about his clients—as people. He wasn't in it for fame or money. He was, above all, a no-bullshit, no-holds-barred advocate for the release of Alan Gross. And now he was worried that his client was giving up.

I couldn't tell Scott that President Obama had created a secret back channel to try to create a new way forward with Cuba, a chance to break through the gridlock and explore a path to a more constructive relationship like those the United States had forged with other longtime enemies, and that slow progress was being made, inch by inch. In my first meeting with the president as secretary of state in 2013, he had told me that he had entrusted his longtime aide Ben Rhodes to take on that delicate assignment, and I was glad to hear it. But that channel had to remain absolutely secret, just as our channel to Iran via Oman had to remain a secret—otherwise those on either side who didn't want to see a change happen could blow up the entire dialogue.

It was too easy in Washington for even those with good intentions to inadvertently spill a secret. I'd learned this lesson the hard way over the years. I know exactly how it happens: you swear one person to secrecy, even tell them that they're the only person you're telling, and confide in them. Then they do the same to someone else. Before you know it, two dozen people all have done the same. There are no secrets in Washington—if you don't want a piece of information to leak out, don't share it beyond those who absolutely need to know, and when you put that rule to the test, you usually realize that very few people actually need to know something! In this case, the stakes were about as high as they get—and so was the level of secrecy.

Cuba had been the third rail of American foreign policy for decades, foolishly so, and almost everyone knew it. Ninety miles from America, the Castro regime had outlasted American president after American president—all of whom had pledged to tighten the screws a little more to bring freedom and democracy to what I still remembered President Kennedy calling an "imprisoned island." It had never worked. All it had succeeded in doing was giving the Castros a convenient rhetorical bogeyman in the United States to distract from the fact that, like the Soviet Union, their experiment in a state-controlled economy had failed. But if the revolution had frozen the Cuban people in time, then our response to it had frozen our freedom of action in our own hemisphere: among Latin American countries, there was always a sense that the United States' policy on Cuba made it harder for them to work with us, the big superpower, and many took an unspoken sense of pride in the way Cuba—this tiny island—held on for so many years thumbing its nose at the United States.

I had never been a fan of the Castros. I didn't buy into the romanticism some attached to them or their revolution. Fidel was a brutal ruler, though I gave his brother Raúl credit for opening up some market-based reforms, if only to keep their communist experiment alive. I had no illusions about them.

I saw Cuba much the way I'd seen Vietnam about twenty years before: as an ideological stalemate that didn't serve any real purpose. The opportunity to perhaps break that dynamic once and for all—to try to begin a new chapter the way John McCain and I had helped presidents do on Vietnam—was promising and overdue.

But just as we could never have moved forward on Vietnam without first investigating and creating closure on the POW/MIA question, there was no solving Cuba without bringing Alan Gross home, free and safe. Sometimes when members of Congress to whom I was quite sympathetic on Cuba policy would come to see me as secretary of state, and they'd ask why the Obama administration wouldn't unilaterally make a policy shift and normalize relations with Cuba—a goodwill gesture—I'd remind them about the lesson we learned on Vietnam. "Just think, guys—we couldn't normalize relations with Vietnam until we'd done the most extensive search for POWs in the history of warfare—when the government believed from day one that none were alive. You think the government's going to change on Cuba when we know for a fact that Alan Gross is very much alive and they won't return him?"

That's exactly where we were stuck in the summer of 2014, as I wrestled with whether we could do anything to help Alan Gross, now in a dark, isolated moment of his life.

I arranged a secret phone call with Cuba's foreign minister, Bruno Rodríguez. He was traveling in Brazil, and I was overseas myself, but we connected for the call and I made another humanitarian appeal for Alan's release given his mother's rapid decline in health and the clock ticking away on Alan's own reservoir of hope. Bruno had served as Cuba's ambassador to the UN for many years. I was no stranger to him. He remembered my visit to the Cuban mission at the United Nations as a senator to appeal for Alan Gross's release shortly after Alan had been arrested. He also remembered that I'd been a voice for opening up relations between our countries over the years. I told him in no uncertain terms that if Alan Gross lost hope and died in prison, the relationship between our countries would not move an inch, and that given the sensitivity, it would make an enormous difference if he could see his way to appeal for Alan to be freed to see his mother before she passed. I didn't know whether Bruno was aware of the back channel, and I didn't dare mention it. But my message was clear: don't let this man die.

Bruno called me back the next day to say that he couldn't resolve Alan's situation on short notice. Twenty-four hours later, Alan's mother slipped away. I was sickened.

I wrote a note by hand to Alan and arranged through the head of the U.S. Interests Section in Havana—a savvy diplomat named Jeff DeLaurentis—to have it delivered to Alan in his cell, sealed, unopened. There weren't a lot of words for a moment like this. I just asked him to hold on—to know that efforts were being made to set him free and to trust that we were going to get there in time for him to be back home with Judy, even if it had come too late for his mother.

I prayed it would not come too late for Alan.

Six months later, eight days before Christmas, I was flying back to the United States from Rome knowing that Alan Gross would soon be walking out of prison a free man, headed home.

On the flight, I called the foreign ministers from our hemisphere and key players in Europe to share the news before it broke officially—to tell them that the president was going to announce not just Alan's release and the return of an actual American intelligence asset in exchange for Cubans convicted in the United States, but also the normalization of relations with Cuba and the start of a new policy. Germany's foreign minister chuckled. "What took you so long?" was all he could say. Our close ally in Colombia was ecstatic—negotiations with the FARC on a peace process were at a critical moment; the Cubans were pivotal players in that engagement, and now we might be welcome to become more involved as well. The sense that we'd restored our own freedom of action in our hemisphere was itself a victory.

But nothing could compare to the sense of closure as our plane landed at Andrews Air Force Base and I saw, not far off on the runway, the plane that had brought Alan Gross home after all these years, home for Hanukkah with Judy and their grown children. I walked inside to the waiting area and standing in front of me was Alan. We embraced. I've never felt more humbled to be able to say to someone, "Welcome home." His sense of peacefulness, the absence of rancor, the lack of any anger about years of indignities and years lost—it was remarkable to be there in his presence.

There has always been something that has fascinated me about those who have been through such struggles and come out the other end with a kind of serenity about life. I'd seen it in Nelson Mandela and his astonishing ability to forgive his captors, seen it in Xanana Gusmão, the Timorese political prisoner and resistance fighter imprisoned by Indonesia during the occupation of East Timor, and I'd seen it most closely of course in John McCain: despite the intensity and the pain of having been unjustly deprived of their freedom for so long, every one of them walked out with a sense of higher purpose and a determination to let go of their anger.

Alan Gross was the same way. Together, we shared one of those surreal, only-in-America kind of moments: we watched from a well-worn airport couch on a big-screen television as the networks interrupted the normally scheduled programming so that President Obama could announce to the American people a new policy—while President Raúl Castro simultaneously did the same in his country. I'd seen so many Americans held in other countries killed. But December 17, 2014—for Alan Gross, and for America, this was a very good day.

Eight months later, I went to Havana to raise the flag above our embassy, the first time the Stars and Stripes would fly there since 1961. I was joined at the flag raising by three men: Larry Morris, Francis "Mike" East and Jim Tracy. They had been Marine guards at our embassy in Havana when we closed it in January 1961. They had lowered Old Glory but they also made a bold promise—that one day they would return to Havana and raise the flag again. And return they did. We brought Larry, Mike and Jim down to Havana for the reopening of the embassy and their presence was a stark reminder of the distance we'd traveled. I invited the three of them to fulfill their pledge by presenting the Stars and Stripes to our current military attachment. It completed a circle that must have been unimaginable when they were last on the island.

Later that day, I met again with Cuban foreign minister Bruno Rodríguez. We remembered our conversations about Alan Gross the summer before and talked about just how much had changed in a year's time. Bruno was extremely disciplined and loyal to the Cuban hard-liners. I spent a lot of time on the phone with Bruno between December 2014 and my first trip to Havana as secretary in August 2015. During those eight months, we had had tough negotiations on how the embassy would function, the freedom of movement for our diplomats, the kind of protection they'd have, and other details. Bruno clearly was not prepared to push the bureaucracy on the issues. He was a man of the system and he saw what happened to colleagues who were less cautious. It was a reminder why the back channel had to be done at the chief executive level, not through the complicated, slow Cuban bureaucracy, in order to succeed.

Nonetheless, I was determined to put diplomacy to the test. I presented Bruno and the Cuban government with a four-stage road map, an attempt to apply lessons learned from past efforts to normalize relations between adversaries to the serious and hard work we needed to do with the Cubans. The road map touched on areas where I thought cooperation was possible, such as law enforcement, the environment and natural disasters. It also tackled more sensitive issues, such as human rights, property claims and fugitive criminals. Establishing diplomatic relations didn't mean that we suddenly agreed on all these issues—quite the contrary. But it created formal channels to communicate and make progress, even if it was slow. Engagement made it easier—not harder—to advance our interests and build support throughout the region for our policies.

The Cuba policy shift was done differently from that with Vietnam and it will proceed differently. We'd begun changing course on Vietnam by lifting the trade embargo, which soon flooded Vietnam with American entrepreneurial energy, which in turn ultimately pressured the regime to embrace greater openness. Congress wasn't about to lift the Cuba embargo; the politics of our institutions forbade it, and that meant we couldn't flood Cuba with American innovation and capitalist spirit. And the Cuban hard-liners were in no hurry for major change; that change may begin on their terms with the post-Castro governments. Change will be more incremental. But change will come. And one thing I've learned in all these years in international affairs remains true: all forms of change are easier when diplomats can pick up the phone to connect, or sit face-to-face, and talk to each other openly on behalf of their two countries.

COLOMBIA IS ANOTHER example proving change is possible when leaders take risks to bring it to pass. It is a lesson that should be taught to aspiring diplomats and might be studied in the Middle East when leaders say change there is impossible because they don't have a partner for peace across the table. Above all, it reflects what Colombians decided they wanted for themselves and their future.

I'd been secretary of state several months when I traveled down to Bogotá in August 2013. My meetings with President Juan Manuel Santos and Foreign Minister María Ángela Holguín were warm and constructive. I'd been a longtime friend to Colombia and an advocate for bilateral trade with the United States. More than that, I had been a veteran of Colombia's struggle in the bad old days when the country teetered on the brink of becoming a narco-state. In the late 1990s, as a member of the Senate Foreign Relations Committee, I had teamed up with Joe Biden and Chris Dodd to work with the Clinton administration in helping to put together what became known as Plan Colombia. I still remember one day in the Senate reacting to the news that most of the supreme court, if not the entire supreme court, had been assassinated. If a democracy fell this way, it would be a dangerous bellwether for the future of democracy in the hemisphere. The insurgency there was one of the longest running in the world. Drug cartels, corruption and surging demand for cocaine in the United States made this not just a foreign policy challenge, but a domestic challenge of the first order. Plan Colombia took the fight to the cartels and, over time, brought Colombia back from the edge of oblivion.

But in 2013, the FARC insurgency was still alive in parts of Colombia. I pledged American support for their peace process, and Santos indicated to me privately that, given the politics of his country at the moment, it wasn't yet time for the United States to play a higher-profile role. But he would come back to me down the road.

Before I left Colombia that day, our embassy organized a game of pickup volleyball with Colombians that would remain fresh in my memory a long, long time. It was a game of wheelchair volleyball with some of the toughest guys I'd ever met. Most were amputees who had lost limbs to FARC booby traps; others had been shot and were paralyzed from the waist down. They were veterans of Colombia's brutal drug wars, and they were on a mission not just to mend their wounds, but their country's as well. They gave me a yellow *numero uno* shirt to wear. I quickly donned the jersey and we played a few rounds. But that day, they taught me a lesson or two in grit and determination, not just on the court but in life. Every single one of them was moving forward in life, not looking backward. They wanted to live with a sense of purpose and drive, and they wanted peace; it was a powerful reminder of the stakes in Colombia's decades-long search for peace, but it was also a reminder of how people who have suffered the most can say most clearly the reasons healing and closure are important.

In December 2014, I went back to Bogotá and met with President Santos again. Four previous attempts to negotiate peace with the FARC had failed. He worried that the process was stalling again and that some of the big issues on security, justice and political participation remained unresolved. He signaled that the time was right for the United States to be more engaged in the peace process. I asked him whether he could welcome a special envoy from our side to help him along. It was something I'd kicked around as an idea in my conversations with Assistant Secretary of State for Western Hemisphere Affairs Roberta Jacobson and Counselor of the U.S. Department of State Tom Shannon, who had held Roberta's job years before. But it would work only if Santos wanted it to happen. He said he was positively disposed to the idea, but that he needed to think more. I suspected I knew why he didn't jump at the opportunity: it was December 12, five days before the world would learn that we were making a fresh start with Cuba. Santos was in the dark. He knew that Cuba had brought the FARC to the table, and he no doubt wondered whether Cuba would balk at the United States—its sworn adversary—suddenly bigfooting the process. Five days later, that would no longer be an obstacle.

When I got back to Washington before Christmas, after the hoopla over Cuba had died down a bit, President Santos sent official word: yes, he welcomed an American envoy. Bernie Aronson had served as President George H. W. Bush's assistant secretary of state for the western hemisphere even though he was a Democrat. He was respected by both political parties and was respected in the region. He had time to give back again through public service. Some in the White House worried: With Cuba, Iran, and so many other issues in the world, did this mean the United States was going to own another crisis? I said, why wouldn't we take advantage of the opportunity that the Cuba opening had created for us in our own neighborhood? The president agreed to give it a shot.

The negotiations weren't easy, but Bernie handled them with patience and diligence. President Santos was understandably concerned whether it was possible to close a deal with the FARC amid so much opposition at home. Two hundred thousand Colombians in a country of forty-eight million had been killed in the conflict. That meant that if your family hadn't lost someone to the violence, you knew a family that had. Making peace was no easy feat.

But President Santos persisted—and he kept in close coordination with Bernie and our team at the State Department. Santos had promised not to ask me to intervene unless he had no other choice; likewise, I promised him that if he asked, I would do my best to say yes. The request came in March 2016. I was headed to Havana with President Obama for his historic trip and quietly peeled off from the presidential delegation because President Santos had asked me to meet with the FARC negotiators. This was the first meeting between a U.S. secretary of state and the FARC, and I intended to put the full weight of American diplomacy behind the push to arrive at a settlement. For decades, the United States had regarded the FARC as a terrorist organization. They had kidnapped several U.S. contractors and held them under brutal conditions. For their part, the FARC regarded the United States as an enemy that had provided matériel, training and intelligence to support the Colombian government's counterinsurgency against them. There was obviously a lot of mistrust on both sides. They weren't good guys. I'd voted to provide the funding over multiple administrations that helped decimate their leadership and dropped pesticides on the coca fields funding their cocaine-backed rebellion. It had once seemed unlikely that we'd ever be looking across a table from each other.

My job that day was to convince the FARC that there was life after revolution and armed violence. But before I could do that, Bernie and I had to rearrange the deck chairs, literally. When we got into the room, we noticed that it was very formal, with big chairs staring at each other across a long table. The setup was all wrong; it would have only created a sense of distance—another barrier to an already complicated conversation. So we started moving the chairs around. When the FARC negotiators arrived, I could tell they were nervous. They read from a prepared statement and then I delivered our message: if they laid down their arms and complied with the peace agreement, the United States would see them as a legitimate actor and there would be a path for them to enter politics. I talked to them about Sinn Féin and Northern Ireland. The meeting injected some confidence into the process at a critical moment. They told me that they were very worried about security. They talked about how in the 1980s, they had laid down their arms, had joined the political party Patriotic Union and were systematically attacked by paramilitary groups. I remember one of them turning to me at the end of the meeting and saying, "Security is not a bodyguard or armored car; what we need is a guarantee against the paramilitaries."

As with negotiations on Middle East peace, I knew that security was a centerpiece of this effort. Bernie suggested that Santos appoint a special subcommittee to examine this issue from every angle. At one point, there was a big disagreement over the name of the subcommittee: the FARC wanted to call it the "paramilitary subcommittee"; the Colombian government wanted it to focus on "post-conflict violence." As usual, Bernie helped defuse the situation with a clever insight from history. He told the FARC leaders about how President Kennedy got two telegrams from the Soviet leader Nikita Khrushchev during the Cuban Missile Crisis: one belligerent and one conciliatory. President Kennedy chose to respond to the latter, and the world was safer for it. Bernie urged the FARC to focus on positive developments—the creation of the subcommittee and the fact that Santos wanted to appoint a respected former head of police to chair it—and avoid squabbling over minor details. Ultimately, the FARC agreed.

So we began a period of constant phone diplomacy with Santos and Bernie. Santos announced the peace agreement in August, and I went to Cartagena the next month for the signing ceremony. It was a promising moment. I had good meetings with Santos and the FARC. We all felt the sense that this was a major diplomatic milestone. But before I could measure its significance, I had to meet with President Nicolás Maduro of Venezuela, who was also there for the peace signing. To go from a meeting focused on ending Latin America's longest-running civil war—one ended because a president put his country's interests first—into the next room to talk with the leader of a country where civil war loomed large, and where failing leadership was taking an entire country into a downward spiral, certainly put things into perspective. It was a powerful reminder that diplomacy requires constant tending and that leadership matters. It was also a harbinger of things to come. The meeting with Maduro ran long and we got stuck in horrendous traffic in the old city in Cartagena. Imagine thirty heads of state trying to depart at the same time. When we finally got to the airport, we found out that our plane had had to park in Barranquilla, a city about eighty miles to the northeast.

We had another hurdle to overcome: a referendum. Under Colombian law, Santos didn't have to submit the peace agreement to a referendum or to congress. To his credit, he wanted a referendum to build popular support for peace. On October 2, by a narrow margin, Colombians voted no. We went into another round of intense shuttle diplomacy to try to salvage the effort. I was on the phone constantly with Santos and former Colombian president Álvaro Uribe, who was strongly opposed to the agreement and whom I'd gotten to know. Uribe and I had a positive history and he knew I cared about his country even if I'd become Santos's stalwart friend in the peace process. Santos worked with the opposition to update the agreement.

Five days after the failed referendum, the world sent a signal to Colombia that it was invested in keeping the peace process alive: the Nobel Prize was awarded to President Santos.

On November 24, the Colombian congress approved a tweaked agreement.

I learned a lot working on this endeavor. I learned just how essential it is to have leaders willing to put their reputations on the line; little is ever accomplished without that much in the equation. But I was also reminded that you aren't defeated unless you decide to throw in the towel. Santos could have accepted the referendum's verdict and given up, and many in other situations—like Brexit—would have advised that he quit and accept the people's judgment. But he was made of stronger stuff than that. He didn't surrender. Neither did we. That was the moment when we leaned in the hardest. At the same time, I remembered all the lessons my dad taught me about diplomacy, starting with the biggest of all: listen. If you convey respect for all sides and listen carefully, even—and especially—when you disagree, you can get a lot done. This was particularly true in my discussions with the FARC, who had spent decades fighting for a cause they believed in deeply, resulting in the deaths of thousands. I could have dismissed them. I could have debated the FARC's concerns. But it wouldn't have helped. My job was to help both sides stay focused on the achievable, not the past. And both came to appreciate the power of diplomacy in putting an end to war and opening some real avenues for peace.

"THAT'S WHERE THE snipers were positioned," said Geoff Pyatt, our Ambassador to Ukraine, pointing to the fog-shrouded vision of the buildings from which the shots came.

Institutskaya Street in Kiev, Ukraine, was still piled with memorial bouquets for the victims, framed photographs of those killed amid the heaps of tires and lumber that had formed makeshift barricades during months of public protests. Barbed wire was everywhere. Bullet holes marked the streetlamps. People hovered beside a barrel with a fire to keep themselves warm.

It was March 2014 and I was in Kiev to show solidarity with the brave people who put their lives on the line to define the future of their country. I announced an initial $16.4 million to help Ukrainians at a moment of difficult transition.

Three months before, peaceful protests took over Kiev's Maidan Square. Thousands of men and women braved long nights, bitter cold and violent crackdowns by their government. They were fed up with the corruption of their president, Viktor Yanukovych, who profited by keeping Ukraine tethered exclusively to Moscow. Ukraine had been part of the Soviet Union. But going back hundreds of years, Ukraine's eastern borders had long been closely connected to Russia. Russian was spoken in much of eastern Ukraine, throughout the Donbass region. Khrushchev had been born in Crimea. Nevertheless, much of the country felt a closeness to Europe. It was a nation with one foot in the West and another in the East. Yanukovych's political patrons in the Kremlin counted on him to keep Ukraine aligned with Russia. But Ukrainians were demanding that Yanukovych broaden the country's engagement with Europe. They urged him to join in trade agreements with the rest of the continent. Yanukovych balked: he signed an exclusive economic relationship with Russia. The popular explosion was immediate. So was Yanukovych's reaction: his snipers shot at protesters from rooftops, cutting down more than one hundred people. But the people refused to go home. It was a Tahrir Square moment unfolding in Europe. Fearing for his life, Yanukovych fled the country in February for the safety of Russia. Ukraine had just undergone a popular revolution.

That March, I walked into a group of Ukrainians spontaneously gathered in the Maidan Square. I listened to their passionate pleas for the right not to go back to life as it was under Viktor Yanukovych. One man told me that after traveling overseas for the first time in his life, he came back to Kiev determined to live as he had seen other people live. One woman explained how poor they were under Yanukovych, how the rich lived well, how those in power took the money and left everyday workers behind. This was real populism, not the politically contrived variety I'd seen in American campaign commercials: it was the impulse of people who wanted a level playing field in life and expected government to be fighting for them.

The people in the Maidan were moving. I was impressed by their courage. They were just like people in so many parts of the world yearning for their rights to be respected and their government to be accountable. As we motorcaded back to the airport, our ambassador pointed out a makeshift memorial on the side of the road where a journalist who dared to criticize Yanukovych was pulled from her car and beaten within an inch of her life. When citizens rummaged through Yanukovych's opulent homes and offices after he fled, they discovered evidence that he personally gave the orders for that journalist to be taken out. I was reminded how some reporters take many risks just to do their jobs and record the truth.

But I was also reminded how complicated a struggle a young Ukraine would face in the months ahead. What to our eyes was an inspiration, to Vladimir Putin was an insult. Yanukovych was Putin's "made" guy. He rose to power on the shoals of Ukraine's "Orange Revolution," a pro-democracy uprising in 2004. Putin backed him against a pro-Western rival, Viktor Yushchenko, who was not-so-mysteriously poisoned and whose face was brutally transfigured. Yanukovych lost that race but made a comeback as prime minister in 2006 and president in 2010, with the help of American campaign consultant Paul Manafort. Yanukovych grew up in Ukraine's hardscrabble east. He looks like a heavyweight boxer, replete with a big, burly frame and a violent reputation. He was locked up twice for assault as a kid and came of age in the rough-and-tumble of the industrial heartland. He grew up speaking Russian and got his shot in Russia's coal-mining industry in eastern Ukraine. Manafort cultivated a rags-to-riches story: Yanukovych—the self-made pol who with a lot of hard work left the coal mines behind him, no mention of his patron in the Kremlin. Manafort burnished Yanukovych's image as a slick strongman who could restore stability at home and put Ukraine on the map abroad. He airbrushed Yanukovych's record of corruption, mismanagement and alleged ties to Russia's KGB. The campaign tactics came from Washington, but the money came from Moscow.

Putin responded to the revolution in Ukraine predictably. He pumped fake news into social media, painting democratic reformers as neo-Nazis. He broadcast propaganda in Russian to try to divide the country. In February 2014, he had ordered Russian troops to invade Crimea, a peninsula in the south of Ukraine. Its largest city, Sevastopol, is the home of Russia's Black Sea Fleet, and many ethnic Russians live in Crimea, giving Putin a ready-made pretext for intervention as well as vital military interests. Once Putin gave the orders, things got ugly fast. Armed militants took over government buildings, wielding Russian weapons and taking the Russian insignia off their uniforms to try to hide in plain sight. By April, Russia and its proxies were conducting attacks across several cities in eastern Ukraine.

Meanwhile, Russian leaders were making outrageous claims to justify their actions. It was nearly impossible to believe Russia could argue that forces occupying buildings, armed to the teeth, wearing brand-new matching uniforms and moving in disciplined military formation, were merely local activists seeking to exercise their legitimate rights. The world knew that peaceful protesters didn't come armed with grenade launchers and automatic weapons, the latest issue from the Russian arsenal, and speaking in dialects that every local knows comes from thousands of miles away.

Putin also unleashed something ugly and destructive in the Donbass: thousands of residential buildings completely destroyed, indiscriminate shelling by separatists hitting hospitals, schools and public areas where civilians wait in line for food and supplies, hundreds of thousands forced to flee, leaving everything behind—if they could even get out. The buses to safety were few and far between, leaving families huddled in the basements of train stations without food, heat or electricity, not knowing when the next vehicle would come or whether they'd be able to get on. It was testament to how much Putin refused to concede Ukraine to its own people.

Russia's denials and obfuscations were absurd, and everyone knew it.

The question was, would the United States and the West stand up to Putin's aggression? Would we help the Ukrainians help themselves, and could we strike the right balance—pulling a reluctant Europe to help Ukraine, but avoiding a new Cold War confrontation? How could we create both a show of strength and a strength of diplomacy that could de-escalate the trouble in Ukraine and empower Kiev to stand on its own two feet?

We led an international response that included bolstering NATO's defenses, reassuring allies and imposing sanctions on Russia that targeted its financial and energy sectors. We called them "scalpel sanctions" because they were more precise than ever before. If we hadn't employed them and ratcheted them up, the Russians could well have ended up in Kiev. The sanctions exacted a heavy toll on Russia's economy. Investor confidence dwindled. Some $70 billion in capital fled the Russian financial system in the first quarter of 2014, more than all the previous year. Growth estimates for 2014 were revised downward by two to three percentage points. Meanwhile, the Russian Central Bank had to spend more than $20 billion to defend the ruble, eroding Russia's buffers against external shocks.

At the same time, we needed to improve security conditions and find a political solution to the conflict. We needed to achieve a breakthrough on the diplomatic front. Our initial approach was to let the Germans, French, Ukrainians and Russians take the lead. This approach had its upsides: it put responsibility on Europe to stay united on Ukraine, and it managed the risk of Putin seeing Ukraine even more conspiratorially through the lens of a U.S.-Russia proxy fight. But those talks dragged on for months with little to show for them, in part because the Russians played divide and conquer. We attempted to insert ourselves in the process, but we were shut out by the participants time and again. It was a source of genuine frustration.

During this period of intense diplomatic activity, Ukraine's democracy was tested over and over again. But what often got lost in the headlines was that Ukraine met those tests. And in fact, it experienced some remarkable democratic successes—from the brave demonstrations in the Maidan to free and fair elections, to the parliament's passage of a strong budget and promising reform plan.

The Obama administration was focused on stopping the violence in eastern Ukraine. I entered into several rounds of intensive talks with Russian foreign minister Sergei Lavrov. I was working closely with our assistant secretary of state for Europe, Victoria Nuland. The Russians knew her as a worthy adversary. Almost everyone who meets Toria is an immediate fan—*almost* everyone. On my first trip as secretary, after Toria had left her post as the department's spokesperson but before the president nominated her for the top Europe position, Sergei Lavrov looked at my staff and said to me, "John, I see you've finally fired that Toria Nuland."

I said, "No, I promoted her!"

He laughed. Before her foreign service days, Toria worked for several months in her early twenties on a Soviet fishing trawler in the Pacific. She brushed up on her Russian and learned how to break the ice with a Stoli. While debating the Russians on Ukraine, there would be days she probably would've been glad to be back on that boat.

We worked together with Susan Rice and the NSC on a detailed diplomatic off-ramp to offer the Russians to decrease the pressure on Ukraine. We negotiated the details in London and Paris. It soon became clear that Lavrov had no room to cut a deal. Putin held the Ukraine card closely because he felt the issue so personally and so viscerally. The talks stalled, but the work we did on decentralization formed a critical bridge between the Minsk I agreement in September and what became known as the Minsk II agreement the following February. To this day, the Minsk approach remains the best possible way to de-escalate the violence and find a lasting political agreement.

Ultimately, that's the only way Russia's standoff with Ukraine can be sustainably resolved. Russia has a simple choice: fully implement Minsk or continue to face economically damaging sanctions. Russia's leaders know exactly what is required: withdraw weapons and troops from the Donbass; ensure that all Ukrainian hostages are returned; allow full humanitarian access to occupied territories, which is required by international law and by several United Nations resolutions; support free, fair and internationally monitored elections in the Donbass under Ukrainian law; and restore Ukraine's control of its side of the international border.

Ukraine's democratic potential is brighter today than it was several years ago, far brighter even than it was before the brave protests in the Maidan. And with transatlantic support, the next years have all the potential possible for Ukraine to prove reform can triumph over corruption and over even the most determined efforts of Russia to thwart Ukraine's determination to embrace modernity. But the struggle that's killed more than six thousand people is not over, not by a long shot. American commitment to lead the West in solidarity with Ukrainians is needed more than ever before.

My time dealing with Putin and Lavrov over Ukraine reminded me just how much America's relationship with Russia has changed since I was a boy riding my bike into Soviet East Berlin, and how much it hasn't. Vladimir Putin is a complicated figure. In one meeting he could be a charming interlocutor, opening bottles of wine and offering bowls of caviar. At other moments, he could employ petty tactics: keeping us waiting for hours just to prove the point that we were on his turf. He could be expansive in one meeting, taciturn in the next. He remembers the Soviet Union with great fondness and sentimentality and believes that the world needs a counterbalance to the United States, yet he presides over a country with no modern economy and invests billions in overseas misadventures in Syria and Ukraine rather than investing in a modern economy. He's a paradox. Putin and Russia were constructive partners on the Iran nuclear negotiations and on Afghanistan among many issues, and yet they were calculated and ruthless on others, from standing with Assad in Syria to assaulting our democracy at home in 2016. It's a mistake to see Russia through either rose-colored glasses or Cold War lenses. For years, Republican and Democratic presidents alike negotiated with the Soviet Union and found ways to make progress. Reagan called it the Evil Empire even as he found ways to eliminate thousands of nuclear weapons between us. Somehow, even when difficult, we must always preserve room to sit down face-to-face, compartmentalize issues as needed, and make progress where we can, even as we disagree where we must. But we can only do that ready to tell the truth, to call out Russia on their malicious activities, from the assault on our elections to the violation of international law in Ukraine. The United States must always lead the effort to hold them accountable.

THERE ARE THOSE who wish that the United States could stand aloof from the world's problems and look inward. But we can't. We know what happens when we do. Leadership isn't a button we push in times of emergency. Leadership is what we have to provide all the time. It isn't easy. It doesn't always work. But if there's one thing I found as secretary of state that permeated my conversations in every region and every corner of the world, it is this: world leaders don't lie awake worrying what will happen if America is present—they worry what will happen if America is absent.

CHAPTER 17

Getting Caught Trying

"JOHN KERRY SPEAKS for me on this issue."

It was March 2013. President Obama had traveled to Israel. He was greeted by big, supportive crowds. We were meeting with Prime Minister Benjamin "Bibi" Netanyahu in Jerusalem. The warm reception made the White House wish the president had traveled there during his first term. The president and prime minister talked about a host of issues—Iran, Islamist extremism, the state of the region two years after the Arab Spring. The two reaffirmed their willingness to again explore negotiations with the Palestinians over a two-state solution. It was then that the president gave me the currency I would need to see if a newly invigorated peace process could lead anywhere: he told Netanyahu that he trusted me and had invested in me to give it a shot.

For decades, peace in the Middle East has eluded presidents, prime ministers, international mediators and, yes, secretaries of state to whom the task of chief mediator or negotiator often falls. I had tracked the process since I came to the Senate in 1985. I had no illusions about the barriers in our way. I was well aware of all the arguments for inaction. But in foreign policy, while it's very easy to speculate about the risks of acting, there's rarely enough focus on the risks of inaction.

That's especially true about peace in the Middle East. Time was not a friend of the peace process. With every past failed effort, the hopes for peace had diminished. Cynicism grew and became self-perpetuating. I worried about the long-term security of our friend Israel. What diplomats call "facts on the ground" and the actions of both Israelis and Palestinians were steadily diminishing the prospects for a two-state solution—separate Israeli and Palestinian states living side by side in peace and security—which is exactly what some on the fringes of each side wanted to prevent.

The Palestinian population was growing increasingly disillusioned. Palestinian social media bubbled over with ugly anti-Israel sentiment, sometimes violent, which the Palestinian leadership did not stop and occasionally encouraged. Extremist Hamas, guilty of the vilest forms of incitement and violence, was gaining traction. War broke out in Gaza every couple of years. The Palestinian population was booming. If Israel remained in control of the Palestinian population from the Jordan River to the Mediterranean Sea, in a handful of years there wouldn't even be a Jewish majority. Under those conditions, how does Israel possibly maintain its character as both a Jewish and democratic state for the long term?

At the same time, settlements were expanding rapidly with little restraint, drawing more Israelis into areas of the West Bank that experts agreed would have to be included in a viable Palestinian state. When Ariel Sharon removed settlers from Gaza during Israel's 2005 unilateral withdrawal, the images were gut-wrenching. That was only eight thousand settlers. But with each passing year, thousands more were moving into the West Bank.

When the Oslo Accords were agreed to in 1993, there were about 110,000 settlers in the West Bank. By the time I became secretary, the number had grown to some 375,000. No one could legitimately argue that the growth and current number didn't represent a major impediment to the creation of a viable, contiguous Palestinian state. Many observers claimed that the settler policy was a purposeful strategy by those in Israel who opposed the creation of a Palestinian state and wanted a "greater Israel" encompassing the West Bank.

Of course, there was always the option of the United States doing nothing, but given the rate at which the dynamics on the ground were changing, that would have been diplomatic malpractice. The window for a two-state solution was closing. Given the extraordinary economic and security benefits of peace for the entire region, and given the growing threat to the dream of a democratic Jewish state for Israel, I believed we bore a fundamental responsibility to give the peace process our best effort. Otherwise, by default, we would have been empowering those on either side who didn't want a Jewish state or a Palestinian state.

Moreover, I didn't think it was a lost cause. Both Prime Minister Netanyahu, in his historic speech at Bar-Ilan University, and President Mahmoud Abbas had clearly expressed their support for the two-state solution. I believed there were such powerful reasons to finally reach a meeting of the minds that if the leaders were determined to get there, we could do it. There were legitimate glimmers of promise for two reasons.

One, years of conversations with Prime Minister Netanyahu and President Abbas convinced me that if they were serious about making peace, the shape of that peace was well known and achievable. Years of negotiations had developed a generally understood outline for peace. The fundamental question was the readiness of both sides to take steps to get there. I had also learned in all those years that very little in the Middle East can be taken at face value. I wanted to believe both leaders but wasn't sure whether they were prepared to back up their words with actions. It was essential, however, to put them to the test.

Two, even though the cause of a Palestinian state wasn't the burning, galvanizing issue it once was for the region, I was convinced that in return for a Palestinian state, Israel's Arab neighbors were ready for a fundamentally different relationship with Israel, including new security arrangements that would benefit everybody. On several occasions, they made that clear to me at the highest level. I thought a new regional realignment would be a huge incentive for Israel and a big reward for the Israeli prime minister willing to make the compromises needed for a two-state solution.

But one lesson in particular informed my approach to the peace process. Incrementalism is an enemy. I know that sounds counterintuitive. In many conflict resolution models, you assume that any step forward is positive and builds confidence. But I didn't think that could any longer work between the Israelis and the Palestinians for the simple reason that it had never succeeded in the past. It had been tried again and again, and intervening events, mostly purposeful, always broke or destroyed any momentum. I believed all the "final status issues" needed to be resolved, at the very least in a broad-brush manner, in one package, even if the implementation took years with tests along the way. Both parties needed to understand the endgame that would satisfy their fundamental aspirations.

Those aspirations could not have been clearer: for Israelis, recognition of Israel as a Jewish state, with Jerusalem as its internationally recognized capital and its security ensured; for Palestinians, a defined, viable Palestinian state with its capital in East Jerusalem and a just resolution of the refugee issue; and for both, a clear path to end the conflict and all claims. In other words, you needed a comprehensive vision of peace, agreed upon in theory between the two sides, or else you left the door wide open for the naysayers to play spoiler. Netanyahu had a great phrase, if an ironic one: he always said "I can't die on a small cross." No leader of either side would be willing to take big risks for small steps.

None of this was an easy sell inside the administration, and I understand why. There were many veterans of the Obama administration who, during the first term, had been through a really tough and demoralizing effort at the peace process. I'm sure some also felt suspicious after many reports in

2012 suggested that Prime Minister Netanyahu had bet big on Mitt Romney. But from all those who didn't think we should launch a new effort at peace, I never heard a workable alternative to the two-state solution. If there wasn't one, how could we afford to disengage when the space for a solution was shrinking? If you punted now, achieving peace would get harder, not easier, down the road.

Despite all the reasons for pessimism, I believed the moment could be ripe for progress. Before I became secretary, King Abdullah of Jordan had invited me to a small gathering of leaders vested in a peace process, held at his royal compound nestled on a beautiful stretch of beach just west of the town of Aqaba, almost on the border of Israel. It provided a perfect venue for discreet, high-level conversations far away from the press and the big entourages. There foreign ministers from most of the Gulf States, former UK prime minister Tony Blair and senior representatives from Russia, the United States and others from the region convened to discuss ways in which regional trends presented new opportunities for peace, security and economic reform. The Arab revolutions had upended the status quo. Regional leaders expressed many more concerns about Iran and the threat of religious extremism than about the Israeli-Palestinian conflict. They saw Iran and radical religious extremism as existential dangers. The Palestinian cause was important to their people, but it was not central to their strategic thinking. However, while they had many reasons to draw closer to Israel, they felt limited in their ability to act on that initiative if the Palestinian issue wasn't resolved.

Peace with the Arab world was always a critical part of any deal for Israel. It was never going to be enough to have peace with the Palestinians. I saw greater possibilities for that kind of regional rapprochement than ever before. And the backing of the Arab world was always going to be necessary for the Palestinians to make peace with Israel anyway.

On security, the new alignment of interests between Israel and the Sunni Arab countries in the region against Iran presented an opportunity to reshuffle the deck. With will and creativity, we could create new alliances. With the right approach, we could help address Israel's security concerns in an integrated way with Egypt, Jordan and other countries in the region.

Economically, Israel's ascendancy as a technological powerhouse presented opportunities for commercial integration that could benefit everyone. Attracting large-scale private sector investment could unleash extraordinary potential for catalyzing sustainable development throughout the Palestinian territories and the wider region.

It would have been a huge missed strategic opportunity to ignore the potential for a rapprochement between Israel and the Sunni Arab nations. Such a regional realignment, more available than ever to the parties, would provide significant enhanced security measures and game-changing economic benefits for Israel, the Palestinians and the region. I was convinced—and remain so—that there was a way to link and leverage these opportunities. We were living in different times and we needed to think accordingly. Different tools were at our disposal.

As ripe as the moment might have been, it ultimately hinged on the two sides themselves. As former U.S. ambassador to Israel Martin Indyk was fond of saying, "You can bring two camels to water in the desert, but you can't make them drink." We couldn't want the peace more than they did. No solutions could be imposed on the parties. No matter how logical something looks, no matter the stakes, no matter the upside and easily tangible benefits, if the politics and personalities are not ready, nothing will make the moment ripe. The principals have to be willing to take risks and be committed to making the outcome they desire come about.

In my many conversations with Prime Minister Netanyahu and President Abbas over the years and in my first months as secretary, both men indicated their understanding of the stakes, the urgency and the opportunities. Both said they were willing to try again if the other side was serious. What I found most promising was Prime Minister Netanyahu's insistence to me personally that he was willing to take risks, willing even to put his governing coalition at risk, to make peace if his conditions were met.

I wanted to put that statement to the test. If the parties were going to get there, the United States had an indispensable role to play as the only country that could give both sides the support and encouragement they needed to make the leap. To me it was worth the risk of getting caught trying. We could not expect Prime Minister Netanyahu and President Abbas to take big risks for peace if we weren't prepared to put ourselves on the line as well.

I set out on this journey with a very personal commitment to Israel. For twenty-eight years, I had the privilege of representing in Massachusetts one of the most civic-minded, active Jewish communities in America. And I had come to know, like and respect Yitzhak Rabin and Shimon Peres. They were extraordinary leaders who believed deeply that Israel would be safer in the long term if there were a Palestinian state. Only through a genuine peace could Israel win recognition as a Jewish state and guarantee its security. Prime Minister Rabin gave his life for that belief.

I'll never forget landing in Tel Aviv on the anniversary of Rabin's assassination. I went straight to Kikar Rabin (Rabin Square) and stood with the late prime minister's daughter, Dalia, at the site of her father's murder. We were just steps away from where the great general, in the last moments of his life, sang the famous lyrics of "Shir LaShalom":

Don't whisper a prayer;
sing a song of peace
in a loud voice.

Don't say the day will come;
bring that day.

Remembering those words brought me back to the chapel at St. Paul's School, where as a boy I sang the anthem "O Pray for the Peace of Jerusalem." I knew Israel as the homeland for the Jewish people—the land of milk and honey. As a kid, I was fascinated watching the 1960 film *Exodus*. I was inspired by the compelling story of liberation: it was the story of a people fighting for a place in the world, a struggle for survival and recognition.

I'd been to Israel many times and I felt a personal connection. On my first trip there in 1986, with my friend the religious and civil rights leader Lenny Zakim and a group of fifteen Jewish friends from Massachusetts, we stood atop the spectacular summit of Masada, where two thousand years ago one thousand martyrs made the ultimate sacrifice in unison and in the name of defending the ancestral homeland of the Jewish people.

Our guide was an intriguing man named Yadin Roman. He was the editor and publisher of *Eretz* magazine and a great student and teacher of history. When we reached the top of Masada, he sat us down in a quiet corner. There he gave us a long explanation of the moment in history when Jews retreated to Masada. He described the details of the long siege that followed. Like any good teacher, he threw enough twists in the tale to create a genuine debate, which I think was his purpose. Did they really all die? There were a number of theories circulating suggesting otherwise. An hour later, we took a vote to decide what the group concluded. It was unanimous—we all agreed that events had happened the way they were described by the Roman historian Flavius Josephus. Then Yadin called us all over to stand at the far precipice, where, on his instruction, we yelled out across the chasm: *"Am Yisrael Chai!"* We shouted and then we listened. Full seconds later, back from the other wall, came a clear and penetrating echo of this Hebrew phrase that means "The people of Israel live! The state of Israel lives!" It was as if, eerily, the voices of past generations were talking to us.

On one visit, I was at Ovda Airbase, in Israel's Negev desert. I had pestered the commanding colonel about whether I'd be allowed to go flying since that had been on my wish list. He told me that Tel Aviv had denied the request, but he would ask again. A few minutes later, he returned and told me we had permission. He handed me a helmet and flight suit. As we went to jump in the jet, he offered me the front cockpit and said, "The minute we're off the ground, it's your plane."

We climbed quickly above ten thousand feet, and I relished the opportunity to see with my own eyes how narrow the borders of Israel are and how that narrowness comes alive in ways it never could on a map. It is the ultimate way to understand the vulnerability of Israel's security. There's simply no margin for error. At one point, the colonel radioed to me and said, "Senator, you better turn faster. You are about to go over Egypt. Turn!" I pulled the aircraft into a tighter turn with tighter gs. I came close that day to violating the airspaces of both Egypt and Jordan. As I flew over the Negev, I asked the colonel for permission to do some aerobatics. With his consent, I gained speed and pulled back on the stick to do a loop. As we turned upside down, all of a sudden I realized the sky was beneath me and the earth above, and I thought, *Wow, finally I'm seeing the Middle East clearly—upside down.*

As secretary of state, every time my plane touched down in Tel Aviv and I walked down the steps of the blue-and-white plane with "United States of America" on the side, I felt like I was visiting a branch of America's family that had made their home in the desert of the Middle East.

Our family's long-buried history underscored just how personal, albeit distant, those connections could be. The *Boston Globe* in 2003 had done compelling genealogical work. Years later, Cam was presented with confirmation that Granny's brother, Otto, and sister, Jenni, had been condemned to the Terezin camp, where Otto died. Jenni was sent on to the Treblinka concentration camp, where she too perished. Yad Vashem's head archivist had shown Cam the chilling records. Cam had converted to Judaism years before when he married his wife, Kathy, a future president of her temple and a skilled lawyer. In 2014, Cam traveled to the Czech Republic and visited Terezin, knowing that our ancesors had gone to the gas chambers because they were Jewish. I thought about both Israel and my own roots in a new light. Early in my time as secretary, on Yom HaShoah, I laid a wreath on behalf of the United States at Yad Vashem. Thinking about the fate of my ancestors who had not escaped and become Kerrys in the New World, I felt even more viscerally the idea of a safe and secure homeland for the Jewish people.

I understand why Israel is, for so many, the shining city on the hill.

On the other side, I really didn't know much about the Palestinians until I went to the U.S. Senate. Most of us in my generation were introduced to Palestinians through the news stories of Yasser Arafat, the PLO and Abu Nidal. In my visits to various Palestinian communities—Ramallah, Jericho—I learned more about Palestinian aspirations, about everyday life. I met some who had become wealthy in business. I met more who had very little, particularly young people. Their plight spoke to my fundamental sense of fairness.

It always bothered me when I drove by Israeli checkpoints and saw long lines of Palestinians, often women and children, waiting for hours just to go from one neighborhood to another in the West Bank. I imagined what it would be like if I couldn't get from downtown Boston to an appointment in Charlestown without waiting in a three-hour line. I talked with people who couldn't visit their relatives a couple of miles away in a land they had lived in for hundreds of years. I listened to them tell stories about sitting at checkpoints, unable to go to work, or the hospital, or the supermarket. I sensed the profound humiliation of their day-to-day lives. And I could see in their eyes a desire for the most basic things that most of us take for granted.

These experiences were a stark reminder that the journey of the Palestinians had left them stateless—if not homeless—and at the mercy of what has been at times a very difficult occupation. While they were human beings who were trying to maintain some sense of dignity in the face of virtually total powerlessness, it was both immoral and counterproductive to resort to terrorism to address their concerns.

To Americans, freedom means the ability to live in a democratic society, to have a voice in your government, to enjoy equal protection under the law. To many Palestinians, freedom means something much simpler. Freedom at the most basic level is the ability to move from one place to another, to travel outside of your country, to provide for your children. It's stamped in the American DNA that we have the right to pursue life, liberty and happiness. For many Palestinians, that is a far-off dream.

As secretary, my primary responsibility was to stand up for and defend our values and interests in the world. That job required me to be invested in Middle East peace on behalf of our country. But I was also personally invested. Israel is our most important ally and the only real democracy in the region. It is a vital U.S. interest to protect and advance Israel's security. That's why the Obama administration provided what Prime Minister Netanyahu himself stressed were "unprecedented" levels of security cooperation and assistance, including the biggest military aid package in history.

I also felt strongly that one of the most important things we could do to support Israel was to help resolve the conflict with the Palestinians once and for all, so they could finally live in peace with their neighbors. Conversely,

I knew that if we were to stand idly by and allow a dangerous dynamic to take hold in a region in which we have vital interests, we would be derelict in our responsibilities.

In short, I wanted to pursue Middle East peace because the stakes were high and there were far too many ordinary Israelis and Palestinians—many of them kids—who had no role in this conflict but were caught in the middle and suffering as a result. No children—Israeli or Palestinian—should have to live like that.

A trip I took as chairman of the Foreign Relations Committee four years before I'd become secretary underscored to me just how dire the situation was—and how difficult the politics would be if I ever got a chance to be more directly involved in the diplomacy. It was 2009, just after a war in Gaza had ended and Israel was on the verge of electing a new prime minister.

I was planning to travel into the Gaza Strip with Teresa. Gaza is one of the most godforsaken corners of the planet, home to one of the world's densest concentrations of people enduring extreme hardships with few opportunities. Out of Gaza's population of 1.8 million, 1.3 million people are in need of daily assistance—food and shelter. Most have electricity less than half the time, and only 5 percent of the water is safe to drink. And yet despite the urgency of these needs, Hamas and other militant groups continue to rearm and divert reconstruction materials to build tunnels, threatening more attacks on Israeli civilians that no government can tolerate.

The people of Gaza were suffering under Hamas rule. I wanted to visit in order to measure the conditions, to understand better if there was a way to stop the escalating cycle of war.

No U.S. delegation had been there during the eight years of the Bush administration. It was deemed physically unsafe. It was politically tricky to go into a territory essentially controlled by a violent foreign terrorist organization. I was aware of the risks, but I also suspected Hamas wouldn't want to risk harm to a U.S. senator. We had worked out a plan to get in with the UN Relief and Works Agency for Palestine Refugees in the Near East (UNRWA).

The night before we left, I sat down for a drink with our ambassador to Israel, Jim Cunningham, and told him that I was planning to go into Gaza the next day. Jim didn't mince words. "We can't support your trip, Senator," he said dryly. "We're officially informing you not to do that," which is diplo-speak for "We think this is a terrible idea, and if things get screwed up, it's not our fault." But a blanket no to an American senator just didn't seem to make sense to me. Other countries' leaders had been to Gaza.

I said to Jim, "I know you're formally required to tell us not to do this. But I'm going into Gaza tomorrow, and I'm just asking you man-to-man—what's the security situation? Am I going to get my ass shot off?" As a career diplomat forced off script, he hesitated for a second, then he looked me in the eye, lowered his voice so nobody in the restaurant would hear and said something along the lines of "Ah, you'll probably be all right. But I didn't just say that."

That was all I needed to hear.

The next day we boarded an Israeli military helicopter with Tzipi Livni, who was the leader most personally interested in pursuing peace with the Palestinians. We flew to Sderot in Israel, which had been the target of thousands of rockets over the last eight years. I wanted to see with my own eyes the life of Israelis under constant threat. Security officials told me that from the moment they know a rocket has been fired from Gaza, people have just fifteen seconds to find safety. We learned about children who had spent literally every day of their lives never more than fifteen seconds from grave danger.

After our briefing, we left Tzipi in Sderot and drove to a gas station on the outskirts of the Kerem Shalom Crossing, from which we would head into the very place where those rockets came from: Gaza.

I left my motorcade of large SUVs, together with all my security team, and climbed into a small UN vehicle—the smallest "convoy" I've ever been in—with virtually no security. We had a UN driver with a small sidearm. Nevertheless, I felt our exposure was an asset, not a danger. I thought the Palestinians would begrudgingly accept—not threaten—a high-level guest who was interested in learning about their situation.

I'm no stranger to seeing the destruction of war, but I was moved by the enormity of the humanitarian crisis. It was like driving around in a postapocalyptic landscape from a *Mad Max* movie—but in a small white UNRWA Toyota.

We visited a bombed-out international school and I thought: How could Hamas possibly justify using places like this to hide weapons or fire at Israel? What monsters could turn a place where little kids are educated into a staging ground for violence? At the same time, I felt deep frustration that so many innocent kids were trapped in a cycle of violence they had nothing to do with. When I passed a young girl playing in the debris on the side of the road, I wondered—as I had in Vietnam and Afghanistan—what do we look like to these people? I didn't want her to see me as an anonymous face behind a bulletproof window, passing through like a ghost on my way to somewhere safer. I wanted to get out of the car and talk to that girl and try to bridge the enormous gap between a kid walking around in rubble in Gaza and a U.S. senator driving around in a convoy. I wanted to look her in the eye, hold her hand and let her know that my country cared about what she was going through.

After a few minutes, I wasn't willing to sit in that car anymore. It made no sense to enter Gaza but not actually see anything up close. I didn't feel threatened. I didn't think I would be attacked among a group of innocent people and in front of the cameras. I got out of the car with Teresa and started walking toward the school. A convoy of Palestinians that had been following us pulled up and jumped out. For a second, I wasn't sure whether they wanted to talk or kick my ass, but then they took out cameras and started asking me questions. I did spontaneous but careful on-air interviews standing in front of the school, much to the concern of my staff. As one of them joked to Teresa, "In the best-case scenario we could be talking to members of a foreign terrorist organization on live TV; in the worst case, we are all about to die."

In the end, that trip had the desired effect. When I later saw President Abbas, he pulled me aside, put his hand on my shoulder and said, "I want to thank you for what you did. That picture of you walking amid the rubble was worth more to the Palestinian people than a thousand statements."

Abbas was a soft-spoken, longtime veteran of the Palestinian cause who had started out as one of Arafat's deputies. Over the course of his career, he had consistently remained committed to achieving a negotiated solution with the Israelis. He actually helped pioneer that effort through the Oslo Accords. Above all, through all the ups and downs of war and divisions within his own political base, he had stayed steadfastly committed to a peaceful Palestinian state. Abbas could be a very frustrating guy to deal with and often said and did things that were entirely counterproductive to his objectives. At the same time, I also understood that he had a very difficult hand to play. He basically had no power with respect to Israel. Nor was he a natural-born politician. While Abbas was a veteran infighter in PLO and Fatah circles, he was not as comfortable with the day-to-day politics of the Palestinian people. He was a proud man, but at times he seemed worn down by years of frustration and beleaguered at his inability to show real progress for his people. Hamas and other extremists were violently acting out the frustrations that many Palestinians were feeling. Abbas was simply not willing to go down that path. For all the frustrations of dealing with him, he remained publicly committed to peaceful coexistence with Israel and, in fact, elevated security cooperation with Israel to its highest level ever.

I wanted President Abbas to know that the United States would try to understand and work fairly with both sides. No progress would ever be made if we didn't have credibility with both parties. President Abbas knew that I was a strong supporter of Israel, but my trip to Gaza helped build trust. The Palestinians needed to know—or at least feel—that I understood their perspective.

The end of the war in Gaza had also brought Israel to a political crossroads, which I witnessed firsthand during that trip. Israelis had just gone to the polls in a tight election. President Shimon Peres had to choose between Bibi Netanyahu and Tzipi Livni to form a coalition. Tzipi had won one more seat in the Knesset than Bibi, which gave her the presumptive first chance to form a new government. But Bibi had the upper hand, because there were more parties on the center-right willing to join him.

The night before I went to Gaza, I had dinner with Bibi at the David Citadel Hotel. We talked about what would follow if he became prime minister. We also talked about opportunities on the Palestinian issue. Bibi expressed his desire to end the conflict, but with his usual skepticism about the Palestinians—and the inevitable qualifying and temporizing about whether an agreement could ever work.

I'd been hearing variations on this subject from Bibi for more than twenty years. We first sat down together when neither of us was in office. He was working in Cambridge, and we sometimes met for coffee in Harvard Square. We always had interesting talks. I enjoyed the give-and-take of a wide-ranging debate with him. He was funny and warm, with a great deep laugh. He was also careful with his words in the way of born politicians. Permeating all our conversations over the years was a genuine fear for Israel's security. I didn't always agree with him about how one achieved that security, but I appreciated his patriotism and commitment to his country. He had lost his brother Yoni in Operation Entebbe in 1976, a successful, daring Israel Defense Forces (IDF) mission to rescue Israeli hostages from their hijackers at an airport in Uganda. The cause of security was forever personal to Bibi. I respected that.

In those years when we were both in the political wilderness, we consistently shared invigorating, fast-moving political and strategic exchanges. I remember once when he said to me, "You know, if we're ever in a position to do things in our governments, I think we could accomplish a lot together."

I never forgot that, particularly when I became secretary of state and he was prime minister.

It was always interesting to compare my conversations with Bibi about the Palestinians with my conversations with Tzipi on the same subject.

Bibi's attitude was "I'm open to solving this problem if I can have all my needs met." That included his political needs with his coalition.

Conversely, Tzipi's attitude was "This problem is eating away at the soul of our country. We need to solve it and I believe it can be done." Bibi was fond of saying, "Take all my excuses away." Tzipi said, "We, Israel, need to solve this problem. And we need your help."

These contrasting perspectives were on my mind when we flew with Tzipi to Sderot in late February 2009. Israel was at a fork in the road—the path of peace or the path of entrenchment. The tension in Israel was palpable.

Peres decided to give the nod to Bibi to form a coalition. I learned the news at the same moment Tzipi did, when we landed in Sderot. She was swarmed by reporters.

I wasn't surprised at Peres's choice. Bibi was one of the better politicians I'd ever met. He was a consummate backroom wheeler and dealer. In a previous life, he could have been a great, old-time Boston ward boss with a cigar in his mouth, cutting deals. Tzipi, on the other hand, was first and foremost an advocate for peace. She was passionate about the policy and her country. Even as Bibi was passionate about Israel's security, he was also passionate about the politics. Peres might have preferred Tzipi's commitment to peace, but as president he could not ignore the fact that Bibi had a better chance of putting together a governing coalition.

As the new government took shape, I sensed immediately that the road to peace with the Palestinians had just gotten a lot longer and a whole lot steeper. I knew from years of talking with Bibi that he was the more ideological of the two leaders. Bibi put together a broad coalition that included many on the Right who did not want a Palestinian state. But I also knew that Bibi cared about history. And I always thought it was worth testing whether—like Ariel Sharon—his bona fides on the Right might bring him to a Nixon to China moment. If I were ever in a position to work on the Middle East peace process directly, I certainly planned to find out.

When I became secretary in 2013, I talked to the Obama administration's special envoy for Middle East peace negotiations, my friend George Mitchell.

I admired George's negotiating skills. His attention to detail and his calm demeanor helped him through many tricky moments. He did a brilliant job negotiating the Good Friday Agreement in Ireland during the Clinton administration. George's experience on the Middle East peace effort raised a number of cautionary flags. Most important, he warned against a massive amount of time and political capital being spent trying to achieve a partial settlement freeze as a precondition to negotiations. He also emphasized the importance of careful choreography in any one-on-one meeting between Bibi and Abbas. It was good advice.

When I first met with President Obama in the Oval Office and expressed my interest in trying to reinvigorate a peace process, he was very skeptical. He had every reason to be. He felt burned from his efforts during the first term. I made the case to him that new regional, security and economic opportunities could change the dynamic. I also talked to him about Bibi's expressed willingness to make tough compromises for a lasting peace. I told the president I thought it was at least worth putting the idea to the test. He listened carefully. He then turned to me and said simply, "Look, I'm skeptical, but you have my support if you want to try." And to his great credit, he always backed me on this issue when I needed it. The president gave me enormous latitude to try to push the process forward.

After decades of starts and stops, near successes and missed opportunities, the basic elements of peace seemed fairly well established. But I knew that just trying the same thing that had been attempted so many times before wasn't going to result in a different outcome. And there were the elements of the process that made the possibilities riper than before: regional support, economic initiative and, most important of all, security. I wanted our peace process to go deeper than ever before on each of these three lines of effort.

First were the regional dynamics. In 2002, King Abdullah of Saudi Arabia announced the Arab Peace Initiative, which offered fully normalized relations between all the Arab states and Israel once a peace agreement was struck with the Palestinians. I remember visiting Arafat's headquarters in Ramallah in January 2002, one and a half years after President Clinton had brought the parties together for the Camp David Summit. A huge hole had been blasted in the side of the headquarters. It was less than two years before he died. He turned to me during the dinner and whispered, "I made a mistake in not accepting Clinton's deal." I already knew that one of the reasons Camp David failed was because the region wasn't sufficiently engaged to give Arafat the political cover he needed. I was also mindful of the story of President Clinton calling then Egyptian president Hosni Mubarak from Camp David the night before everyone was to leave. President Clinton asked for Mubarak's support and, according to Mubarak when he told me the story, he responded, "Support for what?" The message to me was clear. The groundwork had not been sufficiently prepared with Arab leaders in the region.

From the first steps we took, I vowed to make sure the Arab countries were partners every step of the way. It was essential that they be free to move in two directions simultaneously—support the Palestinians and give Israel the peace with the Arab world essential to a final status deal.

During my transition to secretary, I spent a fair amount of time talking with former secretary of state Jim Baker about his efforts on the peace process, particularly his attempt at Madrid in 1991 to bring Arab nations to the table. We agreed that this ingredient of regional cooperation was riper than ever before.

Our team understood the importance of showing Israel a path to peace with its neighbors. Accordingly, one of the first things I did was to bring together the key leaders who were members of the Arab Peace Initiative Follow-up Committee at Blair House in Washington, D.C., for a meeting. I remember feeling a buzz of energy in the room. Everyone there sensed the possibilities that lay ahead. These leaders had a critical role to play and I convened them regularly to ensure they were fully briefed and to enlist their support. The Arab Peace Initiative (API) had laid out a path to Arab-Israeli peace. But there were specific elements of the plan that were problematic for Israel. One was a Palestinian state based on 1967 lines without any reference to land swaps. Swaps were critical for Israel because of the settlements in the West Bank. There were large-scale Israeli developments in three or four areas near the border that almost everyone basically agreed would have to be integrated into Israel. It was a long-accepted premise that there had to be land swaps, but the API didn't reflect that.

It took months of painstaking diplomatic legwork with the Saudis and others, including a one-on-one conversation with the chairman of the API Follow-up Committee, Qatar's foreign minister, to get the deal done. Arab leaders made a gesture that was significant—both substantively and symbolically—in stating publicly for the first time that the final border would include land swaps.

There was another initial significant challenge to overcome, if not just manage: Palestinian cynicism. The Palestinians expressed concern that the Israelis—and we—would cobble together a package of economic initiatives and call that peace. They were adamant that an "economic peace" could never take the place of a real final status agreement. At the same time, we thought improving the Palestinian economy could help build belief in the possibility of peace.

That's why we focused on a major new initiative for the Palestinian economy. The idea was straightforward: a prosperous Palestine would pose less of a security threat. We commissioned McKinsey & Company to analyze the Palestinian economy. McKinsey CEO Dominic Barton agreed to donate the firm's time, putting in eight hundred man-hours or more. The study showed that if the Palestinians were allowed to develop their own economy, the transformation in quality of life could be game changing. But the best possibilities could be fully realized only if there was peace.

The final piece of the puzzle was also the most critical. Again and again, Prime Minister Netanyahu said to me, "Security is the key. Israel must be able to defend itself by itself." He would also remind me of Israel's withdrawal from Gaza: "We pulled out of Gaza and look what we got—rockets and tunnels. We can't turn the West Bank into Gaza." I argued to Bibi that if he actually made peace and reached agreement on the future security relationship of a demilitarized Palestinian state, there was a way to make certain the West Bank would not be Gaza. Meeting Israel's legitimate security needs was our number one priority from the very beginning. As Bibi said to me, "Take all my excuses away." We tried to do just that even when we began to suspect that the list of excuses would never end. We had to think about security in every conceivable way.

We knew it was important to have military professionals design the plan—not politicians. To lead this unprecedented effort, we brought on General John Allen, a four-star retired marine who had commanded U.S. and coalition troops in Afghanistan. John was the perfect man for the job. He was widely respected. I knew he would fully immerse himself in this mission and he would have the respect of his peers in Israel and the Gulf. From day one, John Allen was all in.

Based on prior discussions, Israel had developed dozens of detailed security questions, and the answers would form the essential building blocks of our security initiative. That was our starting point. We coordinated with the Jordanians and Palestinians to create a layered approach that would help guarantee Israel's security while respecting Palestinian sovereignty. King Abdullah of Jordan could not have been more helpful. He was creative. After years of effort, he knew every twist of the issue, all the sensitivities, and as a proven partner of Israel, he was in a position to weigh in with a special stake in the outcome.

We formed a separate team to assess Palestinian security needs in the context of statehood. We anticipated that the United States would continue to play a leading role in helping to build institutional Palestinian capacity, enhancing capabilities to maintain law and order, cooperate in an effective judicial system, combat terrorism and smuggling and manage border security, customs and immigration. We knew that for some period of time this effort would require continued IDF presence in the West Bank. We all recognized, Palestinians included, that there would need to be a comprehensive

Israeli-Palestinian protocol for cooperation, tested over considerable time until Israel could have confidence in the commitment and performance of the Palestinian security services. How long, and under what circumstances, had to be negotiated between the parties. We also developed objective standards by which performance could be measured. We were committed not to leave things to chance. We fully allowed for the time it would take to train, build, equip and test Palestinian institutions. We were determined to ensure that the Palestinians were capable of protecting Palestinian citizens as well as preventing their territory from being used for attacks on Israel. These efforts remained a subject of focus over the next four years.

The run-up to the negotiating process started in earnest when President Obama delivered an important speech in Israel in March 2013, reaffirming the importance of a two-state solution and empowering me to try to give the peace process new life. A few days later, I met with Bibi at the King David Hotel. I will always remember what he told me. He looked me dead in the eye and said, "John, I'm willing to give this effort a try, but there are two things you should know: first, everyone in this region lies all the time and you Americans have a hard time understanding that; second, the most I can do may be less than the least Abbas could ever accept."

That statement really stayed with me. Bibi was raising the bar, perhaps impossibly.

It was clear from the outset that the Palestinians faced a political cost simply for having negotiations with the Israelis. The Palestinians were very skeptical about whether Israel and particularly Prime Minister Netanyahu were serious about peace. His King David Hotel statement raised similar questions with us. We understood Abbas's concern about entering into negotiations that went nowhere, leaving him looking feckless before his skeptical public. Puffing away on cigarette after cigarette, he made it clear that before he could engage in negotiations, Israel had to give him something to bolster his credibility at home and demonstrate Netanyahu's seriousness. He was adamant that before resuming talks Israel had to either release the prisoners from before the Oslo agreement, who had iconic value to the Palestinians—even though some were guilty of heinous terrorist attacks—or agree to negotiate on the basis of the 1967 lines or implement a settlement freeze.

The Israelis refused all three concessions. So that left us with one difficult option: pulling together a package of economic incentives sufficient to permit the Palestinians to say yes to coming back to the table. I made several trips to Jerusalem and Ramallah that spring and summer to haggle over preconditions, which wasted precious time, reinforced skepticism and dissipated hopes.

I had negotiated enough in the Senate and as a prosecutor to know when I was with a party that wanted to get the job done. The Israelis' approach to the negotiation was to make sure they could defend every word that was written and, I sometimes thought, make sure there were so many of them that no one could tell what the hell was going on. The Palestinians figured that if a document leaked they were screwed no matter what, so they wanted to maintain plausible deniability on everything by never writing it down in the first place.

This just reinforced the distrust. The Palestinians believed that the Israelis were building trapdoors and loopholes into every sentence so that any apparent commitment would in fact be vitiated. And Israelis saw Palestinian reluctance to commit to anything in writing as preparing their escape route—which fit the narrative that the Palestinians were always running away from agreements.

In June, after several months of work, we met with Bibi for a critical session at the David Citadel Hotel to put the finishing touches on a package of economic incentives to present to Abbas. When we wrapped up at around 4:30 a.m.—one of the things Bibi and I had in common was a willingness to work late into the night—my longtime Middle East advisor Frank Lowenstein and I took a walk around downtown Jerusalem. Frank's father was Allard Lowenstein, who had been assassinated decades earlier. His father's assassination had left Frank with a sense of tragedy but also with a sense of purpose. He wanted to make the world more just. He was passionate about Middle East peace and came to understand its nuances as well as anybody.

As we walked through the eerily deserted streets of this extraordinary city that was in many ways at the heart of this conflict, the challenge really hit me. I remember shaking my head and telling Frank, "This is absolutely ridiculous. If we have to fight over every word with the Israelis to get agreement on a series of economic steps that we all agree are in everyone's best interests, think about what happens when we get to the big issues!"

By July, it was time to fish or cut bait. We had to determine what the parties' bottom lines really were for resuming talks. This process culminated in four critical days in Amman. There was mounting criticism in the press that I was wasting time on this issue. We'd gone back and forth with both sides more times than I cared to count. I needed to bring this initial process to a close.

I knew neither side would act without a deadline, so I set one and let everyone know that if we didn't get a deal we were done.

I couldn't go back to Israel without raising expectations for a process that I knew might fail. We arranged for an Arab League meeting in Amman as an excuse to go there. I'd finally reached agreement with the Israelis on an economic package to present to the Palestinians. I asked President Abbas to come to U.S. ambassador Stu Jones's residence in Amman. The proposition was straightforward: the Israelis were offering a package of what they viewed as unprecedented economic steps to get Abbas to come back to the table and negotiate final status issues. Abbas was skeptical: he had heard these economic promises in the past and they were of little substantive or political value to him. I kept pushing. He said his right-hand man, Saeb Erekat, would come back the next morning to give Abbas's final answer to the Israeli proposal.

Saeb was one of the more interesting characters I'd come across. I'd known him for over twenty years. He knew the accomplishments and failures of the peace process inside out. He was also held accountable for failure by some, who asked derisively, "What peace has he ever delivered in all his years?"

Saeb had as good an understanding of the issues as anyone I met, but he sometimes let his frustration and accrued mistrust get in the way of compromise. On the plus side, he was steadfastly committed to nonviolence.

He spoke excellent English with endearing malapropisms like "Do I look like I have a neon on my head that says 'stupid'?" But he could also be mercurial, emotional and unpredictable—as charming as he was maddening, with a flair for long diatribes and dramatic pronouncements. In response to my deadline, he told me that Abbas just couldn't sell economic steps to the Palestinian people, who felt like they were half measures designed to buy them off. In their minds, the only issue that really mattered was a state on the land they'd long inhabited.

Moreover, Abbas's main competition was Hamas. Every time he entered into a dead-end negotiation, he looked weak by comparison. Hamas had previously secured the release of hundreds of high-profile Palestinian prisoners in return for Gilad Shalit, a kidnapped IDF soldier. Abbas felt that he couldn't accept anything less than a significant prisoner release to return to the table. He remained adamant that Israel either free the pre-Oslo prisoners or agree to the 1967 lines or implement a settlement freeze.

I called Bibi and said, "Bibi, we're at the end of the line. I've done everything I can. If it doesn't work, it doesn't work. But you have to decide. The only way to get this done is to release the pre-Oslo prisoners. The skepticism just runs too deep. Something has to happen to change the dynamic. Unless you'll agree to the 1967 lines or a settlement freeze, there's just no other option." I knew there was no way Bibi was about to agree to the 1967 lines or a settlement freeze. I told Bibi in no uncertain terms, "If you're not willing to release them, I understand—but this won't work and I'm done with it."

Bibi had insisted all along that Israel was not willing to release any pre-Oslo prisoners. When he was confronted with this deadline, for the first time he said, "Okay, let me see what I can do."

The press was downstairs in the lobby of the hotel in Amman, increasingly aware that we were working on a final push and skeptical that we could get there.

Frank Lowenstein asked whether he should work on a plan B with Saeb and Tzipi in case Bibi wouldn't release the prisoners. But I was determined to keep the pressure on. I told him, "No, absolutely not—if you give either side a way out, they'll take it. Plan B will lead to plan F: failure."

If people claimed that I'd tried and failed, I could live with that, but I wouldn't go through a series of half measures that just let the Israelis and the Palestinians keep dithering.

"Look, if this process isn't serious, I'm just not going to waste any more time on it. And we're going to find that out right now."

The clock was ticking away. Bibi got back to me and said they were willing to do the prisoner release in four separate tranches spread out over the negotiated period. But they needed a firm commitment from President Abbas not to join any international organizations as part of an effort to legitimize the Palestinian state outside the negotiating process. Bibi said he needed settlement building to make his politics work, but the numbers he gave me were much lower than the numbers the Israelis ultimately announced—in part because of their view that no building in East Jerusalem should be considered a settlement, but also because of an arcane, opaque settlement development process that was easily manipulated to serve any argument.

Once I had Bibi's sign-off, I went to Ramallah to see if Abbas would accept the deal. I explained to Abbas the tranches. I said that Israel would be doing some settlement announcements and that we'd try to make them as limited as possible. Abbas, who was surprised we had secured the release of pre-Oslo prisoners, accepted this formulation.

After we left Abbas's residence, we flew to Amman, arriving about an hour and a half before the deadline for our plane to take off. I called the White House, discussed the final terms and then announced at a press conference that the parties had agreed to resume negotiations in principle, pending approval by the Israeli cabinet. Given how far we'd come, this felt like a significant accomplishment. But on the plane ride home, I felt the weight of the previous days: the mutual doubt and mistrust presented a formidable barrier.

The good news was that we had an agreement to resume peace negotiations for nine months. The question then became how to organize those talks. The well had long been poisoned. To manage the process, we needed an experienced negotiator who didn't appear to be in anyone's pocket. I asked Martin Indyk to assume responsibilities as the U.S. special envoy for Israeli-Palestinian negotiations. It would be Martin who would lead the day-to-day negotiations in Israel and the West Bank, while Frank would continue as deputy envoy and my trusted aide in Washington.

They did a superb job under extremely difficult circumstances. Martin is a UK-born, Australian-raised, naturalized American citizen who has made the cause of Israeli-Palestinian peace his life's work. From his service under President Clinton as U.S. ambassador to Israel during Bibi's first term to his work with Secretaries of State Warren Christopher and Madeleine Albright, he brought a keen understanding of diplomacy in the Middle East. In addition to his extraordinary historical perspective and long-standing relationships on both sides—or maybe because of those qualities—Martin had a sharp appreciation of the many ironies of the Middle East. It was good to have a diplomat of Martin's skill join us. Frank and Martin had an easy rapport and shared a mischievous sense of humor.

Above all, Martin was realistic. He brought to the task a healthy skepticism about the willingness of both leaders to make peace. This came from some difficult moments in his relationship with Prime Minister Netanyahu dating back to the Clinton administration, coupled with his knowledge of the Palestinians' ability never to miss an opportunity to miss an opportunity.

After an endless week of working through the last-minute issues, finally the Israeli and Palestinian negotiating teams came to Washington. But the negotiations almost blew up before they even started. We all gathered in an eighth-floor reception room at the State Department for a short meeting before the initial press conference. We read over our statements to make sure we were on the same page. After listening to the expected bromides about the peace process from me and Tzipi Livni, who coheaded the Israeli negotiating delegation with Yitzhak Molho, who represented Bibi, we were all listening with half an ear when Saeb said, "I look forward to having a negotiation on the basis of the 1967 lines," as if he could just casually slip in a critical negotiating point as an aside.

In a nanosecond, everyone went from making small talk to a DEFCON 1 alarm. "What are you doing, Saeb?!" we all asked in unison. Saeb sat there stubbornly, saying, "Of course, this is what we're negotiating about." He wouldn't budge, so I had to take him out to a metaphorical woodshed in the adjoining secretary's ornate private dining room and tell him in no uncertain terms to cut the crap. Needless to say, by the time we got out to meet the press, we were all a bit sobered. If the smiles at that press conference seemed forced, it's because they were.

After the press conference passed without Saeb veering disastrously off script, we all went over to the White House to see President Obama. This was the president's idea, which I naturally welcomed since it would serve to signal his commitment to the process.

In one sense, the meeting was remarkable. It was as if the negotiators, who had just been squabbling over the terms of reference at the State Department, were suddenly transformed by their presence in the Oval Office. They each spoke heartfelt words about their commitment to peacemaking and their common belief that this time it was possible to get it done. As was his practice in such meetings, the president went around the room to make sure everybody had an opportunity to speak before he had the last word. He graciously welcomed the pervasive optimism but then expressed his own skepticism, reminding the negotiators of how difficult their task would be but committing his team to help the parties try again.

After the Palestinians departed, the president told me and the Israelis to finish "the London track."

The London track was a back-channel attempt to draft a framework agreement that would address all the final status issues so everyone knew what the outline of a peace agreement would be. It was a great concept, but closing required the same difficult compromises as the peace process itself.

The track started during President Obama's first term under then national security advisor Tom Donilon and Middle East advisor Dennis Ross. It was a secret negotiation involving senior officials from the United States and Israel and a longtime friend and colleague of Abbas's, Hussein Agha, who lived near London and was not officially a member of the Palestinian team. They had spent over a year working on a lengthy and detailed document addressing all the final status issues, some in more specificity than others.

Tom was still national security advisor when I took over at State. He and the president made it clear to Tzipi and Molho that they wanted them to finish London within a few weeks. The Israelis were invested in London, which they kept calling "the only game in town," because they thought they could make more progress dealing with Agha than with Saeb or any of the other Palestinians. While the London track included Yitzhak Molho, Bibi's closest advisor, it was never clear how much buy-in it had from Abbas. Indeed, as we became more engaged in the negotiations, we grew increasingly concerned that he was using the London track as a mere fishing expedition to determine the extent of Bibi's concessions while he maintained plausible deniability. In any event, apparently he had not told his lead negotiators—Saeb Erekat and Mohammad Shtayyeh—about it. So right from the beginning, we had divergent lines of effort and big secrets.

With the Israelis willing to make compromises only in the context of the secret back channel, the direct negotiations between the Israelis and the Palestinians that Martin was managing were severely handicapped. While it was useful to hear the parties explain their positions on final status issues in depth, there was no real negotiating going on between the two sides.

Meanwhile, we were in hurry-up-and-wait mode on the London track, which was an external process that I couldn't fully control. Despite President Obama making clear he wanted the London track wrapped up in short order, it continued to drag on. It became *Waiting for Godot*. The participants spoke in reverent tones about an almost mystical drafting process, where ideas needed time to "marinate," and the effort simply couldn't be rushed. That's all well and good, but we didn't have the luxury of giving them an unlimited amount of time to finish their work since the nine-month clock was ticking on the other negotiation.

Over time, I grew increasingly frustrated with what felt like a lack of urgency on the London track. At one critical moment, I called to ask when they were next meeting. I was told they weren't planning to meet for another ten days. I gathered them all together at our ambassador's residence in London to see where the document stood. Some members of my team and the White House thought the document was too one-sided in favor of the Israelis. President Abbas had never seen the actual document, whereas Bibi was very familiar with it. One thing that everyone agreed on: it was not done.

While that process was playing itself out, much of our day-to-day focus turned to General Allen's security effort. John continued to report he was having constructive conversations with the IDF. But eventually he realized that people who had been enthusiastically cooperating with him were pulling back. He told me he had gotten as far as he could go with the military people. He was disappointed, detecting a sudden shift in the attitude of his counterparts. John told me directly that the turnaround had been so abrupt, so distinct, there was no doubt in his mind politics had interfered. His counterparts were clearly uncomfortable and limited by the defense minister, Bogie Ya'alon, and the prime minister as to how far he could go in solving the security problem. Knowing that Ya'alon opposed two states, it did not come as a total surprise.

But General Allen had already explored a vast number of possibilities and had narrowed the options. On the basis of the work already completed, we designed a comprehensive security strategy for Israel. We knew the plan had to be decisive, robust and capable of meeting all the IDF's contingencies. One of Israel's major concerns regarding a withdrawal from the Jordan River Valley was the question of what the future might bring in Jordan itself. Bibi expressed great concern about thirty- or even forty-year eventualities should Israel find itself with a swarm of terrorists or another nation's army on the Jordanian border. That—and other questions like it—had to be answered.

The Palestinians had already accepted, as they had previously, that their state would be forever nonmilitarized. Police, but nothing more: no heavy weapons and no air force. In addition, the IDF would be the ultimate failsafe. These were critical up-front terms that immediately put Israel in enhanced security status. But we went significantly further than any previous security discussion.

First, it was clear that the Israelis would never feel safe leaving the West Bank unless they had the right to redeploy in the event of an emergency. The Palestinians understood this position. Further, while America's deterrent capacity has fundamentally been understood to be online on behalf of Israel for decades, we were ready to make that explicit. In addition to proposing joint-force response capacity with Egyptian and Jordanian forces, we agreed that if it took American forces on the ground to provide further deterrence or defense, we would do so. We proposed to put American forces on the Jordanian side, which would also signal a strong commitment by the United States to Jordan's stability. U.S. forces would act as an effective deterrent against any threat from the east. The forces would adopt a low profile and work jointly with the Jordanian military. Peace in the Middle East would be well worth that price.

We also offered to stage American forces on the Palestinian side, and the Palestinians were fully supportive of an indefinite U.S. presence on the border and throughout the West Bank. Moreover, we supported the Israelis maintaining forces on the border for a time to be agreed upon but certainly a number of years and conceivably much longer depending on conditions on the ground.

In addition, we proposed unprecedented extensive upgrades to border security. We envisioned two fences, one on each side of the Jordan River, that would be monitored by video and controlled constantly, effectively creating an approximately two-kilometer no-go zone that would provide ample time to interdict any threats. We provided for Israel's ability to stage rapid-response troops with helicopter scramble authority to respond to any breach within minutes if the Palestinians failed to act effectively. We envisioned two separate staging areas for this rapid Israeli response—one on the northern end of the border in Israel and the second in a nearby settlement—which would have allowed a less than ten-minute response time from warning to troops arriving. And being realistic, long before that kind of scramble would be necessary, Israel and just about everyone else would have detected an enemy mobilization days if not weeks beforehand. This rapid capacity was intended to deal with a supposedly small unit, covert or terrorist activity—and to annihilate that threat, relying on the best of U.S. technical capacity.

Importantly, we never contemplated a sudden withdrawal or immediate turnover of full security responsibility. The Palestinians accepted that their capacity to ensure security had to be proven. They were willing to do that—but understandably, they wanted to do it within an agreement defining their future state. We contemplated testing this plan for as many years as necessary to demonstrate its effectiveness in meeting objective standards, which had to be passed before any IDF withdrawals.

Taken together, these steps would have created the safest border in the world while ensuring that Israel could defend itself by itself always. We believed these integrated and redundant border security systems, along with the U.S. presence, would make it easier for the Palestinians to accept some of the measures necessary to ensure Israel's security needs.

During all this time, our conversations with the Palestinians about security cooperation were constructive. President Abbas agreed to a "forever" commitment to partner with Israel in a long-term, joint counterterrorism coordination. This was intended to be of extraordinary benefit to both Israelis and Palestinians. Both had a shared interest in making certain no terrorist could infiltrate the West Bank. Building the cooperative capacity well beyond what it is today, which Israeli security officials have praised, would enhance stability and security for both peoples.

I described for Bibi the ways we could ensure a long-term program of deep cooperation with Shin Bet, Mossad, the IDF and the Palestinian security services. I emphasized the benefit of that counterterrorism coordination being joined by Jordan, Egypt and the United States. A security envelope could be created that was orders of magnitude stronger than anything ever attempted in the West Bank or between Israelis and Palestinians. If these security measures were implemented together with a peace agreement, the elimination of the occupation over time as conditions were met and a dramatic increase in economic opportunity, there was no reason not to envision Israel's relationship with a Palestinian state on the West Bank being transformed in the same way the relationship between Jordan and Israel was transformed. In 1967, Jordan and Israel were at war. Today, they are partners for peace. Why not the Palestinians too?

When we were finally ready to present the plan, I sat in Bibi's office with Defense Minister Bogie Ya'alon while General Allen walked him through the plan in detail. This was a key moment. If we could resolve Israel's security concerns, I thought we would have solved one of the most difficult problems of all.

We made absolutely clear that at the core of our thinking was a bedrock principle: Israel would not withdraw until it had been clearly and objectively established that the security system would work. Even then, Israeli soldiers would remain in close proximity, ready to return in full force within hours to address any emerging threat. The time frame for the phased IDF withdrawal was left open, entirely dependent on the ability of the security system to meet our agreed-upon criteria. We presented detailed maps showing exactly how the contingencies would unfold, all of which we had coordinated with the Jordanians. We emphasized repeatedly that this would be the most secure sixty miles of border anywhere in the world. I stressed to Bibi, "We have reduced risk to the lowest possible level. With General Allen's enhancements and the border security zone stretching at least a kilometer into Jordan, you'll always have an early-warning system that will give you plenty of time to defend yourself, by yourself, against any threat."

Bibi's initial reaction was positive. I remember him saying, "If this process fails, it won't be because of the envelope," meaning the security of the Jordan River border. I left that night feeling cautiously optimistic.

That optimism was short-lived. The next morning, I met with Bibi to consolidate our progress and talk about how to integrate General Allen's concepts into the London track. Bibi was in a very different mood. He said, "We're never going to leave that area until we, Israel, decide ourselves that it's safe, and that's going to be a very long time." Bibi was willing to accept some of the enhancements we were offering, but he made clear that they wouldn't result in Israel withdrawing the IDF from the West Bank border with Jordan unless they decided in their sole discretion that they were ready. Moreover, while we had been focused on the border, Bibi then began stressing the need for an IDF presence throughout the West Bank. In effect, Bibi was doubling down on a long-term presence in the West Bank, the duration of which would be decided unilaterally by Israel—no standards, no incentives, no goal for the Palestinians to work toward. It was a quick rejection of a security plan that promised extraordinary benefits for Israel and the region.

It was now clear to all of us that Bibi was not interested in actually addressing the security questions in a way that could allow for the eventual withdrawal of the IDF, even with critical benchmarks being met along the way. In fact, he was never going to agree to any kind of realistic process for IDF withdrawal. It seemed to me that this was an article of faith. I kept saying, "Bibi, you can have the entire Israeli army positioned right above the border and U.S. troops on the border." Bibi said, "We don't want U.S. troops getting shot at to protect Israel." I replied, "We don't want to get shot at either. The minute they start shooting at us from across that border, the IDF can come right back in a matter of hours if there is a real threat."

I concluded that this wasn't about security. I wondered what Bogie Ya'alon had said to Bibi the night after we'd left. We had reached a turning point. If Bibi couldn't accept a way to solve the security problem that could work for both sides, it was hard to see how the negotiations would ever succeed.

I let him know I thought he was creating an insurmountable stumbling block if he couldn't accept the best advice of one of his ally's most brilliant military minds. He smiled and said we'd table the discussion for now.

Bibi walked me out of his office, and he pointed to a picture he kept of the two of us on his shelf. "See, I tell everyone you and I are good friends, yours is the only picture I have up here." I laughed. "And I don't take it down when you leave either!" He slapped me on the back, clearly trying to smooth over any ill will from his summary rejection of a security plan that we had spent an enormous amount of time working on.

As the end of 2013 drew near, I insisted that the London group finish their work and present the document to Abbas. The final version had some creative ideas and concepts in it, but on key issues—including Jerusalem—they were unable to agree on anything meaningful.

Moreover, the White House thought the London track was so slanted toward Israel that Abbas would never be willing to negotiate an agreement based on it. The White House was prepared to work with it only if both parties would accept it.

Agha finally showed the London document to Abbas around Christmas. We soon heard back that Abbas wasn't willing to embrace it. Bibi suggested that we turn it into an American paper that both sides would accept "with reservations." So while we were able to incorporate elements of the London effort, we essentially had to create a new document. Critical months had been wasted.

It was at this point that we began intense work on a new U.S. framework. If we were going to put it out as an American document both sides would accept, it had to be balanced. We had a series of intense, secure calls with Bibi and conversations with the Palestinians to get their input. The framework was also informed by lessons learned from the public negotiations and the private track in London.

The Israelis wanted us to negotiate the document with them exclusively and then basically impose it on the Palestinians. Even more problematic, the Israelis were not willing to say anything about a Palestinian capital in East Jerusalem. We knew there was no way the Palestinians would accept final status principles that didn't include a Palestinian capital in East Jerusalem. They couldn't cede to the Israelis sovereignty over the Haram al-Sharif, the third holiest site in Islam. At the same time, Bibi was clear that he was not going to touch that issue. So we had to be prepared to go beyond what the Israelis were willing to do.

In February 2014, we met with Abbas in Paris to update him on the framework. In a private room with Abbas I let him know that we were prepared for the first time publicly to support the international consensus on a Palestinian capital in East Jerusalem as part of a comprehensive solution that addressed the needs of both sides.

I was optimistic that we were putting something significant on the table, but from the second I walked into the room, it was clear his body language was foreboding. Abbas had a cold and appeared exhausted. His mind-set about the entire process was negative. He seemed disengaged and unwilling to have a serious negotiation.

It also didn't help that the Israelis had just made a big announcement of new Israeli housing units in East Jerusalem. These settlement announcements were a profound humiliation to Abbas. I remember him at one point describing being in his office in Ramallah and watching Israeli settlements being constructed right outside his window. This latest announcement had an especially damaging impact on his perception of how serious these negotiations were.

When I explained to Abbas what the United States was prepared to do as part of the framework, he barely reacted at all. It seemed as if the Palestinians had lost faith in the whole process.

A couple of weeks before Abbas came to Washington for a final meeting with President Obama in March 2014, Israeli negotiators argued to Martin Indyk and the team in Israel that Abbas was "running away." They suggested we could put something on the table that leaned further toward the Palestinians than what we had been discussing with them just to test his intentions. We took that as a green light to present our more balanced framework to the Palestinians when Abbas came to town.

When he arrived, I brought Abbas and his senior negotiators to my house in Georgetown. I wanted a more private, personal setting than the State Department. So we ordered Chinese takeout and ate in the dining room. The Palestinians didn't want us to send them a hard copy of the document because, as they explained, they would have been required to share it with the Fatah Central Committee for approval. For certain, the entire document would leak, closing down whatever political space existed. So, I read sections of the document to Abbas later that night; Martin and his team read the whole document to Saeb, which he wrote down word for word.

The next day, when President Obama met with Abbas in the Oval Office, he was clear about what was required as we neared the end of the nine-month negotiating period: "We're running out of time. We need to hear back from you on this as soon as possible—days, not weeks."

Over the next days, the Palestinians continued to say they were studying the proposal, but they never actually responded.

It was clear that they were unwilling to make any concessions as the negotiation period neared its end. Abbas was concerned that any compromises would expose him in front of his people. He was not convinced we could deliver Bibi, so he feared he'd face blowback for making compromises and getting nothing in return.

With the deadline for the release of the last tranche of Palestinian prisoners fast approaching, and the Israelis' firm position that they would not release more prisoners unless there was an extension, it was hard to argue that it was a moment for expenditure of political capital. Thus we turned our attention to that immediate challenge.

The problem with the final tranche of prisoners was that Israel had saved the worst guys for last. As a result, the Israelis needed a real extension of negotiations, not just a few months, in order to accept the political pain of releasing them. In return, the Palestinians wanted additional concessions from the Israelis, especially credible limits on settlement activity, to justify continuing negotiations to their very skeptical public. For that to happen, the Israelis asked us to release the convicted Israeli spy Jonathan Pollard.

The president was deeply skeptical, but he didn't rule out releasing Pollard—I think more because he wanted to support me and his team than because he had any confidence Bibi would follow through. He had been through this exercise with Netanyahu during the first term, when everything collapsed in the face of Bibi's refusal to extend the soft settlement moratorium Hillary Clinton and Senator Mitchell had spent months negotiating. The president and everyone who had worked on it in the first term still bore the scars. President Obama had come to believe that Bibi was not serious about creating a Palestinian state.

I understood the president's perspective. By that time, I shared enormous skepticism about either leader's ability to make peace.

While it was clear to all of us by now that the conditions weren't ripe for a comprehensive agreement, I thought we could still take consequential steps to keep the window from closing on the two-state solution. Since the effort didn't interfere with our other priorities, it was worthwhile trying to keep the parties working, not fighting.

Pollard was nearing the end of his sentence. Still, for very understandable reasons, much of the intelligence community was against any early release. In the end, we had a delicate three-way negotiation to explore whether a deal could be reached that would extend the negotiations and secure additional benefits for the Palestinians in exchange for the release of Pollard.

We went back and forth with the Israelis as Bibi worked to line up political support for concessions he would have to make to extend the negotiations. The Palestinians were losing patience. Their politics were getting difficult. It was a make-or-break moment with Bibi. I urged him to make a credible offer in order to convince President Obama that it was worth keeping Pollard in play and convince Abbas to agree to an extension. I told Bibi point-blank, "You're not doing this for Abbas. You're doing it to empower us to get what you want."

As we were working through the intricacies of the deal, Abbas abruptly informed us he was planning to officially join several international organizations in short order if we did not reach an agreement. This would have violated one of the core promises Abbas had made to the Israelis to get the negotiations started. Basically, it would mean game over.

We negotiated down to the very last minute trying to get the details of the extension and prisoner release worked out. But in the end, the Palestinians ran out of patience with the process.

Abbas stood up at a gathering of Fatah leaders and made a big public showing of signing instruments of accession, which would unilaterally advance their claim to statehood. There was no mistaking the message. Rather than waiting on a process he thought would crater on its own, Abbas was playing to the Palestinian street; he would either force Israel to give him what he needed or be the one who defied Israel with uncharacteristic flamboyance.

In the end, there was simply too much scar tissue from years of failure. Abbas didn't believe the Israeli government was serious about comprehensive negotiations. The Israelis, for their part, were convinced Abbas was looking for a way out. Neither side felt the other was serious enough to merit their taking political heat for difficult decisions. We were caught in a round-robin of mistrust. A cumulative trail of failed expectations and absence of follow-through had broken down faith in any next step.

Near the end of April, we had four or five days left to try to find a last-minute reprieve when we heard reports that Hamas and Fatah had agreed to a national unity government. This was the final nail in the coffin.

I was deeply frustrated with the Palestinians for many reasons. They'd given their critics in Israel all the ammunition they needed: Bibi could blame the Palestinians, saying they chose the path of terror over the path of peace. I was also angry that the Palestinians never even responded to President Obama on his offer; he was the best they could have hoped for and they'd squandered his commitment to them. I was also dismayed that, for all I'd done over the years to build trust with Abbas, he'd avoided the kind of final conversation we deserved.

But I wasn't interested in playing the blame game publicly on this.

As far as I was concerned, both sides had chosen the path of politics over the path of progress. I would forever respect that Bibi had taken the political risk of the prisoner releases, but I believed that he was a willing victim of his politics at home—which Tzipi always pointed out he himself had created. I thought he was more comfortable as the leader of his political party, Likud, vying to be Israel's longest-serving prime minister, than he was risking it all, as Rabin had and as Peres had, trying to be the one who finally made peace.

There is a set of accepted conventional slogans that get thrown around in the process. One of the biggest is that Israel says it doesn't have a partner for peace—and the Palestinians say Israel just wants to use the peace process as cover to continue its inexorable takeover of the West Bank. Both sides get locked into their cynical cycle. I remember saying at one point to Martin, "I feel like I'm having a negotiation with the mayor of Jerusalem and the mayor of Ramallah." In the end, the mistrust was so profound and the narratives of victimization ran so deep on both sides that neither could get to where their populations so desperately needed them to go.

EVEN WITHOUT A peace process, we still had interests in avoiding a conflagration. Our commitment to Israel and our concern for the Palestinians transcended even the deep disappointment of the peace negotiations. So I entered an extended period of trying to manage this conflict. I've always believed that negotiations help to keep a lid on possible violence. And sure enough, soon after negotiations ended in early June 2014, three Israeli teenagers were kidnapped and brutally killed by Hamas operatives in the West Bank. Israel launched a full-scale incursion into the West Bank to find the kidnappers and dismantle the Hamas networks there. As this was going on, Hamas began launching rockets into Israel from Gaza, which escalated into a full-blown shooting war. Bibi's biggest fear—and understandably so—was that Hamas operatives would burrow under the fence from Gaza in order to conduct stealth kidnappings of Israelis. This was a risk Bibi couldn't tolerate, making some type of significant escalation inevitable. As the war spiraled, President Obama asked me to travel to the region to see if we could stop it.

The situation was dire. Hundreds of Palestinian civilians—including women and children—were being killed in the cross fire, often placed there intentionally by Hamas. The human cost to Palestinian civilians in Gaza who were stuck living under the rule of Hamas was gut-wrenching. Of course, we all understood Israel's right to defend itself. I underscored the administration's—the United States'—support. At the same time, we wanted to do whatever we could to end the bloodshed because too many innocent people were suffering on both sides.

Egypt was the logical country to broker an end to the war because of its relationship with Israel and control of the Gaza border crossing. The Israelis were adamant that the Egyptians be the intermediaries to help resolve this war. So my first stop was Egypt. I quickly saw that the Egyptians were working in coordination with the Israelis and shared their overriding desire to crush Hamas. They were not even dealing with the elements of Hamas with the power to bring the war to a close. We had to find somebody who had the leverage to force Hamas to stop firing the rockets. The only countries with that sort of power were Qatar, which provides a lot of funding to Hamas (including sometimes paying the salaries of civil servants in Gaza, with Israel's acquiescence), and Turkey, which is very supportive of them politically.

After a few days in Egypt, I went to Israel. It was at the height of the war. After a Hamas rocket landed near Ben Gurion Airport, the Federal Aviation Administration had announced safety warnings and many U.S. air carriers stopped flying to Israel because the risk was too high. Bibi was furious at this decision. With our pilots and the Air Force's consent, I instructed our plane to land at Ben Gurion Airport. I thought it was important at this moment to make a strong statement of our support for Israel.

We met with Bibi in an underground conference room together with his war cabinet. There he showed us maps identifying the tunnels from Gaza. You could feel the tension. It was one of the few times I saw Bibi very subdued, absent his normal energy and bravado. To see the leader of Israel under siege like that really touched me. I stepped up our efforts to make certain, as part of any resolution of the conflict, that Israel could deal with the tunnel problem. It was imperative. Under attack by terrorists and facing international pressure for killing civilians, Israelis clearly felt that the world had lined up against them. It was as if the worst Israeli narratives were being borne out. I saw Bibi in that moment more vulnerable than I'd ever seen him before. That made me only more determined to make sure that we got the airport open for American carriers as soon as we could. Sure enough, the next day the FAA concluded the airport was safe enough, and that hurdle was behind us.

The focus of our negotiating efforts was Bibi's suggestion that we negotiate a "humanitarian cease-fire." Bibi insisted that Israel couldn't stop the campaign until it finished clearing out the tunnels. That had not yet been accomplished. A normal cease-fire requires the parties to return to the status quo ante; in a humanitarian cease-fire, the parties stay where they are to allow emergency goods to come in. We were trying to shoehorn this concept into an agreement to end the fighting while allowing Israel to finish the work of destroying the tunnels it had already reached behind the lines.

I called the Qataris and Turks and pushed them to force Hamas into accepting this humanitarian cease-fire. They committed to help and did. We eventually produced a draft document that achieved the basic objective of allowing Israel to continue to destroy the tunnels while laying the groundwork for an end to the war. It was a tough sell, but we'd basically gotten much of what Bibi most wanted. Of course, I always knew that the Israelis would have comments on the document and fully understood that there would likely be another round with the Turks and the Qataris as soon as we received Bibi's comments. I called Bibi to arrange for him to receive the document and get back to me with necessary changes. I told him that

I looked forward to talking to him about it. After nine months negotiating with his team, I knew this would take a few rounds. We expected the back-and-forth.

At my instruction, a copy of the paper was sent, clearly marked "DRAFT: CONFIDENTIAL. FOR DISCUSSION PURPOSES ONLY." It was sent directly to the Israeli national security advisor's personal email account so it could be closely held.

I then called Bibi and said, "Have you seen the document?" He said, "Yes, John, I've got a lot of comments on this."

We had just started a conversation when Bibi told me he had to interrupt to attend a cabinet meeting. Two hours later, without any further conversation, without notice, we were looking at Israeli press reports that included the document itself! I was seething. I called Bibi immediately. "I sent you a private document for your comments. I got you what you asked for. Now the document is in the papers with news reports quoting senior Israeli officials saying, 'Kerry is negotiating for Hamas.' You knew this was a draft, Bibi. We were in the middle of negotiating it based on your input. Now I see it in the press? This is outrageous. The humanitarian cease-fire was your idea. And now you leak this document to make it sound like I'm trying to advance Hamas's position?" Bibi mumbled something about how he didn't leak it, that he'd get to the bottom of it and would clear it up with the press. He never did.

I was deeply troubled to see Bibi telling us one thing and telling his cabinet and eventually the press something very different. An element of personal trust had been lost.

Eventually, in early August we did get Israel and Hamas to agree to a humanitarian cease-fire set to start the following morning. Given the difficulty of communications into Gaza and the various factions acting independently, we all understood that the potential cease-fire could come apart before it officially began. Even as our team was heading over for the negotiations, an Israeli soldier was tragically ambushed and killed by Hamas, and another was thought to have been possibly kidnapped. That was the end of the line.

The war dragged on through the end of the summer. Neither side could be seen as backing down. Ending this war was not going to happen with a document or an agreement until each side felt it had achieved its objective.

The question was when both sides would see the futility of continued fighting and decide to stop. The document they wound up agreeing to was incredibly vague and did little more than end the fighting. It was far less strong for Israel than the one I had been negotiating, which included provisions for Israel's security and the importance of seeking a long-term resolution of the crisis.

In the end, Israel did destroy the tunnels, but the cease-fire left all the core issues unresolved.

At a donors' conference for reconstruction in Gaza, held in Cairo in October 2014, I described the tragic dynamic repeating itself once more. This was the third time in less than six years that together with the people of Gaza we had been forced to confront a reconstruction effort. It was the third time in less than six years that we saw war break out and Gaza left in rubble. It was the third time in less than six years that we'd had to rely on a cease-fire to halt the violence.

We were all weary of reconstruction conferences that addressed the aftermath of conflict but did nothing to prevent the next one. None of us had come there to rebuild Gaza only to think that two years later we'd be back at the same table talking about rebuilding Gaza again.

A cease-fire is not peace. Even the most durable of cease-fires is not a substitute for security for Israel and a state for Palestinians.

The March 2015 elections in Israel would not breathe new life into a peace process. We meticulously stayed away from the election. We wanted to avoid any hint of leaning one way or the other. Of course, we followed it from afar. News reports in Israel suggested it was possible Bibi could lose. I remember being in Sharm el-Sheikh for an economic development conference the Friday before the elections. Many attendees were discussing Bibi's prospects. It was clear that Bibi's opponent Isaac "Bougie" Herzog, who headed the center-left, Labor-based Zionist Union, was willing to lean further forward on the peace effort with the Palestinians.

Over the course of the next days, Bibi launched a full-scale effort to save his job. In effect, he cannibalized all the parties on the Right, telling right-leaning voters that a vote for any other right-wing party was a vote for Herzog and Tzipi Livni. Bibi appealed to people's fears that "Israeli Arabs were coming out to vote in droves." In the end, he won with a significant margin and created the most right-wing cabinet in the history of Israel, with a majority of its members opposing the two-state solution. It's no secret that President Obama was not happy with some of Bibi's tactics and statements disavowing the peace process and what sounded like race-baiting on the Palestinians. And he made clear that he didn't think there was any point in getting back to negotiations that Israelis said up front weren't going to work. There's been much speculation about the personal relationship between Bibi and President Obama, but what I saw at times like this were genuine policy disagreements on issues of importance to both our nations.

The president ordered a thorough review to reevaluate all our policies that were based on advancing a two-state solution.

That was a significant turning point that set us on a path for the rest of the administration. While most of our policies didn't actually change, our fundamental view of Israel's intentions with respect to the Palestinians did.

A key element of managing the Israeli-Palestinian conflict was ending the war in Gaza; another was trying to stop war from breaking out in the West Bank and, ultimately, to get the parties to take some steps on the ground that would show that there was progress toward two states. One of the primary sources of tension was around the Temple Mount/Haram al-Sharif compound. With Israel maintaining day-to-day security control, tensions often ran high. In October 2015, those tensions spilled over into a wave of Palestinian violence that threatened to spiral out of control.

King Abdullah had a special interest in this site because of Jordan's historic role in administering it. The Temple Mount/Haram al-Sharif is important to peoples of all three monotheistic faiths—Jews, Muslims and Christians. Of all the issues of incitement, this was the one that could trigger a holy war throughout the region. We spent three grinding days working around the clock in November trying to choreograph statements from both sides. Every word, comma and syllable was the subject of intense negotiations. It was a productive if imperfect outcome. Bibi wound up releasing his statement in English on Facebook at midnight, and King Abdullah never actually said exactly what he was supposed to say. But tensions were reduced and the amount of violence went down. Both sides saw the virtue in leaving well enough alone. In the Middle East, sometimes that's the best you can do.

In the absence of negotiations, we turned our focus to improving the situation on the ground. I thought it was very important to push for steps that would create the conditions for resumption of direct negotiations, while creating a political horizon by starting to craft the reality of the two-state solution.

When Bibi came to Washington to meet with President Obama in November, we had a conversation in which he was very supportive of steps we had taken on the ground. I traveled to Israel to follow up with him a few days later. My argument was that if he took constructive steps to allow the Palestinians to build freely on their land, we could ward off international pressure and get the Palestinians to back off their efforts in international forums. Bibi wouldn't budge. He told me, "I'm not going to

reward these guys in the middle of a wave of attacks against my people."
We went back to Abbas, and, frankly, I had one of the worst meetings with
him that I've ever had. He was clearly fed up, but with Israel under attack
it was not the moment for me to offer him anything. At the same time, it
was very disappointing to us that he wasn't willing to take the stronger
steps that we were pushing him on, including clearly condemning individual acts of violence.

We were getting nowhere with the Palestinians. We had worked very
hard to create a path forward with the Israelis based on steps they had suggested they were willing to take—but now refused to take because of the
violence. I could understand the perspective of both sides; at the same time,
it left us nowhere to go. When we left, I told Bibi—more in sorrow than in
anger—that we were at the end of the line again.

It was clear that we needed to do something significant to change the dynamic. A few days later, I addressed the annual U.S.-Israel Saban Forum at
the Brookings Institution. I wanted to put the onus on those who were arguing against two states to explain how a one-state solution could ever work.
And I wanted to raise awareness among everybody else that this untenable
situation was going to become a permanent reality if serious steps weren't
taken soon. In fact, Israel had increasingly consolidated control over the
majority of the West Bank for its own exclusive use, effectively reversing
the transition to greater Palestinian civil authority that was called for by the
Oslo Accords.

The challenge gets only more daunting as the number of settlers in the
roughly 130 Israeli settlements east of the 1967 lines grows. When I left as
secretary, the settler population in the West Bank alone, not including East
Jerusalem, had increased by nearly 270,000 since Oslo, including 100,000
just since 2009. More than 90,000 settlers were living east of the separation
barrier that was created by Israel itself, and the population of these distant
settlements has grown by 20,000 since 2009. At the same time, thousands
of Israeli settlers have set up some one hundred illegal outposts in the West
Bank with the acquiescence, if not outright support, of successive Israeli
governments.

Even as Israeli settlements and outposts continued to expand, Palestinian development in much of the West Bank had effectively been shut
down and Palestinian structures are being demolished at historically high
rates. Meanwhile, Israeli businesses make vast sums of money in the
West Bank, Israeli farms flourish in the Jordan River Valley and Israeli
resorts line the shores of the Dead Sea, where no Palestinian development
is allowed.

I don't think most people in Israel, and certainly elsewhere in the world, have any idea how broad and systematic this reversal of the Oslo process has become. I began asking a series of questions at Saban and beyond about the implications of this policy for Israel's long-term security. I made the point that these trends were leading toward an irreversible one-state reality on the ground. I think this helped to spark a debate in Israel about the future of the Palestinian Authority and the two-state solution. But it did not result in the kind of broad examination of the creeping one-state reality that I wanted.

So we turned our attention to the one avenue we had left, which was the strong interest of our partners and the international community in finding a way forward. In July 2016, we put the concept of resuming the Oslo transition and specific recommendations for beginning to create a two-state reality on the ground into a report of the Middle East Quartet, a group set up to advance Middle East peace negotiations comprised the UN, the United States, the European Union and Russia. The report was tough on both sides but carefully balanced, and its recommendations gave the international community some constructive steps to point to.

Now what we were left with was the regional front. It was the last card we had to play. From my conversations with Bibi, it was clear that he maintained a keen interest in working on the regional play, which was popular with the Israeli public. I also knew that many Arab and European leaders were prepared to accept a final status agreement that addressed Israel's key concerns, including the need to meet its legitimate security needs. That's where we turned our attention.

To take advantage of all the work we had done during the negotiations and in getting the international community on board with our ideas for resolving the conflict, we set about drafting final status principles—internationally accepted terms of reference for direct negotiations—which had never before been established. The art was to craft language that would be specific enough to be useful and general enough to allow the parties room to negotiate, while reflecting the political sensitivities of both sides and what we could get the international community to support. Based on our two-plus years of conversations with the international community, we knew that most countries, including countries in the region, were willing to accept recognition of Israel as a Jewish state if the overall principles were balanced. We knew that we could get stronger language than ever before on Israel's security. We also effectively made clear that the resolution of the refugee issue could not involve flooding Palestinian refugees back into Israel. We worked closely with the White House to draft the principles. We then set out to create an international consensus around them.

Key to this effort were the Saudis, who carry great weight in the Arab world. A lot of diplomacy takes place behind the scenes, and building those relationships is critical to making progress. I made several trips to Saudi Arabia and hosted countless meetings with the Gulf States, particularly with the Emiratis, who I believed were ready to change their relationship with the Israelis if they could manage the politics.

After I had gotten the Egyptians and Jordanians to accept these final principles—Kerry Principles—and had indications from the Saudis that they were willing to endorse something along those lines, I convened a secret meeting in Aqaba in January 2016 with Bibi, King Abdullah of Jordan and Egyptian president Fattah al-Sisi. It was a remarkable moment. I had key states in the Arab world prepared to meet Israel's core demands, including recognition as a Jewish state and resolution of its security concerns. In particular, the Jordanians and the Egyptians were ready to work directly with Israel and the Palestinians on a comprehensive security strategy in the context of a two-state solution. The Saudis and others had also signaled a willingness to take steps on the path to fulfilling the promise of the Arab Peace Initiative of normalizing relations with Israel.

All Bibi had to do was embrace these proposals. I remember sitting with him on the porch of one of the king's spacious villas in Aqaba. If nothing else, I thought he would be impressed with how far we had moved the world in his direction on these issues. But I could tell right away from his body language that this was not actually what he wanted. Just as I was explaining all this to Bibi, a miniature drone crashed into a tree right next to the terrace where we were sitting. We both laughed a little nervously at what was such an obvious metaphor for where the conversation was headed. Bibi responded, "John, the people of Israel aren't ready for these final status principles. I take care of Jordan's security and Egypt's security, not the other way around." Then Bibi made his counterproposal. He would take small steps on the ground for the Palestinians. And in return for that, he wanted a dialogue with the Saudis and others in the Gulf on the concept of land for peace.

Aqaba was a turning point in my thinking. I realized trying to meet Bibi's requirements wasn't going to work because the goalposts were always moving. Consequently, I focused on convening an international meeting to endorse our final status principles, even though the Israelis and Palestinians had not yet accepted them, in order to create the basis for resumption of negotiations when the parties were ready.

At this point, there were a number of competing initiatives circulating: the Egyptians offered to convene the parties, the Russians were talking about hosting a summit and the French had their own peace conference in the works. I met with the key Arab leaders to get them to agree to publicly endorse the final status principles. All of them said they could support the principles, but they were reluctant to do so publicly because they'd get a lot of blowback. We knew we needed Arab backing to make these principles salable to the Israeli public and to give both sides political cover. It was a delicate balancing act to keep the French, Palestinians and Egyptians fully engaged. As we got closer to the U.S. election, nobody wanted to rock the boat politically so this whole endeavor was shelved until after November.

In September, I received the sad news that one of my heroes, Shimon Peres, passed away. Shimon was one of the founding fathers of Israel and had become one of the world's great elder statesmen. I was proud to call him my friend, and I know that President Obama was as well. I began to reflect on what we had learned—and the way ahead—when I joined President Obama in Jerusalem for the state funeral.

I remembered the first time that I met Shimon in person—standing on the White House lawn for the signing of the historic Oslo Accords. And I thought about the last time, at an intimate one-on-one Shabbat dinner just a few months before he died, when we toasted to the future of Israel and to the peace that he still so passionately believed in for his people.

He summed it up simply and eloquently, as only Shimon could: "The original mandate gave the Palestinians 48 percent, now it's down to 22 percent. I think 78 percent is enough for us."

Then Shimon recalled a discussion he had had with F. W. de Klerk, the former South African president who had ended apartheid. De Klerk said to him that he had saved up enough money to withstand the economic sanctions against his country. They were dug in for the long haul on that. What they could never do, he said, was pay for the moral cost of apartheid. There was no amount of money equal to that task and it was eating away at the soul of his country. Shimon recounted that conversation for me and then said, "If we don't solve this problem, I'm afraid that's what's going to happen to my country."

As we laid Shimon to rest that day, many of us couldn't help but wonder if peace between the Israelis and Palestinians might also be buried along with one of its most eloquent champions.

I was determined not to let that happen. There was simply too much at stake to give in to pessimism. I also believed that the best way to honor Shimon, who never gave up, and his legacy was to keep on fighting to the end ourselves. And his passing made me only redouble my efforts to lay out an internationally accepted set of principles that would create a path to serious negotiations on a two-state solution.

We were a long way from that point. In fact, while we were there for Shimon's funeral, the Israelis advanced the first brand-new settlement in the West Bank in over twenty years. The news of the settlement leaked out just after we left. By the time we were back home, it was all over the news. There's no other way to spin it: to announce a brand-new settlement while the president of the United States was in Israel paying his respects to a fallen Israeli leader, and after we'd just concluded an agreement that gave Israel $38 billion in military assistance, spoke loudly about the governing coalition's attitude toward the administration.

The Palestinians seized the news as an opportunity to circulate a UN Security Council resolution condemning Israeli settlement activity. They knew that if they limited the language to make it consistent with decades-long U.S. policy against settlement activity, it would put us in a very difficult position.

My mind flashed back to Christmas week 2014, when I had spent all my holiday—up through Christmas Eve—making phone calls to persuade other countries to oppose a Palestinian resolution in the Security Council. My only persuasive argument had been that it would destroy the possibility of a meaningful peace process. That wouldn't work any longer.

We all understood the political firestorm we would face if we didn't veto the resolution. At the same time, it was incredibly difficult to imagine that we'd cast our veto to defend an Israeli policy that Israel knew the United States had always strongly opposed and believed was not in their interest or ours.

We had a decision to make.

President-elect Trump had announced he was going to appoint an ambassador to Israel who was a hard-core proponent of the settlements and an avowed opponent of the two-state solution. At the same time, the Israelis had again shown themselves to be completely disdainful of our policy by starting a process of formally legalizing outposts, which was tantamount to annexing significant portions of the West Bank. The proliferation of settler outposts is illegal under Israel's own laws. They're often located on Palestinian land and strategically placed in locations that make a viable Palestinian state impossible. Right-wing politicians in Israel were openly bragging that the two-state solution was dead and they intended to annex the West Bank. We could not defend in the UN Israeli actions that amounted to a massive and unprecedented acceleration of the settlement enterprise.

We had a lot of conversations with the White House focused on the settlement policy and whether to defend it in its most egregious form. There were some who argued for sucking it up because it wasn't worth the political price. President Obama wasn't willing to make a decision that he thought was counter to U.S. interests simply because of the politics. I remember him saying something along the lines of "If we aren't willing to stand up for what we think is right now, what are we doing this job for?"

In the end, we did not agree with every word in the UN resolution. There were important issues that were not sufficiently addressed or even addressed at all. But we could not in good conscience veto a resolution that condemned Palestinian violence and anti-Israel incitement, reiterated the long-standing international consensus on settlements and called for the parties to start taking constructive steps to advance the two-state solution on the ground.

Our UN ambassador, Samantha Power, cast the vote to abstain. I came back to Washington from a brief Christmas holiday with my family to face some predictable criticism.

The Israelis blasted this resolution for calling East Jerusalem occupied territory. But there was absolutely nothing new in the resolution on that issue. It was one of a long line of Security Council resolutions that included East Jerusalem as part of the territories occupied by Israel in 1967, and that includes resolutions passed by the Security Council under Presidents Reagan and George H. W. Bush. Every U.S. administration since 1967, along with the entire international community, has recognized East Jerusalem as among the territories that Israel occupied in the Six-Day War. The Obama administration fully respected Israel's profound historic and religious ties to the city and to its holy sites. But the resolution in no manner prejudged the outcome of permanent status negotiations on East Jerusalem, which must, of course, reflect those historic ties and the realities on the ground.

I felt I had to rebut all these arguments.

I remember sitting with former undersecretary of state Wendy Sherman in my office with a draft of the speech I was planning to give about the resolution. Wendy and I both have strong ties to the Jewish community. She reminded me of what we both understood: "Mr. Secretary, if you give this speech, you're going to lose some friends." I looked out the window of my office over the Mall in Washington and said to Wendy, "I understand that. But I've done a number of things in my life because I thought it was the right thing, not because it was easy. And a lot of other people have done that too—all prepared to accept the consequences. I think this is the right thing to do now and I'm certainly not going to back down because there's going to be political blowback."

I sent the draft speech to President Obama in Hawaii and he wrote back to me: "John . . . I've got your back."

I was satisfied we'd spoken the truth as clearly as we possibly could. What was most disappointing to me about the reaction to this speech was that all the work we'd done on the regional front to establish final status principles had gotten lost in the cacophony of criticism. I had made my argument out of concern for and commitment to Israel. Sometimes you have to say hard truths to friends, and that's a measurement of real friendship.

Before my tenure was up, we had one last chance to get the focus back on the final status principles that we'd worked so hard over the past years to create. We wanted to have clarity about the framework that could lead to peace. We wanted to leave a positive path forward for when the parties were ready to take it. The French were hosting a conference on Middle East peace in January 2017. Heading into the conference, our challenge was to get everyone to sign on to a communiqué that expressly supported our final status principles.

Over the course of the next two days, we had conversations with almost every foreign minister in the room to work out the remaining issues. In the end, we got there. Every country agreed to the communiqué supporting the final status principles, which was accepted by consensus. And following that, a number of foreign ministers acknowledged our work on this. I remember Jean-Marc Ayrault, the French foreign minister who was hosting the conference, saying that "Kerry speaks for all of us on this issue." It was both an incredibly satisfying culmination of two years' worth of effort and a strange anticlimax. Although most people were focused on Donald Trump's election and few paid attention to the significance of the moment, for the first time the international community had come together in support of final status principles to finally end the Israeli-Palestinian conflict.

So where do we go from here?

I am an eternal optimist and I still see only one path forward. Today there are roughly equal numbers of Jews and Palestinians living between the Jordan River and the Mediterranean Sea. They can choose to live together in one state, or they can separate into two states. But here is a fundamental reality: with a one-state solution, Israel can be either Jewish or democratic—it cannot be both—and it won't ever really be at peace. Moreover, the Palestinians will never have the chance to realize their vast potential in a homeland of their own with a one-state solution.

That is why I firmly believe that the Israelis and the Palestinians need to find a fair and sustainable way to separate in the West Bank. Unfortunately, we're heading in the opposite direction. That's one of the most striking realities about the current situation: this critical decision about the future—one state or two states—is effectively being made on the ground every single day, despite the expressed desires of the majority of the people.

I know that among Israelis as well as Palestinians, most people would quickly tell you that as much as they want peace, they think it is a distant dream—something that's just not possible. We simply cannot give in to despair and allow this to become a self-fulfilling prophecy.

For starters, it is important for both sides to take steps that will reverse current trends on the ground. The Palestinians must take much stronger action against violence and incitement that only reinforce Israelis' worst suspicions. President Obama and I made it clear to the Palestinian leadership countless times that all incitement to violence must stop. We condemned violence and terrorism and condemned the Palestinian leadership for not condemning it. And we opposed boycotts and pushed back on efforts to delegitimize Israel in international forums and pursue action against Israel at the International Criminal Court, which only sets back the prospects for peace.

At the same time, the most extreme elements on the Israeli political spectrum risk accelerating a one-state future. If there is only one state, you would have millions of Palestinians permanently living in segregated enclaves in the middle of the West Bank, with no real political rights; separate legal, education and transportation systems; vast income disparities; and under a permanent military occupation that deprives them of the most basic freedoms. Separate and unequal is what you would have. And nobody can explain how that works.

We should never lose sight of the ultimate goal—what President Kennedy described as a genuine peace, "the kind of peace that makes life on earth worth living, the kind that enables men and nations to grow and to hope and to build a better life for their children." That is the future that everybody should be working for. It is up to Israelis and Palestinians to make the difficult choices for peace, but we can all help. For our part, we worked with the international community to create a way forward: steps on the ground that would begin the process of separation and rebuild trust, and final status principles for the parties to accept when they were ready. Whether it is this or some other approach, lasting peace will require difficult choices on both sides. For the sake of future generations of Israelis and Palestinians, for all the people of the region, of the United States and around the world who have prayed for and worked for peace for generations, let's hope that the Israelis and the Palestinians are prepared to make those choices before it's too late.

As for me, my mind returns to the anthem I learned in the chapel in high school: "O Pray for the Peace of Jerusalem." It is a song worth singing, and despite the scars I have, when it came to the effort to make peace between two peoples who desperately deserve it, I will always be proud that I got caught trying.

CHAPTER 18

Preventing a War

IRANIAN FOREIGN MINISTER Javad Zarif walked through the door of a small, windowless room off the side of the UN Security Council chamber that was no bigger than a walk-in closet. The room had just a desk and a couple of chairs. By prearrangement, I was waiting there, having entered from a door on the other side. It was the first meeting of a U.S. secretary of state and an Iranian foreign minister in almost forty years.

By all assessments of our allies, including Israel, and our own experts, Iran was hurtling toward nuclear weapons capability. No one doubted Iran had already mastered the nuclear fuel cycle. From the 164 centrifuges spinning to enrich uranium in the early days of the George W. Bush administration, by 2011 Iran was spinning 19,000 of their 27,000 deployed centrifuges. The Iranians had stockpiled a sufficient amount of enriched uranium, enough for eight to ten bombs if they broke out to make a weapon. They were a few months from commissioning a plutonium reactor that could produce enough weapons-grade plutonium for additional bombs. Our experts assessed that Iran could break out to a weapon in two to three months.

Equally ominous, many of our strongest allies in the region were actively lobbying the United States to bomb Iran's nuclear facilities. For years, prime ministers, kings and presidents in the region had all argued the United States should initiate preemptive strikes.

Iran's behavior in the region greatly complicated the nuclear picture. Iran was testing missiles; supporting Hezbollah, a designated terrorist organization; meddling in Iraq; and threatening Saudi Arabia while supporting civil strife in Yemen. Indeed, the stakes were high.

If the United States was going to bring Iran's nuclear program under appropriate restraints and avoid engaging in a unilateral war of enforcement in the Middle East, we believed it was essential first to exhaust all possible remedies of diplomacy. We have learned through the years that America and the values we represent are stronger when we show the maturity and patience to build a broad coalition of support. That is what George H. W. Bush did in the Gulf War and that is what we did in implementing a strategy to defeat Daesh (more commonly known as ISIS or ISIL). We were well aware of Iran's aggressive behavior in the region. That is precisely why we imposed sanctions for their missile activities, violations of human rights and trafficking in arms.

But for all the problems Iran presented to the world and the region, President Obama and our entire national security team knew it would be easier to deal with Iran and make the world safer if we didn't have the specter of a nuclear weapon hanging over us on all the issues we faced. We had to deal with Iran's nuclear program.

As Zarif and I settled into that small UN meeting room to begin our very first conversation, that stark reality was at the forefront of my mind. The meeting was meant to be a brief exchange.

Javad and I spoke in that closet-sized room for nearly an hour. I had learned as much as I could about him beforehand from friends and colleagues who had worked with him at the UN. It was clear he had done the same, citing my work with the Omanis and other examples of my engagement in the region.

I was immediately struck by Javad's facility with idiomatic English. His American education and years as the Iranian permanent representative to the UN had provided him a huge grounding in American politics. He was well read, educated and intelligent. He was also an articulate, committed spokesperson for an Iranian regime with which we had very fundamental differences.

We talked pleasantries at first—his years in New York, the UN, life in Iran and his family, our politics, my job, the Senate. Then we got down to business. I made it clear that the administration was prepared to be serious but didn't feel either rushed or compelled to reach an agreement on Iran's nuclear program. No deal was better than a bad deal, and it would be vital that Iran be prepared to prove it would live by International Atomic Energy Agency (IAEA) standards and more, or we would be wasting our time. He said Iran was not desperate for a deal. He mentioned the ayatollah's fatwa, made public in 2003, declaring that Iran would not pursue a nuclear weapon. I said we obviously needed one of the most verifiable international agreements ever made. It was understood: we each had clear bottom lines that would never be crossed, but we were also both serious about trying to find a way forward.

Before we departed, we discussed the importance of privacy. From the start, we both acknowledged that our relationship would be essential to success. We needed to have an open line through which we could communicate directly at the break-the-glass, tense moments. For that reason, we pledged in that first meeting to avoid working through disputes publicly, via the press. Instead, we would do all we could to resolve them privately.

The press was well aware that Zarif and I would likely have some kind of conversation that day because we were both scheduled to attend a public meeting of the so-called P5+1—the group formed previously to focus on Iran's nuclear program. The P5+1—the five permanent members of the UN Security Council (China, France, Russia, the UK and the United States) plus Germany—and the European Union had been meeting at lower levels, sporadically, for years, to gauge the possibilities for an agreement that would eliminate the international community's concerns over Iran's growing nuclear program. This was the first time diplomats at the foreign minister or secretary of state level had joined the P5+1 talks. Reporters were packed like sardines in the designated stakeout positions, eager for comments on what unfolded inside the UN Security Council chamber. Zarif and I were well aware of the attention. Forty years of mutual avoidance was erased with our meeting.

All of this unfolded in the middle of the 2013 UN General Assembly—UNGA, as it's known—a power-packed week each September when foreign leaders descend on New York City and New Yorkers avoid the ten-block radius around the UN headquarters in east Midtown for fear of getting caught waiting for one of the hundred-plus motorcades moving through the area. It's controlled chaos. The State Department essentially takes over a few floors of a nearby hotel, converting the guest rooms into offices. It wasn't unusual to have well over a dozen meetings and events on my calendar a day. Each meeting, each movement, is meticulously scheduled and choreographed. Zarif's and my hour-long meeting sent people scurrying to make up for this impromptu encounter.

THE MEDIA REPORTS of that first meeting in New York described it as the opening of a new chapter between the United States and Iran. But our nations' dialogue had actually started well before then.

In May 2011, when I was still chairman of the Senate Foreign Relations Committee, I was introduced to an emissary of Sultan Qaboos of Oman—a man named Salem al-Ismaily. Salem is smart and incisive. He is also soft-spoken and humble—in fact, I'm certain he'd prefer to be excluded from this story. But the fact is his role is too critical to leave out.

Salem first crossed my radar after the Iranian government imprisoned three American hikers who had inadvertently wandered into the Iranian mountains. They were suspected of being spies. When the first of those hikers, Sarah Shourd, was released in September 2010, she publicly highlighted the role Salem had played in her release, thanking her "dear friend Salem al-Ismaily" hours after she cleared Iranian airspace. But several months after Sarah returned home, the other two hikers, Josh Fattal and Shane Bauer, remained in Iran's custody. With the United States and Iran refusing to engage directly on the matter, Sultan Qaboos and Salem were serving as de facto intermediaries for our governments in facilitating Josh's and Shane's release as well.

Salem requested a meeting with me to discuss this issue, offering to fly to Washington from Muscat for the conversation. Despite his record of success in securing Sarah Shourd's release, the sultan doubted whether the administration understood how helpful he intended to be with the Iranians.

Within the first five minutes of meeting Salem, I realized that his objective extended beyond the hikers. We spoke of the importance of getting Josh and Shane home swiftly but he turned quickly to the potential for progress on other fronts as well. At the top of the list was Iran's current path to a nuclear weapon. Salem made clear to me during that first meeting that Sultan Qaboos felt he could be helpful in advancing a mutually agreeable solution. It was also clear that the Omanis were not acting only out of goodwill; they knew that a nuclear-armed Iran would fundamentally undermine the stability of the region. And they were concerned, as we were, that Tehran was getting closer and closer to a weapon.

Shane and Josh were finally released in September 2011, thanks in large part to Oman's efforts. In my view, and in the view of many in the Obama administration, including President Obama himself, Sultan Qaboos had proven his seriousness and his sway with the Iranians.

Having proven their bona fides, I believed it was appropriate to see if they could help bridge the communications divide with the Iranians. We needed greater insight into their thinking. We needed to better assess the possibilities. Salem and I began to talk regularly, both on the phone and, from time to time, in person. We were careful about prying ears and microphones. Knowing there were people in the United States and overseas who advocated military action as the only solution to Iran's nuclear progress, we wanted to be careful not to make a diplomatic solution impossible even before our nations had a chance to sit down and talk.

I shared my discussions only with the smallest number of authorized people in the administration, dealing most of the time with Tom Donilon.

There was general agreement that, given the success of the hikers' release, it was worth at least exploring the potential for progress on the nuclear front. With President Obama's approval, I began planning for a trip to Muscat to meet with Sultan Qaboos in hopes of gaining better insight as to what was really possible. I suggested to President Obama that there was one more person we needed to bring into the circle: Senate majority leader Harry Reid.

It turned out there was only one possible window of time for me to make the trip before the end of the year, and, regrettably, it meant I'd end up missing at least the confirmation vote on Richard Cordray as head of the new Consumer Financial Protection Bureau. I would have to tell Harry he couldn't count on me to be there for the vote. I owed him an explanation as to why.

We met in his office in the Capitol Building. I brought him up to speed on the conversations with Salem and explained that President Obama wanted me to travel to Muscat to meet with the sultan. I started to explain why it was important the trip remain secret, but he stopped me before I got very far—he understood the sensitivity and said he was unlikely to get the nomination through the Senate anyway (Cordray wouldn't be officially confirmed until July 2013).

It was one of the many times I was grateful to have Harry in the leader's office. He was tough as nails on the Senate floor, but behind closed doors, you couldn't find a more supportive colleague. He told me he thought the trip was a good idea. He wanted me to know that he would hold anything I told him in the strictest confidence. And from then until this day he has kept his word. That's the old Senate.

The secrecy also applied to my own staff. Only a couple of my aides were briefed on the full story. When it became clear the Cordray vote would happen while I was gone, we knew the press would inquire about my absence. We never lied to the press, but when the inquiries poured in, my chief of staff told our press team to make no comment and absorb whatever hits followed. Lucky for us, the story died after forty-eight hours.

I arrived at the sultan's palace on the morning of December 8, 2011. I had never met Sultan Qaboos, but I knew his reputation as a thoughtful interlocutor with good relations on both sides of the region's sectarian divide and as a leader who had taken his country from dirt roads to modernity. He had come to power in the 1970s, when Oman had little in the way of infrastructure, health care and education. The sultan used his country's oil revenues to build schools, hospitals and roads and deliver clean water. He had long worked to bridge the divide between Sunni Gulf states and Shia nations like Iran—even at risk to his relationship with his Gulf partners. His impartiality made him one of the few leaders trusted by both the U.S. president and the Iranian supreme leader.

My first visit to Oman was memorable. Not only was it the start of a years-long endeavor, but it was one of the most generous and heartfelt welcomes I had received anywhere. Sultan Qaboos and I sat out on the veranda of one of his spacious, light-stoned palaces overlooking the Gulf, discussing politics, art, music and our shared appreciation of classic cars. Around lunchtime, he escorted me to another part of the palace—this one even larger—where, as we were serenaded by members of the royal orchestra, who played a medley of American songs, we enjoyed a spectacular Middle Eastern feast and turned finally to the topic at the forefront of both our minds: whether the United States and Iran could overcome our respective skepticism and begin to negotiate a solution to the nuclear challenge.

The sultan told me he believed there was a real opportunity at hand. Traditionally, within the Iranian government, the nuclear issue had been managed by hard-liners on the Supreme National Security Council. But the sultan was encouraged because the supreme leader, Ali Khamenei, had decided to transfer oversight to the Ministry of Foreign Affairs, meaning it would be under the purview of then minister Ali Salehi, an MIT-trained nuclear expert. Salehi was the godfather of the Iranian nuclear program, and for that reason, he enjoyed the trust of the supreme leader. But, the sultan argued, Salehi was also one of the biggest advocates in Tehran for giving diplomacy a chance. I would later find out that the sultan's instincts with respect to Salehi were dead-on, as usual.

Notwithstanding the sultan's sense of opportunity, we both understood the very real obstacles to progress. At the top of the list were decades of mutual distrust and deception. Both sides had significant political concerns as well, which, ironically, were not entirely dissimilar: both governments were facing elections and had to appease large constituencies of powerful people who were vehemently opposed to direct talks between the countries. In the broad sweep, to Americans, Iran was a terrorist state, guilty of trashing our embassy and taking hostages, of killing Americans with IEDs and bombs in Iraq and Lebanon, of interfering with governments in the region in furtherance of spreading its "revolution." To Iranians, America was the "Great Satan," untrustworthy overthrower of their government with the CIA, a supporter of the Shah and his torturing secret police, guilty of standing by while Saddam Hussein gassed Iranians and then complaining about Iran's support for Assad. Perceptions and feelings were strong on both sides. There was a lot to work through, and finding a mutually agreeable way forward would be challenging, potentially even impossible.

With that in mind, Sultan Qaboos shared important guidance during that first meeting. "There must be a sense of genuine, mutual respect underlying this negotiation," he told me. "If the Iranians feel bullied or condescended to, they will walk away at once." I took this advice to heart. The talks that followed were often tense, if not heated. But despite huge substantive differences, they were always cloaked in a mantle of respect. It made all the difference.

I LEFT MUSCAT heartened by our conversation and returned to Washington a few days before Christmas. I quickly briefed the White House and State Department. There were still a number of unanswered questions, but President Obama agreed that there appeared to be a basis for real dialogue with the Iranians.

He also agreed that continuing to communicate with the Iranians via messages passed through Muscat wouldn't get us very far; ultimately, we would need to sit down face-to-face with the Iranians themselves. I arranged to return to Muscat on January 3, 2012, to discuss how the Omanis could help bring about such a dialogue.

These initial conversations had energized me. During the Christmas holidays with the family in Ketchum, Idaho, I spent considerable time on the phone with Salem, my staff and others involved in the effort. Now I believed we had a real opportunity to prevent a nuclear arms race in the Middle East. I wanted to make sure we didn't squander it.

I did take some time off. For the past twenty-five years, on Christmas Day, we have played an annual late-afternoon ice hockey game with neighbors in Sun Valley. It's great fun—usually. Kids of all ages play, from four to seventy-four. It isn't "real" ice hockey, though it requires real skating; we play "broom" hockey—small sticks with a shortened blade and a hardened rubber ball. Only a few folks ever wore shin guards or hockey pants. It was purposely pretty tame, although depending on who had the ball, the pace could get fast.

At one point I was chasing the ball, when Tom Hanks—one of our neighbors in Idaho—slipped and fell right in front of me. I was going to either crash into him or try to jump over him and avoid a collision. I opted for the latter. Unfortunately, just as I was halfway over and clearing him, he started to get up, not seeing me coming. As he went up, he caught the shins of my legs, which forced them up and my face down into the ice. My head hit with a crack that was heard from one end of the ice to the other. It happened so quickly there was no time to cushion the face-plant with my arm or hand. I knew instantly I had broken my nose. I went straight to the hospital, where they informed me I would need to wait for the swelling to go down to have it properly set. I wound up with two huge black raccoon eyes and a swollen broken nose complete with beaten boxer look. A week later, when I was scheduled to return to the Middle East, the bruises had barely dissipated. I grabbed a pair of big black sunglasses and off I went.

In Muscat, we got down to business pretty quickly. President Obama relayed a number of concerns, which I conveyed to the sultan. One thing particularly preoccupied the president: How serious were the Iranians? Would whoever they sent to meet with us have authority to actually negotiate, or were they engaged in a stunt to be used against us down the road? Before we would agree to any meeting, we hoped Sultan Qaboos could vouch for Iran's motives. Could he convey confidence in the diplomats charged with negotiating on Iran's behalf? I asked the sultan if he would be willing to visit Iran to take a full personal measure of Iranian intentions. In an extraordinary gesture, the sultan, who seldom traveled officially because of health challenges, made an official visit to Tehran, where he met with the supreme leader Ayatollah Khamenei to discuss the possibilities.

Sultan Qaboos also raised the issue of uranium enrichment, which had been one of the core points of conflict in previous negotiations over Iran's nuclear program. Iran had argued for many years that, as a party to the Nuclear Non-Proliferation Treaty (NPT), it had every right to enrich uranium as long as it stayed fully within the constraints of the NPT. We consistently made clear that the NPT—the central pillar of global nonproliferation efforts—outlines only a right to nuclear power. It does not, and has never, granted parties a defined "right" to enrich uranium themselves. This is a fact I was careful to emphasize from day one in my discussions with the Omanis and by extension the Iranians. Nevertheless, there are thirteen countries, all members of the NPT, including the United States, that have enriching capacity within the constraints of NPT compliance, which includes more rigorous, intrusive accountability than applied to other nations. The Iranians argued that as long as they were in full compliance, they should be allowed to do what other nations were already legally doing. They had a right to peaceful nuclear power and insisted they didn't want to be forced into dependency on the Russians or any other country for their nuclear reactor fuel.

Leaving aside whether Iran had the "right" to enrich, deep down I also understood that unless we were willing to discuss the possibility that Iran's enrichment could continue under carefully defined limits, there was no way we would gain the access, accountability, transparency and restraint necessary to know for certain Iran was not pursuing a weapons program. There might not even be a way to get Iran to the table. The average person in Iran bristles at the notion that his country can't do what other sovereign nations do just because the United States says so. Iranians see that as complete capitulation at the hands of an America that for too long interfered in their sovereignty under the Shah. It's asking too much for even a more moderate Iranian administration to accept.

The position of the United States had long been that any enrichment, however minor, would be a deal breaker. But our P5+1 negotiating partners unanimously moved away from this position. They decided, particularly given what other countries were doing, that some future enrichment would have to be discussed for the Iranians to take any negotiation seriously. I also learned in private conversations that despite its public position, the George W. Bush administration had quietly, privately come to agree with this position, though they had never landed on what structure or levels that might take. Deep down, I agreed too. And, as I came to learn, so did President Obama.

In the weeks that followed, Salem and I remained in close touch, speaking regularly on the phone and occasionally in person in one city or another. One night that spring, we spent hours at a table at Morton's steak house in Georgetown, crafting a detailed blueprint of how a secret back-channel dialogue could work—down to how the delegations would enter and exit the sessions without arousing suspicion, and how many people would be involved.

I believed we had a clear opening for diplomacy.

Most of the National Security Council members agreed that the Omani channel should be explored. Hillary Clinton had some initial doubts about the Omanis. She was not yet convinced they could deliver or that we should trust the track being offered. Everyone acknowledged the difficult history of dealing with Iran but also understood that past opportunities for diplomacy had been squandered. We all remembered reports of an opening the Bush administration rejected in 2003, back when Iran was spinning only 164 centrifuges. Head-to-head talks never happened. In the meantime, despite the aggressive sanctions we put in place, Iran brought more than 1,700 new centrifuges online.

I understood Hillary's caution, even if I disagreed with her. At one point, Tom Donilon convened a meeting in his office. My job, he told me, was to try to convince Hillary that we had to pursue this opportunity. It's not that

she wasn't supportive of diplomacy to address the Iran nuclear challenge—
she was—but she was not confident we had the opening the Omanis
claimed. She had met with Sultan Qaboos about a year before my trip to
Muscat and remained unconvinced that Iran had any desire to reach a deal.
She was worried we'd appear too eager to make a deal and be embarrassed
before anything was resolved. In the end, importantly, she supported the
approach.

The president ultimately agreed to the back channel, though the internal debate had clearly resonated. Early that spring, he set up a call with the
sultan to discuss the details. I don't know exactly what was said, but Salem
called my Senate office shortly after it ended. He was concerned. The leaders' conversation had left Sultan Qaboos anxious, and he wasn't sure the
United States was as committed as I'd conveyed. Would I speak to him? I
called the sultan and reassured him we were on track.

Maintaining momentum would not be easy. For one thing, there seemed
to be a reluctance to settle on a date. The Omanis repeatedly submitted suggestions: April 20? No. April 24? No. May 1 or May 8? Won't work. After a
while, they grew frustrated that an answer did not seem forthcoming.

There was also indecision as to whom the administration would send to
the meeting and whether it made any sense for me to join the delegation.
The sultan had made clear to me that he would be more comfortable with
me there since he and Salem had gotten to know me well, but I also realized
that, as a former nominee for president and a longtime senator with close
ties to the current president, I was too visible for what was supposed to be
a discreet, low-profile exchange. One afternoon, when Tom Donilon and I
were discussing the delegation, he said offhandedly, "Depending on what
happens in the next term, you don't want to be directly communicating with
the Iranians." It was a valid point, though I was surprised. This was a few
months before President Obama pulled me aside during the 2012 campaign
debate prep, where I played Mitt Romney, to let me know someone would
be in touch with me to discuss my potentially taking part in the second-term
administration.

My main concern was that the meeting take place and take place soon,
not who would go. More than a year had passed since my first meeting with
Salem. In the meantime, Iran had continued to march closer to a weapon.
We needed to send a team—any team—to determine whether direct engagement was possible, before we missed the opportunity for good.

President Obama wisely sent Hillary's deputy chief of staff, Jake Sullivan, and National Security Council staffer Puneet Talwar, who would later
become my assistant secretary for political-military affairs, as well as an

IT expert and an interpreter. Jake and Puneet, both smart and capable, were playing key roles on the national security team but were conveniently little known at the time, which made them perfect for the task. They took some extraordinary measures to protect the secrecy of their trip. No one was taking any chances.

The meeting went off without a hitch, but neither side thought it was particularly productive. Jake and Puneet were instructed not to show any latitude on enrichment, which angered the Iranians. In turn, the Iranians showed little willingness to accept even modest restrictions on their program.

And yet, the fact that they showed up at all, with the blessing of the supreme leader, demonstrated that they were taking the prospect of diplomacy seriously. That alone was a significant development—an encouraging sign in the wake of nearly forty years of nothing but invective.

As the summer continued, the external situation grew even more precarious. Israel was sending signals, both publicly and privately, that Iran was approaching a red line, and in response, there were more and more signals that the IDF was prepared to attack. It reached the point where national security experts were examining the phases of the moon for a signal of when it might happen. Common wisdom suggested Israeli military leaders would choose a new moon, when the sky was particularly dark, lending itself to a stealth attack.

The priority at that moment was convincing Israel to refrain from bombing Iran—at least temporarily. The back channel, for all intents and purposes, was put on hold. It would be several months before Iran and the United States reconvened.

THE AGGRESSIVE SANCTIONS regime we and our international partners were pursuing was having a dramatic impact on Iran's economy, without question, but it was simultaneously strengthening the Iranians' resolve to accelerate their nuclear program. Time was running out. We were essentially at the threshold point of a nuclear-armed Iran.

It was time, President Obama determined, to signal to Iran that the United States was willing to discuss the possibility of an agreement in which Iran could continue to enrich uranium on a limited basis. After all, the rest of our P5+1 negotiating partners had already come to that conclusion. We were the only holdouts. At some point, the United States would likely share the blame for the world missing an opportunity to solve the crisis peacefully.

With the Omanis' help, we began to plan for another sit-down with the

Iranians. I was strongly supportive of Bill Burns, the deputy secretary of state, leading the U.S. delegation. Bill, a career Foreign Service officer, was hugely respected at Foggy Bottom. He stood out as one of the most capable career diplomats the department has ever known. I knew he had the respect of former secretary of state Clinton as well as the president. In fact, one of the first things I did when I got to the State Department was ask Bill to postpone his long-planned retirement from the Foreign Service and remain as deputy secretary—in large part because I knew how valuable his expertise would be to the Iran effort. I was fortunate he agreed to do so.

The president and I knew that Bill's involvement in the back channel would serve two goals: first, it would prove how serious we were about the talks, and second, we hoped it would encourage high-level participation on the Iranian side. President Obama also wanted to make sure the meeting was held after I was sworn in as secretary of state. We wanted it to be patently clear that the U.S. government was unified as these talks got under way.

I was sworn in on February 1, 2013. Bill and the rest of the delegation traveled to Muscat in early March. He delivered the message the Iranians needed to hear: the United States would be prepared to explore a limited, exclusively peaceful domestic energy enrichment program, provided Iran would commit to sharp, permanent, verifiable constraints.

THE PROCESS WAS put on hold as Iran's presidential election approached in June 2013. When the more moderate candidate, Hassan Rouhani, won, we were surprised and encouraged. Rouhani had campaigned on repairing Iran's ties with the international community. He had also spent sixteen years as secretary of the Supreme National Security Council. In that role, he had been deeply involved in previous rounds of nuclear negotiations. We didn't know whether that would prove to be helpful or the opposite, but we figured some expertise was preferable to ignorance.

We also took some comfort in Rouhani's appointment of Javad Zarif to serve as foreign minister and oversee the nuclear file. His reputation from his nearly ten years as Iran's permanent representative at the UN was well known. He knew the international playing field as well as anyone. He had spent many years in the United States, was fluent in English and well versed in American culture. In addition, Zarif's predecessor, Ali Salehi, who was essential in setting up the back channel, was appointed to lead Iran's atomic energy program. These appointments seemed to reinforce Iran's serious purpose. I was cautiously optimistic our effort would be reinvigorated—a belief that was confirmed when I heard from Salem that Rouhani's team wasted no time in reaching out to the Omanis with a clear message: they were eager to move forward.

Bill led another delegation to Muscat weeks after Rouhani's inauguration in August. We spoke nightly while he was there. He described a fundamental change in the mood of the talks. For the first time, our delegation perceived a real sense that the Iranians shared our desire to find a way forward. Previously, the meetings had largely been one lengthy speech after another, each person talking past the next. Now there was genuine dialogue.

When Bill returned, I asked him how close we were to finding some common ground. "We're not in the ballpark yet," he said. "But at least we're in the parking lot." Two years of careful back-channel outreach had been worth the risk.

A FEW WEEKS after the 2013 UNGA, Wendy Sherman, our invaluable undersecretary of state for political affairs, traveled to Brussels for a coordination meeting with the political directors of the P5+1 and EU delegations. This was nothing new for Wendy; her experience with multilateral nuclear negotiations dated back to the Clinton administration. Still, she braced herself for a series of tough discussions: it was time to inform our partners of the back channel we had been advancing in secret with Iran.

According to Wendy, no one was shocked. Everyone was pissed off.

The cause of their frustration wasn't so much the secrecy; most people understood our reasons for taking that approach. They were frustrated because they had been trying for years to convince the United States to accept a limited Iranian enrichment program as part of a comprehensive nuclear deal, and we had refused to endorse such a plan. Then we went off on our own and discussed as much with the Iranians without letting our negotiating partners know our position had changed. Sometimes international diplomacy just comes down to people-to-people relationships: the nations we were working with were upset that we had gone around them, and they wanted us to know that they expected to be fully engaged from that point on.

Our partners' negative reaction was understandable, and we had expected it. But there's not a doubt in my mind that it was the right course of action for the United States. Ultimately, the Iranians had to trust that the United States wasn't going to be the spoiler of the talks—that we were as serious as anyone about getting a deal—and we had to get the same sense of certainty with respect to the Iranian position. The back channel had enabled our two nations to reach a baseline of good faith. After noting their frustration for the record, our P5+1 partners accepted that the progress the United

States and Iran had made was fundamentally a good thing. Now the talks could begin in earnest.

Our initial goal was to reach an interim agreement that would give us time to negotiate a comprehensive, longer-term deal. For our part, we knew we couldn't sit at the table as Iran's nuclear program proceeded full steam ahead. At the same time, President Rouhani, who had been elected in large part because he pledged to revive Iran's crippled economy, wanted to get some relief from the tough sanctions that were making life miserable for many of his people. So we needed a temporary arrangement that would, for the duration of our negotiation, freeze Iran's program in place in exchange for modest relief from the nuclear sanctions the world had imposed.

At this point, the United States and Iran had already been discussing in our bilateral talks what this interim agreement could look like. In early November, as Wendy and the other political directors were getting ready to reconvene in Geneva, Wendy called to tell me she thought things were moving along. She thought it was a good time for me to come to Geneva to try to secure the interim agreement.

It wasn't long before the foreign ministers from the other P5+1 nations confirmed their travel to Geneva as well. *Possibly we can build some momentum,* I remember thinking. *Our goal should be to try our hardest to secure an interim agreement but remember always that no deal is better than a bad deal.* None of us anticipated the surprise French foreign minister Laurent Fabius was about to offer.

Upon his arrival at the Geneva hotel, Fabius stopped to talk to the press, which was camped out around the InterContinental hotel, where the talks were being held. "As I speak to you, I cannot say there is any certainty that we can conclude," Fabius told a French radio station in his deep, sonorous voice. France would not accept "a sucker's deal," he warned.

When I heard about Fabius's comments, I was taken aback. I had engaged him in several conversations leading up to the meeting and his team had been involved in all the P5+1 political directors process with Wendy. He hadn't reached out through staff or attempted to talk to me personally or do any of the other things ministers do before airing their grievances to the public. This was not how a cooperative multilateral process should unfold. Regardless, I recognized that I had to do what I could to get things back on track.

I called Fabius and asked to come see him in his room. We were all staying in the same hotel. After initial pleasantries, I asked him to be specific about what language he was concerned about in the draft text. In my memory there was no substantive response. He didn't offer one word or sentence. He had no recommendations for how to improve it. *C'est la vie.*

A little frustrated, I left Fabius and began to prepare for what had just become an even more complicated meeting with Zarif later that evening. Iran was under the impression that the P5+1 countries were coming from a unified place—indeed, that was our strength. Fabius, who was to become a close friend and an important partner in the negotiations, had just made it clear to the world there might be some differences within our own team.

It quickly became evident that we would not be leaving Geneva with an interim agreement, at least not during that visit. The other European nations knew that they could not be seen as weaker than France, so they too had to oppose the text. And in the end, so did the United States. President Obama's guidance was clear: the number one priority was unity among the P5+1. It would be essential, the president believed, both in getting a deal and in protecting that deal once it was reached.

So we stood by France and the rest of our partners, announcing that the gap between Iran and us remained too wide. We were going home. We would try again in a few weeks. As my motorcade pulled up to the tarmac at Geneva Airport, I reached for my cell phone to call the State Department Operations Center. I asked if they could please connect me to Foreign Minister Fabius.

"Laurent," I said, when he was patched through, "I'll see you in a couple of weeks. I look forward to working with you to close any gaps and see to it that everyone is on the same page. I hope you agree that we need to be careful about what we say to the press. If there are any issues, please call me personally." We hung up, and I got out of the car and walked up the tall stairway and into the cabin of the white C-32 U.S. Air Force plane, our home in the sky.

WE RETURNED TO Geneva two weeks later, on Saturday, November 23. Cathy Ashton, the thoughtful EU high representative, and I had been in regular touch since we left Geneva. We agreed on a new game plan: for the time being, I would focus on France and the rest of the P5+1, and she would liaise with Iran. After meeting with Zarif, Cathy presented the updated text of the agreement, which included minor changes to the previous iteration. All nations were more or less on board—except, ironically, my own.

The U.S. delegation agreed with the technical aspects of the text—the steps Iran would take to freeze its program, verification measures, and the process by which we'd provide modest sanctions relief—all of which had largely been negotiated in our secret bilateral channel. Our concerns lay in the preamble to the agreement. We knew that section—the first two paragraphs of the text—would be read most closely and parsed by friends and critics alike. Some might even stop reading after that point. It mattered that we got every word right.

The American delegation quickly dashed the hopes of our partners who were ready for a late-afternoon press conference announcing the deal. We went back and forth with Iran well into the night. It came down to word choice and phrasing. These are the last-minute details over which diplomats pull their hair out. The scene in my hotel room at 3:00 a.m. Sunday morning was like something out of a play: I was in one corner, using the secure phone to explain to National Security Advisor Susan Rice the hiccups and the changes we were working through. Bill was in the adjoining room, on the phone with his counterpart in the secret channel, Majid Takht-Ravanchi, trying to get the Iranians' sign-off, and between us, experts and aides were frantically typing on BlackBerrys, fueled by seemingly endless espresso pods.

Finally, as the clock approached 4:00 a.m., we had an agreement—one we wanted to lock in as airtight and quickly as possible, lest anyone come back later that day with a different view. We woke up the other ministers, who had understandably gone to bed hours earlier, and alerted the press that an announcement was forthcoming.

As we made our way over to the Palais des Nations, where the press conference would be held, Helga Schmid, Wendy's EU counterpart, got a call from Abbas Araghchi, one of Zarif's deputies. The Iranians had four more points they wanted incorporated into the agreement.

Helga passed the phone to Wendy. "Abbas, there are no more points to incorporate," she told him. "The other ministers are now awake, they are making their way to the Palais; the press conference has been advised, and it's done." Abbas understood, and at 5:00 a.m. on Sunday, November 24, 2013—nearly two years after my initial trip to see Sultan Qaboos—the United States, our international partners and Iran announced a preliminary agreement that would enable us to begin direct, comprehensive negotiations. Most important, for the first time in decades, Iran's nuclear program would not be accelerating but frozen in place—and even, in some aspects, rolling back.

I soon boarded our plane and flew home, just in time for Thanksgiving. I thought we all had a lot to be thankful for that year. The world was a little bit safer that morning and a lot of hard work had paid off. But I had no illusions: even harder work was just getting started.

• • •

ON JANUARY 20, 2014, the interim deal—the Joint Plan of Action (JPOA)—went into effect. The Iranians froze production of highly enriched uranium. They stopped installing centrifuges and halted progress on their heavy-water reactor near the city of Arak. In return, we began releasing installments of a total of $4.2 billion of Iran's own money frozen in banks around the world.

Before this step, there was a possibility that Iran would attempt to keep us at the negotiating table for years while it moved closer and closer to a bomb. With the JPOA in place, time could not be used against either side. The situation would not get more dangerous while we were negotiating.

But while that hurdle had been removed, others remained. Critics of the deal on all sides intensified their attacks as the new phase of the talks got under way. A bipartisan group of my former Senate colleagues, led by Senators Mark Kirk, Bob Menendez and Chuck Schumer, was pushing sanctions legislation that, if passed, would torpedo the talks. Their efforts received vocal support from the American Israel Public Affairs Committee (AIPAC), the most powerful pro-Israel lobbying group. Bibi Netanyahu was furious, telling anyone who would listen that the JPOA was a "historic mistake."

By the time our experts got back to the table, politics in both the United States and Iran had made the playing field more complex. In early July, the ayatollah delivered a speech that declared Iran's desire not to cut back its enrichment, as we had been discussing, but to increase its capacity tenfold. In the version of the future the supreme leader described, Iran would be bringing thousands of new centrifuges online in the coming years. It was an outrageous and unexpected assertion—even Zarif claimed to be blindsided—and it gave our critics in the region and on Capitol Hill even more reason to blow their gaskets. The six-month time period we had allotted for the negotiation was wishful thinking. There was no way we were going to reach any agreement by the end of July. We extended the talks, and the JPOA, another four months, to November 24, 2014.

At that point, I stayed in constant communication with our day-to-day negotiating team led by Wendy Sherman, as well as our international partners. Cathy Ashton, Javad and I would meet trilaterally. Then Javad and I would meet bilaterally. The Omanis stepped in to mediate from time to time. We were trying to close the gaps that had emerged, but tensions continued to rise.

In November, just a couple of weeks before the deadline, I stopped in Oman to meet with Javad and his team. I was on my way to China for a

long-scheduled visit but hoped an in-person conversation might help to alleviate some of the tension that had been mounting.

The meeting was a total standoff, with each of us talking straight past
the other. It was so bad that we decided to meet again a few days later, when
I was on my way home from Beijing, but the second meeting was as useless
as the first. Our meetings had always been tough, but until that point they
were calm and respectful. That week in Muscat, we found ourselves shouting across the table. It was the first time we both lost our patience, but it
wouldn't be the last.

As the deadline approached, the experts tirelessly hammered away to
develop solutions to very complex problems. The details were critical. We
were making some headway, but shortly after I arrived in Vienna for the
final stretch, it became clear that we needed more time.

We began to prepare for another extension, but this one would be harder
to explain. In the 2014 midterm elections, the Republicans had won back
the Senate. It would be near impossible to stave off new sanctions legislation much longer. Every delay would give credence to their argument that
talks were futile and a deal was impossible. It would be difficult to sell a
second extension, but if we were able to do it, we'd have to make clear that
this was our last effort. We weren't going to sit at the negotiating table forever.

For several reasons, including scheduling concerns, we agreed to announce two separate deadlines for the talks. We would give ourselves four
months, until March 31, for a political agreement laying out the basic contours of the deal, and, if necessary, we would take another three months,
until June 30, to resolve the technical details.

The night before we announced the extension, I sat in my hotel suite
with a couple of aides, editing my remarks for the press conference we had
scheduled for the following day. I was losing patience with the Iranians.
They were tempting fate by not recognizing the difficulties of the political
playing field in the United States. I wanted to make it crystal clear in my
statement that time was running out. Still, I thought the first cut at the draft
excessively vilified Zarif. It was too harsh. I didn't want hard-liners on both
sides to be able to use my words in defending their assertion that we were
wasting our time with diplomacy. I also knew the Iranians well enough by
that point to understand that if they felt humiliated or condescended to, they
were more likely to dig in than capitulate. I still believed strongly that success was possible, but we'd have to tread carefully. Every move we made—
every word we said—mattered enormously.

The next draft of the remarks was less combative, but I thought it was important to add something about the respect both sides had for each other. Sultan Qaboos had emphasized the importance of respect. I felt strongly that we would gain nothing by venting in public at a critical moment. I told my team, "I've always felt that Javad has been a strong negotiator and he's here in good faith. I want to say that. I know I'll get shit for it, but I want to keep this cordial. Javad's team is working as hard as we are to get to a better place. He deserves some credit for that."

Some critics would attack me for any word of diplomatic nicety I showed to Iran or its foreign minister. That's the world we live in. I was looking at the long-term goal, not one day in the papers. The purpose of the talks was to prevent a country from getting a nuclear weapon, and if it took building "negotiating" respect with a government we had serious disagreements with, so be it. The way to keep the talks on track was for Javad and me to work hard to maintain the civility we had established.

WE HIT THE ground running in 2015. As we crept closer and closer to a deal, our critics got louder and louder. By this point, we were giving regular classified briefings to Congress, our Gulf partners and the Israelis to explain how the talks were evolving and to ensure they understood our thinking. We were making progress, and that sat better with some than others.

During our frequent lengthy and occasionally heated conversations, Prime Minister Netanyahu made his displeasure clear, but we stayed in regular contact. I made sure to call Bibi immediately following each negotiating session to convey where we were. Wendy briefed the Israeli security community often in person and in depth. While Bibi and those closest to him were opposed to what we were doing, most of the high-level leadership of the Israeli security forces supported the outcome of the agreement and would continue to do so even after President Obama left office.

On January 19, 2015, in the late afternoon, I met with Israel's ambassador to the United States, Ron Dermer, in my office in Washington. I'd known him a long time and even weighed in on his behalf when some in the White House were concerned about agreeing to his appointment. After I became secretary, we continued to have an open and respectful relationship. I had enjoyed a wonderful Passover Seder at his home. On this January afternoon, as the Iran negotiations were hitting what felt like the home stretch, I sat with Ron for a solid hour, talking about the future of the region and, of course, the progress made between the P5+1 countries and Iran.

The next morning, Speaker of the House John Boehner announced that Prime Minister Netanyahu had accepted his invitation to visit Washington in March to address a joint session of Congress. I was stunned. Ron sat in my office the day before knowing this announcement was coming and without giving me even a subtle heads-up that he had been working with the Speaker to engineer such a visit. I was blindsided, along with the president and everyone else in the administration.

It was a total departure from protocol and tradition; in the past, the White House and Congress consulted each other before extending this kind of invitation to a foreign leader. In this case, Congress purposely left President Obama out of the loop, in part because Prime Minister Netanyahu was invited precisely to undercut the administration's diplomatic efforts. It was another troubling indication that on foreign policy, Congress was operating no longer as an institution belonging to the country and history, but on behalf of a party and the moment.

I knew that Israel's mistrust in Iran's leaders ran deep—we all shared it—but in accepting congressional Republicans' invitation, the Israeli government revealed its disrespect for President Obama. The relationship between the two presidents never recovered.

In early March, as Bibi made his way to the U.S. Capitol, I was in Montreux, Switzerland, for a series of negotiations with the Iranians. I braced myself for what he would say.

The speech was broadcast live internationally, including in Switzerland. A few of us were in the middle of a tense session with the Iranians, so I missed it, but much of the delegation watched and reported the highlights. I read it later and caught a few snippets on the news. Bibi passionately told Congress that the deal "doesn't block Iran's path to the bomb. It paves Iran's path to the bomb." It was no surprise that Netanyahu grossly distorted the agreement. He delivered a well-crafted but purely political statement, not an honest analysis of nonproliferation strategy or a substantive argument for how one would in fact make Israel safer without the agreement. But then again, everyone understood that the speech was an appeal to the gut—an emotional screed calculated to mobilize his supporters in the United States and scare senators from approving the agreement.

As an unwavering supporter of Israel who always viewed my differences with Bibi through a political, not personal lens, I was disappointed in him. For my entire Senate career, I had loyally supported Israel, and as secretary, I continued in countless ways to help Israel avoid attacks in international organizations, to intervene on unfair resolutions and to recommend vetoes at the UN. President Obama had done as much, if not more, to support Israel than any other president. We had consistently acted with Israel's best interest at heart in international forums. I thought we deserved better than a speech that hit below the belt. We were vilified alongside the Iranians, which was strange indeed. For those of us gathered in Montreux that day, it was one of the more inexplicable moments of the journey.

We had gotten used to the steady stream of third-party vitriol by that time. We'd walk out of an intense, even heated meeting with the Iranians, only to catch wind of an angry statement released by someone who was ostensibly on our side. I'd spend three hours trying to convince Javad that an offer on a particular item was the best he could hope for, only to dial into a call with a counterpart from the region who wanted to give me a completely inaccurate and even fanciful earful on how much I was giving away. Fighting for a good deal on multiple flanks simultaneously made the entire task much more difficult.

A few days after Bibi's speech, Senator Tom Cotton, a Republican from Arkansas, led forty-six of his Senate colleagues in sending a letter to the Iranian government. The letter essentially argued that the Obama administration didn't speak for the United States. It warned Iran against trusting us, suggesting that any deal would be undone "with the stroke of a pen" as soon as Obama was out of office.

I had served in the Senate for twenty-eight years, as chairman of the Foreign Relations Committee for the last four of them. I knew how unprecedented it was for a member of Congress to intervene directly with foreign leaders and try to undermine a sitting president in the middle of a negotiation, let alone one where the stakes were so high. It was irresponsible and reckless. I could only imagine what the response of the Republicans would have been if Democrats had ever done that to President Reagan during his negotiations with the Soviet Union.

I saw Zarif the following day. I had barely said hello before he pulled out a copy of the letter. I explained the inaccuracies in Cotton's statement and urged him to remain focused on narrowing the gaps between our sides. We were getting too close to allow distractions to shake us. After all, there would be no better way to shut up the naysayers than to come home with a good deal in hand.

BY THE END of 2014, I had more or less succeeded in convincing Javad there was no way President Obama would agree to a deal that didn't expand Iran's so-called breakout time to at least a year. This key principle became a central tenet that guided the talks from that point on. Translated, it meant we needed U.S. nuclear experts to be confident that if the Iranians decided to break out of the deal and ramp up their enrichment, it would take at least a year for them to acquire enough fissile material to power a bomb. In our view, a year was more than enough time for the United States and our allies to pursue "alternative" (read: military) means of preventing a nuclear-armed Iran.

Breakout time is calculated based on a number of factors, from the size of the existing stockpile of enriched uranium, to how many centrifuges would be spinning, to how advanced those centrifuges were, to how they would be configured. The trouble was certain inputs our experts used to crunch those numbers were classified. There was only so much we could explain to the Iranians about why individual proposals were more, or less, acceptable to us. This frustrated Zarif. Much of what could clarify the choice of one approach over another was dependent on mathematics and science rather than politics. Perhaps because neither of us was a scientist, it was difficult to persuade each other of the efficacy of one position over another.

Just before we walked into the Situation Room one afternoon for an NSC meeting, Wendy received an email from Abbas. The Iranians notified us they were sending Ali Salehi to the next round of talks to oversee the more technical negotiations. Salehi was one of Iran's top nuclear physicists and served as the head of the country's Atomic Energy Organization. Abbas wanted to know whom we would send to serve as Salehi's interlocutor.

Wendy pulled Susan Rice and me aside and read the email off her Black-Berry. In unison, the three of us spoke the obvious answer: Ernie.

Like all secretaries of energy, Ernie Moniz oversaw the U.S. nuclear arsenal. But unlike other secretaries of energy, he also had a PhD and decades of experience in nuclear physics. While Salehi and Moniz had never met, they had overlapped for a few years at MIT in the 1970s. This turned out to have consequence: Salehi was very proud of his MIT education. And Ernie was a professor there by the time Salehi was working toward his degree. Ernie not only had the appropriate clearances, but was fully briefed on the most sensitive aspects of the negotiations. He had frequently weighed in on our internal discussions. He was ready to jump right in.

Moments after Wendy read out Abbas's email, Ernie made his way into the Situation Room. As the NSC meeting got under way, Susan and I broke the news to him. "Hopefully you don't have plans this weekend," we said. "You're going to Switzerland."

We didn't know initially if Salehi had been sent to try to get a deal or to prevent one. As such, he was extremely close to Ayatollah Khamenei. At first, most of our nuclear folks thought it was a bad sign that the Iranians were deciding to send him in. He was viewed as the guy who would say no.

In their estimation, he would be reluctant to take any steps that might undermine the country's nuclear program that he had built from scratch.

I was among those who thought his presence could be positive. I didn't believe the Iranians would send Salehi if their only goal was to obstruct progress. There were plenty of ways to do that. To me his participation meant they wanted to get the solution right. It meant they were serious about reaching a deal.

I turned out to be right. On the surface, Salehi and Moniz could not have been more different. Salehi, who wore wire-rimmed glasses and an impeccably groomed beard, was soft-spoken and serious. Moniz, whose hair fell to just above his shoulders, was gregarious and easygoing. But their differences were irrelevant. They spoke the same scientific language. With them on hand to hammer through the more technical elements with mutually understood authority, the rest of us could focus on the bigger picture. The talks began to accelerate.

WITH OUR INITIAL deadline fast approaching, we arrived in the Swiss city of Lausanne on March 26, 2015, with the goal of finally concluding the political agreement we had promised the world.

We took over the Beau-Rivage, a hotel on the shore of Lake Geneva. It had seen its fair share of diplomacy in the past, including the signing of the Treaty of Lausanne in 1923, which dissolved the Ottoman Empire. Zarif was all too familiar with this history. "If we have an announcement to make at the end of this, we can't do it at the Beau Rivage," he joked. "Too much baggage."

The U.S., French, British, German, Chinese, Russian, EU and Iranian delegations each had office space in the hotel. The U.S. delegation room was occupied around the clock. The experts—from nuclear experts to sanctions experts to experts in international law—were meeting regularly with their foreign counterparts, and in between those meetings, they were on standby to be pulled into one of our minister-level sessions. Our communications team was stationed at the conference table, eager for updates from me or Wendy Sherman or one of the other negotiators. (They were also seeking refuge from the press, who were sectioned off in another part of the hotel, not so patiently waiting for details to feed to their editors in every part of the world.) It was crunch time, and everyone was aware of the ticking clock.

We were also in regular touch with Washington. At night, when it was midafternoon in D.C., a few of us would pack into a small tent where our

IT team had set up a secure video conference. We'd update the president, Susan Rice, Treasury Secretary Jack Lew and others on the progress, or lack thereof, we had made and we'd discuss the strategy for the following day.

These virtual meetings were some of the most productive I've ever experienced. President Obama's leadership was clear and important. He was well briefed on every aspect of the agreement, asking all the right questions and making tough decisions whenever he was required to do so. But he also trusted us. He would defer to Ernie or Jack or me if he thought we had a better sense of what could be accomplished. We knew exactly where he stood and exactly how much freedom we had to maneuver in the negotiating room. It was a paradigm for how an administration should function, and I wish that kind of administration-wide collaboration was more common.

But now it was time to see whether we could reach a deal or whether we should call it quits. Unfortunately, progress was met by almost daily backsliding. I don't know if the Iranians were engaging in a deliberate strategy or whether they were getting pushback from leaders in Tehran after they reported on the day's deliberations. Either way, it became somewhat debilitating. We'd arrive at a decent place one evening, and by the next morning, the Iranians would walk back some of the progress we'd made the night before. It was three steps forward and two steps back, and it was an unproductive use of our limited time.

"Thank goodness the real deadline is in June, not March," Chinese foreign minister Wang Yi said to me at one point. "We'd never make it otherwise." But the Chinese didn't have to deal with a Congress that was eager to do mischief. To the U.S. delegation, the March deadline was as real as it gets: the Republican majority was ready at the first sign of weakness to implement new sanctions against Iran and in effect blow up the talks. So, in an effort to ensure each negotiating session built off the previous one, we minimized the amount of time between our meetings. We worked until late in the night, every night. One night we worked straight through until 9:00 a.m. the following morning. Then we slept for two or three hours and immediately came back to the table.

President Obama said that if we were getting close, we were not to get up from the table simply because the clock struck midnight. He told us to be mindful of the deadline, but to work through the following day or two, if we thought it meant we could get where we needed to be.

We did exactly that. The gaps continued to narrow. We started to build some momentum with a sense that an agreement was within reach. Before we knew it, we were discussing the political realities each side faced in making an announcement. Until that moment, we had refrained from putting anything on paper, in hopes of preventing leaks or premature dissection by talking heads. Wendy had the creative idea of bringing in a large dry-erase board, where we highlighted each component of the agreement, facilitating an overview that proved helpful.

We were mindful that if there was to be an announcement, it would be vital to explain clearly in layman's terms precisely what was agreed. Steadily, we pulled together a document outlining the agreed-upon points, the wording of which prompted yet another hours-long negotiation.

When we were all of us finally comfortable, I assured Javad we wouldn't put the document out until after we had a joint press conference the following day. "Wait a minute!" he exclaimed. "This document isn't meant to be public!"

I couldn't believe what I was hearing. "Javad," I said, "it's four o'clock in the morning. We just spent eighteen hours negotiating every single word of this thing. If you don't want another round of sanctions, this has to be public. Of course it's going to be public!"

If we had returned to the United States claiming to have agreement on a series of principles, but told Congress and the public that we couldn't show them what those principles were, we would have been ridiculed. More important, we wouldn't have a shred of credibility with Congress to keep it from passing sanctions. And the negotiations would not survive additional sanctions, which the Iranian leadership would regard as bad faith, to say the least.

The next morning I went to see Zarif and explain this reality to him. If we couldn't put out a fact sheet, I told him, we might as well go home.

Finally, he conceded. "Please be careful how you word it," he said. "Don't go overboard. Make it clear this is an agreement, not something you're forcing us to accept. Otherwise, it will be very difficult to move forward."

We honored his request, in the fact sheet as well as in my public statement to the press. For example, we were careful to say, "Iran has agreed to do X," instead of "Iran must do X." I understood that Javad had his own political reality. If we were perceived to be taking victory laps at the expense of the Iranians, hard-liners in his country would pull the plug before we got any further.

That evening, April 2, 2015, we announced a detailed framework, essentially the broad outline of the agreement but with key details to be filled in during the ensuing months. It was an important milestone, but we still faced very difficult negotiations ahead of us. None of us wanted to go public with a framework agreement. We were forced to do so because of the congressional threat of sanctions. More sanctions would have killed the process, but releasing the framework also made the road ahead much more difficult, because it showed how far we had gotten and how real the possibility of a final agreement was. We knew that was sure to bring out the opponents on both sides.

The delegation went to a nearby Italian restaurant for dinner at eleven o'clock that night, just in time for us to catch our 2:00 a.m. ride back to Washington. Ernie proposed a toast, but I wasn't ready to celebrate. "We're not there yet," I reminded the team. I was a killjoy and I knew it, but to me, celebration felt premature. After all, we had deferred until the next round some of the toughest issues, like the timing of sanctions relief and what kind of research and development Iran's nuclear program would be permitted to undertake. A comprehensive deal was far from certain.

It had been imperative to announce our progress in Lausanne. The only way to hold on to the gains we achieved was to release as many details as possible; opponents of the talks were ready to pull the plug if we didn't. It would have been far more effective if we could have completed the entire agreement before announcing an unfinished product. Congress didn't give us any choice.

The framework announced in Lausanne was well received. It was far more ambitious than most people expected. It was applauded by experts, some of whom had been publicly skeptical until that point. But we knew that the positive response—and the extra time it bought us—would come at a steep price.

Every detail we put out served as a target for the opponents. Critics were already calculating what might turn out to be the weakest aspects of the deal, given what was left to be negotiated, and they began to target their criticism accordingly.

At the same time, the praise the P5+1 received in the press outraged and embarrassed the Iranians. It was clear from the moment the headlines were printed that, in the next round, the Iranians would try to compensate for those things they were criticized for by the opponents to a deal at home. Sometimes I wished Americans could have read or heard some of the vicious criticism Javad Zarif and his colleagues were subjected to; perhaps they might have thought a bit more clearly about what we were accomplishing in Lausanne. Both sides were left extremely exposed.

• • •

As EXPECTED, THE momentum from Lausanne faded almost immediately. Republicans began an immediate push for legislation to require congressional review of the final text of the deal. Given Congress's inability to pass much of anything, the Obama administration viewed a formal congressional ratification process to be a death sentence. After an intense series of negotiations led by Senate Foreign Relations Committee chairman Bob Corker, Republican from Tennessee, a bill was passed. Under this legislation, which President Obama signed into law that May, if we completed the deal by July 9 as planned, Congress would have a month to review it, and senators would then be permitted to vote to prevent President Obama from lifting the sanctions. If we completed the deal after July 9, which ended up being the case, Congress would have sixty days to review the deal. If two-thirds of the Senate agreed to reject the agreement, they could stop the president from implementing the deal.

This was key: It wouldn't be necessary for us to convince a sweeping majority of senators to vote in support of the deal, which might have been impossible, given the aggressive anti-Iran lobbying campaign from groups like AIPAC and others. Instead, we would need thirty-four senators *not* to vote to reject the deal in order to uphold the president's inevitable veto and forty-one to prevent filibuster of the legislation that would stop it from passing altogether. Securing those votes would be an enormously difficult task in its own right, but this legislation, which the Senate passed near unanimously, gave us a fighting chance.

Of course, we did not yet have a final agreement to defend. In late May, we had a particularly tense meeting with the Iranians and the EU at the InterContinental hotel in Geneva. In the wake of the Lausanne agreement and its reception, Ayatollah Khamenei had put forward a number of new parameters that we judged to be off the wall, from breakout-time calculations to centrifuge numbers. I understood that the Iranians were reacting to the storm of criticism they had received at home, but I felt they were undermining everything we had achieved just a few weeks prior. At one point, I was angry enough at what I heard that I banged my hand down on the table, hard. The pen I was holding accidentally bounced out of my hand and flew straight at Abbas Araghchi, landing near his chest. Everyone was silent for a moment; it was the most demonstrative any of them had ever seen me. I apologized to Abbas at once, but the moment surprised us all and punched a reset, bringing us back to a respectful and reasonable, if not terribly productive, conversation. That six-hour meeting ranked up with Muscat as the worst we had, but it was necessary. Sometimes in diplomacy, you need to have a meeting where absolutely nothing positive happens. It forces everyone to go home, take a breath and reexamine the reasons for negotiating in the first place. Often enough, I've found, the least productive meetings set the stage for the most productive ones.

In this case, however, our meeting was followed by a setback of a different kind. The next morning, a Sunday, I went for a bike ride—something I tried to do on long trips to get some outdoor exercise and clear my head for an hour or two. We drove an hour out of Geneva to the small town of Cluses, just over the border in France. I was about to embark on a mountain climb, the Col de la Colombière at the foot of the French Alps—a short section of the Tour de France. I was just getting started, moving pretty slowly, while maneuvering to clear a police motorcycle to my left. With my head turned in that direction, my bike crashed into a barely visible curb, knocking me over on my right side. My leg was crunched under me. When I tried to get up, nothing worked. I couldn't get my leg to react. I put both hands on my thigh and watched while one hand went in one direction and the other the opposite direction. I turned to the security guys who had run over to help and said, "I've broken my leg." The leverage between the curb and the street had created exactly the wrong angle, snapping my femur.

I was in pain but the main thing I felt was frustration. I was pissed at myself for letting this happen and hugely disappointed at not being able to enjoy the day and make the climb. More important, we had the last, critical weeks of negotiation ahead of us to get a deal. I was determined not to let my injury get in the way.

From Geneva, I had been scheduled to head to Spain and then Paris to chair an important meeting of the global coalition we were leading against ISIL. I still fully intended on doing those stops, as soon as my leg was wrapped up, but after the Swiss doctors examined me, they said that I was in no condition to do much of anything. The break, they said, was an inch from my femoral artery, just below my hip—a dangerous place for a shattered bone. I needed surgery right away.

President Obama called me when he heard the news. I assured him I would not miss a beat. I'm not sure what he believed, but he could not have been more supportive, then and in the days to come.

I flew back to Boston on a C-17 along with Dr. Dennis Burke, the superb orthopedic surgeon who had performed my hip replacement a number of years before. He had graciously flown to Geneva to examine me and accompany me home for the operation. My deputy chief of staff, Tom Sullivan; my senior advisor for strategic communication, Glen Johnson; my longtime aide, Jason Meininger; and a few members of my security detail stayed with me on the flight back as well. As we were crossing the Atlantic,

Dennis told me that I had to take it easy for a few weeks, or I'd be out of commission for a lot longer than I needed to be.

When we arrived at Logan International Airport, I was transported by ambulance from the plane to Massachusetts General Hospital—about a five-minute walk from my home in Boston. I heard what the doctors told me, and I listened. But I had business to conduct. The morning of my surgery was the anti-ISIL coalition meeting I was scheduled to attend in Paris. I woke up at 4:30 a.m. to call into the meeting. (Later my foreign minister friends told me how important it was that this disembodied voice was piped into their meeting to encourage additional efforts to rapidly crush ISIL.) For the next ten days, I made as many calls and conducted as many virtual meetings as I could from my hospital bed.

I also worked my ass off on physical therapy. At first, my doctors were skeptical I'd be able to fly overseas to conclude the Iran negotiations at the end of the month. I'd be on crutches at least a couple of months, and there were risks involved with flying too quickly after the surgery. But the Iranians couldn't come to the United States, and it simply wouldn't have been possible to negotiate such a deal over the phone. I knew I had to get well enough to be cleared for a transatlantic flight. I worked every single day toward that goal. Finally, the verdict came back from the doctors: I was good to go. I boarded the plane for Vienna at Andrews Air Force Base the morning of June 26. A hydraulic lift elevated me up to the door of the plane since I couldn't climb the stairs.

THE FINAL ROUND of negotiations was held at the Palais Coburg, a massive residence-turned-hotel with a history (and a wine cellar) that dates back to the sixteenth century. Its centuries-old foundation meant the floor plans were a bit convoluted; going from one office to another often meant switching elevators and navigating long, mazelike hallways. Thankfully, the other delegations and the hotel management were understanding of my condition, and I was able to spend non-negotiating time in a suite right off the elevator on the second floor.

Summer was in full swing, and Vienna was scorching hot. At the Coburg, the top-floor suite in which the delegation spent most of its time crunching numbers and fine-tuning statements had subpar air-conditioning, but the superb team from the U.S. mission to Vienna brought in several fans and taped plastic tarps over the windows to keep the cool air inside. The embassy team were unsung heroes: they worked to ensure we didn't miss a beat thousands of miles away from the nerve center in Foggy Bottom, monitoring updates and intelligence reports from around the world, facilitating meetings and transportation logistics at a moment's notice and even keeping the fridge stocked and the coffee flowing around the clock.

The various experts so essential to our delegation were heroes as well. Many of them had been working in Vienna, away from their families, for weeks longer than the rest of us. They missed weddings, anniversaries, funerals, children's birthdays—every aspect of family life was sacrificed to achieve a vital public policy goal. But no one complained or even asked for a break. Every single member of the team was deeply committed to the mission. It was among the most professional, capable group of people I've ever worked with.

As June turned to July, it soon became clear we would also miss whatever Fourth of July plans any of us had made. Roland, the cheerful and flamboyant manager of the Coburg, tried to make the best of it. He wore star-spangled pants all day and hosted a quick barbecue on the terrace of the hotel, complete with hot dogs and hamburgers. It was a nice and rare reprieve from the marathon talks.

Back in the negotiating room, however, things were getting tougher. As we narrowed down the issues, the latitude for concession also narrowed. We continued to argue over numbers, configurations, documents and timelines.

One evening Ernie Moniz and I met with Zarif and Salehi in the prime negotiating room on the second floor. We wondered if the Iranians were stalling, uncertain about their direction and intent, or waiting for instructions from Tehran. We found ourselves raising voices yet again. One of my aides came into the room and informed us that we were echoing down the hall for the whole floor to hear. I ran into German foreign minister Frank-Walter Steinmeier shortly afterward, and he quipped that, from what he was able to hear, my meeting with Zarif "sounded constructive."

It wasn't. The following day I relayed our lengthy conversation to the rest of the P5+1 ministers, and we spent hours working up a proposal with ideas on a number of sticking points that we thought would help to close some of the gaps between the two sides.

We invited Zarif into the large conference room, and about thirty seconds after we walked him through what we had come up with, he dismissed it out of hand.

"This is insulting. You're trying to threaten me!" he exclaimed, getting up to leave. "Never threaten an Iranian."

A brief silence followed, before Russian foreign minister Sergei Lavrov broke the tension: "Or a Russian!"

There was some nervous laughter at Lavrov's quip, but the meeting was over. Disappointed, I headed to the Coburg's dining room for dinner with the U.S. negotiating team. We took over a large, round table and, as we ate our sixth Wiener schnitzel of the week, debriefed what had just happened. For the first time since these talks began, I thought it could well be necessary to leave Vienna without a deal. We began talking about how we would explain the failure—how we could describe how unreasonable the Iranians were being in a way that wouldn't give immediate confidence to those advocating military action, inadvertently sparking a larger conflict.

I went to bed that night hoping the Iranians would see the value of what we had proposed. The next morning, I visited Javad in his suite. I wanted to talk to him one-on-one to see if we really had reached an impasse.

"Javad," I began. "This is it. Do you want to make this work, or don't you?" We talked for some time about the stakes and the road we had taken to get where we were. Javad told me he had talked with Tehran. He thought they had responded constructively to some ideas he had, and he wanted to get together to see if we could pull back from the brink. I told him I was willing to listen but that there were certain things we couldn't move away from. I left that conversation with a feeling that Javad had reflected overnight and resolved problems he had thought were insurmountable.

We remained in Vienna for several more days. I believe the Iranians may have thought they could hold us over the barrel that Congress had created, which triggered a longer period of congressional review if we didn't finish by the July 9 deadline established in the Corker legislation. We didn't let the deadline scare us. We weren't willing to sacrifice anything just to meet an arbitrary congressional deadline, even if it meant Congress would ultimately have twice as long to review the agreement.

Every day, we were getting closer, but Zarif still couldn't seem to bring himself to say yes. On the evening of July 13, our seventeenth night in Vienna, I invited Zarif, Lavrov and the new EU high representative, Federica Mogherini, to the American suite at the Coburg. Federica had succeeded Cathy Ashton and had already gotten to know Lavrov and Zarif pretty well. I sat there with my bum leg propped up on an ottoman, and we listened to Zarif tick off all the reasons the deal we had been working toward wasn't good enough for Iran. Around midnight, Lavrov, who was eager to depart on a trip to Uzbekistan the following day, interrupted him. "Javad, is it that you don't have the authority to make a deal? If that's the case, then please, just tell us. You are wasting our time."

Zarif was furious at Lavrov's goading. Angry, he rose off the sofa and started to move toward the door, forcefully objecting to Lavrov's taunt. I jumped up as fast as I could and hobbled over on my crutches to intercept him. "I know Sergei didn't mean to insult you," I told Zarif, trying to calm him down. We'd been at it for long, difficult hours. Tension was understandably high. "We just don't think there's anything else we can do. This is the deal. It's the moment of truth. Are you taking it or leaving it?"

After a moment, he acknowledged that he was prepared to accept the agreement, but he needed one more thing—of several he had asked for—that from his point of view would make it fair.

I moved as quickly as I could into the adjoining room, where Robert Malley from the NSC, Jon Finer, Wendy Sherman and a few others were waiting for an update.

I told them, "We're not moving away from anything on the substance, but let's find something that gets him over the hump without costing us. That's all that's standing in the way. Thoughts?" I looked around to shrugged shoulders from all.

Chris Backemeyer, our sanctions lead, cautiously began to speak. "There's one thing . . ."

The Treasury Department had already been prepared to remove a dozzen additional people from the list of Iranians we had been sanctioning. We held this back for a moment like this—a card the United States had kept in our back pocket. It was time to play it.

"They're small players," Chris advised. "They may not be enough." But I was convinced that what mattered was the gesture and respect for the difficult choices the Iranians had made. I had grabbed my crutches and headed for the door.

I reentered the room where Sergei and Javad were seated. I told Javad we were willing to take one more step to bring this to a close. I offered him the handful of additional names we were prepared to delist from sanctions. "Do we have a deal?" I asked.

He paused for what seemed like an eternity. "We have a deal."

It was after midnight, and there wasn't much time—or energy—for celebration. After a few handshakes, I returned to my room, where I called the president to deliver the news. He thanked me, I thanked him, and I told him I was gearing up for the fight we had ahead of us on Capitol Hill. We had gotten the deal we wanted; now we had to keep it.

WHEN THE CORKER legislation passed, some suggested the less time Congress had to consider the deal the better off we'd be. I came to believe the opposite was true. Most members took the process incredibly seriously, and

we were grateful to have sixty days to brief them thoroughly and answer any questions they had.

The hearings were vicious. Corker told me I had been "fleeced." Others said we were "bamboozled" and called the agreement "ludicrous." But I was more confident in the merits of that deal than anything I'd ever worked on. Outside the public eye, Wendy, Ernie, Jack Lew and I went up to the Hill to meet with senators privately. We had the support of some essential allies—including Senators Dick Durbin, Chris Murphy and Jeanne Shaheen—who were constantly whipping votes and pointing us toward senators in need of persuasion. We didn't take a single vote for granted, and we tried to turn even the staunchest opponents. It was an all-hands-on-deck affair, complete with a "war room" setup at the White House, and it was an ensemble effort drawing on the best of every relevant agency, the intelligence community and the team at the White House, including Susan Rice. Chris Backemeyer was practically living on Capitol Hill. Undecided senators were reading the text with a fine-tooth comb and seeking answers to all the questions they had. Senator Barbara Mikulski, who was struggling with the vote, actually traveled to Vienna to meet with the IAEA and get a better understanding of the transparency and verification aspects of the agreement directly from the international experts. Slowly, more and more senators announced that they would vote on our side. On September 2, upon her return from Vienna, Barbara Mikulski became the thirty-fourth senator to announce her support for the agreement, giving us enough votes to sustain a veto. In the end, forty-two senators voted with us. The Iran agreement would go forward.

THE JCPOA WAS to go into effect on the appropriately if not creatively named "Implementation Day." There was no specific date attached to it in the text; rather, it would be the date on which the IAEA certified that Iran had completed a series of steps to roll back its nuclear program, and in return, the United States, the EU and the UN would suspend their nuclear-related sanctions. Given the number of actions Iran had to take—for example, shipping nearly all of its enriched uranium out of the country, removing most of the centrifuges from the Fordow facility, allowing inspectors to ensure it no longer conducted nuclear activities at a military site called Parchin and deactivating its heavy-water reactor at Arak—we expected the Iranians would take about nine months to complete their part, which would put Implementation Day somewhere in March 2016. But Iran worked quickly, perhaps, as some suspected, in hopes of obtaining the sanctions relief before the country's February 2016 elections. By mid-December, the IAEA informed us that Implementation Day could be weeks, not months, away.

Two unrelated negotiations between the United States and Iran, each led by entirely separate teams, but catalyzed by the nuclear breakthrough, came to a head at around the same time.

The first involved our long-standing efforts to secure the release of four Iranian American citizens unjustly imprisoned in Iran. Not a meeting would go by without our pressing at some point for the release of the Americans. In response, the Iranians would spout talking points about the severity of the charges against them and vaguely mention that there were a number of Iranians in U.S. prisons that they would like freed as well. By the end of 2014, we realized there might be real potential for an exchange. We didn't think it would be appropriate to negotiate their release in the same track as the nuclear talks because we didn't want the Iranians to make their lives a bargaining chip for a lesser nuclear agreement. Accordingly, both countries appointed entirely separate teams to explore a potential exchange. We tapped Brett McGurk, an experienced diplomat who had recently helped secure a peaceful political transition in Iraq, to lead the U.S. delegation. Brett and a small group of colleagues began to meet monthly in Geneva with their Iranian counterparts. The talks were held in secret, given the obvious sensitivity involved. In fact, most of our nuclear negotiators, and even many senior officials in our administration, had no idea they were happening.

It took a while for any progress to be made. At first, the Iranians gave us an absurd list of prisoners whom they wanted released; it was dozens of names long and included people with charges related to terrorism and other violent crimes. President Obama was clear that only those with nonviolent charges would even be considered for release. After the nuclear deal, the negotiations gained some steam, and by the fall of 2015, the negotiators had come up with a list of seven Iranians, all of whom had been charged with nonviolent crimes, whom we were willing to release in exchange for the Americans' freedom. At one point, it looked like we might have our guys home by Thanksgiving, but unfortunately the process hit a few more speed bumps, delaying the exchange until mid-January.

Back in the 1970s, before the Iranian Revolution, the United States sold our then ally hundreds of millions of dollars' worth of military equipment. The Shah's government fell far behind in its required payments, and the parties reached an agreement in early 1979 to restructure the sales. Once Ayatollah Khomeini seized power and took our embassy personnel hostage, the United States obviously wasn't going to provide those weapons to Iran. The only problem was, Iran had already paid for many of them. That money was sitting in an account with the U.S. Treasury. Iran had long demanded that we return the money—with interest. Tehran filed claims with an international court at The Hague for $10 billion, plus interest, including return of those funds. They had a solid legal case for this portion of its claim, and hearings were slated to begin. The court could stick the United States with an enormous bill. The administration eventually agreed to settle the claim for those funds, as prior administrations had settled other claims with Iran, and did so for less than a fifth of what they were attempting to claim: $1.7 billion. This figure was derived from the amount of funds in the Iranian account at the treasury, plus an amount to account in part for interest.

While $1.7 billion is still a lot of money, it is a hell of a lot better than $10 billion. Before the United States paid the money, however, there were a few other things to consider. First and foremost, President Obama wanted to make certain the decision to move forward with the payment was a good deal for the country on the merits, not a concession. He asked all the relevant cabinet members to carefully consider whether they thought this settlement made sense at face value, and to send him their individual written recommendation. He would move forward, he explained, only if there was unanimous consent to do so. We all agreed that the settlement was fair and likely to save taxpayers billions of dollars. The State Department's career lawyers, who led this negotiation, told me it was a better deal than they thought possible.

After the president decided that we would move forward, there was the question of timing. While the settlement had no connection to the prisoner exchange, neither of our governments could ignore the fact that both agreements had been reached and that the execution of either one—or political backlash in either country—could interfere with the other. Despite the diplomatic breakthroughs, we still had zero trust in each other. The prisoner exchange, we knew, mattered more to us than it did to them, so it would have been foolish to make the payment before the Americans were released, just in case they decided to renege on the swap. Rouhani had been elected president to improve an economy starved of cash by our sanctions, so finalizing the Hague settlement was a major priority. While we never discussed it, I suspect the Iranians worried that if the Americans were released before the settlement was paid, we might go back on our word and try to delay paying what was agreed.

In the end, for all these reasons, both sides decided that it made the most sense to bring everything to a close at once: we would implement the nuclear deal, pay the settlement and exchange the prisoners simultaneously. We knew that all these moving parts would be difficult to coordinate. We also knew that the optics would be bad; we were giving an opening for politically motivated people to attack it. With that in mind, we were immediately transparent about the fact that the payment was made and why. Still today, however, plenty of critics will argue we delivered a secret ransom and tried to hide it from the American people. That is simply not true, as many of those who spread that lie know.

As 2015 became 2016, the IAEA was preparing to certify that Iran had met all the required rollbacks to its nuclear program. It was time for Implementation Day. I made plans to join Zarif and Mogherini in Europe to sign the appropriate paperwork on January 16.

All of our various teams spent hours hammering out the details of what was to be a tightly choreographed day of diplomacy, involving complicated transactions, legal and political steps in a half dozen countries—when planes would take off, when documents would be signed, who would be on hand for what, etc. But as Robert Burns reminds us, the best-laid plans of mice and men often go awry. This was no exception. In retrospect, given the complexity, it was almost inevitable.

The day before Implementation Day, we awoke to news that the non-nuclear issues we had hoped to resolve that day were hitting snags. The plane carrying the first tranche of the settlement money we intended to deliver to Iran would be delayed for several hours. Ironically, because the sanctions we had implemented were so effective, it was almost impossible to electronically transfer the funds we owed in a reasonable amount of time. We agreed to make the payments in cash instead, which became another source of baseless conspiracy theories. All of this meant the entire exchange would be delayed several hours.

And there were plenty of other last-minute hurdles to come.

For one thing, the Swiss military flight that was supposed to take the newly freed Americans from Iran to Switzerland was having trouble getting approval from some countries to fly through international airspace. Three countries refused to green-light the pilot's request, since the flight originated in Tehran and they were concerned that permitting it would violate our own international sanctions regime. We fired off a series of urgent phone calls and emails to our ambassadors, asking them to immediately communicate to their host governments the sensitive humanitarian purpose for the flight from Tehran and to urge them to approve the flight path without delay.

We landed in Vienna around lunchtime, and I headed straight for the Palais Coburg. It was odd to walk through the hotel where we had spent so many late nights around the negotiating table. It was virtually empty, absent the palpable energy that existed during those midsummer talks. The beautiful building felt enormous and cold. As I walked past the dining hall, where we had devoured so much Wiener schnitzel months before, I noticed it was dark and unused. The hallways felt eerily quiet, and for a moment I worried that it might be an omen.

In between our JCPOA discussions, we learned of another significant hiccup back in the United States: one of the Iranians we had agreed to release was no longer interested in taking the deal. He had a multimillion-dollar forfeiture judgment that he wanted expunged, and he wanted a pardon, not a commutation, from President Obama. That wasn't going to happen, but without his cooperation, the entire exchange might have been at risk. And so began a major and ultimately successful lobbying effort from his government, our government and members of his own family—all trying to talk some common sense into him. The Iranians also tried to get us to guarantee that their citizens, who were to be released from prisons across the United States, would return to Iran, presumably for some PR-driven welcome. We said no, this wasn't part of the deal—and as it turned out, none of them wanted to go back.

Back in Vienna, as we prepared to finalize the JCPOA paperwork, Federica Mogherini received word that the French foreign minister, Laurent Fabius, had new questions he wanted answered before she signed on the dotted line on behalf of the EU. It was surprising, as he had previously signed off on everything he now objected to, but he had similarly raised last-minute "concerns" in Geneva, Lausanne and Vienna the last time around. But this time, there was some risk in delay. Javad was receiving regular photos of President Rouhani and his entire cabinet waiting for the implementation announcement with stern looks on their faces. They were beginning to suspect that we were purposely delaying the JCPOA's implementation for some reason. Nerves were fraying, to say the least.

Federica worked diligently to try to persuade Laurent, who was in Paris, of the merits of what had been proposed (and long agreed to). She spent over an hour on the phone with him, and by 9:30 p.m., she thought she had inched him closer, but he wasn't fully on board. I realized that the clock was ticking, and things could get messy very quickly, so, in an attempt to expedite the process, I brought Javad and Federica into my suite. Together, we called Laurent. After passing my iPhone around in circles, I finally put it on speaker and placed it in the middle of the coffee table. The three of us heard him out before carefully suggesting that instead of altering the deal, which was impossible, we could put new language into the joint EU-Iran statement to be released during the press conference. We explained how we thought our fixes would assuage his concerns—and then we paused to gauge his comfort with the plan. Javad finally said, "Do we have a deal, Laurent?" After a beat, Fabius's distant voice said, "Yes."

Minutes after Javad and Federica left my Coburg suite to head to the press center, I sat down to sign the documents lifting the U.S. nuclear-related sanctions on Iran. As I was signing, Jon Finer's phone rang. It was Brett, calling from Geneva. We had a problem: *Washington Post* reporter Jason Rezaian, one of the Americans being released by Iran, had been told his wife, a journalist named Yeganeh Salehi, couldn't accompany him out of the country. Apparently, she too had an outstanding judicial charge against her, and the Iranians on the ground said that made it impossible for them to send her home. I couldn't believe it. We had an explicit agreement that spouses would be permitted to accompany the released prisoners home. I called Zarif as soon as I could, but he was already onstage at the press conference. We hustled over to the press center, and I grabbed Zarif as soon as he walked offstage to explain what I had learned from Brett. His face dropped. To his credit he understood immediately how serious this situation was. He assured me he would take care of it right away and proceeded to immediately light a fire under his colleagues back in Tehran.

Before we took off for Washington, I called Zarif one more time to confirm Jason's wife was cleared to leave. He assured me it was settled. Officials ultimately went to a judge's home in the middle of the night so he could sign an order to permit Yeganeh to leave.

Our flight had barely taken off before we got another call from Brett: both Yeganeh and Jason's mother, Mary, who had been visiting from the United States, were missing. No one could track them down. Murphy's law at work overtime. I was ready to bang my head into the airplane bulkhead, convinced no one could script such a day if they tried. Another flurry of frantic phone calls and emails commenced. Finally, Brett got in touch with Jason's brother, Ali, who indicated that he had been in contact with the women. They were holed up in an apartment, scared and not sure whom to trust—a reasonable reaction given everything they had experienced. Ali gave Brett a phone number where they could be reached and a code phrase ("mango sticky rice") to indicate to them that they could trust him. When he got Yeganeh on the phone, Brett took down her address and told her Giulio Haas, the Swiss ambassador to Iran, who was an essential partner on the ground in Tehran, would come to escort her to the aircraft. Haas arrived a few minutes later and took the women to the runway, and a short while after that they were on a Swiss military aircraft heading first to Zurich and then back home to the United States. Finally, Jason, who had been released from prison, was really free: he was in the arms of the love of his life again.

MORE THAN TWO years of intense, complicated effort and an agreement was finally in place. What had we achieved? We had certainly avoided war, until or unless Iran decides to try to break out. We had already witnessed Iran take major steps to freeze and dismantle its program. But more important, Iran committed to six other nations and the UN Security Council that it would forever live up to the Nuclear Non-Proliferation Treaty—that for the lifetime of the agreement it would adhere to the Additional Protocol of the treaty mandating inspection of any facility suspected of being used for illicit nuclear purposes; that its stockpile of enriched uranium would be restricted for 15 years to 300 kilograms, physically too little to make a bomb; that its tens of thousands centrifuges would be dismantled and limited to 5,000 and all centrifuge production would be monitored 24 hours a day, 7 days a week, 365 days a year, for 20 years; that Iran's uranium enrichment level would be restricted to 3.67 percent—far too low to power a bomb; that the country's only plutonium reactor would be destroyed; that all mining of uranium in Iran would be tracked from cradle to grave for 25 years; that Iran would accept 130 additional inspectors living and working every day in Iran to guarantee compliance with each and every provision of the agreement; that for at least a decade, it would take Iran a year or more to break out of our agreement and move toward a bomb.

Here's the bottom line: it would be impossible for Iran to build a bomb for at least the next decade and a half—at least—and if, after that, it began to try, we would know immediately and have enough time to deploy every single option then that was available to us before the agreement went into effect—and perhaps more. We always maintained our ability to bomb Iran if they didn't comply.

Given the situation we faced when I first sat down with Javad Zarif that afternoon in New York—where Iran had mastered the nuclear fuel cycle and was a month or two away from a weapon—the limitations we put in place bought us important time and offered the best chance for peace, even as we maintained security and all our military options. To me, that's a damn good deal, and it made the United States, Israel, the region and the world safer.

CHAPTER 19

The Open Wound

THE TINY BOY in the maroon T-shirt wasn't much older than my grandson. His arm was awkwardly contorted, twitching back and forth uncontrollably. His eyes stared ahead, unfocused, empty, as he moaned. The hospital floor was packed, every inch of it, with the bodies of mothers, fathers, grandparents, boys and girls, stretched out, arms across their chests. Parents sobbing, refusing to let go of their children's lifeless pajama-clad bodies. Innocent people unable to control the spasms jerking their bodies into unnatural positions. Agony. Despair. Death. Fourteen hundred people, a third of them children, indiscriminately murdered.

The scene could have easily been mistaken for the aftermath of traditional combat or a natural disaster, with one haunting exception: there wasn't a single drop of blood visible anywhere. No scratches, bruises, cuts or outward signs of physical violence. But violence it was. The life had been squeezed out of the dead and dying by poison gas.

Local doctors reported that the victims all evidenced symptoms consistent with exposure to nerve gas. Each symptom described the prelude to a horrible death: suffocation; constricted, irregular and infrequent breathing; involuntary muscle spasms; nausea; frothing at the mouth; fluid coming out of nose and eyes; convulsing; dizziness; blurred vision; red and irritated eyes and pinpoint pupils.

There was no mistaking what had happened. Early that morning, around 2:00 a.m. local time in Syria, rockets armed with chemical weapons were fired from regime-controlled areas and released deadly fumes over several suburbs of Damascus—an area held by the opposition to Bashar al-Assad's regime.

Thousands of miles away in the comfort of my wood-paneled, private office on the seventh floor of the Harry S Truman Building, I was sickened and seething. I took a pause from watching the video and scrolling through the classified photos and maps on my secure iPad. I looked out the window. Washington is deserted in August, and the city felt eerily empty. It was 7:00 a.m. The rising sun lit up the Lincoln Memorial, wrapping it in a warm orange glow. It was almost hard to imagine that the same sun rising peacefully over Washington had risen that morning over Ghouta, Syria, casting the soft morning light on abject horror. Imagine: parents had tucked their children into bed the night before, some entire families never to wake again.

Bashar al-Assad had flagrantly violated not just international law, but every idea or norm of human decency. Audio intercepts proved high-level Syrian government coordination in the attack. It wasn't a war crime committed by a rogue military unit. It was official regime policy carried out mercilessly.

Assad's regime had been murdering its own people in increasingly insidious ways since the uprisings began in 2011. When I became secretary of state, already more than one hundred thousand Syrians had been killed. Assad possessed the world's largest stock of undeclared chemical weapons. Almost exactly one year before, President Obama had publicly warned Assad against using them. The admonition was intended to prevent this kind of atrocity. The president threatened "serious consequences" if the line was crossed. Now, on this sultry August day, Assad, increasingly on defense on the battlefield, had overtly and arrogantly barreled right through the red line of American warnings, international law and civilized behavior.

I wondered what combination of desperation, miscalculation, weakness and bloodless evil had led him to this point. I'd probably spent more hours with Assad in 2009 than any American other than, perhaps, the American ambassador. Assad always seemed slightly in over his head. I wondered whether he had been led into this barbaric act by his family or if this was his initiative to regain battlefield momentum and remake the brutal playbook his father had used in the Hama massacre, when twenty thousand of his Syrian countrymen were wiped out.

But given the willful choice of weapon, the why didn't matter all that much. Assad, who once seemed like an accidental authoritarian, had committed an atrocity and nothing about it was accidental. He was an undeniable, irredeemable war criminal presiding over the gruesome destruction of his country. We now knew Assad was capable of using his chemical weapons arsenal indiscriminately.

It was exactly the scenario that had most worried us in the U.S. government. A few months before, the U.S. experts had determined the regime was likely using the nerve agent sarin in small-scale, isolated actions. It precipitated my first trip to Moscow as secretary in May 2013. President Obama wanted me to make clear to President Putin that we knew definitively what Assad was doing. It was in Putin's interests to rein in his proxy. We didn't specify what would happen if he did not. My meeting with Putin was instructive. He lamented America's response to the Arab Awakening, particularly our "abandonment" of "reliable" authoritarians in Egypt and Libya. Growing extremism in post-Gaddafi Libya, Putin warned, was evidence of what happens when strong rulers fall without knowing who will replace them.

I argued to President Putin that in Syria the world had a chance to galvanize an orderly transition now. Assad's dangerous acts of desperation underscored the urgency. Putin was mercurial. He said he feared both the implosion of the Syrian state and Assad's penchant for miscalculation, but added that this was no time for "social engineering" in sovereign countries. He made clear that if there was a dangerous moment—institutions of the state collapsing and stockpiles of the world's worst weapons unsecured— we might work together to seek their safe removal.

I warned the Russians that we would take action in response to the regime's chemical weapons misdeeds, however isolated. Not long afterward, the White House announced we would increase the scope and scale of support to Assad's opposition.

Now it was late August and Assad had made a clear and criminal statement to the world about how far he would go to preserve his regime. It was imperative that we respond rapidly to reinforce the red line. We needed to hold the war criminal accountable before the world, and we simultaneously needed to send a message to Moscow and Tehran that our word meant something. The phone calls and meetings started right away, as the national security team tried to shape the most effective response.

I believed President Obama would decide he had to strike and that, therefore, Assad had made a huge miscalculation. He had invited the world to put him on his heels. I believed that military strikes could achieve a number of goals. They would send an unequivocal message that the United States stood by the red line and would enforce it with or without our allies. They would signal that international norms regarding the use of weapons of mass destruction were ironclad and that we would defend them, an important message for a number of regimes, including Iran, to hear loud and clear. And I believed they might finally give us leverage to change Assad's calculation, beginning by making it plain to him just how badly he'd misjudged the world's tolerance for his barbarity. I also thought that these strikes could create a diplomatic opening and bring countries together around an endgame that could lead to a post-Assad Syria with the institutions of the state preserved. Assad's protectors in Iran and Russia would learn there were limits to Assad's freedom of action and ability to gain advantage on the ground. I knew Assad had acted out of weakness, not strength. There was no military solution to the war, but the opposition was doing well enough to worry him.

I believed that if Russia's calculation changed, they might encourage either a negotiated exit for Assad and the creation of a transition government (more acceptable regime elements alongside secular opposition representatives) or an election in which the people of Syria would select their future leader. Most of all, Assad might see that he couldn't gas his way out of a civil war. A targeted, surgical military response was proportional to Assad's atrocity, but I believed its bigger potential value was in initiating diplomacy.

I conveyed all this to my colleagues in conversations that afternoon and the next day, during a three-and-a-half-hour meeting in the White House Situation Room. Susan Rice, who had recently started as the president's national security advisor, led the meeting. There was broad agreement around the table that a military response was appropriate. I was encouraged because, prior to this event, the military leadership had been reluctant to get more engaged in Syria. Now there seemed to be unanimity that we had to respond forcefully, even with uncertainty about the next step. The question was what and when.

Chairman of the Joint Chiefs of Staff General Martin Dempsey and Secretary of Defense Chuck Hagel both expressed their support for limited military action. It was the first time since I had arrived in February that they did so. The president's chief of staff, Denis McDonough, was wary, concerned it was not in our strategic interest to get pulled into Syria. He and the team's veterans of the first term all bore the scars of having seen Libya descend into chaos after a humanitarian no-fly zone simultaneously neutered a dictator's military advantage, led to his death at the hands of his own people and plunged the country into tribal chaos. Some worried we might wind up sending more refugees into neighboring countries already struggling to keep up with the steady stream of displaced families. In fairness, no argument on either side was illogical. It was a question of weighing difficult options, all of which promised uncertain outcomes. That's exactly what the National Security Council is there for—to air different perspectives, each of which informs the president, the ultimate decider.

What I could not predict as easily, because I had not been part of the administration the year before, was where the president's thinking would fall. He had declared a Syria red line in 2012, but I'd seen in my first months on the job that the president was careful and methodical. He based judgments on current information. He always demanded comprehensive analysis of potential unintended consequences. I admired his thoughtful approach. Over the years, America had lost a lot more service members as a result of a president's rash, ideological decision than it ever had to carefully considered, fact-based ones.

Likewise, in my six months on the job, I had experienced some teachable moments. Earlier that spring, as we sat around the same conference room table and debated how to support the Syrian opposition, I had inadvertently walked into a small hornet's nest. I argued that, since the administration had declared in 2012 that "Assad must go," and repeated it many times since, we risked looking weak if we didn't increase support to the opposition. Saying Assad must go and doing little to help those trying to make it happen would seem feckless. My remark was not intended as an insult to anyone; it was the obvious backdrop to whatever decisions we recommended.

I hit a nerve with Denis McDonough. "If you're saying the president looks weak, I take umbrage at that," Denis said tensely. That was not what I said. But I did believe that if you said you were going to do something, it was important to follow through. There was a clear distinction. I tried to smooth over the tension with Denis. Deputy Secretary Bill Burns explained to me that there was a long history: many in the White House believed that past administrations' worries about looking "weak" had sometimes become excuses for bad decisions that weren't in America's interests, especially in the Middle East.

I had lived more than my share of that history; presidents had driven us deeper into Vietnam for fear that correcting course would look weak at home and overseas. But in my judgment, we weren't debating a deep military entanglement. We weren't on the brink of a quagmire. Nothing anyone was proposing would have put us on a slippery slope. We were merely discussing ways to back up the policy the president had set a year before. We were also enforcing a globally accepted norm for behavior in conflict. I wondered if scar tissue remained from the way in which the Arab Spring had morphed into an autocratic winter, or if the murder of our diplomats in Benghazi the year before had taken a toll on how the White House now looked at deepening our engagement elsewhere. There was a lot of internal history preceding my arrival at the Situation Room table.

Still, as we met in August in the aftermath of the chemical weapons atrocities, I thought military action was inevitable and that it was better to act quickly—for many reasons, including denying Assad time to place innocent civilians into key targets to deter us from hitting them. Surprise and speed were assets, I figured.

It became quickly clear neither was on the agenda.

Martin Dempsey talked us through various military options, including launching Tomahawk missiles from destroyers already deployed in the Mediterranean. A contingency target list had been assembled by the Pentagon weeks beforehand, including military facilities and government-owned buildings.

We reconvened the next day with the president. The conversation focused on how—not whether—we would strike. The military options were relatively straightforward; we debated whether we would be on solid legal ground. Russia would veto any meaningful response at the UN Security Council. After all, in a remarkable display of churlish contrarianism and propagandist posturing, Russia was still claiming Assad had not even carried out the attack. It seemed they treated everything as a game, but their veto at the UN gave them a strong hand to play.

Our internal discussions bogged down over legal precedent. There are three basic legal green lights for a nation's use of force: one, you are acting in self-defense; two, you are acting pursuant to an invitation from the legitimate government of a nation; and three, you are acting pursuant to a UN Security Council resolution. Those are essentially uncontestable. Then there is action within the "color" of law—something that may, depending on the circumstances, be arguable but if sufficiently compelling will most likely get by. In the late 1990s, President Clinton and our NATO allies used military force to stop Slobodan Milošević's ethnic cleansing in Kosovo. Clinton knew he would not receive UN Security Council support, given that Russia supported Milošević. Instead, the administration justified its actions based on the "legitimacy" of action.

What Assad had done to those innocent, sleeping children was without question a humanitarian emergency with far broader security consequences for the region and beyond. I believed it would be a dangerous precedent for international law if any government could gas its citizens with impunity, with Putin holding final veto over what was legal and what wasn't. There were other multilateral organizations that could lend their imprimatur to action, including, as it had on Libya, the Arab League and possibly NATO.

President Obama raised the question of engaging Congress. Vice President Biden, Defense Secretary Chuck Hagel and I—three former senators—were in favor of consulting Congress. We knew everything would be easier with the Hill on our side. But I argued that sudden, surgical military action, rather than months of bombing, shouldn't require the time to wait for formal authorization from Congress, particularly since it was scheduled to be on recess until September 9. Swift action was imperative.

In between our internal deliberations and domestic outreach, I was on the phone with foreign counterparts. There was reluctance among some Europeans based on questions of legality. They feared acting without UN approval. But Jordan pushed for action, noting that the attack had been mere miles from the Jordanian border. Saudi Arabia warned that our credibility was on the line.

Russia, as expected, was a through-the-looking-glass conversation. Sergei Lavrov balked at the idea that the Assad regime was to blame. He told me we couldn't rule out the possibility the rebels somehow amassed the chemicals without our knowledge and used them on their own communities in an attempt to rally international sympathy. If Assad had nothing to hide, I told Sergei, he should let UN inspectors come examine the site in question immediately, while the evidence was fresh. Rather than welcoming the inspectors with open arms, Assad continued to shell the rebel-held areas where the attacks transpired, destroying evidence by the hour and making any eventual findings increasingly less credible.

With each succeeding day, the Russians joined the Syrians in sowing public doubt. One Russian member of parliament told reporters that the United States was " 'convinced' that Assad used chemical weapons, and earlier they were 'convinced' that there were weapons of mass destruction in Iraq. It's the same old story."

Susan Rice and I thought the absurd Russian propaganda effort demanded a response. You don't let charges go unanswered. We had lived my 2004 campaign together—Susan was a senior leader of the general election effort. Neither of us thought Assad or Russia should be allowed to rewrite history with impunity. So, on Monday morning, August 26, at the president's direction, I went to the press briefing room on the second floor of the State Department to respond to the Russians. I told the reporters that based on the evidence we had gathered already, including open-sourced information like the number and location of the victims, the symptoms of those killed or injured and the firsthand accounts of the humanitarian organizations on the ground, there was no doubt that Assad was responsible and that the regime was actively working to cover it up. It was beyond debate.

The president hadn't shared a final, formal decision, but the discussions inside the Situation Room left me confident we were a few days, not weeks, away from air strikes.

Because Congress was still out of session, Susan Rice, Director of National Intelligence Jim Clapper and I held a conference call to brief members on both sides of the aisle on the evidence and why the administration believed a response was warranted. We were getting our ducks in a row. The chairs and ranking members of the relevant national security committees seemed supportive. I got the sense that the Senate leaders actually preferred we act without more than this congressional consultation, because they had a busy legislative schedule that fall. But several members did ask if we planned to come to them for authorization.

The only note of concern I heard was from Republican representative Hal Rogers of Kentucky, chairman of the House Appropriations Committee. He was supportive of strikes against Assad but wary of the global politics. "If Russia's not with you, and the UN isn't with you, aren't you better off if the Congress is with you?" It was sincerely constructive advice. But it probably assumed a functional Congress that no longer existed. Rogers was one powerful member of the House; but his colleague, the junior senator from Kentucky, Rand Paul, was already prone to describing American support for the Syrian opposition as "arming al-Qaeda." Politics hadn't stopped at the water's edge in a long time. Still, Rogers's words stuck in my mind.

I bounced back and forth between talking to Capitol Hill and talking to our allies. Already we were working hand in glove with Chuck Hagel and his military counterparts in key Arab countries to build a broad coalition representative of the region, not just the West. We were also mindful of avoiding the appearance that it was the Sunni world ganging up against a Shia government.

Foreign Secretary William Hague from the United Kingdom, among the foreign ministers most frequently on my speed dial, reiterated Prime Minister David Cameron's commitment to act in lockstep with the United States. Cameron had cut short his vacation and returned to London. But suddenly there was a wrinkle: without any prior notice to us, Cameron announced he would seek Parliament's approval before moving forward. Cameron was confident he'd win the vote, and in a parliamentary system that's usually the case. But this time, Cameron had miscalculated—badly. On August 29, the vote failed in Parliament. The shadow of Prime Minister Tony Blair's buddy routine with George W. Bush on the misadventure of Iraq still poisoned politics in Great Britain. Cameron, chastened, conceded that he would respect the verdict of Parliament.

I was on the phone almost immediately to Foreign Minister Laurent Fabius of France. He confirmed that President François Hollande remained committed, with or without the United Kingdom. For France, perhaps, there might even be some bragging rights in carrying the banner for an always competitive Europe.

Nonetheless, I worried we were losing momentum. Time was passing. It had been eight days since the attacks, and we learned Assad was taking countermeasures that put civilian lives at risk.

The vote in London sent shock waves through our politics at home. It revived overnight memories of the Iraq War. The Russians were also laying a trap, publicly arguing that no military steps be taken before completion of a UN investigation. They were just trying to run out the clock and hope that the sense of urgency evaporated: the UN investigation was charged only with concluding whether chemical weapons had been used, not who used them. And, of course, at the end of any investigation a Russian veto awaited in the Security Council.

We couldn't afford to wait. We needed to fight back against efforts to change the subject.

I'd been pushing for our administration to release a declassified report on the chemical weapons attack, to help the country judge for itself what had happened and to debunk the distortions of Assad's allies in Moscow. To accompany it, I was asked to make a public statement that was factual but forceful.

As someone who had lived through the Iraq debate in 2002, I wanted to be certain that my case would stand the test of truth. Secretary Colin Powell's infamous speech on Iraq's weapons of mass destruction at the UN forever haunted him. I was not going to speak a word I wasn't sure was accurate. But I also wanted every American watching at home to know the truth: We didn't suspect, we didn't surmise. We *knew* what had happened in the Damascus suburbs.

Along with my chief of staff and Deputy Secretary Bill Burns, I worked through the night and all morning up to a few minutes before my remarks, trading edits and honing the text. The White House signed off on it. The case I was about to make was precise, down to the last word. I wanted to lay out the facts much as I used to when I was a prosecutor. It seemed very similar to a closing statement in a trial: here's what we know, and here's why it matters. I felt a moral clarity about the argument in the same way I had felt moral clarity when I testified to the Foreign Relations Committee in 1971.

I entered the Treaty Room and began a live television broadcast. After walking through all the evidence, I said, "The primary question is no longer what do we know. The question is what is the free world going to do about it?" I was thinking of a different leader who used gas to murder his own people when I said, "As previous storms in history have gathered, when unspeakable crimes were within our power to stop them, we have been warned against the temptations of looking the other way. History is full of leaders

who have warned against inaction, indifference and especially against silence when it mattered most." But this was not simply a case of keeping
faith with the 1,459 lives lost days before in Syria; even longer-standing
principles were at stake. I reminded the country that "it matters that nearly a
hundred years ago, in direct response to the utter horror and inhumanity of
World War I, that the civilized world agreed that chemical weapons should
never be used again. That was the world's resolve then. And that began
nearly a century of effort to create a clear red line for the international community." I didn't want the predictable cable coverage to gloss over the fact
that this wasn't President Obama's red line alone—it was the world's red
line and it had been drawn nearly a century before.

Late that night, I was home reading my briefing book when, at about
9:30, the State Department Operations Center called: "The president would
like to speak with you on a secure line." As I made my way upstairs to the
small area where my secure phone was installed, I braced myself for the
conversation we were about to have. I assumed that Tomahawk missiles
were about to be launched.

Instead, the president told me he had been thinking more and had talked
about it at length during a walk around the White House grounds with Mc-
Donough. He absolutely believed a response was warranted but wanted
Congress to authorize the use of force so that they'd be in it for the duration.
It was clear he had made up his mind. He wanted to gather the National Security Council in the morning. I told the president we would do all we could
to win the authorization.

I hung up the phone. My mind flashed back to the previous days of
phone calls consulting Congress. I hadn't been opposed to putting anything
to a vote. But no one had indicated that was the track we might be traveling,
and I had assumed the president saw the advantage in striking fast and preventing opposition from building up. To this day, I don't know every nuance
of the president's thinking, but I do know so many of us missed where the
president's decision was headed.

Perhaps since I was new to the job I wasn't yet familiar with the president's approach. Susan Rice was also new as national security advisor, and
she had argued forcefully for action now. Perhaps I hadn't yet mastered
how to read Barack Obama. Perhaps we didn't realize how strong his reluctance was to take the plunge deeper on Syria without Congress. Perhaps
he had seen that, with an opposition party which on many days even equiv-
ocated on whether he was born in America, acting without Congress could
invite all kinds of trouble, maybe even calls for impeachment.

None of the "perhapses" really mattered. The president had made the decision to bomb, but he wanted Congress with him in the effort. My job was to do all I could to help ensure he got their support.

THERE WAS LOGIC in going to Congress for authorization, legally and practically. Similar interventions in Panama, Haiti, Kosovo, Bosnia and Libya had all been undertaken without congressional authorization. But you're always strongest speaking as one country. After David Cameron lost the vote in Parliament, it was harder to justify bypassing Capitol Hill. Dempsey argued the air strikes would be as effective in three days or three weeks. I did not agree with that, but so much time had already passed that any element of surprise was already gone. And I assumed we would receive congressional consent.

In hindsight, Susan Rice was the only one of us who correctly predicted the mood of Congress. Seeking formal authorization was a dead end: she warned that the Republicans wouldn't authorize *anything* for Obama. My respect for the Senate Foreign Relations Committee and Senate preroga-tives in particular made me think otherwise; surely, I thought, with Israel supporting military action, and given the brutality of Assad's attacks and the narrow scope we were discussing, Congress would vote to hold Assad accountable. I did caution the president that the Republican Congress could always decide to screw him just for the sake of politics, and if they did it would have lasting consequences for his presidency. Republicans could make the president look like a lame duck. But I concluded that Congress would have to do exactly what most of its members had been saying they wanted to do in Syria for two years now. Hagel and Biden agreed. We Sen-ate veterans were wrong. Susan was the only one who pegged it.

Denis McDonough had an expression that was especially relevant to our discussion: he called it "wearing the jacket." It was about shared respon-sibility at both ends of Pennsylvania Avenue. It was important for the Hill to wear the jacket with us. For many on the Hill who had been urging the United States to do more on Syria, this should have been their chance to prove they were as effective at rounding up votes as they were at talking on the Sunday shows.

Together with General Dempsey and Secretary Hagel, I spent a full week on the Hill in testimony in front of four different committees, answer-ing more than twenty hours of questions. It felt like two hundred. In retro-spect it was a no-win argument: we had to convince half the Congress we wouldn't do too much in Syria and convince the other half we wouldn't do too little.

Some in Congress clearly didn't want to vote on anything that could be portrayed as "siding" with Barack Obama. Senator Marco Rubio had been a hawk in the Senate, a neoconservative who had ripped President Obama for "dithering as innocent Syrians die at the hands of a merciless regime." Now he said it was "too late." Too late for what? I wondered. Too late to make it clear a dictator couldn't gas children with impunity? The only thing that had changed was that now Marco was gearing up to run for president in 2016 and he was worried about the politics of a conservative electorate who hated the president.

On the Democratic side, many in Congress had been elected because President Bush's Iraq War had been such a disaster. Some worried about giving any president a "blank check" ever again, anywhere. The fact that we were talking about a limited, targeted operation without boots on the ground didn't make a difference. They may have heard the word "Syria," but all they saw was Iraq. George W. Bush and Dick Cheney's foreign policy hangover was still infecting our decision-making. It was the American equivalent of the backlash Cameron had faced in Great Britain.

For others, there was a general numbness to what had occurred in Syria. Senator Susan Collins of Maine, a moderate Republican, wondered whether there was really a difference between Assad's attacks on his own people with bombs as opposed to an atrocity committed with poison gas. I was stunned to hear how quickly and easily a serious senator had forgotten that chemical weapons had been banned by the civilized world for a reason.

As we tried to persuade Democrats that the operation would be targeted in scope, conservatives lamented we weren't doing more. My friends John McCain and Lindsey Graham didn't bring any votes with them for a much greater intervention, but they did a hell of a good job criticizing our approach. I was personally disappointed. John and Lindsey wanted to see Assad gone. So did I. The three of us had talked privately almost weekly about my efforts to ratchet up pressure on Assad. They knew I was in an uphill battle internally. But they refused to accept that punishing air strikes putting Assad on his heels were the most this president and this Congress could possibly achieve right now. Rather than meeting us halfway, John and Lindsey were more comfortable picking apart our strategy. It was an interesting experience fighting friends and opponents at the same time.

At each hearing, progressive protesters from Code Pink held up posters while chanting, "Don't bomb Syria," and "Blood on your hands." When the chairman tried to gavel them to silence, I defended their right to protest, remembering my own years as an activist. But I wondered: Where were the posters of children whose lives were snuffed out by a weapon banned ever since we had witnessed its horror in World War I? Had they no sense of moral outrage against a dictator who had killed hundreds of families while sleeping in their beds? Did the scars of the Iraq War run so deep that no one could differentiate between force that was justified and a war of choice that should never have been fought at all? The person with real blood on his hands was a butcher in Damascus who must have been quite comforted by the sight of dysfunction in Congress.

The first test vote on a resolution to authorize the use of force came in the Senate Foreign Relations Committee, which I had chaired less than a year before. It passed, but only by a vote of 10–7. Even my former colleague from Massachusetts Ed Markey, my friend who had taken over my seat when I became secretary, did not vote to support the president's action. He voted "present," explaining he was still haunted by his vote to authorize the war in Iraq. He confided in me that had his friend whom he trusted not been secretary of state, he would have voted no.

Joe Biden and I compared notes and numbers: We both concluded that we could lose the final vote in Congress. That outcome would be a devastating setback for the international prohibition against chemical weapons, for American credibility and for the president's broader agenda.

As the domestic debate continued, I was working the phones around the clock to all my counterparts who had a stake in Syria. Sergei Lavrov and I spoke regularly, and our calls tested my patience. I would try to convince him our intelligence was unimpeachable. Assad was clearly culpable. He would try to convince me military action would have severe repercussions and there was no way we could know what had actually happened in Ghouta.

The day after the Foreign Relations Committee vote, he again questioned our intelligence findings. "There's no doubt," I told him. "Believe me, Chuck Hagel and I remember Iraq."

He responded that even if we were correct, military action would be too risky.

"I don't believe that, Sergei," I said. "There are always things we can do. For example, if Assad agreed to have the full stock of chemical weapons shipped out—"

"It's too risky," Lavrov interrupted. He contended that the extremists might get their hands on them as they were being transported. In Moscow in May, Lavrov had sounded optimistic about a joint effort to remove chemical weapons. Now he wanted no part of it.

"You don't think we could work with the UN to plan for safe passage?" I asked.

He told me he didn't know and then continued to lecture me about American military meddling without the support of the international community or the U.S. Congress.

I rolled my eyes at Sergei's sudden claims to understand the Obama administration's domestic political constraints.

That evening a call request from Lavrov came through.

President Obama had been in St. Petersburg with President Putin for the G20. Putin broached the possibility of having the international community step in to secure the chemical weapons stockpile in Syria and transport it out of the country to be destroyed. Susan Rice had called me to report the conversation.

I told Lavrov I'd speak with President Obama. Sergei already knew I thought the idea was worth exploring. He was sending me a message: there was potential for progress.

PRESIDENT OBAMA WASN'T optimistic, but he did think Lavrov and I should continue to discuss it, particularly since it seemed increasingly unlikely we would succeed in Congress. The Syrians hadn't even publicly admitted that they had chemical weapons; it seemed like a long shot that we could convince them not only to acknowledge their weapons but to abandon them.

Almost three weeks had passed since Assad's night of terror.

I was in London holding a press conference with Foreign Secretary William Hague when Margaret Brennan from CBS News asked the key question: "Is there anything, at this point, that Assad's government could do or offer that would stop an attack?"

"Sure," I replied, my conversations with Lavrov fresh in my mind. "He could turn over every single bit of his chemical weapons to the international community in the next week. Turn it over, all of it, without delay, and allow a full and total accounting."

I voiced skepticism, putting the bait out and pulling it back a bit to cover us. "But he isn't about to do it," I added, "and it can't be done, obviously."

Flying back to Washington from London, we had barely hit cruising altitude when I received word Lavrov wanted to talk with me urgently. He and Putin had conferred. They were prepared to make a statement taking me up on my offer to press Assad to get the chemical weapons out of Syria. I made it clear we weren't interested in gauzy declarations, only in outcomes that were both verifiable and achievable. I immediately related the conversation to Susan Rice.

While it was a welcome possibility, I worried we were losing the mo-

ment I'd hoped for most of all: the chance to turn air strikes into leverage
for diplomacy in Syria. By failing to authorize the use of force, Congress
was effectively taking the power out of our hands and undermining the authority of the commander in chief.

The president instructed me to put the chemical weapons removal initiative to the test. The following evening, he gave a prime-time address aimed
at galvanizing public support for action against Assad. He amended his remarks, stating that the U.S.-Russian initiative "has the potential to remove
the threat of chemical weapons without the use of force." He continued: "I
have, therefore, asked the leaders of Congress to postpone a vote to authorize the use of force while we pursue the diplomatic path."

TWO DAYS LATER, I was en route to Geneva, along with a team of diplomats and lawyers with chemical weapons, nonproliferation and regional
expertise. We're blessed to have career Foreign Service officers and civil
servants on duty around the clock to marshal technical expertise for any
issue, no matter how complex. They are a national treasure. From the moment the war broke out, our team had been examining the chemical weapons problem. They had already gamed out possible avenues to removing the
weapons. We were ready to deal with anything the Russians might throw
at us.

Amazingly, however, the Russian delegation didn't even make a pitch.
They had come to Geneva without any specific language as a starting point.
I think the Russians were surprised by the granularity we brought to the
task. Our team was well prepared.

Lavrov and I spent hours in a conference room at the InterContinental hotel discussing the scope of the Syrian stockpile, technical options for
destroying the weapons, best ways to monitor and verify that destruction,
and how to protect the personnel trusted to conduct this work. Meanwhile,
American specialists took over a block of rooms and, in concert with their
Russian counterparts, began hammering away at the details. Russia—a
country still publicly pretending to believe Assad hadn't used chemical
weapons at all—came much closer to our position than we had ever anticipated.

Still, divisions emerged, chiefly on how the agreement would be enforced. Both sides agreed that the text we hashed out together would have
to be codified by the UN Security Council. But Russia did not agree that
the resolution that the Security Council ultimately passed should be legally
binding. We didn't trust the Syrian regime and believed they'd try to hide

some weapons or chemical agents. So we pushed for as much access and transparency as possible. Assad would try to cheat, and we wanted to be sure Syria could be punished for violating the deal.

I would spend hundreds of hours negotiating with Lavrov in four years as secretary. He's clever, calculating and idiosyncratic. He's also famous for little stunts and mind games to seek some small advantage at the bargaining table. After many hours of arguing whether the resolution would be legally binding, a member of my team slipped me a note: the Russian delegation had placed their bags out in the hotel hallway, ostensibly to be loaded for departure. It was a ham-handed tactic to imply they were about to walk away. We were in the home stretch; I knew they weren't about to get up and leave.

"Sergei, the press is reporting that you're leaving. Are you leaving? Are we wasting our time right now?"

Sergei admitted they weren't leaving Geneva, lit another cigarette and got back to work without the contrived pressure.

By the next morning, less than a week after my press conference in London, Lavrov and I were able to announce a detailed U.S.-Russia framework for eliminating Syria's *declared* chemical weapons. When we presented the text to the full Security Council on September 27, it passed unanimously, 15–0. Some wondered if it could be a turning point in the international response to the Syria crisis. It was not a turning point; at best it was the high point amid the many tragic low points that would follow.

SYRIA WAS ALWAYS going to be difficult. The risks were obvious: left to its own devices, the civil war could be an incubator of regional violence, a testing ground for jihadis, a proxy terrain for Iran and Russia, a safe harbor for enemies of our ally Israel, a playing field for Kurd aspirations and a dumping ground for various Sunni countries to keep extremists at a distance. All these dangers combined to make it a place with unavoidable strategic consequences for us and our allies.

Given the secular complexity of the country, time was never on our side: Syria would only get worse so long as either side and their proxies believed they could win on the battlefield. Because the United States almost always ends up owning the aftermath of the world's conflicts, we had an interest in the war ending sooner. When I had appeared before the Senate Foreign Relations Committee in January 2013 for my confirmation hearing, I talked about the dangerous dynamic.

"Right now, President Assad does not think he is losing," I explained, "and the opposition thinks it is winning." I told the committee what I believed throughout my time as secretary: "We need to change Bashar Assad's calculation." I explained that we needed to make Assad "see the die is cast, the handwriting is on the wall," so he would "save lives and hold the state together in a transition." Assad wasn't concerned the United States would actually engage. At the same time, most experts believed Assad was weak. He was suffering major defections from both high-level military and political players. I thought the moment was ripe to ramp up the pressure. But both in the administration and on the Hill, while there was deep concern for what was happening, there was deeper concern for what might happen if we did more. Syria was difficult in every way, made more so by our failure to make choices that gave us greater leverage.

After the agreement was reached in Geneva, we faced the immediate task of ensuring the removal of tons of the world's most devastating, insidious weapons from stockpiles all over the country, in the middle of a bloody civil war.

First, we had to identify, secure, collect and move the weapons to the port of Latakia, from where they could be shipped out of the country. Then we had to figure out the best place to destroy them. During the first phase—removing the weapons from Syria—we relied on Russia to pressure the Syrians to comply. The Syrians were trying to milk the process for everything they could. They would tell us they needed massive, unnecessary military equipment—the vehicles used to move tanks—to help move the weapons. Nine out of ten of their requests were absurd, and even the Russians told them so.

The second phase—destroying the weapons—was a challenge because we couldn't find a place to do it. We tried to convince Jordan and Turkey, in hopes of limiting the distance the weapons would have to travel, but neither was willing to take the risk of gas accidentally killing its people. The United States was too far away. Russia told us there was a law on its books that prevented it from bringing foreign chemical weapons into the country. Albania agreed to host the destruction, but shortly after it agreed, the prime minister called me. I could hear protesters chanting in the background as he explained, "Listen to what I'm facing. I wanted to do this. I just can't. I'm sorry."

Finally, we came up with a plan to destroy the weapons at sea. One of the ways to destroy Assad's chemicals was to water them down, creating a big tank of sludge that could then be incinerated. The chemical weapons experts from the Organisation for the Prohibition of Chemical Weapons (OPCW) developed a prototype of an incinerator that was small enough to fit on a ship, found a mothballed ship, retrofitted it with the special incinerator, trained a crew and then deployed it. It was creative problem-solving at its best.

By July 2014, the teams had removed roughly thirteen hundred tons of chemical weapons and destroyed them by September. For the first time ever in the middle of a conflict, weapons of mass destruction were removed as an asset in the hands of a warring party. Thirteen hundred tons of chemical weapons were no longer available to Assad or to extremists who, as they swept across the Syrian landscape, would almost certainly have secured some somewhere. In a country that shares a border with Israel, mitigating that massive threat was itself progress. For those reasons alone, the agreement we reached in Geneva was valuable. But it also carried its burden of tragedy.

For one thing, we always believed Assad would find a way to avoid declaring his full stockpile. After all, the OPCW and the world were working off best estimates. While it was a huge accomplishment to remove the thirteen hundred tons, we worried he would hide chemical agents somewhere. Proving so was nearly impossible even though we set out immediately at the UN to try.

But more important, the world had witnessed public, grotesque evidence of what a ruthless murderer Bashar al-Assad had become. Murderers should be punished, not just stripped of their killing arsenal. To the members of the opposition and many of the nations that supported them, Assad was getting away with murder. If the horrifying attack didn't inspire the world's intervention, they said, nothing would. They thought Assad and Russia could now see just how war-weary America was; they had little to fear. They weren't entirely wrong. The impunity with which Assad acted destroyed people's hope that he could be brought to heel and belied the institutions established to maintain respect for the rule of law. Assad belonged behind bars at The Hague. Everyone knew it, but those most able to do something—ourselves included—were mired in internal gridlock.

I worried that the longer the fighting continued, the more it invited the worst elements of the region into Syria in greater numbers as jihadis. As the number of refugees exploded, I feared the increasingly destructive impact on the social fabric and politics of Europe. I underscored to the opposition that I was not giving up on trying to end the conflict that was shattering Syria. Even lacking the leverage that military force would have given us, we needed to do everything possible to end the war. I promised them I would try to secure additional support to change the reality on the battlefield.

In fact, the battlefield did begin to change—and not for the better. The regime intensified its attacks, taking Homs and other cities. The opposition made headway down the eastern side of the country. The seesaw battles meant thousands were dying every month. Hundreds of thousands were displaced. More than a million people were forced to flee their homes in 2013 alone.

At the other end of the globe, it was like *Groundhog Day* in Washington, D.C., the same debates replaying every time we convened. "Diplomacy isn't working because we don't have enough leverage." "We need more options. Should we consider direct strikes?" "What would direct strikes look like?" "If we don't do strikes, what could we do short of that?" "Will that be enough to change Assad's calculus?" "We need more options." The debate was endless and circular.

BASHAR AL-ASSAD WAS "a one-man super-magnet for terror," I said with emphasis. It was January 23, 2014. Foreign ministers from across the world had convened in Geneva, Switzerland, under UN auspices to focus on the Syrian civil war. Syria's foreign minister, Walid Muallem, had just delivered a reprehensible speech branding all opposition to Assad as terrorists. It was a sickening insult to average Syrians who had stood up to Assad's brutality and in return, for close to two years, had been gassed, barrel-bombed, starved and turned into refugees. Now the murderous autocrat was blaming his own people for the scourge of foreign fighters taking advantage of the lawless chaos in Syria, moving back and forth across the Iraqi-Syrian border with ease.

Thousands of miles away in Washington, there was a low-grade skirmish within the National Security Council between those who saw only bad options in Syria and didn't think we could change the outcome and those of us who wanted to make the most of bad options and thought we should not only try but could make a difference. I argued additional pressure could be brought to bear in ways that didn't dig us irretrievably into Syria, but did change the dynamics for the better. It was a belief argument, not a provable fact. And I never succeeded in persuading the president the belief was worth acting on, that the risks, such as they were, were worth taking.

Complicating any analysis, the war continued to change. There were now at least two wars being fought with equal brutality: the Syrian civil war between Assad and the homegrown opposition (alongside its proxy fight between Assad's sponsors in Tehran and Moscow and the Sunni countries), and the increasing incursion of foreign terrorists into both Syria and Iraq.

Fighting Assad in Syria had become a cause célèbre for aspiring jihadis from the region and from Europe, abetted by some of our Sunni friends, who were glad to see angry young men fight the Shia apostate regime. Social media played a shockingly effective role as recruiter in chief for all of it. In Iraq, long-boiling sectarian resentments between Sunni and Shia found a violent synergy with weak, divisive leadership. Prime Minister Nouri al-Maliki clumsily helped create the environment that allowed for the rise of Daesh by consolidating power among the Shia elite instead of uniting Iraq. His government was in disarray. His military was in shambles.

Even as the overall equation was becoming far more complicated, the Syrian civil war had morphed into a magnet for something else: a threat that, unlike Assad himself, galvanized a remarkable response from the United States. It would go by multiple names: ISIL. ISIS. Daesh. But it was pure evil. Radical, violent extremists launched an assault across Iraq's Anbar Province and captured the city of Fallujah and parts of Ramadi, the province's capital. Our experts warned that this group was "al-Qaeda on steroids"—capable, radicalized and well-funded enough to accumulate and hold territory, inching closer to cities like Baghdad and Erbil.

They called themselves the Islamic State of Iraq and Syria. Countries in the region called them Daesh, an Arabic acronym that the terrorists despised. But no matter what you called them, we needed a policy that would ensure they never achieved the full-fledged caliphate they sought so brazenly. We would need to attack them every way necessary before they permanently reordered the Middle East in their ugly and hateful image.

In early June, Mosul, the second-largest city in Iraq, fell, with the Iraqi army crumbling as soon as it was confronted by the extremist fighters. Prime Minister Maliki desperately requested American air strikes. President Obama was in a tough situation. We all were. Iraq was gravely threatened. But because Maliki was hopeless, we knew air strikes alone weren't a solution. You couldn't defeat Daesh with Maliki at the helm in Baghdad.

Careful about not repeating history, we were genuinely committed to the proposition that only the Iraqis themselves could decide to change their leadership. Nothing else could produce success. We engaged immediately in delicate, under-the-radar diplomacy to encourage a peaceful transition. Vice President Biden and I made separate trips to Baghdad in June to meet with Maliki. The vice president had developed great expertise on Iraq, both as chairman of the Senate Foreign Relations Committee and in the White House. His former aide Tony Blinken was instrumental in helping our team to navigate the waters of transition. We were playing a difficult hand—we knew the strategic military imperative was growing to push back on Daesh, but we also knew doing so would relieve the political pressure on Maliki. We didn't want short-term progress to condemn us to failure in the long term. Timing was critical.

Maliki understood the magnitude of the crisis with one-third of his country under Daesh's control, but at first he gave no indication that he would depart. American diplomats met quietly with Iraqi leaders to confirm their distrust of Maliki and convey our own. We sent a message: the sustained support they needed was unlikely to come with Maliki in charge. Iraq needed a leader who would govern in an inclusive, nonsectarian manner. The Iraqis landed on Haider al-Abadi. In early August, Iraq's president formally requested that Abadi replace Maliki and form a new coalition government as prime minister. Maliki was defiant at first but within a few days relented, once he understood that Shia Iran didn't support his remaining in office any more than the Americans. Daesh was a threat to Iran as well.

While we helped Iraq put its political house in order, empowering it on multiple fronts to repel the terrorists, Daesh gave the world fresh evidence of its barbarity.

James Foley was a young journalist from New Hampshire. I had met his family in 2011 after he was captured and held in Libya, where he was covering the Arab Spring. As chairman of the Foreign Relations Committee, I did what I could then to work with the State Department and encourage his release. That story had a happy ending: he was freed. Now, two years later, as secretary, I learned Jim had been kidnapped again—this time covering the war in Syria. My heart sank. He was one of a handful of Americans—journalists, humanitarian aid workers—who had crossed the border into Syria to make a difference and had been taken prisoner by extremists. I met many of their parents. The wear and strain on their faces communicated more than words ever could. I made dozens of phone calls and talked directly to foreign ministers from the Gulf about using their influence, if they had any, to locate and free the captured Americans. One family from Massachusetts was lucky: with Qatar's intervention, their loved one was released alive.

President Obama went to extraordinary lengths to plan and authorize a rescue mission that put American boots on the ground in Syria where we believed the Americans were being held by Daesh. At the White House, we listened to this mission unfold in real time in the Situation Room. I will never forget the sinking feeling when we all heard the disembodied voice of a courageous special operator on the ground in Syria, inspecting rooms at the location where we were informed the hostages were held: "Dry hole. It's a dry hole." The hostages weren't there.

On August 19, I was in a meeting when a note was passed to me by an aide, his face ashen: a video had appeared on YouTube claiming to show the beheading of James Foley at the hands of a masked, cowardly thug cloaked from head to toe in black. I watched it alongside my chief of staff, who had also come to know the family. My profound feeling of injustice and sadness turned to anger. Something was horribly, unimaginably sick and wrong in the world. I closed my eyes. I wanted this brave young journalist to be home with his family, safe and alive. I wanted Daesh extinguished from the face of the earth. But now I could help accomplish only one of those things.

In real time there was urgent evidence that Daesh's threat was existential for the region. Not far from the Turkish border, the extremists terrorized a religious minority, the Yazidi families. They murdered the men and enslaved the women. The siege sent the Yazidis fleeing their homes and eventually left tens of thousands stranded on Mount Sinjar, without access to food, water or medicine. It was genocide in the making. Daesh was closing in on Erbil, the Kurdish city where we have a major consulate.

We sat in the Situation Room weighing military options. President Obama was calm and reasoned as usual. Unspoken but palpable in the room was the reality that a president who had been elected in 2008 promising to get the United States out of a war in Iraq had no choice but to order air strikes in that country again—to save the Yazidis and fight off the Daesh incursion. He gave the lonely order. Air strikes rained down to repel Daesh near Sinjar mountain on August 7. The Daesh killers scattered like roaches confronted by the beam of a flashlight.

But the president rightfully wanted to know, before deepening our involvement anymore, that the United States was pursuing a carefully designed, comprehensive strategy above and beyond air strikes. Before deploying our military to fight Daesh in a sustained way, the president outlined three conditions that had to be met: better governance in Iraq, a regional coalition and a comprehensive diplomatic strategy.

We had laid some of the groundwork already, but I went to work immediately, convening the State Department's top experts to make certain there were no gaps in our approach. Three days later, I delivered a memo to the president. In addition to military support, we would go after Daesh's financial lifeline, clamping down on any institutions from which money and oil flowed to the terrorists; we would go after Daesh's ability to recruit foreign fighters, exchanging relevant data and intelligence with nations around the world and expanding the Department of Homeland Security's ability to prevent recruitment in the United States; and we would go after Daesh's extremist propaganda, working with partners in the region to counter the hateful rhetoric of the terrorists and amplify the voices of peaceful Muslim leaders. We would devote significant resources to improving the humanitarian situation for those who had suffered at Daesh's hands. But most important, we would galvanize the broadest possible coalition. Our military commitment would give me leverage to deliver on all these other requisite steps. It wouldn't be America alone.

The president embraced the strategy in full. The memo became the foundation of our approach from that point forward. I felt unleashed, fully empowered to put together a decisive coalition that could rescue our friends from the clutches of extremist horror. It was energizing to know we were deploying all our assets in one enterprise with the full support of everyone.

Chuck Hagel and I together secured the commitment of our NATO allies. We also moved to line up the Arab states as rapidly as possible. It was obvious to all of us that we needed a united Islamic front to counter whatever degree of Islamic authority Daesh was claiming for its campaign of terror. We couldn't afford any daylight between us and the Islamic world. I'd been a senator for two wars in Iraq. We were still living the consequences of the second one in an Iraq torn by internal strife. But the first Iraq war was a model to be emulated: Desert Storm, executed by a broad coalition of nations, particularly those in the Middle East. Secretary James Baker personally traveled to dozens of countries to win their engagement. I needed to do the same, relying on personal relationships invested in over years as a senator and now as secretary.

Support from the Gulf was far from automatic. Persuading Sunni leaders to commit their military and their voices to a war against Sunni extremists who were fighting their sworn enemies in Syria and fighting for a return to Sunni dominance in Iraq was not without its own complications. I remember one meeting of foreign ministers in Istanbul where some of my friends from the region talked openly about supporting the toughest fighters to accelerate Assad's departure and then fighting the "second" war down the road when Assad was gone. But we needed them to all move in the same direction simultaneously. The second war was now.

Many in the region would take their lead from the kingdom of Saudi Arabia. The Saudis were still angry that the United States had not gone after Assad, following the chemical weapons attack. Nonetheless, I hoped that building a coalition to fight Daesh might also provide a diplomatic realignment that could ultimately end the larger war in Syria. Assad, after all, had been the one attracting the extremists into Iraq and Syria. But first we had to work together to build a coalition against the extremists.

In Saudi Arabia, because of the extraordinary heat, meetings often happen at night when it cools off a bit. Late one night, I made my way to the summer palace in Jeddah, a magical spot right on the edge of the Red Sea. I was ushered in for an audience with King Abdullah, ninety, and Prince Saud al-Faisal, the longest-serving foreign minister in the world. Saud al-Faisal was a proud Princeton graduate whose wisdom and grace came from an incredible tenure of over forty years as the kingdom's foreign minister. He had become a good friend. Parkinson's disease was slowing his voice, but his mind was sharp as ever and his smile just as warm.

The king himself was not well at that time. He was courageously carrying out his responsibilities, but you couldn't predict when exactly he could meet or how strong he would be. I appreciated that he made the effort and that he spent as much time with me as he did. We talked for hours about Syria, Iraq, the region. King Abdullah would never let go of his disappointment over the failure to bomb Syria, but he did take a long view about the friendship between the United States and the kingdom, one that began under Franklin Roosevelt in 1945 and had endured through moments as painful as 9/11. He expressed his concern that the forces of Sunni extremism presented a long-term threat to the very kingdom he would one day pass on to others in the House of Saud, and to Islam itself. In the background we could hear the soft music of prayers played always in the palace. He fingered prayer beads in his hand.

The king had planned to convene a group of regional leaders with me to discuss the coalition. Iraq was not invited; the wounds between the nations were still healing. But I asked the king if Prime Minister Abadi could send his new foreign minister. He agreed. Such an invitation would have been unthinkable just a month earlier.

We were, slowly but surely, building a coalition in reality, not just on paper.

City by city, mile by mile, we began taking back territory in Iraq, our actions welcomed by the new government. But in Syria, Daesh was accumulating more and more territory with near impunity. We had to eliminate the sanctuary the group was creating there.

The president authorized air strikes to wallop Daesh in and around Raqqa, the group's self-proclaimed capital, and Kobane, a town in northern Syria near the Turkish border. That very first night, our military flew alongside forces from Saudi Arabia, the UAE, Bahrain, Jordan and Europe. It was the first time our militaries collaborated to fight Sunni extremists— a milestone in the war against terrorism.

By early 2015, the coalition had swelled to more than sixty member nations from every part of the world. Between launching thousands of air strikes, disrupting Daesh's command structure, undermining its propaganda, squeezing its financing, damaging its supply networks, dispersing its personnel and forcing the group to change tactics regularly, we had retaken the initiative.

Iraqi forces retook the Mosul and Haditha dams and territory near the city of Tikrit. In Syria, we smashed Daesh's command facilities, damaged its oil infrastructure and blocked its siege of Kobane. The long-beleaguered opposition actually gained remarkable ground and was pushing into Latakia, the regime's heartland. Assad was nervous.

But Daesh held on to its foothold in Syria, in large measure because of a powerful recruiting tool: it claimed to be bringing the fight to Assad. We were compartmentalizing—going after Daesh first, with the intention of dealing with Assad second. But on the Sunni street, many wondered why those who claimed to oppose Assad were fighting the jihadis who said they too were fighting him.

It was messy. And in the fall of 2015, it got even messier.

I had hoped the opposition's progress combined with our military intervention against Daesh might finally force the regime back to the bargaining table. Instead, Assad's backers—Iran and Hezbollah—seeing that the opposition had made some gains, doubled down. They were well aware that our engagement was limited to stopping Daesh—a fight they shared with us—and to helping the opposition. When their doubling down still didn't improve Assad's situation, an even bigger backer played the biggest hand of all: on September 30, 2015, the Russian military launched its first air strikes against the opposition in Syria. The conflict was fundamentally and irretrievably changed.

THE RUSSIANS TOLD us they were sending their military into Syria in a typical Russian manner—which is to say, they didn't tell us at all. President Obama and I met with President Putin in New York the day before their strikes launched. We discussed Syria at length. Putin gave us no indication of what was coming.

The next morning, as soon as I learned the news, I caught up to Sergei Lavrov in the hallway of the UN. I said, "Sergei—you guys are now bombing in Syria and moving troops? What's up?" He looked surprised and at first said, "No way—what do you mean?" I showed him the media reports. He blanched slightly and hurried off, subsequently seen talking on his cell phone. Maybe Sergei was bluffing, but Putin was known to hold his cards close to the vest on issues like Syria and Ukraine, which are especially personal to him.

Either way, the Russians had upped the ante to a degree that they knew we would not match. Sometimes "diplomatic leverage" is just a fancy way of defining who has the greatest stake. For Putin, Syria was a longtime client state dating back to the Cold War, the site of Russian naval bases, his country's only foothold in the Middle East. No cost was too large for him to pay to protect his investment. I couldn't persuasively make the same case in the Situation Room.

A week or two later, Teresa and I went home to Boston for a rare long weekend away from Washington. But I was restless. I couldn't sleep. Syria haunted me. Until that point, our strategy had been to apply pressure on Assad through our assistance to the opposition, in hopes of forcing him to the negotiating table. With Russia's military now all in, whatever marginal leverage we might have possessed was eviscerated. The regime was reinvigorated. The opposition could expect a bloody winter.

I asked myself a different question: What if we focused foremost on ending the bloodshed and getting humanitarian aid to those who need it? If a genuine cease-fire was in place, perhaps then we could make progress on the political track.

Russia's engagement on each of these steps would be essential—and unavoidable.

The White House was skeptical. Why would Russia support a cease-fire, let alone spearhead a negotiated political transition? It was a fair question. Maybe we couldn't get it done, I admitted. But I thought there were reasonable answers. For one thing, both Iran and Russia had accepted principles similar to ours as to how a political transition could take place. I believed they might welcome a legitimate cease-fire to pursue a reasonable political outcome. In Afghanistan in the 1980s, Russia had learned a bitter lesson about quagmires. Putin had been a young KGB colonel in the years when Russia's best and brightest military officers ran into a meat grinder fighting an unwinnable occupation. The Russians would not want to bleed forever in Syria. They might be amenable to an exit strategy that protected their interests.

But most of all, I asked, what was our alternative? Did anyone see a viable answer we could impose unilaterally, while Russia was flying planes over Syria? I knew I didn't have the best hand to play, but I'd rather play that hand than just sit back and "admire the problem" while the number of displaced persons grew by the day, while barrel bombs were being dropped indiscriminately on schools, while the fabled city of Aleppo was being destroyed, while the international community seemed powerless before the world to hold atrocity accountable.

In the late fall, Lavrov accepted my proposal to assemble a group of nations that came to be known as the International Syria Support Group (ISSG). No solution would work unless all the major parties were part of the process, including Iran. It took weeks of work, but ultimately, when we convened the first meeting, the foreign ministers from Iran and Saudi Arabia sat at the same table with Turkey, Iraq and Egypt. Given the tensions between all the parties, that in and of itself felt like a milestone, if not momentum. All thirty-one nations eventually came to agreement on a statement regarding the shape of the potential peace.

By December 2015, we had agreed on a series of principles to guide the peace process, later codified unanimously in UN Security Council Resolution 2254, a new road map leading to a transitional Syrian government and democratic, UN-hosted elections within a year. Planning for a cease-fire and increased humanitarian access would begin immediately.

On February 11, 2016, in Munich, ISSG reconvened to talk about a cease-fire—and humanitarian progress. The meeting lasted hours longer than it was supposed to, as usual. The opposition to Assad vehemently objected to the word "cease-fire." They thought it implied they were giving up the fight against Assad. "Cessation of hostilities" was easier to swallow. I didn't care what we called it; I cared about what it might do. Could it stop the violence and allow humanitarian help to be delivered? Could it open up breathing room for leaders to bring the parties to a real negotiation for a political settlement?

At midnight, on February 27, 2016, the cessation of hostilities began. It held for twenty-four hours. Then forty-eight. Then a week. Then two. Then three.

Then it started fraying—slowly at first, and then more rapidly. The regime claimed to be bombing terrorists, when they were mainly hitting the more moderate rebels. Every action has a reaction, so the opposition would understandably attack regime forces. Before too long the violence was as bad as it had been before the cessation of hostilities and, in some places, worse. No one was holding either Assad or the opposition accountable. Worse, the extremists—al-Qaeda, now called al-Nusra, were commingled with our so-called moderate opposition, an uncomfortable fact a number of the opposition's supporters were unwilling to confront.

For some of my colleagues in Washington, this was enough. There was nothing more we could try to do, they believed. I disagreed. We had the right principles on the table, and we needed to find a new way to make them work. I wasn't about to stop trying unless President Obama asked me to stop. He never did.

But I never succeeded in persuading him to give me the tool I wanted most: greater leverage. Not boots on the ground or a large-scale operation; even a small strike on an appropriate target would send a message.

Oddly, it was not even easy to engage the Pentagon in a discussion of bolder military options. One meeting sticks out in my memory. We had just finished the umpteenth meeting on options for Syria. A number of small steps had been agreed to. I then asked everyone assembled in the Situation Room a basic question: "Let's all be honest with each other. Does anyone here think any of these options will actually change anything for Assad or Russia?" Everyone agreed that none of the existing options could truly change the state of play. I turned to the video screen, where then CENTCOM commander General Lloyd Austin was conferencing in from Tampa.

"General, if the commander in chief said to you, 'I want to end this agony in Syria within the next six to nine months'—if he said that, are there options you could suggest that would achieve that goal?"

General Austin responded, "Mr. Secretary, I don't think that's where the president's head is at."

"Okay, but I didn't ask you where the president's head is at," I said. "I want to know: Do realistic military options exist that could end this war in six to nine months?"

"Of course there are options. But the president doesn't want . . ."

Susan Rice jumped in and saved me from my own palpable frustration. I owed her. "The president has always been clear that he wants new ideas. If there are additional options that have not already been submitted, please write them up for the boss."

I wasn't the only one calling for more forceful interventions. Samantha Power, ambassador to the UN, and to some extent CIA director John Brennan also believed the risks of inaction outweighed those of using limited military force. But the Pentagon—and, more important, the president—remained as unconvinced as ever that overt military action to support the Syrian opposition, however limited, was worth pursuing.

The Defense Department was just as opposed to the only other alternative: working directly with Russia to de-escalate the conflict. We all knew by now that a cease-fire and humanitarian access could only work if Assad's air force was grounded. The regime's air strikes were the primary reason the cease-fire failed, the primary driver of refugees from Syria and the primary source of the military advantage that left the moderate opposition feeling as though they were sitting ducks. President Putin and Lavrov told me they were willing and able to keep Assad's planes on the ground. In return, they wanted military-to-military cooperation in fighting Daesh and al-Nusra. I thought, *If Daesh and al-Nusra are our enemy and we're supposedly targeting both anyway, why would we not be willing to carefully coordinate with Russia the more rapid destruction of Daesh with a better chance of securing a political settlement?* After all, we had agreed publicly on the outlines of a settlement. Given the level of killing, the length of the war and the negative impacts on the region and Europe, and given the threat of Daesh, which every day it existed exacerbated all the other challenges we faced in the region, why would we not want to put the proposition of killing Daesh and al-Qaeda faster to the test? If it worked, together we'd be fighting the actual terrorists, while Russia would have given us veto power over any air strike. If it didn't work, we'd have eliminated the confusing back-and-forth about who was responsible for what. We would have exposed the Russians. What was the downside?

The new secretary of defense, Ash Carter, dismissed the idea out of hand. He didn't like the appearance of the United States working with the Russians on any issue. He didn't trust Russia, and he believed that, from a military perspective, they had more to gain than we did. It was true that we had very publicly suspended all military cooperation with Moscow in 2014, after they'd annexed Crimea. But sanctions in place against Russia over Ukraine would remain intact. I was willing to tolerate Russia claiming some pyrrhic public relations victory from military cooperation if it meant Assad's air force wasn't killing Syrians and if we could destroy the terrorists faster.

I couldn't and still don't understand Ash's rigidity. He wouldn't budge. He had no proposal of his own to end the Syrian civil war, but he was openly scornful of the one idea on the table.

After much debate, the president gave us the go-ahead to organize a detailed proposal.

By design, the plan was simple. The cease-fire would start immediately, and Assad's forces would stop flying. Humanitarian convoys would enter besieged areas. If this proceeded smoothly for forty-eight hours, the U.S. military would begin coordinating with the Russians through what we named the Joint Implementation Cell. Once that was up and running successfully, negotiations for an end to the war would begin.

It made sense to me. Ash disagreed. He argued that we needed not two, but seven days of calm before we could start working with the Russians to kill terrorists.

I was baffled. Seven days of calm was impossible. There were too many spoilers—from Assad to Daesh and al-Nusra—all of whom would want this effort to fail. Why? Because part of the deal was that Russia would keep Assad's air force from flying, which Assad didn't want, and the other part was that we and Russia would jointly target al-Nusra and Daesh, which they didn't want. Giving the worst actors seven days to disrupt the calm was a poison pill. But Ash dug in. The president signed off on my overall plan but accepted Ash's condition: seven days. The plan was doomed before we walked out of the Situation Room.

The Russians met us in Geneva to review and finalize the proposal. We reached an agreement around noon on Friday, September 9, but because Washington was six hours behind, they still needed to review the final text. Nine hours after we sent the text back to Washington, Washington wanted one line added. Lavrov said it was redundant. I explained that Washington was adamant. Sergei predictably flipped out. "Are you fucking kidding me? That's already in the fucking agreement! We already have that covered!"

I repeated that we needed the extra line. Eventually, Lavrov relented. "Fine. We can make that addition, on one condition: we also have to add, right after that new sentence, 'as it already says below, in the same fucking paragraph.'" We left out the swear word, but otherwise agreed. The final text of the September 9 agreement includes both Washington's and Lavrov's additions.

The agreed-upon seven days of "calm" began quietly in mid-September, right before the world headed to New York for the UN General Assembly, my last one as secretary of state. On September 17, an alarming wire story popped up as a news alert on my phone: an American air strike had accidentally killed seventy uniformed Syrian regime troops.

I reached Lavrov as soon as I could. He was furious. The Russians accused us of targeting the Syrians on purpose. In a perverse nod to our war-fighting abilities, they did not believe the U.S. military could make such a mistake. They outright accused the military of not wanting to work with them and therefore purposely killing the possibility. Publicly and privately I vehemently defended our action as the purest of accidents, but nothing I said could convince him of the truth that it was a horrible accident.

Two days later, a humanitarian convoy was bombed as it tried to make its way to deliver aid to civilians in Aleppo. The Syrians and Russians were the only ones with any flights in the vicinity, and eyewitness reports as well as technical tracking of aircraft pointed to Assad's air force. The opposition had no aircraft. Everything I predicted had played out. We had spent months negotiating the path of that convoy. Bombing the aid workers was not only despicable, it was the final shredding of the diplomatic process into which so many had put so much. We never got to test whether cooperating on anti-extremist efforts and enforcing the cease-fire against Assad together with a veto on Russian and Syrian flights would have brought everyone to the table.

Two days later, Lavrov and I sat several seats away from each other at a UN Security Council session. He spoke before me, and as I listened, I could hardly contain my incredulity. The rapid disintegration of the agreement that began with our unfortunate accident and followed by the humanitarian convoy bombing had clearly put the Russians squarely back to status quo tactics. It was an appropriate moment of the surreal for all that had transpired. Despite the attack on the convoy, Lavrov called for the inter-Syrian political talks to resume quickly, "without any preconditions." He called for a "thorough and impartial" investigation into the bombing. He denied that either the Russians or the Syrians had attacked the convoy when evidence and common sense proved otherwise. He asked that his counterparts "refrain from emotional responses."

Then it was my turn.

"I listened to my colleague from Russia," I began. "He said that nobody should have any preconditions to come to the table. . . . How can people go sit at a table with a regime that bombs hospitals and drops chlorine gas again and again and again and again and again and again, and acts with impunity? Are you supposed to sit there and have happy talk in Geneva . . . when you've signed up to a cease-fire and you don't adhere to it?"

I wanted the talks to continue more than anyone, but I couldn't let Russia get away with this Orwellian doublespeak.

"Just think about what happened in the last couple of days," I argued. "President Putin's press secretary . . . claims that the attack on the humanitarian convoy was somehow a necessary response to an alleged offensive by al-Nusra elsewhere in the country. That's the first claim. Then a Russian ambassador said that Russian and Syrian forces were not bombing the area, but they were targeting Khan Tuman. Then we heard a completely different story. The defense ministry said that the aid convoy had been accompanied by militants in a pickup truck with a mortar. We've seen no evidence of that. But that, in any case, would not justify a violation of the cessation of hostilities. . . . Then the defense ministry switched completely, and it denied Russia's involvement. It said, according to spokesman Igor Konashenkov, 'Neither Russia nor Syria conducted air strikes on the UN humanitarian convoy in the southwestern outskirts of Aleppo.'

"Then Konashenkov went further and he said the damage to the convoy was the direct result of the cargo catching fire. The trucks and the food and the medicine just spontaneously combusted. Anybody here believe that?"

As I walked out of the Security Council chamber, I felt for the first time that we had arrived at the end of the road. If the Russians were going to speak from a script of alternative facts, negotiation had gone from improbable to impossible.

In November, after Donald Trump's victory in the presidential election, I tried to make one last attempt to achieve some measure of progress, even if it was incremental. Trump had said Assad deserved an A for leadership, so I figured our Gulf partners might have added incentive to be cooperative in the last months of the Obama administration. More than that, we had all worked effectively on a number of imperfect cease-fires that had saved some lives, and we had delivered humanitarian assistance to places that had received none in four years. Small steps were still steps. One life saved was still one less tragedy in a cascade of horror. I hosted my counterparts from Russia, Iran, Saudi Arabia, Qatar, Turkey, Iraq and Egypt in Lausanne. All we could do was negotiate the evacuation and surrender of Aleppo to the regime. I've never had such a sinking sense of futility.

Diplomacy to save Syria was dead for our administration, and the wounds of Syria remained open.

I think every day about how we might have closed them and how the world might close them still.

CHAPTER 20

Protecting the Planet

ONE BY ONE the sleek BMW police motorcycles escorted motorcade after motorcade to a precisely designated place at the gate to the exhibition hall at Le Bourget Airport, not far from the exact spot where Charles Lindbergh had touched down in the *Spirit of St. Louis* after his epic transatlantic flight in 1927. Black limousine after black limousine then broke away from the motorcade to roll up to a grand entrance with a huge red carpet, where the leaders of the world, one after the other, stepped out of their cars to be formally greeted by President François Hollande of France. A bank of cameras focused on each arrival as the leaders turned to pose for photographs, a steady, repetitive moment in the sun to satisfy each home audience and history.

President Obama arrived in the oversized, overweight limo called "the beast." I suppose that arriving at the Conference of the Parties (COP) for the Global Climate Change meeting in Paris, we might have thought twice about rolling up in a gas-guzzling behemoth that allegedly gets 3.7 miles to the gallon, but the Secret Service doesn't factor climate or messaging into presidential security. The president stepped onto the red carpet while the rest of us went around the official greeting party.

One after the other, the cavalcade continued. President Xi of China. Prime Minister Narendra Modi of India. President Putin of Russia. King Abdullah of Jordan. Presidents, prime ministers, kings and princes—150 strong had all come to Paris because the world appeared to be finally galvanizing around the urgency of addressing climate change. I can't think of any other meeting or event, other than the UN General Assembly, that commanded such attendance, and unlike the UNGA in New York, this was all happening at the same time, all on the same day, compressed within a few hours. It was an extraordinary assemblage. It was also a moment of solidarity with France. Just a couple of weeks earlier, homegrown Islamic extremists had blown themselves up and unleashed torrents of gunfire inside a Paris concert hall, at the soccer stadium and outside bars and restaurants, murdering 130 innocent people and wounding hundreds more. Worries about security forced cancellation of a long-planned march for the planet. What a startling juxtaposition: Paris paralyzed by those who wanted to destroy civilization itself, while hundreds of leaders were gathering to try to save it from a different existential threat.

Inside the exhibition hall, heads of state posed together for what is known as the "family photo," all standing dutifully next to one another on a dais, posing for a class picture. They greeted each other like old friends whether they had met before or hated each other. Even Bibi Netanyahu and Mahmoud Abbas shook hands for the first time in five years. Some issues are so important that even enemies are able to work in common cause.

Then, in another departure from the usual protocol of such a meeting, everyone milled around and slowly shuffled their way through a tent corridor into the plenary chamber, which was a large hard-frame tent set up for the conference. It was a rare moment of egalitarian opportunity to corral one leader or another, whether they wanted to talk or not. I chuckled watching the body language of some leaders as they were importuned unexpectedly and others expansively holding forth, obviously enjoying the conversation. None of us had ever seen such an assemblage of world leaders sauntering through a hallway like high school kids moving from one class to another.

This was the formal opening of the Twenty-First Conference of the Parties to the UN Framework Convention on Climate Change (UNFCCC). The first day would be consumed by heads of state speeches to the plenary. One by one, they described their country's particular concerns and urged the conference to act before it was too late.

The road to this meeting was not as easy as the vast assemblage seemed to suggest. For many of the attendees, there were still tricky issues to be resolved. Less developed nations wanted more clean energy technology donated to their impoverished countries, particularly since they were barely contributing to the problem. Island nations wanted to be saved from disappearing beneath a rising ocean. Oil-producing countries wanted to protect their economic life source as they transitioned to a new economy. Every region had its own survival instincts. And, of course, the twenty major polluting nations bearing responsibility for 80 percent of global greenhouse gas emissions faced huge pressure from powerful economic interests.

I thought back to a night in the weeks before I was confirmed as secretary. I was enjoying a dinner with my Senate chief of staff, at Las Placitas, a hole-in-the-wall Salvadoran restaurant on Capitol Hill. He would join me as my chief of staff at the State Department. We were talking through the workload and agenda while enjoying terrific guacamole, salsa and margaritas, a pleasant way to plan the future.

Former secretary James Baker had previously shared with me how important it was to set two or three top priorities and never lose sight of them. I pulled out my Senate legal pad and made the short list and the long list. In 2013, there were the obvious, enduring challenges for any American secretary of state: nuclear weapons, war, terrorism, religious extremism. But I wanted to elevate another priority, just as urgent and existential, yet woefully under-resourced at the State Department and astonishingly not accepted in all quarters as a crisis at all. I wanted to do for the environment what my predecessor, Hillary Clinton, had done for global women's issues. Why was I so focused on the environment? Quite simply, because even as a person of faith, I believe in science, and after a quarter century working on the issue, I knew as a matter of scientific fact that climate change is an existential threat. There is no Planet B.

It is nothing less than extraordinary to me that in the United States, without evidence, without factual, scientific inquiry, charlatans get away with arguing that climate change is not hugely aggravated by man-made choices. It is beyond Orwellian, beyond the old disinformation of the Cold War. It is even more disturbing that the current president of the United States has eagerly assumed the role of cheerleader in chief for capricious choices that will cost lives and treasure.

The profound environmental concern I brought to public life came directly from my mother's choices and environmentalist Rachel Carson's inspiration. My mother never shoved the environment at any of us, but her example was powerful and sublime at the same time. At Potomac School, she was a principal mover in the creation of the nature walk where we buried my Cairn terrier, Sandy. She could identify countless birds and even rose early sometimes to go bird-watching. She was one of the original recyclers. She served on the health committee of her local community. She taught us to respect our surroundings, pick up trash, not pollute. She was my early indoctrination in the meaning of an ecosystem.

Of course at Naushon Island we were surrounded by a natural habitat that, from my earliest years, required respect, even reverence. Because the Woods Hole Oceanographic Institution was based just across from the island, we would not only visit and be mesmerized by Marine species in tanks and stories of exploration, but we would often bump into researchers gathering specimens off the shores of the island. My mother was a huge Jacques Cousteau fan. Watching the Cousteau specials on TV was regular fare.

When *Silent Spring* was published in 1962, my freshman year at Yale, Rachel Carson instilled in me and a whole generation a sense of moral urgency. Her story of corporate connivance and government complicity in hiding the killer impacts of pesticides on humans was an eye-opener at the time. We hadn't yet grown so cynical that we expected either corporations or government to mislead the consumer. It was a rude awakening to what we now have come to expect as just the way it is. The cigarette companies hid the evidence that smoking gives you cancer; the Woburn dump hid the leaching that could give people cancer; the coal companies denied any responsibility for acid rain—the examples are plentiful. Because of Rachel Carson sounding the alarm, I was privileged to be involved in the takeoff of the modern environmental movement.

Now, in 2013, forty-three years after the first Earth Day, as well as my many efforts on oceans, fisheries, acid rain and climate legislation in the Senate, I was excited that as secretary of state I could represent a president and administration deeply committed to reaching a global agreement on climate change at the 2015 COP in Paris.

To get there, I was convinced the essential first step was finding a way to cooperate with China. Regrettably, China and the United States had been adversaries on this issue for decades. It was time to change the dynamic. I shared this thought with President Obama during our first meeting after he nominated me. He was enthusiastic. He had his own hopes for what we could do on climate change in his second term, but we both knew how tough it would be.

Four years before, in December 2009, I attended the UN climate negotiations in Copenhagen. The goal of the conference was to reach a global agreement on each nation's reduction of greenhouse gas emissions. I had been to many of these conferences since the 1992 Rio conference. In Copenhagen, there was a new optimism about the United States' engagement. But optimism wasn't an outcome. While President Obama's passion for climate action was a welcome change, there were tough issues to work through. First and foremost was the bifurcation of countries into "developed" and "developing" nations.

One of the principal reasons the 1997 Kyoto Protocol had failed is that it required much more from the United States and other developed nations and essentially nothing from developing countries, including major emitters like China and India. At the time, China was already the world's number two polluter. Even though China promised it would undertake serious efforts, not signing up for a measurable—if not enforceable—reduction schedule simply wouldn't do. We didn't need all countries to take the exact same steps, but we certainly needed all countries to be taking some action toward a low-carbon future.

Another major hurdle was transparency. There was a huge trust deficit. Most delegates were not comfortable letting countries sign up for emissions reduction levels and then trusting them to follow through. We had experienced this starkly with the very first climate agreement, reached at the 1992 UNFCCC in Rio, which relied entirely on voluntary commitments and thus quickly fell apart. Ensuring that countries were transparent about the actions they were taking, and that their efforts were verifiable by third parties, was essential, we realized. This didn't sit well with China, which informally led the bloc of developing nations. China viewed robust transparency measures as an infringement on its sovereignty.

While I was not part of the official negotiating team at Copenhagen— that was the prerogative of the State Department—as chairman of the Senate Foreign Relations Committee, I had a number of meetings with negotiators from both the American and foreign delegations. Their frustration was palpable. On every one of the major issues, they were making little progress. I knew from experience it wasn't going to be easy—when you're dealing with nearly two hundred countries, how can it be?—but the negotiations were even more constipated than I anticipated. The talks just weren't going anywhere.

President Obama's team had hoped a deal would be in hand by the time he touched down. Instead, he arrived in Copenhagen to find his work cut out for him. China and the so-called G77—the seventy-seven developing nations of the world—were stubbornly avoiding responsibility for major reductions. The president was forced to literally rush from meeting to meeting. He was conducting whirlwind personal diplomacy. To try to salvage some success in Copenhagen, he even crashed a meeting between the leaders of China, India, Brazil and South Africa. President Obama was able to convince his counterparts at least to come together around a list of principles. It became known as the Copenhagen Accord. But it was not the full-fledged agreement he intended.

In the environmental community, Copenhagen was generally deemed a failure. It did not augur well for urgently needed emissions reductions. But it did achieve two critical goals: First, the world's major economies— developed and developing alike—agreed to make national commitments to reduce pollution. Second, they agreed to be transparent. This would at least be a building block for subsequent efforts.

Previous negotiations had established the next major deadline for agreement in Paris in 2015. The parties committed to try again for a global reduction of emissions. Achieving an agreement in Paris became the focus of all our energy.

During the years I was chairman of the Senate Foreign Relations Committee, I consistently talked to the Chinese about climate change. I met frequently with Xie Zhenhua, the Chinese minister in charge of climate negotiations. We met in China, in the United States, at conferences around the world, all of which steadily built a trusting, personal relationship. On one occasion, we actually met at a transient airport restaurant because of our travel schedules. In addition, I met with a number of high-level Chinese government officials, including Xi Jinping, who would soon become the nation's president. They insisted that China grasped the urgency of the problem and was ready to be a partner. I know talk is cheap, but these many conversations made me believe there was an opening. I sensed a real partnership was possible.

Now I wanted to put it to the test as secretary of state.

When formally sworn in on February 1, 2013, one of my earliest meetings was with Todd Stern, the president's climate envoy, and his team. I immediately asked for input on how we could expand climate cooperation between the United States and China. Todd was supportive, but when he realized I was talking about the expanded cooperation beginning in a matter of weeks or months, not years, he expressed skepticism. He argued that the UNFCCC process didn't work like that—and neither did the Chinese. We had to start with baby steps—a decision to begin exploring areas of cooperation, for example—negotiated on the staff level, and then eventually the process would reach Todd's level, and then, perhaps, it would be appropriate for the senior-most government officials to get involved. Danny Russel, who would a few months later become my assistant secretary for Asia, also warned that the Chinese way of doing anything was slow, steady and incremental. The Chinese tended to resist sudden, high-level decision-making. I valued their caution, but we didn't have the luxury of time.

From my own experience, I knew China had a time-honored approach, but I also believed China was ready to do more. When then Chinese foreign minister Yang Jiechi reached out to congratulate me shortly after I was sworn in, I took the opportunity to explain my thinking. "China and the U.S. represent more than 45 percent of global emissions," I told him. "If we find constructive ways to approach this, we can set an example for the world." He agreed that U.S.-China climate cooperation would be good for

both countries and the world. "I share your interests," he said. "We need to work together."

I spoke to Minister Yang again in the weeks before my first trip to China in April 2013. I told him I planned to come to Beijing with some thoughts on what we might be able to accomplish together.

I asked Todd and the team to draft a memo describing how China and the United States could embark on a special journey together. Todd politely said that I misunderstood how things worked, arguing that the Chinese wouldn't want to be blindsided by our ideas in an in-person meeting with Yang, who by that point had been promoted to state councilor. Instead, Todd explained, they'd want any suggestions vetted with staff at lower levels. I worried that this was an invitation to bureaucratic inertia. It may have been the way things had been working, but I thought we needed to change the dynamic. I thought it would be a mistake to allow my first major bilateral visit to China to come and go without making real progress.

Todd relented. He sent me the memo I'd requested. I departed for China prepared to present it. On the flight out, as Danny Russel and I were reviewing the proposal, Danny again raised the risks of rushing the Chinese. I said I was comfortable with the conversation I had had with Yang. I trusted the relationship and personally believed we were not rushing them beyond their tolerance level.

When we arrived in China, I presented the ideas to Yang. To my delight, he was indeed receptive. By the end of that trip, two months into my tenure, together we launched the U.S.-China Climate Change Working Group (CCWG), a commitment of the world's two largest emitters and economies to work together to significantly reduce the growth of global emissions. Three months after that, China and the United States approved five joint initiatives for the CCWG, focusing on a range of climate challenges, from the emissions of heavy-duty vehicles to the development of smart grids. Finally, we were approaching this global threat not as rivals, but as teammates.

It was a start. We had mended some of the wounds from years past. But I still felt we needed a major joint achievement to set us up for success two years later in Paris. I wanted us to be able to stand with the Chinese and announce a cooperative approach that could help lead the G77 and the developed world to success in Paris. One of our team members came up with a variation on that—building on the previous U.S. proposal that nations put forward their own individual emissions reductions targets before the 2015 COP. What if the United States and China set the bar for these targets by

announcing our respective, ambitious goals together, when our presidents were scheduled to meet in Beijing late in 2014. I thought that could work, providing that the Chinese were prepared to make a sufficient effort.

It would reinforce the principle already adopted in prior negotiations of "common but differentiated" responsibility—an acceptance by the developed world that many countries were simply not able to afford the same approaches they could. We would each announce the best we could do. That would set the example we were looking for to all other nations. We would establish measurable but achievable goals, thereby inviting all countries to participate. It would also mean the United States would have to expedite the internal process for setting our own target, but if we were able to pull it off, the gridlock of developed versus developing could be behind us. We would come to Paris united, making our shared goal of reaching a comprehensive, global climate agreement much easier to achieve.

President Obama agreed, assuming, of course, we were able to convince the Chinese to develop ambitious targets so that we wouldn't lose our established credibility. As long as their target was real and appropriate, we would be helping them to transition away from international criticism. Sharing the spotlight with the United States in such a positive way would also help to cement China's journey to leader on the world stage. And most important, people in both nations would benefit from the elevated ambition—as would the world, providing we were setting the bar high enough. The Chinese like to frame policy proposals as win-wins, but sometimes what they put on the table is a win-lose in China's favor. But on this occasion, our cooperation could produce a victory for everyone.

We spent the summer and early fall negotiating in secret. If anything leaked prematurely, the entire initiative might fall apart. In October 2014, a month before President Obama's trip to China, I invited Yang Jiechi to Boston for a few days. I wanted his visit to be as productive and personal as possible. Some of us were worried that our efforts wouldn't be complete in time for the president's Beijing stop. After a morning work session, I hosted State Councilor Yang for lunch at Legal Sea Foods on the docks of Boston Harbor. I asked Todd Stern and John Podesta, President Obama's counselor who was leading the White House preparations for the trip to China and was a principal advisor to the president on climate, to join us.

The luncheon location was not an accident. Just a few decades earlier, the harbor was a national environmental scandal, mocked by George H. W. Bush in his campaign for president in 1988. Fishing or swimming there was an invitation to disease. Now, after a $2 billion cleanup, the harbor was an economic asset for the city. I wanted to show Yang Jiechi that an environmental disaster could be transformed into an economic engine.

We met in a private room upstairs with a handful of other government officials. Standing on the balcony above the dock, we took in a spectacular view of the harbor. Then over lunch, we discussed our shared responsibility, given the size and power of our nations, to lead the world in responding to the threat of climate change. We spent hours together that afternoon, and while we had known each other for many years, after that, I think we both felt as though there was a new level of understanding between us. The Boston meeting helped crystallize preparations for the presidents to meet and make a powerful announcement. There were last-minute tensions over the targets, but with hard work from the State Department and important input from the White House, including a subsequent visit to China, the gaps were closed.

A month later, on Veterans Day, when President Obama and I were in Beijing, he and President Xi stood side by side and announced the respective target emissions reductions of our two nations. It was quite a moment: two countries that had long led opposing camps with respect to climate change standing together as partners in the face of the shared threat. There we were in one of the grand rooms of the Great Hall of the People, with the two most powerful presidents in the world making an improbable announcement. After so many years of hearing people say this could never happen and we were naive for even trying, after so many years of effort traveling to one COP after another, I finally felt we had reached a moment of turning. The crashes of Rio, Kyoto and Copenhagen melted into the past. Now, in Beijing, there was a real sense of possibility. We believed this day would galvanize countries everywhere to follow suit with their own ambitious targets. We wanted to send them a message: success in Paris was possible. The roadblocks we had hit for decades were finally starting to be removed.

As the December 2015 date for convening in Paris approached, our goal was to keep up the momentum. The EU announced its target shortly after our U.S.-China joint announcement, which meant the three largest polluters in the world were out in front—a positive sign. But that still left the vast majority of the world's countries silent. It became a top priority to get as many nations as possible to put their targets on the table in advance of Paris. Obviously, some nations lacked the resources necessary to develop ambitious and realistic targets, let alone craft and implement policies that would actually help them achieve those targets. Luckily, the United States was able to mobilize a deep bench of climate experts to assist those countries. We made extensive technical assistance available to help foreign governments arrive at emissions reduction levels, develop targets and devise strategies for sustainable development. We did this with the understanding that emissions anywhere threaten the future for people everywhere. We had a national interest in making sure the most ambitious targets possible were being set in every corner of the world.

The State Department team was able to track countries' progress closely. I made sure it was on my counterparts' radars as well, raising climate change in nearly every bilateral meeting I attended. At first, I would get funny looks from some of the ministers since, for many of them, climate change was not a topic dealt with by the foreign ministry. But, given the global security implications of climate change, in my view, it was an issue that should rise to the highest levels of all governments. With that conviction, each September I convened an annual climate-focused meeting of foreign ministers on the margins of the UN General Assembly. Before long, it was rare for me to find an interlocutor who wasn't fully briefed on climate issues. It even reached the point where, frequently, I wasn't the first to raise the topic.

As the date for the Paris talks neared, it was imperative we ensure our own house was in order as well. By this point, President Obama recognized there was little hope for a legislative fix in the United States to reduce carbon emissions. He decided he had no choice but to use his executive authority to launch the Clean Power Plan. That decision, in addition to other policies such as the Corporate Average Fuel Economy standards targeting vehicles' fuel consumption and the tax breaks for renewable energy investments, helped make certain we were on our way to cutting domestic emissions dramatically.

But we also needed to make changes to our climate change approach from a broader policy perspective. I had observed how our climate team essentially operated in its own silo at the State Department. Most of the regional bureaus didn't have a thorough understanding of the issue, let alone the negotiations. One of the tools available to a secretary of state is the issuance of policy guidance cables that can be distributed to the entire department. I took immediate advantage of this practice to make climate change the focus of my first guidance cable. I set out my expectation that all diplomats become relatively fluent on the issue and directed all posts and bureaus to make the issue a priority in their day-to-day diplomatic work.

I also made the department's work on climate change a key pillar of the Quadrennial Diplomacy and Development Review, which is designed to guide State Department planning from one administration to the next. This has resulted in, for example, climate-related modules being added to the training of new Foreign Service officers.

In the years to come, climate change will present an enormous number of challenges to our Foreign Service officers and posts all around the world. There will likely be large numbers of climate refugees as a result of drought, more intense storms, food shortages caused by catastrophic failure of crops, fires, water shortages, fish stock failures, sea-level rise, migration of species including human beings impacted by killer heat, new communicable diseases and failure of health systems to cope—just to name some of the challenges already manifesting themselves. And I was driven by the stark reality that even today, no country in the world is doing enough to live sustainably.

Because of our economic power, our military might and our values, all of which contribute to the responsible role we play in the world, the United States has traditionally led efforts to respond to global crises. Climate change is without question high on the list. The State Department needs to prioritize this threat. Every person in it needs to see the interconnection of all these issues. Choices that other governments make—all at the heart of diplomacy—will affect our country and our citizens.

WHEN THE WORLD gathered in Paris at the end of 2015, everyone knew the heads of state would not attend for the full negotiation. They were there to create momentum and kick-start the negotiating process. In addition to the opening day speech, President Obama spent a couple of days on the ground, meeting with a number of his counterparts, including, of course, President Xi of China and Prime Minister Modi of India. But, as expected, it's hard to have productive conversations and manage the different agendas of 150 heads of state. It's hard just to navigate the facilities and coordinate their staffs and security details. Most of the heads of state departed Paris within a day or two to leave us to our daily negotiating.

I was scheduled to be on hand for as much of the talks as possible. I had slugged it out at too many COPs over the years and waited a long time for the ripeness of this moment, to which we had already contributed by bringing China to the table. I did have to depart briefly for a couple of days in the middle of the two weeks in order to attend the annual NATO ministerial meeting in Brussels, at which we discussed our Afghanistan policy, and the Organization for Security and Co-operation in Europe ministerial meeting in Belgrade—but I returned immediately. Paris was the top priority with the promise for greatest global impact. We couldn't lose the moment. All the parties were aware that the call to Paris had established a two-week period for the negotiations. The conference would conclude on December 11. The pressure was on.

When it came to expertise, the United States was armed to the teeth. In addition to my direct staff, Todd was there with the entire climate team. They were an extraordinary, dedicated band of devotees to the cause, having worked tirelessly for years to shepherd each step of the journey. Without them, there was no possibility of securing an agreement. We also had experts from the Environmental Protection Agency; the Departments of Treasury, Energy and Agriculture; and the U.S. Trade Representative's Office. A number of White House officials remained on-site as well, including Brian Deese, who had succeeded John Podesta as Obama's senior advisor on climate issues. I had first met Brian when he interned for me in the Senate. He had risen high and fast on smarts and good judgment. I was happy to be working with him again. Our team was a brilliant cadre, each person with his or her own unique proficiency. I couldn't have been more confident in who was sitting behind the U.S. flag.

We knew coming in to Paris what the remaining biggest hurdles would be. But as the talks got under way, we got a feel for the developing dynamic. Every large negotiation like this gets caught in certain currents driven by regional leaders or by big countries with big interests. As we had hoped, the developing versus developed country dynamic was different from past COPs, but new challenges presented themselves. Instead of a head-to-head standoff between the United States and China, with everyone else casting their lot in one of our camps, our two nations were more or less in agreement. But that led some countries—in particular, the low-lying island states for which climate change was an existential threat—to worry that we would pursue a weak agreement that met our nations' needs but not those of poorer nations.

It was a valid fear. Allaying it required careful diplomacy. I had met several times with the leaders of the small islands, as had President Obama. We had taken every opportunity possible to reassure them of our commitment to their future. To emphasize this, we also joined a coalition of nations spearheaded by the Marshall Islands, with a stated goal of reaching an ambitious agreement.

Still, while the United States certainly understood its responsibility as the world's wealthiest nation and largest historical emitter, and we fully supported the so-called UN Green Climate Fund to help poorer nations grapple with climate change, we knew that we couldn't return home with an agreement that legally required the United States to pay anything resembling reparations for the pollution we emitted before we fully understood the consequences. That was the ultimate nonstarter.

Resolving this issue was essential, but the U.S. negotiating team found Tuvalu's chief negotiator to be particularly dug in. He was utterly intractable on the matter. The country's prime minister, Enele Sopoaga, was seen to be more reasonable, but Sopoaga seemed to be held in check by his chief negotiator, who was typically in the meetings. Little progress was made. So we agreed that I should request to meet with him one-on-one, with no staff, and see if we could work something out.

I met with him and suggested we honor their need to take note of the loss-and-damage language, so important to them, by acknowledging it in the agreement, as Tuvalu and its negotiating partners wanted, but it would be placed in a different section of the agreement from where they had proposed. We would put the liability-and-compensation language, so important to us, front and center in the decision, where it was critical to make clear we were not creating a new cause of action exposing the developed world to a rash of lawsuits.

This compromise sounds simple now, but it was harder for some nations to swallow than others. As you would imagine, passions ran high among less developed nations, particularly island states whose existence was at stake but which had contributed next to nothing to the problem. They believed the most developed countries owed them compensation for damages. While we acknowledged that bad decisions—originally made out of ignorance, then in a stubborn refusal to accept facts—had contributed to the global problem, there was no way any wealthy country or soon-to-be wealthy country was going to sign up for liability and compensation. The breakthrough with Tuvalu was critical and welcome.

As the scheduled end of the talks approached, the French, who were not only hosting the conference but also serving as the rotating COP president, released initial drafts of agreement text. We raced to make copies and distribute them to all our experts, who took a half hour to read through it. Then the senior members of the delegation joined a dozen issue-area experts around the table in the U.S. office space and carefully analyzed what worked for the United States and what didn't. While I wasn't expected to be present, I found it particularly helpful to listen to the experts debate the impact of one provision or another. Hearing from the people who lived and breathed each of the respective sections was the best way for me to understand where we might have "give" and where we needed "take."

Together, we continued to work toward the Friday, December 11, deadline. I connected with Todd in the morning and talked through which countries I needed to lobby that day. President Obama remained engaged from Washington, placing calls as needed to his counterparts, including Prime Minister Modi of India and President Dilma Rousseff of Brazil.

But by Thursday night, the progress we had been making stalled, and in some cases, we seemed to be going backward. I returned to my hotel around 11:00 p.m. to make a secure call to Washington, but the team, frustrated by what they were hearing in the negotiating hall, asked me to return there around midnight. Once I got there, I understood why: a meeting of all the parties had devolved once again into a debate over whether developed and developing countries should have different requirements. For a brief instant I feared the same argument that kept us divided for so many years and that the China outreach was meant to forever bury was now at the eleventh hour going to rear its ugly head. I sat among the delegates and listened for a while. Many of the faces around the table were new to the debate. Less developed countries were expressing their outrage that they were paying the price for developed nations whose economies had developed without regard to the impact of fossil fuels on the environment. Furthermore, now that everyone was negatively impacted, they didn't believe the richer countries were bearing enough of the burden. To them, "common but differentiated" responsibility meant primarily defining the burden of the developed world. I sensed the potential for things to stay stuck.

We were seated around an enormous rectangular table, each of the sixty or so negotiators with several of their staff seated behind them in an outer ring around the table. I caught the eye of the chairperson and asked to be recognized. "I'm troubled by some of what I've been hearing," I told them. I spoke, energized by all the years we had been through these arguments and by the stakes. I began by reminding people that for those of us who had been to prior COPs, this was an old debate. "It was in fact an argument that had produced nothing over the years. When we were in Kyoto we tried to have mandatory reductions in which the developed states did more than anyone, which was appropriate because they had indeed contributed more to the problem. But that crashed and burned because many countries—mine included—balked at the reality that certain states would do nothing even though they were increasingly contributing to the damage. Unless we share and all recognize responsibility, we will all unwittingly join in a suicide pact." I then went on to the most critical point: "It was ludicrous to suggest that the agreement we are poised to adopt lacks differentiation to account for each country's individual circumstances. The contributions we're discussing are completely voluntary. They are determined by each nation.

This agreement is actually the greatest monument to differentiation that you could imagine. Every nation decides for itself what it is willing to do and capable of doing!" We were so close. I urged the negotiators not to nitpick the agreement to death. "We are closer to something reasonable that all nations can accept than we have ever been before. Don't let the 'perfect' be the enemy of the good."

I went back to the hotel around 2:30 a.m. The talks were continuing at the expert level, so I requested my chief of staff, Jon Finer, stay behind to help keep things on track and call me if I needed to come back. The negotiations continued until 5:00 a.m. When Jon finally returned to the hotel, he was optimistic the text would come together within the next twenty-four hours. It seemed that the delegates drifted back to the core organizing principle of the Paris Agreement: each country would define its best efforts. We would not again make ourselves prisoners of mandatory reduction targets even though we all knew the urgency argued for them.

The next day was consumed by last-minute efforts to build consensus. It happened to be my birthday, and no one had any question about what I wanted. Minister Piyush Goyal of India, one of their chief negotiators, thoughtfully dropped by our office with a massive, tall bouquet of flowers. It was a wonderful gesture and even an indicator that we might get over our last hurdle with India. The negotiating continued into Friday night. Effectively we stopped the clock at midnight Friday and allowed ourselves to drift into Saturday. Then, around lunchtime on Saturday, December 12, the French released the final version of the agreement. As usual, we made copies, passed them around and sat quietly to review the text.

Todd was the first one to spot the error. On page twenty-one, a sentence that was supposed to read that developed nations "should" reduce emissions by whatever amount they proposed, instead read that developed nations "shall" reduce emissions by that amount. "Should" is an ambiguous word, without legal implications for missing our target. "Shall" means that coming short of our target would be a legal violation of the agreement, and by accepting that language, we would be crossing a line with Congress, which would not agree to mandatory reductions.

The should-for-shall swap was shocking and had to have been done purposely by someone, since we had spent ample time negotiating that very sentence—and all parties were ostensibly okay with "should" in the end. I immediately called Laurent Fabius, the French foreign minister, who was chairing the negotiations, and explained our alarm. He seemed genuinely surprised. He assured me he would fix the mistake immediately and look into how it happened.

Still, as we arrived in the main conference hall around 6:00 p.m., we weren't sure what to expect. Had other countries been briefed on the last-minute should/shall debacle? Would anyone challenge it from the floor? I quickly found Minister Xie, the lead negotiator from China, who assured me they were okay with the text. India and South Africa were comfortable as well.

I noticed the head of the Nicaraguan delegation, Paul Oquist, at the front of the room, arguing with Fabius. Apparently, he wanted to take advantage of the opportunity to block the agreement, which he believed did not go far enough to help countries like his address the climate challenge. I talked to the Russians and Chinese and asked them to try to talk him off the ledge. They and others talked with him quietly on the side of the plenary. I then called the State Department Operations Center from my cell phone, which eventually connected me to the First Lady of Nicaragua. I explained the scene her representative was causing and softly reminded her that it would be unfortunate if Nicaragua was the only nation standing in the way of success in Paris. I don't know whether she ended up reaching Oquist, but he ceased making a public spectacle. Shortly thereafter, Fabius grew tired of his antics and joined President Hollande and UN secretary-general Ban Ki-moon onstage. He quickly explained the should/shall change to the plenary, made brief remarks about the text and said, finally, "I hear no objection."

With that, he banged his gavel on the podium. "The Paris climate accord is adopted."

I felt a swell of emotion as soon as the words left his mouth. Years of work for a lot of folks came to fruition at that moment. The floor of the plenary erupted, everyone shaking hands, hugging, offering congratulations. I looked around and saw elation on the faces of several thousand delegates and various advocates who had been laboring away for a long time. Somehow, we had done it. I posed for selfie after selfie as members of various delegations approached us. I shared congratulations with Secretary-General Ban Ki-moon, Al Gore, Laurent Fabius and his team, with whom we had worked so closely. Laurent had been focused and disciplined as the chair, managing many delegations with skill and good diplomacy.

When the exuberance on the floor dulled down to a steady murmur, the chair recognized a few of us to speak to the moment. When my turn arrived, I cautioned the room that for all the accomplishment and significance of what we achieved, we needed to remind ourselves: we were not leaving Paris with a guarantee that we would hold Earth's temperature increase to two degrees centigrade—the goal we set in the agreement. The real importance of our achievement was the message we were sending to the world's private sector that 196 nations were now committed to move in the same direction on energy policy. That message, we hoped, would unleash a torrent of investment into sustainable, alternative and renewable energy. Why? Because the solution to climate change is energy policy, and the technology we have today could, if deployed rapidly enough, solve the crisis. We were betting on the genius of the entrepreneur to recognize that public policy was reinforcing the largest market the world has ever known, a market today of four to five billion energy users worth multitrillions of dollars, which would be growing over the next thirty years to nine billion users and worth multiples of those trillions. No burden was placed by government on anyone. It was an invitation to the marketplace to get the job done and make money doing it. That was the real success of the Paris Agreement. Paris was inviting the private sector to save us from ourselves.

I returned to my hotel around 11:00 p.m. to scarf down a quick dinner before heading to a TV studio nearby to pretape a round of interviews with the hosts of the various Sunday news shows. It was important to define for ourselves what had been accomplished—and what had not—rather than having others do it for us. I was exhausted, but we had just concluded an agreement decades in the making. I was happy to share the good news.

For a moment, I wondered why we couldn't do the interviews live the following day, but then I remembered that I was scheduled to be on my way to Rome at 7:00 a.m. for meetings on the deteriorating political situation in Libya. From there, it was on to Moscow to discuss Syria.

As was often the case during my four years as secretary of state, a good night's sleep would have to wait.

A FEW MONTHS later, on April 22, 2016—Earth Day—I was at the UN in New York to formally sign the Paris Agreement on behalf of President Obama and the United States. It was a deeply emotional day—made more so by the fact that my daughter Alex, who lived in New York at the time, was there to share it with me, along with my two-year-old granddaughter, Isabelle.

Before I arrived at the UN, I stopped for a moment to reflect on the history that brought us to that day. I thought about the first Earth Day in 1970, when I joined with millions of Americans in teach-ins to educate the public about the environmental challenges we faced. I thought about the inaugural UN climate conference in Rio, where I first talked at length with my future wife, Teresa. I thought of the urgency we all felt back then in 1992. And of course, I thought about the many ups and downs in the climate fight that led us to that December night at Le Bourget, when it seemed—for the first time—that the world had finally found the path forward.

But as I sat and played with my granddaughter in the green room behind the lectern, waiting for my turn to go out and sign the agreement, I wasn't thinking of the past. I thought about the future. Her future. The world her children would one day inherit.

I was holding Isabelle in my arms, joking with her, when I was told the United States of America had been called to sign the document. Before her mom knew it, Isabelle and I ventured out onstage. A wave of applause surprised me as people reacted to Isabelle's presence. They were responding just as I had a few moments earlier. This was about her and the nearly two billion children around the world under the age of fifteen. Isabelle never flinched. She didn't cringe at the sudden exposure to a full General Assembly Hall. She seemed fascinated by it all. With Isabelle sitting on my left knee, I signed the document, stood up and walked over to the edge of the stage, where her mother was observing. When I put Isabelle back in her mother's open arms, Isabelle announced firmly, "Mummy, I no sign paper," somehow thinking she got cheated out of her role. Little did she or any of us know the impact she had without her signature.

Since then, people from all walks of life, all over the world, have told me how that moment moved them too. They were reminded of their own children and grandchildren, they explained. They too thought of the future.

MY LOVE AFFAIR with the ocean began when I was three years old. I've seen a number of photos of myself at that age, playing in the light waves near the shore of Naushon with a small plastic shovel and bucket. I was mesmerized by the live snails, the razor clams and the occasional schools of shrimp washing in and out with the rhythm of the water. My mother had to drag me in for dinner. As I got older, I lived in a bathing suit. I loved the smell of the sea air, the screeching squawk of seagulls swooping in to scavenge dead fish or exposed clams at low tide. There was a perceptible pattern to life by the sea. At a remarkably young age I formed a bond with the ocean that eventually led me to the Navy and life always near the water.

While I was introduced early to the beautiful complexity of the world under the sea—three-quarters of the planet is covered by oceans—it wasn't until my work on climate change that I began to fully understand the complex synergy that makes up this yet to be fully understood relationship between man and ocean.

What I do know is that the oceans are responsible for life as we know it: 51 percent of the oxygen we breathe comes from the ocean. The currents of the ocean are critical to temperature and weather. The greenhouse effect it-self is the temperature regulator of Earth, which until recently helped keep Earth's temperature at a livable average of 57 degrees Fahrenheit.

Now all of that is changing. The water is warming. The ice is melting. Spawning grounds for fisheries are being overrun by rising sea levels. Acid-ity from increased greenhouse gas emissions is bleaching coral, killing reefs and changing the basic ecosystem. Almost every major fishery is at peak fishing or fished out because there is too much money chasing too few fish.

It's not just climate change that needs urgent attention. The oceans are at risk. I know that seems implausible because they are so vast and powerful. But the reality is humans are dumping so much garbage, plastic, chemicals, raw sewage and runoff from agriculture and development that the oceans are in increasing numbers of places just overwhelmed. There are over five hundred dead zones in the oceans today—and increasing. The danger is that we don't fully understand the impact of all that we are doing, but since it is a living ecosystem, the last thing we should be willing to tolerate would be passing a tipping point. We are strip-mining the oceans. We are exploit-ing the fish stocks that have sustained life for generations. On the high seas, there is no enforcement.

Just as with climate change, the threats facing our ocean can only be ad-dressed with widespread global cooperation. I was determined to try to ad-vance that cooperation as secretary. We traveled a huge distance to elevate awareness of the oceans—to make them a matter of international govern-mental focus—not just the domain of nongovernmental voices struggling to be heard.

Shortly after I arrived at Foggy Bottom, I asked the team to begin plan-ning a global summit that would help to bring the world together to drive that kind of cooperation. I envisioned a high-level conference, with every partic-ipant bringing a concrete commitment to the table—whether it be a plan to detect and prosecute illegal fishing, a new policy to help reduce plastic pol-lution or expanded research programs to help us better understand the chem-ical changes the ocean is experiencing because of climate change.

This wasn't a directive the State Department's career employees had been anticipating, and at first there was some confusion about what, exactly, I was thinking. They tried hard to accommodate my unusual request. We worked together to develop a conference that would be different—not just to beat the drum for those who were already focused on ocean protection, but to elevate the health of our oceans to the highest levels of government. Much as we were doing with climate change, we wanted to sound the alarm on the dire state of the ocean and drive real action—the kind of action that could only come with high-level attention in capital cities from pole to pole and around the equator.

The team at the State Department embraced the mission. Getting my foreign counterparts to pay attention was another challenge. Some—like Norwegian foreign minister Børge Brende—were eager to join from the start. He was already a leader. But it wasn't an issue area many foreign ministries were accustomed to handling. It took persuasion and recruitment.

We hosted the first Our Ocean conference at the State Department in 2014, and it was more successful than I had anticipated, with governments committing to formally protect more than four million square kilometers of ocean water, among other things. Chile volunteered on the spot to host the second Our Ocean conference in Valparaíso in 2015, and I held the third conference back at the State Department in 2016, which President Obama keynoted and which more than two dozen foreign ministers or heads of state attended. By the time we left, the Our Ocean conferences generated more than $9 billion in pledges to protect the ocean from everything from plastic pollution to illegal, unregulated and unreported fishing. Nations also set aside an additional ten million square kilometers as formal Marine protected areas—collectively, a swath of ocean water roughly the size of the United States. We attacked illegal fishing and created a digital tracking system to ensure accountability on the high seas.

The most auspicious thing to come out of those conferences, however, was the momentum they generated: in 2017, the EU hosted the fourth annual Our Ocean conference, and Indonesia, Norway and Palau have each committed to hosting future iterations of the conference, ensuring that year after year global leaders will come forward to take stock of the progress made to date and put forth new commitments. The health of our oceans is getting international attention; it is up to everyone now to sustain it.

DURING HIS FINAL year in office, President Obama made it clear to the cabinet he expected us to "run through the tape." That certainly included our efforts on climate change. For the next several months, we worked hard to corral China and as many of our international partners as possible to quickly bring the Paris Agreement permanently into force. We accomplished our goal less than a year after it was gaveled in—far faster than even the most optimistic among us might have predicted.

The Paris Agreement will last beyond what any one U.S. president chooses to do because it addresses a growing threat understood and acknowledged by responsible leaders around the world and, most important, gives each nation the opportunity to design its own approach. Precisely for that reason, many argue it doesn't go far enough because we are currently on track to hit *four degrees centigrade* in this century. But it does give us a foundation of nationally determined climate goals on which we can build. It provides support to countries that need help meeting the targets. It leaves no country to weather the storm of climate change alone. It marshals an array of tools in order to help developing nations invest in infrastructure and technology and the science to get the job done. It supports the most vulnerable countries so they can better adapt to the climate impacts that many of those countries are already confronting. And it enables us to ratchet up ambition over time as technology develops and as the price of clean energy comes down. The agreement calls on the parties to revisit their national pledges every five years in order to ensure that we keep pace with the technology and that we accelerate the global transition to a clean energy economy. This process—a cornerstone of the Paris Agreement—gives us a framework that is built to last and a degree of global accountability that has never before existed.

The environmental progress we made in 2016 alone extends well beyond Paris. For example, international aviation wasn't covered by what we did in Paris. If that sector were a country, it would rank among the top dozen greenhouse gas emitters in the world. So in early October 2016, with U.S. support, the International Civil Aviation Organization (ICAO) established a sector-wide agreement for carbon-neutral growth.

A few weeks later, I traveled to Kigali, Rwanda, to work with representatives from nearly two hundred countries to phase down the global production and use of hydrofluorocarbons, greenhouse gases that are less common but thousands of times more potent than carbon dioxide. In part because much of the world was paying little attention to the negotiations, they were tougher than we had anticipated. I remember one particularly prickly meeting with the Indian delegation. The rest of the parties had essentially agreed on the text, but the Indians were pushing hard for what we viewed as a totally unreasonable change. Finally, I told their minister, "President Obama is going to call Prime Minister Modi later today. He can either call to explain how the Indian delegation single-handedly prevented the nearly two hundred parties from reaching an agreement, or he can call to thank him for his cooperation in addressing a matter of such global concern." In the end, we resolved the dispute, but tensions had been so high that when we realized we finally had a deal, both of our delegations spontaneously broke into applause in the small room in which we had been cloistered. In the end, we succeeded—and the so-called Kigali Amendment could single-handedly help us avoid an entire half-degree centigrade of warming by the end of the century, while at the same time opening up new opportunities for growth in a range of industries.

Our last year in office, 2016, was a banner year for climate diplomacy. With Paris, Kigali and ICAO, we hit an environmental trifecta. It was the single most effective year for the environment I can remember since groundbreaking legislation was passed in the early 70s. President Obama's focus paid off. Every one of these steps combined to move the climate discussion in the right direction. Global leaders finally seemed to wake up to the enormity of the climate challenge. There was hope the international community might actually do what is necessary to meet this generational test.

I SPENT ELECTION Day 2016 on our military plane, headed to New Zealand with my team. Our communications were shoddy as we flew over the Pacific, but from time to time my friends in Boston or Washington would email me the latest exit polls. Every so often I'd wander out into the main cabin and share the news with my senior staff. "I know a thing or two about exit polls," I reminded them. "Let's see how it goes."

By the time we landed in Christchurch, it was clear that Donald J. Trump was going to be our next president. As a few members of my team and I watched his victory speech in my hotel suite, I tried to process what a Trump victory would mean for so much of the progress we had made during the Obama administration. More than anything else, I was worried about what President Trump would do—or not do—to fight climate change. The prospect of a climate change denier in the White House was the last thing the planet needed.

A few days after the 2016 election, I was headed to Marrakesh, Morocco, for the first COP since Paris. My speechwriter and I had been working on a "tough love" speech—a "don't think the hard work is behind you" speech—underscoring the need for countries to hold one another accountable to the goals we had set the previous year. Obviously, that would no longer work. The United States had just elected as president a man who described climate change as a "hoax perpetrated by the Chinese." The world's climate experts and negotiators needed to hear why they should have any faith at all that the agreement would endure.

So we rewrote the speech. And when I got to Marrakesh, I reminded the climate community of how far we had come together and how impossible it would be for any one leader to reverse the transition toward clean energy—a transition that, thanks in large part to Paris, was already under way. I expressed my hope that perhaps a President Trump would be more responsible than a candidate Trump had been. And I stressed to them why our shared efforts were so important: nothing less than the future world our children and grandchildren will inherit is at stake. "It's important to remind ourselves that we are not on a preordained path to disaster," I told the packed room. "It's not written in the stars. This is about choices—choices that we still have. This is a test of willpower, not capacity. It's within our power to put the planet back on a better track. But doing that requires holding ourselves accountable to the hard truth. It requires holding ourselves accountable to facts, not opinion; to science, not theories that can't be proven—and certainly not to political bromides."

I was on the ground in Morocco for less than twenty-four hours, but while I was there, I asked Jonathan Pershing (no relation to Dick), who had by then replaced Todd as our special envoy for climate change, if he could gather the whole U.S. negotiating team together. I wanted to talk to them.

When I walked into the room Pershing had reserved, I looked around at the amazing group of public servants who had dedicated so much of their careers to solving this challenge. The excited smiles I had seen on their faces in Paris had been replaced by solemn expressions. They didn't know what to expect.

I was candid with them. I said that I didn't know what to expect either. But I told them that even if Trump followed through on his campaign pledge to abandon the Paris Agreement—even if he walked away from renewable energy and started subsidizing coal and other fossil fuels—even if he took every step imaginable to reverse the progress we had made, as was his prerogative—even then, so much of what we had achieved would continue. In 2017, 75 percent of the new electricity coming online in the United States came from solar. Coal contributed 0.2 percent. Even a President Trump cannot undo what the marketplace is doing.

The energy market was moving in the right direction. The international community was committed. Prime ministers and presidents everywhere understood the challenge like never before—and so, by the way, did American mayors and governors and business leaders. The world would take on the climate threat, with or without the support of the president of the United States.

TODAY I FEEL myself growing increasingly angry as ideology and cheap, lowest-common-denominator politics destroy what is left of America's leadership on this issue. I feel as if someone else's ignorance and demagoguery is stealing the future from my children and grandchildren, from the planet itself.

My mind keeps flashing back to my trip to Antarctica. To really see and understand the full magnitude of the climate threat, you have to go there. I was the first secretary of state and the highest-ranking U.S. official to ever make the trip. I flew by helicopter over the West Antarctic Ice Sheet. I walked out onto the Ross Sea ice shelf. I flew to McMurdo Station in Antarctica to see and understand even better what is taking place.

Antarctica contains multiple ice sheets that are, in some places, three miles deep or more. If we are irresponsible about climate change and all that ice melts, then sea levels would rise somewhere between one hundred and two hundred feet in the next couple of centuries. For the past fifty years, climate scientists have believed just the West Antarctic Ice Sheet alone is a sword of Damocles, hanging over our entire way of life. Large chunks, including one the size of Rhode Island, have already broken off and drifted out to sea. Should the entire ice sheet break apart and melt into the sea, it alone could raise global sea levels by four to five meters.

Standing there, the power of God's creation was unmistakable. Each of the three great Abrahamic faiths (Judaism, Islam and Christianity) calls on believers to protect creation. Every values-based approach to life, every philosophy, talks of our responsibility to each other and to creation. The first inhabitants of North America, Native Americans, maintained a beautiful balance with elements around them.

But if religion isn't enough to stir your conscience, science certainly must. In Antarctica, I listened to the scientists who are on the front lines, not politicians or pundits, but people whose entire lives are dedicated to extensive research and who draw conclusions based on facts, not ideology. They were all clear: the more they learn, the more alarmed they become about the speed with which these changes are happening.

A scientist from New Zealand named Gavin Dunbar described what they're seeing as the "canary in the coal mine" and warned that some thresholds, if we cross them, cannot be reversed. The damage we inflict could take centuries to undo, he said, if it can be undone at all.

The scientists in Antarctica told me that they are still trying to figure out how quickly this change is happening. But they know for certain that it is happening, and it's happening faster than they previously thought possible. An American glacial geologist, a fellow whose name is appropriately enough John Stone, didn't mince words when he told me, "The catastrophic period could already be under way."

For anyone who cares about the world and our future, those words should be more than sobering; for a diplomat or a leader, no matter who is in the White House, science and fact must be motivating—while there's still time to act.

Afterword

JULY 4, 2018. As I wrote this book, I tried hard to fight the numbing power of nostalgia. A memoir is a tempting venue to look back and see the good outcomes in life as preordained. It's always easy to believe things were better "back when." My parents instilled in me great respect for history. I was encouraged to live it—and perhaps even to help make some of it. But history—real history, not the phony demagoguery about the mythical past calculated and propagated to mobilize unthinking retro movements— inspires because it reminds us that times weren't always easy. The winter soldiers of Valley Forge inspire not because they knew they'd win; their determination is more awesome because they had every reason to believe they might end up at the end of a British rope, and yet they persevered.

It's easy to put on rose-tinted glasses, look back at earlier days and say "those were better times" or easier times, when the truth is, they weren't. I tried to avoid those traps in writing my story.

I share this because I was tempted to write that I was born into a gentler or simpler era at home and abroad. But, on reflection, I wasn't. The *Leave It to Beaver* America of the 1950s had much to admire. For most, jobs came with pensions and economic security. We were an optimistic country. But we were also a country where Jim Crow was still the law and "Whites Only" signs dotted the landscape in half our country, and were unspoken but just as real in the other half. Women were devalued and LGBT Americans had to be invisible to avoid persecution.

It took years, until I was in college, for Congress to pass bedrock civil rights legislation.

Joe McCarthy trampled on civil liberties and invoked a fact-free Red Scare at home, which divided and distracted us in dangerous ways. Overseas, we were basking in the afterglow of victory in World War II and through the Marshall Plan we were rebuilding the economies of our former enemies. But World War II had been succeeded by a perilous Cold War. We soon awakened from the euphoria of 1945 to find America's sons dying in

Korea in a proxy conflict with the Soviet Union. A decade later, I watched on a grainy black-and-white television set as President Kennedy led us through the Cuban Missile Crisis and the very real danger of nuclear holocaust. Our tragic misinterpretation of Cold War reality led us into a quagmire in Southeast Asia for which nearly sixty thousand Americans paid the ultimate price. And Richard Nixon brought us domestic spying on dissenters, abuse of the Department of Justice for political purposes, attacks on the free press, a presidential "enemies list" and the mire of what President Gerald Ford called "our national nightmare." I learned the hard way at twenty-seven what it was like to be a target of a rogue White House. Pipe bombs were exploding in public places; riots saw blocks of cities set on fire; irreplaceable leaders were assassinated. The list goes on.

I've told much of this story in these pages for a reason: not to relive a difficult past, but to remember how we changed the course of our country. Good people believed the world—at home and abroad—could be different and better. Citizens organized. People fought for something. We marched. We voted. We got knocked down and we got back up.

No, "the good old days weren't always good." That's not an insult to America, that's an affirmation of America: an America that makes itself stronger when, despite long odds and searing setbacks, everyday citizens stand up and decide that the way things are isn't the way things have to be.

My life has been a story of faith in America tested and redeemed not by being passive, but by being passionate about our country and its promise. It is the story of a journey begun in the latter half of the twentieth century and lived now in the morning of the twenty-first: two different eras of staggering transformation in how we live, learn, work and relate to each other, two different eras where old assumptions were constantly challenged and confounded and when faith in institutions came under intense scrutiny. This is also a story about how we listen and how we learn, how we face problems, how we try to embrace a vision of the future that meets our best hopes and aspirations.

In the end, I believe it is a story of optimism, but clearly a story that doesn't unfold on autopilot. It's not an automatic. It's optimism earned the hard way.

In my life, I've seen things that were hard to imagine—if not regarded as impossible—happen again and again—and I learned from people who bent history. I wanted to share their stories as well as mine.

All of this recounting and retelling also reminded me that the world has always been complicated. Truly complicated. Leaders have always been imperfect, some even downright malevolent, others too small for the moment. The fight at home has always been a struggle.

That is what makes me all the more optimistic about today: because I've seen with my own eyes that the institutions the Founders created to hold America together have worked best when America needed them the most. I have the scars to prove it, and I know that while we've often faced daunting challenges, in the end, we have met them.

I'm an optimist because America has a pretty good, 242-year record of turning difficult passages into landmark progress. I'm an optimist because of the people I've met and what life has taught me.

How could I not be? I began my service to country in a war, a bitter war that frayed and nearly shredded the fabric of America. I finished my last tour of service to country in a mission of peace. In the final month of my service as secretary of state, I was back in Vietnam one more time, on the Mekong Delta where the rivers I'd patrolled in combat had become rivers the United States was now protecting from environmental degradation.

Back on the Bay Hap River, where almost forty-eight years before I'd come face-to-face with my own mortality, staring down the business end of a Viet Cong B-40 rocket launcher, I met a man whose mission that day in 1969 was to kill me and my crew. We were the same age. He was short and sinewy, not an ounce of fat, his face lined with the years and the hardship, but with a smile of welcome, devoid of hatred or malice. I looked at him and thought, *How crazy is this?* Years ago, when we were young, we were both heeding the call of our leaders, trying to kill each other. But now we stood there in peace, a peace I had been privileged in some small way to help make real by first making peace at home. If that doesn't make you an optimist, nothing will.

That's why I wrote this book: to share with you that the abiding truth I've learned in my journey is you can change your country and you can change the world. You may fail at first, but you can't give in. You have to get up and fight the fight again, but you can get there. The big steps and the small steps all add up. History is cumulative. We all can contribute to change if we're willing to enter the contest for the future, often against the odds.

Why this book and why now? Not just because I have finished my time as secretary of state and in the Senate, but because the causes that have defined my life until now have never been more at risk. Our democracy is challenged. But I remain confident in our ability to reclaim it because our democracy is as alive as any person who lives in it. It is constantly changing, growing and reinventing itself. But its well-being always—always—depends on citizens to keep it alive. The strength of the United States is derived not from a party, not from a leader, but from a natural resource that is truly renewable: the resolve of our citizens and their commitment to make the American ideal a reality.

Even after an amazing journey, I'm still learning, and still fighting. If you take nothing else away from the American journey I describe in these pages, I hope it's this: there's nothing wrong with America and the world today that can't be fixed by what's right with our citizens and with people around the globe. As John Kennedy said when he sought and won the first breakthrough in nuclear arms control, "Our problems are man-made—therefore they can be solved by man."

My hope is that as you finish reading these pages, you will believe more in the possibilities and less in the hurdles, and that more of you will dare to try more. I will keep using my extra days to do my part—and I see so many others now fighting on the front lines of our history. Extra days aren't just a gift for those who served in war; they are a gift for all of us fortunate to be blessed with the freedom to stand up and seek the best America and a better world.

Onward.

Acknowledgments

I HAVE BEEN LUCKY beyond words to have had extraordinary people by my side to guide, advise, caution, exhort, challenge, tolerate, teach and love me through a grand adventure, with more to come, I hope.

This book is a sweep through almost three-quarters of a century. I say sweep because I have been blessed with a life so full that I could write a separate book about individual stops on the journey—growing up, the war in Vietnam, the years as an activist fighting to stop it, the District Attorney's Office and practicing law, Massachusetts politics, twenty-eight fascinating years in the Senate, and four post-to-post, packed years as secretary of state. *Every Day Is Extra* logs the entire journey under one cover in a way that shares with you who I am and what has motivated me. It is honest and comprehensive, even as it is by necessity compacted.

The challenge of thanking those who made both the journey and its retelling possible is a daunting one; it is too easy to leave someone out or inadvertently give short shrift to one period over another. My life in politics didn't begin as lieutenant governor or senator, and my immersion in diplomacy didn't begin at the State Department. I hope that those who were there for the journey to and through all these destinations spot their reflection in the lessons that prepared me to arrive there and contribute after I did. When I look back, I remember the words of Tennyson: "I am a part of all that I have met." The many, many people whom I have met, worked with, been inspired by and come to respect are a part of me and a part of this book forever. I am, at seventy-four, well-aware that there's truth to the maxim "If you see a turtle on a fencepost, you know it didn't get there on its own."

I start with the book itself. I am grateful to my small, loyal team that has worked with me over the last year and a half to help me write, research, fact-check and edit my usually longer than necessary descriptions. Stephanie Epner and Andrew Imbrie both worked with me at the State Department, where they were talented members of the Policy and Planning team. They traveled with me extensively in our petri dish flying machine, tolerating grueling hours, researching and writing their way around the world. They agreed to extend that journey and come with me after I left the State Department, and both did an outstanding job of researching and organizing massive amounts of material and helping me to reduce the clutter (I hope). They're both going to contribute to the public debate in America for a long time.

I could never have tackled this book without the skill of my friend and collaborator David Wade. He was my chief of staff both in the Senate and in the State Department. He knows my voice and my life. His wife, Elizabeth, and their two young sons, Robert and Alec, gave up a lot of time with Dad to make this happen.

Matt Summers has been an unsung hero on my team since he came to work for me as a Senate intern, and climbed the ladder of numerous jobs to become invaluable. He's fiercely loyal and incalculably capable, someone who handles sensitive assignments and small details with equal commitment. Julie Wirkkala has been my scheduler since 2003. Her fifteen years probably feel like dog years; she's helped organize my life and move me around the globe with calm and precision. Together, their loyalty and constant vigilance on my behalf make my continued public life possible today.

I thank Simon & Schuster for believing this was a life story worth publishing. Jonathan Karp's enthusiasm helped me believe the time and effort was worthwhile. His words of encouragement kept me writing. Bob Bender, my patient and superb editor, believed in this book from the very beginning. As an editor citizen, Bob has lived most of the issues raised in this chronicle. He weighed in with practical, sometimes tough assessments about clichés and drivel. His skill was invaluable in helping to excise the excess and home in on the important. Bob doesn't blow smoke at you. You have to earn approval, and it was fun trying to do so. I am grateful for his knowledgeable guidance.

Simon & Schuster is blessed with a talented team. I hope I have met the high standards of Johanna Li, Associate Editor; Jonathan Evans, Manager of Copyediting; Richard Rhorer, Associate Publisher; Cary Goldstein, Publicity Director; Julia Prosser, Deputy Director of Publicity; and Jackie Seow, Vice President and Executive Director of Trade Art. I'm also forever grateful to the two gifted photographers who captured two distinct moments in my life: George Butler, whose photos appear on the cover and inside, and Kelly Campbell, whose photo appears on the back cover.

To Bob Barnett, with gratitude not just for helping me navigate the path to Simon & Schuster, but also for endless enthusiasm about everything that's followed. I got to know Bob really well in 2012 when I was assigned the task of playing the Republican presidential nominee in debate prep. This was a much more familiar environment to get to know him better!

In the final weeks I asked a few of my oldest friends to read through key chapters and a couple of folks to read from start to finish. My profound thanks to my former chief of staff in the Senate and head of Policy Planning at State, a character in this book and an extraordinary ally in life, Ambassador David McKean, and my friend of forty-five years, Robert Shrum, both of whom dropped everything to read the manuscript and made thoughtful, insightful suggestions. David McKean is a terrific writer in his own right who penned five books in the years he worked for me, and Bob Shrum's gift for the written word is exceeded only by his gift for friendship. I also want to thank my close friend Tim Collins for his astute observations both on sections written about and some things not said. Tim's agile and inquisitive mind keeps pushing limits, and I am grateful for the intellectual and personal relationship.

To Evelyn Small, thank you for serving as such an invaluable sounding board and sharing years of wisdom.

I wanted to make certain the geography of South Vietnam and our missions was traceable in an understandable form. My thanks to the team at the Yale University Library, as well as David Medieros at the Stanford Geospatial Center, who worked to make that happen.

Any writing determined to accurately reflect events as they unfolded requires reference to government documents and coordination with the State Department. I thank Behar Godani, who was unbelievably helpful in making space available at the State Department, locating my personal notes, and working with us to ensure any sensitive references were handled appropriately.

A group of fellows at Yale contributed time, thinking and research skill. I thank Chris Haugh for helping to organize those efforts.

The list of friends who have been part of this journey is far too long to include them all here. But I am blessed with special journeymen and -women who are directly involved in every page, every step, by name or by contribution. I love them all and thank my lucky stars for such company. There's my brother, Cam, and sisters, Peggy and Diana, and our many cousins who have enriched our lives. I have leaned on friends from growing up, from high school to college, including David Thorne, Dan Barbiero, Harvey Bundy, Lewis Rutherfurd, a great group of friends from Yale, from my fraternity, extracurricular activities, athletic teams, debating and Jonathan Edwards College.

I put my life in the hands of those I served with on PCF-44 and PCF-94 and we remain brothers to this day: Bill Zaladonis, Jim Wasser, David Alston, Drew Whitlow, Del Sandusky, Fred Short, Gene Thorson and Mike Medeiros—and two crewmates we lost too soon, Tommy Belodeau and Steve Hatch. They are heroes each and all, and I'm forever grateful to all of those who served in Swift boats and for all we gave each other on those rivers.

I have brothers and sisters also from the movement to stop the war, friends to this day: Tommy Vallely, Chris Gregory, John Hurley and George Butler. There are classmates from Boston College Law School who made a difference in my life, especially, my moot court partners Ronna Schneider and Tom Haynes, and Paul Kane, our advisor, and my study group. There are friends from every step of my political journey, whether in the 1972 campaign and beyond, including John Marttila, Tom Kiley and Dan Payne, the district attorney's office, lieutenant governor's campaign, Governor Michael Dukakis and Kitty who were so supportive and such loyal friends.

To twenty-eight years of senate friends, including but not limited to Chris Greeley, Patty Foley, Kaaren Hinck, Ayanna Pressley, Greg Stewart, Meaghan Carroll, Setti Warren, Roger Lau, Dan Gross, Brendan "B-Man" O'Donnell, Larry Carpman, Jim Shaer, Mary Anne Marsh, Roger Fisk and so many more who worked with me in Massachusetts on behalf of state and country. And to those we've lost—Mary Pappey, Jeanette Boone, Bill Bradley, Louise Etheridge and Gene Heller. Thank you Drew O'Brien— my savvy Massachusetts right-arm for so many years. And those in Washington who stood by me and pushed me, from some already mentioned to Ron Rosenblith, Jonathan Winer, Frances Zwenig, Tricia Ferrone, Nancy Stetson, Jim Jones, Pat Gray, Heather Zichal, John Phillips, George Abar, Gregg Rothschild, Tim Barnicle, Scott Bunton, David Leiter and so many more I wish I had the space to thank—including the late Jayona Beal.

Thank you to those who worked so hard on my presidential campaign. I wish I could thank you all individually, but I would like to especially thank Jim Jordan, Mary Beth Cahill, John Sasso, Michael Whouley, Jack Corrigan, Stephanie Cutter, Amy Dacey, Jeanne and Billy Shaheen, Harold Schaitberger, John Sweeney (former president of the AFL-CIO) and the leaders of organized labor, Jerry Crawford, Jim Margolis, Tom Keady, Mike McCurry, Marcus Jadotte, Nick Clemons, Jill Alper, Judy Reardon, Ken Robinson, Tad Devine, Mike Donilon, John Norris and, of course, Marvin Nicholson. From the extraordinary team that kept the lights on in campaign after campaign, I thank Peter Maroney, the late Bob Farmer, Jackson Dunn, Leigh Garland, Lou Susman, Bob Crowe, Alan Solomont, Anne Finucane, Joan Lukey, Bernie Schwartz, Jack Manning and Lyle Howland. To Jon

Macks, thank you for the common sense and good humor. And I'm forever grateful to those who saddled up again after the presidential campaign.

There's the dedicated team at the State Department who worked under difficult circumstances to make our country stronger. Thank you to three great deputy secretaries of state: Bill Burns, Heather Higginbottom and Tony Blinken; to our Ambassador to the United Nations, Samantha Power, and my colleagues at the NSC and the White House, including Susan Rice, Tom Donilon, Valerie Jarrett, Denis McDonough and Pete Rouse. Thank you to Vice President Biden, who will always be a trusted friend.

Thank you to my senior State team, who worked around the clock without complaint to make our mission a success: Jon Finer, my exceptionally capable chief of staff and head of policy and planning; Wendy Sherman, Tom Shannon, Lisa Kenna, Jen Psaki and John Kirby, Frank Lowenstein, Kristie Kenney, Pat Kennedy, Julia Frifield, Joe MacManus and John Bass. To John Natter, Claire Coleman, Joe Semrad, Nick Christiansen, Chris Flanagan, Cindy Chang and all of my "S Specials"—thank you for all you did to keep the trains on Mahogany Row running. Thank you to Glen Johnson— who was both hardworking and great company on a global journey. To Jason Meininger, a jack-of-all-trades who was always by my side through thick and thin in both the Senate and at State. Thank you for your friendship, loyalty and the many early-morning bike rides. To the Operations Center and to "The Line"—the lifeblood of the department. Thank you to Diplomatic Security, who protects not only the secretary of state but our embassies and consulates around the world. And finally, thank you to all the men and women of the Foreign Service, who constantly uproot their lives and family and move around the globe—often to dangerous corners of the world—missing special milestones and holidays with loved ones, all in the name of diplomacy.

In addition to working with the talented people who represent our country, one of the extraordinary privileges of serving as secretary of state is to get to know as colleagues and friends the people who represent their own countries with equal skill and passion. They include diplomats like Britain's Lady Cathy Ashton or Jordan's Nasser Judeh; Norway's Borge Brende, a committed environmentalist; Sheikh Abdullah bin Zayed Al Nahyan of UAE or Adel al-Jubeir of the Kingdom of Saudi Arabia; savvy emissaries like Salem al-Ismaily or leaders of countries like Sultan Qaboos of Oman; and religious leaders whose lives of faith remind me of the universal truths that bind us, including the Archbishop of Canterbury Justin Welby, the Aga Khan, or Cardinal Pietro Parolin of the Holy See. I was privileged to work closely on a variety of critical issues with many of my European counterparts like Philip Hammond and William Hague of the United Kingdom, Frank-Walter Steinmeier of Germany, Laurent Fabius of France, Federica Mogherini, the High Representative to the European Union, and many others. There are many more, too many to mention, all of whom were on speed dial those four years and many who remain so today, but their friendship and camaraderie will always be fresh in my memory.

Thank you to the many people from the different parts of my life who were so helpful throughout the writing process: Martin Indyk, Will Imbrie, Tom Sullivan, Danny Russell, Bernie Aronson, Dan Feldman, Rick Stengel, Doug Frantz, Rob Malley, Salman Ahmed, Brett McGurk, Tom Countryman, Perry Cammack, Anthony Weir, Sue Biniaz, Melanie Nakagawa, Kathleen Frangione and Toria Nuland.

To my friends in the Senate and House who continue the fight, thank you for your service and your friendship. To my Senate colleagues who are no longer with us—Teddy Kennedy, John Glenn, Dan Inouye and Robert Byrd—thank you for your mentorship and your countless contributions to our country.

To the people of Massachusetts—thank you for allowing me to represent you for almost three decades in the U.S. Senate. I hope I kept faith with your aspirations. It was the honor of a lifetime.

To President Obama—thank you for the opportunity to serve as our nation's sixty-eighth secretary of state and for your commitment to pursue peace as a first resort. Your trust made all the difference.

To my daughters, Alexandra and Vanessa, and their husbands, I hope you always know how grateful I am for the gift of our family. And to the extended Heinz family, Johnny, Andre and Chris, their families and the Pickle Mafia—thank you for supporting my adventure, putting up with the intrusions that came with it and helping to blend families, never an easy task.

Teresa, your gift of caring and your quiet way of calming, and your compass, which values what's most important in life—precious time—has taught me to grab the important moments and always appreciate what we have. You've been amazingly supportive through all of it, and always you've been there when the road is steepest.

John Kerry

Index

Image Credits